COMPUTATIONAL BUSINESS ANALYTICS

Chapman & Hall/CRC
Data Mining and Knowledge Discovery Series

AIMS AND SCOPE

This series aims to capture new developments and applications in data mining and knowledge discovery, while summarizing the computational tools and techniques useful in data analysis. This series encourages the integration of mathematical, statistical, and computational methods and techniques through the publication of a broad range of textbooks, reference works, and handbooks. The inclusion of concrete examples and applications is highly encouraged. The scope of the series includes, but is not limited to, titles in the areas of data mining and knowledge discovery methods and applications, modeling, algorithms, theory and foundations, data and knowledge visualization, data mining systems and tools, and privacy and security issues.

PUBLISHED TITLES

ADVANCES IN MACHINE LEARNING AND DATA MINING FOR ASTRONOMY
Michael J. Way, Jeffrey D. Scargle, Kamal M. Ali, and Ashok N. Srivastava

BIOLOGICAL DATA MINING
Jake Y. Chen and Stefano Lonardi

COMPUTATIONAL BUSINESS ANALYTICS
Subrata Das

COMPUTATIONAL INTELLIGENT DATA ANALYSIS FOR SUSTAINABLE DEVELOPMENT
Ting Yu, Nitesh V. Chawla, and Simeon Simoff

COMPUTATIONAL METHODS OF FEATURE SELECTION
Huan Liu and Hiroshi Motoda

CONSTRAINED CLUSTERING: ADVANCES IN ALGORITHMS, THEORY, AND APPLICATIONS
Sugato Basu, Ian Davidson, and Kiri L. Wagstaff

CONTRAST DATA MINING: CONCEPTS, ALGORITHMS, AND APPLICATIONS
Guozhu Dong and James Bailey

DATA CLUSTERING: ALGORITHMS AND APPLICATIONS
Charu C. Aggarawal and Chandan K. Reddy

DATA CLUSTERING IN C++: AN OBJECT-ORIENTED APPROACH
Guojun Gan

DATA MINING FOR DESIGN AND MARKETING
Yukio Ohsawa and Katsutoshi Yada

DATA MINING WITH R: LEARNING WITH CASE STUDIES
Luís Torgo

FOUNDATIONS OF PREDICTIVE ANALYTICS
James Wu and Stephen Coggeshall

GEOGRAPHIC DATA MINING AND KNOWLEDGE DISCOVERY, SECOND EDITION
Harvey J. Miller and Jiawei Han

HANDBOOK OF EDUCATIONAL DATA MINING
Cristóbal Romero, Sebastian Ventura, Mykola Pechenizkiy, and Ryan S.J.d. Baker

INFORMATION DISCOVERY ON ELECTRONIC HEALTH RECORDS
Vagelis Hristidis

INTELLIGENT TECHNOLOGIES FOR WEB APPLICATIONS
Priti Srinivas Sajja and Rajendra Akerkar

INTRODUCTION TO PRIVACY-PRESERVING DATA PUBLISHING: CONCEPTS AND TECHNIQUES
Benjamin C. M. Fung, Ke Wang, Ada Wai-Chee Fu, and Philip S. Yu

KNOWLEDGE DISCOVERY FOR COUNTERTERRORISM AND LAW ENFORCEMENT
David Skillicorn

KNOWLEDGE DISCOVERY FROM DATA STREAMS
João Gama

MACHINE LEARNING AND KNOWLEDGE DISCOVERY FOR ENGINEERING SYSTEMS HEALTH MANAGEMENT
Ashok N. Srivastava and Jiawei Han

MINING SOFTWARE SPECIFICATIONS: METHODOLOGIES AND APPLICATIONS
David Lo, Siau-Cheng Khoo, Jiawei Han, and Chao Liu

MULTIMEDIA DATA MINING: A SYSTEMATIC INTRODUCTION TO CONCEPTS AND THEORY
Zhongfei Zhang and Ruofei Zhang

MUSIC DATA MINING
Tao Li, Mitsunori Ogihara, and George Tzanetakis

NEXT GENERATION OF DATA MINING
Hillol Kargupta, Jiawei Han, Philip S. Yu, Rajeev Motwani, and Vipin Kumar

RAPIDMINER: DATA MINING USE CASES AND BUSINESS ANALYTICS APPLICATIONS
Markus Hofmann and Ralf Klinkenberg

RELATIONAL DATA CLUSTERING: MODELS, ALGORITHMS, AND APPLICATIONS
Bo Long, Zhongfei Zhang, and Philip S. Yu

SERVICE-ORIENTED DISTRIBUTED KNOWLEDGE DISCOVERY
Domenico Talia and Paolo Trunfio

SPECTRAL FEATURE SELECTION FOR DATA MINING
Zheng Alan Zhao and Huan Liu

STATISTICAL DATA MINING USING SAS APPLICATIONS, SECOND EDITION
George Fernandez

SUPPORT VECTOR MACHINES: OPTIMIZATION BASED THEORY, ALGORITHMS, AND EXTENSIONS
Naiyang Deng, Yingjie Tian, and Chunhua Zhang

TEMPORAL DATA MINING
Theophano Mitsa

TEXT MINING: CLASSIFICATION, CLUSTERING, AND APPLICATIONS
Ashok N. Srivastava and Mehran Sahami

THE TOP TEN ALGORITHMS IN DATA MINING
Xindong Wu and Vipin Kumar

UNDERSTANDING COMPLEX DATASETS: DATA MINING WITH MATRIX DECOMPOSITIONS
David Skillicorn

COMPUTATIONAL BUSINESS ANALYTICS

SUBRATA DAS

Machine Analytics, Inc.

Belmont, Massachusetts, USA

CRC Press
Taylor & Francis Group
Boca Raton London New York

CRC Press is an imprint of the
Taylor & Francis Group, an **informa** business

A CHAPMAN & HALL BOOK

The author can be requested at sdas@machineanalytics.com for a demonstration version of any of the three Machine Analytics tools used to perform case studies in the two penultimate chapters of the book. It will be the sole discretion of the author to provide tools upon a satisfactory analysis of the requestor's usage intention. Use of the tools is entirely at their own risk. Machine Analytics is not responsible for the consequences of reliance on any analyses provided by the tools. Licensing details for commercial versions of these tools can be obtained by sending an email to admin@machineanalytics.com.

CRC Press
Taylor & Francis Group
6000 Broken Sound Parkway NW, Suite 300
Boca Raton, FL 33487-2742

Printed on acid-free paper
Version Date: 20131118

International Standard Book Number-13: 978-1-4398-9070-7 (Hardback)

Visit the Taylor & Francis Web site at
http://www.taylorandfrancis.com

and the CRC Press Web site at
http://www.crcpress.com

Contents

Preface

According to the Merriam-Webster dictionary[1], analytics is "the method of logical analysis." This is a very broad definition of analytics, without an explicitly stated end-goal. A view of analytics within the business community is that analytics describes a process (a method or an analysis) that transforms (hopefully, logically) raw data into actionable knowledge in order to guide strategic decision-making. Along this line, technology research guru Gartner defines analytics as methods that "leverage data in a particular functional process (or application) to enable context-specific insight that is actionable" (Kirk, 2006). Business analytics naturally concerns the application of analytics in industry, and the title of this book, *Computational Business Analytics*, refers to the algorithmic process of analytics as implemented via computer. This book provides a computational account of analytics, and leaves such areas as visualization-based analytics to other authors.

Each of the definitions provided above is broad enough to cover any application domain. This book is not intended to cover every possible business vertical, but rather to teach the core tools and techniques applicable across multiple domains. In the process of doing so, we present many examples and a selected number of challenging case studies from interesting domains. Our hope is that practitioners of business analytics will be able to easily see the connections to their own problems and to formulate their own strategies for finding the solutions they seek.

Traditional business analytics has focused mostly on descriptive analyses of structured historical data using myriad statistical techniques. The current trend has been a turn towards predictive analytics and text analytics of unstructured data. Our approach is to augment and enrich numerical statistical techniques with symbolic Artificial Intelligence (AI)[2] and Machine Learning (ML)[3] techniques. Note our usage of the terms "augment" and "enrich" as opposed to "replace." Traditional statistical approaches are invaluable in data-rich environments, but there are areas where AI and ML approaches provide better analyses, especially where there is an abundance of subjective knowledge. Benefits of such augmentation include:

[1] http://www.merriam-webster.com/

[2] AI systems are computer systems exhibiting some of form human intelligence.

[3] Computer systems incorporating ML technologies have the ability to learn from observations.

- Mixing of numerical (e.g., interest rate, income) and categorical (e.g., day of the week, position in a company) variables in algorithms.
- "What-if" or explanation-based reasoning (e.g., what if the revenue target is set higher, explain the reason for a customer churn).
- Results of inferences (are) easily understood by human analysts.
- Efficiency enhancement incorporating knowledge from domain experts as heuristics to deal with the "curse of dimensionality," for example.

Though early AI reasoning was primarily symbolic in nature (i.e., the manipulation of linguistics symbols with well-defined semantics), it has moved towards a hybrid of symbolic and numerical, and therefore one is expected to find both probabilistic and statistical foundations in many AI approaches.

Here are some augmentation/enrichment approaches readers will find covered by this book (not to worry if you are not familiar with the terms): we enrich principal component and factor analyses with subspace methods (e.g., latent semantic analyses), meld regression analyses with probabilistic graphical modeling, extend autoregression and survival analysis techniques with Kalman filter and dynamic Bayesian networks, embed decision trees within influence diagrams, and augment "nearest-neighbor" and k-means clustering techniques with support vector machines and neural networks. On the surface, these extensions may seem to be replacements of traditional analytics, but in most of these cases a generalized technique can be reduced to the underlying traditional base technique under very restrictive conditions. The enriched techniques offer efficient solutions in areas such as customer segmentation, churn prediction, credit risk assessment, fraud detection, and advertising campaigns.

Descriptive and Predictive Analytics together establish current and projected situations of an organization, but do not recommend actions. An obvious next step is Prescriptive Analytics, which is a process to determine alternative courses of actions or decision options, given the situation along with a set of objectives, requirements, and constraints. Automation of decision-making of routine tasks is ubiquitous (e.g., preliminary approval of loan eligibility or determining insurance premiums), but subjective processes within organizations are still used for complex decision-making (e.g., credit risk assessment or clinical trial assessment). This current use of subjectivity should not prohibit the analytics community from pursuing a computational approach to the generation of decision options by accounting for various non-quantifiable subjective factors together with numerical data. The analytics-generated options can then be presented, along with appropriate explanations and backing, to the decision-makers of the organization.

Analytics is ultimately about processing data and knowledge. If available data are structured in relational databases, then data samples and candidate variables for the models to be built are well-identified. However, more than eighty percent of enterprise data today is unstructured (Grime, 2011), and there is an urgent need for automated analyses. Text analytics is a framework to enable an organization to discover and maximize the value of information within large quantities of text (open source or internal). Applications include sentiment analysis, business intelligence analysis, e-service, military intelligence analysis, scientific discovery, and search and information access. This book covers computational technologies to support two fundamental requirements for text analyses, information extraction and text classification.

Most analytics systems presented as part of case studies will be "hybrid" in nature, in combinations of the above three approaches, namely statistics-, AI-, and ML-based. Special emphasis is placed on techniques handling time. Examples in this book are drawn from numerous domains, including life status estimation, loan processing, and credit risk assessment. Since the techniques presented here have roots in the theory of statistics and probability, in AI and ML, and in control theory, there is an abundance of relevant literature for further studies.

Readership

The book may be used by designers and developers of analytics systems for any vertical (e.g., healthcare, finance and accounting, human resources, customer support, transportation) who work within business organizations around the world. They will find the book useful as a vehicle for moving towards a new generation of analytics approaches. University students and teachers, especially those in business schools, who are studying and teaching in the field of analytics will find the book useful as a textbook for undergraduate and graduate courses, and as a reference book for researchers. Prior understanding of the theories presented in the book will be beneficial for those who wish to build analytics systems grounded in well-founded theory, rather than ad hoc ones.

Contents

The sixteen chapters in this book are divided into six parts, mostly along the line of statistics, AI, and ML paradigms, including the parts for introductory materials, information structuring and dissemination, and tools and case studies. It would have been unnatural to divide along the three categories of analytics processes, namely, descriptive, predictive, and prescriptive. This is mainly due to the fact that some models can be used for the purpose of more than one of these three analytics. For example, if a model helps to discriminate a set of alternative hypotheses based on the available information, these hypotheses could be possible current or future situations, or alternative courses of actions. The coverage of statistics and probability theory in this book is far from comprehensive; we focus only on those descriptive and inferential techniques that are either enhanced via or used within some AI and ML techniques. There is an abundance of books on statistics and probability theory for further investigation, if desired.

PART I – Introduction and background

Chapter 1 details the concepts of analytics, with examples drawn from various application domains. It provides a brief account of analytics modeling and some well-known models and architectures of analytics. Chapter 1 is written in an informal manner and uses relatable examples, and is crucial for understanding the basics of analytics in general.

Chapter 2 presents background on mathematical and statistical preliminaries, including basic probability and statistics, graph theory, mathematical logic, performance measurement, and algorithmic complexity. This chapter will serve as a refresher for those readers who have already been exposed to these concepts.

PART II – Statistical Analytics

Chapter 3 provides a detailed account of various statistical techniques for descriptive analytics. These include relevant discrete and continuous probability distributions and their applicability, goodness-of-fit tests, measures of central tendency, and dispersions.

Chapter 4 is dedicated to Bayesian probability and inferencing, given its importance across most of the approaches. We analyze Bayes's rule, and discuss the concept of priors and various techniques for obtaining them.

Chapter 5 covers inferential statistics for predictive analytics. Topics include generalization, test hypothesis, estimation, prediction, and decision. We cover various dependence methods in this category, including linear and logistics regressions, polynomial regression, Bayesian regression, auto-regression, factor analysis, and survival analysis. We save the Decision Tree (DT) learning techniques Classification and Regression Tree (CART) for a later chapter, given its close similarity with other DT techniques from the ML community.

PART III – Artificial Intelligence for Analytics

Chapter 6 presents the traditional symbolic AI approach to analytics. This chapter provides a detailed account of uncertainty and describes various well-established formal approaches to handling uncertainty, some of which are to be covered in more detail in subsequent chapters.

Chapter 7 presents several probabilistic graphical models for analytics. We start with Naïve Bayesian Classifiers (NBCs), move to their generalizations, the k-dependence Naïve Bayesian Classifiers (kNBCs), and, finally, explore the most general Bayesian Belief Networks (BNs). The chapter presents various evidence propagation algorithms. There is not always an intuitive explanation of how evidence is propagated up and down the arrows in a BN model via abductive (explanation-based) and deductive (causal) inferencing. This is largely due to the conditional independence assumption and, as a consequence, separation among variables. To understand evidence propagation behavior and also to identify sources of inferencing inefficiency, readers are therefore encouraged to go through in as much detail as they can the theory underlying BN technology and propagation algorithms.

Chapter 8 describes the use of the Influence Diagram (ID) and symbolic argumentation technologies to make decisions using prescriptive analytics. The BN and rule-based formalisms for hypothesis evaluation do not explicitly incorporate the concepts of action and utility that are ubiquitous in decision-making contexts. IDs incorporate the concepts of action and utility. Symbolic argumentation allows one to express arguments for and against decision hypotheses with weights from a variety of dictionaries, including the probability dictionary. Arguments are aggregated to rank the considered set of hypotheses to help choose the most plausible one. Readers must go through the BN chapter to understand IDs.

Chapter 9 presents our discussion of models in the temporal category. We present several approaches to modeling time-series data generated from a dynamic environment, such as the financial market, and then make use of such models for forecasting. We present the Kalman Filter (KF) technique for estimating the state of a dynamic environment, then present the Hidden Markov Model (HMM) framework and the more generalized Dynamic Bayesian Network (DBN) technology. DBNs are temporal extensions of BNs. Inference algorithms for these models are also provided. Readers must understand the BN technology to understand its temporal extension.

Chapter 10 presents sampling-based approximate algorithms for inferences in non-linear models. The algorithms that we cover are Markov Chain Monte Carlo (MCMC), Gibbs sampling, Metropolis-Hastings, and Particle Filter (PF). PF algorithms are especially effective in handling hybrid DBNs containing both categorical and numerical variables.

PART IV – Machine Learning for Analytics

Chapter 11 covers some of the most popular and powerful clustering techniques for segmenting data sets, namely, hierarchical, k-means, k-Nearest Neighbor (kNN), Support Vector Machines (SVM), and feed-forward Neural Networks (NNs). The first three have their roots in traditional statistics, whereas the latter two developed within the ML community.

Chapter 12 presents supervised and unsupervised techniques for learning trees, rules, and graphical models for analytics, some of which have been presented in the previous chapters. We start with algorithms for learning Decision Trees (DTs), and then investigate learning of various probabilistic graphical models, namely, NBC, kNBC, and BN. Finally, we present a general rule induction technique, called Inductive Logic Programming (ILP).

PART V – Information Structuring and Dissemination

Chapter 13 deals with the analytics of unstructured textual data. The two fundamental tasks that provide foundations for text analytics are information extraction and text classification. This chapter briefly introduces some popular linguistic techniques for extracting structured information in the form of Resource Description Framework (RDF) triples, then details an array of techniques for learning classifiers for text corpus, such as NBC, *k*NBC, Latent Semantics Analysis (LSA), probabilistic LSA (PLSA), and Latent Dirichlet Allocation (LDA). PLSA and LDA are particularly useful for extracting latent topics in a text corpus in an unsupervised manner.

Chapter 14 presents standardized semantics of information content to be exchanged in order to be comprehended as consumers by various entities, whether they are computer-based processes, physical systems, or human operators. We present the Semantic Web technology to serve such a purpose.

PART VI – Analytics Tools and Case Studies

Chapter 15 presents three analytics tools that are designed and conceived by the author: 1) Intelligent Decision Aiding System (*i*DAS), which provides implementations of a set of ML techniques; 2) Environment for 5th Generation Applications (E5), which provides a development environment in declarative languages with an embedded expert system shell; and 3) Analysis of Text (*a*Text) for information extraction and classification of text documents. Demo versions of *i*DAS, E5, and *a*Text can be obtained by purchasing a copy of the book and then emailing a request to the author. The chapter presents very briefly a handful of commercial and publicly available tools for analytics, including R, MATLAB, WEKA, and SAS.

The author can be contacted at sdas@machineanalytics.com or subrata@skdas.com to request a demonstration version of any of the above three Machine Analytics tools used to perform case studies in the two penultimate chapters of the book. It will be the sole discretion of the author to provide tools upon a satisfactory analysis of the requestor's usage intention. Use of the tools is entirely at his or her own risk. Machine Analytics is not responsible for the consequences of reliance on any analyses provided by the tools. Licensing details for commercial versions of these tools can be obtained by sending an email to admin@machineanalytics.com.

Chapter 16 presents four detailed case studies, namely, risk assessment for both individual and commercial lendings, life status estimation, and sentiment analysis, making use of all three tools, *i*DAS, E5, and *a*Text. The demo versions of the tools (see above) come with data from these case studies for readers to run on their own. The chapter also describes various types of fraud detection problems that can be solved by using various modeling and clustering technologies introduced in the book.

The scope of analytics is broad and interdisciplinary in nature, and is likely to cover a breadth of topic areas. The aim of this book is not to cover each and every aspect of analytics. The book provides a computational account of analytics, and leaves areas such as visual analytics, image analytics, and web analytics for other authors. Moreover, the symbolic thrust of the book naturally puts less emphasis on sub-symbolic areas, such as neural networks.

Notable omissions are case-based reasoning and blackboard approaches to prescriptive analytics, though technologies presented in the book can provide the foundations of such alternative approaches. I have made my best effort to make this book informative, readable, and free from mistakes, and I welcome any criticism or suggestions for improvement.

Tutorials Source

Much of the material in this book is based on the slides of two series of tutorials that I have been delivering over the past few years: one series is on Analytics and Business Intelligence, and the other series is on Multi-sensor Data Fusion. Conference organizers, institutions, and government and commercial organizations interested in on- or off-site tutorials based on the content of this book may contact the author directly (subrata@skdas.com or sdas@machineanalytics.com).

Subrata Das

Machine Analytics, Inc.
Belmont, MA

Acknowledgements

Thanks to my wife, Janique, my son, Sébastien, and my daughter, Kabita, for their love, patience, and inspiration throughout the preparation of this book. My sincere thanks go to Jessica Volz for her careful reading of the first draft of the manuscript. Many thanks to Chapman and Hall/CRC Press, especially Randi Cohen, Acquisitions Editor, and the anonymous reviewers for their help in producing the book from the beginning.

There are academic and analytics practitioners in government and industry from around the world with whom I have had valuable technical discussions and arguments that helped me to understand and appreciate better the fusion area. Thanks to all of my colleagues here at Machine Analytics in Belmont, Massachusetts, and also at Xerox Research Center Europe in Grenoble, France, and at Milcord in Waltham, Massachusetts, with whom I have had numerous technical discussions on various aspects of this book.

Finally, I thank my parents, brothers, sisters, and other family members back in one of many thousands of small villages in India for patiently accepting my absence and showing their encouragement and support through many phone calls.

Author

Dr. Subrata Das is the founder and president of Machine Analytics®, a company in the Boston area providing analytics and data fusion consultancy services for clients in government and businesses. The company develops practical but theoretically well-founded customized solutions using a combination of in-house, commercial-off-the-shelf, and publicly available tools. Dr. Das is often consulted by companies of all sizes to develop their analytics and data fusion strategies.

Dr. Das possesses applied and deep technical expertise in a broad range of computational artificial intelligence and data mining/machine learning techniques with foundations in the theory of probability of statistics, mathematical logic, and natural language processing. Specific technical expertise includes regression and time series analyses, cluster analyses, Bayesian and neural networks, Monte Carlo simulations, rules and argumentation, intelligent agents, subspace methods, and probabilistic and other formalisms for handling uncertainty. Dr. Das is proficient in multiple programming languages including Java, C++, and Prolog, scripting language such R and Matlab, and various database and cloud computing technologies. He has conceived and developed in-house Machine Analytics® tools *a*Text, *i*DAS and RiskAid.

Dr. Das spent two years in Grenoble, France, as the lab manager of more than forty researchers in the document content laboratory at the Xerox European Research Centre. Dr. Das guided applied analytics research and development in the areas of unstructured data analyses, machine translation, image processing, and decision-making under uncertainty. Dr. Das was one of the five-members in the high-profile Xerox task force Knowledge Work 2020, working alongside colleagues from the Palo Alto Research Center (PARC) to explore a strategic vision of the future of work.

Before joining Xerox, Dr. Das held the chief scientist position at Charles River Analytics in Cambridge, MA, where he led many fusion and analytical projects funded by DARPA, NASA, and various branches within the US Department of Defense (DoD), including the Army, the Office of Naval Research (ONR) and the Air Force Research Lab (AFRL). He has also collaborated extensively with various universities around the world. In the past, Dr. Das held research positions at Imperial College and Queen Mary and Westfield College, both part of the University of London, where he conducted research in the health informatics domain. He received his PhD in computer science from Heriot-Watt University in Scotland, a Master's in mathematics from the University of Kolkata, and an M.Tech from the Indian Statistical Institute.

Dr. Das is the author of the books *Foundations of Decision Making Agents: Logic, Modality, and Probability*, published by the World Scientific/Imperial College Press, *High-Level Data Fusion*, published by the Artech House, and *Deductive Databases and Logic Programming*, published by Addison-Wesley. Dr. Das has also co-authored the book entitled *Safe and Sound: Artificial Intelligence in Hazardous Applications*, published by the MIT Press (Nobel laureate Herbert Simon wrote the foreword of the book).

Dr. Das served as a member of the editorial board of the *Information Fusion* journal, published by Elsevier Science. He has been a regular contributor, a technical committee member, a panel member, and a tutorial lecturer at various international conferences. Dr. Das has published many conference and journal articles, edited a journal special issue, and regularly gives seminars and training courses based on his books.

Dr. Das can be contacted at sdas@machineanalytics.com or subrata@skdas.com.

CHAPTER 1

Analytics Background and Architectures

The objective of this chapter is to provide readers with a general background in analytics. The chapter surveys and compares a number of analytics architectures and related information and processes, including the well-known data-information-knowledge hierarchy model. The chapter also draws a parallel between analytics and data fusion, to benefit from well-established data fusion techniques in the literature.

1.1 ANALYTICS DEFINED

Analytics is the process of transforming raw data into actionable strategic knowledge in order to gain insight into business processes, and thereby to guide decision-making to help businesses run efficiently. An analytics process can be categorized into one of three categories:

- *Descriptive Analytics* looks at an organization's current and historical performance.
- *Predictive Analytics* forecasts future trends, behavior, and events for decision support.
- *Prescriptive Analytics* determines alternative courses of actions or decisions, given the current and projected situations and a set of objectives, requirements, and constraints.

To concretely illustrate the above categories, consider a very simple scenario involving a company who recently entered into the telecommunication services business. FIGURE 1.1 shows some of the analytics questions that can be asked by the management to analyze the company's performance to date. The questions that fall into the descriptive analytics category ask about past monthly sales performance and about valuable customers. The predictive analytics questions ask for projected sales and identification of customers that are likely to leave. Finally, the prescriptive analytics questions ask for recommendations to increase sales and for kinds of incentives that can be offered to encourage customer retention/loyalty.

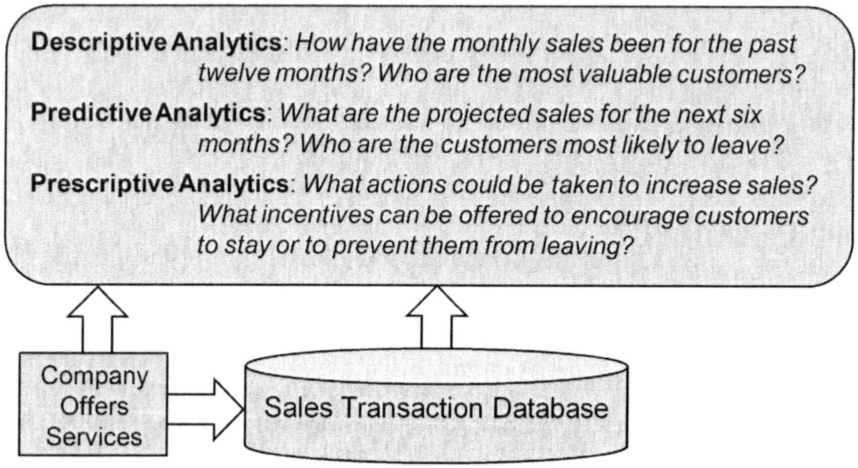

FIGURE 1.1 : Example analytics questions

The underlying database to support answering these questions contains sales transaction information, and hence is temporal in nature. Various charts and statistics can be generated and visualized to answer the descriptive analytics questions. A temporal analysis, such as an examination of monthly sales trends, can be drawn as part of both descriptive and predictive analytics, but there is a fundamental difference between the two. A trend as part of descriptive analytics is merely a plot of past data. Plotting a future trend as part of prescriptive analytics requires intelligent algorithms to accurately compute the trend. The recommendation for future action under prescriptive analytics can be based on both descriptive and predictive analyses.

Now, we take a wider view of analytics and concretely formulate a set of representative questions that are usually posed by business analysts, working in a variety of application domains, to fulfill their analytics requirements:

- *Customer Relationship Management*: How to best and most profitably classify and visualize customers into category A (most valuable), B and C (descriptive)? How to determine the probability that a customer will be lost within the next two years (predictive)?
- *Telecommunication*: How to cluster customers on the basis of collected historic data points (e.g., calls, text messages, multi-media messages, website navigation, and email exchanges) and then offer tailored messages and offers to each cluster?

- *Banking*: How to determine the credit-worthiness of new clients on the basis of historic data of past clients? How to determine credit card usage fraud based on usage patterns?
- *Insurance*: How to estimate the probability of a claim (e.g., car accident) by an existing customer or by a new applicant, using historical personal data? How to identify patterns that reveal the likelihood of an insured to buy other insurance policies?
- *Marketing*: How to compute the likelihood of existing customers to purchase a new product, in order to launch an effective advertising campaign for the product? How to predict the likelihood of success of a new product in early stages of product development?
- *Medical and Pharmaceutical*: How to determine possible side effects of a drug given to a patient, and the associated factors? How to determine the current and future clinical state of a subject, possibly via remote monitoring?
- *Quality Assurance Management*: How to find out combinations of production parameters that have an important influence on the final product to achieve six sigma objectives?
- *Logistics Supply Chain*: How to predict the number of goods to be consumed in different places?
- *Call Center*: How to assign the most appropriate agent to an incoming call requiring specialized expertise?
- *Human Resource*: How to predict the financial impact of fundamental strategies such as pay differentiation, pay-at-risk, total rewards mix, and organizational structure?
- *Stock Market*: How to predict market trends (bull vs. bear)? How to recommend the associated actions?
- *Fraud Detection*: How to identify various types of fraud in a variety of domains, including insurance claims, credit card usage, medical billing, and money laundering?

The underlying generic problem in the majority of the above cases is one of how to aggregate a group of interrelated objects and events to accurately produce an aggregate property (e.g., credit-worthiness) or to predict a property (e.g., drug side effects, goods consumption, incoming call type) or the likelihood of an event (e.g., a purchase, an insurance claim).

Analytics processes consume both structured and unstructured data. Structured data refers to computerized information which can be easily interpreted and used by a computer program supporting a range of tasks. Information stored in a relational database is structured, whereas texts, videos, and images, and web pages containing any of these are unstructured. Data can also be temporal (dynamic) in nature. In other words, the behavior of recorded attributes in a temporal database changes over time. An employee's id, for example, is static, whereas their salary is temporal. We will present techniques specifically designed to handle temporal data.

Texts are sometimes categorized as semi-structured. Text analytics is a process to enable an organization to discover and maximize the value of information within large quantities of text (open-source or internal). Applications of text analytics include sentiment analysis, business intelligence, e-service, intelligence analysis, scientific discovery, and search and information access. Two aspects of text analytics, namely, text classification and information extraction, are the foundations for any text analytics application. Here are some concrete examples of text analytics:

- *Customer Satisfaction*: Customer surveys include structured fields (e.g., rating, postal code) and text fields (e.g., customer views). Find the most frequently occurring terms or topics in free-text fields and identify how those topics evolve over time.

- *Customer Retention*: Data includes demographic and transactional information as well as customer calls. Extract the most important concepts from customer calls and notes from call center agents to input into the prediction model.

- *Manufacturing*: Car or complex machine manufacturers analyze repair reports from repair shops to understand the root cause of frequent failures. This analysis provides early warning indicators to avoid costly product recalls.

- *Life Science*: To study the risk of patients who suffer from heart disease, both structured data (e.g., blood pressure, cholesterol, age) and unstructured textual information (e.g., alcohol consumption) from a patient's medical history are relevant. With the additional information extracted from text, some patients might be eligible for exemption from further intensive and expensive medical supervision and control.

There are also other types of analytics: 1) Web Analytics: Analytics of internet usage data for purposes of understanding and optimizing web usage, and business and market research; 2) Visual Analytics: Analytics facilitated by interactive visual interfaces; 3) Image Analytics: Analyze real-world videos and images to extract information with machine performance comparable to humans; 4) Cross-lingual Analytics: Analytics with contents in multiple languages. Though we do not cover these areas in this book, various computational techniques that are presented can be used to build analytical systems for these areas.

1.2 ANALYTICS MODELING

Our approach to analytics is model-based (see FIGURE 1.2). Inferences for description, prediction, and prescription, in the context of a business problem, are made through a combination of symbolic, sub-symbolic, and numerical representations of the problem, together forming what we call a *computational model*. Structured input in the form of transactions and observations is fed into an inference engine for the model to produce analytical results. If the input is textual (as opposed to structured relational tables), structured information needs to be extracted. A traditional knowledge-based or rule-based expert system falls into this category, as structure relational data in the form of facts, and computational models in the form of rules, together form the knowledge base. Structured relational data is an explicit representation of knowledge, and rules help to derive implicit facts.

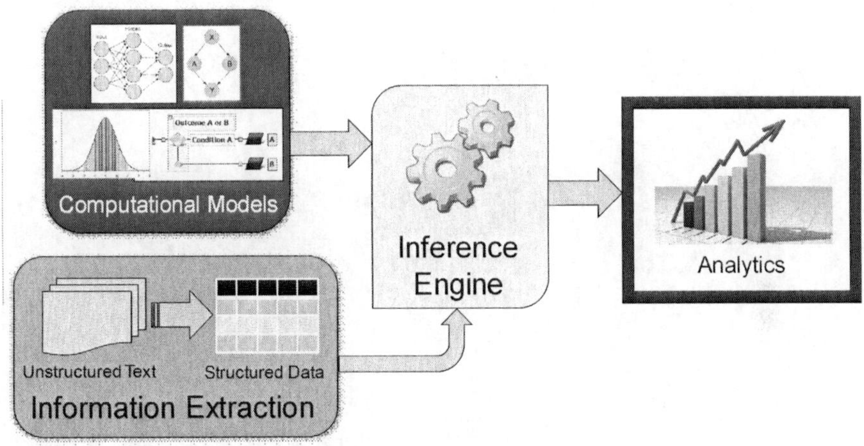

FIGURE 1.2 : Model-based analytics

Our special emphasis on building temporal models reflects the fact that we are not only dealing with current situation descriptions of an organization, but also their evolution and trend. Moreover, models are not necessarily static, prebuilt and monolithic, but will be adapted over time via learning from significant events as they occur.

So how do we build these models? Traditional statistical models are in the form of mathematical equations such as regression analysis and probability density functions. We expand this narrow view by including models that are internal to human analysts, with the hope of mimicking human reasoning at super-human speeds. By observing various business processes and events as they unfold, and by interacting with peers and with business processing systems (such as transaction and information processing systems and decision support systems), business analysts form internal mental models of things they observe and with which they interact. These mental models require more expressive graphical constructs and linguistics variables for their representation. They provide predictive and explanatory power for understanding a specific situation at hand, for which there may not be any mathematical formulae. This implies that one needs to capture the mental model of an analyst in order to "automate" the situation-understanding and prediction process. Computational models can also be viewed as patterns that are embedded within huge volumes of transactional data continuously generated by many business processing systems. Such models can therefore be extracted or learned via automated learning methods. For example, a regression equation is extracted automatically from observations of the dependent and independent variables. We will be dealing with a variety of models built on graphical constructs and linguistics variable symbols.

In the consideration of capturing a business analyst's mental model or in learning models automatically from large volumes of data, one must consider the following steps, as depicted in FIGURE 1.3:

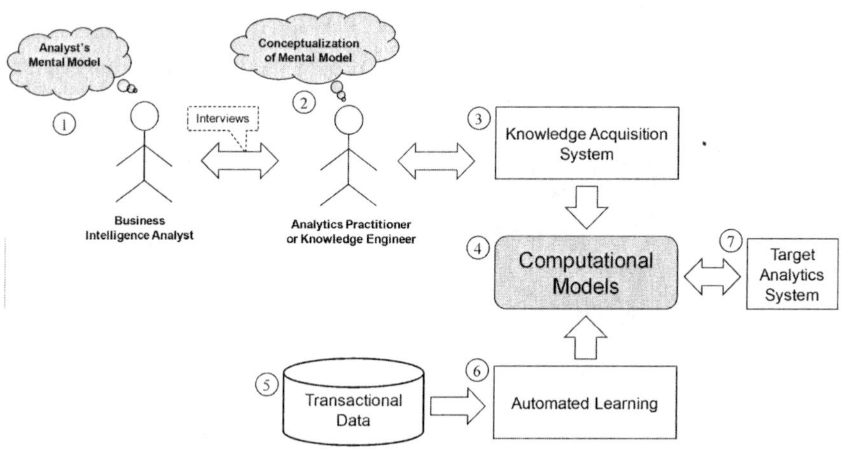

FIGURE 1.3 : Steps in building a model-based system for analytics

1. The business analyst's mental model;
2. The analyst practitioner or knowledge engineer's conceptualization of that mental model;
3. The knowledge acquisition system that captures the analyst's mental model for description, prediction, and explanation of situations;
4. The computational models for the target analytics system;
5. Input transactional data, if it exists;
6. The automated learning system to be used or created to extract computational models from input transactional data; and

7. The target analytics system that uses the computational models.

As shown in FIGURE 1.3, the knowledge engineer helps to transform an analyst's mental model into the computational model of a target system. However, this transformation process, via knowledge acquisition, is a serious bottleneck in the development of knowledge-intensive systems, and in AI systems in general. Computational representations that are complex in structures and semantics do not naturally lend themselves to easy translation from mental models.

Computational models (or, simply, models) for analytics to be presented in this book are in the four categories as shown and explained in TABLE 1.1: statistics-based, AI-based (or knowledge-rich), temporal, and ML-based (or knowledge-lean). For example, an analytic system built on a knowledge-rich AI model is unable to detect unusual activities or movements in the market or sentiments expressed in surveys that have not been explicitly modeled. This suggests that an effective detection system should hybridize AI models with data-based models such as statistics or ML, for example, including a test of normality or unsupervised clustering to indicate that there is something else going on.

TABLE 1.1: : Approaches to modeling analytics

Paradigm	Overall Approach	Technologies
Statistical	Non-deterministic relationships between variables are captured in the form of mathematical equations and probability distributions	Test hypothesis, regression analyses, probability theory, sampling, inferencing
Artificial Intelligence (AI)	Domain experts provide knowledge of system behavior, and knowledge engineers develop computational models using an underlying ontology	Logic-based expert systems, fuzzy logic, Bayesian networks
Temporal	Linear/nonlinear equations specify behavior of stochastic processes or of dynamic systems as state transitions and observations	Autoregression, survival analysis, Kalman filters, Hidden Markov Models, Dynamic Bayesian Networks
Machine Learning (ML)	System input/output behavior is observed, and machine learning techniques extract system behavior models	Clustering, neural network, and various linear, nonlinear, and symbolic approaches to learning

A temporal analytical approach models time explicitly. The variables in a temporal model change their state over time and thus are suitable for modeling market dynamics, for example, in order to build trading systems. Representation and propagation of uncertainty, in both data and knowledge, is a common problem that we address extensively in this book.

1.3 ANALYTICS PROCESSES

This section presents several well-known information and information-processing hierarchies that will let us conveniently divide analytics into modularized processes.

1.3.1 Information Hierarchy

The traditional DIKW (Data, Information, Knowledge and Wisdom) hierarchy (FIGURE 1.4) organizes data, information, knowledge, and wisdom in layers, with an increasing level of abstraction and addition of knowledge, starting from the bottom-most data layer. Various analytical systems help to transform content from one layer to a higher one so as to be better comprehended by analysts.

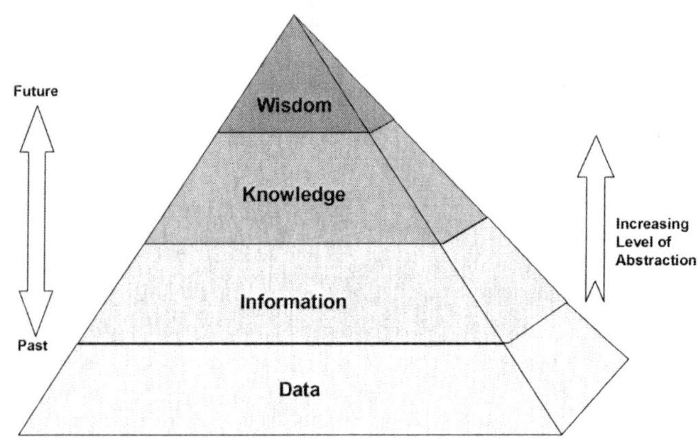

FIGURE 1.4 : Information hierarchy

Data Layer

Data are transactional, physical, and isolated records of activity (e.g., business transactions, customer interactions, facts or figures obtained from experiments or surveys). Data are, for example, numbers, texts, images, videos, and sounds, in a form that is suitable for storage or processing by a computer. Data are the most basic level and by themselves have little purpose and meaning.

Information Layer

Information is the semantic interpretation of data, and may represent relationships among data with meaning and purpose (e.g., a customer called for a specific type of support). Information therefore has been organized and presented in a systematic fashion to clarify the underlying meaning.

Knowledge Layer

Knowledge is the general awareness or possession of information, facts, ideas, truths, or principles. Knowledge is generally personal and subjective. Knowledge can also be extracted from underlying information by applying some form of induction (e.g., call volume is usually high during the period immediately after lunch).

Wisdom Layer

Wisdom is the knowledge of what is true or right coupled with just judgment as to action. Wisdom requires a specific kind of knowledge and experience to make the right decisions and judgments in actions.

Thus "data" is the basic unit of "information," which in turn is the basic unit of "knowledge," which in turn is the basic unit of "wisdom." The term "information" is sometimes used in a generic sense, representing any of the four layers of the DIKW hierarchy.

1.3.2 Information Processing Hierarchy

In coherence with the information hierarchy, we present here an information processing hierarchy (as shown in FIGURE 1.5) with examples drawn from a variety of functional areas. The processing is organized in layers with an increasing level of abstraction of input knowledge, starting from the bottom-most data layer. We have attached well-known business processing systems appropriate to these processing layers for illustrative purposes.

A Transaction Processing System (TPS) is an information processing system that collects, stores, updates, and retrieves the daily routine transactions necessary to conduct a business. A TPS transforms raw data into information by storing it with proper semantics, such as in relational databases where the schema of a database defines its semantics.

A Management Information System (MIS) is an information processing system that analyzes relationships among people, technology, and organizations to aid in running businesses efficiently and effectively. An MIS transforms information into knowledge which is descriptive in nature.

An Executive Information System (EIS) is an information processing system that supports decision-making needs of management by combining information available within the organization with external information in an

Level	Functional Area	Finance and Accounting	Customer Support	Human Resources	Information Support	Manufacturing	Sales and Marketing
Action (Prescriptive)	Decision Support System (DSS)	Budget adjustment	Support staff reorganization	Pay differentiation	Support planning	Load balancing	Sales strategy
Wisdom (Predictive)	Executive Support System (ESS)	Profit planning, cost and budget forecasting	Call volume forecasting	Pay at risk, analyses, personnel planning	Load forecasting	Future operating plan	Trend Analysis, promotion effects
Knowledge (Descriptive)	Management Information System (MIS)	Pricing and profitability, investment, annual budgeting, cost	Customer call volume, habits and preferences, fraud	Organizational and Pay structures, personnel distribution	Load and usage	Inventory, production schedule	Order, marketing
Information	Transaction Processing System (TPS)	Payroll, billing, accounts payable and receivable	Customer requests	Personnel records, training, compensation	User login, resource usage	Machine and plant controls	Order tracking, order Processing
Data							

FIGURE 1.5 : Information processing hierarchy

analytical framework. An EIS transforms knowledge into wisdom or actionable intelligence that is predictive in nature.

A Decision Support System (DSS) is an information processing system that generates a set of alternative decision options based on predictions and then recommends the best course of action by maximizing some utility in the context. A DSS therefore supports prescriptive analytics.

1.3.3 Human Information Processing Hierarchy

The Artificial Intelligence (AI) thrust of this book obligates us to consider analytics in the way humans process information, and thereby allows us to implement AI systems for analytics more faithfully. Here we choose a human-processing hierarchy that resembles the DIKW hierarchy presented above. Rasmussen's well-known three-tier model of human information processing (Rasmussen, 1983 and 1986) is shown in FIGURE 1.6. The arch in Rasmussen's SRK (Skill, Rule, Knowledge) model represents the flow of information through the human decision-maker. The left side of the arch corresponds to stimulus processing, and the right side corresponds to motor processing. Processing is divided into three broad categories, corresponding to activities at three different levels of complexity.

Skill-Based Processing

At the lowest level is skill-based sensorimotor behavior, such as perceptual feature extraction and hand-eye coordination. This level represents the most automated, largely unconscious level of skilled performance (e.g., identification of market trends just by looking at the raw values of various indices).

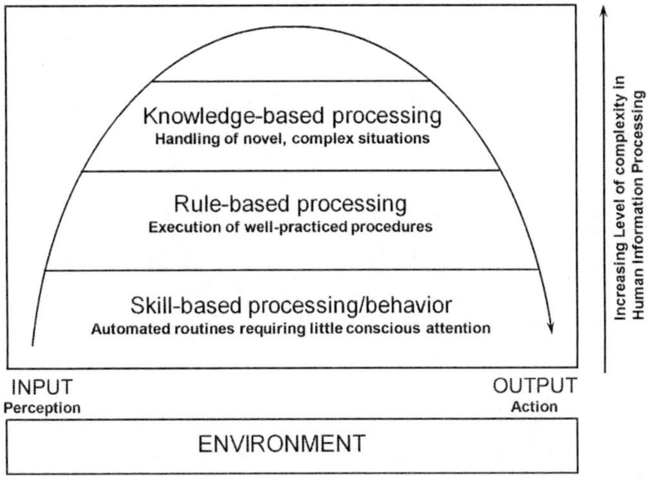

FIGURE 1.6 : Rasmussen's hierarchy of human information processing

Rule-Based Processing

At the next level is rule-based behavior, exemplified by procedural skills for well-practiced tasks such as the identification of a credit-card fraud transaction based on its purchase location, value, type of goods purchased, and other relevant information.

Knowledge-Based Processing

Knowledge-based behavior represents the most complex cognitive processing used to handle novel, complex situations where no routines or rules are available to be applied. Examples of this type of processing include the interpretation of unusual behavior by a competitor and the decision on whether or not to launch a product based on the quality, market completion, revenue potential, etc.

The Generic Error Modeling System (GEMS) (Reason, 1990), an extension of Rasmussen's approach, describes the competencies needed by workers to perform their roles in complex systems. GEMS outlines three major categories of errors: skill-based slips and lapses, rule-based mistakes, and knowledge-based mistakes. See Das and Grecu (2000) for an instantiation of the information processing hierarchy required to implement an agent that amplifies human perception and cognition.

1.4 ANALYTICS AND DATA FUSION

Data fusion is a "process dealing with the association, correlation, and combination of data and information from single and multiple sources to achieve refined position and identity estimates, and complete and timely assessments of situations and threats, and their significance (White, 1987)." Barring the terms such as "position," "identity," and "threat," which are typical of the defense-domain jargon in which the field originated, the rest of the processing concepts in the definition constitute analytics processes. High-level data fusion, a sub-field of data fusion, is defined as the "study of relationships among objects and events of interest within a dynamic environment (Das, 2008b)," and combines the descriptive and predictive analytics processes. The closeness of these two fields (the author views as "two sides of the same coin") motivates us to introduce some basic concepts of fusion, starting with the well-known Joint Directors of Laboratories (JDL) model (Hall and Llinas, 2001).

1.4.1 JDL Fusion Model

The most influential data fusion model to date is from the Joint Directors of Laboratories (JDL) and is shown in FIGURE 1.7. The so-called JDL functional model (White, 1988) was intended to facilitate communication among data fusion practitioners, rather than to serve as a complete architecture detailing various processes and their interactions.

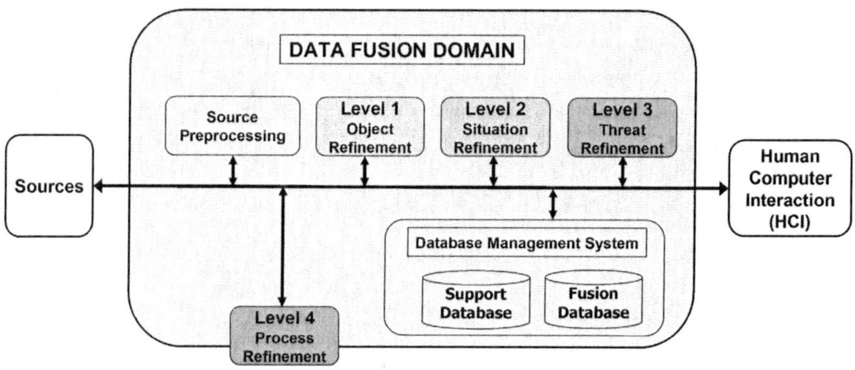

FIGURE 1.7 : JDL data fusion model (White, 1988)

Sources on the left of the figure include local and remote sensors accessible to the data fusion system, information from the reference system, and human input. The main task of Source Preprocessing involves analysis of individual sensor data to extract information or improve a signal-to-noise ratio, and preparation of data (such as spatiotemporal alignment) for subsequent fusion processing. The JDL model has the following four functional levels of fusion:

Level 1: Object Refinement

This level combines sensor data to obtain the most reliable and accurate tracking and estimation of an entity's position, velocity, attributes, and identity. Although this level is not considered part of the high-level fusion, entity-tracking is analogous to tracking a phenomenon, such as the price of a stock. In fact, we will make use of the Kalman Filter, which is a popular technique for entity-tracking, to track and predict a stock price.

Level 2: Situation Refinement

The Situation Refinement level develops a description of current relationships among entities and events in the context of their environment. This is analogous to descriptive analytics.

Level 3: Threat Refinement

This level projects the current situation into the future to draw inferences about enemy threats, friend and foe vulnerabilities, and opportunities for operations. This is analogous to predictive analytics.

Level 4: Process Refinement

Process Refinement monitors the overall data fusion process to assess and improve real-time system performance (it has been placed on the edge of the data fusion domain in FIGURE 1.7 due to its meta-level monitoring characteristics).

The Human Computer Interaction (HCI) block provides an interface to allow a human to interact with the fusion system. The Database Management System block provides management of data for fusion (sensor data, environmental information, models, estimations, etc).

The DIKW hierarchy bears some resemblance to the JDL data fusion model in the sense that both start from raw transactional data to yield knowledge at an increasing level of abstraction. Steinberg et al. (1998) revised and expanded the JDL model to broaden the functionality and related taxonomy beyond the original military focus. The distinction between Level 2 and Level 3 is often artificial. Models for Level 2 fusion are temporal in many cases, and thus both the current situation and its projection to the future come from a single temporal model. The definition of Level 2 fusion along the lines of Steinberg et al. (1998) is more appropriate: the "estimation and prediction of relations among entities, to include force structure and cross force relations, communications and perceptual influences, physical context, etc." The Level 2 fusion is also called Situation Assessment (SA), a term equally appropriate for business domains. Moreover, drawing inferences about enemy threats, friend and foe vulnerabilities, and opportunities for operations requires generations of Courses of Action (COAs). Here we take the hypotheses evaluation approach, where COAs are overall actions and their suitabilities need to be evaluated via some arguments of pros and cons and expected utility measures.

Llinas et al. (2004) discuss issues and functions considered to be important to any further generalization of the current fusion model. Their remarks and assertions include a discussion of quality control, reliability, and consistency in data fusion; the need for coprocessing of abductive, inductive, and deductive inferencing processes; and the case of distributed data fusion. These extensions, especially various types of inferencing, are mostly covered given our AI and ML thrusts. Blasch and Plano (2002, 2003) add Level 5 user refinement into the JDL model to support a user's trust, workload, attention, and situation awareness. Analytics analogous to Level 5 is not within the scope of this book.

1.4.2 OODA Loop

One of the first C4I (Command, Control, Communications, Computers, and Intelligence) architectures is the OODA (Observe-Orient-Decide-Act) Loop (2001), shown in FIGURE 1.8.

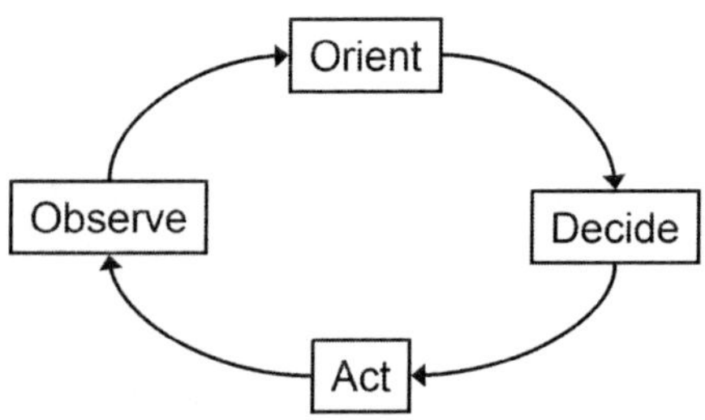

FIGURE 1.8 : Boyd's OODA loop

The OODA architecture was developed during the Korean War by Col. John Boyd, USAF (Ret), and refers to the abilities possessed by successful combat fighter pilots. "Observations" in OODA refers to scanning the environment and gathering information from it, "orientation" is the use of the information to form a mental image of the circumstances, "decision" involves considering options and selecting a subsequent course of action, and "action" refers to carrying out the conceived decision.

The Orient step in the OODA loop encapsulates both descriptive and predictive analytics, whereas the Decide step corresponds to prescriptive analytics. An example instantiation of the OODA loop in the business domain is as follows: 1) observation is declining revenue figures; 2) orientation is to identify causes for declining revenue and to fully understand the company's overall financial situation and other relevant factors; 3) decision could be to enhance a marketing campaign, upgrade products or introduce new products; and 4) action is the marketing campaign or new product launch. An action in the real world generates further observations such as the increased revenue or customer base as a result of the marketing campaign.

1.5 FURTHER READING

More on Rasmussen hierarchy can be found in (Rasmussen, 1983 & 1986). Llinas et al. (2004) is a good read on data fusion in general. Consult (Das, 2008b) for a detailed account of high-level fusion. Steinberg et al. (1998) and Llinas et al. (2004) are helpful in understanding deficiencies in the current JDL model and needed enhancements.

CHAPTER 2

Mathematical and Statistical Preliminaries

This chapter provides the background mathematical notations and concepts needed to understand the rest of the book. The topics discussed in this chapter include basic probability theory and statistics, fundamentals of linear algebra covering the notions of eigenvalues and eigenvectors, propositional and first-order mathematical logics for representing rules, graphs and trees for representing Bayesian networks and influence diagrams, notions of performance measurements for use in classifier algorithms, and a concise introduction to the theory of algorithmic complexity to analyze expected runtime performance of evidence propagation algorithms. Appendix A details our conventions for symbol usage.

2.1 STATISTICS AND PROBABILITY THEORY

Statistics and probability theory are two intimately related fields. Statistics is the study and analysis of empirical observations on variables known as *populations*. From a given population, we compute what we call "statistics" to be used to compute or estimate population parameters. For example, we can compute the parameters of mean, median, mode and standard deviation from empirical observations of the variable representing total daily rainfall. These parameters index the underlying probability density function of the population, such as the normal density function. A probability density can then be used to compute the probability of a future observation of rainfall, for example. So, loosely speaking, probability theory provides a mathematical foundation for statistics.

The understanding of the concept of probability is fundamental to the theory of probability. Probabilities are defined in terms of likely outcomes of random experiments. A repetitive process, observation, or operation that determines the results of any one of a number of possible outcomes is called a *random experiment.* An *event* is an outcome of a random experiment. The set of all possible outcomes of an experiment is called the *sample space* or *event space.*

Example

Random experiments and outcomes include: tossing a coin a hundred times to determine the number of heads, rolling a pair of dice a couple of hundred times to determine the number of times the sum of the upturned faces is 7, observing the weather throughout the month of March to determine the number of sunny mornings, and recording daily temperatures over a month to determine the number of hot days. Therefore, tossing a head, rolling a six and a three, a sunny morning, and a hot day are example events. The sets $\{head, tail\}$, $\{(1,1),(1,2),...,(6,6)\}$, $\{sunny, rain, snow\}$, and $\{t : t \in [0^{o}\mathrm{C}, 100^{o}\mathrm{C}]\}$ are, respectively, examples of sample spaces for these experiments.

A *probability* provides a quantitative description of the likely occurrence of a particular event. The probability of an event x, denoted as $p(x)$, is conventionally expressed on a scale from 0 to 1, inclusive.

Example

In the single die experiment, the probability of rolling a six is $1/6$. There are 36 possible combinations of numbers when two dice are rolled. The sample points for the two events x and y consisting of sums of 7 and 10 are, respectively, $x = \{(1,\ 6),(2,\ 5),(3,\ 4),(4,\ 3),(5,\ 2),(6,\ 1)\}$ and $y = \{(4,\ 6),(5,\ 5),(6,\ 4)\}$. Hence, we have $p(x) = 6/36$, $p(y) = 3/36$.

As defined above, an event consists of a single outcome in the sample space. Let us generalize this definition by calling it a *simple event* (or *elementary event* or *atomic event*), and by defining a *compound event* as an event that consists of multiple simple events. In general, an event is either a simple event or a compound event. Set theory can be used to represent various relationships among events. For example, if x and y are two events (which may be either simple or compound) in the sample space S then:

- $x \cup y$ means either x or y occurs (or both occur).
- $x \cap y$ (or xy) means both x and y occur.
- $x \subseteq y$ means if x occurs then so does y.
- $\bar{x}$ means event x does not occur (or equivalently, the complement of x occurs).
- Φ represents an impossible event.
- S is an event that is *certain* to occur.

Two events x and y are said to be *mutually exclusive* if $x \cap y = \Phi$. (The occurrence of both x and y is impossible, and therefore the two events are mutually exclusive.) On the other hand, two events x and y are said to be *independent* if $p(x \cap y) = p(x) \times p(y)$. As a result, when dealing with independent events x and y in an event space, the sets x and y must have a point (event) in common if both x and y have nonzero probabilities. Mutually exclusive, non-impossible events x and y cannot be independent as $x \cap y = \Phi$, so that $p(x \cap y) = 0$, but $p(x) \times p(y) \neq 0$.

Example

Suppose in the two-dice experiment we want to find the probability that the first die shows even and the second die shows odd. We consider the event x as the set of all sample points with the first element even and event y as the set of all sample points with the second element odd. Therefore, x is $\{(2,1), (2,2), ..., (6,6)\}$ and y is $\{(1,1), (2,1), ..., (6,5)\}$. Each of these two events has 18 points and the two sets have 9 points in common. Hence, $p(x) = 18/36$, $p(y) = 18/36$, and $p(x \cap y) = 9/36$. Therefore, $p(x \cap y) = p(x) \times p(y)$ holds. So by definition, x and y are independent.

There are three approaches that provide guidelines on how to assign probability values to events:

- The classical approach
- The relative frequency approach
- The axiomatic approach

In the *classical approach*, the probability of an event x in a finite sample space S is defined as follows:

$$p(x) = \frac{n(x)}{n(S)}$$

where $n(X)$ is the cardinality of the (finite) set X. Since $x \subseteq S$, $0 \leq p(x) \leq 1$ and $p(S) = 1$.

In the *relative frequency* approach, the probability of an event x is defined as the ratio of the number (say, n) of outcomes or occurrences of x to the total number (say, N) of trials in a random experiment. The choice of N depends on the particular experiment, but if an experiment is repeated at least N times without changing the experimental conditions, then the relative frequency of any particular event will (in theory) eventually settle down to some value. The probability of the event can then be defined as the limiting value of the relative frequency:

$$p(x) = \lim_{N \to \infty} \frac{n}{N}$$

where n is the number of occurrences of x and N is total number of trials.

For example, if a die is rolled many times then the relative frequency of the event "six" will settle down to a value of approximately $1/6$.

In the *axiomatic* approach, the concept of probability is axiomatized as follows:

- $p(x) \geq 0$, where x is an arbitrary event.
- $p(S) = 1$, where S is a certain event (i.e., the whole event space).
- $p(x \cup y) = p(x) + p(y)$, where x and y are mutually exclusive events.

Note that while the axiomatic approach merely provides guidance on how to assign values to probabilities, the classical and relative frequency approaches specify what values to assign.

A *Bayesian* or *subjective probability* describes an individual's personal judgment about how likely a particular event is to occur. It is not based on any precise computation, but is an assessment by a subject-matter expert based on his or her experience. We present Bayesian probability at length later in Chapter 4.

Now we turn to formally defining random variables and probability distributions, the concepts central to the development of probabilistic models for decision-making. A *random variable* is a function defined over an event space (that is, the domain of a random variable consists of random events from the sample space), and its value is determined by the outcome of an event. The *range* of a random variable is the set of values it can assume. A *discrete random variable* is a random variable whose range is finite or denumerable. The elements in the range (i.e., possible values) of a random variable are called its *states*.

Example

Consider the process of rolling a pair of dice, whose sample space is $\{(1,1), (1,2), ..., (6,6)\}$. Consider the random variable *Dice* defined over this sample space, where its values are determined by the sum of the upturned faces, that is, $Dice(i,j) = i + j$, for each sample point (i,j). For example, $Dice(2,3)$ is equal to 5. Therefore, *Dice* is discrete, with a range of $\{2, 3, 4, ..., 12\}$. Consider another random variable *Weather* defined over the sample space of the morning weather conditions in a particular month, where the current weather determines its value on a particular morning. The possible values of the discrete random variable *Weather* might be $\{sunny, rain, snow\}$. The domain $\{t : t \in [0^{O}\text{C}, 100^{O}\text{C}]\}$of the random variable *Temperature* is continuous, and the range could be kept the same as the domain. If the range is considered as, for example, $\{hot, warm, normal, cold, freezing\}$ then it becomes a discrete random variable.

When X is a random variable, $p(X)$ means the probability of an event that the variable X represents. Since an event is characterized by its outcome, we write $p(X)$ as $p(X = x)$, where x is an outcome. So we can say $p(Weather = sunny)$. Following are some important probability rules that follow from this definition, where X_i and Y_i are random variables, ***joint probability*** $p(X,Y)$ or $p(XY)$ is the probability that the two events X and Y are occurring together, and the ***conditional probability*** $p(X|Y)$ is the probability of X given Y.

Multiplication Rule

Rule: $p(X_0, X_1, ..., X_n) = p(X_0)\, p(X_1|X_0)\, p(X_2|X_0X_1) ...p(X_n|X_0X_1...X_{n-1})$, if $p(X_0, X_1, ..., X_n) > 0$.

Special Case: $p(X,Y) = p(X)\, p(Y|X)$.

Total Probability Rule

Rule: $p(X) = \sum_{i=1}^{n} p(X|Y_i)\, p(Y_i)$, given $p(Y_i) > 0$, for every i, and given $\sum_{i=1}^{n} p(Y_i) = 1$.

Special Case: $p(X) = p(X|Y)\, p(Y) + p\left(X|\overline{Y}\right) p\left(\overline{Y}\right)$, if $0 < p(Y) < 1$.

Marginalization Rule

Rule: $p(X) = \sum_{i=1}^{n} p(X, Y_i)$, given $p(Y_i) > 0$, for every i, and given $\sum_{i=1}^{n} p(Y_i) = 1$.

Special Case: $p(X) = p(X,Y) + p\left(X,\overline{Y}\right)$, if $0 < p(Y) < 1$.

Bayes' Rule

Rule: $p(Y_j|X) = \frac{p(X|Y_j)p(Y_j)}{\sum_{i=1}^{n} p(X|Y_i)p(Y_i)}$, if $p(X) > 0$ and $p(Y_i) > 0$, for every i, and $\sum_{i=1}^{n} p(Y_i) = 1$.

Special Case: $p(X|Y) = \frac{p(Y|X)p(X)}{p(Y)}$, if $p(X) > 0$and $p(Y) > 0$.

2.2 LINEAR ALGEBRA FUNDAMENTALS

We represent a vector-valued random variable X of length or dimension n as an $n \times 1$ matrix as follows:

$$X = \begin{bmatrix} X_1 \\ X_2 \\ \dots \\ X_n \end{bmatrix}$$

or its transpose $[X_1, X_2, ..., X_n]^T$ or $[X_1, X_2, ..., X_n]'$, where each X_i is a random variable. A value of a vector-valued random variable is a *vector* of dimension n and can be thought of as a point in the n-dimensional Euclidean space. A vector X of dimension n can be transformed to a vector Y of dimension m via a *matrix transformation* as

$$Y = AX$$

where A is an $m \times n$ matrix. A rotation transformation matrix rotates a vector.

Example

Consider the matrix

$$\begin{bmatrix} \cos(\theta) & -\sin(\theta) \\ \sin(\theta) & \cos(\theta) \end{bmatrix}$$

The unit axis vector $\begin{bmatrix} 1 & 0 \end{bmatrix}^T$ can be rotated by 30° by multiplying with the rotation matrix as follows:

$$\begin{bmatrix} \sqrt{3}/2 & -1/2 \\ 1/2 & \sqrt{3}/2 \end{bmatrix} \begin{bmatrix} 1 \\ 0 \end{bmatrix} = \begin{bmatrix} 0.866 \\ 0.5 \end{bmatrix}$$

Rotation matrices are orthonormal, i.e., $AA^T = I$, where I is the identity matrix. Usually, the direction and the magnitude of a vector changes upon a transformation except in some special cases. If a transformation via an $n \times n$ square matrix A on a vector X takes the following form

$$AX = \lambda X$$

where λ is a scalar value, then X is an *eigenvector* of A and λ is the associated *eigenvalue*.

Example

The matrix

$$A = \begin{bmatrix} 2 & 1 \\ 4 & 3 \end{bmatrix}$$

has the eigenvectors

$$X = \begin{bmatrix} -0.539 \\ 0.842 \end{bmatrix}$$

with eigenvalue $\lambda_1 = 0.438$, and

$$X' = \begin{bmatrix} -0.364 \\ -0.932 \end{bmatrix}$$

with eigenvalue $\lambda_2 = 4.562$ since $AX = \lambda_1 X$ and $AX' = \lambda_2 X'$.

The *trace* of a matrix A is equal to the sum of its diagonal elements, which is also equal to the sum of its eigenvalues. For example, the trace of the matrix A in the above example is 5, which is equal to $\lambda_1 + \lambda_2$. Any scalar multiple of an eigenvector is also an eigenvector. Hence eigenvectors are only unique up to scalar multiplications. Eigenvectors of a matrix are linearly independent, i.e., one eigenvector cannot be expressed as a linear combination of the rest. The *rank* of a matrix is the number of linearly independent column vectors of the matrix which are equal to the number of non-zero eigenvalues. A square $n \times n$ matrix is *singular* if its rank is less than n.

An *orthogonal* matrix is a square matrix and its column vectors are an *orthonormal basis*, that is, each column has length one and columns are linearly independent. The rows of an orthogonal matrix are also an orthonormal basis. Hence for an orthogonal matrix A, $AA^T = A^T A = I$. A real, symmetric square matrix has real eigenvalues, with eigenvectors forming an orthonormal basis. A *positive semi-definite* matrix is such a matrix with all non-negative eigenvalues. Positive semi-definite matrices include correlation, covariance, and cross-product matrices.

Because eigenvectors corresponding to different eigenvalues are orthogonal to each other, it is possible to store all of the eigenvectors of a matrix A in an orthogonal matrix, say E. Thus

$$AE = E\Lambda$$

where Λ is the diagonal matrix of the eigenvalues of A. If A is positive semi-definite then we have its *eigenvalue decomposition*

$$A = E\Lambda E^T$$

where $EE^T = I$ for normalized eigenvectors else EE^T is a diagonal matrix.

Example

The positive-definite matrix

$$A = \begin{bmatrix} 2 & 1 & 1 \\ 1 & 3 & 2 \\ 1 & 2 & 4 \end{bmatrix}$$

can be decomposed as

$$
\begin{aligned}
A &= E\Lambda E^T \\
&= \begin{bmatrix} -0.328 & 0.737 & 0.591 \\ -0.591 & 0.328 & -0.737 \\ -0.737 & -0.591 & 0.328 \end{bmatrix} \begin{bmatrix} 6.049 & 0 & 0 \\ 0 & 1.643 & 0 \\ 0 & 0 & 1.308 \end{bmatrix} \\
&\quad \begin{bmatrix} -0.328 & -0.591 & -0.737 \\ 0.737 & 0.328 & -0.591 \\ 0.591 & -0.737 & 0.328 \end{bmatrix}
\end{aligned}
$$

and

$$
\begin{bmatrix} -0.328 & 0.737 & 0.591 \\ -0.591 & 0.328 & -0.737 \\ -0.737 & -0.591 & 0.328 \end{bmatrix} \begin{bmatrix} -0.328 & -0.591 & -0.737 \\ 0.737 & 0.328 & -0.591 \\ 0.591 & -0.737 & 0.328 \end{bmatrix} = \begin{bmatrix} 1 & 0 & 0 \\ 0 & 1 & 0 \\ 0 & 0 & 1 \end{bmatrix}
$$

More generally, the ***singular value decomposition*** (SVD) transforms any $m \times n \quad (m \geq n)$ matrix A to the product of three matrices:

$$
A = UDV^T
$$

where U is an $m \times n$ orthonormal (has orthogonal, unit length columns), V is an $n \times n$ orthonormal, and D is an $n \times n$ diagonal whose elements $d_1, ..., d_n$ are called the singular values of A satisfying $d_1 \geq ... \geq d_n \geq 0$.

Example

The matrix

$$
A = \begin{bmatrix} 1 & 2 \\ 3 & 4 \\ 5 & 6 \end{bmatrix}
$$

is decomposed as

$$
A = UDV^T = \begin{bmatrix} 0.230 & 0.883 \\ 0.525 & 0.241 \\ 0.820 & -0.402 \end{bmatrix} \begin{bmatrix} 9.526 & 0 \\ 0 & 0.514 \end{bmatrix} \begin{bmatrix} 0.620 & 0.785 \\ -0.785 & 0.620 \end{bmatrix}
$$

where

$$
U^T U = \begin{bmatrix} 0.230 & 0.525 & 0.820 \\ 0.883 & 0.241 & -0.402 \end{bmatrix} \begin{bmatrix} 0.230 & 0.883 \\ 0.525 & 0.241 \\ 0.820 & -0.402 \end{bmatrix} = \begin{bmatrix} 1 & 0 \\ 0 & 1 \end{bmatrix}
$$

$$
VV^T = \begin{bmatrix} 0.620 & 0.785 \\ -0.785 & 0.620 \end{bmatrix} \begin{bmatrix} 0.620 & -0.785 \\ 0.785 & 0.620 \end{bmatrix} = \begin{bmatrix} 1 & 0 \\ 0 & 1 \end{bmatrix}
$$

For symmetric positive definite matrices, the eigenvalue decomposition and the SVD are equal. *Principal component analysis* (PCA) converts a set of measurements of possibly correlated variables into a set of values of linearly uncorrelated variables called principal components. PCA can be done by eigenvalue decomposition or by SVD as defined above.

2.3 MATHEMATICAL LOGIC

This section presents a very brief introduction to the classical logics for developing approaches to logic-based (more specifically, rule-based) analytics. We start with classical propositional logic and then move to first-order logic. We omit detailed explanations for the sake of relevance and space. References provided at the end of the chapter enable the reader to find further details, such as the model theoretic semantics of the logics, the soundness and completeness theorems, resolution theorem-proving, logic programming, and the logic programming language Prolog.

Mathematical logic is a study of valid arguments. Arguments are represented in logical syntaxes such as propositional and first-order. A *proposition* is a declarative sentence that is either *true* or *false*, but not both. Examples of propositions related to marketing a product are:

Sale is high
Demand is heavy

Propositions will be symbolized as, for example, $P, Q, R, ...$, and are called atoms or atomic formulae. Compound propositions are formed by modifying with the word "not" or by connecting sentences via the words/phrases "and," "or," "if ... then," and "if and only if." These five words/phrases are called logical connectives and are usually symbolized as shown in TABLE 2.1.

TABLE 2.1: : Standard logical connectives

Connective	Symbol
not	$\neg$
and	$\wedge$
or	$\vee$
if ... then	$\rightarrow$
if and only if	$\leftrightarrow$

Example

Examples of compound propositions are as follows:

If demand for a product is heavy then the sale is high
Demand is not heavy

Competition is stiff or demand is heavy

The above composite propositions are symbolized respectively in the *propositional language* as:

$$P \to Q$$
$$\neg P$$
$$R \vee P$$

where:

P stands for "Demand is heavy"
Q stands for "Sale is high"
R stands for "Competition is stiff"

Each of these compound propositions is called a *Well-Formed Formula* (WFF) or *formula* as part of the propositional language, and the symbols occurring in the formulae are part of the propositional alphabet. Formal definitions of these terms are given below.
A *propositional alphabet* consists of the following:

- Two parentheses "(" and ")"
- A set of propositional variables $P, Q, R, \ldots$ as atoms
- A set of logical connectives $\neg, \wedge, \vee, \to$, and $\leftrightarrow$

Well-Formed Formulae or *formulae* in propositional logic are defined as follows:

- An atomic formula is a formula, for example, $P, Q, R, \ldots$, as mentioned previously.
- If F is a formula, then $(\neg F)$ is a formula.
- If F and G are formulae, then $(F \wedge G)$, $(F \vee G)$, $(F \to G)$, and $(F \leftrightarrow G)$ are formulae.

Given a propositional alphabet, the *propositional language* comprises the set of all formulae constructed from the symbols of that alphabet. An expression is a formula only if it can be shown to be a formula by the above three conditions. A formula of the form $(\neg F)$ is called the *negation* of the formula F. Formulae of the forms $(F \wedge G)$ and $(F \vee G)$ are called the *conjunction* and *disjunction*, respectively, of the formulae F and G. A formula of the form $(F \to G)$ is called a *conditional* formula; F is called the *antecedent* and G is called the *consequent*. A formula of the form $(F \leftrightarrow G)$ is called a *biconditional* formula. We will see later that disjunctions are one way that uncertain knowledge can be represented.

The following conventions are used to avoid using parentheses in a formula.

The connective $\neg$ is applied to the smallest formula following it, then $\wedge$ is to connect the smallest formulae surrounding it, and so on for the rest of the connectives $\vee$, $\rightarrow$, and $\leftrightarrow$ in that order.

Example

If parentheses are restored in the formula

$$\neg P \wedge Q \rightarrow R \leftrightarrow Q \vee R \wedge P$$

then the resulting formula would be

$$((((\neg P) \wedge Q) \rightarrow R) \leftrightarrow (Q \vee (R \wedge P)))$$

We are especially interested in assessing the "truth" of a formula as a function of the "truth" of its atoms. To do this, we first assign a ***truth value*** to each atom; that is, we assign "true" (denoted as $\top$) or "false" (denoted as $\perp$) to the symbolized atomic propositions that occur in a formula. Then we compute the truth value of the formula using special rules to handle the logical connectives. So for every assignment of truth values $\top$ or $\perp$ to the symbolized atomic propositions that occur in a formula, there corresponds a truth value for the formula. This can be determined using the ***truth table*** of the formula.

Example

TABLE 2.2 is the combined truth table for the fundamental formulae $\neg P$, $P \wedge Q$, $P \vee Q$, $P \rightarrow Q$, and $P \leftrightarrow Q$; it shows how to compute truth values for a formula containing these logical connectives. Using this basic truth table, the truth table for any formula can then be constructed; for example, the truth table for $(\neg P \leftrightarrow Q) \rightarrow (P \wedge (Q \vee R))$ is displayed in TABLE 2.3.

TABLE 2.2: : Truth table in propositional logic

P	Q	$\neg P$	$P \wedge Q$	$P \vee Q$	$P \rightarrow Q$	$P \leftrightarrow Q$
$\top$	$\top$	$\perp$	$\top$	$\top$	$\top$	$\top$
$\top$	$\perp$	$\perp$	$\perp$	$\top$	$\perp$	$\perp$
$\perp$	$\top$	$\top$	$\perp$	$\top$	$\top$	$\perp$
$\perp$	$\perp$	$\top$	$\perp$	$\perp$	$\top$	$\top$

TABLE 2.3: : Truth table for $(\neg P \leftrightarrow Q) \rightarrow (P \wedge (Q \vee R))$

P	Q	R	$\neg P$	$\neg P \leftrightarrow Q$	$Q \vee R$	$P \wedge (Q \vee R)$	$(\neg P \leftrightarrow Q) \rightarrow (P \wedge (Q \vee R))$
$\top$	$\top$	$\top$	$\bot$	$\bot$	$\top$	$\top$	$\top$
$\top$	$\top$	$\bot$	$\bot$	$\bot$	$\top$	$\top$	$\top$
$\top$	$\bot$	$\top$	$\bot$	$\top$	$\top$	$\top$	$\top$
$\top$	$\bot$	$\bot$	$\bot$	$\top$	$\bot$	$\bot$	$\bot$
$\bot$	$\top$	$\top$	$\top$	$\top$	$\top$	$\bot$	$\bot$
$\bot$	$\top$	$\bot$	$\top$	$\top$	$\top$	$\bot$	$\bot$
$\bot$	$\bot$	$\top$	$\top$	$\bot$	$\top$	$\bot$	$\top$
$\bot$	$\bot$	$\bot$	$\top$	$\bot$	$\bot$	$\bot$	$\top$

Given a formula F, suppose $P_1, P_2, ..., P_n$ are all atomic formulae occurring in F. Then an *interpretation* of F is an assignment of truth values to $P_1, P_2, ..., P_n$, where no P_i is assigned both $\top$ and $\bot$. Hence every row in a truth table for a formula F is an interpretation of F.

A formula F is a *tautology* or is *valid* (denoted as $\models F$) if its value is $\top$ under all possible interpretations of F.

Example

The formula $P \rightarrow (P \vee Q)$ is a tautology according to TABLE 2.4.

TABLE 2.4: : A tautology

P	Q	$P \vee Q$	$P \rightarrow (P \vee Q)$
$\top$	$\top$	$\top$	$\top$
$\top$	$\bot$	$\top$	$\top$
$\bot$	$\top$	$\top$	$\top$
$\bot$	$\bot$	$\bot$	$\top$

A formula F is *false* (or *inconsistent* or a *contradiction*) if and only if its value is $\bot$ under all possible interpretations.

Example

The formula $P \vee Q \leftrightarrow \neg P \wedge \neg Q$ is false by TABLE 2.5.

TABLE 2.5: : A contradiction

P	Q	$\neg P$	$\neg Q$	$P \vee Q$	$\neg P \wedge \neg Q$	$P \vee Q \leftrightarrow \neg P \wedge \neg Q$
$\top$	$\top$	$\bot$	$\bot$	$\top$	$\bot$	$\bot$
$\top$	$\bot$	$\bot$	$\top$	$\top$	$\bot$	$\bot$
$\bot$	$\top$	$\top$	$\bot$	$\top$	$\bot$	$\bot$
$\bot$	$\bot$	$\top$	$\top$	$\bot$	$\top$	$\bot$

There are various kinds of arguments that cannot be conveniently stated in the language of propositional logic. Consider the following argument as an example:

The demand for the newly launched product is heavy
Heavy demand for every product makes its sale volume high
Therefore, the sale volume of the newly launched product is high

The above argument is a valid argument. However, if the three premises are symbolized as P, Q, and R, respectively, it is not possible to prove R from P and Q within the framework of propositional logic, unless the second premise "Heavy demand for every product makes its sale volume high" is instantiated specifically for the newly launched product. The correctness of the above argument relies upon the meaning of the expression "every," which has not been considered in the propositional logic. However, first-order logic handles this kind of argument, and also extends the propositional logic by incorporating more logical notations, such as terms, predicates, and quantifiers. The set of symbols (the *first-order alphabet*) in the case of first-order logic is defined as follows:

- Delimiter: , (comma)
- Parentheses: (,)
- Primitive connectives: $\neg$ (negation), $\rightarrow$ (implication)
- Universal quantifier: $\forall$ (for all)
- Individual variables: $x, y, z, x_1, y_1, z_1, ...$
- Individual constants: $a, b, c, a_1, b_1, c_1, ...$
- For each natural number n, n-ary predicate symbols: $P, Q, R, P_1, Q_1, R_1, ...$
- For each natural number n, n-ary function symbols: $f, g, h, f_1, g_1, h_1, ...$

Terms are expressions which are defined recursively as follows:

- A variable or an individual constant is a term.

- If f is an n-ary function symbol and $t_1, t_2, ..., t_n$ are terms then $f(t_1, t_2, ..., t_n)$ is a term.
- An expression is a term if it can be shown to be so only on the basis of the above two conditions.

A *predicate* is a function which evaluates to either true or false, or a statement about a relation that may be true or false. If P is an n-ary predicate symbol and $t_1, t_2, ..., t_n$ are terms, then $P(t_1, t_2, ..., t_n)$ is an *atomic formula* (or *atom* or *positive literal*). A *negative literal* is a formula of the form $\neg A$, where A is an atom. A *literal* is either positive or negative. Based on these primitive notions, the *Well-Formed Formulae* (WFFs) or *formulae* of first-order logic are recursively defined as follows:

- Every atomic formula is a formula.
- If F is a formula then $\neg F$ is a formula.
- If F is a formula and x is a variable then $\forall x(F)$ is a formula.
- If F and G are formulae then $F \rightarrow G$ is a formula.
- An expression is a formula only if it can be generated by the above four conditions.

For convenience and improved readability of formulae, the other logical connectives, $\wedge$, $\vee$, and $\leftrightarrow$, are also introduced and defined in terms of $\neg$ and $\rightarrow$ just as in the case of propositional logic. Additionally, an *existential quantifier*, denoted as $\exists$, is introduced and defined as follows:

$$\exists x(F) \equiv \neg(\forall x(\neg F))$$

In the formulae $\exists x(F)$ and $\forall x(G)$, F and G are called the *scope* of the quantifiers $\exists x$ and $\forall x$ respectively. As in the case of propositional calculus, the same convention is made about the omission of parentheses in a formula. A formula in propositional logic can be considered as a formula in first-order logic (where the atoms are 0-ary predicates, and there are no variables, functions, or quantifiers). Hence all the results established so far in connection with propositional logic are also applicable to the set of all quantifier- and variable-free formulae in first-order logic. Each ground atomic formula (no occurrence of variables) occurring in this set is considered as a propositional symbol.

Given a first-order alphabet, the *first-order language* comprises the set of all formulae constructed from the symbols of the alphabet. Using the first-order language, a symbolization of the first two premises of the argument presented in the beginning of this subsection is as follows:

$$\begin{array}{l} HeavyDemand\,('newly\,launched\,product') \\ \forall x\,(HeavyDemand\,(x) \rightarrow Sale\,(x, high)) \\ Sale\,('newly\,launched\,product', high) \end{array}$$

where *HeavyDemand* and *Sale* are unary and binary predicate symbols respectively, and *'newly launched product'* and *high* are constants. The representation of demand for a product via the unary predicate *HeavyDemand*, as opposed to a binary predicate such as *Demand*, is the matter of modeling style and requirements dictated by the application at hand. This symbolization is within the framework of *first-order logic*. An axiomatic deduction or inferencing of the conclusion of the argument appears as follows:

Step 1: $\forall x\,(HeavyDeamnd\,(x) \rightarrow Sale\,(x, high))$, Given Premise
Step 2: $HeavyDemand\,('newly\,launched\,product')$, Given Premise
Step 3: $HeavyDemand\,('newly\,launched\,product') \rightarrow$
$Sale\,('newly\,launched\,product', high)$, Particularization of Step 1
Step 4: $Sale\,('newly\,launched\,product', high)$,
Modus Ponens on Steps 2 & 3.

The premises in steps 1 and 2 are considered *proper axioms*. The above deduction is a *proof* of the conclusion $Sale\,('newly\,launched\,product', high)$ and therefore is a *theorem* that follows from the first-order system with the two proper axioms. Step 3 is derived from step 1 by particularization of the first premise. If the first premise is true for all products, then it is also true for the newly launched product. Step 4 is arrived at by the application of Modus Ponens (i.e., B is derived from A and $A \rightarrow B$). These steps demonstrate the basic *axiomatic* theorem-proving approach.

A procedure for determining whether or not a formula is a theorem of a particular theory K is called a *theorem proving procedure* or *proof procedure* for the theory K. Theorem proving procedures deal with formulae in standard forms, for example, prenex normal form, Skolem conjunctive normal form, and clausal form. This section provides tools for obtaining these forms from given formulae.

A formula is said to be in *prenex normal form* if it is of the form

$$Q_1 x_1 Q_2 x_2 ... Q_n x_n B$$

where each Q_i is either $\forall$ or $\exists$, and the formula B is quantifier-free. The formula B is called the *matrix*. A prenex normal form formula is said to be in *Skolem conjunctive normal form* if it has the form

$$\forall x_1 \forall x_2 ... \forall x_n B$$

where the matrix B is in conjunctive normal form, that is, B is a conjunction of a disjunction of literals. Such a Skolem conjunctive normal form formula is said to be a *clause* if it has the form

$$\forall x_1 \forall x_2 ... \forall x_n \,(L_1 \vee L_2 \vee ... \vee L_m)$$

where each L_i is a literal and $x_1, x_2, ..., x_n$ are the variables of the disjunction $L_1 \vee L_2 \vee ... \vee L_m$. A formula is said to be in *clausal form* if it is a clause.

For the sake of convenience, a clause is rewritten as the disjunction $L_1 \vee L_2 \vee ... \vee L_m$ of literals without its quantifiers or as the set $\{L_1, L_2, ..., L_m\}$ of literals. Thus when a disjunction $L_1 \vee L_2 \vee ... \vee L_m$ or a set $\{L_1, L_2, ..., L_m\}$ is given as a clause C, where each L_i is a literal, then C is regarded as being of the form $\forall x_1 \forall x_2 ... \forall x_n (L_1 \vee L_2 \vee ... \vee L_m)$, where $x_1, x_2, ..., x_n$ are all the variables occurring in all the L_is. The clausal form of $\forall x (HeavyDemand(x) \rightarrow Sale(x, High))$ is $\neg HeavyDemand(x) \vee Sale(x, High)$.

Every arbitrary first-order formula F can be transformed to its equivalent formula G in Skolem conjunctive normal form by applying the appropriate transformation steps. For example, the Skolem conjunctive normal form of the formula

$$\forall x (\neg R(x) \rightarrow P(a) \wedge \neg \exists z \neg Q(z, a)) \wedge \forall x (P(x) \rightarrow \exists y Q(y, x))$$

is

$$\forall x \forall z \forall x_1 ((R(x) \vee P(a)) \wedge (R(x) \vee Q(z, a)) \wedge (\neg P(x_1) \vee Q(f(x_1), x_1)))$$

where each conjunct in

$$\{R(x) \vee P(a), R(x) \vee Q(z, a), \neg P(x_1) \vee Q(f(x_1), x_1)\}$$

is a clause or in clausal form.

2.4 GRAPHS AND TREES

The fundamental modeling tools known as graphs and trees are introduced in this section. Graphs and trees are most often presented graphically (hence their names) as in the examples below; we give their formal nongraphical definitions here, as this background is useful for issues such as theoretical discussions and algorithm development.

A *simple graph* G is a pair $\langle \mathbf{V}, \mathbf{E} \rangle$, where $\mathbf{V}$ is a nonempty set of elements called *vertices* (or *nodes*), and $\mathbf{E}$ is a set of unordered pairs of distinct elements of $\mathbf{V}$ called *edges*. Edges are denoted as $N_i N_j$, where $N_i, N_j \in \mathbf{V}$. The definition of a *directed graph* (or *digraph*) is given in the same way as a graph except that the set $\mathbf{E}$ is a set of ordered pairs ($N_i N_j \neq N_j N_i$) of elements of $\mathbf{V}$ called *directed edges*. A simple graph is said to have been *obtained* from a directed graph by removing the direction of each of its edges.

A *path* (of length m) in a simple graph $\langle \mathbf{V}, \mathbf{E} \rangle$ is a finite sequence of edges of the form

$$N_0 N_1, N_1 N_2, ..., N_{m-1} N_m$$

where $N_i N_{i+1} \in \mathbf{E}$ for each term in the sequence, and where the $N_i \in \mathbf{V}$ are distinct vertices (except possibly $N_0 = N_m$). Informally, a path consists of a sequence of "hops" along edges of the graph to distinct vertices. The sequence above can be written in abbreviated form as

$$N_0 - N_1 - N_2 - ... - N_{m-1} - N_m$$

Therefore, if $N_0 - N_1 - ... - N_m$ is a path in a simple graph then $N_m - N_{m-1} - ... - N_0$ is also a path in the graph. Similarly, a *path* (of length m) in a directed graph $\langle \mathbf{V}, \mathbf{E} \rangle$ is a finite sequence of directed edges of the form

$$N_0 \to N_1 \to N_2 \to ... \to N_{m-1} \to N_m$$

where each ordered pair $N_i N_{i+1} \in \mathbf{E}$ in the sequence is understood to be a directed edge of the digraph.

Two nodes are *connected* if there is a path between them. A *cycle* (of length $m+1$) in a simple graph $\langle \mathbf{V}, \mathbf{E} \rangle$ is a finite sequence of edges of the form $N_0 - N_1 - N_2 - ... - N_m - N_0$, where $m \geq 1$. A *cycle* (of length $m+1$) in a directed graph $\langle \mathbf{V}, \mathbf{E} \rangle$ is a finite sequence of edges of the form $N_0 \to N_1 \to N_2 \to ... \to N_m \to N_0$. Thus, if $N_0 = N_m$ in a path then we return to our starting point, and the path is called a *cycle* (or directed cycle in the case of a digraph).

Example

The graph on the left side of FIGURE 2.1 represents a simple graph $\langle \mathbf{V}, \mathbf{E} \rangle$, where $\mathbf{V} = \{N_1, N_2, N_3, N_4, N_5\}$ and $\mathbf{E} = \{N_1N_2, N_1N_3, N_2N_4, N_3N_4, N_3N_5\}$. Since each edge is an unordered pair of elements, $N_iN_j = N_jN_i$, for all i, j. An example path of length 3 in this simple graph is $N_1 - N_2 - N_4 - N_3$. An example path of length 4 in this simple graph is $N_1 - N_2 - N_4 - N_3 - N_1$.

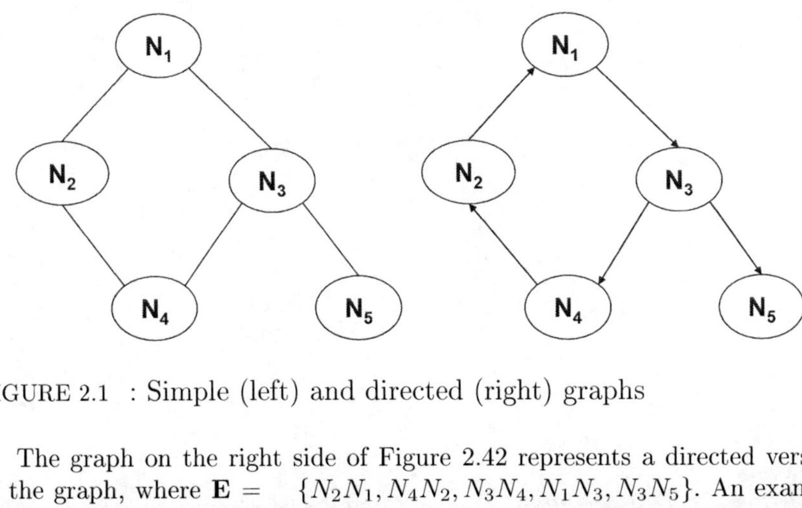

FIGURE 2.1 : Simple (left) and directed (right) graphs

The graph on the right side of Figure 2.42 represents a directed version of the graph, where $\mathbf{E} = \{N_2N_1, N_4N_2, N_3N_4, N_1N_3, N_3N_5\}$. An example path of length 3 in this directed graph is $N_1 \to N_3 \to N_4 \to N_2$. An example path of length 4 in this directed graph is $N_1 \to N_3 \to N_4 \to N_2 \to N_1$.

A simple graph is said to be *acyclic* if it has no cycles. A directed graph is said to be *acyclic* (or a *directed acyclic graph* or simply a DAG) if it has no cycles. Neither of the simple and directed graphs in FIGURE 2.1 is acyclic. Examples of simple and directed acyclic graphs are shown in FIGURE 2.2.

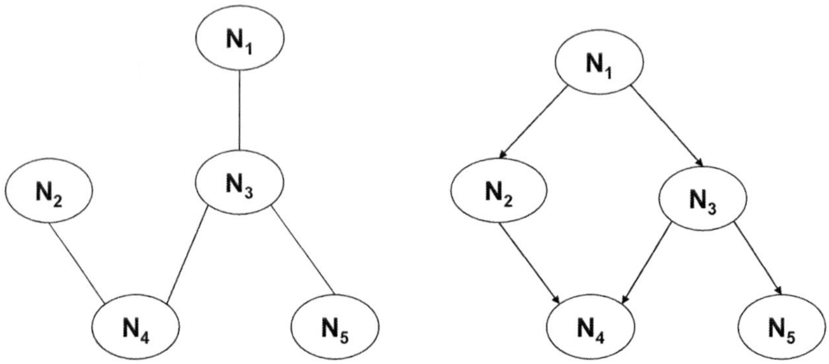

FIGURE 2.2 : Simple (left) and directed (right) acyclic graphs

A simple graph is a *polytree* if and only if any two vertices of the graph are connected by exactly one path. A directed graph is a *polytree* if and only if its underlying simple graph is a polytree. Example polytrees are shown in FIGURE 2.3.

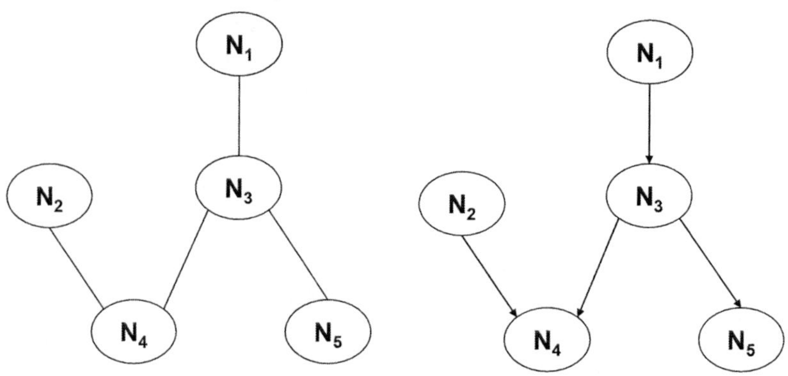

FIGURE 2.3 : Simple (left) and directed (right) polytrees

Suppose $N_0 \to N_1 \to N_2 \to ... \to N_{m-1} \to N_m$ is a path of a directed graph. The vertices occurring in this path are described in genealogical terms as follows:

- N_{i+1} is a *child* of N_i, for $0 \le i < m$
- N_{i-1} is a *parent* of N_i, for $0 < i \le m$

- N_i is an *ancestor* of N_j, for $0 \leq i < j \leq m$
- N_j is a *descendant* of N_i, for $0 \leq i < j \leq m$

A *leaf* of a directed polytree is a node without any children in any path of the tree containing the node. A *root* of a directed tree is a node without any parent in any path of the tree containing the node.

Example

The graph on the left side of FIGURE 2.3 is a simple polytree and the graph on the right side of FIGURE 2.3 is a directed polytree. Consider the directed polytree in the figure: N_3 is the only child of N_1; N_4 and N_5 are the children of N_3; N_2 and N_3 are the parents of N_4; and N_3 is a parent of N_4 and N_5. N_3, N_4, and N_5 are the descendants of N_1; N_1 and N_3 are the ancestors of N_4 and N_5; N_1 and N_2 are the root nodes; and N_4 and N_5 are the leaf nodes.

A directed graph is a *tree* if it is a polytree with only one root node. The *level* of a vertex in such a tree is the number of edges in the path between the vertex and the root. The *depth* of such tree is the maximum level of the vertices in the tree. The level of the root in a tree is 0. Example trees are shown in FIGURE 2.4.

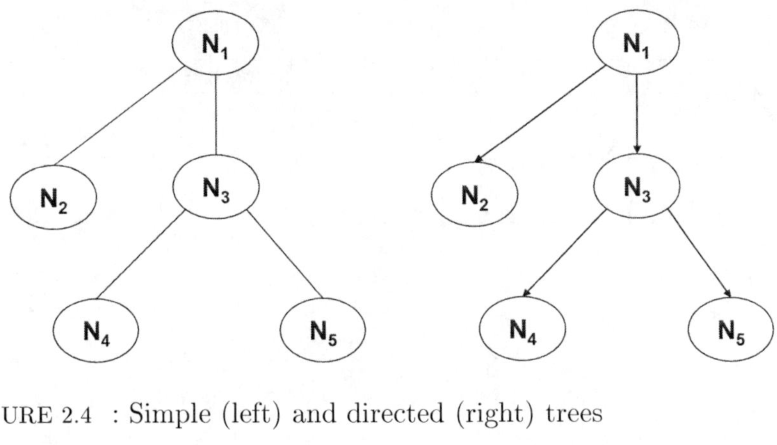

FIGURE 2.4 : Simple (left) and directed (right) trees

The root and leaf nodes of a simple polytree are not well defined, as its edges are undirected. For example, the node N_4 in the simple polytree of FIGURE 2.3 can be taken as a root node as well as a leaf node. To resolve this kind of ambiguity, we can designate a set of such vertices as root nodes and convert a simple polytree into a *rooted tree*. For example, the nodes N_1 and N_2 in the simple polytree of FIGURE 2.3 can be designated as roots. Unless otherwise stated, each reference in this book to the term "tree" will be implicitly regarded as "rooted tree."

Example

The graph on the left side of FIGURE 2.4 is a simple tree and on the right is a directed tree. Vertex N_1 is the root node of the directed tree, whereas the vertex N_1 has been designated as the root of the simple tree. The levels of the vertices N_1, N_2, N_3, N_4, and N_5 are 0, 1, 1, 2, and 2 respectively. Therefore the depth of each of these two trees is 2.

2.5 MEASURES OF PERFORMANCE

In a supervised learning system for classification, a training set of examples or instances with labels are given, along with a test set of examples whose labels are unknown to the system. The task of the classification system is to make predictions of class labels for newly arrived instances, and the test examples are used to evaluate its performance. A *confusion matrix* is a square matrix that contains information about actual and predicted classifications of the test data done by a classification system. Performance of the classification systems is then evaluated using the data in the matrix. The size of the confusion matrix is as many as the number of classes. TABLE 2.6 shows the confusion matrix for a two-class classifier (i.e., a classifier with two classes called Positive and Negative).

TABLE 2.6: : Actual and predicted classifications in a two-class classifier

	Positive	**Negative**
Positive	True Positive (TP) (Hit)	False Positive (FP) (False Alarm or Type I Error)
Negative	False Negative(FN) (Miss or Type II Error)	True Negative (TN) (Correct Rejection)

- True Positive (TP) (or Hit) is the number of test instances that are labeled as positive and are classified as positive by the classifier.
- False Positive (FP) (or False Alarm or Type I Error) is the number of negative instances that are classified as positive.
- False Negative (FN) (or Miss or Type II Error) is the number of positive instances that are classified as negative.
- True Negative (TN) (or Correct Rejection) is the number of negative instances that are classified as negative.

The total of the four entries, $TP + TN + FP + FN = n$, is the number of test examples. Many different summary statistics can be computed from these entries depending on the application.

In the domain of medical diagnosis, for example, *sensitivity* is a measure of how likely it is for a test to pick up the presence of a disease in a person who has it. *Specificity* is a measure of how likely that the test says a person does not have the disease when in fact the person is disease-free. Thus,

$$Sensitivity = \frac{TP}{TP+FN}$$
$$Specificity = \frac{TN}{FP+TN}$$

A *False Positive Rate* measures how likely it is for a test to pick up the presence of a disease in a person who is free of the disease. A *False Negative Rate* measures how likely it is for a test to miss the presence of a disease in a person who has the disease. Thus we have the following:

$$False\,Positive\,Rate = \frac{FP}{FP+TN}$$
$$False\,Negative\,Rate = \frac{FN}{TP+FN}$$

In the domain of information retrieval, for example, *precision* is the fraction of retrieved instances that are relevant, while *recall* is the fraction of relevant instances that are retrieved. Thus,

$$Precision = \frac{TP}{TP+FP}$$
$$Recall = \frac{TP}{TP+FN}$$

The *F-score* can be used as a single measure of performance of the test:

$$F = 2 \times \frac{Precision \times Recall}{Precision + Recall}$$

A Receiver Operator Characteristic (ROC) curve is a plot with the FP rate on the x-axis and the TP rate on the y-axis. The point (0, 1) is the perfect classifier as it classifies all positive cases and negative cases correctly. Usually a classifier has a parameter that can be adjusted to increase TP at the cost of an increased FP or decrease FP at the cost of a decrease in TP. Each parameter setting provides an (FP, TP) pair, and a series of such pairs can be used to plot an ROC curve.

2.6 ALGORITHMIC COMPLEXITY

An algorithm is a program that is guaranteed to give a correct answer to a problem within a certain time. We say an algorithm runs in *polynomial time* when there is a polynomial

$$p(x) = a_0 + a_1x + a_2x^2 + ... + a_kx^k$$

such that the time taken to run the algorithm is less than or equal to $p(x)$, where x is the "input length" (essentially, the amount of data needed to describe an instance of the problem), and $a_0, a_1, a_2, ..., a_k$ are nonnegative integers. Formally, if an algorithm runs in polynomial time, then we say that the algorithm complexity (or simply, the algorithm) is "*of order* x^k" or $O(x^k)$, where k is the highest power in $p(x)$ above. This theory of computational complexity started with Cook's paper (Cook, 1971), and its close relationship to combinatorial optimization can be found in (Karp, 1972).

Relationships among complexity classes are shown in FIGURE 2.5. A problem for which an algorithm of order x^k exists is said to be in the *polynomial class* or P *class*. Unfortunately, time-complexity functions are not always bounded this way; for example, some algorithms belong to the *exponential* class, or *EXP* class. These algorithms have "exploding" time functions which contain exponential factors, like 2^n or $n!$ (where n is again the input length of the problem). They grow extremely quickly, much faster than any polynomial function. A problem with time complexity bounded by a polynomial function is considered *tractable*; otherwise, it is *intractable*.

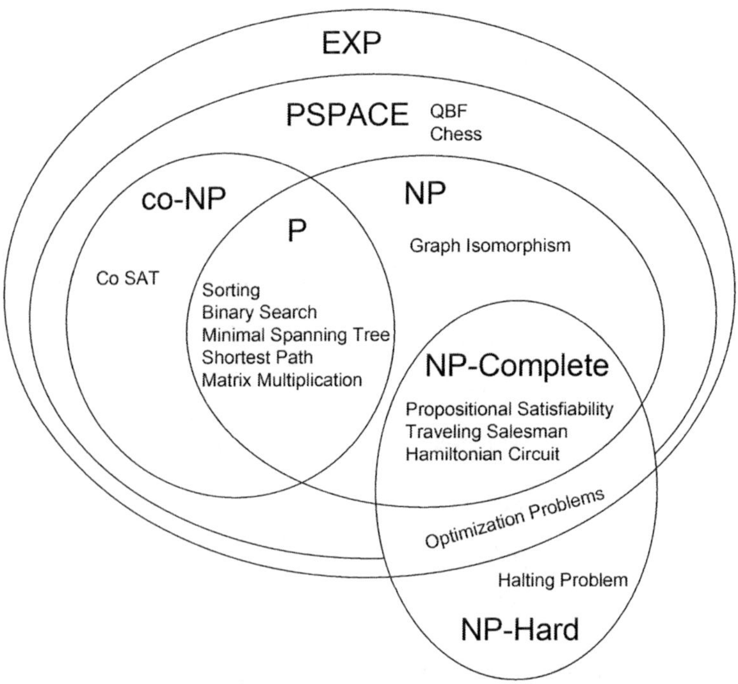

FIGURE 2.5 : Relationships among complexity classes

A decision problem (or recognition problem) is one that takes the form of a question with a "yes" or "no" answer. Consider, for example, the Traveling Salesman Problem (TSP), which decides if there is some tour or circuit in a complete weighted graph that visits every node exactly once, with total path weight less than some given value. This differs from the corresponding optimization problem of finding the shortest tour of all the cities, which requires exponential running time. We say that a decision problem belongs to the NP (*Nondeterministic Polynomial*) complexity class if every "yes" instance has a certificate whose validity can be checked in polynomial time. For example, if the TSP decision problem has the answer "yes" then one certificate is a list of the orders in which the nodes should be visited. It takes only time $O(x)$ to add up the length of this tour and check that it is less than the given value. By reversing the roles played by "yes" and "no" we obtain a complexity class known as *Co-NP*. In particular, for every decision problem in NP there is an associated decision problem in Co-NP obtained by framing the NP question in the negative, for example, the question "Do all traveling salesman tours have a length greater than a certain value?" For Co-NP problems, every "no" instance has a certificate whose validity can be checked in polynomial time.

The complexity class NP-complete is the set of decision problems that are the hardest problems in NP, in the sense that they are the ones most likely not to be in P. Formally, a problem is *NP-complete* if

- It is in NP, and
- Every NP problem can be reduced to it in polynomial time.

An optimization problem for which the related decision problem is NP-complete is termed *NP-hard*. Such a problem is at least as hard as or harder than any problem in NP. Thus an NP-hard problem is any problem such that every NP problem can be converted to it (reduced to it) in polynomial time. Therefore, if we are given an algorithm that solves an NP-hard problem, then the algorithm can also be used to solve any problem in NP with no more than $O\left(x^k\right)$ extra time. The class of NP-complete problems is the intersection of the classes of NP-hard and NP problems. The running time of a P *problem* on a deterministic Turing machine has a polynomial-length input, and NP problems are the polynomial-time problems on nondeterministic Turing machines.

The set of all P problems is contained in the set of all NP problems, which, in turn, is contained in the set of all EXP problems. Some examples of P problems are sorting, binary search, minimal spanning tree, shortest path, and matrix multiplication. The most well-known NP-complete problem is the propositional satisfiability (SAT) problem which determines whether a given propositional formula is satisfiable. SAT has 2^N possible solutions if there are N propositional variables, and so has exponential time complexity (assuming we must check them all to determine if there is a solution). But a possible solution is easy to check in polynomial time, and therefore it is an NP-complete problem. Another NP-complete problem is the Hamiltonian Circuit Problem, which finds a circuit in a graph that passes through each vertex exactly once. The most famous outstanding question in complexity theory is whether P = NP, that is, whether the NP problems actually do have polynomial-time solutions that haven't yet been discovered. Although there is strong suspicion that this is not the case, no one has yet been able to prove it.

As mentioned previously, decision problems are associated with optimization problems. For example, for the TSP, the associated optimization question is "What is the length of the shortest tour?" If an optimization problem asks for a certain type of structure with the minimum "cost" among such structures, we can associate with that problem a decision problem that includes a numerical bound B as an additional parameter and that asks whether there exists a structure of the required type having a cost no more than B. The problem of finding the best clique tree (which will be defined in the context of junction tree algorithms in the chapter on BNs) is such an optimization problem which is NP-hard.

The *graph isomorphism problem* (Are two graphs isomorphic?) is suspected to be neither in P nor NP-complete, though it is obviously in NP. There exists no known P algorithm for graph isomorphism testing, although the problem has also not been shown to be NP-complete. The *subgraph isomorphism problem* (Is a graph isomorphic to a subgraph of another graph?) is NP-complete. The *halting problem* (Given an algorithm and an input, will the algorithm ever stop?) is a decision problem, but is not NP-complete; it is an NP-hard problem.

The following types of algorithms are used in practice to deal with intractable problems and problems not admitting reasonably efficient algorithms:

- Approximation algorithms that settle for less than optimum solutions;

- Heuristic algorithms that are probably efficient for most cases of the problem;

- Randomized algorithms that are probably correct in typical problem instances.

For *undecidable* problems, there is no algorithm that always solves them, no matter how much time or space is allowed. The halting problem is an undecidable problem. In general, it cannot be solved in finite time. First-order logic (discussed in the last section) is also undecidable in the sense that, in general, there is no effective procedure to determine whether a formula is a theorem or not.

The *space complexity* of an algorithm is concerned with the amount of memory used but not time. The difference between space complexity and time complexity is that space can be reused. Space complexity is not affected by determinism or nondeterminism, as deterministic machines can simulate nondeterministic machines using a small amount of space (Savitch's theorem). A problem is said to be in the class PSPACE if it can be solved in space polynomial in the size of its input. Clearly, a Turing machine that uses polynomial time also uses at most polynomial space. However, a Turing machine that uses polynomial space may use an exceedingly large amount of time before halting. Therefore, NP is a subset of PSPACE. A problem is said to be PSPACE-complete if it is in PSPACE and if every other PSPACE problem is polynomial-time reducible to it. It is widely believed that PSPACE-complete problems are strictly harder than the NP-complete problems. Proving the validity of Quantified Boolean Formulae (QBF) and perfect chess-playing are examples of PSPACE-complete problems.

2.7 FURTHER READING

There are plenty of well-written text books in each of the areas covered in this chapter. Here I provide only a few popular ones. Two good books on probability are Feller (1968) and Chung (2000).

There are dozens of good textbooks on classical logics, of which three excellent ones are Copi (1979), Mendelson (1987), and Stoll (1963). Robinson's paper (1965) is highly recommended as a foundational reading on theorem proving. Chang and Lee (1973) provide a thorough coverage of automated theorem proving. For a more recent account on automated theorem proving, see Gallier (2003). The author's own book (Das, 1992) and (Lloyd, 1987) present a detailed overview of logic programming and its related field deductive databases.

The graph theory book by Deo (1974) is one of the first comprehensive texts on graph theory with applications to computer science and engineering. Wilson's book (1996) is another good introductory book on graph theory.

There are many books on linear algebra covering eigenvalues and eigenvectors. An elementary, self-contained, and easy-to read-book is (Strang, 2009).

Finally, Papadimitriou (1993) is a good textbook on complexity theory.

CHAPTER 3

Statistics for Descriptive Analytics

This chapter makes use of statistics for descriptive analytics. Specifically, we use descriptive statistics that concisely summarize the information content of collected observational data via distributions, measures of central tendency, and measures of dispersion. A *distribution* is a summary of the frequency of individual values or ranges of values for a variable. Analysts and researchers often need to know the distribution of a population of interest for certain applications. Once the distribution of a population is known, it can then be used to compute the probability of a future observation. Distributions aid exploratory data analyses to maximize insight into a data set, uncover underlying structures, and extract important information. Here we present the most commonly used distributions for analytics, along with the ones used to build some of the AI and ML techniques covered in this book.

The central tendency of a distribution locates the center of a distribution of values. The three major types of estimates of parameters for central tendency are the mean, the median, and the mode. Dispersion is the spread of values around the central tendency. There are two common measures of dispersion, range and standard deviation. Wherever appropriate, these parameters are derived for the distributions presented in this chapter.

When describing a given population via a probability distribution, we want to choose the distribution with the best fit. In many circumstances, a population is assumed to be Gaussian by default without performing some form of parametric tests. Here we present various goodness-of-fit tests for verifying that a given sample comes from a population with some known distribution.

3.1 PROBABILITY DISTRIBUTIONS

The *probability distribution* of a random variable is a function whose domain is the range of the random variable (that is, the set of values the variable can assume), and whose range is a set of values associated with the probabilities of the elements of the domain. The probability distribution of a discrete random variable is called a *discrete probability distribution.* The probability distribution of a continuous random variable is called a *continuous probability distribution.*

The probability distribution of a random variable is described through its *probability mass function* (or *probability density function*, or PDF). A PDF f of a discrete random variable X with *states* $\{x_1, ..., x_n\}$ is defined as follows: $f(x_i)$ is the probability that X will assume the value x_i. The expected value or expectation of variable X is defined by

$$\mu = E[X] = \sum_i x_i p(X = x_i)$$

Examples

Consider the random variable *Dice* defined as the sum of the upturned faces of two dice, therefore having the range $\{2, 3, 4, ..., 12\}$. Now, $\{(i, j) \in \{(1,1), (1,2), ..., (6,6)\} : i + j = 5\}$ is equal to $\{(1,4), (2,3), (3,2), (4,1)\}$. Therefore, $p(Dice = 5) = 4/36$. Similarly, we have the following:

$$p(Dice = 2) = 1/36, \quad p(Dice = 3) = 2/36, \quad p(Dice = 4) = 3/36$$
$$p(Dice = 5) = 4/36, \quad p(Dice = 6) = 5/36, \quad p(Dice = 7) = 6/36$$
$$p(Dice = 8) = 5/36, \quad p(Dice = 9) = 4/36, \quad p(Dice = 10) = 3/36$$
$$p(Dice = 11) = 2/36, \quad p(Dice = 12) = 1/36.$$

Also, the sum of all the probabilities is equal to 1, that is,

$$\sum_{x \in \{2,3,...,12\}} p(Dice = x) = 1.$$

The expected value of the sum of the upturned faces is therefore

$$\begin{aligned} & E[Dice] \\ & \quad = 2 \times \tfrac{1}{36} + 3 \times \tfrac{2}{36} + 4 \times \tfrac{3}{36} + 5 \times \tfrac{4}{36} + 6 \times \tfrac{5}{36} + 7 \times \tfrac{6}{36} + \\ & \qquad 8 \times \tfrac{5}{36} + 9 \times \tfrac{4}{36} + 10 \times \tfrac{3}{36} + 11 \times \tfrac{2}{36} + 12 \times \tfrac{1}{36} \\ & \quad = 6.7 \end{aligned}$$

Consider the random variable *Weather* with range $\{sunny, rain, snow\}$. Define

$$\begin{gathered} p(Weather = sunny) = 0.55 \\ p(Weather = rain) = 0.15 \\ p(Weather = snow) = 0.30 \end{gathered}$$

FIGURE 3.1 represents the graphs of the two PDFs associated with the random variables *Dice* and *Weather*. Such a graphical depiction of a probability mass function is called a *probability histogram*.

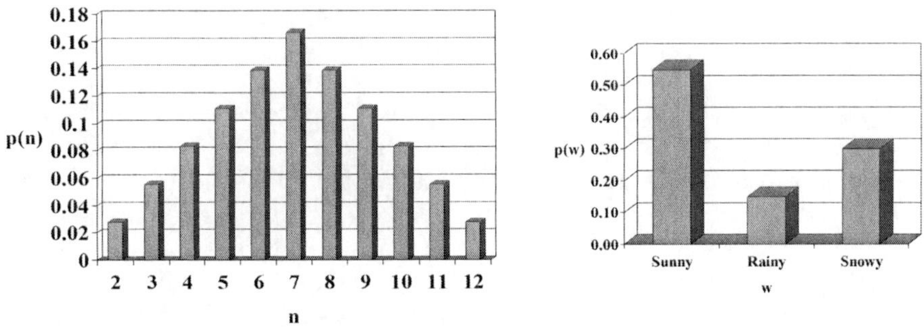

FIGURE 3.1 : Probability density functions (PDFs) for the random variables Dice and Weather

The *joint probability distribution* of two discrete random variables X and Y, denoted as $p(X,Y)$ or $p(XY)$, is a function whose domain is the set of ordered pairs (x,y) of events, where x and y are, respectively, possible values for X and Y. The range of the function is the set of probability values corresponding to the ordered pairs in its domain. Such a probability is denoted by $p(X=x,Y=y)$ (or simply $p(x,y)$ when X and Y are clear from the context) and is defined as

$$p(x,y) = p(X=x, Y=y) = p(X=x \text{ and } Y=y)$$

The definition of the joint probability distribution can be extended to three or more random variables. In general, the joint probability distribution of the set of discrete random variables $X_1, ..., X_n$, denoted as $p(X_1, ..., X_n)$ or $p(X_1 ... X_n)$, is given by

$$p(x_1, ..., x_n) = p(X_1 = x_1, ..., X_n = x_n) = p(X_1 = x_1 \text{ and} ... \text{and } X_n = x_n)$$

The notion of conditional probability distribution arises when one wants to know the probability of an event, given the occurrence of another event. An example conditional probability is the probability of snowy weather later today given that the current temperature is freezing. Formally, the *conditional probability distribution* of the two random variables X and Y, denoted as $p(X|Y)$, is a function whose domain is the set of ordered pairs (x,y), where x and y, respectively, are possible values for X and Y. The range of the function is the set of probability values corresponding to the ordered pairs. The conditional probability distribution is defined as follows:

$$p(X|Y) = \frac{p(XY)}{p(Y)}, \quad \text{if } p(Y) > 0$$

Two random variables X and Y are *independent* if $p(X|Y) = p(X)$ and $p(Y|X) = p(Y)$, that is, they convey no information about each other. Consequently, $p(XY) = p(X)p(Y)$, when variables X and Y are independent. A sequence $X_1, ..., X_n$ of random variables is *independent and identically distributed* (i.i.d.) if each random variable X_i has the same probability distribution as the others and $X_1, ..., X_n$ are mutually independent (i.e., pairwise independent).

The probability distribution of a continuous random variable is also described through its *probability density function*, or PDF. A PDF f of a continuous random variable X with domain D is defined as follows: $f(x), x \in D$, is the probability that X will assume the value d, and its integral over the domain D is equal to one.

$$\begin{array}{l} f(x) \geq 0, \ x \in D \\ \int\limits_D f(x)dx = 1 \end{array}$$

The *expected value* or *expectation* of variable X is defined by

$$\mu = E[X] = \int\limits_D xf(x)dx$$

The *variance* of the random variable X is defined as

$$var(X) = \sigma^2 = E[X - E[X]]^2 = E\left[X^2\right] - E[X]^2$$

The expected value of a variable is known as its *population mean*. The *sample mean* is an estimator for the population mean and is commonly known as *average*. Its value depends on the data values chosen. A continuous random variable X with domain $(-\infty, +\infty)$ is said to follow a (univariate) *normal* or *Gaussian distribution* with parameters μ and σ if it has the following PDF:

$$f(X) = \frac{1}{\sigma\sqrt{2\pi}} e^{-\frac{(X-\mu)^2}{2\sigma^2}}$$

We write $X \sim N\left[\mu, \sigma^2\right]$ when X is Gaussian with parameters μ and σ. As shown in the left of FIGURE 3.4, the PDF is a symmetrical bell-shaped curve with center at its expected value μ. The variance of a Gaussian random variable is σ^2.

3.2 DISCRETE PROBABILITY DISTRIBUTIONS

Two discrete distributions are presented in this section. The first one is multinomial distribution, of which binomial distribution is special case. The second one is Poisson distribution. Both have applications in various analytics techniques presented in the subsequent chapters. We also introduce the Poisson process as a generalization of Poisson distribution.

3.2.1 Binomial and Multinomial Distributions

Suppose the probability of success and failure in any one trial is given by the fixed probabilities p and $q = 1 - p$. Binomial distribution provides the probability of the number of successes and failures in n such independent 2-outcome trials. The probability density function of binomial distribution is

$$f(X; n, p) = \binom{n}{X} p^X (1-p)^{n-X}$$

The mean of the distribution is np and the variance is $np(1-p)$. FIGURE 3.2 shows a binomial distribution plot with $n = 4$ and $p = 0.5$.

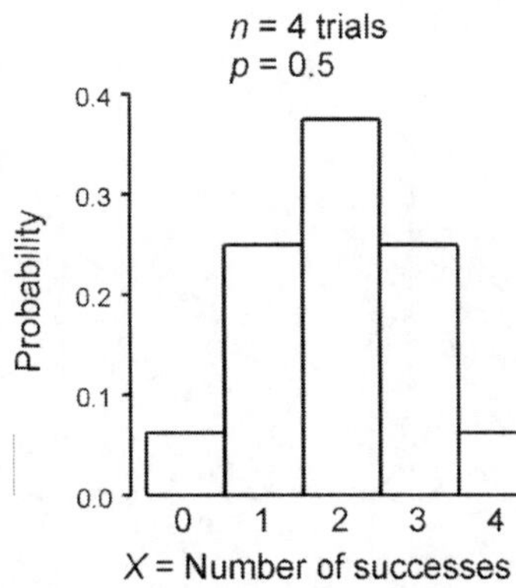

FIGURE 3.2 : Binomial distribution

Suppose the probability of each outcome in any one k-outcome trial is given by the fixed probabilities $p_1, ..., p_k$. The multinomial distribution is a generalization of the binomial distribution giving the probability of each combination of outcomes in n independent trials of such a k-outcome process. Distribution of each n k-outcome trials:

$$f(X_1, ..., X_k; n, p_1, ..., p_k) = \frac{n!}{X_1! ... X_k!} p_1^{X_1} ... p_k^{X_k},$$

$$X_i \geq 0, p_i \geq 0 \text{ and } \sum_i p_i = 1$$

Later in the chapter dealing with text classification and topic extraction, topics for documents in corpus or words under a particular topic are assumed to be multinomial.

3.2.2 Poisson Distribution and Process

The *Poisson distribution* is used to model the number of events occurring within a given time interval, such as the number of calls received during the first hour in a call center and the number of customers arriving at a supermarket over the weekend. The length of a document in a large corpus also can be modeled as a Poisson distribution with constant parameters. A discrete random variable X is said to follow a *Poisson distribution* with parameter λ, if it has the following PDF:

$$f(X;\lambda) = \frac{\lambda^X}{X!}e^{-\lambda}, \ \lambda > 0, \ X = 0, 1, 2, ...$$

where λ represents the mean of the distribution representing the average number of events in the given time interval. The mean and variance of the distribution is λ. FIGURE 3.3 shows Poisson distributions for various values of λ.

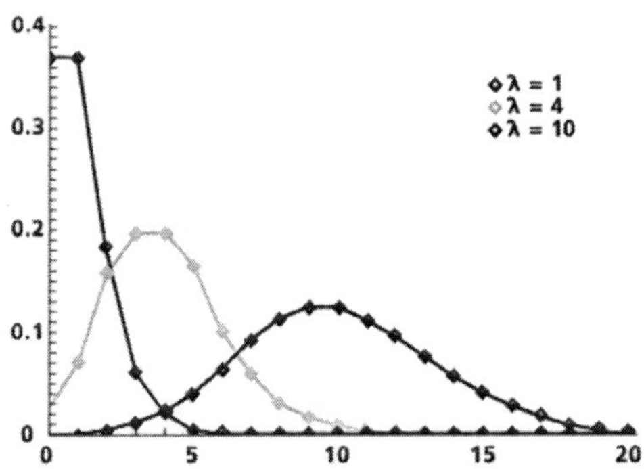

FIGURE 3.3 : Poisson distribution

A Poisson process is a stochastic process where events occur continuously and independently of each other. Poisson processes can be used to model the arrival of customers at a supermarket, telephone calls received in a call center, and occurrences of natural disasters in a given area. Underlying assumptions of Poisson distributions are: 1) Probability of observing a single event over a small interval is approximately proportional to the size of that interval; 2) Probability of two events occurring in the same narrow interval is negligible; 3) Probability of an event within a certain interval does not change over different intervals; and 4) Probability of an event in one interval is independent of the probability of an event in any other non-overlapping interval.

A Poisson process models the number of events in a given time interval. The number of arrivals $X(t)$ (X is a function of t) in a finite interval of length t obeys the Poisson distribution

$$f(X;t,\lambda) = \frac{(\lambda t)^X}{X!}e^{-\lambda t}, \ X = 0, 1, 2, ...$$

where λ is the mean arrival rate, i.e., the probability of arrival per unit time. As a consequence, the inter-arrival times are independent and follow the exponential distribution $e^{-\lambda t}$. Note that the numbers of arrivals in non-overlapping intervals are independent.

3.3 CONTINUOUS PROBABILITY DISTRIBUTIONS

The continuous probability distributions that we present in this section include univariate and multivariate normal distributions, beta and Dirichlet distributions, and lognormal, Weibull, exponential, and gamma distributions. Some of these distributions are just special cases of others.

3.3.1 Gaussian or Normal Distribution

A continuous random variable X with domain $(-\infty, +\infty)$ is said to follow a (univariate) *normal* or *Gaussian distribution* with parameters μ and σ if it has the following PDF:

$$f\left(X;\mu,\sigma^2\right) = \frac{1}{\sigma\sqrt{2\pi}} e^{-\frac{(X-\mu)^2}{2\sigma^2}}$$

As shown in the left of FIGURE 3.4, the PDF is a symmetrical bell-shaped curve with center at its expected value μ. The variance of a Gaussian random variable is σ^2.

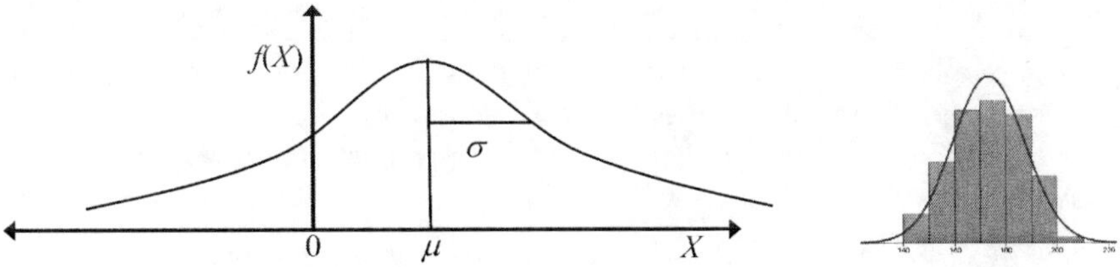

FIGURE 3.4 : Gaussian distribution

When a random variable X is distributed normally with mean μ and variance σ^2, we write $X \sim Normal\left(\mu,\sigma^2\right)$ or simply $X \sim N\left(\mu,\sigma^2\right)$.

An analytics application (e.g., classifier) deals with the attributes of an object (e.g., customer or document) arranged as a vector. A *vector-valued random variable* is an n-dimensional vector consisting of n random variables that are all associated with the same event. An example 3-dimensional random variable consists of the name, email address, and telephone number of a customer:

$$X = \begin{bmatrix} name \\ email \\ tel \end{bmatrix}$$

The *multivariate normal distribution* model extends the univariate normal distribution model to fit vector observations. An n-dimensional random variable X is said to follow a multivariate normal distribution if it has the following PDF:

$$f(X;\mu,\Sigma) = \frac{1}{(2\pi)^{p/2}|\Sigma|^{1/2}} e^{-\frac{1}{2}(X-\mu)'\Sigma^{-1}(X-\mu)}$$

where μ is the vector of mean and Σ is the covariance matrix of X, that is, $\Sigma_{ij} = Cov(X_i, X_j)$. We write $X \sim N_n(\mu, \Sigma)$.

Special case (standard normal distribution): $\mu = 0, \sigma^2 = 1$. Normal is a limiting case of n in a discrete binomial distribution (illustrated in the right of FIGURE 3.4).

The product of two Gaussian distributions is also a Gaussian distribution. So if $X_1 \sim N(\mu_1, \sigma_1^2)$ and $X_2 \sim N(\mu_2, \sigma_2^2)$ then it can be shown that

$$Z = X_1 X_2 \sim N\left(\frac{\mu_1\sigma_2^2 + \mu_2\sigma_1^2}{\sigma_1^2+\sigma_2^2}, \frac{\sigma_1^2\sigma_2^2}{\sigma_1^2+\sigma_2^2}\right)$$

The sum of two independent Gaussian distributions is Gaussian. So if $X_1 \sim N(\mu_1, \sigma_1^2)$ and $X_2 \sim N(\mu_2, \sigma_2^2)$ and X_1 and X_2 are independent (i.e., $p(X_1X_2) = p(X_1)p(X_2)$), then it can be shown that

$$Z = X_1 + X_2 \sim N(\mu_1+\mu_2, \sigma_1^2+\sigma_2^2)$$

3.3.2 Lognormal

A random variable X is distributed lognormally if the logarithm of X, $\ln(X)$, is normally distributed. Lognormal distribution, as shown in FIGURE 3.5, is good for modeling the lives of units whose failure modes are of a fatigue-stress nature. Say $X' = \ln(X)$ and μ' and σ' are respectively mean and variance of X':

$$f(X';\mu',\sigma'^2) = \frac{1}{\sqrt{2\pi}\sigma'} e^{-\frac{1}{2}\left(\frac{X'-\mu'}{\sigma'}\right)^2}$$

Given equal probabilities under the normal and lognormal PDFs, incremental areas should also be equal:

$$f(X)\,dX = f(X')\,dX'$$

Relation between $f(X)$ and $f(X')$:

$$X' = \ln(X) \Rightarrow dX' = \frac{1}{X}dX \Rightarrow f(X) = \frac{f(X')}{X}$$

Therefore, the density function of the lognormal distribution is

$$f(X;\mu',\sigma'^2) = \frac{1}{X\sqrt{2\pi}\sigma'} e^{\frac{1}{2}\left(\frac{\ln(X)-\mu'}{\sigma'}\right)^2}, \; X \geq 0, \; f(X) \geq 0$$

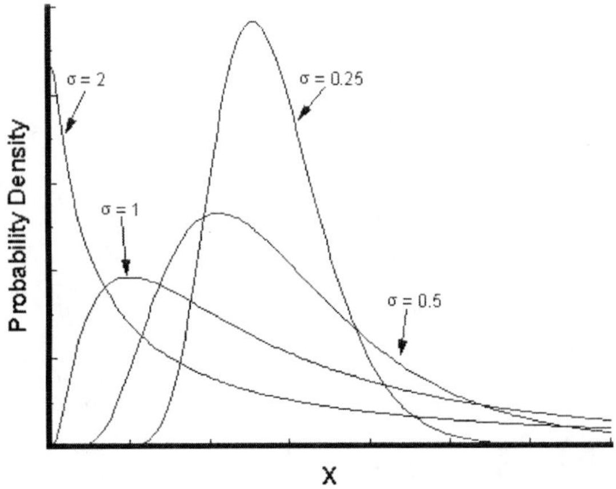

FIGURE 3.5 : Lognormal Distribution

3.3.3 Exponential Distribution

The exponential distribution can be used in modeling reliability with a constant failure rate λ. Exponential distribution, as shown in FIGURE 3.6, can also be used to model the amount of time X a customer support agent spends on a phone call or a customer spends in a bank. If this time is assumed to be exponentially distributed with a mean of 5 minutes, then the rate $\lambda = 1/5$. The density function of the exponential distribution with parameter λ is

$$\begin{aligned} f(X;\lambda) & \\ = \lambda e^{-\lambda X} & \quad X \geq 0 \\ = 0 & \quad X < 0 \end{aligned}$$

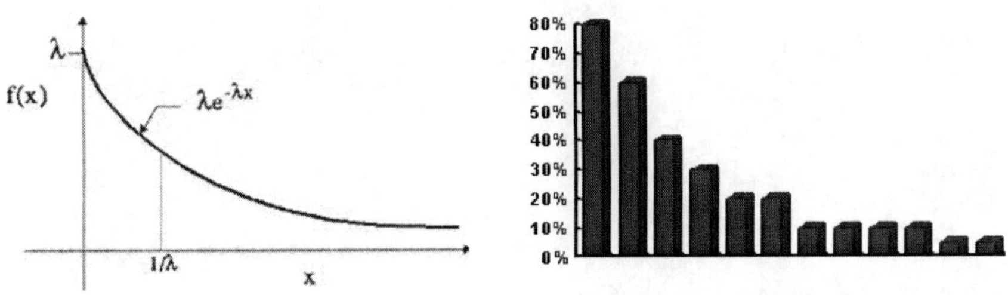

FIGURE 3.6 : (left) Exponential distribution; (right) Exponentially distributed call center duration.

The standard exponential distribution is when λ =1, that is, e^{-X}. The mean and variance of the distribution is

$$E[X] = \frac{1}{\lambda}, Var[X] = \frac{1}{\lambda^2}$$

The CDF of exponential distribution is

$$\begin{aligned} &F(X;\lambda) \\ &= 1 - e^{-\lambda X} \qquad X \geq 0 \\ &= 0 \qquad\qquad\quad X < 0 \end{aligned}$$

The exponential distribution is memory-less, which means the conditional probability has the form

$$p(X > s + t | X > s) = p(X > t)$$

It can be proven as shown below:

$$\begin{aligned} &p(X > s + t | X > s) \\ &= \frac{p(X>s+t, X>s)}{p(X>s)} \\ &= \frac{p(X>s+t)}{p(X>s)} \\ &= \frac{1-\left(1-e^{-\lambda(s+t)}\right)}{1-(1-e^{-\lambda s})} \\ &= e^{-\lambda t} = p(X > t) \end{aligned}$$

So the probability that an agent will spend more than 10 minutes on a call is e^{-2}, and the probability that an agent will spend more than 15 minutes on a call given that he is still on the call after 10 minutes is e^{-1}.

3.3.4 Weibull Distribution

The density function of the Weibull distribution is:

$$f(X;\beta,\eta,\gamma) = \frac{\beta}{\eta}\left(\frac{X-\gamma}{\eta}\right)^{\beta-1} e^{-\left(\frac{X-\gamma}{\eta}\right)^{\beta}}, X \geq \gamma$$

where β is the shape parameter, η is the scale parameter, and γ is the location parameter. FIGURE 3.7 shows Weibull distributions with varying shape (β), scale (η), and location (γ).
Some special cases of Weibull distribution are as follows:

- $\beta = 1$: Exponential distribution
- $\beta = 2$: Rayleigh distribution
- $3 \leq \beta \leq 4$: Approximates normal distribution

Example

We consider the data set of recorded daily fastest-mile wind speeds for the

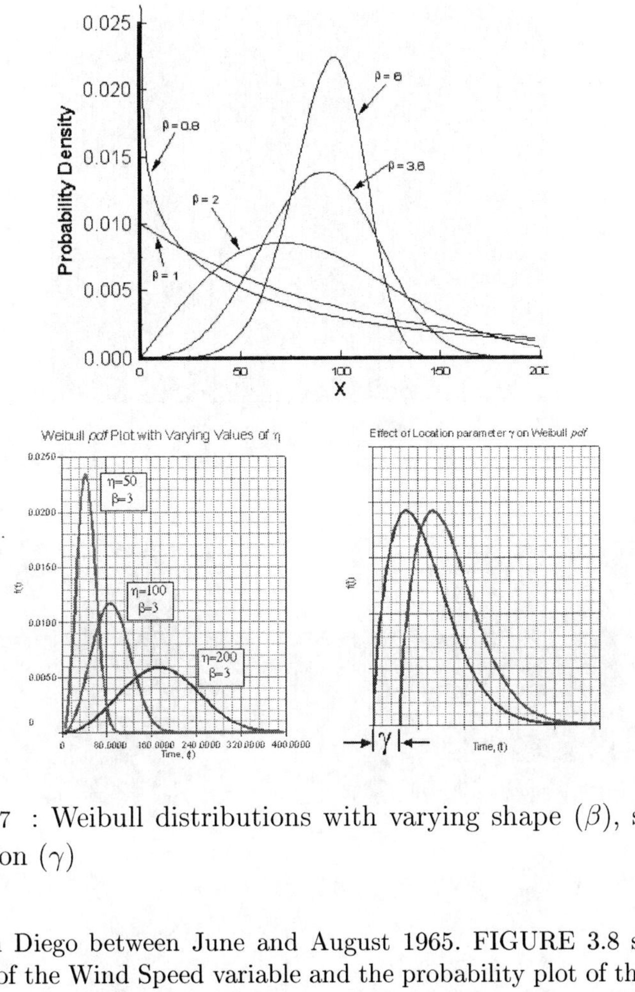

FIGURE 3.7 : Weibull distributions with varying shape (β), scale (η), and location (γ)

city of San Diego between June and August 1965. FIGURE 3.8 shows the histogram of the Wind Speed variable and the probability plot of the Weibull distribution. Two more probability plots, normal and lognormal distributions, are considered for comparison. It seems both Lognormal and Weibull are good fit for the data.

3.3.5 Beta and Dirichlet Distributions

Beta distribution is used to model continuous data with values between 0 and 1. The distribution function for the beta distribution has no closed form solution. The density for the standard univariate beta distribution is

$$f(X;\alpha,\beta) = \frac{X^{\alpha-1}(1-X)^{\beta-1}}{\mathrm{B}(\alpha,\beta)} \quad 0 \le X \le 1$$

where

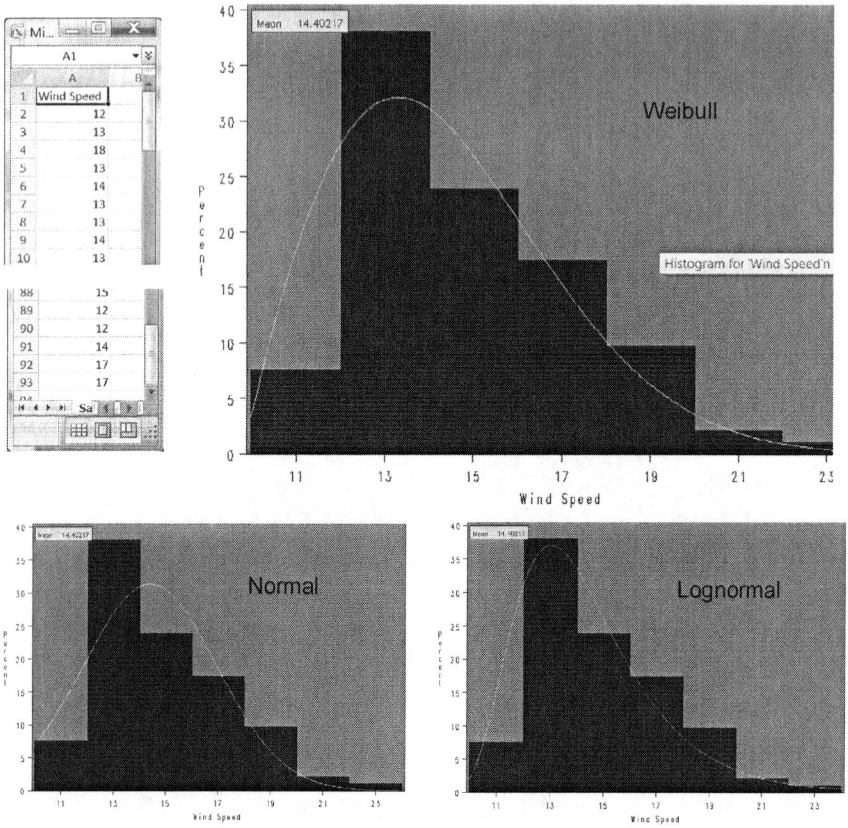

FIGURE 3.8 : Weibull distribution for San Diego Wind Speed Data Jun-Aug 1965 (Ref: http://www.itl.nist.gov/div898/winds/daily.htm)

$$\mathrm{B}(\alpha,\beta) = \frac{\Gamma(\alpha)\Gamma(\beta)}{\Gamma(\alpha+\beta)}$$

When variable X has beta distribution, we write $X \sim Beta(\alpha, \beta)$. The mean and variance of Beta distribution are as follows:

$$\mu = \mathrm{E}[X] = \tfrac{\alpha}{\alpha+\beta},$$
$$\sigma^2 = Var[X] = \tfrac{\alpha\beta}{(\alpha+\beta)^2(\alpha+\beta+1)}$$

FIGURE 3.9 shows several Beta distributions with varying permutations of the parameters α and β.

Dirichlet distribution is a generalization of Beta distribution as defined

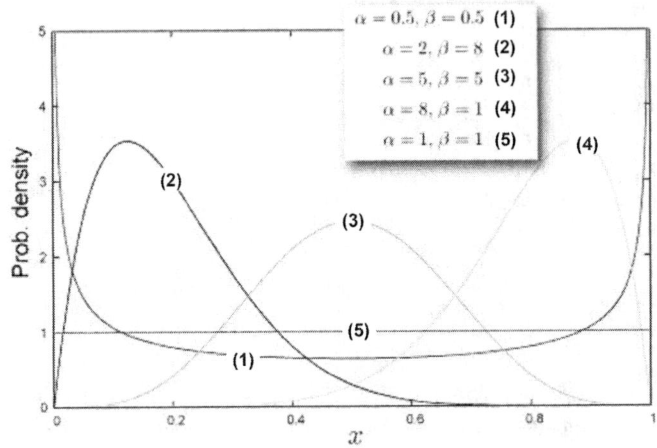

FIGURE 3.9 : Beta distributions with varying parameters

below:

$$f(X_1, ..., X_n; \alpha_1, ..., \alpha_n) = \frac{1}{Beta(\alpha_1, ..., \alpha_n)} \prod_{i=1}^{n} X_i^{\alpha_i - 1},$$

$$X_i \geq 0, \alpha_i \geq 0 \text{ and } \sum_i X_i = 1$$

The parameter α_i can be interpreted as the prior observation counts for events governed by the probability representing the variable X_i. The normalization constant $Beta(\alpha_1, ..., \alpha_n)$ is:

$$Beta(\alpha_1, ..., \alpha_n) = \frac{\prod_{i=1}^{n} \Gamma(\alpha_i)}{\Gamma\left(\sum_{i=1}^{n} \alpha_i\right)}$$

The mean and variance of the Dirichlet distribution is:

$$\mu_i = \mathrm{E}[X_i] = \frac{\alpha_i}{\alpha_1 + ... + \alpha_n} = \frac{\alpha_i}{\sum_j \alpha_j}$$

$$\sigma_i^2 = Var[X_i] = \frac{\alpha_i \left(\sum_j \alpha_j - \alpha_i\right)}{\left(\sum_j \alpha_j\right)^2 \left(\sum_j \alpha_j + 1\right)}$$

In the context of text corpus classification and topic extraction discussed in a later chapter, every topic is a distribution over the terms of the vocabulary, and every document is a distribution over the topics. These distributions are sampled from Dirichlet distributions.

3.3.6 Gamma Distribution

The density of Gamma distribution over parameters α and β is

$$f(X;\alpha,\beta) = \frac{X^{\alpha-1}e^{-\frac{X}{\beta}}}{\beta^{\alpha}\Gamma(\alpha)}, \; X \geq 0, \; \alpha > 0, \; \beta > 0$$

where the Gamma function $\Gamma(\gamma)$ is defined by:

$$\Gamma(\gamma) = \int_{0}^{\infty} x^{\gamma-1}e^{-x}dx, \; \gamma \in (0,\infty)$$

The parameter α is called the *shape* parameter and the parameter β is called the *scale* parameter. The mean of Gamma distribution is $\alpha\beta$ and the variance is $\alpha\beta^2$. The density of the standard univariate Gamma distribution is

$$f(X;\alpha) = \frac{X^{\alpha-1}e^{-X}}{\Gamma(\alpha)}, \; X \geq 0, \; \alpha > 0$$

FIGURE 3.10 shows several standard Gamma distributions varying the shape parameter α.

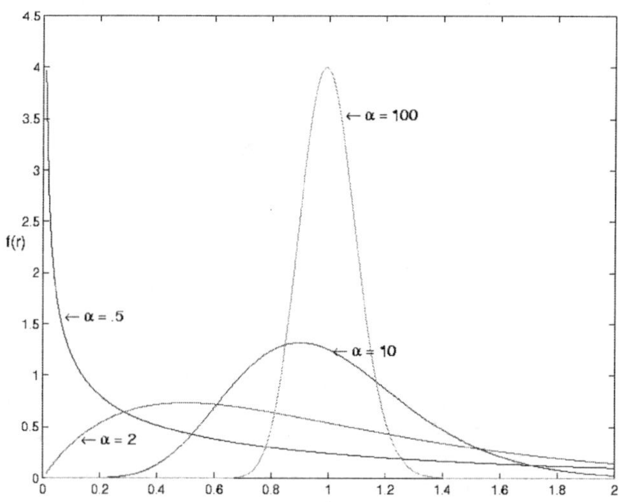

FIGURE 3.10 : Standard Gamma distributions varying the shape parameter

Some important properties of Gamma function:

$$\Gamma(\gamma+1) = \gamma\Gamma(\gamma), \quad \gamma > 0$$

$\Gamma(k) = (k-1)!$, k is a positive integer

$$\Gamma\left(\frac{1}{2}\right) = \sqrt{\pi}$$

Gamma distributions are good for modeling highly skewed variables. Gamma distribution simplifies to the exponential when the shape parameter is set to 1, and the scale parameter to the mean interval between events. The distribution simplifies to Chi-Squared distribution when the shape parameter is set to the degrees of freedom divided by two and the scale parameter is set to 2.

3.4 GOODNESS-OF-FIT TEST

This section presents one-way or one-sample goodness-of-fit tests to verify whether a given sample comes from a population with some known distribution or not. The section also presents a two-way or two-sample test to verify if two populations have the same distribution.

We make use of *hypothesis testing* to determine if a given goodness-of-fit hypothesis is true. A statistical hypothesis is an assumption about a population parameter. The testing of a hypothesis means to either verify or reject the hypothesis on a random sample of the population. A null hypothesis H0 is formed (e.g., two population means are not equal), reflecting a common view that a researcher or an analyst tries to reject. The alternative hypothesis H1, which is a logical negation of H0, reflects what the researcher really thinks is the cause or phenomenon. If one or more significance tests generate 95% or 99% likelihood that the results do not fit the null hypothesis, then it is rejected, favoring the alternative.

3.4.1 Probability Plot

Probability plotting is a graphical technique for testing whether or not a sample approximately follows a given distribution. The vertical of a plot is the ordered response values of the variable and the horizontal axis is the percentile, which is the value of the variable below which a certain percent of observations fall. If the sample is consistent with a sample from a given distribution, the points should fall close to a straight line. The greater the variation of the points from this line, the greater the indication of departure from the distribution. The normal probability plot is useful for testing whether or not a sample is approximately normally distributed.

Example

Consider the Temperature column in the Play-Tennis example in Appendix B. FIGURE 3.11 and FIGURE 3.12 show the histograms of the variable Temperature and three probability plots of lognormal, normal and exponential distributions.

Temperature
75
80
85
72
69
72
83
64
81
71
65
75
68
70

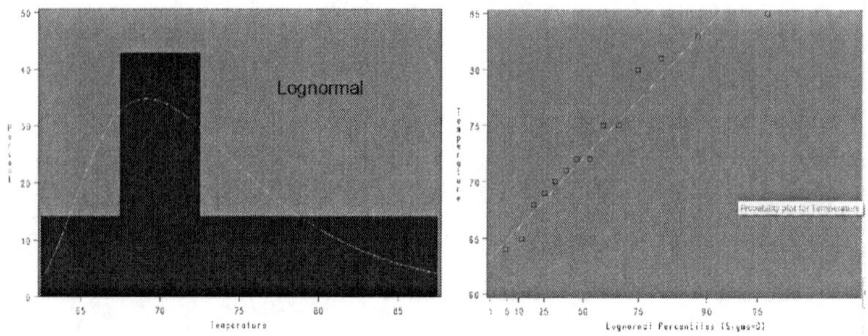

FIGURE 3.11 : Probability plots of Temperature for Lognormal distribution

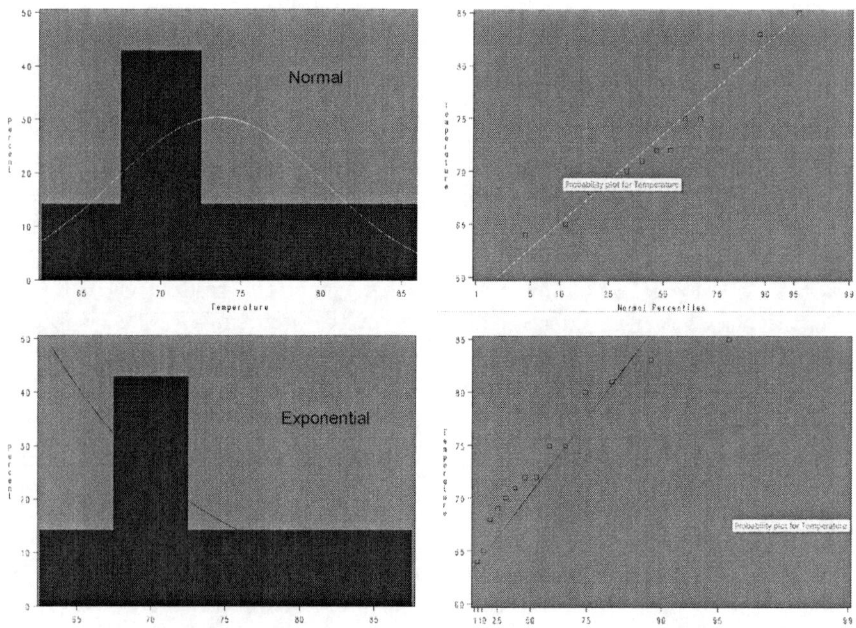

FIGURE 3.12 : Probability plots of Temperature for Normal and Exponential distributions

It's quite obvious from the plots that the sample distribution is closer to the lognormal distribution than to the normal or exponential. If the distribution is right-skewed with a long tail to the right, as is the case here, the plotted points will appear to bend up and to the left of the line. If the distribution is left-skewed, the plotted points will appear to bend down.

3.4.2 One-Way Chi-Square Goodness-of-Fit Test

Chi-Square (χ^2) is a non-parametric test to investigate whether distributions of categorical variables differ from one another. The one-way or single-sample chi-square goodness-of-fit is to determine whether a significant difference exists between an observed and some theoretically expected distribution (frequencies of occurrence).

Example

Let us suppose that the expected and observed distribution of the variable Outlook is as shown in TABLE 3.1.

TABLE 3.1: : Distribution of variable Outlook

Outlook	Expected	Observed
sunny	5	6
overcast	4	3
rain	5	5

The null hypothesis H0 here is that the observed and expected distributions of the variable Outlook are not the same. The two bar diagrams shown in FIGURE 3.13 provide a visual comparison of the expected and observed values:

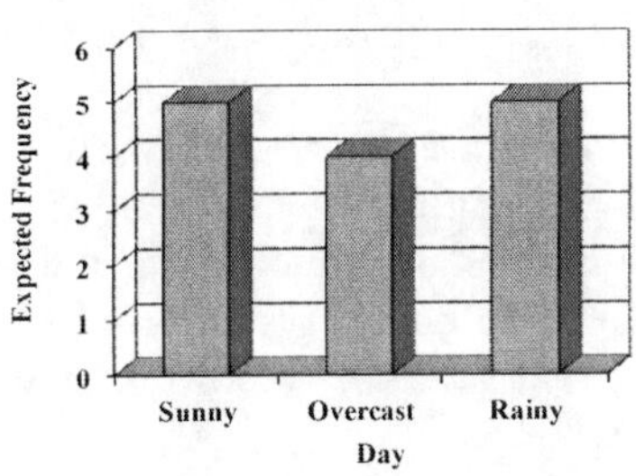

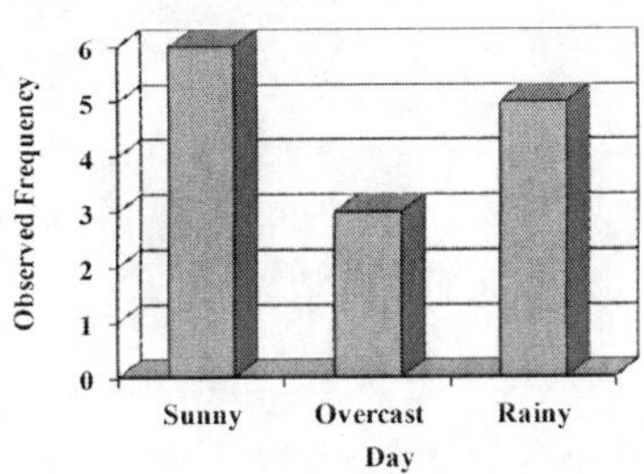

FIGURE 3.13 : Comparison of expected and observed frequency

It is difficult to quickly distinguish differences between the observed and expected counts by eye. A better visual representation is shown in FIGURE 3.14, which plots differences between the observed and expected counts divided by the square root of the expected counts. The question is whether, given this statistic, the observed values are likely, under the assumed distribution of the expected.

The chi-square test statistic is defined as:

$$\sum_i \frac{(O - E)^2}{E}$$

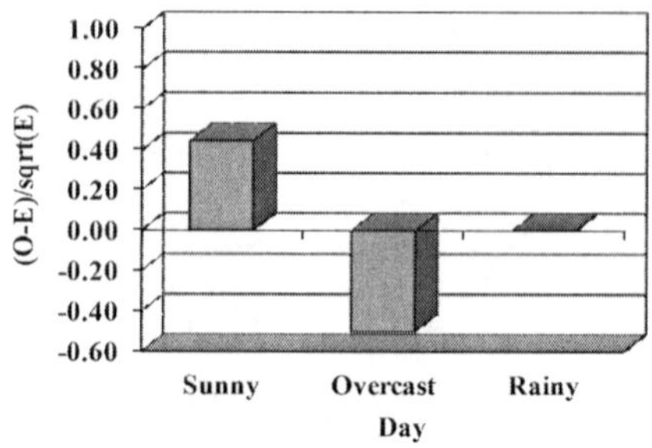

FIGURE 3.14 : Difference between the observed and expected distributions

If the computed test statistic is large, then the observed and expected values are not close and the model is considered a poor fit to the data. H0 is rejected if this value exceeds the upper critical α value of the $\chi^2(k)$ distribution, where α is the desired level of significance and k is the degree of freedom. Here we consider 95% as the predetermined level of significance.

Degrees of freedom can be described as the number of classes that are free to vary. Suppose we observe the weather over a period of 14 days and classify it as sunny, overcast or rainy. If we observe 8 sunny days and 2 overcast days, then the number of rainy days must be 4. In this example, 2 classes are free to vary while the third is not. Therefore, there are 2 degrees of freedom in the observation.

A random variable is said to have a *chi-square distribution* with k degrees of freedom if it is the sum of the squares of k independent standard normal random variables. Therefore, the square of a single standard normal random variable has a chi-square distribution with one degree of freedom. The table in FIGURE 3.15 contains values of test statistics for some combinations of probability values and degrees of freedom.

Example

Consider the expected and observed distribution of the variable Outlook as shown in TABLE 3.1. Now,

$$\sum_i \frac{(O-E)^2}{E} = \frac{(6-5)^2}{5} + \frac{(3-4)^2}{4} + \frac{(5-5)^2}{5} = 0.45.$$

The probability corresponding to the value 0.45 with 2 degrees of freedom is 0.8, which is less than 0.95. Hence the null hypothesis that the two distributions are not the same is accepted and the difference in observed vs. expected weather is considered to be true.

Degrees of Freedom	Probability										
	0.95	0.90	0.80	0.70	0.50	0.30	0.20	0.10	0.05	0.01	0.001
1	0.004	0.02	0.06	0.15	0.46	1.07	1.64	2.71	3.84	6.64	10.83
2	0.10	0.21	0.45	0.71	1.39	2.41	3.22	4.60	5.99	9.21	13.82
3	0.35	0.58	1.01	1.42	2.37	3.66	4.64	6.25	7.82	11.34	16.27
4	0.71	1.06	1.65	2.20	3.36	4.88	5.99	7.78	9.49	13.28	18.47
5	1.14	1.61	2.34	3.00	4.35	6.06	7.29	9.24	11.07	15.09	20.52
6	1.63	2.20	3.07	3.83	5.35	7.23	8.56	10.64	12.59	16.81	22.46
7	2.17	2.83	3.82	4.67	6.35	8.38	9.80	12.02	14.07	18.48	24.32
8	2.73	3.49	4.59	5.53	7.34	9.52	11.03	13.36	15.51	20.09	26.12
9	3.32	4.17	5.38	6.39	8.34	10.66	12.24	14.68	16.92	21.67	27.88
10	3.94	4.86	6.18	7.27	9.34	11.78	13.44	15.99	18.31	23.21	29.59
	Nonsignificant								Significant		

FIGURE 3.15 : χ^2table

3.4.3 Kolmogorov-Smirnov Test

The Kolmogorov-Smirnov (K-S) test can be used to answer the question "Are the data from an X distribution?" where X could be normal, lognormal, exponential, etc. One of the advantages of the K-S test is that it leads to a graphical presentation of the data, which enables the user to detect normal and other distributions.

The K-S test is based on empirical Cumulative Distribution Function (CDF) values of continuous observations. Given an ordered set of n data points $x_1, ..., x_n$, the empirical CDF is defined by the following fraction:

$$\hat{F}(x) = \frac{\#(i : x_i < x)}{n}$$

Given a known CDF F_0, the null hypothesis to be tested is:

$$H_0 : F(x) = F_0(x), \quad for\, all\, x$$

The K-S test statistic is

$$D_n = \sup_x \left| \hat{F}(x) - F_0(x) \right|$$

A null distribution of the statistic D_n can be approximated by simulation or, for large samples, by using the K-S's distribution function. Test statistic D_n can be compared to the critical value from a statistical table. If D_n is larger than the critical value, then we reject the hypothesis that the data set was drawn from the theoretical distribution F_0; otherwise, we do not reject the hypothesis.

Example

Consider the Temperature column in the Play-Tennis example in Appendix B. The ordered values are given below:

$$Temperature = \left\{ \begin{array}{l} 64,\ 65,\ 68,\ 69,\ 70,\ 71,\ 72, \\ 72,\ 75,\ 75,\ 80,\ 81,\ 83,\ 85 \end{array} \right\}$$

Since there are two duplicate pairs, $n = 12$. The mean and standard deviation of the above temperature values are $\mu = 73.57, \sigma = 6.57$. Are the temperatures sampled from $N\left(\mu, \sigma^2\right)$? The null hypothesis is $H_0 : F(x) = F_0(x)$, where $F_0(x)$ is the CDF of $N\left(\mu, \sigma^2\right)$. We need to compute the empirical CDF $\hat{F}(x)$ first.

No data point lies strictly below 64, 1/14 (0.07) of the data is strictly smaller than 65, 2/14 (0.14) of the data is strictly smaller than 68, 3/14 (0.21) of the data is strictly smaller than 69, and so on. There are 10 data points smaller than 80, and hence we would say that the cumulative fraction of the data smaller than 80 is 10/14 (0.71). For any data point x, the cumulative fraction is the fraction of the data that is strictly smaller than x. Hence the empirical CDF $\hat{F}(x)$ of the ordered temperature values are given below:

$$\hat{F}(x) = \begin{cases} 0 & x < 64 \\ 0.07 & 64 \leq x < 65 \\ 0.14 & 65 \leq x < 68 \\ 0.21 & 68 \leq x < 69 \\ 0.28 & 69 \leq x < 70 \\ 0.35 & 70 \leq x < 71 \\ 0.43 & 71 \leq x < 72 \\ 0.57 & 72 \leq x < 75 \\ 0.71 & 75 \leq x < 80 \\ 0.78 & 80 \leq x < 81 \\ 0.85 & 81 \leq x < 83 \\ 0.93 & 83 \leq x < 85 \\ 1.0 & x \geq 85 \end{cases}$$

We compute $\left|\hat{F}(x) - F_0(x)\right|$ in TABLE 3.2 below to compute the K-S test statistics. Therefore, $\sup_x \left|\hat{F}(x) - F_0(x)\right| = 0.1645$ and thus D_{12} gets the value $d = 0.1645$.

TABLE 3.2: : K-S test statistics

x	$\hat{F}(x)$	$F_0(x)$	$\left\|\hat{F}(x) - F_0(x)\right\|$
64	0.07	0.0726	0.0026
65	0.14	0.0961	0.0439
68	0.21	0.1983	0.0117
69	0.28	0.2433	0.0367

TABLE 3.2: : K-S test statistics

70	0.35	0.2934	0.0566
71	0.43	0.3478	0.0822
72	0.57	0.4055	0.1645
75	0.71	0.5860	0.1240
80	0.78	0.8360	0.0560
81	0.85	0.8708	0.0208
83	0.93	0.9423	0.0123
85	1.0	0.9590	0.0410

FIGURE 3.16 is the plot of the cumulative fraction for our control data. Each step in the plot corresponds to a data point. The plot of $F_0(x)$ is a normal CDF for the values of the continuous variable Temperature. On the same graph we also plot $\hat{F}(x)$, the control cumulative fraction. We use a thick line to display $\hat{F}(x)$. The K-S test is based on the maximum distance d between these two curves.

Temperature
64
65
68
69
70
71
72
72
75
75
80
81
83
85

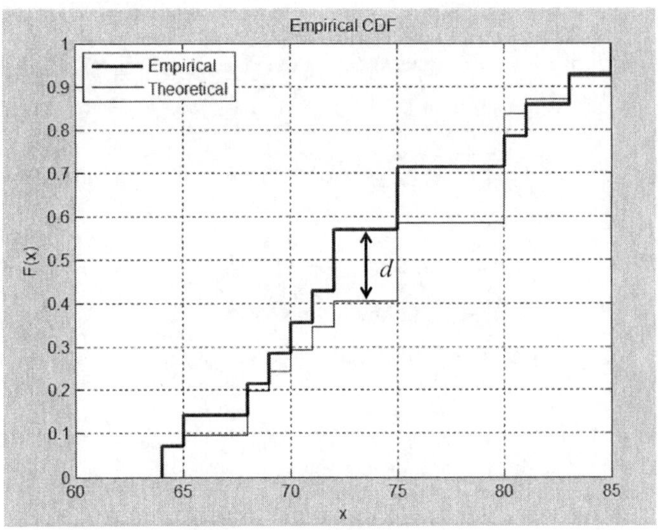

FIGURE 3.16 : Plot of normal CDF and cumulative fraction

It can be seen that the two plots span much the same range of values. But for most values of x, the fraction of the temperature values that is strictly less than x is clearly less than the fraction of the control group that is less than x. For $n = 12$ and the level of significance $\alpha = 0.05$, the critical value from the statistical table is 0.33815. Since our computed value $d = 0.1645$ for normal distribution is less than the critical value 0.33815, the data set was drawn from the normal distribution.

Independently, FIGURE 3.17 shows SAS output of various goodness-of-fit tests of the continuous variable Temperature for normal, lognormal, and exponential distributions. In each of the three cases, the value of d is below the critical value of 0.33815. The d value for the Lognormal distribution is the lowest of the three distributions. This suggests that the Lognormal distribution is the best fit for the temperature data, a conclusion which is also evident in FIGURE 3.11.

Goodness-of-Fit Tests for Normal Distribution

Test		Statistic		p Value
Kolmogorov-Smirnov	D	0.16592298	Pr > D	>0.150
Cramer-von Mises	W-Sq	0.05096146	Pr > W-Sq	>0.250
Anderson-Darling	A-Sq	0.30214105	Pr > A-Sq	>0.250

Goodness-of-Fit Tests for Lognormal Distribution

Test		Statistic		p Value
Kolmogorov-Smirnov	D	0.11385708	Pr > D	>0.500
Cramer-von Mises	W-Sq	0.03099351	Pr > W-Sq	>0.500
Anderson-Darling	A-Sq	0.24558213	Pr > A-Sq	>0.500

Goodness-of-Fit Tests for Exponential Distribution

Test		Statistic		p Value
Kolmogorov-Smirnov	D	0.22553608	Pr > D	0.157
Cramer-von Mises	W-Sq	0.14975221	Pr > W-Sq	0.103
Anderson-Darling	A-Sq	0.78160576	Pr > A-Sq	0.116

FIGURE 3.17 : Kolmogorov-Smirnov tests of Temperature for Normal, Lognormal and Exponential distributions (from left to right)

3.5 FURTHER READING

Two comprehensive books on probability distributions are (Feller, 1968) and (Grimmett and Stirzaker, 2001).

CHAPTER 4

Bayesian Probability and Inference

The traditional frequentist approach to determining the probability of an event is to calculate a ratio of the number of occurrences of an event to the total number of trials. The Bayesian approach is a different way of thinking about probability; it is based instead on a subjective interpretation of probability. In the Bayesian approach, it is assumed that there is a *prior* probability or "belief" that a person already holds about the likelihood of occurrence of an event, even before gathering information about the event. The person then changes his or her own belief based on new information, and obtains a *posterior* probability. The objective here will be to explore the way in which updating prior probabilities takes place in light of new information. The foundation underlying this belief-updating inferencing is known as *Bayes' rule*. If the prior probability follows a certain distribution, Bayesian inferencing can be made by summarizing this new information in a probability distribution. Having the correct assumptions about a prior probability is crucial in the absence of any concrete evidence. We devote a section to the state-of-the-art in constructing priors, and we emphasize inferencing based on conjugate priors in particular.

4.1 BAYESIAN INFERENCE

Recall that the multiplication rule gives the following joint probabilities of two events X and Y:

$$p(X,Y) = p(X)\,p(Y|X)$$
$$p(Y,X) = p(Y)\,p(X|Y)$$

Together the above two formulae yield Bayes' rule as

$$p(X|Y) = \frac{p(Y|X)\,p(X)}{p(Y)}$$

In Bayesian inference, one of the two events is the hypothesis H and the other is data D. The Bayesian inferencing problem is to decide on the relative truth of the hypothesis, given the data. According to Bayes' rule above

$$p(H|D) = \frac{p(D|H)\,p(H)}{p(D)}$$

The conditional probability $p(D|H)$ is known as the *likelihood function*, that is, the probability of observed data given the hypothesis. The probability $p(H)$ is known as the *prior*, and the conditional probability $p(H|D)$ is known as the *posterior*. The transformation from prior to posterior in Bayes' rule captures what is learned from the data about the hypothesis under consideration.

If there are n mutually exclusive and exhaustive sets of hypotheses $H_1, ..., H_n$ under consideration, and H is any one of them, then we have

$$p(H|D) = \frac{p(D|H)\,p(H)}{\sum\limits_{i=1}^{n} p(D|H_i)\,p(H_i)}$$

The denominator of the right-hand side of the above equation is known as the normalizing constant. One can therefore write $p(H|D) \propto p(D|H)\,p(H)$.

Example

A random quality-assurance test for a product being made in a factory finds that about 2% of the products are defective. However, the test is not perfect. It is about 95% correct (i.e., positive) for identifying defective products, and about 99% correct (i.e., negative) for identifying non-defective products. A positive outcome doesn't necessarily mean the product is defective, and a negative outcome doesn't necessarily mean the product is non-defective. The test is observed to be positive for a new sample. What is the posterior probability that a sample is defective?

$$H = Sample\,is\,defective$$
$$D = Test\,is\,positive$$

$$\begin{aligned}
&\mathrm{p}(H|D) = ?\\
&\mathrm{p}(H) = \;\; 0.02\\
&\mathrm{p}(D|H) \;\; = \;\; 0.95\\
&\mathrm{p}(not\,D|not\,H) = \;\; 0.99\\
&\mathrm{p}(D|not\,H) = \;\; 1.0 - 0.99 \;\; = \;\; 0.01
\end{aligned}$$

$$\begin{aligned}
&\mathrm{p}(H|D)\\
&\quad = \frac{\mathrm{p}(D|H) \times p(H)}{p(D)}\\
&\quad = 0.95 \;*\; 0.02 \;/\; (0.95 \;+ 0.01) \;\; = \;\; 0.19/0.96\\
&\quad = 0.0198
\end{aligned}$$

So the posterior probability that a sample is defective is 0.0198 given the test is positive for the sample. So the new $p(H)$ is 0.0198.

Example

One of the most popular applications of Bayesian probability is parameter estimation of a dynamic system where noisy observations are obtained via sensors. Suppose a physician is remotely monitoring a patient's heart rate X and the observation Z is being captured by an instrument and sent over the internet. The observation equation is

$$Z = X + e$$

where the noise variable e follows Gaussian distribution with zero mean and variance σ_e^2. The physician has to give his or her best guess for X given an observed value Z. In other words, if the conditional probability $p(X|Z)$ is known as a function, then the best guess $\hat{X}$ of X is the one that maximizes $p(X|Z)$:

$$\hat{X} = \arg\max_X p(X|Z)$$

But Bayes' rule gives $p(X|Z) \propto p(Z|X)\,p(X)$. Hence,

$$\hat{X} = \arg\max_X p(Z|X)\,p(X)$$

We must use subjective knowledge of the prior. Since the patient has been known to the physician for a while, the physician comes up with the mean value of X as 80 and variance as σ_X^2, based on experience in conjunction with previously recorded measurements from the patient. The prior is approximated as a Gaussian distribution.

$$p(X) = \frac{1}{\sqrt{2\pi}\sigma_X} e^{-\frac{(X-80)^2}{2\sigma_X^2}}$$

Since the noise is a zero-mean Gaussian

$$p(Z|X) = p(X+e|X) = \frac{1}{\sqrt{2\pi}\sigma_e} e^{-\frac{(Z-X)^2}{2\sigma_e^2}}$$

$$p(X|Z) \propto \arg\max_X e^{-\frac{(Z-X)^2}{2\sigma_e^2} - \frac{(X-80)^2}{2\sigma_X^2}}$$

The value of X that maximizes $p(X|Z)$ is the same as the one that minimizes

$$\frac{(Z-X)^2}{2\sigma_e^2} + \frac{(X-80)^2}{2\sigma_X^2}$$

Hence,

$$\hat{X} = \frac{Z\sigma_X^2 + 80\sigma_e^2}{\sigma_X^2 + \sigma_e^2}$$

The above can also be derived from the fact that $\hat{X}$ is the mean of the product of the two distributions $p(Z|X)$ and $p(X)$, and if $X_1 \sim N(\mu_1, \sigma_1^2)$ and $X_2 \sim N(\mu_2, \sigma_2^2)$ then

$$X_1 X_2 \sim N\left(\frac{\mu_1\sigma_2^2 + \mu_2\sigma_1^2}{\sigma_1^2 + \sigma_2^2}, \frac{\sigma_1^2\sigma_2^2}{\sigma_1^2 + \sigma_2^2}\right)$$

So if the prior and likelihood distributions are considered normal, then the posterior is normal. The normal distribution is a conjugate prior to itself. We will discuss more general conjugate priors in the following section for other distributions.

4.2 PRIOR PROBABILITIES

By definition, Bayesian probability is highly subjective, and one expects that all priors will be subjective. However, many disagree with this notion of subjectivity for prior distributions, and thus various objective or non-informative priors are considered. Following are various ways an analyst can cope with a prior probability required to apply Bayesian inferencing to the task at hand:

1. *Informative priors*: The analyst has a strong prior belief about the distribution of the parameter of interest and wishes to influence the analysis task at hand with such a belief.

2. *Conjugate priors*: The analyst can make use of conjugate priors for mathematical convenience, wherein the prior has the same analytical expression as the posterior.

3. *Non-informative priors*: The analyst has no prior belief and does not wish to influence the analysis task with the prior. A non-informative prior is expected to have minimal impact on the posterior distribution of the parameters.

A *flat prior* does not prefer any particular value over any other value. A flat prior is not non-informative in general. The *uniform prior* is an example of a flat prior. The trouble with the flat prior is that a probability statement that is non-informative on one scale might take a very different shape when we transform the statement to another scale. Here is an example that illustrates that the flat prior is not transformation-invariant.

Suppose X is our variable of interest and $p(X) = 1$. The infinitesimal mass element of probability for X to be in the interval dX is the absolute value of $p(X)\,dX$. The transformation invariance requires that the mass element $p(X)\,dX$ remains unchanged when expressed in terms of Y as follows:

$$p(X)\,dX = p(Y)\,dY$$

Consider the transformation

$$Y = e^X$$

An example of this kind of transformation is that if m is the mortality rate then the annual survival rate is $S = e^{-m}$. Some analysts may prefer to use m for modeling and others may prefer S, but the inference should not depend on this arbitrary parameterization. Since $X = \log(Y)$, $p(Y) = \frac{1}{Y}$, which is not flat. Another example is the logit function $\phi = \log\left(\frac{p}{1-p}\right)$ which transforms a probability statement from the scale $0 < p < 1$ to another scale $-\infty < \varphi < \infty$.

The method described by Jeffreys (1946) for finding invariant non-informative priors does not take the structure of the problem into account. Another well-known class of non-informative priors is the "reference prior" described by Bernardo (1979) and then further developed by Berger and Bernardo (1992). This reference prior method is based on the notion of maximizing the information provided by the observed data in the resulting analysis.

4.2.1 Conjugate Priors

The Bayesian approach suffers from the problem of choosing a prior probability distribution. There is always a tradeoff between a realistic prior vs. a mathematical function that simplifies the analytic computation of the posterior so that the posterior belongs to the same functional family as the prior. TABLE 4.1 shows some examples of conjugate priors.

TABLE 4.1: : Conjugate priors

Conjugate Prior ***p(X)***	***Likelihood*** ***p(Z/X)***	***Posterior*** ***p(X/Z)***
$Normal\left(\mu_1, \sigma_1^2\right)$	$Normal\left(\mu_1, \sigma_2^2\right)$ with known σ_2^2	$Normal\left(\frac{\mu_1\sigma_2^2+\mu_2\sigma_1^2}{\sigma_1^2+\sigma_2^2}, \frac{\sigma_1^2\sigma_2^2}{\sigma_1^2+\sigma_2^2}\right)$
$Beta\,(p;\ r,\ s)$	$Binomial\,(n;\ N,\ p)$	$Beta\,(p; r+n, s+N-n)$
$Gamma\,(\lambda;\ r,\ s)$	$Poisson\,(\lambda;\ n)$	$Gamma\,(\lambda; r+n, s+1)$
$Dirichlet$ $(p_1, ..., p_k; \alpha_1, ..., \alpha_k)$	$Multinomial$ $(n_1, ..., n_k; p_1, ..., p_k)$	$Dirichlet\begin{pmatrix} p_1, ..., p_k; \\ n_1+\alpha_1, ..., \\ n_k+\alpha_k \end{pmatrix}$
$Gamma\,(\lambda;\ r,\ s)$	$Exponential\,(\lambda;\ n)$	$Gamma\begin{pmatrix} \lambda;\ r+n, \\ s+\sum X_i \end{pmatrix}$

Example

Consider the following density of Beta distribution as the prior distribution of variable p representing the probability of a head in a coin flip:

$$f\left(p;\alpha,\beta\right)=\frac{\Gamma\left(\alpha+\beta\right)}{\Gamma\left(\alpha\right)\Gamma\left(\beta\right)}p^{\alpha-1}\left(1-p\right)^{\beta-1},\ 0\leq p\leq 1$$

The likelihood for obtaining n heads with the probability of a head being p is binomial:

$$f\left(n;N,p\right)=\left(\begin{array}{c}N\\ n\end{array}\right)p^{n}\left(1-p\right)^{N-n}$$

The posterior is Beta:

$$f\left(p;\alpha+n,\beta+N-n\right)=$$
$$\frac{\Gamma(\alpha+n+\beta+N-n)}{\Gamma(\alpha+n)\Gamma(\beta+N-n)}p^{\alpha+n-1}\left(1-p\right)^{\beta+N-n-1},\ 0\leq p\leq 1$$

Conjugate priors are computationally tractable, but unlike a non-informative prior, can strongly influence the posterior distribution objective.

4.2.2 The Jeffreys Prior

The Jeffreys prior is based on the principal of invariance. The prior in a one dimensional case is

$$p_J\left(\theta\right)\propto\left|I\left(\theta\right)\right|^{\frac{1}{2}}$$

where I is the Fisher information, defined as the second derivative of the log likelihood as follows:

$$I\left(\theta\right)=-E_{\theta}\left[\frac{\partial^2}{\partial\theta^2}\log p\left(X|\theta\right)\right]$$

If θ is a multivariate then

$$I\left(\theta\right)=-E_{\theta}\left[\frac{\partial^2}{\partial\theta_i\partial\theta_j}\log p\left(X|\theta\right)\right]_{n\times n}$$

It can be shown that for any re-parameterization $\varphi=f\left(\theta\right)$ if we first compute $p_J\left(\theta\right)$ and then transform variables from θ to ϕ in the likelihood function to compute $p_J\left(\phi\right)$, the following property holds:

$$p_J\left(\phi\right)d\phi=p_J\left(\theta\right)d\theta$$

Thus the Jeffreys prior is indeed independent of re-parameterization.

Example

Suppose variable X is binomially distributed, that is, $X\sim Bin\left(n,\theta\right)$. So the likelihood function of parameter θ is

$$L(\theta) = p(X|\theta) = \begin{pmatrix} n \\ X \end{pmatrix} \theta^X (1-\theta)^{n-X}$$

We derive Fisher information from log likelihood to obtain the Jeffreys prior for θ as follows:

$$\begin{aligned} &\log L(\theta) = \log \begin{pmatrix} n \\ X \end{pmatrix} + X \log \theta + (n-X) \log (1-\theta) \\ &\tfrac{\partial}{\partial \theta} \log L(\theta) = \tfrac{X}{\theta} - \tfrac{n-X}{1-\theta} \\ &\tfrac{\partial^2}{\partial \theta^2} \log L(\theta) = -\tfrac{X}{\theta^2} - \tfrac{n-X}{(1-\theta)^2} \end{aligned}$$

So the Fisher information $I(\theta)$ is given below:

$$\begin{aligned} &I(\theta) \\ &\quad = -E\left[\tfrac{\partial^2}{\partial \theta^2} \log L(\theta)\right] \\ &\quad = E\left[\tfrac{X}{\theta^2} + \tfrac{n-X}{(1-\theta)^2}\right] \\ &\quad = \tfrac{n\theta}{\theta^2} + \tfrac{n-n\theta}{(1-\theta)^2}, \text{since } E[X] = np \text{ for } X \sim Bin(n, \theta) \\ &\quad = \tfrac{n}{\theta(1-\theta)} \end{aligned}$$

Therefore, the Jeffreys prior $p_J(\theta) = |I(\theta)|^{\frac{1}{2}} \propto \theta^{-\frac{1}{2}} (1-\theta)^{-\frac{1}{2}}$. Thus, $p_J(\theta)$ is of the form of $Beta\left(\frac{1}{2}, \frac{1}{2}\right)$ as opposed to the flat prior $Beta(1,1)$.

Example

Suppose variable X is normally distributed, that is, $X \sim N(\mu, \sigma^2)$. We want to compute priors in the following three cases:

Case 1: The parameter σ^2 is known.

So the likelihood function of parameter μ is

$$L(\mu) = p(X|\mu) = \frac{1}{\sqrt{2\pi\sigma^2}} e^{-\frac{(X-\mu)^2}{2\sigma^2}}$$

The partial derivative with respect to μ gives

$$\frac{\partial^2}{\partial \mu^2} \log L(\mu) = -\frac{1}{\sigma^2}$$

which is a constant when the parameters are X and μ. So the Fisher information $I(\mu)$ is given below:

$$I(\mu) = -E\left[\frac{\partial^2}{\partial \mu^2} \log L(\mu)\right] = -E\left[\frac{1}{\sigma^2}\right] = -\frac{1}{\sigma^2}$$

Since σ^2 is known, the Jeffreys prior is the flat prior:

$$p_J(\mu) = |I(\mu)|^{\frac{1}{2}} \propto 1$$

This prior is improper since

$$\int_{\mu} p_j(\mu) d\mu = \infty$$

To compute the posterior, suppose $x_1, ..., x_n$ are i.i.d from $N(\mu, \sigma^2)$, where σ^2 is known and the prior $p(\mu) = 1$. Consider the following derivation of posterior:

$$\begin{aligned}
& p(\mu | x_1, ..., x_n) \\
& \quad \propto p(x_1, ..., x_n | \mu) \times p(\mu) \\
& \quad = p(x_1|\mu) \times ... \times p(x_n|\mu) \times 1 \\
& \quad \propto e^{-\frac{(x_1-\mu)^2}{2\sigma^2}} \times ... \times e^{-\frac{(x_n-\mu)^2}{2\sigma^2}} \\
& \quad = e^{-\frac{\sum_i (x_i-\mu)^2}{2\sigma^2}} \propto e^{-\frac{n\mu^2 - 2\mu \sum_i x_i}{2\sigma^2}} \\
& \quad \propto e^{-\frac{(\mu-\bar{x})^2}{2\times\frac{\sigma^2}{n}}}, \; where \, \bar{x} = \frac{1}{n}\sum_i x_i
\end{aligned}$$

$$\mu | x_1, ..., x_n \sim N\left(\bar{x}, \frac{\sigma^2}{n}\right)$$

Hence the posterior is also a normal distribution.

Case 2: The parameter μ is known.
So the likelihood function of parameter σ^2 is

$$L(\sigma^2) = p(X|\sigma^2) = \frac{1}{\sqrt{2\pi\sigma^2}} e^{-\frac{(X-\mu)^2}{2\sigma^2}}$$

The partial derivative with respect to σ^2 gives

$$\frac{\partial^2}{\partial^2_{\sigma^2}} \log L(\sigma^2) = -\frac{1}{4(\sigma^2)^2} - \frac{(X-\mu)^2}{(\sigma^2)^3}$$

So the Fisher information $I(\sigma^2)$ is given below:

$$\begin{aligned}
& I(\sigma^2) \\
& \quad = -E\left[\frac{\partial^2}{\partial^2_{\sigma^2}} \log L(\sigma^2)\right] \\
& \quad = -E\left[-\frac{1}{4(\sigma^2)^2} - \frac{(X-\mu)^2}{(\sigma^2)^3}\right] \\
& \quad = \frac{1}{(\sigma^2)^2}, \text{Since } E\left[(X-\mu)^2\right] = \sigma^2
\end{aligned}$$

Therefore, $p_J(\sigma^2) = \left|I(\sigma^2)\right|^{\frac{1}{2}} \propto \frac{1}{\sigma^2}$

Given $x_1, ..., x_n$ are i.i.d from $N(\mu, \sigma^2)$, where μ is known and the prior $p(\sigma^2) \propto \frac{1}{\sigma^2}$, the posterior in this case is as follows:

$$\sigma^2 | x_1, ..., x_n \sim \frac{1}{(\sigma^2)^{\frac{n}{2}+1}} e^{-\frac{\sum_i (x_i-\mu)^2}{2\sigma^2}}$$

Case 3: The parameters μ and σ^2 are unknown.

So the likelihood function of parameter μ and $\sigma^2$is

$$L\left(\mu, \sigma^2\right) = p\left(X|\mu, \sigma^2\right) = \frac{1}{\sqrt{2\pi}\left(\sigma^2\right)^{\frac{1}{2}}} e^{-\frac{(X-\mu)^2}{2\sigma^2}}$$

The Fisher information $I\left(\mu, \sigma^2\right)$ is given below (variable v is σ^2):

$$\begin{aligned} & I\left(\mu, \sigma^2\right) \\ & = -E\left[\begin{array}{cc} \frac{\partial^2}{\partial\mu^2}\log L\left(\mu, \sigma^2\right) & \frac{\partial^2}{\partial\mu\partial v}\log L\left(\mu, \sigma^2\right) \\ \frac{\partial^2}{\partial v\partial\mu}\log L\left(\mu, \sigma^2\right) & \frac{\partial^2}{\partial v^2}\log L\left(\mu, \sigma^2\right) \end{array}\right] \\ & = \left[\begin{array}{cc} -\frac{1}{\sigma^2} & 0 \\ 0 & \frac{1}{(\sigma^2)^2} \end{array}\right] \end{aligned}$$

Therefore, $p_J\left(\mu, \sigma^2\right) = \left|I\left(\mu, \sigma^2\right)\right|^{\frac{1}{2}} \propto \frac{1}{(\sigma^2)^{\frac{3}{2}}}$

Given $x_1, ..., x_n$ are i.i.d from $N\left(\mu, \sigma^2\right)$, where the prior $p\left(\sigma^2\right) \propto \frac{1}{(\sigma^2)^{\frac{3}{2}}}$, the posterior in this case is as follows:

$$\mu, \sigma^2|x_1, ..., x_n \sim \frac{1}{\left(\sigma^2\right)^{\frac{n}{2}+1}} e^{-\frac{n(\mu-\bar{x})^2+\sum_i (x_i-\bar{x})^2}{2\sigma^2}}$$

4.3 FURTHER READING

A comprehensive book on Bayesian probability and inference is by Gelman et al. (2003). For further reading on the Jeffreys prior, please consult the original paper (Jeffreys, 1946) and his book (Jeffreys, 1961).

CHAPTER 5

Inferential Statistics and Predictive Analytics

Inferential statistics draws valid inferences about a population based on an analysis of a representative sample of that population. The results of such an analysis are generalized to the larger population from which the sample originates, in order to make assumptions or predictions about the population in general. This chapter introduces linear, logistics, and polynomial regression analyses for inferential statistics. The result of a regression analysis on a sample is a predictive model in the form of a set of equations.

The first task of sample analysis is to make sure that the chosen sample is representative of the population as a whole. We have previously discussed the one-way chi-square goodness-of-fit test for such a task by comparing the sample distribution with an expected distribution. Here we present the chi-square two-way test of independence to determine whether significant differences exist between the distributions in two or more categories. This test helps to determine whether a candidate independent variable in a regression analysis is a true candidate predictor of the dependent variable, and to thus exclude irrelevant variables from consideration in the process.

We also generalize traditional regression analyses to Bayesian regression analyses, where the regression is undertaken within the context of the Bayesian inference. We present the most general Bayesian regression analysis, known as the Gaussian process. Given its similarity to other decision tree learning techniques, we save discussion of the Classification and Regression Tree (CART) technique for the later chapter on ML.

To use inferential statistics to infer latent concepts and variables and their relationships, this chapter includes a detailed description of principal component and factor analyses. To use inferential statistics for forecasting by modeling time series data, we present survival analysis and autoregression techniques. Later in the book we devote a full chapter to AI- and ML-oriented techniques for modeling and forecasting from time series data, including dynamic Bayesian networks and Kalman filtering.

5.1 CHI-SQUARE TEST OF INDEPENDENCE

The one-way Chi-Square (χ^2) goodness-of-fit test (which was introduced earlier in the descriptive analytics chapter) is a non-parametric test used to decide whether distributions of categorical variables differ significantly from predicted values. The two-way or two-sample chi-square test of independence is used to determine whether a significant difference exists between the distributions of two or more categorical variables. To determine if Outlook is a good predictor of Decision in our play-tennis example in Appendix B, for instance, the null hypothesis H0 is that two distributions are not equal; in other words, that the weather does not affect if one decides to play or not. The Outlook vs. Decision table is shown below in TABLE 5.1. Note that the row and the column subtotals must have equal sums, and that total expected frequencies must equal total observed frequencies.

TABLE 5.1: : Outlook vs. Decision table

Outlook	Decision play	Decision don't play	Row Subtotal
sunny	2	3	5
overcast	4	0	4
rain	3	2	5
Column Subtotal	9	5	Total = 14

Note also that we are computing expectation as follows with a view that the observations are assumed to be representative of the past

$$\begin{aligned}
&Exp\,(Outlook = sunny\ \&\ Decision = play)\\
&\quad = 14 \times p\,(Outlook = sunny\ \&\ Decision = play)\\
&\quad = 14 \times p\,(Outlook = sunny) \times p\,(Decision = play)\\
&\quad = 14 \times \left(\sum_{Decision} (p\,(Outlook = sunny) \times p\,(Decision)) \right) \times\\
&\qquad \left(\sum_{Outlook} (p\,(Decision = play) \times p\,(Outlook)) \right)\\
&\quad = 14 \times (p\,(sunny) \times p\,(play) + p\,(sunny) \times p\,(don't\,play)) \times\\
&\qquad (p\,(play) \times p\,(sunny) + p\,(play) \times p\,(overcast) + p\,(play) \times p\,(rain))\\
&\quad = 14 \times (\text{Row subtotal for } sunny/14) \times (\text{Column subtotal for } play/14)\\
&\quad = (5 \times 9)\,/14
\end{aligned}$$

The computation of Chi-square statistic is shown in TABLE 5.2.

TABLE 5.2: : Computation of Chi-square statistic

Joint Variable	Observed (O)	Expected (E)	$(\text{O-E})^2/\text{E}$
sunny & play	2	3.21	0.39
sunny & don't play	3	1.79	0.82
overcast & play	4	2.57	0.79
overcast & don't play	0	1.43	1.43
rainy & play	3	3.21	0.01
rainy & don't play	2	1.79	0.02

Therefore, Chi-square statistic $= \sum_i \frac{(O-E)^2}{E} = 3.46$
The degree of freedom is $(3-1) \times (2-1)$, that is, 2. With 95% as the level of significance, the critical value from the Chi-square table is 5.99. Since the value 3.46 is less than 5.99, so we would reject the null hypothesis that there is significant difference between the distributions in Outlook and Decision. Hence the weather does affect if one decides to play or not.

5.2 REGRESSION ANALYSES

In this section, we begin with simple and multiple linear regression techniques, then present logistic regression for handling categorical variables as the dependent variables, and, finally, discuss polynomial regression for modeling nonlinearity in data.

5.2.1 Simple Linear Regression

Simple linear regression models the relationship between two variables X and Y by fitting a linear equation to observed data:

$$Y = a + bX$$

where X is called an *explanatory variable* and Y is called a *dependent variable.* The *slope* b and the *intercept* a in the above equation must be estimated from a given set of observations. "Least-squares" is the most common method for fitting equations, wherein the best-fitting line for the observed data is calculated by minimizing the sum of the squares of the vertical deviations from each data point to the line.

Suppose the set $(y_1, x_1), ..., (y_n, x_n)$ of n observations are given. The expression to be minimized is the sum of the squares of the residuals (i.e., the differences between the observed and predicted values):

$$\sum_{i=1}^{n} (y_i - a - bx_i)^2$$

By solving the two equations obtained by taking partial derivatives of the above expression with respect to a and b and then equating them to zero, the estimations of a and b can be obtained.

$$\hat{b} = \frac{\sum_{i=1}^{n}(x_i-\bar{X})(y_i-\bar{Y})}{\sum_{i=1}^{n}(x_i-\bar{X})^2} = \frac{\sum_{i=1}^{n} x_i y_i - \frac{1}{n}\sum_{i=1}^{n} x_i \sum_{j=1}^{n} y_j}{\sum_{i=1}^{n} x_i^2 - \frac{1}{n}\left(\sum_{i=1}^{n} x_i\right)^2} = \frac{Cov(X,Y)}{Var(X)}$$

$$\hat{a} = \bar{Y} - \hat{b}\bar{X}$$

The plot in FIGURE 5.1 shows the observations and linear regression model (the straight line) of the two variables Temperature (Fahrenheit degree) and Humidity (%), with Temperature as the dependent variable. For any given observation of Humidity, the difference between the observed and predicted value of Temperature provides the residual error.

Temperature (°F)	Humidity (%)
75	70
80	90
85	85
72	95
69	70
72	90
83	78
64	65
81	75
71	80
65	70
75	80
68	80
70	96

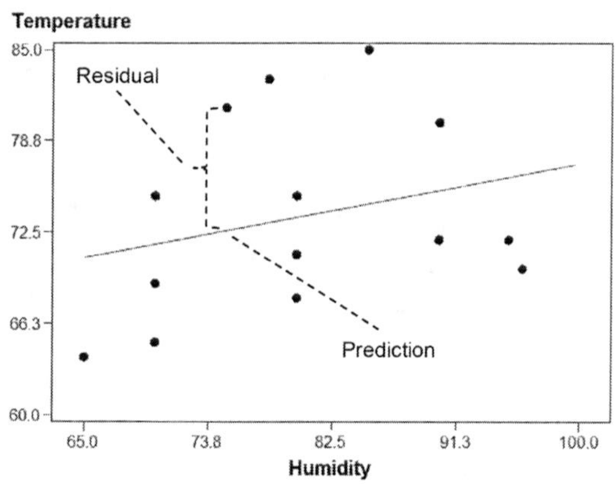

FIGURE 5.1 : Example linear regression

The correlation coefficient measure between the observed and predicted values can be used to determine how close the residuals are to the regression line.

5.2.2 Multiple Linear Regression

Multiple linear regression models the relationship between two or more response variables X_i and one dependent variable Y as follows:

$$Y = a + b_1 X_1 + ... + b_p X_p$$

The given n observations $(y_1, x_{11}, ..., x_{1p})$, ..., $(y_n, x_{n1}, ..., x_{np})$ in matrix form are

$$\begin{bmatrix} y_1 \\ y_2 \\ \ldots \\ y_n \end{bmatrix} = \begin{bmatrix} a \\ a \\ \ldots \\ a \end{bmatrix} + \begin{bmatrix} b_1 \\ b_2 \\ \ldots \\ b_p \end{bmatrix}^T \begin{bmatrix} x_{11} & x_{21} & \ldots & x_{n1} \\ x_{12} & x_{22} & \ldots & x_{n2} \\ \ldots & \ldots & \ldots & \ldots \\ x_{1p} & x_{2p} & \ldots & x_{np} \end{bmatrix}$$

Or in abbreviated form

$$\mathbf{Y} = A + B^T\mathbf{X}$$

The expression to be minimized is

$$\sum_{i=1}^{n} (y_i - a - b_1 x_{i1} - \ldots - b_p x_{ip})^2$$

The estimates of A and B are as follows:

$$\hat{B} = \left(\mathbf{X}^T\mathbf{X}\right)^{-1} \mathbf{X}^T\mathbf{Y} = \frac{Cov(\mathbf{X},\mathbf{Y})}{Var(\mathbf{X})}$$
$$\hat{A} = \bar{\mathbf{Y}} - \hat{B}\bar{\mathbf{X}}$$

5.2.3 Logistic Regression

The dependent variable in logistic regression is binary. In order to predict categorical attribute Decision in the play-tennis example in Appendix B from a new category Temperature, suppose the attribute Temp_0_1 represents a continuous version of the attribute Decision, with 0 and 1 representing the values "don't play" and "play" respectively. FIGURE 5.2 shows the scatter plot and a line plot of Temperature vs. Temp_0_1 (left), and a scatter plot and logistic curve for the same (right). The scatter plot shows that there is a fluctuation among the observed values, in the sense that for a given Temperature (say, 72), the value of the dependent variable (play/don't play) has been observed to be both 0 and 1 on two different occasions. Consequently, the line plot oscillates between 0 and 1 around that temperature. On the other hand, the logistic curve transitions smoothly from 0 to 1. We describe here briefly how logistic regression is formalized.

Since the value of the dependent variable is either 0 or 1, the most intuitive way to apply linear regression would be to think of the response as a probability value. The prediction will fall into one class or the other if the response crosses a certain threshold or not, and therefore the linear equation will be of the form:

$$p(Y = 1|X) = a + bX$$

However, the value of $a + bX$ could be > 1 or < 0 for some X, giving probabilities that cannot exist. The solution is to use a different probability representation. Consider the following equation with a ratio as the response variable:

$$\frac{p}{1-p} = a + bX$$

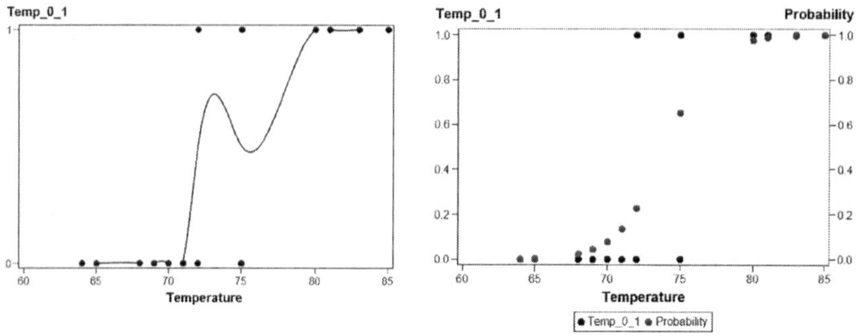

FIGURE 5.2 : (left) Scatter and line plots of Temperature vs. Temp_0_1, and (right) scatter plot and logistic curve for the same

The ratio ranges from 0 to ∞ for some X but the value of $a + bX$ would be below 0 for some X. The solution is to take the log of the ratio:

$$\log\left(\frac{p}{1-p}\right) = a + bX$$

The logit function above transforms a probability statement defined in $0 < p < 1$ to one defined in $-\infty < a + bX < \infty$. The value of p is as follows:

$$p = \frac{e^{a+bX}}{1+e^{a+bX}}$$

A maximum likelihood method can be applied to estimate the parameters a and b of a logistic model with binary response:

- $Y = 1$ with probability p
- $Y = 0$ with probability $1 - p$

For each $Y_i = 1$ the probability p_i appears in the likelihood product. Similarly, for each $Y_i = 0$ the probability $1 - p_i$ appears in the product. Thus, the likelihood of the sample $(y_1, x_1), ..., (y_n, x_n)$ of n observations takes the following form:

$$\begin{aligned} &L\left(a, b; (y_1, x_1), ..., (y_n, x_n)\right) \\ &= \prod_{i=1}^{n} p^{y_i} (1-p)^{1-y_i} \\ &= \prod_{i=1}^{n} \left(\frac{e^{a+bx_i}}{1+e^{a+bx_i}}\right)^{y_i} \left(\frac{1}{1+e^{a+bx_i}}\right)^{1-y_i} \\ &= \prod_{i=1}^{n} \frac{\left(e^{a+bx_i}\right)^{y_i}}{1+e^{a+bx_i}} \end{aligned}$$

Alternatively, we can maximize the log likelihood, $\log\left(L\left(a, b; Data\right)\right)$, to solve for a and b. In the example above, the two values of a and b that maximize the likelihood are 45.94 and -0.62, respectively. Hence the logistic equation is:

$$\log\left(\frac{p}{1-p}\right) = 45.94 - 0.62X$$

FIGURE 5.2 (right) shows the logistics curve plotted for the sample.

5.2.4 Polynomial Regression

The regression model

$$Y = a_0 + a_1X + a_2X^2 + ... + a_kX^k$$

is called the k-th order polynomial model with one variable, where a_0 is the Y-intercept of X, a_1 is called the *linear effect parameter*, a_2 is called the *quadratic effect parameter*, and so on. The model is a linear regression model for $k = 1$. This model is non-linear in the X variable, but it is linear in the parameters a_0, a_1, a_2, ... and a_k. One can also have higher-order polynomial regression involving more than one variable. For example, a second-order or quadratic polynomial regression with two variables X_1 and X_2 is

$$Y = a_0 + a_1X_1 + a_2X_2 + a_{11}X_1^2 + a_{22}X_2^2 + a_{12}X_1X_2$$

FIGURE 5.3 (left) shows a plot of 7 noisy, evenly-spaced random training samples $(x_1, y_1), ..., (x_7, y_7)$ drawn from an underlying function f (shown in dotted line). Note that a dataset of $k+1$ observations can be modeled perfectly by a polynomial of degree k. In this case, a six-degree polynomial will fit the data perfectly, but will "over-fit" the data and will not generalize well for test data. To decide on the appropriate degree for a polynomial regression model, one can begin with a linear model and include higher-order terms one by one until the highest-order term becomes non-significant (determined by looking at p-values for the t-test for slopes). One could also start with a high-order model and exclude the non-significant highest-order terms one by one until the remaining highest-order term becomes significant. Here we measure fitness with respect to the test data of eight evenly-spaced samples as shown plotted in FIGURE 5.3 (right).

FIGURE 5.4 shows six different polynomial regressions of degrees 1 to 6 along with the sample data. Note that the polynomial regression of degree 6 goes through all seven points and fits perfectly.

The closest fit to the sample training data is based on the R2 measure in Excel. FIGURE 5.5 (left) shows this measure of fitness between the training data and the predictions of each polynomial model of certain degree. As shown in the figure, the polynomial of degree 6 has the perfect measure of fitness 1.0. The test error is based on the error measure

$$\sum_{i=1}^{8} |y_i - f(x_i)|$$

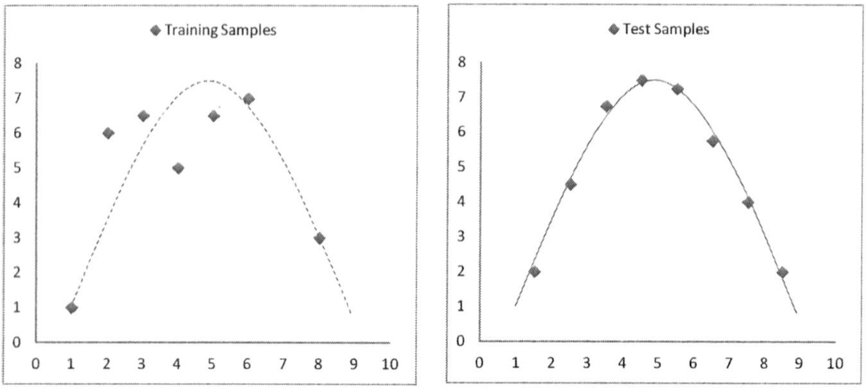

FIGURE 5.3 : Sample (left) and test data (right) from a function

between the test data and the six polynomial regressions corresponding to degrees 1 to 6. We can see in FIGURE 5.5 (left) that while the measure of fitness is steadily increasing towards 1.0, the test error in FIGURE 5.5 (right) reaches a minimum at degree 2 (hence the best fit) and then increases rapidly as the models begin to over-fit the training data.

5.3 BAYESIAN LINEAR REGRESSION

Bayesian linear regression views the regression problem as introduced above as an estimation of the functional dependence between an input variable $\mathbf{X}$ in $\Re^d$ and an output variable Y in $\Re$ as shown below:

$$\begin{aligned} Y(\mathbf{X}) & \\ &= \sum_{i=1}^{M} w_i \phi_i (\mathbf{X}) + \varepsilon \\ &= \mathbf{w}^T \Phi (\mathbf{X}) + \varepsilon \end{aligned}$$

where $\mathbf{w}^T \Phi (\mathbf{X})$ (e.g., $\Phi(\mathbf{X}) = \left(1, x, x^2, ...\right)$) is a linear combination of M pre-defined nonlinear basis functions $\phi_i (\mathbf{X})$ with input in $\Re^d$ and output in $\Re$. The observations are additively corrupted by i.i.d. noise with normal distribution

$$\varepsilon \sim N\left(0, \sigma_n^2\right)$$

that has zero mean and variance σ_n^2.

The goal of Bayesian regression is to estimate the weights w_i given a training set $\{(\mathbf{x}_1, y_1), ..., (\mathbf{x}_n, y_n)\}$ of data points. In contrast to classical regression, a Bayesian linear regression characterizes the uncertainty in $\mathbf{w}$ through a probability distribution $p(\mathbf{w})$. We use a multivariate normal distribution as prior on the weights as

$$p(\mathbf{w}) = N(\mathbf{0}, \Sigma_w)$$

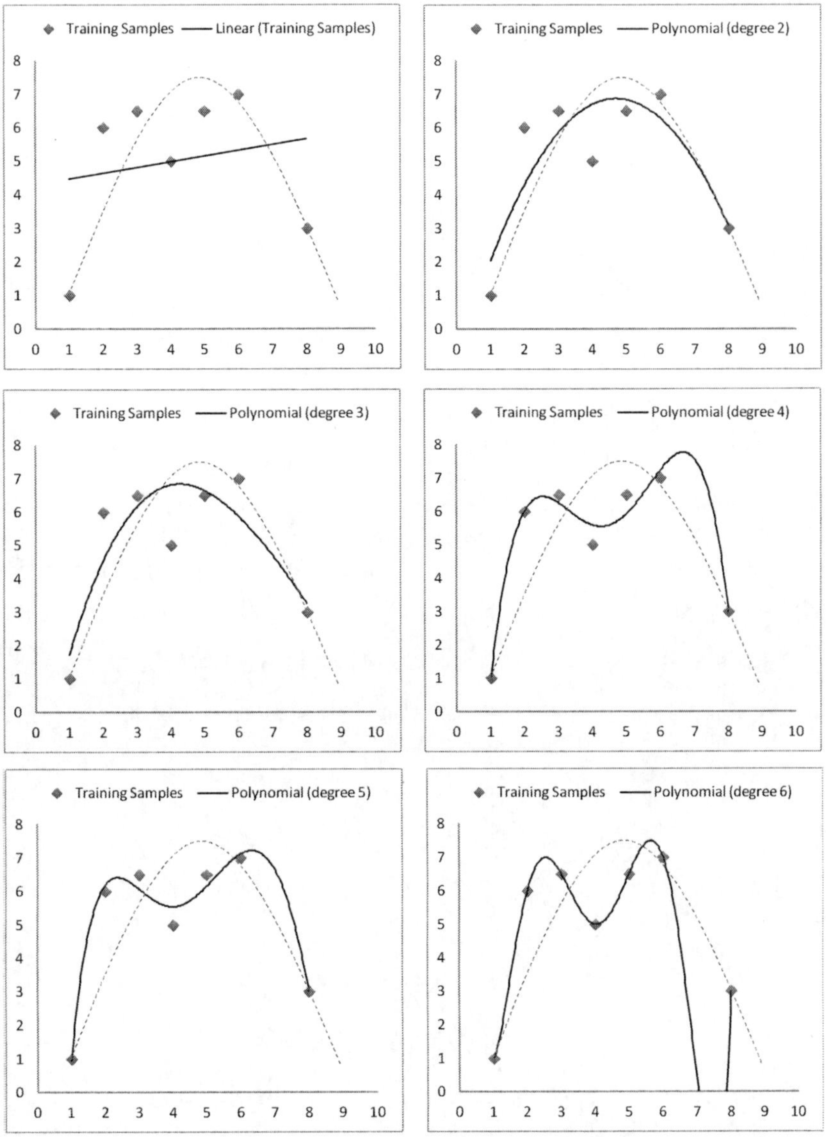

FIGURE 5.4 : Fitting polynomials of degrees 1 to 6

with zero mean and Σ_w as an $M \times M$ -sized covariance matrix. Further observations of data points modify this distribution using Bayes' theorem, with the assumption that the data points have been generated via the likelihood function. Let us illustrate Bayesian linear regression as

$$Y = \mathbf{w}^T \mathbf{X} + \varepsilon$$

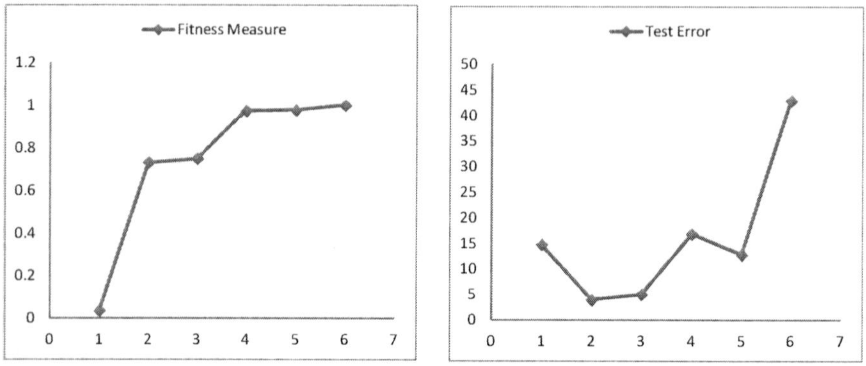

FIGURE 5.5 : Plots of fitness measures (left) and test errors (right) against polynomial degrees

Suppose $\mathbf{D}$ is the $d \times n$ matrix of input $\mathbf{x}$ vectors from this training set and $\mathbf{y}$ is the vector of y values. We have a Gaussian prior $p(\mathbf{w})$ of parameters $\mathbf{w}$, and the likelihood of the parameters is

$$p(\mathbf{y}|\mathbf{D},\mathbf{w}) = N\left(\mathbf{w}^T\mathbf{D}, \sigma_n^2\mathbf{I}\right)$$

According to Bayes' rule, the posterior distribution over $\mathbf{w}$ is

$$\begin{aligned} &p(\mathbf{w}|\mathbf{y},\mathbf{D}) \\ &\quad \propto p(\mathbf{y}|\mathbf{D},\mathbf{w})\, p(\mathbf{w}) \\ &\quad = N\left(\tfrac{1}{\sigma_n^2}\mathbf{A}^{-1}\mathbf{D}\mathbf{y}, \mathbf{A}^{-1}\right), \text{ where } \mathbf{A} = \Sigma_{\mathbf{w}}^{-1} + \tfrac{1}{\sigma_n^2}\mathbf{D}\mathbf{D}^T \end{aligned}$$

The predictive distribution is

$$\begin{aligned} &p(Y|\mathbf{X},\mathbf{y},\mathbf{D}) \\ &\quad = \int_{\mathbf{w}} \left(\mathbf{w}^T\mathbf{X}\right) p(\mathbf{w}|\mathbf{y},\mathbf{D})\, d\mathbf{w} \\ &\quad = N\left(\tfrac{1}{\sigma_n^2}\mathbf{X}^T\mathbf{A}^{-1}\mathbf{D}\mathbf{y}, \mathbf{X}^T\mathbf{A}^{-1}\mathbf{X}\right) \end{aligned}$$

The multivariate normal distribution above can be used for predicting Y given a vector input $\mathbf{X}$.

5.3.1 Gaussian Processes

A Gaussian process is a collection of random variables, any finite subset of which has a joint Gaussian distribution. Gaussian processes extend multivariate Gaussian distributions to infinite dimensionality. A regression technique starts with a set of data points, $\{(\mathbf{x}_1, y_1), ..., (\mathbf{x}_n, y_n)\}$, consisting of input-output pairs. The task is then to predict or interpolate the output value y given an input vector $\mathbf{x}$. As we observe the output, the new input-output pair is added to the observation data set. Thus the data set grows in size over time. Any number of observations $y_1, ..., y_n$ in an arbitrary data set can be viewed as a single point sampled from some multivariate Gaussian distribution. Hence, a regression data set can be partnered with a Gaussian process where the prediction always takes into account the latest observations.

We consider a more general form of regression function for interpolation

$$Y = f(\mathbf{X}) + N\left(0, \sigma_n^2\right)$$

where each observation $\mathbf{X}$ can be thought of as related to an underlying function f through some Gaussian noise model. We solve the above for the function f. In fact, given n data points and new input $\mathbf{X}$, our objective is to predict Y and not the actual f since their expected values are identical (according to the above regression function). We can obtain a Gaussian process from the Bayesian linear regression model:

$f(\mathbf{X}) = \mathbf{w}^T\mathbf{X}$ with $\mathbf{w} \sim N(0, \Sigma_{\mathbf{w}})$
where the mean is given by

$$E[f(\mathbf{X})] = E\left[\mathbf{w}^T\right]\mathbf{X} = \mathbf{0}$$

and the covariance is given by

$$E\left[f(\mathbf{x}_i)^T f(\mathbf{x}_j)\right] = \mathbf{x}_i^T E\left[\mathbf{w}\mathbf{w}^T\right]\mathbf{x}_j = \mathbf{x}_i^T \Sigma_{\mathbf{w}} \mathbf{x}_j$$

It is often assumed that the mean of this Gaussian process is zero everywhere, but one observation is related to another observation via the covariance function

$$k(\mathbf{x}_i, \mathbf{x}_j) = \sigma_f^2 \times e^{\frac{-|\mathbf{x}_i - \mathbf{x}_j|^2}{2l^2}} + \sigma_n^2 \times \delta(\mathbf{x}_i, \mathbf{x}_j)$$

where the maximum allowable covariance is defined as σ_f^2, which should be high (and hence not zero) for functions covering a broad range on the Y axis. The value of the kernel function approaches its maximum if $\mathbf{x}_i \approx \mathbf{x}_j$. In this case $f(\mathbf{x}_i)$ and $f(\mathbf{x}_j)$ are perfectly correlated. This means the neighboring points yield very close functional values, making the function smooth, and distant observations will have a negligible effect during interpolation of f at a new $\mathbf{x}$ value. The length parameter$l$ determines the effect of this separation. $\delta(\mathbf{x}_i, \mathbf{x}_j)$ is known as the *Kronecker delta* function ($\delta(\mathbf{x}_i, \mathbf{x}_j) = 0$ if $\mathbf{x}_i \neq \mathbf{x}_j$ else 1).

For Gaussian process regression, suppose the observation set is $\{(\mathbf{x}_1, y_1), ..., (\mathbf{x}_n, y_n)\}$ and a new input observation is x_* We capture the covariance functions $k(\mathbf{x}_i, \mathbf{x}_j)$ for all possible $\mathbf{x}_i, \mathbf{x}_j$, and x_* in the following three matrices:

$$\mathbf{K} = \begin{bmatrix} k(\mathbf{x}_1, \mathbf{x}_1) & k(\mathbf{x}_1, \mathbf{x}_2) & ... & k(\mathbf{x}_1, \mathbf{x}_n) \\ k(\mathbf{x}_2, \mathbf{x}_1) & k(\mathbf{x}_2, \mathbf{x}_2) & ... & k(\mathbf{x}_2, \mathbf{x}_n) \\ ... & ... & ... & ... \\ k(\mathbf{x}_n, \mathbf{x}_1) & k(\mathbf{x}_n, \mathbf{x}_2) & ... & k(\mathbf{x}_n, \mathbf{x}_n) \end{bmatrix}$$

$$\mathbf{K}_* = \begin{bmatrix} k(\mathbf{x}_*, \mathbf{x}_1) & k(\mathbf{x}_*, \mathbf{x}_2) & \ldots & k(\mathbf{x}_*, \mathbf{x}_n) \end{bmatrix}$$
$$\mathbf{K}_{**} = k(\mathbf{x}_*, \mathbf{x}_*)$$

Note that $k(\mathbf{x}_i, \mathbf{x}_i) = \sigma_f^2 + \sigma_n^2$, for all i. As per the assumption of a Gaussian process, the data set can be represented as a multivariate Gaussian distribution as follows:

$$\begin{bmatrix} \mathbf{y} \\ y_* \end{bmatrix} \sim N\left(\mathbf{0}, \begin{bmatrix} \mathbf{K} & \mathbf{K}_*^T \\ \mathbf{K}_* & \mathbf{K}_{**} \end{bmatrix}\right)$$

We are interested in the conditional distribution $p(y_*|\mathbf{y})$ which is given below:

$$y_*|\mathbf{y} \sim N\left(\mathbf{K}_*\mathbf{K}^{-1}\mathbf{y}, \mathbf{K}_{**} - \mathbf{K}_*\mathbf{K}^{-1}\mathbf{K}_*^T\right)$$

Therefore the best estimate for y_* is the mean $\mathbf{K}_*\mathbf{K}^{-1}\mathbf{y}$ of the above distribution.

Example

To illustrate the Gaussian process, consider the sample data set of seven points in TABLE 5.3, a plot of which was shown earlier in FIGURE 5.3.

TABLE 5.3: : Sample data set

X	Y
1	1
2	4.5
3	6.5
4	6
5	6.7
6	7
8	3
7.5	?

Considering the covariance function:

$$k(\mathbf{x}_i, \mathbf{x}_j) = e^{\frac{-|\mathbf{x}_i - \mathbf{x}_j|^2}{2l^2}}$$

With the value of l as 0.8 in the function k above, we calculate the covariance matrix $\mathbf{K}$ as shown in TABLE 5.4.

TABLE 5.4: : Matrix of covariance functions

1	0.457833	0.043937	0.000884	3.73E-06	3.29E-09	2.37E-17
0.457833	1	0.457833	0.043937	0.000884	3.73E-06	6.1E-13
0.043937	0.457833	1	0.457833	0.043937	0.000884	3.29E-09
0.000884	0.043937	0.457833	1	0.457833	0.043937	3.73E-06
3.73E-06	0.000884	0.043937	0.457833	1	0.457833	0.000884

TABLE 5.4: : Matrix of covariance functions

3.29E-09	3.73E-06	0.000884	0.043937	0.457833	1	0.043937
2.37E-17	6.1E-13	3.29E-09	3.73E-06	0.000884	0.043937	1

It is clear from the above table that the closer the X values are to each other, the higher the values of the covariance function are. We also have $\mathbf{K}_*$as shown in TABLE 5.5.

TABLE 5.5: : Vector of covariance functions

4.62E-15	5.45E-11	1.35E-07	6.98E-05	0.007576	0.172422	0.822578

The formula $\mathbf{K}_*\mathbf{K}^{-1}\mathbf{y}$ provides 3.23 as the mean of the predicted y-value for $x = 7.5$.

5.4 PRINCIPAL COMPONENT AND FACTOR ANALYSES

Principal component analysis (PCA) converts a set of measurements of possibly correlated variables into a set of values of linearly uncorrelated variables called principal components. PCA can be done by eigenvalue decomposition or SVD as introduced earlier in the background chapter.

Example

Consider the data set in FIGURE 5.6 with 6 variables and 51 observations of the US Electoral College votes, population, and area by state. The full data set is given in Appendix B.

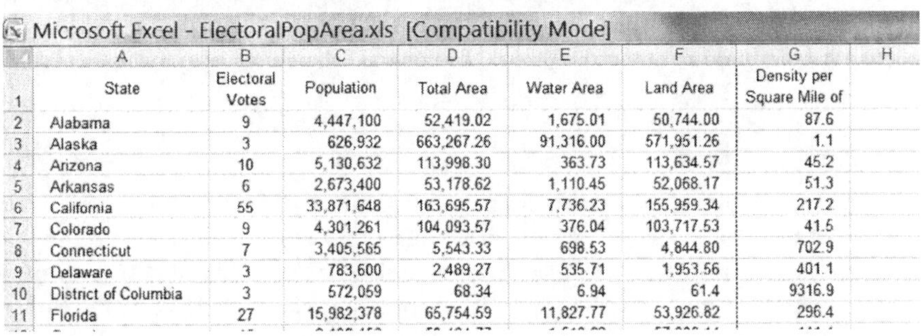
Microsoft Excel - ElectoralPopArea.xls [Compatibility Mode]

	A	B	C	D	E	F	G
1	State	Electoral Votes	Population	Total Area	Water Area	Land Area	Density per Square Mile of
2	Alabama	9	4,447,100	52,419.02	1,675.01	50,744.00	87.6
3	Alaska	3	626,932	663,267.26	91,316.00	571,951.26	1.1
4	Arizona	10	5,130,632	113,998.30	363.73	113,634.57	45.2
5	Arkansas	6	2,673,400	53,178.62	1,110.45	52,068.17	51.3
6	California	55	33,871,648	163,695.57	7,736.23	155,959.34	217.2
7	Colorado	9	4,301,261	104,093.57	376.04	103,717.53	41.5
8	Connecticut	7	3,405,565	5,543.33	698.53	4,844.80	702.9
9	Delaware	3	783,600	2,489.27	535.71	1,953.56	401.1
10	District of Columbia	3	572,059	68.34	6.94	61.4	9316.9
11	Florida	27	15,982,378	65,754.59	11,827.77	53,926.82	296.4

FIGURE 5.6 : United States Electoral College votes, population, and area by state

The correlation matrix in FIGURE 5.7 clearly indicates two groups of correlated variables. The fact that the number of electoral votes is proportional to the population gives rise to the first set of correlated variables. The second set of correlated variables is the set of all areas.

Correlation Matrix						
	Electoral Votes	Population	Total Area	Water Area	Land Area	Density per Square Mile of Land
Electoral Votes	1.0000	0.9996	0.1090	0.0510	0.1148	-.0757
Population	0.9996	1.0000	0.1100	0.0528	0.1156	-.0779
Total Area	0.1090	0.1100	1.0000	0.8276	0.9960	-.1679
Water Area	0.0510	0.0528	0.8276	1.0000	0.7739	-.0692
Land Area	0.1148	0.1156	0.9960	0.7739	1.0000	-.1783
Density per Square Mile of Land	-.0757	-.0779	-.1679	-.0692	-.1783	1.0000

FIGURE 5.7 : Correlation matrix for the data in FIGURE 5.6

All six eigenvalues and eigenvectors are shown in FIGURE 5.8, of which the first three are dominating as expected, given the two groups of correlated variables as shown in FIGURE 5.7 and the only remaining variable for density. The first principal component PRIN1 shows the domination of the coefficients corresponding to the three variables related to the areas. The second principal component PRIN2 shows the domination of the coefficients corresponding to Electoral Votes and Population.

Eigenvalues of the Correlation Matrix				
	Eigenvalue	Difference	Proportion	Cumulative
1	2.83831733	0.90006486	0.4731	0.4731
2	1.93825247	0.97029922	0.3230	0.7961
3	0.96795324	0.71288651	0.1613	0.9574
4	0.25506673	0.25465650	0.0425	0.9999
5	0.00041023	0.00041023	0.0001	1.0000
6	0.00000000		0.0000	1.0000

Eigenvectors						
	PRIN1	PRIN2	PRIN3	PRIN4	PRIN5	PRIN6
Electoral Votes	0.195980	0.676606	0.058914	-.019591	-.707066	-.000000
Population	0.196790	0.676325	0.057041	-.023601	0.707141	0.000000
Total Area	0.570839	-.159819	0.044632	0.304680	0.000564	-.744163
Water Area	0.510240	-.187209	0.150926	-.818979	-.002452	0.105344
Land Area	0.562499	-.150401	0.026248	0.474510	0.001028	0.659639
Density per Square Mile of Land	-.142331	-.039750	0.983776	0.101702	0.001665	0.000000

FIGURE 5.8 : Eigenvalues and eigenvectors of the correlation matrix in FIGURE 5.7

FIGURE 5.9 shows the principal component plot of the data set in FIGURE 5.6 with the first two components. It is clear from the plot that the component PRIN1 is about the area and PRIN2 is about the population. This is the reason why the state of Alaska has a large PRIN1 value but very little PRIN2, and DC is just opposite. The state of California has large values for both PRIN1 and PRIN2.

Factor analysis (Anderson, 2003; Gorsuch, 1983) helps to obtain a small set of independent variables, called *factors* or *latent variables*, from a large set of correlated observed variables. Factor analysis describes the variability among observed variables in order to gain better insight into categories or to provide a simpler prediction structure. For example, factor analysis can reduce a large number of financial ratios into categories of financial ratios on

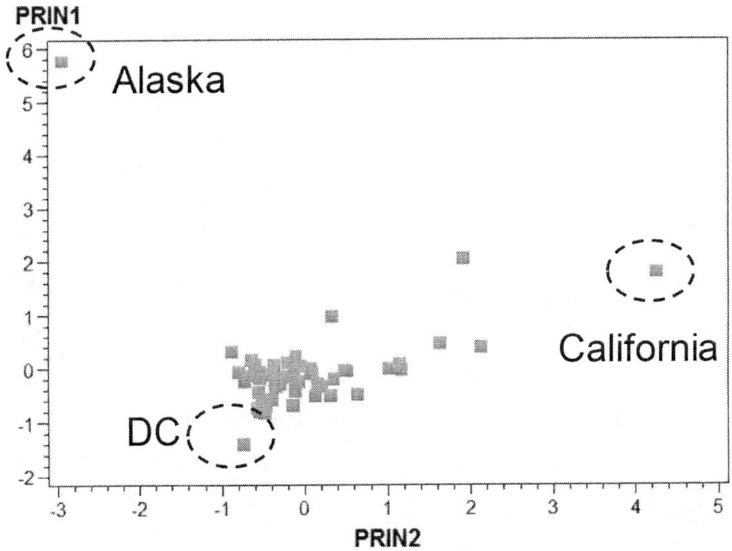

FIGURE 5.9 : Principal component plot of the data set in FIGURE 5.6

the basis of empirical evidence. It can help with finding contributing factors affecting, for example, prices of groups of stocks, GDPs of countries, and water and air qualities. For *exploratory factor analysis* (EFA), there is no predefined idea of the structure or dimensions in a set of variables. On the other hand, a *confirmatory factor analysis* (CFA) tests specific hypotheses about the structure or the number of dimensions underlying a set of variables.

The factor model proposes that observed responses $X_1, ..., X_n$ are partially influenced by underlying common factors $F_1, ..., F_m$ and partially by underlying unique factors $e_1, ..., e_n$.

$$
\begin{aligned}
X_1 &= \lambda_{11}F_1 + \lambda_{12}F_2 + ... + \lambda_{1m}F_m + e_1 \\
X_2 &= \lambda_{21}F_1 + \lambda_{22}F_2 + ... + \lambda_{2m}F_m + e_2 \\
&... \\
X_n &= \lambda_{n1}F_1 + \lambda_{n2}F_2 + ... + \lambda_{nm}F_m + e_n
\end{aligned}
$$

The coefficients λ_{ij} are called the *factor loadings*, so that λ_{ij} is the loading of the ith variable on the jth factor. Factor loadings are the weights and correlations between each variable and the factor. The higher the loading value, the more relevant the variable is in defining the factor's dimensionality. A negative value indicates an inverse impact on the factor. Thus a given factor influences some measures more than others, and this degree of influence is determined by loadings. The error terms $e_1, ..., e_n$ serve to indicate that the hypothesized relationships are not exact. The ith error term describes the residual variation specific to the ith variable X_i. The factors are often called the *common factors* while the residual variables are often called the *unique* or *specific factors*.

The number of factors m should be substantially smaller than n. If the original variables $X_1, ..., X_n$ are at least moderately correlated, the basic dimensionality of the system is less than n. The goal of factor analysis is to reduce the redundancy among the variables by using a smaller number of factors.

To start an EFA, we first extract initial factors, using principal components to decide on the number of factors. Eigenvalue is the amount of variance in the data described by the factor, and eigenvalues help to choose the number of factors. In principal components, the first factor describes most of the variability. We then choose the number of factors to retain, and rotate axes to spread variability more evenly among factors. Redefining factors that loadings tend to make very high (-1 or 1) or very low (0) makes sharper distinctions in the interpretations of the factors.

Example

We apply the principal component-based factoring method on the data in FIGURE 5.6. The eigenvalues and the factor patterns are shown in FIGURE 5.10.

Eigenvalues of the Correlation Matrix: Total = 6 Average = 1				
	Eigenvalue	Difference	Proportion	Cumulative
1	2.83831733	0.90006486	0.4731	0.4731
2	1.93825247	0.97029922	0.3230	0.7961
3	0.96795324	0.71288651	0.1613	0.9574
4	0.25506673	0.25465650	0.0425	0.9999
5	0.00041023	0.00041023	0.0001	1.0000
6	0.00000000		0.0000	1.0000

Factor Pattern					
	Factor1	Factor2	Factor3	Factor4	Factor5
Electoral Votes	0.33017	0.94198	0.05796	-0.00989	-0.01432
Population	0.33154	0.94159	0.05612	-0.01192	0.01432
Total Area	0.96171	-0.22250	0.04391	0.15388	0.00001
Water Area	0.85962	-0.26063	0.14849	-0.41362	-0.00005
Land Area	0.94766	-0.20939	0.02582	0.23965	0.00002
Density per Square Mile of Land	-0.23979	-0.05534	0.96788	0.05136	0.00003

FIGURE 5.10 : Eigenvalues and factor patterns for the data in FIGURE 5.6

Now we apply the orthogonal Varimax rotation (maximizes the sum of the variances of the squared loadings) to obtain rotated factor patterns, as shown in FIGURE 5.11, and the revised distribution of variance explained by each factor, as shown in FIGURE 5.12. The total variance explained remains the same and gets evenly distributed between the major two factors.

Example

Here is an artificial example to check the validity and robustness of factor analysis. The data from the Thurstone box problem (Thurstone, 1947), as shown in FIGURE 5.13, measures 20 different characteristics of boxes, such as individual surface areas and box inter-diagonals. If these measurements are only linear combinations of the height, width, and depth of the box, then the

	Factor1	Factor2	Factor3	Factor4	Factor5
Electoral Votes	0.05001	0.99821	-0.02916	0.00444	-0.01432
Population	0.05057	0.99811	-0.03131	0.00657	0.01433
Total Area	0.98552	0.05696	-0.07507	0.14095	0.00000
Water Area	0.74351	0.01089	0.00056	0.66864	0.00001
Land Area	0.99306	0.06252	-0.08477	0.05223	0.00000
Density per Square Mile of Land	-0.09193	-0.04217	0.99487	-0.00145	-0.00001

FIGURE 5.11 : Rotated factor patterns from factors in FIGURE 5.10

Factor1	Factor2	Factor3	Factor4	Factor5
2.5237450	2.0016895	1.0044198	0.4697354	0.0004102

FIGURE 5.12 : Variance explained by each factor in FIGURE 5.11

data set could be reproduced by knowing only these dimensions and by giving them appropriate weights. These three dimensions are considered as factors.

i	x	y	z	i	x2	y2	z2	xy	xz	yz	sqrt(x2+y2	sqrt(x2+z2	sqrt(y2+z2	2(x+y)	2(x+z)	2(y+z)	logx	logy	logz	xyz	sqrt(x2+y2+z2)	ex	ey	ez
1	3	2	1	1	9	4	1	6	3	2	3.605551	3.162278	2.236068	10	8	6	0.477121	0.30103	0	6	3.741657387	20.08554	7.389056	2.718282
2	3	2	2	2	9	4	4	6	6	4	3.605551	3.605551	2.828427	10	10	8	0.477121	0.30103	0.30103	12	4.123105626	20.08554	7.389056	7.389056
3	3	3	1	3	9	9	1	9	3	3	4.242641	3.162278	3.162278	12	8	8	0.477121	0.477121	0	9	4.358898944	20.08554	20.08554	2.718282
4	3	3	2	4	9	9	4	9	6	6	4.242641	3.605551	3.605551	12	10	10	0.477121	0.477121	0.30103	18	4.69041576	20.08554	20.08554	7.389056
5	3	3	3	5	9	9	9	9	9	9	4.242641	4.242641	4.242641	12	12	12	0.477121	0.477121	0.47712	27	5.196152423	20.08554	20.08554	20.08554
6	4	2	1	6	16	4	1	8	4	2	4.472136	4.123106	2.236068	12	10	6	0.60206	0.30103	0	8	4.582575695	54.59815	7.389056	2.718282
7	4	2	2	7	16	4	4	8	8	4	4.472136	4.472136	2.828427	12	12	8	0.60206	0.30103	0.30103	16	4.898979486	54.59815	7.389056	7.389056
8	4	3	1	8	16	9	1	12	4	3	5	4.123106	3.162278	14	10	8	0.60206	0.477121	0	12	5.099019514	54.59815	20.08554	2.718282
9	4	3	2	9	16	9	4	12	8	6	5	4.472136	3.605551	14	12	10	0.60206	0.477121	0.30103	24	5.385164807	54.59815	20.08554	7.389056
10	4	3	3	10	16	9	9	12	12	9	5	5	4.242641	14	14	12	0.60206	0.477121	0.47712	36	5.830951895	54.59815	20.08554	20.08554
11	4	4	1	11	16	16	1	16	4	4	5.656854	4.123106	4.123106	16	10	10	0.60206	0.60206	0	16	5.744562647	54.59815	54.59815	2.718282
12	4	4	2	12	16	16	4	16	8	8	5.656854	4.472136	4.472136	16	12	12	0.60206	0.60206	0.30103	32	6	54.59815	54.59815	7.389056
13	4	4	3	13	16	16	9	16	12	12	5.656854	5	5	16	14	14	0.60206	0.60206	0.47712	48	6.403124237	54.59815	54.59815	20.08554
14	5	2	1	14	25	4	1	10	5	2	5.385165	5.09902	2.236068	14	12	6	0.69897	0.30103	0	10	5.477225575	148.4132	7.389056	2.718282
15	5	2	2	15	25	4	4	10	10	4	5.385165	5.385165	2.828427	14	14	8	0.69897	0.30103	0.30103	20	5.744562647	148.4132	7.389056	7.389056
16	5	3	2	16	25	9	4	15	10	6	5.830952	5.385165	3.605551	16	14	10	0.69897	0.477121	0.30103	30	6.164414003	148.4132	20.08554	7.389056
17	5	3	3	17	25	9	9	15	15	9	5.830952	5.830952	4.242641	16	16	12	0.69897	0.477121	0.47712	45	6.557438524	148.4132	20.08554	20.08554
18	5	4	1	18	25	16	1	20	5	4	6.403124	5.09902	4.123106	18	12	10	0.69897	0.60206	0	20	6.480740698	148.4132	54.59815	2.718282
19	5	4	2	19	25	16	4	20	10	8	6.403124	5.385165	4.472136	18	14	12	0.69897	0.60206	0.30103	40	6.708203932	148.4132	54.59815	7.389056
20	5	4	3	20	25	16	9	20	15	12	6.403124	5.830952	5	18	16	14	0.69897	0.60206	0.47712	60	7.071067812	148.4132	54.59815	20.08554

FIGURE 5.13 : 20 variable box problem data set (Thurstone, 1947)

As shown in FIGURE 5.14, the three dimensions of space are approximately discovered by the factor analysis, despite the fact that the box characteristics are not linear combinations of underlying factors but are instead multiplicative functions. Initial loadings and components are extracted using PCA.

The question is how many factors to extract in a given data set. Kaiser's criterion suggests that it is only worthwhile to extract factors which account for large variance. Therefore, we retain those factors with eigenvalues equal to or greater than 1.

There are 20 observations, each a function of x, y or z or one of their combinations. In FIGURE 5.14, Proportion indicates the relative weight of each factor in the total variance. For example, $12.6149/20 = 0.6307$. So the first factor explains about 63% of the total variance. Cumulative shows the total amount of variance explained, and the first six eigenvalues explain almost 99.6% of the total variance. From a factor analysis perspective the first three eigenvalues suggest a factor model with three common factors. This is because the first two eigenvalues are greater than unity and the third one is closer to unity and together they explain over 98% of the total variance.

	Eigenvalue	Difference	Proportion	Cumulative
1	12.6149281	8.5779579	0.6307	0.6307
2	4.0369702	1.0555741	0.2018	0.8326
3	2.9813961	2.8658323	0.1491	0.9817
4	0.1155639	0.0243452	0.0058	0.9874
5	0.0912187	0.0161426	0.0046	0.9920
6	0.0750761	0.0212835	0.0038	0.9958
7	0.0537926	0.0336045	0.0027	0.9984
8	0.0201881	0.0096911	0.0010	0.9995
9	0.0104970	0.0102092	0.0005	1.0000
10	0.0002878	0.0002478	0.0000	1.0000
11	0.0000400	0.0000124	0.0000	1.0000
12	0.0000276	0.0000164	0.0000	1.0000
13	0.0000112	[illegible]	0.0000	1.0000

		Factor1	Factor2	Factor3
x2	x2	0.65429	-0.64243	0.39829
y2	y2	0.73494	-0.07609	-0.67280
z2	z2	0.66029	0.69102	0.27622
xy	xy	0.87500	-0.34749	-0.32152
xz	xz	0.83048	0.34552	0.41593
yz	yz	0.83741	0.53072	-0.04473
sqrt(x2+y2)	sqrt(x2+y2)	0.86147	-0.50000	-0.06145
sqrt(x2+z2)	sqrt(x2+z2)	0.84659	-0.26776	0.45159
sqrt(y2+z2)	sqrt(y2+z2)	0.87070	0.28522	-0.38836
2(x+y)	2(x+y)	0.88297	-0.42891	-0.18507
2(x+z)	2(x+z)	0.88467	0.03195	0.46089
2(y+z)	2(y+z)	0.87804	0.40991	-0.23776
logx	logx	0.66268	-0.63904	0.36671

FIGURE 5.14 : Factor analysis of the data in FIGURE 5.13 shows the eigenvalues for variance explained by each factor and three retained factors

Rotating the components towards independence, rather than rotating the loadings towards simplicity, allows one to accurately recover the dimensions of each box and also to produce simple loadings. FIGURE 5.15 shows the factors of FIGURE 5.14 after an orthogonal Varimax rotation. The total of eigenvalues for the factors remains the same, but variability among factors is evenly distributed.

There are some differences between EFA and PCA and they will provide somewhat different results when applied to the same data. EFA assumes that the observations are based on the underlying factors, whereas in PCA the principal components are based on observations. The rotation of components is part of EFA but not PCA.

5.5 SURVIVAL ANALYSIS

Survival analysis (Kleinbaum and Klein, 2005; Hosmer et al., 2008) is a time-to-event analysis that measures the time from the beginning of a study to a terminal event, conclusion of the observation period, or loss of contact/with-

Variance Explained by Each Factor		
Factor1	Factor2	Factor3
6.8439524	6.5329085	6.2564335

		Factor1	Factor2	Factor3
x2	x2	0.65429	-0.64243	0.39829
y2	y2	0.73494	-0.07609	-0.67280
z2	z2	0.66029	0.69102	0.27622
xy	xy	0.87500	-0.34749	-0.32152
xz	xz	0.83048	0.34552	0.41593
yz	yz	0.83741	0.53072	-0.04473
sqrt(x2+y2)	sqrt (x2+y2)	0.86147	-0.50000	-0.06145
sqrt(x2+z2)	sqrt (x2+z2)	0.84659	-0.26776	0.45159
sqrt(y2+z2)	sqrt (y2+z2)	0.87070	0.28522	-0.38836
2(x+y)	2 (x+y)	0.88297	-0.42891	-0.18507
2(x+z)	2 (x+z)	0.88467	0.03195	0.46089
2(y+z)	2 (y+z)	0.87804	0.40991	-0.23776
logx	logx	0.66268	-0.63904	0.36671

FIGURE 5.15 : Factors of FIGURE 5.14 after an orthogonal Varimax rotation

drawal from the study. Survival data consist of a response variable that measures the duration of time (event time, failure time, or survival time) until a specified event occurs. Optionally, the data may contain a set of independent variables that are possibly associated with the failure time variable. Examples of survival analysis include determining the lifetime of a device (the time after installation until the device breaks down), the time until a company declares bankruptcy after its inception, the length of time an auto driver stayed accident-free since becoming insured, the length of time a person stayed on a job, the retention time of customers, and the survival time (or time until death) for organ transplant patients since transplant surgery.

The *censoring* problem in survival analysis arises due to incomplete observations of survival time during a period of study. Some subjects of study have censored survival times because they may not be observed for the full study period due to drop-out, loss to followup, or early termination of the study. A censored subject may or may not have an event of interest if it occurs before the end of the study but their data is incomplete.

Example

FIGURE 5.16 illustrates the survival histories of six subjects in an example of a study that could be measuring implanted device lifetimes or post-organ transplant outcomes.

In the figure, the terminal event of interest is "breakdown" or "death" which motivates a study of survival time. Not all devices will cease to work during the 325 days of the study period, but all will break down eventually. In the figure, the solid line represents an observed period at risk, while the broken line represents an unobserved period at risk. The letter "X" represents an

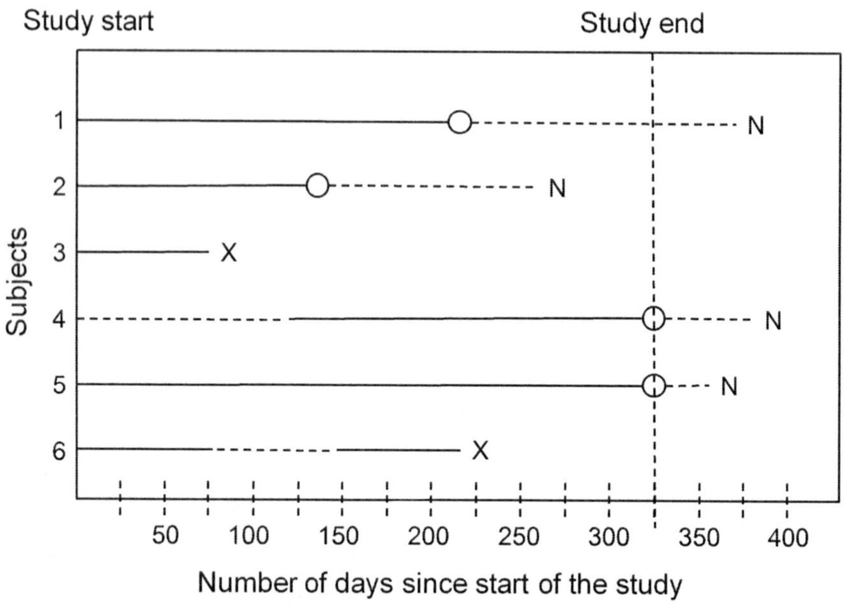

FIGURE 5.16 : Survival histories of subjects for analysis

observed terminal event, the open circle represents the censoring time, and the letter "N" represents an unobserved event.

An observation that is *right-censored* means the relevant event has not yet occurred at the time of observation. An observation that is *left-censored* means the relevant event has occurred before the time of observation but the exact time is not known. An observation is *interval-censored* if the event occurs at an unknown point in a time interval. Right-censored observations are the most common kind.

Example

In FIGURE 5.16, the observation of subject 5 is right-censored. Subject 4 joined the study late. Subject 6 is lost to observation for a while. Subject 2 joined the study on time but was lost to observation after some time, and died before the study period ended, but it is not known exactly when.

Consider the random variable T representing the survival time with density $f(t)$. The cumulative distribution function is $F(t) = p(T \leq t)$, which represents the probability that a subject survives no longer than time t. $S(t)$ is the survival function or the probability that a subject survives longer than time t, that is,

$$S(t) = p(T > t) = 1 - F(t) = \int_{t}^{\infty} f(s)\,ds.$$

A typical question to be asked is "What is the probability of the device lasting past 300 days?" and the answer is $S(300)$. The hazard function is defined as

$$h(t) = \frac{f(t)}{S(t)}.$$

Methods for estimating survival function include *life table analysis*, *Kaplan-Meier product-limit estimator*, and *Cox's semi-parametric proportional hazard model*, of which the life table is the least complicated way to describe the survival in a sample. A straightforward multiple regression technique is not suitable for survival analysis because of the problem of censoring and the survival time dependent variable, as well as the fact that other independent variables are not normally distributed.

In the life table analysis, the distribution of survival times is divided into a certain number of intervals. For each interval we can then compute the number and proportion of cases or objects that entered the respective interval, the number and proportion of terminal events, and the number of cases that were lost or censored in the respective interval. Several additional statistics can be computed based on these numbers and proportions, especially the estimated probability p_i of failure in the respective interval. This probability p_i of the ith interval is computed per unit of time as $(n_i - n_{i+1})/t_i$, where n_i is the estimated cumulative proportion surviving at the beginning of the ith interval, n_{i+1} is the cumulative proportion surviving at the end of the ith interval, and t_i is the width of the ith interval. Since the probabilities of survival are assumed to be independent across the intervals, the survival probability up to an interval is computed by multiplying out the probabilities of survival across all previous intervals.

The life table gives us a good indication of the distribution of survival over time. However, for predictive purposes it is often desirable to understand the shape of the underlying survival function in the population. The two major distributions that have been proposed for modeling survival or failure times are the exponential and the Weibull distribution.

The Kaplan-Meier product-limit estimator (1958) is a life table analysis in which each time interval contains exactly one case. The method arranges the data in increasing order of the observed values, noting the censored cases. It then computes the proportion of subjects who left the study after each change in the ordering. The advantage of using this estimator is that the resulting estimates do not depend on the grouping of the data into a certain number of time intervals. Cox's proportional hazards model determines the underlying hazard rate as a function of the independent variables.

Example

We undertake a retrospective analysis of 863 records (part displayed in FIGURE 5.17) of patients who underwent a kidney transplant during a certain period of time. The patient population examined contains males and females, and both black and white subjects.

```
Data on 863 kidney transplant patients
See Section 1.7
Data can be read in free format. The variables represented in the dataset are as follows:

Observation number
Time to death or on-study time
Death indicator (0=alive, 1=dead)
Gender (1=male, 2=female)
Race (1=white, 2=black)
Age in years
THE DATA
   1        1        0        1        1       46
   2        5        0        1        1       51
   3        7        1        1        1       55
   4        9        0        1        1       57
   5       13        0        1        1       45
   6       13        0        1        1       43
   7       17        1        1        1       47
   8       20        0        1        1       65
   9       26        1        1        1       55
  10       26        1        1        1       44
  11       28        1        1        1       49
  12       32        0        1        1       52
  13       32        0        1        1       31
```

FIGURE 5.17 : Example data for survival analysis (Ref: http://www.mcw.edu/FileLibrary/Groups/Biostatistics/Publicfiles/DataFromSection/DataFromSectionTXT/Data_from_section_1.7.txt)

Survival studies were calculated using the Kaplan-Meier Product-Limit method. The outcome endpoints were alive and dead. The data were grouped by the gender and race variables and hence there were four groups. The survival functions for both white and black females are shown in FIGURE 5.18.

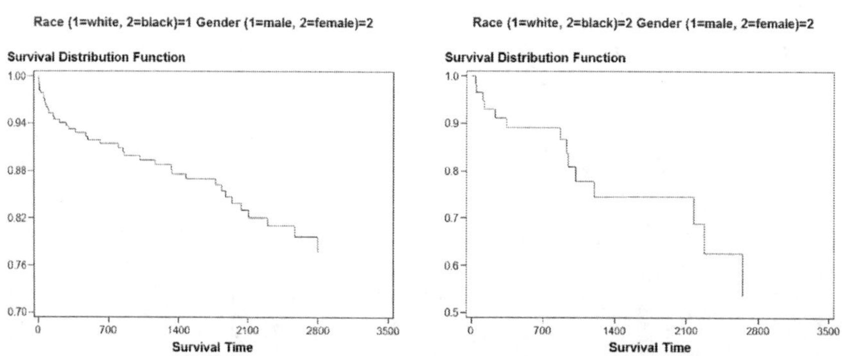

FIGURE 5.18 : An example survival analysis plots

It's clear from the figure that the average survival time is higher for the population representing the distribution function on the left than on the right. Similar other conclusions can be drawn by studying and comparing the two distribution functions.

5.6 AUTOREGRESSION MODELS

A process is stochastic if it evolves in time according to probabilistic laws. In this section, we introduce three types of stochastic processes, Autoregressive (AR), Moving Average (MA), and Autoregressive and Moving Average (ARMA), which are a special type of Gaussian process for modeling time-series data. A simple AR process, AR(1), is recursively defined as follows:

$$X_t = aX_{t-1} + \varepsilon_t$$

where a is the coefficient, ε_t is white noise with $\varepsilon_t \sim N\left(0, \sigma^2\right)$ and ε_i and ε_j are independent for $i \neq j$. By repeated substitution,

$$X_t = \varepsilon_t + a\varepsilon_{t-1} + a^2\varepsilon_{t-2} + ...$$

Therefore, $E\left[X_t\right] = 0$ and $Var\left[X_t\right] = \sigma^2\left(1 + a^2 + a^4 + ...\right) = \frac{\sigma^2}{1-a^2},\ if\ |a| < 1$. More generally, an autoregression model of order p, AR(p), is defined as :

$$X_t = a_1X_{t-1} + ... + a_pX_{t-p} + \varepsilon_t$$

where X_t can be obtained by linear regression from $X_{t-1}, ..., X_{t-p}$.

The MA process represents time series that are generated by passing the white noise through a non-recursive linear filter. The general MA process of order q, MA(q), is defined as follows:

$$X_t = \varepsilon_t + b_1\varepsilon_{t-1} + ... + b_q\varepsilon_{t-q}$$

where b_is are coefficients and ε_i is white noise with $\varepsilon_i \sim N\left(0, \sigma^2\right)$. AR(p) and MA(q) processes can be combined to define ARMA(p, q) as

$$X_t = \underbrace{a_1X_{t-1} + ... + a_pX_{t-p}}_{\text{Autoregressive (AR)}} + \underbrace{\varepsilon_t + b_1\varepsilon_{t-1} + ... + b_q\varepsilon_{t-q}}_{\text{MovingAvergae (MA)}}$$

Example

FIGURE 5.19 is an autoregressive plot of forecasts of the closing values of Intuit stock for seven days in the first half of January 2006. The order of the autoregressive process is 5 and the process employs a maximum likelihood estimator method. The figure also shows the 3 standard deviations from the mean as the Lower Control Limit (LCL) and Upper Control Limit (UCL) values.

Note from the figure that the autoregression process takes a time-step or two to predict a steep ascension or decline in the observed data.

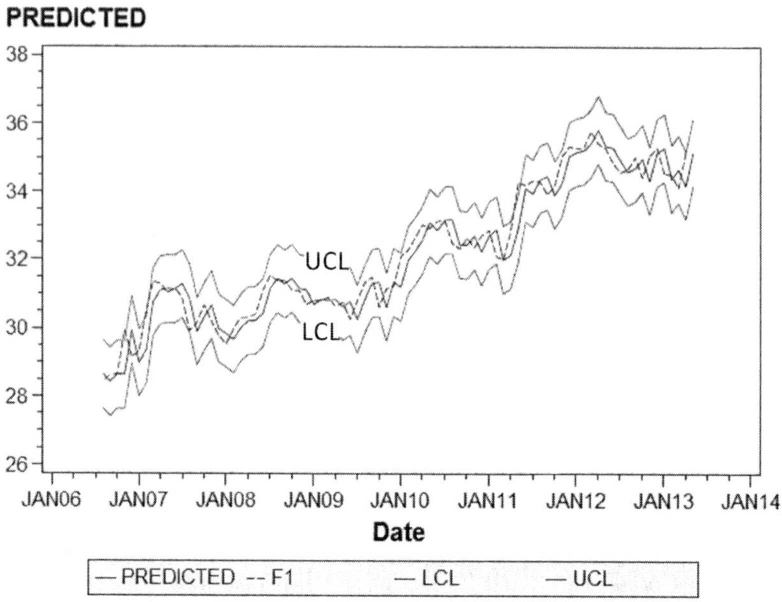

FIGURE 5.19 : Plot of forecasts by autoregression

5.7 FURTHER READING

Two very comprehensive books on applied regression analyses are (Gelman and Hill, 2006) and (Kleinbaum et al., 2007). A great tutorial on survival analysis can be found in (Kleinbaum and Klein, 2005).

CHAPTER 6

Artificial Intelligence for Symbolic Analytics

This chapter presents the traditional artificial intelligence (AI) approach to analytics, which we term *symbolic analytics*. The reasoning involves manipulation of symbols which are fundamental constructs for expressing facts or models constituting the underlying knowledge of a problem.

Handling of uncertain information is at the core of any analytics system. Uncertainty can occur at the level of data, information, or knowledge (as in the knowledge pyramid presented earlier). Some questions to be addressed include how to express or quantify uncertainty, and how to aggregate or discount uncertain pieces of information. So far in this book, we have addressed these questions by using probability to quantify uncertainty. This chapter takes a broader view of uncertainty by surveying and categorizing different types of uncertainty and ways of expressing uncertainty. We then categorize various approaches to handling uncertainty and present computational formalism from each of the categories. Some of these formalisms will be described in much more detail in subsequent chapters to solve various analytics-related problems.

6.1 ANALYTICS AND UNCERTAINTIES

This section explains the origin of uncertainty, and surveys and categorizes different types of uncertainty and ways of expressing uncertainty.

6.1.1 Ignorance to Uncertainties

Ignorance can be generally characterized as lack of information. Different types of information may be lacking in data and knowledge bases, and consequently give rise to different kinds of uncertainty. Here we present a survey of certain common forms of ignorance (Bonissone and Tong, 1985; Smets, 1991) and of the mathematical techniques that have been suggested to quantify ignorance. We then discuss interrelationships among these techniques in the next section.

- *Incompleteness*: Incomplete information refers to cases where the value of a variable is missing. Consider a database of car owners populated with parsed information from their social network posts or blogs. Each record should include information about, among others, location of the owner or blogger (city or zip code), category (gas, battery, or hybrid), brand (Ford, Toyota, Honda, or Volkswagen), and price (in dollars). Such information can be used to personalize sidebar advertisements for accessories. It is expected that some of the fields would be missing because a user may not have provided all the information in a blog. If, for example, the value of the variable representing the category is missing from a record, the information in the record becomes incomplete, but the rest of the information in the record is precise and certain (i.e., the user from zip code 12345 owns a Toyota).

- *Imprecision*: Imprecise information refers to cases where the value of a variable is given, but not with enough meaningful clarity. Imprecision can occur due to the parsing ambiguity in natural languages. Suppose the value of the variable representing the brand of a blogger at a certain location is "Ford" or "Honda." This can happen when the blogger compares the car that he owns with another car. The information is complete because the values of each of the three variables representing the blogger's position, car category, and brand are given, but the information is imprecise because there is some ambiguity as to the exact brand of the car owned by the blogger.

- *Uncertainty*: Uncertain information refers to cases where the information is complete and precise, but it might be wrong. This type of ignorance appears when the limitation of the observer (human, sensor, or an automated parsing agent) is taken into account. It is the observer who is not certain about the available information. Someone who is listed as owning a hybrid and posts about owning a hybrid, yet has their car listed as a Suzuki, may trigger uncertainty about the information, since Suzuki does not produce hybrid cars. The blogger may have posted about having a hybrid bicycle, for instance, and the automated agent may have automatically labeled the blogger as a hybrid car owner with a brand mentioned in another context.

Usually a database variable (i.e., a column attribute for a relational database) is constrained either by a domain, when the variable is qualitative or categorical, or by a range, when the variable is numeric. The variables representing the brand and category of a car are qualitative variables, whereas the variable representing the price of a car is a numeric one. Then it might be argued that incomplete information on qualitative variables is just a special case of imprecision.

Moreover, imprecision and incompleteness are context-dependent in the sense that information that is imprecise or incomplete in one context may be precise or complete in another context. For example, the imprecise information "Toyota or Honda" is sufficient for a marketing campaign to target any Japanese car, but insufficient for determining only those cars assembled within the USA. Similarly, if the campaign is to target any car with a price range of \$20,000, then the information "a car is under \$15,000" is sufficient to determine that the car is a target. But if the campaign is to target any car within the price range \$12,000 then that piece of information is not sufficient to determine whether it is a target or not. TABLE 6.1 presents types of uncertainty and subtypes, and example instances. The rest of the section discusses how traditional classical and non-classical logics and the theory of probability fail to handle some of these uncertainties. Specific techniques for handling these uncertainties will then be discussed in the next section.

TABLE 6.1: : Classification of uncertainties and examples

Type	Subtype	Example
Incompleteness	Existential	A social network user owns a hybrid car at a certain location, but its brand is unknown
	Universal	All the cars that have been owned so far at certain locations are in the gas category, but their brands are unknown
Imprecision	Disjunctive	The category is gas or hybrid
	Negation	The category is not battery
	Interval-valued	A car is priced between \$12,000 and \$15,000
	Fuzzy-valued	The price of a car of certain brand is very high
Uncertainty	Probability	The chance of the brand of the car being Ford is 70%
	Possibility	It is possible that the price of the car is \$15,000
	Credibility	0.8 is my degree of belief that the brand of the car is Volkswagen

A technique for handling uncertainty must offer a syntax for representing uncertain information. Such a technique based on classical logic will be able to express some of the uncertainties in the table. For example, existential and universal incompleteness in a knowledge base can be represented using quantifiers of first-order logic. Disjunction and negation types of imprecision can be represented using connectives of both propositional and first-order logics. First-order logic needs to be expanded with the axioms and inference rules of arithmetic to deal with intervals. There is no natural way of expressing fuzzy-valued imprecision in classical logic other than considering phrases such as "very fast" as a term of the underlying syntax of the logic. Fuzzy logic (Zadeh, 1965) has been developed to handle such imprecision. Moreover, coarse-grained two-valued representation of truth in classical logic is not sufficient to express the last category of uncertainties in the table.

The probability theory is the predominant paradigm for handling uncertainty, especially Bayesian probability, where interpretation of a probability value relies on a subject's degree of belief. In the Bayesian approach, as we have explained in the chapter on Bayesian probability, the probability is not based on any precise computation, but describes an individual's personal judgment (degree of belief) about how likely a particular event is to occur, based on his or her own experiences. But the probability theory fails to represent, for example, a disjunction naturally. One has to distribute the total probability of a disjunction among its constituent disjuncts.

Here we contrast the probabilistic and fuzzy-valued approaches to handling uncertainty. Fuzzy logic handles fuzzy-valued uncertainty by allowing truth to be a matter of degree (as in the membership degree in fuzzy sets). In the probabilistic approach, the information is complete, precise, but uncertain since it might be wrong. For example, if one source asserts that a company's yearly revenue reached $100m, then the information is complete and precise, but not certain since the source might be wrong. If the probability quantifying uncertainty in this case is 0.9, it would be interpreted as "there is a 90% chance that the company's yearly revenue reached $100m." Note that this is not equivalent to approximating the yearly revenue to a value such as $90m. On the other hand, in fuzzy logic there is no uncertainty about the yearly revenue reaching $100m, but the uncertainty is about the degree to which the observed revenue figure matches the $100m mark. The degree 0.9 is the company's degree of membership in the fuzzy set of all the companies reaching $100m yearly revenue. In other words, if we order the elements of this fuzzy set, the target will be positioned 90% of the way to the maximum revenue.

Two forms of possibility have been described in the literature: the epistemic and the physical (Smets, 1994). The first form, "possible that," which we have considered here, is related to our state of knowledge and is called epistemic. The second form, "possible for," deals with actual abilities independently of our knowledge about them. The distinction is similar to the one between the epistemic concept of probability and the traditional one based on chance. Modal logics (Lemmon, 1977; Chellas, 1980; Hughes and Cresswell, 1996) and their epistemic interpretations (Hintikka, 1962; Meyer and van der Hoek, 1995) can be used to represent and reason with the epistemic possibility. However, this coarse-grained representation of the knowledge of possibilities about assertions via this type of logic is quite inadequate for practical applications. That is to say, if two assertions are possible in the current world, they are indistinguishable in the modal formalism, even if an agent knows that one of them is true in twice as many possible worlds (Kripke, 1963). Therefore, any epistemic interpretation of the modal operators for necessity and possibility would fail to incorporate the notion of the decision maker's "degree of belief" into its epistemic states (Fox and Das, 2000). We have decided not to include discussion of the Possibility Theory and Possibilistic Logic in this book.

The Dempster-Shafer theory of belief function (Shafer, 1976) converts source credibility into probability intervals representing second-order uncertainty. Such an interval provides upper and lower bounds of the true probability.

6.1.2 Approaches to Handling Uncertainties

The general context of the uncertainty-handling problem in this book can formally be stated as follows. Suppose a decision-maker (e.g., an analyst) has the universe of discourse $\Omega = \{w_1, ..., w_n\}$ at hand as the set of likely hypotheses for a given decision-making problem. These hypotheses need to be associated with some values, such as probabilities, possibility measures, or other qualitative terms suitably defined by the decision-maker, representing the decision-maker's quantified degree of belief in their likely occurrence based on the available uncertain evidence. The last section broadly discussed various approaches to handling uncertainty. Specific technologies proposed for handling uncertainties can be categorized as shown in TABLE 6.2 (along the line of Pearl (1990)). This self-explanatory table provides motivation and definition of each category, along with examples of seminal technology for the category.

TABLE 6.2: : Approaches to handling uncertainties

Category	**Motivation**	**Definition**	**Technologies**
Neo-Logicist	Monotonicity in classical logics is not suitable for handling commonsense knowledge	Deals with non-numerical nonmonotonic inferencing for handling uncertainty in negation	Negation as Failure
Neo-Probabilist	Traditional framework of probability is not suitable for handling large number of variables	Remains within the traditional framework, but provides computational facilities to perform analytics	Bayesian Belief Networks

TABLE 6.2: : Approaches to handling uncertainties

Neo-Calculist	Probability calculus is inadequate for capturing uncertainty	New calculus for handling uncertainty	Theory of Belief Functions, Certainty Factors
Neo-Granularist	Coarse-grained two-valued representation of truth is not sufficient to model practical applications	Nothing is a matter of degree in two-valued Boolean logic	Probabilistic Logic, Fuzzy Logic

The monotonic nature of classical logics is not suitable for handling commonsense knowledge and related uncertainty. Neo-logicists provide nonmonotonic logics (Ginsberg, 1987) to support defeasible inferencing, the kind of inference of everyday life in which conclusions are drawn tentatively, reserving the right to retract them in the light of further information. Various types of nonmonotonic logics have been studied over the years, of which Reiter's Default Logic (Reiter, 1980) is the most prominent one. Closed World Assumption (CWA) (Reiter, 1978) is the one adopted in relational databases. Program Completion (Clark, 1978) and Circumscription (McCarthy, 1980) infer negative information from the proof-theoretic point of view. Program Completion is the theoretical foundation of the Negation as Failure (NAF) rule of the logic programming language Prolog (Bratko, 2000). CWA and NAF rules provide semantics of negative information in the rule-based knowledge bases to be considered in this book. For a detailed discussion on the semantics of negative information in databases and knowledge bases, see Das (1992).

The traditional framework of probability is not suitable for handling large numbers of variables due to the difficulty in maintaining joint distribution, and thereby computation, of probabilities of interest. Neo-probabilist approaches remain within the traditional framework but provide computational facilities to perform analytics. Bayesian Belief Network (BN) (Pearl, 1988; Jensen, 1996) technology, for example, exploits the conditional independence assumption and causalities among variables to represent joint distributions into manageable forms. Proposals such as Markov logic networks (Richardson and Domingos, 2006) and probabilistic relational models (Friedman et al., 1999) make use of the full expressive power of first-order logic, representing the formalism of first-order logic by factor graph models or Bayesian networks. Inference in such models is performed using belief propagation.

The Theory of Belief Functions (Shafer, 1976) and Certainty Factors (Shortliffe, 1976) are prime examples of new calculus for handling uncertainty. The *Theory of Belief Function*, or *evidence theory*, was initiated by Arthur P.

Dempster in a series of articles in the 1960s and was later developed by Shafer (1976); it is also known as the Dempster-Shafer Theory. The theory uses two related measures, called belief and plausibility measures, as upper and lower probabilities. The probability measure is a special case of the belief and plausibility measures. Certainty Factors (Shortliffe and Buchanan, 1975; Heckerman and Shortliffe, 1992) is one of the early approaches to handling uncertainty in expert systems.

Coarse-grained two-valued representation of truth is not sufficient to model practical applications. Early work in the area of many-valued logics (Lukasiewicz, 1970) deals with a multi-valued representation of truth. To break the coarse-grained granularity of Boolean-type truth-value, we embed numbers from the dense set $[0, 1]$ to represent degrees of uncertainty with two semantics in mind: 1) classical probability; and 2) mass values, as in the Dempster-Shafer theory. To determine ranking among a set of decision options by aggregating incoming evidence, we apply the Bayesian formula to compute posterior probabilities in the case of probability semantics, and apply the Dempster combination rule to compute overall degrees of belief in the case of belief semantics.

Zadeh proposed Fuzzy Sets (1965) as a way of extending two-valued membership of ordinary sets. Fuzzy Logic allows truth to be a matter of degree, as in the case of membership degree in fuzzy sets. Zadeh (1978) introduced the Possibility Theory as an extension of fuzzy sets and fuzzy logic. Possibilistic Logic (Dubois and Prade, 1988) extends the Possibility Theory with a richer representation of domain knowledge via logical sentences. The Possibility Theory is a natural tool to model imprecision and uncertainty when they occur together in ordinary language, such as in the statement "It is likely that the vehicle is moving fast." The probability and possibility measures are special cases of the belief and plausibility measures.

The technologies listed under the four categories of TABLE 6.2 are described in the following four sections. A technology for handling uncertainty that is model-based (see the first chapter for model-based approaches) has two components: the knowledge component describes an analyst's state of belief given the information available to the analyst, and the inferencing component explains how to update beliefs given new pieces of information that become available. The knowledge component for the underlying BN technology, for example, is represented in terms of causal graphs that provide prior distribution of variables in the graph. Inferencing via a propagation algorithm computes posterior distributions of the variables in a graph. For rule-based expert systems, the knowledge component consists of rules and facts and the inferencing is a backward- or forward-chaining.

6.2 NEO-LOGICIST APPROACH

This section explains a special subset of classical logics that takes the form of conditional *if-then* type rules and applies the "nation-as-failure rule" in that context to implement a nonmonotonic reasoning. The if-then type syntax provides domain experts a natural way of expressing their knowledge, be it as arguments for or against carrying out actions or as simple conditional statements for deriving implicit knowledge from observations. Unlike definite rules handled in a typical rule-based expert system, the syntax of rules considered in this section allows negative consequents for representing arguments against certain options. We begin the presentation of this section with an introduction of how the if-then type rule syntax evolved from the syntax of classical logics.

6.2.1 Evolution of Rules

Earlier in the chapter covering mathematical preliminaries, we mention the procedure for converting an arbitrary first-order sentence to its equivalent conjunctive normal form, where each conjunct is a clause or is in clausal form. Such a clause is then interpreted as various types of program clauses or if-then type rules. A non-empty clause can be rewritten as

$$M_1 \vee ... \vee M_p \vee \neg N_1 \vee ... \vee \neg N_q, p+q \geq 1$$

where M_is and N_js are positive literals, and variables are implicitly and universally quantified over the whole disjunction. Every closed well-formed formula can be transformed into this clausal form. The above clause can be written in the form of a *program clause* as

$$M_1 \vee ... \vee M_k \leftarrow N_1 \wedge ... \wedge N_q \wedge \neg M_{k+1} ... \wedge \neg M_p, k \geq 1, p \geq 0, q \geq 0$$

or in the form of a *goal* as

$$\leftarrow N_1 \wedge ... \wedge N_q \wedge \neg M_1 \vee ... \vee \neg M_p, p+q \geq 1$$

Thus, a program clause (or simply *clause*) is a formula of the form

$$A_1 \vee ... \vee A_m \leftarrow L_1 \wedge ... \wedge L_n, m \geq 1, n \geq 0$$

where $A_1 \vee ... \vee A_m$ is the *head* (or *conclusion* or *consequent*) of the program clause and $L_1 \wedge ... \wedge L_n$ is the *body* (or *condition* or *antecedent*) . Each A_i is an atom and each L_j is either an atom (a *positive condition*) or a negated atom (a *negative condition*). Any variables in $A_1, ..., A_m, L_1, ..., L_n$ are assumed to be universally quantified over the whole formula. Each A_i (and respectively, each L_j) is said to have *occurred* in the head (or for L_j, in the body) of the clause. The various forms of the clause $A_1 \vee ... \vee A_m \leftarrow L_1 \wedge ... \wedge L_n$ with m and n values of interest are the following:

- $m = 1$, $n = 0$. That is, the clause has the form

$$A \leftarrow \ (or\ simply A)$$

in which the body is empty and the head is a single atom. This clause is called a *unit clause* or *unit assertion.*

- $m = 1,\ n \geq 0$, and each L_i is an atom. That is, the clause has the form

$$A \leftarrow B_1 \wedge ... \wedge B_n$$

in which A and B_is are atoms. This clause is called a *definite clause.*

- $m = 1,\ n \geq 0$. That is, the clause has the form

$$A \leftarrow L_1 \wedge ... \wedge L_n$$

in which A is an atom and L_is are literals. This is a *normal clause* (or simply *clause*).

- $m = 0,\ n \geq 1$, and each L_i is an atom. That is, the clause has the form

$$\leftarrow B_1 \wedge ... \wedge B_n$$

in which B_is are atoms. This clause is called a *definite goal.*

- $m = 0,\ n \geq 1$. That is, the clause has the form

$$\leftarrow L_1 \wedge ... \wedge L_n$$

in which L_is are literals. This clause is a *normal goal* (or simply *goal*).

- $m > 1,\ n \geq 0$. That is, the clause has the form

$$A_1 \vee ... \vee A_m \leftarrow L_1 \wedge ... \wedge L_n.$$

This clause is called an *indefinite clause.*

Thus a unit clause is a special form of a definite clause; a definite clause is a special form of a normal clause; and a definite goal is a special form of a normal goal. The following example contains various types of clauses involved with the problem of representing numbers.

Example

The clauses and their types in square brackets are given below:

C1. $Owner\,(Tom, Hybrid)$ [Unit]
C2. $Market\,(x, y) \leftarrow Owner\,(x, z) \wedge Accessory\,(z, y)$ [Definite]
C3. $Conversion\,(x, y) \leftarrow Demand\,(x, y) \wedge \neg Competition\,(x)$ [Normal]
C4. $Conversion\,(x, y) \vee Competition\,(x) \leftarrow Demand\,(x, y)$ [Indefinite]

Clause $C1$ represents that Tom is the owner of a hybrid type of car. Clause $C2$ represents that if x is the owner of a car of type z and y is an accessory needed by the same type of car, then market z to x. Clause $C3$ represents that if the level of demand for a certain type of product x is y (e.g., high) and there is no market competition for the product then the level of conversion for the type of product x is y. Clause $C4$ represents that if the level of demand for a certain type of x is y then the conversion level for x is y or there is competition for x. Although clauses $C3$ and $C4$ are logically equivalent, the semantics of a logic program, which includes clause $C3$, may be different if the program replaces $C3$ by $C4$. In such cases, the use of the negation symbol "$\neg$" becomes the NAF in our case.

Here we do not deal with indefinite clauses with consequent $A_1 \vee ... \vee A_m$ with $m > 1$. The main argument against such considerations is not only to avoid reasoning complexity, but also that the coarse level of uncertainty that an indefinite clause can represent via its disjunction sign will be subsumed by a more general modeling technique that attaches probabilities or mass values to clauses as their degrees of uncertainty.

A *subgoal* of a goal G is a literal occurring in G. A *definite program* is a finite set of definite clauses. A *normal program* (or simply *program*) is a finite set of normal clauses. A definite program is therefore a special form of a normal program. In writing a set of clauses to represent a program, the same variables may be used in two different clauses. If there are any common variables between two different clauses, they are renamed before they are used.

Example

Consider the following program:

C1. $Conversion\,(x, y) \leftarrow Demand\,(x, y) \wedge \neg Competition\,(x)$
C2. $Campaign\,(x, Aggressive) \leftarrow Demand\,(x, High) \wedge Strategic\,(x)$
C3. $Profit\,(x, y) \leftarrow Conversion\,(x, y)$
C4. $Demand\,(Hybrid, High)$
C5. $Demand\,(Gas, Medium)$
C6. $Competition\,(Gas)$

The clause $C1$ makes the above program normal. In this program, $Campaign\,(x, y)$ means the level of campaign is y for the product x, and $Strategic\,(x)$ means the product x is strategic to the company.

FIGURE 6.1 shows the overall evolution of rules along with examples. Expert system rules and Prolog (Bratko, 2000; Clocksin and Mellish, 2003) rules based on logic programming (Kowalski, 1979) are just the definite version of general if-then-type rules with attached uncertainty values. By definite we mean if the condition of a rule is true then the conclusion is definite rather than a disjunction. Arguments are more general than these rules and will be considered in the Neo-granularist section below. An argument can have a negation symbol at its consequent representing an argument against a hypothesis. Rules normally used in rule-based expert systems to represent expert knowledge are restricted to propositional syntax to avoid reasoning complexity and to enhance efficiency. Each such rule has an associated degree of uncertainty represented by elements from dictionaries (for example, probability values drawn from $[0, 1]$ or certainty factor values drawn from the dictionary $[-1, +1]$ or values drawn from a qualitative dictionary such as

$\{high,\ medium,\ low\}$). Arguments are more general than definite rules since the syntax of an argument against an option requires a negative consequent.

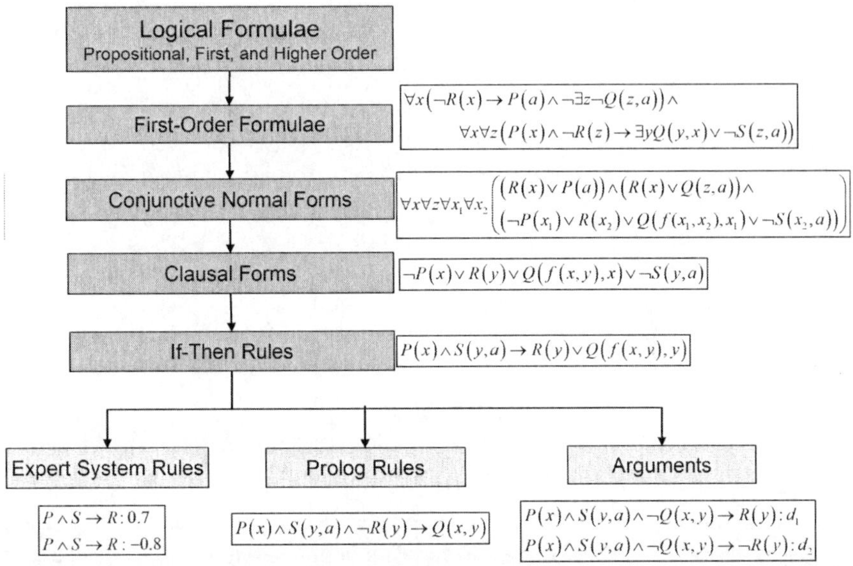

FIGURE 6.1 : Evolution of rules with examples

The if-then type rules in the decision-making context we will be dealing with in the neo-granularist section have the following general form:

IF Events
THEN *Hypothesis* (D)

The above rule is interpreted as "If *Events* occur, then *Hypothesis* follows with a certain degree of uncertainty D." In the expert system rule syntax as shown in FIGURE 6.1, the above rule is

$$Events \rightarrow Hypothesis : D$$

In the absence of D, the rule becomes a definite rule, and reasoning with such rules can be performed using any of the resolution principles without the need to handle uncertainty. If D is a probability value, then the rule is interpreted as "If *Events* occur, then the probability that *Hypothesis* will follow is D." *Events* is a conjunction of propositional symbols, each representing an event, and *Hypothesis* can be the state of a variable representing a *property* as in

IF the demand for a product is high
THEN the competition is stiff (0.8)

or an action as in

IF the competition is stiff
AND the product is strategic to the company
THEN campaign aggressively (0.9)

But the logical reasoning presented here does not distinguish between a property symbol and an action symbol. Degrees of uncertainty can be drawn from a quantitative dictionary (for example, $[0,1]$ or $[-1,+1]$) or a qualitative dictionary (for example, $\{high,\ medium,\ low\}$). Our objective here is to interpret rules upon receiving evidence (for example, evidence on the state of competition) and then compute aggregated evidence on individual decision options (for example, campaign aggressively or keep campaign level low-key) by handling uncertainty appropriately. We present two approaches to handling uncertainty in rules: Bayesian probability theory in the neo-probabilist section and the Dempster-Shafer theory of belief function in the neo-calculist section. But here we present inferencing via the Negation As Failure (NAF) rule.

6.2.2 Inferencing in Rule-based Systems

All logical consequences of a program can be considered as positive information. Declarative, procedural, and fixpoint semantics are sometimes concerned only with the positive information about a program that can be derived from that program. The negative information is not explicitly stored in a program but is assumed by default. This additional implicit negative information cannot be proved from the program by normal inference rules such as modus ponens. *Rules for inferring negative information* are rules that infer this additional implicit negative information. Hence a rule for inferring negative information defines the *semantics for negative information* in the program and is given in either a declarative or a procedural manner. This rule will be studied alongside the other three kinds of semantics mentioned above.

Example

Consider the following program **P**:

$$\begin{array}{l} Conversion\,(x,y) \leftarrow Demand\,(x,y) \\ Demand\,(Hybrid, High) \\ Competition\,(Gas) \end{array}$$

The semantics for the above program can be represented by the set

$$\mathbf{S} = \left\{ \begin{array}{c} Demand\,(Hybrid, High)\,, Conversion\,(Hybrid, High)\,, \\ Competition\,(Gas) \end{array} \right\}$$

The semantics for negative information generates the set

$$HB(\mathbf{P}) - \mathbf{S}$$

where $HB(\mathbf{P})$ is the Herbrand Base of the program **P** (basically, all possible ground instantiations of all the predicates). Therefore, $Competition\,(Hybrid)$ is taken as false in the context of **P** according to the semantics for negative information. Note that the logical representation above is not typed. Hence, $Demand\,(High, Hybrid)$ and $Competition\,(High, Hybrid)$, for example, are valid representations, but they are false according to the semantics.

The above-mentioned declarative and procedural semantics for programs are only concerned with the positive information that can be derived from the program. *Closed World Assumption* (CWA) and *Negation As Failure* (NAF) rules are provided below for studying the semantics of negative information in definite programs. Each of these is consistent for the class of definite programs and can be used in conjunction with the other two semantics introduced above to obtain the complete meaning of a definite program.

Given a program **P** and $A \in HB(\mathbf{P})$, one of the ways to say that $\neg A$ may be inferred from **P** is if A is not a logical consequence of **P**. This declarative definition for inferring negative information is what is called the closed CWA, and hence is considered a rule for inferring negative information from a program. Thus

$$CWA(\mathbf{P}) = \{A | A \in HB(\mathbf{P}) \text{ and } A \text{ is not a logical consequence of } \mathbf{P}\}$$

If A is not a logical consequence of **P**, then each branch of a proof tree (called SLD tree, see (Das, 1992)) for $\mathbf{P} \cup \{\leftarrow A\}$ is either finitely failed or infinite. This operational aspect of the CWA provides a new rule for inferring negative information from a program and is called the NAF rule. The rule can be formally stated as follows. Given a program **P** and $A \in HB(\mathbf{P})$, if $\mathbf{P} \cup \{\leftarrow A\}$ has a finitely failed proof tree, then A is not a logical consequence of **P** and hence $\neg A$ can be inferred from **P**. Thus

$$\begin{aligned} NAF(\mathbf{P}) = \{A | A \in HB(\mathbf{P}) \text{ and } \\ \mathbf{P} \cup \{\leftarrow A\} \text{ has a finitely failed proof tree}\} \end{aligned}$$

Naturally CWA is more powerful from the point of view that A may not be a logical consequence of **P** but every proof tree for $\mathbf{P} \cup \{\leftarrow A\}$ has an infinite branch. Consider, for example, the program $\mathbf{P} = \{P(a) \leftarrow P(a)\}$. Clearly $P(a)$ is not a logical consequence of **P** and hence CWA infers $\neg P(a)$ from **P**. But the only branch of the tree for $\mathbf{P} \cup \{\leftarrow P(a)\}$ is infinite. If a system implementing the proof resolution procedure is not capable of detecting such infinite branches, then a task for finding whether A is a logical consequence or not would be incomplete in that system. As far as the properties of rules for negative information are concerned, both CWA and NAF are consistent for definite programs.

6.2.3 Advantages and Disadvantages of Rule-Based Systems

Subject-matter experts usually express their predictive and actionable domain knowledge in terms of expressions such as "this action should be taken under that condition," "this situation means that," and so on. Such knowledge, with clearly separated antecedent and consequent parts, can be easily transformed to rules. Moreover, each rule is a self-documented, independent piece of knowledge that can be acquired and maintained in a local context without analyzing its global impact.

Rule-based systems provide both data-driven reasoning (that is, forward chaining) and goal-driven reasoning (that is, backward chaining). A derivation via each such reasoning method is transparent in the sense that derivation steps can be laid out in sequence to provide a basis for explaining an answer to a query. Rules can be attached with supports drawn from various types of qualitative and quantitative dictionaries, other than just probabilities, provided appropriate algebras exist for manipulating dictionary terms (for example, mass values in Dempster-Shafer and certainty factors). Rules can also be learned, given sufficient training instances, using standard machine learning techniques such as decision trees for learning propositional rules and inductive logic programming for learning first-order rules. These learning algorithms are part of the tool *i*DAS to be presented later in the chapter on analytics tools.

Since each rule is self-documented, a special reasoning procedure is required to implement abductive or diagnostic reasoning (this kind of reasoning is an integral part of evidence-propagation algorithms for belief networks). Moreover, a knowledge base consisting of many isolated rules does not provide a global view of the domain that it is modeling in terms of links and relationships among variables.

6.3 NEO-PROBABILIST

A Bayesian Belief Network (BN) (Pearl, 1988; Jensen, 2002) is a graphical, probabilistic knowledge representation of a collection of variables describing some domain, yielding a domain model. The nodes of the BN denote the variables and the links denote causal relationships among the variables. The topology encodes the qualitative knowledge about the domain. Conditional Probability Tables (CPTs) encode the quantitative details (strengths) of the causal relationships. The BN of FIGURE 6.2 encodes the relationships over the domain consisting of the binary relations *Demand*, *Quality*, *Conversion*, *Reputation*, and *Profit*. The topology of the BN captures the commonsense knowledge relating to a new product launch in terms of cause-effect relationships. Specifically, the BN encodes that:

- *Demand* and *Quality* of a product together cause its *Conversion* level.
- The level of *Conversion* determines the *Profit* level.
- *Quality* of a product has an effect on the *Reputation* of the company.

As shown in FIGURE 6.2, a CPT specifies the probability of each possible value of a child variable conditioned on each possible combination of its parent variable values. For example, the probability of increased reputation with a good quality product launch is 0.90, whereas the probability of decreased reputation with a bad quality product launch is 0.95.

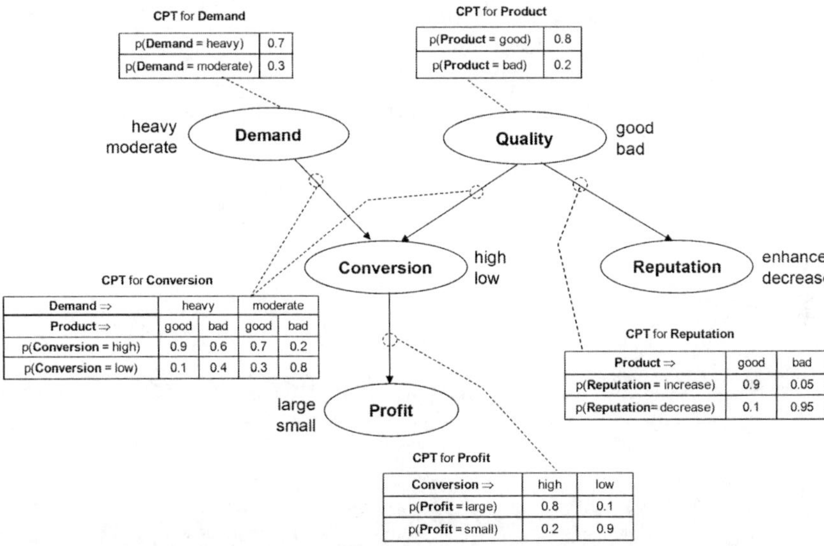

FIGURE 6.2 : An example BN

The chance that a node of a BN is in a particular state is termed its "belief" in the state, reflecting the probability that the node is in that state given all the previous evidence received. The structure of a BN encodes other information as well. Specifically, the lack of links between certain variables represents a lack of direct causal influence, indicating conditional independence relations. This BN encodes many conditional independence relations, for example,

- *Reputation* is independent of *Conversion* given *Quality*, and
- *Profit* is independent of *Demand* and *Quality* given *Conversion.*

That is, once the value of *Quality* is known, the value of *Reputation* adds no further information about *Conversion.* Similar conditional independence assertions hold for the other variables.

When new evidence is posted to a variable in a BN, that variable updates its own belief vector (i.e., belief represented as a vector) and then sends out messages indicating updated predictive and diagnostic support vectors to its child and parent nodes respectively. These messages are then used by other nodes to update their belief vectors and to propagate their own updated support vectors. The separation of evidence yields a propagation algorithm for polytree-type BNs (Pearl, 1988), such as the one in FIGURE 6.2, in which update messages need only be passed in one direction between any two nodes following posting of evidence. Thus, the algorithm's complexity is proportional to the number of links in the network. This separation also prevents the possibility of double-counting evidence. Details on more complex algorithms are in the chapter on probabilistic graphical models.

FIGURE 6.3 an implementation of the BN in FIGURE 6.2 on the HUGIN platform. The panel on the right displays the BN structure and the panel on the left displays the current beliefs of all the variables given all the evidence so far, which is the likelihood of enhanced reputation with certainty. Thus, for example, we have

$$p(Profit = large|Reputation = enhanced) = 0.68$$

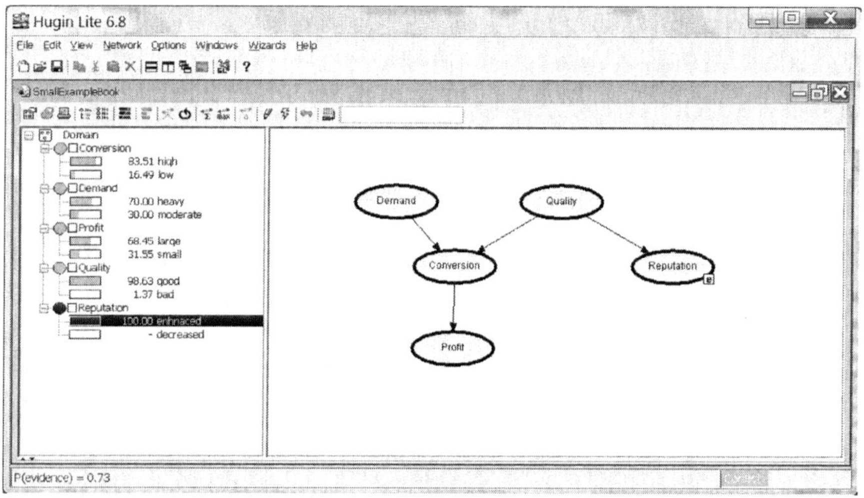

FIGURE 6.3 : An implementation of the BN in FIGURE 6.2

There are many commercial and publicly available BN tools. The most notable of these tools is GeNIe (http://genie.sis.pitt.edu/) from the University of Pittsburgh.

6.4 NEO-CALCULIST APPROACH

In this section, we present certainty factors and the Dempster-Shafer theory of belief function.

6.4.1 Certainty Factors

One of the early approaches to handling uncertainty in expert systems is Certainty Factors (Shortliffe and Buchanan, 1975; Heckerman and Shortliffe,

1992). This formalism provides a number to measure the decision-maker's degree of confirmation or belief in a hypothesis, where the maximum value for belief is +1.0 (definitely true), and the minimum value is −1.0 (definitely false). An intuitive interpretation of qualitative terms into certainty factors is shown in TABLE 6.3:

TABLE 6.3: : Qualitative interpretations of certainty factors

Qualitative Term	**Certainty Factor**
Definitely	+1.0
Almost certainly	+0.8
Probably	+0.6
Maybe	+0.4
Unknown	[−0.2, +0.2]
Maybe not	−0.4
Probably not	−0.6
Almost certainly not	−0.8
Definitely not	−1.0

In the certainty factor formalism, unlike in the theory of probability, a piece of evidence E could support a hypothesis H without necessarily supporting the complement of that hypothesis. In other words, although the property

$$p(H|E) = 1 - p(\neg H|E)$$

holds in probability theory, the certainty formalism rejects the following:

$$belief\,(H|E) = f\,(belief\,(\neg H|E))$$

The approach creates the following measures of belief and disbelief:

$$MB\,(H,E) = \begin{cases} 1 & \text{if } p\,(H) = 1 \\ \frac{p(H,E)-p(H)}{1-p(H)} & \text{otherwise} \end{cases}$$

$$MD\,(H,E) = \begin{cases} 1 & \text{if } p\,(H) = 0 \\ \frac{p(H)-p(H|E)}{p(H)} & \text{otherwise} \end{cases}$$

The value $1-p\,(H)$ represents the decision-maker's total doubt in the hypothesis, and thus the measure of belief *MB* based on evidence E computes the reduction in the decision-maker's disbelief. Similarly, the measure of disbelief *MD* based on evidence E computes the reduction in the decision-maker's belief. The measure of belief is then computed as follows:

$$cf = \frac{MB - MD}{1 - \min\,(MB, MD)}$$

Different values of cf are interpreted as follows:

- *cf is positive*: evidence supports the hypothesis since $MB > MD$.
- *cf is 1.0*: evidence definitely supports the hypothesis.
- *cf is 0.0*: either there is no evidence or the belief is canceled out by the disbelief.
- *cf is negative*: evidence favors negation of the hypothesis since $MB < MD$.

The certainty factor assigned by a rule is propagated through the reasoning chain. It involves establishing the net certainty of the rule consequent when the evidence in the rule antecedent is uncertain. Given the rule

$$\text{IF } E \text{ THEN } H(cf)$$

and given $CF(E)$, the combined belief in the hypothesis is computed by propagating the certainty factor as follows:

$$CF(H, E) = CF(E) \times cf$$

The following are the certainty factor propagation rules for conjunctions and disjunctions:

$$\begin{array}{l} CF(E_1 \wedge ... \wedge E_n) = \max[CF(E_1), ..., CF(E_n)] \\ CF(E_1 \vee ... \vee E_n) = \min[CF(E_1), ..., CF(E_n)] \end{array}$$

Finally, one needs to combine certainty factors for a hypothesis implicated by more than a rule as below:

$$\begin{array}{ll} \text{IF } E_1 \text{ THEN } H & (cf_1) \\ \text{IF } E_2 \text{ THEN } H & (cf_2) \end{array}$$

The combination of cf_1 and cf_2 for H given both E_1 and E_2 is

$$CF(cf_1, cf_2) = \begin{cases} cf_1 + cf_2 \times (1 - cf_1) & \text{if}\, cf_1 > 0\, \text{and}\, cf_2 > 0 \\ \frac{cf_1 + cf_2}{1 - \min[|cf_1|, |cf_2|]} & \text{if}\, cf_1 < 0\, \text{or}\, cf_2 < 0 \\ cf_1 + cf_2 \times (1 + cf_1) & \text{if}\, cf_1 < 0\, \text{and}\, cf_2 < 0 \end{cases}$$

A natural requirement for any formalism for handling uncertainty is that the evidence combination rule should be associative. However, this rule for the certainty factor formalism is not associative. The rule should never be applied if E_1 and E_2 are deduced from a common piece of evidence E_0. To illustrate, suppose we have the following rules:

$$\begin{array}{ll} \text{IF } E_0 \text{ THEN } E_1 & (1.0) \\ \text{IF } E_0 \text{ THEN } E_2 & (1.0) \\ \text{IF } E_1 \text{ THEN } H & (1.0) \\ \text{IF } E_2 \text{ THEN } H & (1.0) \end{array}$$

Let the certainty factor of E_0 be α, then both E_1 and E_2 have a certainty factor equal to α. A blind application of the combination rule leads to a certainty factor of $2\alpha - \alpha^2$ for H. The result is wrong as the set of four rules can be reduced into

$$\text{IF } E_0 \text{ THEN } H \quad (1.0)$$

and therefore the certainty factor of H given E_0 should be α. This example shows the danger of using ad hoc models blindly.

6.4.2 Dempster-Shafer Theory of Belief Function

Dempster-Shafer theory of belief functions (Shafer, 1976) is a slight departure from the probability thrust of this book is a generalization of the Bayesian theory of subjective probability (mainly by virtue of its explicit definition of the concept of ignorance) to combine accumulative evidence or to change prior opinions in the light of new evidence. Whereas the Bayesian theory requires probabilities for each question of interest, belief functions allow us to base degrees of belief for one question (for example, whether the product has low conversion) on probabilities for a related question. Arthur P. Dempster set out the basic ideas of the theory (Dempster, 1966), and Glenn Shafer developed the theory further (Shafer, 1976). Briefly, the theory may be summarized as follows.

Suppose expert X (for example, a market analyst, product manager, or marketing manager) says that the conversion for a product is not high due to low demand. The decision-maker's subjective probabilities for expert X being reliable or unreliable are 0.7 and 0.3. Now, expert X's statement must be true if reliable, but not necessarily false if unreliable. The expert's testimony therefore justifies 0.7 "degrees of belief" that the conversion is not high, but only a zero (not 0.3) degree of belief that the conversion is high. The numbers 0.7 and 0 together constitute a belief function.

Suppose subjective probabilities were based on the decision-maker's knowledge of the frequency with which experts like X are reliable witnesses. 70% of statements made by reliable witnesses would be true, $n\%$ by unreliable witnesses would be true, and $(30 - n)\%$ by unreliable witnesses would be false. 0.7 and 0 are the lower bounds of true probabilities $(70 + n)/100$ and $(30 - n)/100$ respectively. Thus a single belief function is always a consistent system of probability bounds, but may represent contradictory opinions from various experts. For example, consider the belief function 0.7 and 0 from expert X's opinion of the conversion not being high, and 0.8 and 0 from expert Y's opinion of the conversion being high. The lower bound of the true probability for the conversion not being high in the first case is 0.7, but the upper bound is 0.2 in the second case, yielding contradiction.

Let Ω be a finite set of mutually exclusive and exhaustive propositions, called the *frame of discernment*, about some problem domain ($\Omega = \{High, \neg High\}$ in our example decision making problem) and $\Pi(\Omega)$ is to be the power set of Ω. A *basic probability assignment* (BPA) or *mass function* is the mapping

$$m : \Pi(\Omega) \rightarrow [0,1]$$

which is used to quantify the belief committed to a particular subset A of the frame of discernment, given certain evidence. The probability number $m(A)$, the *mass* of A, says how much belief there is that some member of A is in fact the case, where

$$m(\Phi) = 0 \text{ and } \sum_{A \subseteq \Omega} m(A) = 1$$

The value 0 indicates no belief and the value 1 indicates total belief, and any values between these two limits indicate partial beliefs. If the probability number p for only a partial set A of hypotheses is known, then the residual complementary probability number $1-p$ is assigned to the frame of discernment, thus allowing the representation of ignorance. A basic probability assignment m is Bayesian if $m(A) = 0$ for every non-singleton set A. For any set $A \subseteq \Omega$ for which $m(A) \neq 0$, A is called a *focal element.*

The measure of total belief committed to $A \subseteq \Omega$ can be obtained by computing the *belief function Bel* for $A \subseteq \Omega$ which simply adds the mass of all the subsets of A:

$$Bel(A) = \sum_{B \subseteq A} m(B)$$

A *single* belief function represents the lower limit of the true probability and the following plausibility function provides the upper limit of the probability:

$$Pl(A) = \sum_{B \cap A \neq \Phi} m(B) = 1 - Bel(A^c)$$

Mass can be recovered from belief function as follows:

$$m(B) = \sum_{A \subseteq B} (-1)^{|A-B|} Bel(A)$$

So there is a one-to-one correspondence between the two functions m and *Bel.* Two independent evidences expressed as two basic probability assignments m_1 and $m_2$can be combined into a single joined basic assignment $m_{1,2}$ by Dempster's rule of combination:

$$m_{1,2}(A) = \begin{cases} \dfrac{\sum_{B \cap C = A} m_1(B) m_2(C)}{1 - \sum_{B \cap C = \Phi} m_1(B) m_2(C)}, & A \neq \Phi \\ 0, \quad A = \Phi \end{cases}$$

Example

In order to illustrate the Dempster-Shafer theory in the context of our example, we consider only the following three different expert rules for the level of conversion for a product with the degrees of reliability on experts from whom the rules have been acquired:

Rule 1:
IF *Stiff Competition* THEN *Low Conversion*
Expert: Market Analyst; Reliability: 0.7

Rule 2:
IF *Bad Quality* THEN *Low Conversion*
Expert: Product Manager; Reliability: 0.8

Rule 3:
IF *Winter Season* THEN *Low Conversion*
Expert: Marketing Manager; Reliability: 0.9

Note that Dempster-Shafer theory requires that evidences to be combined must be independent. In the above set of rules, the potential usable evidences (level of competition, product quality, and season) are essentially so.

In case of stiff competition, the values 0.7 and 0 together constitute a belief function. The focal element is $\{Low\,Conversion\}$ and the mass distribution is $m_1(\{Low\,Conversion\}) = 0.7$. We know nothing about the remaining probability so it is allocated to the whole frame of discernment as $m_1(\Omega) = 0.3$, where $\Omega = \{Low\,Conversion, \neg Low\,Conversion\}$. Evidence of bad-quality product provides the focal element $\{Low\,Conversion\}$ other than Ω, with $m_2(\{Low\,Conversion\}) = 0.8$. The remaining probability, as before, is allocated to the whole frame of discernment as $m_2(\Omega) = 0.2$. Dempster's rule can then be used to combine the masses as shown in TABLE 6.4.

TABLE 6.4: : Combination of masses by Dempster's rule

$LC - Low\,Conversion$	$m_2(\{LC\}) = 0.80$	$m_2(\Omega) = 0.20$
$m_1(\{LC\}) = 0.70$	$m_{1,2}(\{LC\}) = 0.56$	$m_{1,2}(\{LC\}) = 0.14$
$m_1(\Omega) = 0.30$	$m_{1,2}(\{LC\}) = 0.24$	$m_{1,2}(\Omega) = 0.06$

Now, $Bel(\{Low\,Conversion\}) = 0.56 + 0.24 + 0.14 = 0.94$. Therefore, the combined belief and plausibility are computed in TABLE 6.5.

TABLE 6.5: : Computation of belief and plausibility

Focal Element (A)	$Bel(A)$	$Pl(A)$
$\{Low\,Conversion\}$	0.94	1.0
Ω	1.0	1.0

Example

Here is a more interesting example with a third decision option for the product to have medium conversion. Therefore, the *frame of discernment* is

$$\Omega = \left\{ \begin{array}{l} High\,Conversion\,(HC), Medium\,Conversion\,(MC), \\ Low\,Conversion\,(LC) \end{array} \right\}$$

We consider the following set of expert rules along with the degrees of reliability:

Rule 1:
IF *No Competition* THEN NOT *Low Conversion*
Expert: *Market Analyst*; Reliability: 0.6

Rule 2:
IF *Bad Quality* THEN *Low Conversion*
Expert: *Product Manager*; Reliability: 0.8

Rule 3:
IF *Winter Season* THEN NOT *High Conversion*
Expert: *Marketing Manager*; Reliability: 0.7

Here also the potential usable evidences (competition, product quality, and season) are considered independent.

In case of evidence of no competition, the conversion not being low (that is, high or medium) and the values 0.7 and 0 together constitute a belief function. The focal element other than Ω is $\{HC, MC\}$ and the mass is distributed to it as $m_1(\{HC, MC\}) = 0.6$. We know nothing about the remaining probability, so it is allocated to the whole frame of discernment as $m_1(\Omega) = 0.4$.

There is also evidence of winter season, resulting in 0.6 subjective probability that the conversion will not be high in this situation. The new evidence suggests the focal element $\{MC, LC\}$ other than Ω with $m_2(\{MC, LC\}) = 0.7$. The remaining probability, as before, is allocated to the whole frame of discernment as $m_2(\Omega) = 0.3$. Considering that the market competition and season are independent of each other, Dempster's rule can then be used to combine the masses as shown in TABLE 6.6.

TABLE 6.6: : Combination of masses by Dempster's rule

	$m_2(\{MC, LC\}) = 0.70$	$m_2(\Omega) = 0.30$
$m_1(\{HC, MC\}) = 0.60$	$m_{1,2}(\{MC\}) = 0.42$	$m_{1,2}(\{HC, MC\}) = 0.18$
$m_1(\Omega) = 0.40$	$m_{1,2}(\{MC, LC\}) = 0.28$	$m_{1,2}(\Omega) = 0.12$

Therefore the combined belief and plausibility are computed in TABLE 6.7.

TABLE 6.7: : Computation of belief and plausibility

Focal Element (A)	$Bel(A)$	$Pl(A)$
$\{MC\}$	0.42	1.0
$\{MC, LC\}$	0.70	1.0
$\{HC, MC\}$	0.60	1.0
Ω	1.0	1.0

The basic probability assignments m_1 and m_2 are different but consistent, and therefore the degrees of belief in both $\{MC, LC\}$ and $\{HC, MC\}$being true (that is, that the product has medium conversion) is the product of $m_1(\{MC, LC\})$ and $m_2(\{HC, MC\})$, or 0.42.

Finally, bad product quality suggests low conversion and thus the focal element $\{LC\}$ and Ω with $m_3(\{LC\}) = 0.8$ and $m_3(\Omega) = 0.2$. The Dempster rule of combination applies as before, but with one modification. When the evidence is inconsistent, the products of masses are assigned to a single measure of inconsistency, say k, as shown in TABLE 6.8.

TABLE 6.8: : Combination of masses by Dempster's rule

	$m_3(\{LC\}) = 0.8$	$m_3(\Omega) = 0.20$
$m_{1,2}(\{MC\}) = 0.42$	$k = 0.336$	$m(\{MC\}) = 0.084$
$m_{1,2}(\{MC, LC\}) = 0.28$	$m(\{LC\}) = 0.224$	$m(\{MC, LC\})$ $= 0.056$
$m_{1,2}(\{HC, MC\}) = 0.18$	$k = 0.144$	$m(\{HC, MC\})$ $= 0.036$
$m_{1,2}(\Omega) = 0.12$	$m(\{LC\}) = 0.096$	$m(\Omega) = 0.024$

The total mass of evidence assigned to inconsistency k is $0.336 + 0.144 = 0.48$. The normalizing factor is $1 - k = 0.52$. The resulting masses of evidence are as follows:

$$
\begin{aligned}
&m(\{LC\}) = (0.224 + 0.096)/0.52 = 0.62 \\
&m(\{MC\}) = 0.084/0.52 = 0.16 \\
&m(\{MC, LC\}) = 0.056/0.52 = 0.11 \\
&m(\{HC, MC\}) = 0.036/0.52 = 0.07 \\
&m(\Omega) = 0.024/0.52 = 0.04
\end{aligned}
$$

Therefore, the combined belief and plausibility are computed in TABLE 6.9.

TABLE 6.9: : Computation of belief and plausibility

Focal Element (A)	$Bel(A)$	$Pl(A)$
$\{LC\}$	0.62	0.73
$\{MC\}$	0.16	0.38

TABLE 6.9: : Computation of belief and plausibility

$\{MC, LC\}$	0.89	1.0
$\{HC, MC\}$	0.23	0.38
Ω	1.0	1.0

Hence, the most likely hypothesis is the low conversion of the product.

Let us consider two examples to illustrate two special cases for evidence aggregation.

Example

Hypothetically, consider the case when the set of focal elements of the basic probability distribution $m_2$is exactly the same as m_1. The evidence combination table is shown TABLE 6.10.

TABLE 6.10: : Combination of masses by Dempster's rule

	$m_2(\{LC, MC\}) = 0.60$	$m_2(\Omega) = 0.40$
$m_1(\{LC, MC\}) = 0.70$	$m_{1,2}(\{LC, MC\}) = 0.42$	$m_{1,2}(\{LC, MC\}) = 0.28$
$m_1(\Omega) = 0.30$	$m_{1,2}(\{LC, MC\}) = 0.18$	$m_{1,2}(\Omega) = 0.12$

Now,

$$\begin{aligned} & Bel(\{LC, MC\}) \\ & \quad = 0.42 + 0.18 + 0.28 \\ & \quad = 0.88 \\ & \quad = 0.6 + 0.7 - 0.6 \times 0.7 \end{aligned}$$

In general, when two mass distributions m_1 and m_2 agree on focal elements, then the combined degree of belief on a common focal element is $p_1 + p_2 - p_1 \times p_2$, where p_1 and p_2 are mass assignments on the focal element by the two distributions.

As opposed to agreeing on focal elements, if m_2 is contradictory to m_1, then an example evidence combination is shown in TABLE 6.11.

TABLE 6.11: : Combination of masses by Dempster's rule

	$m_2(\{HC\}) = 0.60$	$m_2(\Omega) = 0.40$
$m_1(\{LC, MC\}) = 0.70$	$k = 0.42$	$m_{1,2}(\{LC, MC\}) = 0.28$
$m_1(\Omega) = 0.30$	$m_{1,2}(\{HC\}) = 0.18$	$m_{1,2}(\Omega) = 0.12$

In this case,

$$Bel(\{LC, MC\}) = 0.28/(1 - 0.42) = 0.70(1 - 0.60)/(1 - 0.42)$$

In general, when two mass distributions m_1 and m_2 are contradictory, the combined degree of belief on the focal element for m_1 is $p_1(1 - p_2)/(1 - p_1 \times p_2)$ and the combined degree of belief on the focal element for m_2 is $p_2(1 - p_1)/(1 - p_1 \times p_2)$, where p_1 and p_2 are mass assignments on the focal element by the two distributions.

6.5 NEO-GRANULARIST

In this section, we present probabilistic logic and fuzzy logic as neo-granularist approaches.

6.5.1 Probabilistic Logic

In this approach, degrees of uncertainty are represented as a probability value from $[0, 1]$. This approach describes the decision options from an application as a set of possible outcomes, termed "hypotheses." Bayesian inference requires an initial (prior) probability for each hypothesis in the problem space. The inference scheme then updates probabilities using evidence. Each piece of evidence may update the probability of a set of hypotheses calculated via the Bayesian rule, which is defined in the following:

$$p(A|B) = \frac{p(B|A)p(A)}{p(B)}$$

where A and B are events that are not necessarily mutually exclusive, $p(A|B)$ is the conditional probability of event A occurring given that event B has occurred, $p(B|A)$ is the conditional probability of event B occurring given that event A has occurred, $p(A)$ is the probability of event A occurring, and $p(B)$ is the probability of event B occurring. In general, if there are m mutually exclusive and exhaustive hypotheses $H_1, ..., H_m$ (that is, $\sum_{i=1}^{m} p(H_i) = 1$) and n possible events $E_1, ..., E_n$ that can occur, then the probability of a hypothesis given some evidence is computed as follows:

$$p(H_i|E_j) = \frac{p(E_j|H_i)p(H_i)}{\sum_{k=1}^{m} p(E_j|H_k)p(H_k)}$$

The Bayesian inference mechanism is illustrated in the following example.

Example

Consider a knowledge base consisting of the following three rules describing the chances of low conversion of a product based on a variety of evidence:

IF $StiffCompetition$ THEN $Low\,Conversion$ (0.7)
IF $Bad\,Quality$ THEN $Low\,Conversion$ (0.8)
IF $Winter\,Season$ THEN $Low\,Conversion$ (0.9)

The two mutually exclusive and exhaustive hypotheses are:

$$\begin{aligned} H_1 &= Low\,Conversion \\ H_2 &= \neg Low\,Conversion \end{aligned}$$

Three independent events on which evidence can be gathered are:

$$\begin{aligned} E_1 &= StiffCompetition \\ E_2 &= Bad\,Quality \\ E_3 &= Winter\,Season \end{aligned}$$

Below, we illustrate how posterior probabilities of the hypotheses are updated as evidence on competition, product quality, and season is gathered.

Initial State

Conditional probabilities $p(H_i|E_j)$ for the hypotheses are inferred as follows from the three rules of the knowledge base and the relation $p(H_1|E_j) + p(H_2|E_j) = 1$:

$$\begin{aligned} p(H_1|E_1) &= p\,(Low\,Conversion\,|Stiff\,Competition) = 0.7 \\ p(H_2|E_1) &= p((\neg Low\,Conversion\,|Stiff\,Competition) = 0.3 \end{aligned}$$

$$\begin{aligned} p(H_1|E_2) &= p\,(Low\,Conversion\,|Bad\,Quality) = 0.8 \\ p(H_2|E_2) &= p\,(\neg Low\,Conversion\,|Bad\,Quality) = 0.2 \end{aligned}$$

$$\begin{aligned} p(H_1|E_3) &= p\,(Low\,Conversion\,|Winter\,Season) = 0.9 \\ p(H_2|E_3) &= p\,(\neg Low\,Conversion\,|Winter\,Season) = 0.1 \end{aligned}$$

Given prior probabilities $p(E_j)$ and $p(H_i)$ are listed below:

$$\begin{aligned} p(E_1) &= p\,(Stiff\,Competition) = 0.2 \\ p(E_2) &= p\,(Bad\,Quality) = 0.1 \\ p(E_3) &= p\,(Winter\,Season) = 0.01 \end{aligned}$$

$$\begin{aligned} p(H_1) &= p\,(Low\,Conversion) = 0.2 \\ p(H_2) &= p\,(\neg Low\,Conversion) = 0.8 \end{aligned}$$

The following conditional probabilities $p(E_j|H_i)$ for evidence are computed via the application of the Bayesian rule:

$$\begin{aligned} p(E_1|H_1) &= p\,(Stiff\,Competition\,|\,Low\,Conversion) = 0.7 \\ p(E_1|H_2) &= p\,(Stiff\,Competition\,|\neg Low\,Conversion) = 0.075 \end{aligned}$$

$$p\,(E_2|H_1) = p\,(Bad\,Quality\,|Low\,Conversion) \;= 0.4$$
$$p\,(E_2|H_2) = p\,(Bad\,Quality\,|\neg Low\,Conversion) = 0.025$$

$$p\,(E_3|H_1) = p\,(Winter\ Season\,|Low\,Conversion) \;= 0.045$$
$$p\,(E_3|H_2) = p\,(Winter\ Season\,|\neg Low\,Conversion) = 0.001$$

Evidence of Stiff Competition

Assume that we first receive confirming evidence e on E_1 (that is, stiff competition). Then the probability $p\,(Low\,Conversion\,|Stiff\,Competition)$ directly provides the posterior probability 0.7 for low conversion of the product, which is a significant increase from the prior probability $p\,(Low\,Conversion) = 0.2$. If you are not completely sure about low conversion, then soft evidence e can be encoded as the following likelihood:

$$\begin{bmatrix} p\,(e|Stiff\,Competition) \\ p\,(e|\neg Stiff\,Competition) \end{bmatrix} = \begin{bmatrix} 0.95 \\ 0.05 \end{bmatrix}$$

The posterior probability of E_1 upon receiving e is computed as shown below (α is the normalizing constant):

$$\begin{aligned} &p\,(Stiff\,Competition|e) \\ &\quad = \alpha \times p\,(e|Stiff\,Competition) \times p\,(Stiff\,Competition) \\ &\quad = \alpha \times \begin{bmatrix} 0.95 \\ 0.05 \end{bmatrix} \times \begin{bmatrix} 0.2 \\ 0.8 \end{bmatrix} = \begin{bmatrix} 0.83 \\ 0.17 \end{bmatrix} \end{aligned}$$

You can then compute the posterior probability of the hypotheses as follows:

$$\begin{aligned} &p\,(Low\,Conversion|e) = \\ &\quad p\,(Low\,Conversion|Stiff\,Competition) \times p\,(Stiff\,Competition|e) + \\ &\quad p\,(Low\,Conversion|\neg Stiff\,Competition) \times p\,(\neg Stiff\,Competition|e) \end{aligned}$$

But we have

$$\begin{aligned} &p\,(Low\,Conversion|\neg Stiff\,Competition) \\ &\quad = \frac{p(\neg Stiff\,Competition|Low\,Conversion) \times p(Low\,Conversion)}{p(\neg Stiff\,Competition)} \\ &\quad = \frac{(1 - p(Stiff\,Competition|Low\,Conversion)) \times p(Low\,Conversion)}{1 - p(Low\,Conversion)} \\ &\quad = \frac{(1-0.7) \times 0.2}{1-0.2} = 0.07 \end{aligned}$$

Therefore,

$$p\,(Low\,Conversion|e) = 0.7 \times 0.83 + 0.07 \times 0.17 = 0.59$$
$$p\,(\neg Low\,Conversion|e) = 0.41$$

Note that the probability that the product has low conversion has increased significantly from the earlier prior value 0.2, but not as much as to 0.7 when evidence on E_1 was certain.

Evidence of Bad Quality

In addition to the confirming evidence on E_1, suppose now we observe confirming evidence on E_2 (that is, bad product quality). The posterior probabilities are computed using the following formulae:

$$p(H_i|E_1E_2) = \frac{p(E_1E_2|H_i) \times p(H_i)}{\sum_{j=1}^{2} p(E_1E_2|H_j) \times p(H_j)}, \qquad i = 1, 2$$

Since E_1 and E_2 are independent, $p(E_1E_2|H_i) = p(E_1|H_i) \times p(E_2|H_i)$. Therefore,

$$p(Low\,Conversion\,|Stiff\,Competition, Bad\,Quality) \\ = \frac{0.7\times0.4\times0.2}{0.7\times0.4\times0.2+0.075\times0.025\times0.8} = 0.97$$

$$p(\neg Low\,Conversion\,|Stiff\,Competition, Bad\,Quality) \\ = \frac{0.075\times0.025\times0.8}{0.7\times0.4\times0.2+0.075\times0.025\times0.8} = 0.03$$

Note that the posterior probability of the low conversion has increased further (from 0.7 to 0.97) due to evidence of both stiff competition and bad product quality. This process of probability revision continues as evidence arrives.

When the requisite initial assumptions (for example, prior probabilities and event independence) are fairly accurate, the Bayesian approach typically provides optimal results. However, there is always some question as to how accurate our a priori assumptions are for any given situation we are modeling. Under such circumstances, where a priori assumptions are inaccurate, Bayesian methods may perform poorly. The Dempster-Shafer theory was specifically developed to mitigate these weaknesses.

6.5.2 Fuzzy Logic

Fuzzy logic provides a foundation for approximate reasoning by extending traditional Boolean logic and by allowing truth to be a matter of degree (as in the case of membership degree in fuzzy sets). It is applicable to problems where the expressive power of words is greater than that of numbers. For example, an expert reported that the market size of a particular product is small, without knowing the exact market size in dollars. Words like "small" are less precise than numbers, but imprecision can be tolerated to achieve robustness. The four facets of fuzzy logic are shown in FIGURE 6.4.

Here is an example of traditional logic-based exact reasoning just to contrast with fuzzy reasoning:

IF Market Size is big

THEN Profit is large

Market Size is big

Therefore, Profit is large

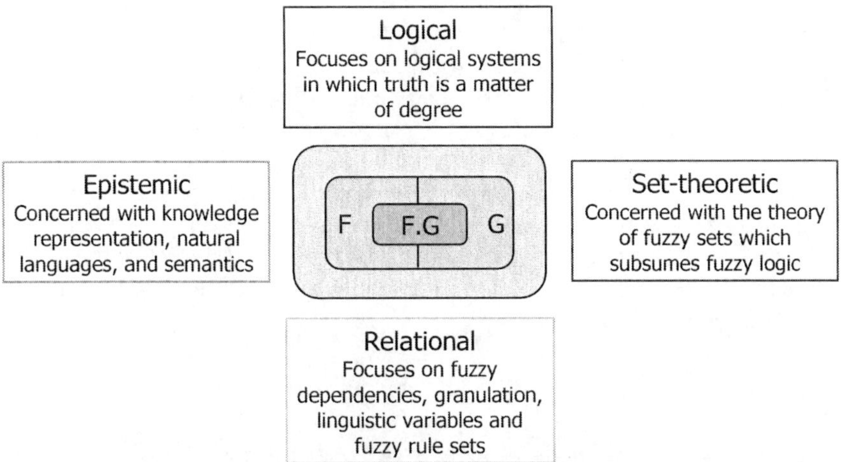

FIGURE 6.4 : Facets of fuzzy logic (Zadeh, 2002)

In the case of fuzzy reasoning, the concept of a linguistic variable plays a central role. In the reformulation of fuzzy reasoning of the above exact reasoning, the linguistic variables are *Market Size* and *Profit*. Values of linguistic variables are words or sentences in a natural or synthetic language, and are constructed by composing primary terms or predicates with modifiers. In the case of the variable *Market Size*, primary terms or predicates are, for example, *big*, *medium*, *small*, ..., and modifiers are, for example, *not*, *very*, *quite*, *rather*, ... Thus, linguistic values of the variable *Market Size* are *rather big*, *not small*, *very big*, and so on. A numerical or "crisp" value of the variable *Market Size* is in its universe of discourse, which is the interval $[0, 60]$ of values in million dollars. Modifiers fall into two classes:

- *Fuzzy Truth Qualifier*: quite true, very true, more or less true, etc.
- *Fuzzy Qualifier*: many, few, almost

An example fuzzy proposition is "Market Size is very big." Fuzzy expressions or formulae are built using fuzzy propositions, logical connectives, and quantifiers. Here is an example fuzzy formula:

IF Market Size is medium
AND Campaign is low-key
THEN Profit is small

where the linguistic variables are *Market Size*, *Campaign*, and *Profit*. A fuzzy proposition can have its truth value in the interval $[0, 1]$ defined by a membership function.

In proposition "X is P," $P(X)$ (or simply P when X is clear from the context) is a fuzzy set and the membership function $\mu_P(X)$ (or simply μ_P) defines the degree of membership in the set. Truth values of fuzzy propositions are defined by membership functions. Consider the three values, namely *big*, *medium*, and *small*, of the linguistic variable *Market Size*. Then the truth value of the proposition "Market Size is medium" is defined by μ_{medium}.

A generic fuzzy reasoning architecture is shown in FIGURE 6.5. The Fuzzification component computes the membership degrees for each input variable with respect to its linguistic terms. The Fuzzy Reasoning component yields the output fuzzy set using computed membership degrees and the fuzzy rules, via rule matching, inference, and aggregation. Finally, the Defuzzification component determines a crisp value from the output membership function as the final result of the solution.

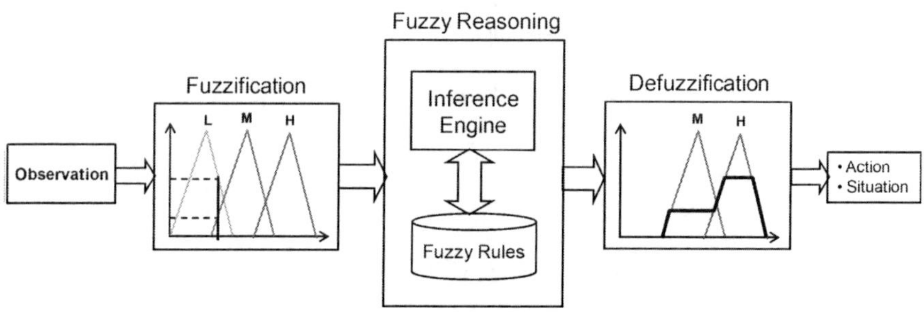

FIGURE 6.5 : Generic fuzzy engine

We illustrate the fuzzy reasoning process in the context of an example scenario involving estimation of a product's profit which is affected by its market size and campaign. There are three linguistic variables: *Market Size*, *Campaign*, and *Profit*. The underlying fuzzy rule base relating these variables is captured in the table shown in the table in FIGURE 6.6. Each entry in the table is a value of the variable *Profit* given the value of the two variables *Market Size* and *Campaign* in the corresponding column and row, respectively. For example, the shaded cell corresponds to the following rule:

IF Market Size is big
AND Campaign is lowkey
THEN Profit is large

There will be altogether nine rules corresponding to the nine cells containing the values of the variable *Profit*. The set of rules are shown in FIGURE 6.7 when traversing the cells row-by-row starting from the left.

Campaign \ Market Size (Profit)	big	medium	small
none	small	none	none
lowkey	large	small	none
aggressive	large	large	small

FIGURE 6.6 : Fuzzy rule base in tabular form

R1: IF Market Size is big AND Campaign is none THEN Profit is small
R2: IF Market Size is medium AND Campaign is none THEN Profit is none
R3: IF Market Size is small AND Campaign is none THEN Profit is none
R4: IF Market Size is big AND Campaign is lowkey THEN Profit is large
R5: IF Market Size is medium AND Campaign is lowkey THEN Profit is small
R6: IF Market Size is small AND Campaign is lowkey THEN Profit is none
R7: IF Market Size is big AND Campaign is aggressive THEN Profit is large
R8: IF Market Size is medium AND Campaign is aggressive THEN Profit is large
R9: IF Market Size is small AND Campaign is aggressive THEN Profit is small

FIGURE 6.7 : Fuzzy rule base

The membership functions for each of three variables are shown in FIGURE 6.8. Note that the membership function for $\mu_{medium}(Market\ Size)$ is Gaussian with mean 28.0 and variance 6.0.

In the fuzzification stage, one needs to determine, given the value of an input variable, the degree of membership for each term of the variable. Given the campaign cost is \$1.52M and the market size is \$40M, FIGURE 6.9 illustrates the determination of membership degrees and the resultant values are the following:

$$\begin{array}{ll} \mu_{none}(15.2) = 0 & \mu_{small}(40) = 0 \\ \mu_{lowkey}(15.2) = 0.25 & \mu_{medium}(40) = 0.1 \\ \mu_{aggressive}(15.2) = 0.70 & \mu_{big}(40) = 0.60 \end{array}$$

We then calculate the firing strength of every rule by combining the individual membership degree for all terms involved in the antecedent of a rule. Consider the rule

IF Market Size is big
AND Campaign is lowkey
THEN Profit is large

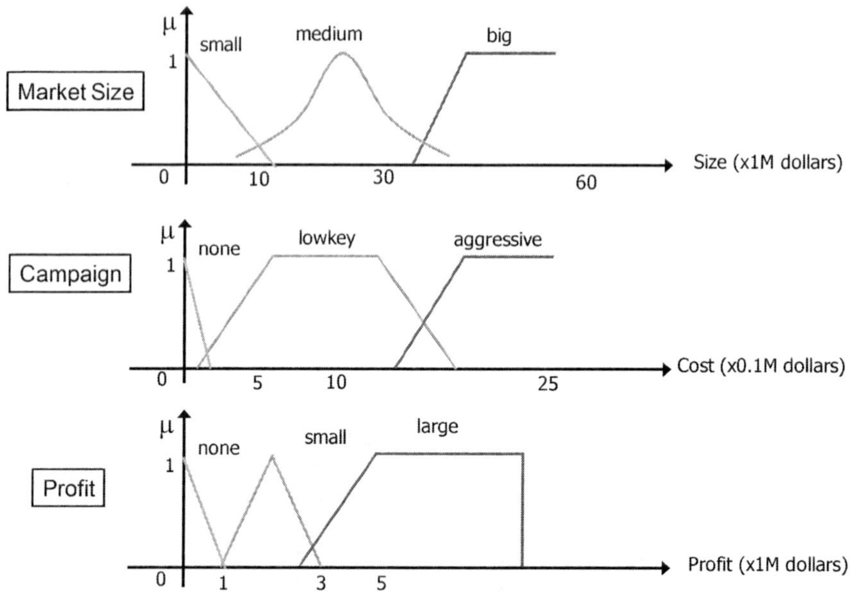

FIGURE 6.8 : Fuzzy sets of the variables Market Size, Campaign, and Profit

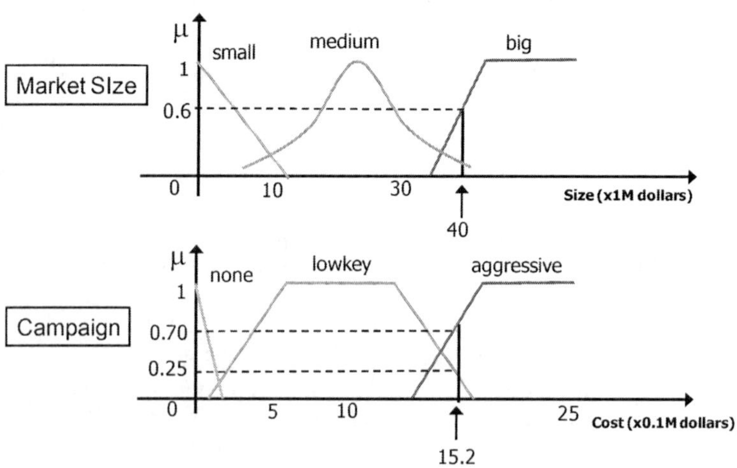

FIGURE 6.9 : Degrees of membership for a value of the input variable

Since we have $\mu_{big}\,(Market\ Size) = 0.60$ and $\mu_{lowkey}\,(Campaign) = 0.25$, and the antecedent of the rule is a conjunction, the combined membership degree is

$$\min\{\mu_{big}(40), \mu_{lowkey}(15.2)\} = 0.25$$

The next step is, for each rule, to apply the firing strength to modify its consequent fuzzy set, resulting in a new fuzzy set as the result of applying the rule. Consider again the above rule as an example. The modification of its consequent fuzzy set with the firing strength 0.25 is shown in FIGURE 6.10.

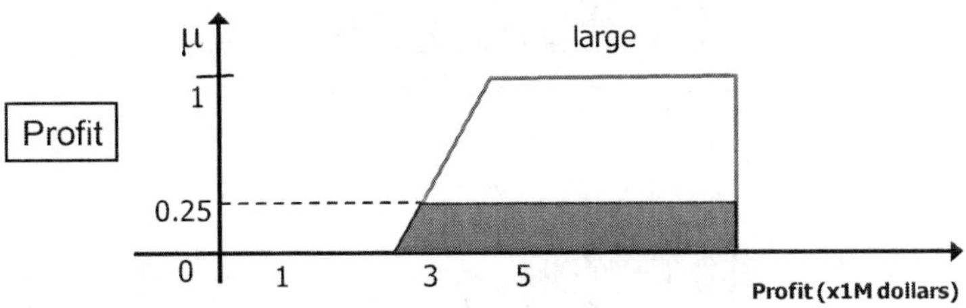

FIGURE 6.10 : Modification of a rule's consequent fuzzy set

This modification essentially reduces the degree of membership for every value of the variable *Profit* in the conclusion. What we are interested in is the shaded area underneath. There will be nine such modifications corresponding to the consequents of the nine rules in the fuzzy rule base, and all such modifications need to be aggregated. This involves the combination of responses of individual rules to yield an overall output fuzzy set using the max-operator (i.e., superimpose the shaded areas). An example aggregation involving just the three types of modifications is shown in FIGURE 6.11.

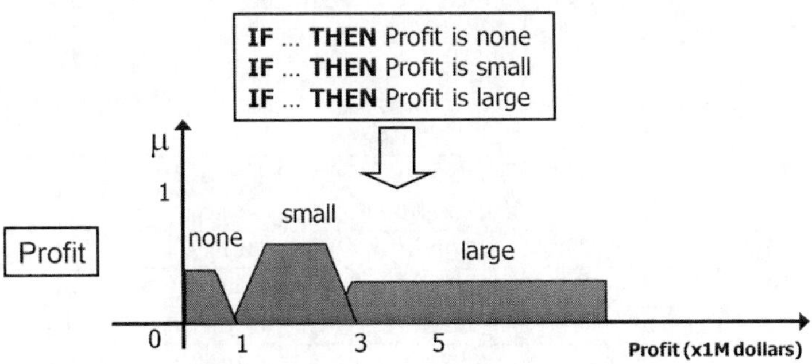

FIGURE 6.11 : Aggregation of modified fuzzy sets

The final defuzzification process determines crisp values from the output membership function. Two of the more common defuzzification techniques are the Centroid and Maximum methods. In the Centroid method, the crisp value of the output variable is computed by finding the variable value of the center of gravity of the membership function for the fuzzy value. In the Maximum method, one of the variable values at which the fuzzy subset has its maximum truth value is chosen as the crisp value for the output variable.

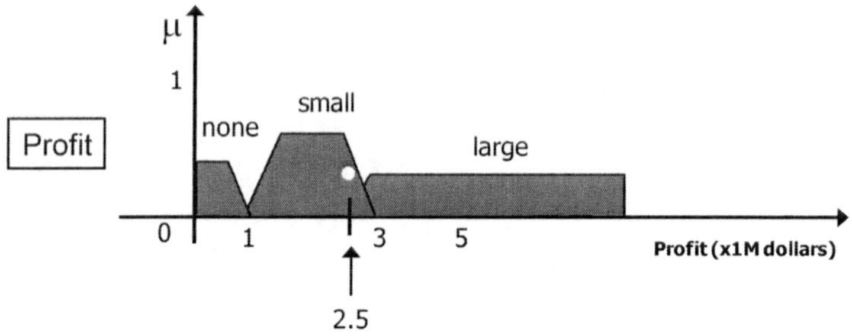

FIGURE 6.12 : Defuzzification

FIGURE 6.12 shows the projection of the center of gravity of the aggregated membership function onto the time-axis, yielding the crisp value of \$2.5M. This value is the estimated profit given the crisp values for the market size and the level of campaign.

6.5.3 Fuzzy Logic for Customer Segmentation

A credit card company segments its customers into gold, silver, and red categories, depending on their average monthly spending, usage frequency, and payment delay. The red customers are likely to default in the future. Some example fuzzy rules for segmenting customers are shown in TABLE 6.12 below. These rules are likely to have been acquired from experts working in the credit card processing department.

TABLE 6.12: : Fuzzy rules for customer segmentation

	Amount Spent	Usage Frequency	Payment Delay	Customer Segment
Rule 1	large	medium	short	silver
Rule 2	very large		none	gold
Rule 3	low	high	none	silver
Rule 4	large	low	none	gold
Rule 5	large		long	red

The first row in the table, for example, states the rule

IF Amount Spent is large
AND Usage Frequency is medium
AND Payment Delay is short
THEN Customer Segment is silver

FIGURE 6.13 shows the various stages of a classification system for the example problem. Possible inputs to a fuzzy logic-based classification system are the average amount spent, usage frequency, and payment delay of the customer we intend to segment. An input is fuzzified in the first step. This means that for each linguistic variable the degree to which the input fulfills it is determined. This is done by evaluating the values of the corresponding membership functions. For example, for the input amount spent=\$2500 the degree of "medium" is $\mu_{medium}(2500) = 0.55$. The degree of the rule antecedents is then computed by taking the minimum of all such degrees.

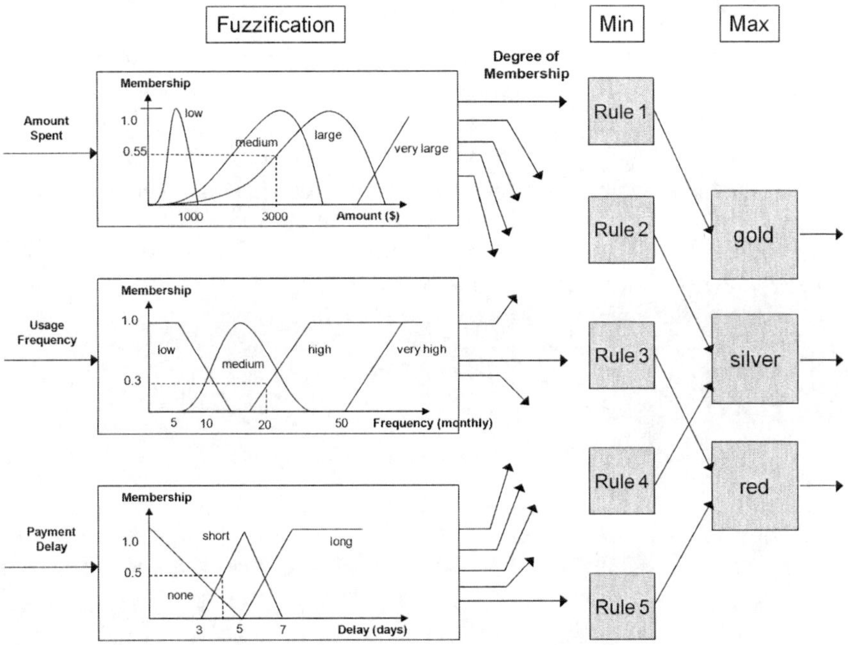

FIGURE 6.13 : Flow of computation in a fuzzy logic-based customer segmentation

Consider, for example, the first rule. For the input values \$2500, 20/month, and 4 days for a customer, respectively, of the variables *Amount Spent*, *Usage Frequency*, and *Payment Delay*, the following degrees are obtained:

$$\mu_{l\,arg\,e}(3000) = 0.55$$
$$\mu_{medium}(20) = 0.3$$
$$\mu_{short}(4) = 0.5$$

So the degree of rule antecedent is $\min\{0.55, 0.3, 0.5\} = 0.3$, which is the degree with which the rule is fulfilled, i.e., the degree with which the customer belongs to the class *silver*. The degree with which the customer belongs to each of the three classes is then computed by taking the maximum of all the rules describing the class as follows:

$$\begin{aligned} \text{degree}\,(gold) &= \max\{\text{degree}\,(\text{Rule }1)\} \\ \text{degree}\,(silver) &= \max\{\text{degree}\,(\text{Rule }2)\,,\ \text{degree}\,(\text{Rule }4)\} \\ \text{degree}\,(red) &= \max\{\text{degree}\,(\text{Rule }3)\,,\ \text{degree}\,(\text{Rule }5)\} \end{aligned}$$

The output class is then the class corresponding to the maximum of these three degrees.

6.6 FURTHER READING

A good book on AI with broad coverage is (Russell and Norvig, 2009). Maturity and a high level of interest in the area of rule-based expert systems have culminated dozens of text books. (Jackson, 1998) provides a good background of the subject. Shafer's own book (1976) and the edited volume by Yager et al. (1994) are good sources on the Dempster-Shafer theory of belief function. See (Smets, 1991) for various other formalisms for handling uncertainty, including fuzzy logic (Zadeh, 1965) and possibility theory (Zadeh, 1978; Dubois and Prade, 1988), and their relations to the theory of belief function. The next chapter provides many references to Bayesian networks.

CHAPTER 7

Probabilistic Graphical Modeling

This chapter presents three probabilistic graphical modeling paradigms in an increasing order of generality, and associated Bayesian inferencing techniques to compute posterior probabilities given some evidence. A graphical model has nodes representing some variables of a domain, and arcs between nodes representing probabilistic relationships among variables. A graphical model can be built in consultation with subject-matter experts. We start with Naïve Bayesian Classifier (NBCs), move to their generalizations k-dependence Naïve Bayesian Classifier (kNBCs) and, finally, explore the most general Bayesian Belief Networks (BNs). An NBC is a kNBC with $k = 0$, and a kNBC is also a BN with limited relationships among variables. Structures of NBCs and kNBCs are considerably simpler than BNs, and inferencing in them does not require complex evidence propagation algorithms. Given their foundations in Bayesian probability, these graphical models are perhaps most suitable as a stepping stone from traditional statistical analytics to the model-based AI paradigm for analytics, allowing human expertise to be incorporated easily into graphical models. Unless otherwise stated, variables are assumed to be categorical in this section.

This chapter covers model structures and inference algorithms. The machine learning chapter will present techniques for automated learning of these models from data. For the section on BNs, which is the bulk of the chapter, we begin by defining and illustrating the concept of conditional independence. We then present the concepts of evidence, belief, and likelihood. Next, we present two propagation algorithms to compute variables' posterior probabilities based on evidence: one for the class of networks without cycles, and another for a class of networks with restrictive cycles, and then analyze the complexities of these two algorithms. We provide some guidance for acquiring network probabilities, including the "noisy-or" technique. We summarize the overall advantages and disadvantages of BN technology and point to its application to analytics in various domains. Finally, we conclude the chapter by providing a selected list of commercially available BN tools and packages.

7.1 NAIVE BAYESIAN CLASSIFIER (NBC)

The most frequent use of NBC models is to separate a set of unlabeled data into a set of classes $C = \{c_1, ..., c_n\}$. NBCs are networks in which there is exactly one parent for the whole network, as shown in FIGURE 7.1. An NBC, and classifiers in general, can be viewed as computing or learning a discriminant function (and more)

$$f : D \to C$$

where D is an unlabeled data or instance space (e.g., relational tables, documents, articles, emails, surveys) that needs to be classified and, for $d \in D$, $f(d) = c_k$ means d is in class c_k. In an NBC, each child node or variable V_j in the network corresponds to an attribute or feature with some possible values. For a relational table, these attributes correspond to the columns of the table. For example, Outlook is an attribute of the play-tennis relational table in Appendix B, and its possible values are sunny, overcast, and rain. For text-based document indexing, these attributes usually indicate the presence or absence of a word in a sample of text. The parent node determines the output of the discriminant function, which is the class to which the example belongs. Here we focus on the application of NBC to handle structured data in the form of relational tables for classification or decision-making. NBC for unstructured text document classification will be discussed later in the chapter on unstructured data handling.

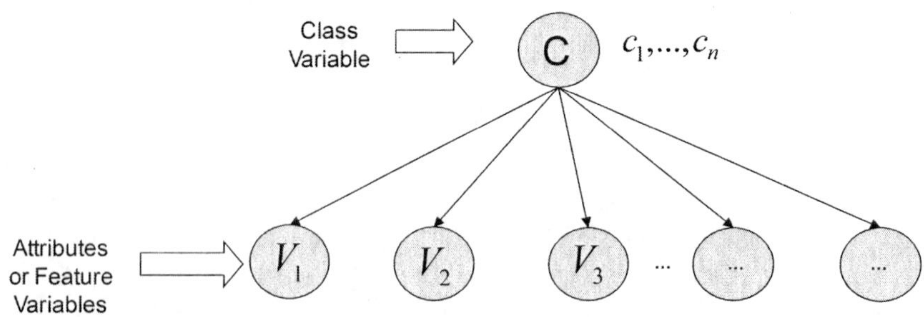

FIGURE 7.1 : Generic structure of an NBC

Let $d = (v_1, v_2, ...)$ be a structured record (a record in a relational table) that we want to classify, where v_js are the values of the attributes V_js in the record d. Suppose the given set of classes is $C = \{c_1, ..., c_n\}$. We want to compute $p(c_i|d)$, for every i. Now,

$$p(c_i|d) = \frac{p(c_i)\,p(d|c_i)}{p(d)} = \frac{p(c_i)\prod_j p(v_j|c_i)}{\sum_{k=1}^{n} p(c_k)\prod_j p(v_j|c_k)}$$

The product of conditional probabilities comes from the assumption that values in a record are independent given the record class. Note that the conditional independence assumption of features does not hold in most cases.

To compute the above posteriors $p(c_i|d)$, one would of course require the prior and conditional probabilities $p(c_i)$and $p(v_j|c_i)$, which can either be obtained from domain experts or determined based on the value frequencies in the table as detailed in the machine learning chapter. We don't need the estimated posterior $p(c_i|d)$ to be correct. Instead, we only need

$$\arg\max_{c_i} \{p(c_i|d)\},\ \text{i.e., } \arg\max_{c_i} \left\{ p(c_i)\prod_j p(v_j|c_i) \right\}$$

The score for each class can be expressed in the following tractable form for analytical purposes:

$$\log(p(c_i)) + \sum_j \log(p(v_j|c_i))$$

The score is not a probability value, but is sufficient for the purpose of determining the most probable class. It reduces round-off errors due to a product of small fractions caused by a large number of tokens.

Example

An example NBC is shown in FIGURE 7.2, which is based on the play-tennis example in the Appendix B. The example considers the two numerical attributes Temperature and Humidity as categorical, with possible values of high, medium, and low. The existing categorical attributes Outlook and Windy are also considered. The root node corresponds to the last (decision) column in the class node with two mutually exclusive and exhaustive sets of hypotheses (i.e., play vs. don't play). The four children nodes of the network correspond to the remaining four columns of the table.

Suppose $d = (sunny,\ medium,\ medium,\ weak)$. For each value c_i of the class Decision, the following expression needs to be computed and normalized to obtain $p(c_i|d)$:

$$\begin{aligned}&p(Decision = c_i) \times \\ &p(Outlook = sunny|Decision = c_i)\,p(Temp = medium|Decision = c_i) \\ &p(Humidity = medium|Decision = c_i)\,p(Windy = weak|Decision = c_i)\end{aligned}$$

In the chapter on machine learning, we will learn the constituent probabilities

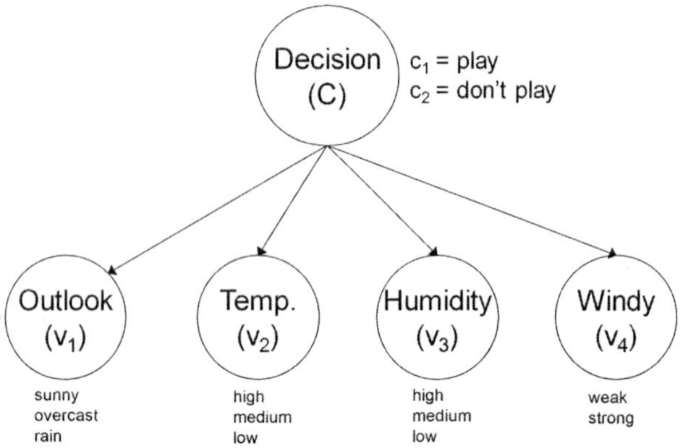

FIGURE 7.2 : An example NBC for the play-tennis example

in the above expression from the rows in the table in Appendix B. Given the learned NBC:

$$p\,(Decision = play|\,(sunny,\ \ medium,\ \ medium,\ \ weak)) = 0.58$$
$$p\,(Decision = don't\,play|\,(sunny,\ \ medium,\ \ medium,\ \ weak)) = 0.42$$

So the probability of the decision to play is 0.58 given the weather is sunny, the temperature is medium, the humidity is medium, and the wind is weak. The probability of the decision not to play is 0.42.

7.2 K-DEPENDENCE NAIVE BAYESIAN CLASSIFIER (KNBC)

NBC generally ignores dependencies among different features, but there are variations of NBC that do consider the dependence among features. For example, a general framework for limited dependence BNs, called k-dependence NBC, has been presented in Sahami (1996). A kNBC, as shown in FIGURE 7.3, contains the structure of the NBC and allows each feature v_i to have a maximum of k feature nodes as parents, where features v_js are tokens in document d. By varying the value of k one can define models that move smoothly along the spectrum of feature dependence.

Let d be a record that we want to classify, and the given set of classes is $C = \{c_1, ..., c_n\}$. We want to compute $p\,(c_i|d)$, for every i:

$$p\,(c_i|d) = \frac{p\,(c_i)\,p\,(d|c_i)}{p\,(d)} = \frac{p\,(c_i)\prod\limits_j p\,(v_j|c_i, \Pi\,(v_j))}{\sum\limits_{k=1}^{n} p\,(c_k)\prod\limits_j p\,(v_j|c_k, \Pi\,(v_j))}$$

where $\Pi\,(v_j)$ are the values of the parent variables of V_j. Note that the computation of the posterior $p\,(c_i|d)$ after propagation of evidence e involves only

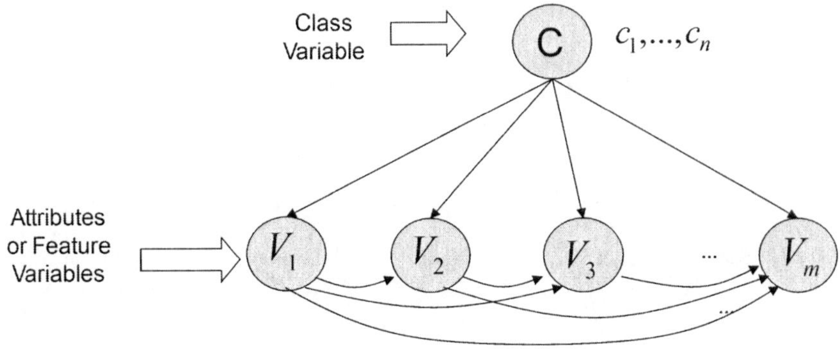

FIGURE 7.3 : Generic structure of a k-NBC

a multiplication of the relevant entries from the probability tables, without requiring full belief propagation as in Bayesian networks (to be presented next). One requires the prior and conditional probabilities $p(c_i)$and $p(v_j|c_i, \Pi(v_j))$, which can either be obtained from domain experts or determined based on the frequencies of attribute values in records. As in NBC, we don't need the exact estimation of posterior $p(c_i|d)$. Instead, we only need $\arg\max_{c_i} p(c_i|d)$ without having to compute the denominator of $p(c_i|d)$.

Example

An example kNBC based on the example NBC in FIGURE 7.2 is shown in FIGURE 7.4.In the kNBC structure of FIGURE 7.3, an edge from V_i to V_j implies that the influence of V_i on the assessment of the class variable also depends on the value of V_j. In the example in FIGURE 7.4, the influence of the attribute Windy on the class Decision (C) depends on the value of Outlook, while in the equivalent NBC (i.e., without the edge among children) the influence of the attribute Windy on the class variable is independent of other attributes, including the attribute Outlook. This presence of additional edges among children in a kNBC affects the classification process, in that a value of Windy that is unsurprising (i.e., weak) results in the unsurprising classification of the value of its correlated attribute, Outlook, as also unlikely (i.e., sunny). In this situation, the NBC will overpenalize the probability of the class variable by considering two unsurprising observations (i.e., weak wind and sunny outlook), while the augmented network of FIGURE 7.4 will not.

In NBC, $p(Decision = play|(sunny,\ medium,\ medium,\ weak)) =$ 0.58, but 0.39 in kNBC. Therefore, the classification by kNBC in this case is more discriminatory than NBC since 0.39 is further away from the most ambiguous split at 0.5 in comparison with 0.58.

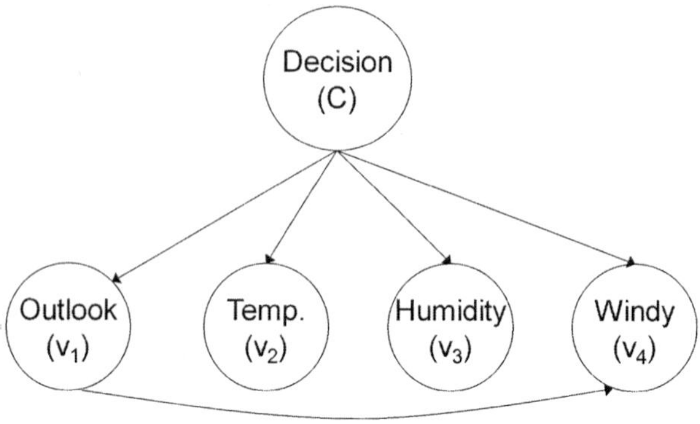

FIGURE 7.4 : An example k-NBC for the play-tennis example

7.3 BAYESIAN BELIEF NETWORKS

A Bayesian Belief Network (BN) is a network (that is, a graph consisting of nodes and links) with the following interpretation:

- Each node in the network represents a random variable that can take on multiple discrete values; these values are mutually exclusive events constituting the sample space over which the random variable is defined. The terms *node* and *variable* are synonymous in the context of a BN and are often used interchangeably.
- Each link in the network represents a relation or *conditional dependence* between the two variables it connects, and an associated *conditional probability table* (CPT) quantifies the relation associated with the link.
- There is a notion of causality between two linked variables, so links with explicit direction (represented by arrows) are drawn from "cause" nodes to "effect" nodes.
- The network is based on some *marginal* and *conditional independence* assumptions among nodes. These assumptions are described in the next section.
- The state of a node is called a *belief*, and reflects the posterior probability distribution of the values associated with that node, given all the a priori evidence.

The probabilities in a CPT are typically acquired from subject-matter experts in the domain, but can also be learned automatically given a large enough number of training instances (details on BN learning are in Chapter 10). The causality restriction can sometimes be relaxed by allowing links between a pair of nodes that are simply correlated, and the direction of the arrow between the two nodes is decided based on the ease of acquisition of the probabilities in the CPT. A typical causal relationship between two variables inevitably brings the temporal dimension into the modeling problem. We avoid building any formal dynamic or temporal BNs within which the state of a variable is allowed to change over time by modeling a simple snapshot of the problem domain at a particular time (dynamic BNs are discussed later in the chapter on time-series modeling).

Example

An example BN is shown in FIGURE 7.5. It illustrates causal influences on whether or not a company adopts a product and needs to start a marketing campaign, and how many conversions and how much profit is going to occur if it does, given the current level of competition, demand, product quality, and other related sources of evidence. Note that there are many ways to approach modeling an analytics problem with BNs. The selection of random variables and their granularities and interdependences is largely subjective, but should be driven by the problem-solving requirements. (Please note that we are not emphasizing any specific modeling methodology; the specific BN structure in FIGURE 7.5 is constructed to illustrate the technology via a single unified example. The conditional probabilities that will follow are examples only and may not accurately reflect reality.)

Each node in the BN in FIGURE 7.5 and its associated mutually exclusive and exhaustive states (possible values of the random variable representing the node) are described below (from top to bottom):

- *Demand*: Overall demand of the product condition during the marketing campaign – *heavy*, *moderate*, *low*. A demand state is heavy if it is neither moderate nor low.
- *Supply*: Company's ability to supply the product to keep up with the demand – *adequate*, *shortage*.
- *Competition*: Level of competition in the market for the product – *stiff*, *moderate*, *none*.
- *Strategic*: Whether or not the product to be adopted has strategic value to the company – *yes*, *no*.
- *Campaign*: Whether the marketing campaign for the product is to be aggressive or low-key – *aggressive*, *lowkey*. The variable provides a recommendation to the campaign manager to make an appropriate decision about the level of campaign.
- *Quality*: Quality of the product – *good*, *bad*.
- *Conversion*: Level of conversion of the product – *high*, *medium*, *low*.
- *Profit*: Amount of profit as a result of conversion – *large*, *small*, *none*.

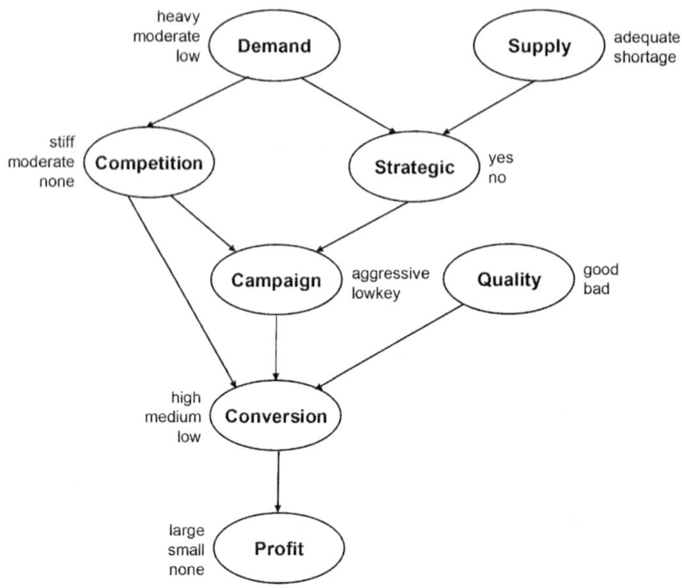

FIGURE 7.5 : An example BN

All states in the random variable *Demand*, for example, are mutually exclusive, that is, the overall demand for the product cannot be both heavy and moderate at the same time. But a probability density function f of the variable *Demand* with the domain $\{heavy,\ moderate, low\}$ can be defined and interpreted as "$f(x)$ is the probability that *Demand* will assume the value x." One such function can be defined as follows:

$$f\,(heavy) = 0.80, f\,(moderate) = 0.05, f\,(low) = 0.15$$

The causal influences by numbers (as shown in FIGURE 7.6) along the directions of the arrows are defined as follows:

- Demand for a product determines the level of competition. For example, a heavy demand for a product attracts many companies to enter the market and will cause stiff competition.

- Demand for a product and the company's ability to supply it together determine the strategic value of the product for the company. For example, heavy demand and the company's ability to supply adequate product together influence the product's strategic nature.

- Market competition the product faces and the product's strategic value for the company together determine the level of campaign for the product. For example, an aggressive marketing campaign is required for a product with stiff competition and with strategic value for the company. A product that has no competition may not require an aggressive campaign, irrespective of its strategic value.

- Market competition, level of campaign, and the product quality together determine the level of conversion.

- Conversion level determines the amount of profit. A low conversion may not yield any profit at all due to a fixed cost for product launch and campaign.

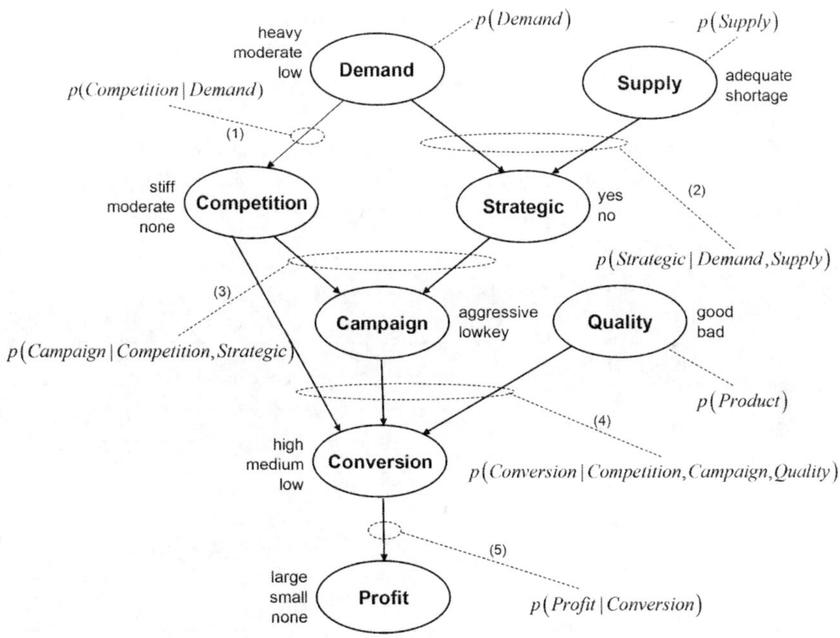

FIGURE 7.6 : BN with prior and conditional probabilities

The three prior probabilities corresponding to the three nodes without parents, namely, Demand, Supply, and Quality, are shown in TABLE 7.1, TABLE 7.2, and TABLE 7.3, respectively.

TABLE 7.1: : $p\,(Demand)$

Demand	heavy	0.55
	moderate	0.15
	low	0.3

TABLE 7.2: :$p\,(Supply)$

Supply	adequate	0.99
	shortage	0.01

TABLE 7.3: : $p\,(Quality)$

Quality		
Quality	good	0.6
	bad	0.4

The five conditional probabilities of the BN in FIGURE 7.6 corresponding to the five nodes Competition, Strategic, Campaign, Conversion, and Profit are shown in TABLE 7.4, TABLE 7.5, TABLE 7.6, TABLE 7.7, and TABLE 7.8, respectively. This BN and its associated CPTs are used throughout the rest of this chapter to illustrate algorithms and other related concepts. Note that the CPT in TABLE 7.8 is in the form of an identity matrix, and guarantees the perfect causal relationship between the states of *Profit* and *Conversion* variables.

TABLE 7.4: : $p\,(Competition|Demand)$

Demand		heavy	moderate	low
Competition	stiff	0.9	0.7	0.8
	moderate	0.09	0.2	0.15
	none	0.01	0.1	0.05

TABLE 7.5: : $p\,(Strategic|Demand, Supply)$

Demand		heavy		moderate		low	
Supply a – adequate s – shortage		a	s	a	s	a	s
Strategic	yes	0.95	0.6	0.3	0.1	0.4	0.2
	no	0.05	0.4	0.7	0.9	0.6	0.8

TABLE 7.6: : $p\,(Campaign|Competition, Strategic)$

Competition		stiff		moderate		none	
Strategic		yes	no	yes	no	yes	no
Campaign	aggressive	0.99	0.1	0.8	0.1	0.01	0
	lowkey	0.01	0.9	0.2	0.9	0.99	1

TABLE 7.7: : $p(Conversion|Competition, Campaign, Quality)$

Competition		stiff				moderate				none			
Campaign		aggr.		lowkey		aggr.		lowkey		aggr.		lowkey	
Quality g – good b – bad		g	b	g	b	g	b	g	b	g	b	g	b
Conv.	high	0.9	0.8	0	0	0.2	0.1	0	0	0.09	0	0	0
	med.	0.1	0.2	0	0	0.8	0.9	0	0	0.9	0.9	0	0
	low	0	0	1	1	0	0	1	1	0.01	0.1	1	1

TABLE 7.8: : $p(Profit|Conversion)$

Conversion		high	medium	low
Profit	large	1	0	0
	small	0	1	0
	none	0	0	1

7.3.1 Conditional Independence in Belief Networks

Two random variables Y and Z are said to be (marginally) *independent*, denoted as $Y \perp Z$, if

$$p(Y, Z) = p(Y)\, p(Z)$$

for any combination of values for the variables Y and Z. The variable Y is *conditionally independent* of Z given another variable X, denoted as $Y \perp Z|X$, if

$$p(Y, Z|X) = p(Y|X)\, p(Z|X)$$

Therefore,

$$p(Y|Z, X) = \frac{p(Y, Z|X)}{p(Z|X)} = \frac{p(Y|X)\, p(Z|X)}{p(Z|X)} = p(Y|X)$$

Similarly, $p(Z|Y, X) = p(Z|X)$. Note that marginal independence (no conditioning) does not imply conditional independence; nor does conditional independence imply marginal independence.

FIGURE 7.7 represents conditional independence in a chain fragment of a BN where a node X is between two other nodes $Y$and Z. We factorize the joint probability distribution of the variables X, Y, and Z as follows:

$$p(X, Y, Z) = p(Z|X, Y)\, p(X, Y) = p(Z|X)\, p(X|Y)\, p(Y)$$

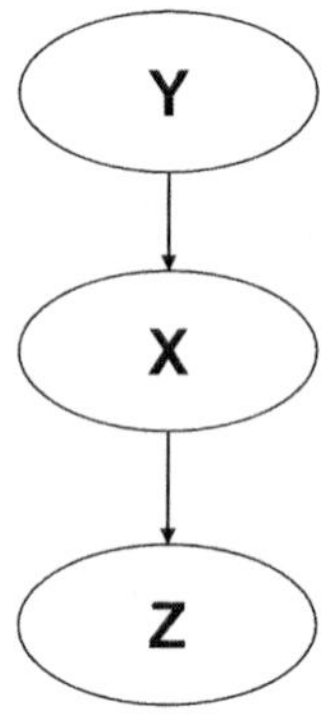

FIGURE 7.7 : Conditional independence in a chain fragment: Z is conditionally independent of Y given X

Example

FIGURE 7.8 shows an example instantiation of conditional independence in a chain network fragment as shown in FIGURE 7.7.

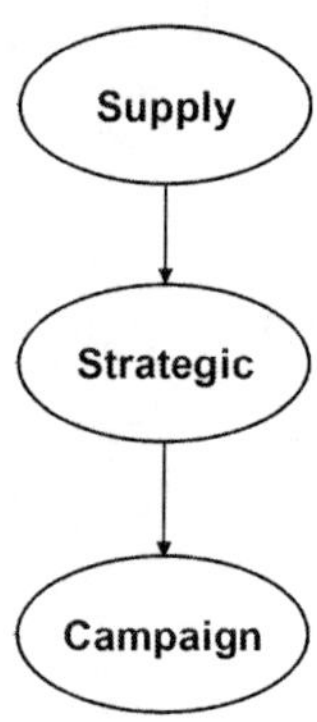

FIGURE 7.8 : Example conditional independence in a chain network fragment: Supply and Campaign are conditionally independent given Strategic

The variables X, Y, and Z represent the company's ability to supply a product, the strategic value of the product, and the level of campaign for the product, respectively. If we observe with complete certainty that the product has strategic value, then the probability distribution among the different levels of campaign is determined. Therefore, confirmation that the company adequately supplies the product or not will not change the probability of the campaign status, and vice versa.

FIGURE 7.9 represents conditional independence in a tree network fragment of a BN where the node X is the parent of two other nodes Y and Z. In this case, we factorize the joint probability distribution of the variables X, Y, and Z as follows:

$$p(X,Y,Z) = p(Z|X,Y)\,p(X,Y) = p(Z|X)\,p(Y|X)\,p(X)$$

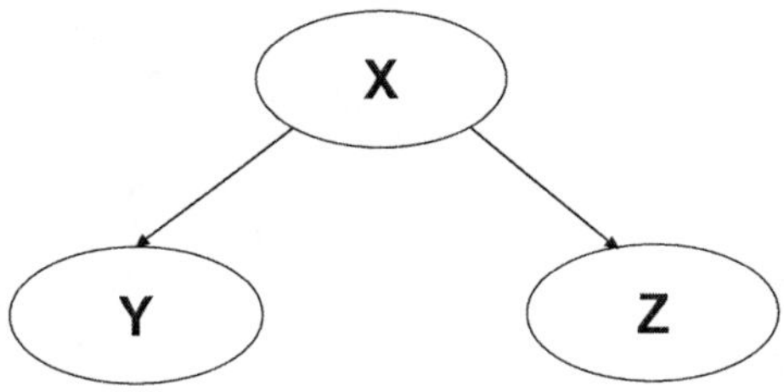

FIGURE 7.9 : Conditional independence in a tree network fragment: Z is conditionally independent of Y given X

Example

FIGURE 7.10 shows an example instantiation of conditional independence in a tree network fragment. The variables X, Y, and Z represent the demand for a product, market competition for the product, and the product's strategic value to the company, respectively. If we observe heavy demand, the probabilities of the market competition being stiff and the product having no strategic value are determined, and confirmation of the competition being stiff will not change the probability of the product having no strategic value, and vice versa.

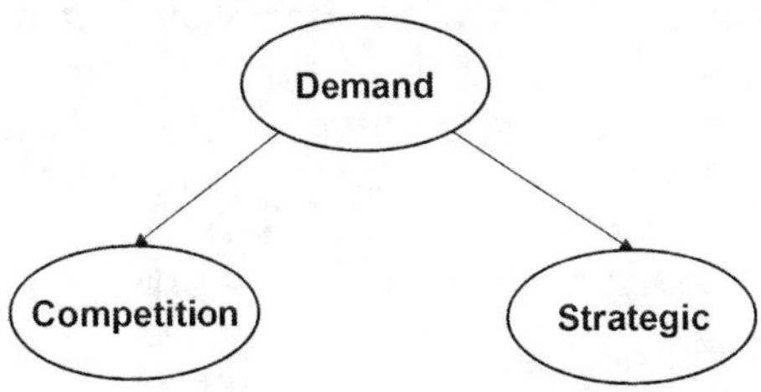

FIGURE 7.10 : Example conditional independence in a tree network fragment: Competition and Strategic are conditionally independent given Demand

FIGURE 7.11 shows conditional dependence in a polytree network fragment between the nodes Y and Z, given that we know about X; the two variables are marginally independent if we know nothing about X. For a polytree fragment as shown in FIGURE 7.11, the probability distribution of the variables Y, Z, and X can be factorized as follows:

$$p(X,Y,Z) = p(X|Y,Z)\,p(Y,Z) = p(X|Y,Z)\,p(Y)\,p(Z)$$

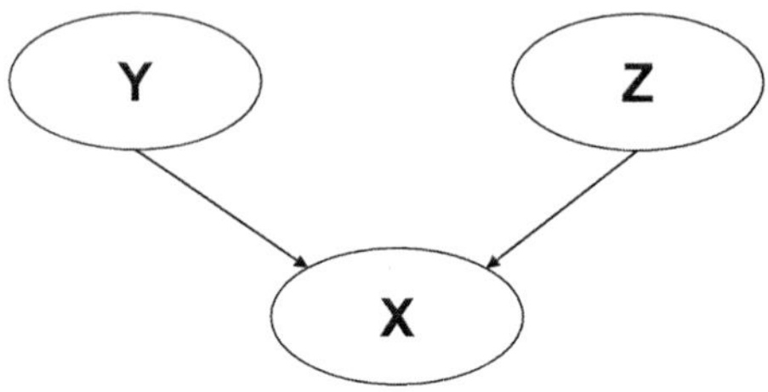

FIGURE 7.11 : Conditional dependence in a polytree fragment: Y is conditionally dependent on Z given X

Example

FIGURE 7.12 shows an example instantiation of the conditional dependence in a polytree network fragment. Both the demand for a product and the company's ability to supply the product can affect its overall strategic value to the company. Before any evidence is obtained on the strategic value, the probability of the demand for the product to be in a particular state is independent of the probability of the company's ability to supply. However, once some evidence on the strategic value, say high strategic value, is obtained, the state of demand may influence the probability of the product supply. For example, observation of heavy demand (thus explaining why the strategic value is high) may decrease the probability of the company's ability to supply (note that if a company decides to put a high strategic value on a product, perhaps the decision is based at least in part on the ability to supply the product.) This phenomenon is termed *explaining away*. In other words, observation of the status of one parent "explains away" the other, given a value of the child node.

In view of the joint distribution formulae for these three types of network fragments, the joint probability distribution in a directed acyclic graph (DAG) ("directed" means the links have an explicit direction represented by arrows, and "acyclic" means that the arrows may not form a directional cycle in the network) network can be factored into conditional probabilities, where each factor involves only a node and its parents. This is stated through the following result:

Proposition 7.31: Consider a network consisting of variables $X_1, X_2, ..., X_n$.

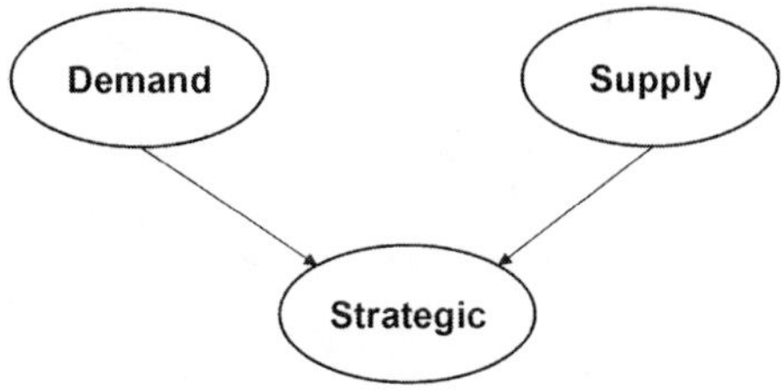

FIGURE 7.12 : Example conditional independence in a polytree network fragment: Demand is conditionally dependent on Supply given Strategic

The joint probability distribution $p(X_1, X_2, ..., X_n)$ is the product of all conditional probabilities specified in the network:

$$p(X_1, X_2, ..., X_n) = \prod_{i=1}^{n} p(X_i | pa(X_i))$$

where $pa(X_i)$ denotes the parent variables of X_i.

Example

Consider the network shown in FIGURE 7.5. For any combination of values d, su, co, st, ca, q, cn, p of the variables *Demand*, *Supply*, *Competition*, *Strategic*, *Campaign*, *Quality*, *Conversion*, and *Profit*, respectively, the joint probability is

$$p(d, su, co, st, ca, q, cn, p) = \\ p(d)\,p(su)\,p(co|d)\,p(st|d, su)\,p(ca|co, st)\,p(q)\,p(cn|co, ca, q)\,p(p|cn)$$

Influence in a BN is only allowed to flow along the links given in the network. Therefore, independence between two nodes is represented by the absence or blockage of links between the two nodes. Whether a link between a pair of nodes exists or not is determined by a property called *d-separation.* Before we formally define d-separation, we need to introduce three kinds of connections between a node X and two of its neighbors Y and Z. The three possibilities are shown in FIGURE 7.7, FIGURE 7.9, and FIGURE 7.11. Their example instantiations are shown in FIGURE 7.8, FIGURE 7.10, and FIGURE 7.12, respectively.

In FIGURE 7.7, there are links from Y to X and from X to Z. In other words, Y has an influence on X, which in turn influences Z. The connection or path between Y and Z is called *linear.* In this case, causal or deductive evidence from Y will change the belief of X, which then changes the belief of Z. Similarly, diagnostic or abductive evidence from Z will change the belief of X, which then changes the belief of Y. But if the state of X is known, then the connection between Y and Z is blocked and they cannot further influence each other. Thus, Y and Z become independent given X. We say that Y and Z are d-separated given X.

In FIGURE 7.9, there are links from X to Y as well as from X to Z. In other words, X has influence on both Y and Z, and Y and Z will influence each other via X. The connection or path between Y and Z is called *diverging* and the node X is said to have diverging arrows. As in the linear case, if the state of X is known then Y and Z cannot further influence each other, and we say that Y and Z are d-separated given X.

The third case, shown in FIGURE 7.11, is the opposite of the previous case. In this case, there are links from Y to X as well as from Z to X. In other words, both Y and Z have influence on X. The connection or path in this case is called *converging* and the node X is said to have converging arrows. In this case, if nothing is known about X then Y and Z are independent, and therefore cannot influence each other. But if the state of X is known then Y and Z can influence each other. In other words, Y and Z are already d-separated, but not when X is given.

In general, two nodes Y and Z in a DAG-type of network are d-separated if, for all paths between Y and Z, there is an intermediate node X such that either

- The path between Y and Z is serial or diverging at node X and the state of X is known, or
- The path between Y and Z is converging at node X and neither X nor any of its descendants has received evidence.

Two nodes Y and Z in a DAG are d-connected if they are not d-separated. The following proposition establishes a connection between conditional independence and d-separateness.

Proposition 7.32: If any two nodes $Y$and Z in a DAG are d-separated with evidence e entered, then Y and Z are conditionally independent given e(i.e., $Y \perp Z | e$ or $p(Y|Z, e) = p(Y|e)$).

Example

Consider the network shown in FIGURE 7.5. Let $Y = \mathit{Competition}$ and $Z = \mathit{Supply}$. The two paths between the nodes Y and Z are:

$$\mathit{Competition} \leftarrow \mathit{Demand} \rightarrow \mathit{Strategic} \leftarrow \mathit{Supply}$$
$$\mathit{Competition} \rightarrow \mathit{Campaign} \leftarrow \mathit{Strategic} \leftarrow \mathit{Supply}$$

The first path contains a diverging node (*Demand*) and the second path contains a converging node (*Campaign*). If the state of the variable *Demand* is known and the variable *Campaign* and its descendants *Conversion* and *Profit* have not received evidence, then the nodes *Competition* and *Supply* are d-separated. Alternatively, if the variable *Strategic* and its descendants *Campaign*, *Conversion*, and *Profit* have not received evidence, then the nodes *Competition* and *Supply* are d-separated.

The above definition of d-separation between two nodes takes into account the evidence entered into the network. Here we present a more generalized definition of d-separation that identifies a set of nodes, instead of a single node, that could potentially separate two nodes in a network. Moreover, the definition provided here is between two sets of nodes rather than between two nodes.

For any three disjointed node subsets S_X, S_Y, and S_Z, S_X is said to *d-separate* S_Y and S_Z if for every path between a node in S_Y to a node in S_Z there is a node X satisfying one of the following two conditions:

- X has converging arrows and none of X or its descendants is in S_X, or
- X does not have converging arrows and X is in S_X.

Example

Consider the network shown in FIGURE 7.5. Let S_Y be $\{Competition\}$ and S_Z be $\{Supply\}$. The set of all paths from a node in S_Y to a node in S_Z is:

$$Competition \leftarrow Demand \rightarrow Strategic \leftarrow Supply$$
$$Competition \rightarrow Campaign \leftarrow Strategic \leftarrow Supply$$

Suppose $S_X = \Phi$. The first path contains node *Strategic* with converging arrows and none of its three descendants *Campaign*, *Conversion*, and *Profit* is in S_X. The second path contains the node *Campaign* with converging arrows and none of its two descendants *Conversion* and *Profit* is in S_X. Therefore, S_Y and S_Z are d-separated by the empty set. But, if we consider S_X as $\{Conversion\}$, the first path contains the node *Strategic* with converging arrows and its descendant *Conversion* is in S_X. Also, the second path contains the node *Campaign* with converging arrows and its descendant *Conversion* is in S_X. Although the first path contains the node *Demand* without converging arrows, the node does not belong to S_X. Therefore, $\{Conversion\}$ does not d-separate S_Y and S_Z. Note that Φ does not d-separate $\{Competition\}$ and $\{Strategic\}$, but $\{Demand\}$ does, and so does $\{Demand, Conversion\}$.

The generalized set-theoretic definition of d-separation above yields the following proposition:

Proposition 7.33: For any three disjoint subsets S_X, S_Y, and S_Z of variables in a DAG, S_X d-separates S_Y and S_Z if and only if S_Y and S_Z are conditionally independent given S_X (that is, $S_Y \perp S_Z | S_X$).

Once we have built BNs, either with the help of domain experts or via automated learning from past observations, we need to reason with them, that is, to examine how the variables in a network change their beliefs when observations are propagated into the network as evidence.

7.3.2 Evidence, Belief, and Likelihood

Evidence on a variable is a statement of certainties of its states based on certain observations. Since the states of a BN variable are mutually exclusive, such a statement of certainty of a state variable is usually made with a percentage that represents the chance of being in that state. If the statement constituting evidence for a variable gives the exact state of the variable (that is, 100%), then it is *hard* evidence (which is also called *instantiation*); otherwise, the evidence is called *soft*. As an example, consider the variable *Demand* whose states are *heavy*, *moderate*, and *low*. If the evidence e is based on someone's direct observation of the market and states that the demand is heavy, then it is hard evidence and is denoted by $Demand = heavy$. In general, if $E = \{X_1, ..., X_n\}$ is the set of all variables whose values are known as $X_1 = a_1, ..., X_n = a_n$ then

$$e = \{X_1 = a_1, ..., X_n = a_n\}$$

where each a_i is hard evidence of the state of X_i. For example, if

$$E = \{Demand, Competition, Campaign\}$$

and the evidence states that the demand is heavy, the competition is moderate, and the campaign is aggressive, then

$$e = \left\{ \begin{array}{l} Demand = heavy, Competition = moderate, \\ Campaign = aggressive \end{array} \right\}$$

On the other hand, consider the situation when the source of evidence on the variable Demand is based on the observation by a market expert. The statement constituting evidence states that there is an 80% chance that the demand is heavy, 15% chance that the demand is moderate, and 5% chance that the demand is low. The evidence in this case is inexact and is therefore soft. Evidence on a variable X yields a likelihood vector, denoted as $\lambda(X)$, expressed in terms of probability measures. For example, the above soft evidence on the variable Demand yields the likelihood vector

$$\lambda(Demand) = \begin{bmatrix} 0.80 \\ 0.15 \\ 0.05 \end{bmatrix}$$

The hard evidence $e = \{Demand = heavy\}$ yields the likelihood $\left[\begin{array}{ccc} 1 & 0 & 0 \end{array}\right]^T$.

Usually, the total evidence accumulated on the states of a variable is expected to be more or less than 100%. An example of such type of evidence obtained by listening to a market expert (for example, the expert indicates green for heavy demand, blue for moderate, and red for low; ambiguities may occur because of an error in judgment or a noisy environment producing incorrect market indicators on which the expert relies) states that there is a

70% chance that the demand is heavy, a 50% chance that the demand is moderate, and a 15% chance that the demand is low. The likelihood vector for this evidence is the following:

$$\lambda\left(Demand\right) = \begin{bmatrix} 0.70 \\ 0.50 \\ 0.15 \end{bmatrix}$$

The above evidence states that if all 100 market circumstances similar to the current one indicate heavy demand for the product, the expert is likely to be correct 70 times; if all are moderate, the expert is likely to be correct 50 times; and if all are low, the expert is likely to be correct 15 times.

How do we then relate evidence to probability? Observe that $70:50:15$ is the ratio of the number of times the expert is likely to produce e_{Demand} if all 100 market circumstances are of heavy demand, to the number of times it is likely to produce e_{Demand} if all 100 are moderate, to the number of times it is likely to produce e_{Demand} if all 100 are low. This relation yields the following likelihood ratio:

$$p\left(e_{Demand}|Demand = heavy\right) : p\left(e_{Demand}|Demand = moderate\right) :$$
$$p\left(e_{Demand}|Demand = low\right) = 70:50:15$$

This ratio gives the following likelihood:

$$\lambda\left(Demand = heavy\right) = p\left(e_{Demand}|Demand = heavy\right) = 0.70$$
$$\lambda\left(Demand = moderate\right) = p\left(e_{Demand}|Demand = moderate\right) = 0.50$$
$$\lambda\left(Demand = low\right) = p\left(e_{Demand}|Demand = low\right) = 0.15$$

The likelihood vector $\lambda\left(Demand\right)$ is $p\left(e_{Demand}|Demand\right)$, and we therefore have the following:

$$\lambda\left(Demand\right) = p\left(e_{Demand}|Demand\right) = \begin{bmatrix} 0.70 \\ 0.50 \\ 0.15 \end{bmatrix}$$

If the expert indicates green when the demand is heavy, then the above likelihood vector changes to

$$\lambda\left(Demand\right) = \begin{bmatrix} 1.0 \\ 0.50 \\ 0.15 \end{bmatrix}$$

But, conversely, the green indication does not necessarily mean the demand *is* heavy, though it certainly indicates a high probability of heavy demand.

The CPTs of a BN remain unchanged upon the arrival of evidence. When evidence is ***posted*** to the designated node to compute posterior probabilities of the nodes in the networks, the ***node state certainties***, or ***probability distributions***, change. After receiving evidence e, the posterior probability of node X

is $p(X|e)$. The *belief* of the node X of a BN, denoted as $Bel(X)$, is the overall belief of the node X contributed by all evidence so far received. Therefore, if e is the evidence received so far then $Bel(X) = p(X|e)$.

Consider the network fragment as shown in FIGURE 7.13. Suppose e_X^+ and e_X^- are the total evidence connected to X through its parents and children, respectively. In other words, e_X^+ and e_X^- are the evidence contained in the upper and lower sub-networks with respect to the node X. We then define the following two π and λ vectors:

$$\pi(X) = p\left(X|e_X^+\right)$$
$$\lambda(X) = p\left(e_X^-|X\right)$$

The vectors $\pi(X)$ and $\lambda(X)$ represent the distributions of the total supports among the states of X through its parents and children, respectively. If the network that contains the fragment is a tree, then the vectors $\pi(X)$ and $\lambda(X)$ represent the distributions of the total causal and diagnostic supports among the states of X by all its ancestors and descendants, respectively.

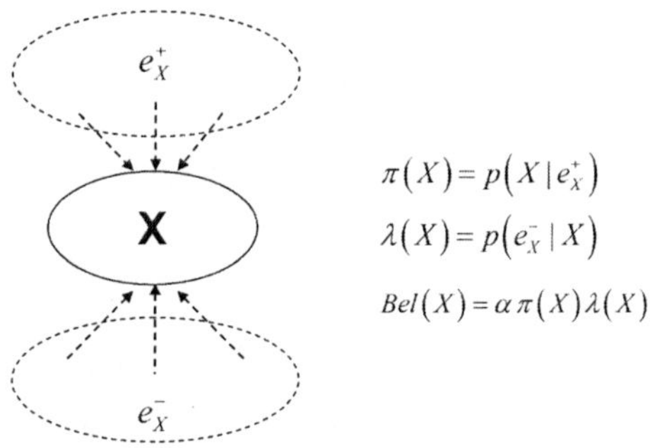

FIGURE 7.13 : Network fragment containing node X

7.3.3 Prior Probabilities in Networks without Evidence

Evidence propagation and belief updating start with "fresh" networks without any observed evidence. Then the π and λ vectors of the variables, and hence the belief vectors, are updated incrementally as evidence is accumulated. In this section, we detail how the initial vectors of these variables are computed in a fresh network.

If no evidence has yet been propagated in a network, then for every variable X in the network, $\pi(X)$ is $p(X)$, since e_X^+ is empty. Therefore, $\pi(X)$ is simply the prior probability of the variable X. Since e_X^- is the empty set, $\lambda(X)$ is $p(\Phi|X)$. Since Φ is a constant, each $p(\Phi|x)$ is equal to $\frac{1}{n}$, where n is the number of states of X. For the purpose of simplicity, we will write an initial λ vector simply as a nonnormalized n-vector $(1, 1, ..., 1)$.

Recall that the relationships among the variables in a network are quantified via CPTs of the form $p(X|U_1, U_2, ..., U_n)$ for a variable X with parents

$U_1, U_2, ..., U_n$. Therefore, if X has no parent (that is, X is a *root node*) then its CPT is just $p(X)$, which is its prior probability. With this in mind, we present a simple recursive routine to compute the beliefs and the π and λ vectors in a fresh network.

First we mark all the root nodes. Then we recursively compute $p(X)$ of a node X, each of whose parents is already marked, and mark the node Xitself. If X has parents $U_1, U_2, ..., U_n$ then

$$\begin{aligned} p(X) & \\ &= \sum_{U_1,...,U_n} p(X|U_1, ..., U_n) p(U_1, ..., U_n) \\ &= \sum_{U_1,...,U_n} p(X|U_1, ..., U_n) p(U_1|U_2, ..., U_n) \ldots p(U_{n-1}|U_n) \, p(U_n) \end{aligned}$$

Since $U_1, U_2, ..., U_n$ are marginally independent

$$p(X) = \sum_{U_1,...,U_n} p(X|U_1, ..., U_n) \prod_{i=1}^{n} p(U_i)$$

Thus, $p(X)$ can be computed using its CPT and the prior probabilities of its parents.

Example

Consider the network in FIGURE 7.14, along with the prior probabilities $p(Competition)$ and $p(Strategic)$ of the root nodes *Competition* and *Strategic*, respectively, and the two CPTs $p(Campaign|Competition, Strategic)$ and $p(Conversion|Campaign)$ of the two other nodes of the network. The network also shows the initial π and λ vectors, and hence belief vectors, of each of the two root nodes.

The prior probability of the node *Campaign* and then of the node *Conversion* is computed as follows:

$$\begin{aligned} p(Campaign) & \\ &= \sum_{\substack{Competition, \\ Strategic}} \left(\begin{array}{l} p(Campaign|Competition, Strategic) \times \\ p(Competition) \, p(Strategic) \end{array} \right) \\ &= \begin{bmatrix} 0.67 \\ 0.33 \end{bmatrix} \end{aligned}$$

$$\begin{aligned} p(Conversion) & \\ &= \sum_{Campaign} p(Conversion|Campaign) p(Campaign) \\ &= \begin{bmatrix} 0.50 \\ 0.17 \\ 0.33 \end{bmatrix} \end{aligned}$$

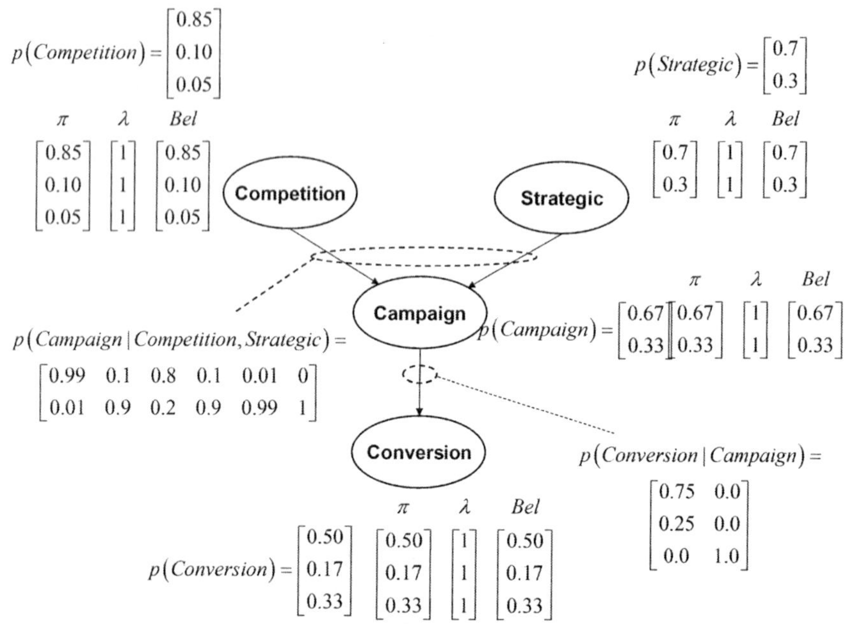

FIGURE 7.14 : Initial probabilities, beliefs, and π and λ vectors

7.3.4 Belief Revision

In this section, we describe how a node revises its own beliefs upon receiving evidence on itself. Suppose a node X receives evidence e_X and the probability vector $p(X)$ is its current state certainties. Then its posterior probability is defined as:

$$p(X|e_X) = \frac{p(X)\,p(e_X|X)}{p(e_X)} = \alpha\, p(X)\,\lambda(X)$$

where the normalizing constant α is computed by summing over mutually exclusive and exhaustive states of the variable X (that is, $\sum_{X=x} p(X) = 1$):

$$\alpha = \frac{1}{p(e_X)} = \frac{1}{\sum_X p(X, e_X)} = \frac{1}{\sum_X p(e_X|X)\,p(X)}$$

Therefore, the belief of the node X after receiving evidence e_X becomes the normalized product of its prior probability vector $p(X)$ with the likelihood vector $\lambda(X)$.

Example

Consider the node *Demand* whose prior probability $p(Demand)$ and posted evidence e_{Demand} are shown in FIGURE 7.15. A particular evidence e_X on a variable X in a network will be hypothetically considered as a binary child node of the node X, where the CPT $p(e_X|X) = \lambda(X)$.

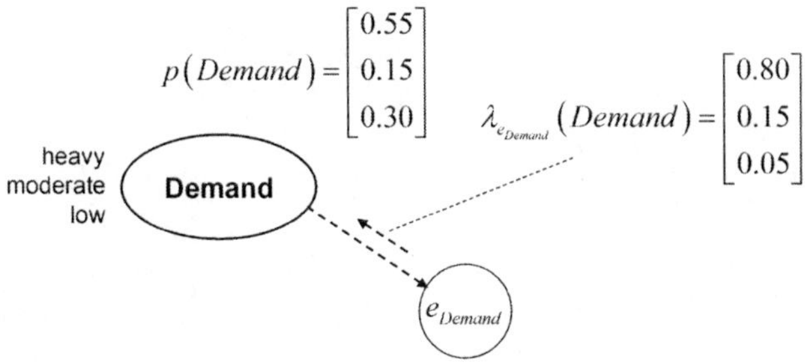

FIGURE 7.15 : Posting evidence on a node

The posterior probability of the variable *Demand*, for example, is computed as follows:

$$p(Demand|e_{Demand}) = \begin{bmatrix} \alpha \times 0.55 \times 0.80 \\ \alpha \times 0.15 \times 0.15 \\ \alpha \times 0.30 \times 0.05 \end{bmatrix} = \begin{bmatrix} 0.92 \\ 0.05 \\ 0.03 \end{bmatrix}$$

where

$$\alpha = \frac{1}{0.55 \times 0.80 + 0.15 \times 0.15 + 0.30 \times 0.05} = 2.09.$$

Now consider belief revision in the case illustrated in FIGURE 7.13. The posterior probability of the node X upon receiving all the evidence is computed as follows:

$$\begin{aligned} & Bel(X) \\ & = p(X|e_X^+, e_X^-) = \frac{p(e_X^+, e_X^-, X)}{p(e_X^+, e_X^-)} \\ & = \frac{p(e_X^-|e_X^+, X)\, p(X|e_X^+)\, p(e_X^+)}{p(e_X^+, e_X^-)} \\ & = \alpha\, p(X|e_X^+)\, p(e_X^-|X) \\ & = \alpha\, \pi(X)\, \lambda(X) \end{aligned}$$

where

$$\begin{aligned} \alpha &= \frac{p(e_X^+)}{p(e_X^-, e_X^+)} = \frac{1}{p(e_X^-|e_X^+)} \\ &= \frac{1}{\sum_{X=x} p(e_X^-|e_X^+, X) p(X|e_X^+)} \\ &= \frac{1}{\sum_{X=x} \pi(X)\lambda(X)} \end{aligned}$$

Note that $p(e_X^-|e_X^+, X) = p(e_X^-|X)$ because X separates e_X^+ and e_X^-. The node belief is therefore the normalized product of its λ and π vectors, which can be factorized as follows.

Consider a concrete instantiation of the above case as shown in FIGURE 7.16. The node X has parents U, V, and W, through which it received evidence e_U^+, e_V^+, and e_W^+ respectively. Node X has children Y, Z, and Q, through which it received evidence e_Y^-, e_Z^-, and e_Q^-, respectively. Thus,

$$
\begin{aligned}
e_X^+ &= \{e_U^+, e_V^+, e_W^+\} \\
e_X^- &= \left\{e_Y^-, e_Z^-, e_Q^-\right\}
\end{aligned}
$$

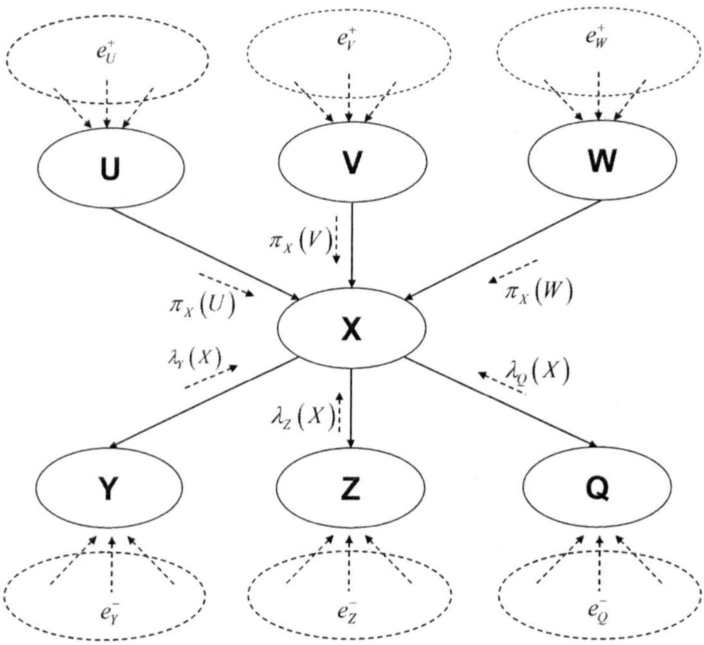

FIGURE 7.16 : Node X has multiple parents and children

$$
\begin{aligned}
&\pi(X) \\
&\quad = p\left(X|e_X^+\right) \\
&\quad = p\left(X|e_U^+, e_V^+, e_W^+\right) \\
&\quad = \sum_{U,V,W} p\left(X|U,V,W,e_U^+, e_V^+, e_W^+\right) p\left(U,V,W|e_U^+, e_V^+, e_W^+\right) \\
&\quad = \sum_{U,V,W} p(X|U,V,W) p\left(U|V,W,e_U^+, e_V^+, e_W^+\right) \\
&\qquad\qquad p\left(V|W,e_U^+, e_V^+, e_W^+\right) p\left(W|e_U^+, e_V^+, e_W^+\right) \\
&\quad = \sum_{U,V,W} p(X|U,V,W) p\left(U|e_U^+\right) p\left(V|e_V^+\right) p\left(W|e_W^+\right) \\
&\quad = \sum_{U,V,W} p(X|U,V,W) \pi_X(U) \pi_X(V) \pi_X(W)
\end{aligned}
$$

The above derivation uses the conditional assumption since U, V, and W

separate X from e_U^+, e_V^+, and e_W^+, respectively. The derivation also uses independence relationships, such as U is independent of V, W, e_V^+, and e_W^+; V is independent of U, W, e_U^+, and e_W^+; and W is independent of U, V, e_U^+, and e_V^+. Similarly,

$$\begin{aligned}\lambda(X) &= p\left(e_X^-|X\right)\\ &= p\left(e_Y^-, e_Z^-, e_Q^-|X\right)\\ &= p\left(e_Y^-|e_Z^-, e_Q^-, X\right)p\left(e_Z^-|e_Q^-, X\right)p\left(e_Q^-|X\right)\\ &= p\left(e_Y^-|X\right)p\left(e_Z^-|X\right)p\left(e_Q^-|X\right)\\ &= \lambda_Y(X)\,\lambda_Z(X)\,\lambda_Q(X)\end{aligned}$$

This derivation uses the conditional independence assumptions that given X, e_Y^- is independent of e_Z^- and e_Q^-, and e_Z^- is independent of e_Q^-.

Now consider the case shown in FIGURE 7.17, when a given node X receives evidence e_X. In addition, suppose e_X^+ and e_X^- are the total evidence connected to X through its parents and children, respectively. Then the revised $\lambda(X)$ can be computed by using the conditional independence assumption derived from the fact that X separates e_X and e_X^-:

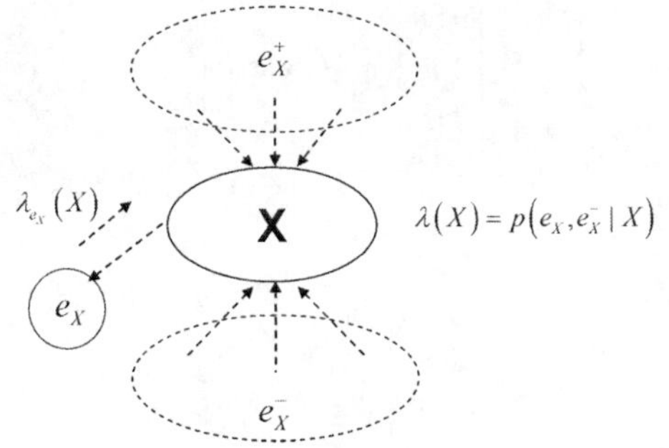

FIGURE 7.17 : Node X receives evidence $\mathbf{e_X}$

$$\begin{aligned}&\lambda_{new}(X)\\ &\quad= p\left(e_X\, e_X^-|X\right)\\ &\quad= p\left(e_X^-|e_X, X\right)p\left(e_X\,|X\right)\\ &\quad= p\left(e_X^-|X\right)p\left(e_X\,|X\right)\\ &\quad= \lambda(X)\,\lambda_{e_X}(X)\end{aligned}$$

Thus, a node revises its λ vector by multiplying its λ vector with the likelihood vector for the evidence. Note that $\pi(X)$ remains unchanged as e_X^+ is unchanged. The revised belief of X is computed as follows, using the necessary independence assumption derived from the fact that X separates e_X^+ from e_X^-, and e_X:

$$
\begin{aligned}
& Bel_{new}(X) \\
& \quad = p\left(X | e_X^+, e_X^-, e_X\right) \\
& \quad = \frac{p\left(e_X^+, e_X^-, e_X, X\right)}{p\left(e_X^+, e_X^-, e_X\right)} \\
& \quad = \frac{p\left(e_X^-, e_X | e_X^+, X\right) p\left(X | e_X^+\right) p\left(e_X^+\right)}{p\left(e_X^+, e_X^-, e_X\right)} \\
& \quad = \alpha\, p\left(X | e_X^+\right) p\left(e_X^-, e_X | X\right) \qquad \left[\text{where } \alpha \text{ is } \frac{1}{p\left(e_X^-, e_X | e_X^+\right)}\right] \\
& \quad = \alpha\, \pi(X)\, \lambda_{new}(X)
\end{aligned}
$$

Therefore, the revised belief is simply the product of the revised $\lambda(X)$ with unchanged $\pi(X)$.

Example

Consider the network fragment at the top half of FIGURE 7.18 along with the π, λ, and belief vectors.

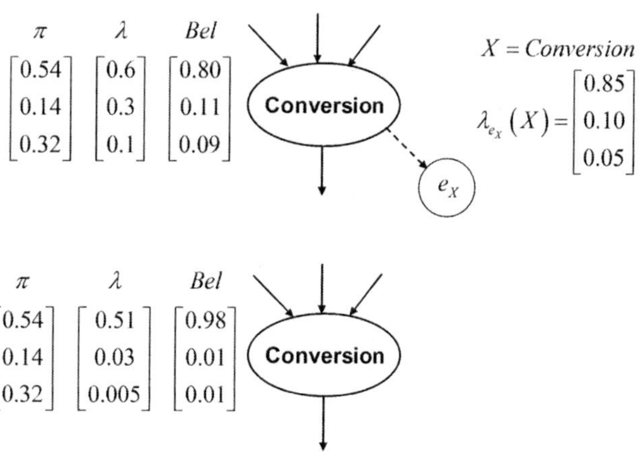

FIGURE 7.18 : Example of a belief revision

As shown in the figure, evidence e_X has been posted into the node *Conversion.* Then the revised λ and belief vectors are computed below (also shown at the bottom half of the figure).

$$
\lambda_{new}(X) = \lambda(X)\, \lambda_{e_X}(X) = \begin{bmatrix} 0.6 \\ 0.3 \\ 0.1 \end{bmatrix} \begin{bmatrix} 0.85 \\ 0.10 \\ 0.05 \end{bmatrix} = \begin{bmatrix} 0.51 \\ 0.03 \\ 0.005 \end{bmatrix}
$$

$$
\pi(X) = \begin{bmatrix} 0.54 \\ 0.14 \\ 0.32 \end{bmatrix}
$$

$$Bel(X) = \alpha\pi(X)\lambda_{new}(X) = \alpha \begin{bmatrix} 0.54 \\ 0.14 \\ 0.32 \end{bmatrix} \begin{bmatrix} 0.51 \\ 0.03 \\ 0.005 \end{bmatrix} = \begin{bmatrix} 0.98 \\ 0.015 \\ 0.005 \end{bmatrix}$$

7.3.5 Evidence Propagation in Polytrees

In the previous section, we detailed how a node updates its own beliefs upon receiving evidence on itself. This section discusses how a node X in a polytree updates its own beliefs when evidence is observed on one of its neighboring nodes, and how it propagates the effects of that evidence to the neighboring nodes to help update their beliefs. We consider six different cases corresponding to possible polytree fragments around the node X that contain its immediate neighbors:

- *Upward propagation in a linear fragment*: X has only one parent U, and one child Y, and the child Y receives evidence.
- *Downward propagation in a linear fragment*: X has only one parent U, and one child Y, and the parent U receives evidence.
- *Upward propagation in a tree fragment*: X has only one parent U, and three children Y, Z, and Q, and one of the children, say Y, receives evidence.
- *Downward propagation in a tree fragment*: X has only one parent U, and three children Y, Z, and Q, and the parent U receives evidence.
- *Upward propagation in a polytree fragment*: X has parents U, V, and W, and three children Y, Z, and Q, and one of the children, say Y, receives evidence.
- *Downward propagation in a polytree fragment*: X has parents U, V, and W, and three children Y, Z, and Q, and one of the parents, say U, receives evidence.

7.3.5.1 Upward Propagation in a Linear Fragment

This case is illustrated in Figure 7.315, where the node X has only one parent U, and one child Y, and the child Y receives evidence e_Y. The node Y updates its belief and sends the message $\lambda_Y(X)$ to X. The node X updates its belief upon receiving the message from Y and, in turn, sends the message $\lambda_X(U)$ to U to help update its belief. All the π vectors remain unchanged, as there is no new causal evidence. Next, we compute the values of $\lambda_Y(X)$, $\lambda_X(U)$, and their relations to the new beliefs of X and U.

Let e_Y^- be the total evidence connected to Y, but not through its parent X. If Y now receives evidence e_Y, then

$$\lambda_{new}(Y) = p\left(e_Y, e_Y^- | Y\right)$$

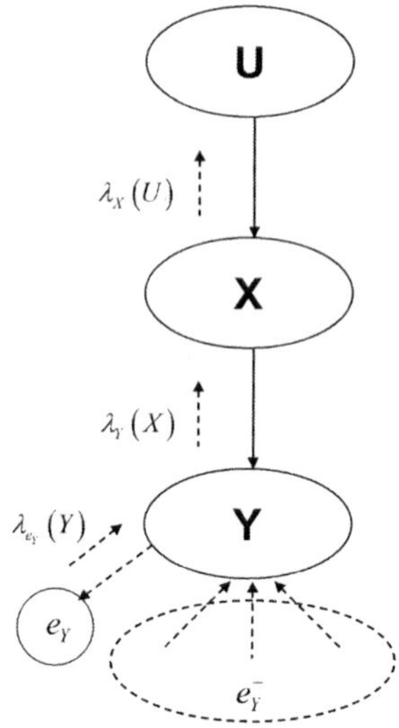

FIGURE 7.19 : Upward propagation of evidence $\mathbf{e_Y}$ in a linear fragment

Since Y separates X from $e_Y$and e_Y^-, the revised $\lambda(X)$ can now be computed as follows:

$$\begin{aligned}&\lambda_{new}(X)\\ &\quad= p\left(e_Y\, e_Y^- | X\right)\\ &\quad= \sum_Y p\left(e_Y\, e_Y^- | Y,\, X\right) p\left(Y|X\right)\\ &\quad= \sum_Y p\left(e_Y\, e_Y^- | Y\right) p\left(Y|X\right)\\ &\quad= \sum_Y \lambda_{new}(Y)\, p\left(Y|X\right)\end{aligned}$$

Therefore, the revised $\lambda(X)$ can be computed at the node Y by taking the product of the revised $\lambda(Y)$ and the CPT $p(Y|X)$. The revised value $\lambda_{new}(X)$ is then sent to the node X from Y as the message $\lambda_Y(X) = \lambda_{new}(X)$. Note that $\pi(X)$ remains unchanged as e_X^+ is unchanged. Since X separates e_X^+ from e_Y and e_Y^-, the node X revises its belief as follows:

$$\begin{aligned}&Bel_{new}(X)\\ &\quad= p\left(X|e_Y, e_Y^-, e_X^+\right)\\ &\quad= \alpha\, p\left(X|e_X^+\right) p\left(e_Y, e_Y^-|X\right)\\ &\quad= \alpha\, \pi(X)\, \lambda_{new}(X)\end{aligned}$$

Therefore, X revises its belief by multiplying the revised $\lambda(X)$, sent as a message by Y, with its unchanged $\pi(X)$. The revised $\lambda(U)$ can now be computed as follows:

$$\lambda_{new}(U) = \sum_X \lambda_{new}(X)\, p\left(X|U\right)$$

X sends $\lambda_{new}(U)$ as a message $\lambda_X(U)$ to U.

Example

Consider the linear fragment shown in FIGURE 7.20 along with the π, λ, and belief vectors.

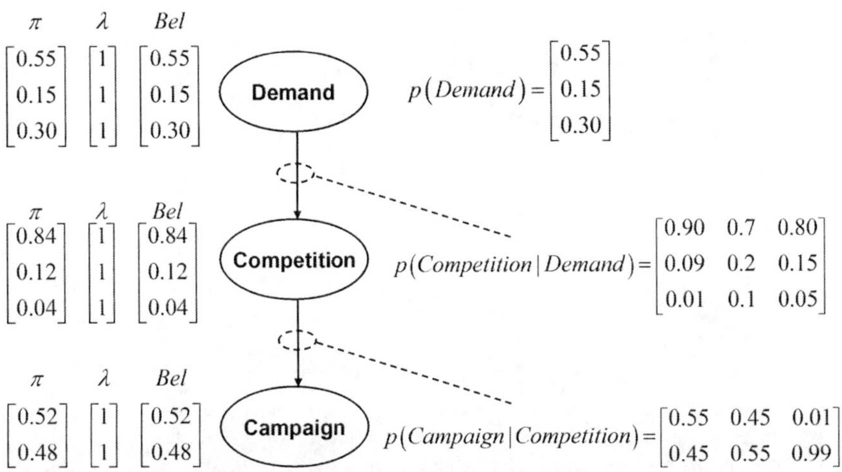

FIGURE 7.20 : Example linear fragment

The upward propagation of evidence due to the posting of evidence $e_{Campaign}$ at the node *Campaign* is shown in FIGURE 7.21.

The two λ-values $\lambda_{Campaign}(Competition)$ and $\lambda_{Competition}(Demand)$ in the figure are computed as follows:

$$
\begin{aligned}
&\lambda_{Campaign}(Competition) \\
&\quad = \lambda_{new}(Competition) \\
&\quad = \sum_{Campaign} \lambda_{new}(Campaign)\, p(Campaign|Competition) \\
&\quad = \begin{bmatrix} 0.9 \times 0.55 + 0.1 \times 0.45 \\ 0.9 \times 0.45 + 0.1 \times 0.55 \\ 0.9 \times 0.01 + 0.1 \times 0.99 \end{bmatrix} = \begin{bmatrix} 0.54 \\ 0.46 \\ 0.11 \end{bmatrix}
\end{aligned}
$$

$$
\begin{aligned}
&\lambda_{Competition}(Demand) \\
&\quad = \lambda_{new}(Demand) \\
&\quad = \sum_{Competition} \lambda_{new}(Competition)\, p(Competition|Demand) \\
&\quad = \begin{bmatrix} 0.54 \times 0.90 + 0.46 \times 0.09 + 0.11 \times 0.01 \\ 0.54 \times 0.7 + 0.46 \times 0.2 + 0.11 \times 0.1 \\ 0.54 \times 0.80 + 0.46 \times 0.50 + 0.11 \times 0.05 \end{bmatrix} = \begin{bmatrix} 0.53 \\ 0.48 \\ 0.51 \end{bmatrix}
\end{aligned}
$$

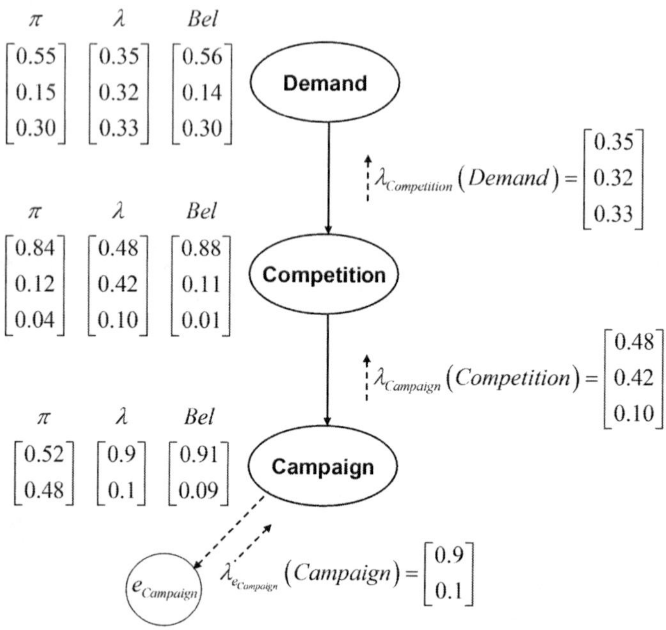

FIGURE 7.21 : Example upward propagation in a linear fragment

7.3.5.2 Downward Propagation in a Linear Fragment

This case is illustrated in FIGURE 7.22, where the node X has only one parent U, and one child Y, and the parent node U receives evidence e_U. The node U updates its belief and sends the message $\pi_X(U)$ to X. The node X updates its belief upon receiving the message from U and, in turn, sends the message $\pi_Y(X)$ to $X$to help update its belief. Next, we compute the values of $\pi_X(U)$, $\pi_Y(X)$, and their relations to the new beliefs of X and Y, respectively.

Let e_U^+ be the total evidence connected to U but not through its child X. If Unow receives evidence e_U, then $\lambda_{new}(U) = \lambda_{e_U}(U)\lambda(U)$. Note that $\pi(U)$ remains unchanged since there is no change in evidence connected through the parents of U. The revised $\pi(X)$ can now be computed as follows:

$$
\begin{aligned}
\pi_{new}(X) &= p\left(X|e_U, e_U^+\right) \\
&= \sum_U p\left(X|U, e_U, e_U^+\right) p\left(U|e_U,\ e_U^+\right) \\
&= \sum_U p(X|U) p\left(U|e_U, e_U^+\right) \qquad [U \text{ separates } X \text{ from } e_U \text{ and } e_U^+] \\
&= \sum_U \pi_X(U)\, p(X|U)
\end{aligned}
$$

where $\pi_X(U) = p\left(U|e_U, e_U^+\right)$ is simplified as follows:

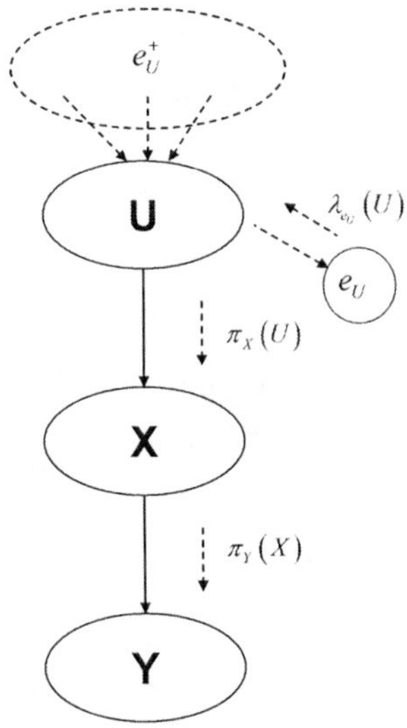

FIGURE 7.22 : Downward propagation of evidence $\mathbf{e_U}$ in a linear fragment

$$
\begin{aligned}
\pi_X(U) &= p\left(U|e_U\, e_U^+\right) \\
&= \frac{p\left(e_U, e_U^+, U\right)}{p\left(e_U, e_U^+\right)} \\
&= \frac{p\left(e_U|e_U^+, U\right) p\left(U|e_U^+\right) p\left(e_U^+\right)}{p\left(e_U, e_U^+\right)} \\
&= \alpha\, p\left(U|e_U^+\right) p\left(e_U|U\right) \qquad \left[\text{since } U \text{ separates } e_U \text{ and } e_U^+\right] \\
&= \alpha\, \pi(U)\, \lambda_{e^U}(U) \qquad \left[\alpha \text{ is } \frac{1}{p\left(e_U|e_U^+\right)}\right]
\end{aligned}
$$

The node U can compute $\pi_X(U)$ by multiplying its likelihood vector for the evidence with its π vector. Therefore, the revised $\pi(X)$, $\pi_{new}(X)$, can be computed at the node X by taking the product of $\pi_X(U)$ and the CPT $p(X|U)$. The revised value $\pi_{new}(X)$ is then sent to the node Y from X as the message $\pi_Y(X)$. Note that $\lambda(X)$ remains unchanged since e_X^- is unchanged. The node X revises its belief as follows:

$$
\begin{aligned}
Bel_{new}(X) &= p\left(X|e_U, e_U^+, e_U^-\right) \\
&= \alpha\, p\left(e_U, e_U^+|X\right) p\left(X|e_U^-\right) \qquad \left[\text{since } X \text{ separates } e_U^- \text{ from } e_U \text{ and } e_U^+\right] \\
&= \alpha\, \pi_{new}(X)\, \lambda(X) \\
&= \alpha\, \pi_X(U)\, p(X|U)\, \lambda(X)
\end{aligned}
$$

Therefore, X revises its belief by multiplying message $\pi_X(U)$ sent by U, with its unchanged λ vector $\lambda(X)$ and the CPT $p(X|U)$. Similarly, X sends a message $\pi_Y(X)$ to Y to help revise its belief.

Example

Consider the linear fragment shown in FIGURE 7.23 along with the π, λ, and belief vectors.

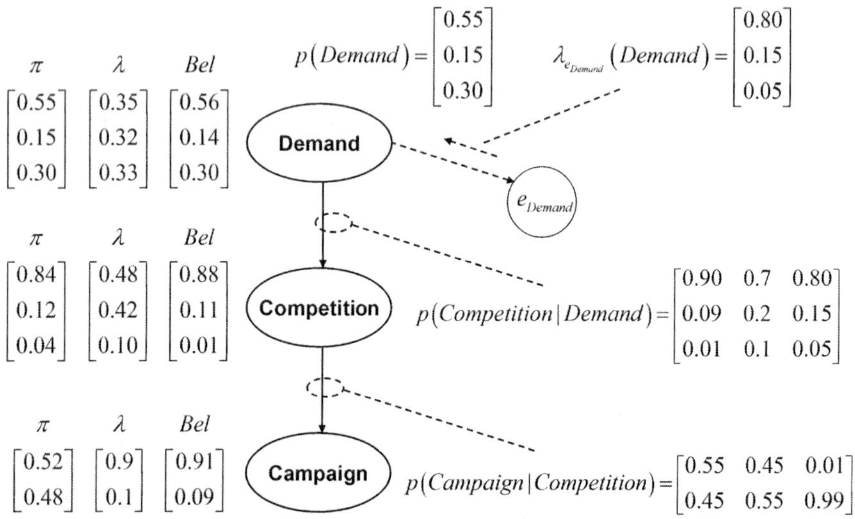

FIGURE 7.23 : Example linear fragment

The downward propagation of evidence due to the posting of evidence e_{Demand} at the node *Demand* is shown in FIGURE 7.24.

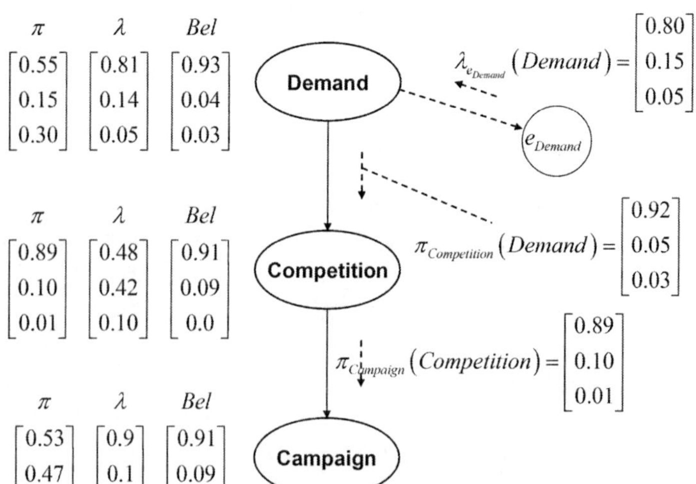

FIGURE 7.24 : Example downward propagation in a linear fragment

7.3.5.3 Upward Propagation in a Tree Fragment

This case is illustrated in FIGURE 7.25, where the node X has only one parent U, and three children Y, Z, and Q, and the child Y receives evidence e_Y. The node Y updates its belief and sends the message $\lambda_Y(X)$ to X. The node X updates its belief upon receiving the message from Y and, in turn, sends the diagnostic message $\lambda_X(U)$ to U and the causal messages $\pi_Z(X)$ and $\pi_Q(X)$ to Z and Q, respectively, to help update their beliefs. The messages $\lambda_Y(X)$ and $\lambda_X(U)$ are computed as above in the case of upward propagation in a linear fragment. Next, we compute $\pi_Z(X)$, $\pi_Q(X)$, and their relations to the new beliefs of Z and Q.

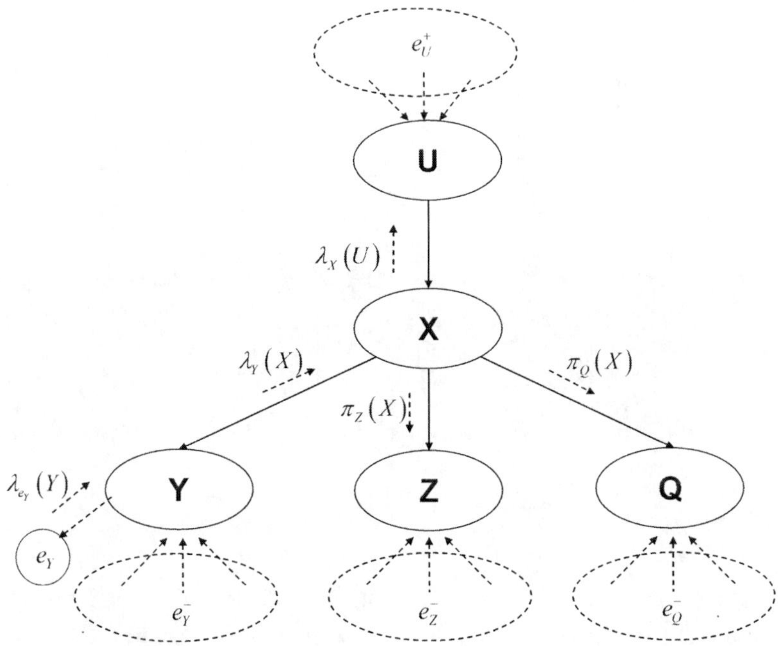

FIGURE 7.25 : Upward propagation of evidence $\mathbf{e_Y}$ in a tree fragment

Let e_Y^-, e_Z^-, and e_Q^- be the total diagnostic evidence associated with Y, Z, and Q, respectively, that is not obtained through their parent X, and e_U^+ be the total causal evidence associated with U that is not obtained through its child X.

$$\begin{aligned}\pi_{new}(Z) &= p\left(Z|e_Y, e_Y^-, e_Q^-, e_U^+\right)\\ &= \sum_X p\left(Z|X, e_Y, e_Y^-, e_Q^-, e_U^+\right) p\left(X|e_Y, e_Y^-, e_Q^-, e_U^+\right)\\ &= \sum_X p\left(Z|X, e_Y, e_Y^-, e_Q^-\right) p\left(X|e_Y, e_Y^-, e_Q^-, e_U^+\right)\\ &\qquad \left[\text{given } X,\ Z \text{ is independent of } e_U^+\right]\\ &= \sum_X p(Z|X)\, \pi_Z(X)\\ &\qquad \left[\text{given } X,\ Z \text{ is independent of } e_Y, e_Y^-, e_Q^-\right]\end{aligned}$$

where

$$\begin{aligned}\pi_Z(X) &= p\left(X|e_Y, e_Y^-, e_Q^-, e_U^+\right) = \frac{p\left(e_Y, e_Y^-, e_Q^-, e_U^+, X\right)}{p\left(e_Y, e_Y^-, e_Q^-, e_U^+\right)}\\ &= \frac{p\left(e_Y, e_Y^-|e_Q^-, e_U^+, X\right) p\left(e_Q^-|e_U^+, X\right) p\left(X|e_U^+\right) p\left(e_U^+\right)}{p\left(e_Y, e_Y^-, e_Q^-, e_U^+\right)}\\ &= \alpha p\left(e_Y, e_Y^-|e_Q^-, e_U^+, X\right) p\left(e_Q^-|e_U^+, X\right) p\left(X|e_U^+\right)\\ &\qquad \left[\alpha = \frac{1}{p\left(e_Y, e_Y^-, e_Q^-|e_U^+\right)}\right]\\ &= \alpha p\left(e_Y, e_Y^-|X\right) p\left(e_Q^-|e_U^+, X\right) p\left(X|e_U^+\right)\\ &\qquad \left[X \text{ separates } e_Y, e_Y^- \text{ from } e_Q^-, e_U^+\right]\\ &= \alpha p\left(e_Y, e_Y^-|X\right) p\left(e_Q^-|X\right) p\left(X|e_U^+\right) \qquad \left[X \text{ separates } e_Q^- \text{ from } e_U^+\right]\\ &= \alpha\, \lambda_Y(X)\, \lambda_Q(X)\, \pi(X)\\ &= \alpha \frac{\lambda_Y(X)\lambda_Z(X)\lambda_Q(X)\pi(X)}{\lambda_Z(X)}\\ &= \alpha \frac{Bel_{new}(X)}{\lambda_Z(X)}\end{aligned}$$

Therefore, the revised $\pi(Z)$ can be computed at the node Z by taking the product of the message $\frac{Bel_{new}(X)}{\lambda_Z(X)}$, sent by its parent X, and the CPT $p(Z|X)$. Similarly, X sends $\frac{Bel_{new}(X)}{\lambda_Q(X)}$ to Q to update its belief. Note that $\lambda(Z)$ remains unchanged since e_Z^- is unchanged. The node Z revises its belief as follows:

$$\begin{aligned}Bel_{new}(Z) &= p\left(Z|e_Y, e_Y^-, e_Q^-, e_U^+, e_Z^-\right)\\ &= \alpha p\left(Z|e_Y, e_Y^-, e_Q^-, e_U^+\right) p\left(e_Z^-|Z\right)\\ &\qquad \left[\text{since } Z \text{ separates } e_Z^- \text{ from } e_Y, e_Y^-, e_Q^-, e_U^+\right]\\ &= \alpha \pi_{new}(Z)\, \lambda(Z)\\ &= \alpha \pi_Z(X)\, p(Z|X)\, \lambda(Z)\end{aligned}$$

Therefore, Z revises its belief by multiplying the message $\pi_Z(X)$, sent by its parent X, with its unchanged λ vector $\lambda(Z)$ and its CPT $p(Z|X)$.

7.3.5.4 Downward Propagation in a Tree Fragment

This case, which is illustrated in FIGURE 7.26, is similar to the case of downward propagation in a linear fragment presented earlier.

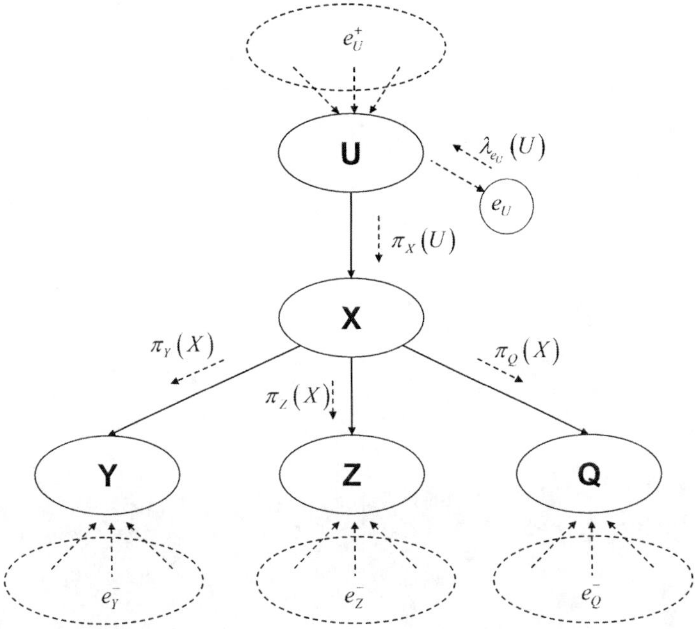

FIGURE 7.26 : Downward propagation of evidence $\mathbf{e_U}$ in a tree fragment

7.3.5.5 Upward Propagation in a Polytree Fragment

This case is illustrated in FIGURE 7.27, where the node X has three parents U, V, and W, and three children Y, Z, and Q, and the child Y receives evidence e_Y. The node Y updates its belief and sends the message $\lambda_Y(X)$ to X. The node X updates its belief upon receiving the message from Y and, in turn, sends the causal messages $\pi_Z(X)$ and $\pi_Q(X)$ to Z and Q, respectively, to help update their beliefs. The messages $\pi_Z(X)$ and $\pi_Q(X)$ are $\frac{Bel_{new}(X)}{\lambda(Z)}$ and $\frac{Bel_{new}(X)}{\lambda(Q)}$ computed as above in the case of upward propagation in a tree fragment. In the following, we show how U, V, and W update their beliefs upon receiving the messages $\lambda_X(U)$, $\lambda_X(V)$, and $\lambda_X(W)$, respectively, from their common child X.
The revised $\lambda(U)$ can now be computed as follows:

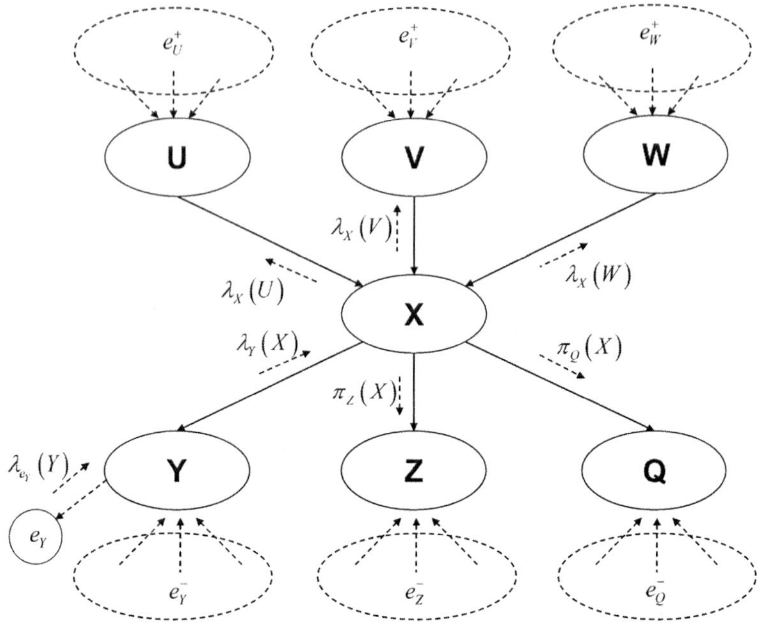

FIGURE 7.27 : Upward propagation of evidence $\mathbf{e_Y}$ in a polytree fragment

$$\begin{aligned}
\lambda_{new}(U) &= p\left(e_Y, e_Y^-, e_Z^-, e_Q^-, e_V^+, e_W^+ | U\right) \\
&= \sum_X \sum_V \sum_W p\left(e_Y, e_Y^-, e_Z^-, e_Q^-, e_V^+, e_W^+ | U, V, W, X\right) p\left(V, W, X | U\right) \\
&= \sum_X \sum_V \sum_W \; p\left(e_Y, e_Y^-, e_Z^-, e_Q^- | e_V^+, e_W^+, U, V, W, X\right) \\
&\qquad p\left(e_V^+, e_W^+ | U, V, W, X\right) p\left(V, W, X | U\right)
\end{aligned}$$

$$\begin{aligned}
&= \sum_X \sum_V \sum_W \; p\left(e_Y, e_Y^-, e_Z^-, e_Q^- | X\right) p\left(e_V^+ | e_W^+, U, V, W, X\right) \\
&\qquad p\left(e_W^+ | U, V, W, X\right) p\left(V, W, X | U\right) \\
&\qquad \left[\text{since } X \text{ separates } e_Y, e_Y^-, e_Z^-, e_Q^- \text{ from } e_V^+, e_W^+, U, V, W\right] \\
&= \sum_X \sum_V \sum_W \lambda_{new}(X)\, p\left(e_V^+ | e_W^+, V, W\right) p\left(e_W^+ | V, W\right) p\left(V, W, X | U\right) \\
&\qquad \left[\begin{array}{l}\text{since } V \text{ separates } e_V^+ \text{ from } U,\ X, \text{ and} \\ W \text{ separates } e_W^+ \text{ from } U, X\end{array}\right] \\
&= \sum_X \lambda_{new}(X) \sum_V \sum_W p\left(e_V^+, e_W^+ | V, W\right) p\left(X | V, W, U\right) p\left(V, W | U\right)
\end{aligned}$$

Since U, V, and W are marginally independent, $\lambda_{new}(U)$ can further be simplified as follows:

$$\begin{aligned}
\lambda_{new}(U) &= \alpha \sum_X \lambda_{new}(X) \sum_V \sum_W \frac{p(V,W|e_V^+,e_W^+)}{p(V,W)} p(X|V,W,U) p(V,W) \\
&= \alpha \sum_X \lambda_{new}(X) \sum_V \sum_W p(V|W,e_V^+,e_W^+)\, p(W|e_V^+,e_W^+)\, p(X|V,W,U) \\
&= \alpha \sum_X \lambda_{new}(X) \sum_V \sum_W p(V|e_V^+)\, p(W|e_W^+)\, p(X|V,W,U) \\
&= \alpha \sum_X \lambda_{new}(X) \sum_V \sum_W \pi_X(V)\, \pi_X(W)\, p(X|V,W,U)
\end{aligned}$$

Therefore, the message $\lambda_X(U)$, which will be sent to U from X as the new λ vector for U, is the above expression computed at X. Note that $p(X|V,W,U)$ is the CPT of X stored at the node X. The revised belief of U is obtained by multiplying its unchanged π vector with the above λ vector. The messages that are sent to V and W are the following:

$$\begin{aligned}
\lambda_X(V) &= \alpha \sum_X \lambda_{new}(X) \sum_U \sum_W \pi_X(U)\, \pi_X(W)\, p(X|U,W,V) \\
\lambda_X(W) &= \alpha \sum_X \lambda_{new}(X) \sum_U \sum_V \pi_X(U)\, \pi_X(V)\, p(X|U,V,W)
\end{aligned}$$

Example

Consider the network fragment shown in FIGURE 7.28 along with the π, λ, and belief vectors, where the two CPTs for the nodes *Conversion* and *Profit* are the same as the two CPTs in TABLE 7.7 and TABLE 7.8, respectively, in our main BN example.

The upward propagation of evidence due to the posting of evidence e_{Profit} at the node *Profit* is shown in FIGURE 7.29.

7.3.5.6 Downward Propagation in a Polytree Fragment

This case is illustrated in FIGURE 7.30, where the node X has three parents U, V, and W, and three children Y, Z, and Q, and the parent U receives evidence e_U. Node U updates its belief and sends the causal message $\pi_X(U)$ to X. Node X updates its belief upon receiving the message from Y and, in turn, sends the messages $\pi_Y(X)$, $\pi_Z(X)$, and $\pi_Q(X)$ to Y, Z, and Q, respectively, to help update their beliefs. The messages $\pi_Y(X)$, $\pi_Z(X)$, and $\pi_Q(X)$ are $\frac{Bel_{new}(X)}{\lambda(Y)}$, $\frac{Bel_{new}(X)}{\lambda(Z)}$, and $\frac{Bel_{new}(X)}{\lambda(Q)}$, respectively, computed as above in the case of upward propagation in a tree fragment. Next, we show how V and W update their beliefs upon receiving, respectively, the messages $\lambda_X(V)$ and $\lambda_X(W)$ from their common child X.

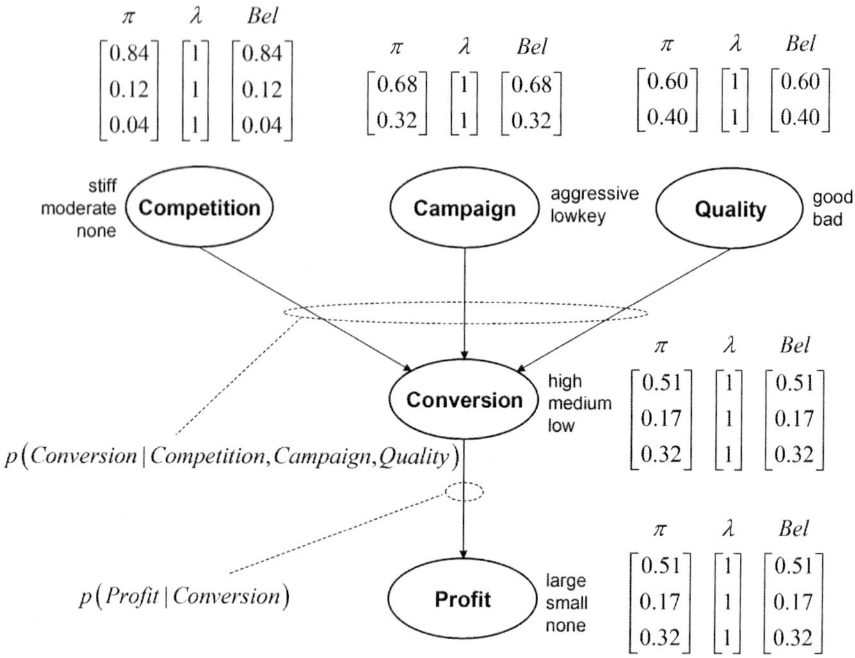

FIGURE 7.28 : Example polytree fragment

$$
\begin{aligned}
\lambda_{new}(V) &= p\left(e_U, e_U^+, e_W^+, e_Y^-, e_Z^-, e_Q^- | V\right) \\
&= \sum_X \sum_U \sum_W p\left(e_U, e_U^+, e_W^+, e_Y^-, e_Z^-, e_Q^- | V, U, W, X\right) p(U, W, X | V) \\
&= \sum_X \sum_U \sum_W \; p\left(e_Y^-, e_Z^-, e_Q^- | e_U, e_U^+, e_W^+, V, U, W, X\right) \\
&\qquad p\left(e_U, e_U^+, e_W^+ | V, U, W, X\right) p(U, W, X | V) \\
&= \sum_X \sum_U \sum_W \; p\left(e_Y^-, e_Z^-, e_Q^- | X\right) p\left(e_U | e_U^+, e_W^+, V, U, W, X\right) \\
&\qquad p\left(e_U^+, e_W^+ | V, U, W, X\right) p(U, W, X | V) \\
&\qquad \left[\text{since } X \text{ separates } e_Y^-, e_Z^-, e_Q^- \text{ from } e_U, e_U^+, e_W^+, U, V, W\right]
\end{aligned}
$$

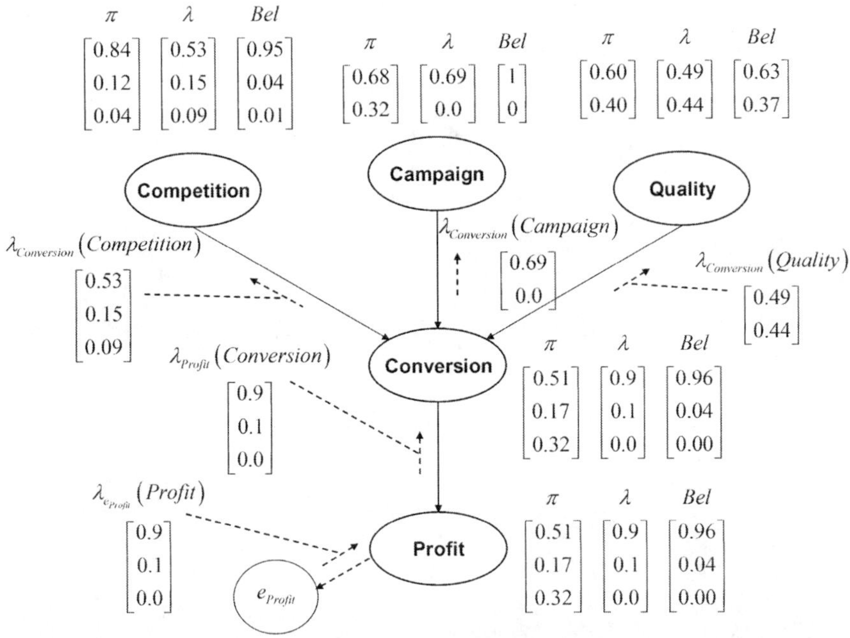

FIGURE 7.29 : Example upward propagation in a polytree fragment

$$= \sum_X \sum_U \sum_W \lambda(X)\, p(e_U|U)\, p\left(e_U^+, e_W^+|U,W,V\right) p(U,W,X|V)$$

$$\left[\begin{array}{l}\text{since } U \text{ separates } e_U \text{ from } e_U^+, e_W^+, X, V, W, \text{ and} \\ \text{since } U,\ W \text{ separate } e_U^+, e_W^+ \text{ from } V, X\end{array}\right]$$

$$= \sum_X \lambda(X) \sum_U \sum_W \begin{array}{l}\lambda_{e_U}(U)\, p\left(e_U^+|U\right) \\ p\left(e_W^+|W\right) p(U,W|V)\, p(X|U,W,V)\end{array}$$

$$\left[\text{since } e_U^+, e_W^+ \text{ are independent of each other given } U \text{ or } W\right]$$

$$= \alpha \sum_X \lambda(X) \sum_U \sum_W \lambda_{e_U}(U)\, \pi_X(U)\, \pi_X(W)\, p(X|U,W,V)$$

$$[\text{since } U \text{ and } W \text{ are marginally independent}]$$

Note that if X did not receive any diagnostic evidence from its descendants Y, Z, and Q, then the λ vector for X would still be $(1,1,...,1)$. In this case, the above message sent to V from X due to the evidence on U would still be $(1,1,...,1)$, making no impact on the belief of V. This is consistent with the network marginal independence property, which says that U, V, and W are independent of each other if neither X nor any of its descendants received evidence. This is illustrated below.

Suppose $x_1,...,x_n$ (n states) are all possible instantiations of X. Then, from the CPT of X, U, V, W, we have for any u, v, w:

$$\sum_i p(x_i|u,v,w) = 1$$

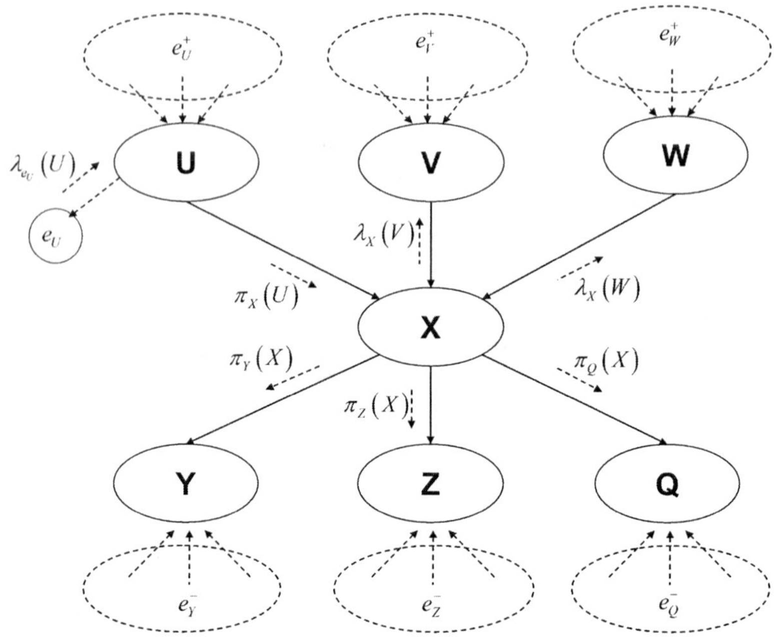

FIGURE 7.30 : Downward propagation of evidence $\mathbf{e_U}$ in a polytree fragment

If the variable X did not receive any evidence from its descendants then $\lambda(x_i) = 1$, for every i. If the variable V has m states and $v_1, ..., v_m$ are all possible instantiations of V, then from the derivation of $\lambda_{new}(V)$ above,

$$\begin{aligned}
\lambda_X(v_j) &= \alpha \sum_i \lambda(x_i) \sum_U \sum_W \lambda_{e_U}(U)\, \pi_X(U)\, \pi_X(W)\, p(x_i|U, W, v_j) \\
&= \alpha \sum_i \sum_U \sum_W \lambda_{e_U}(U)\, \pi_X(U)\, \pi_X(W)\, p(x_i|U, W, v_j) \\
&= \alpha \sum_U \sum_W \lambda_{e_U}(U)\, \pi_X(U)\, \pi_X(W) \sum_i p(x_i|U, W, v_j) \\
&= \alpha \sum_U \sum_W \lambda_{e_U}(U)\, \pi_X(U)\, \pi_X(W)
\end{aligned}$$

Therefore, each $\lambda_X(v_j)$ has the same value, making the vector $\lambda_X(V)$ a unit vector that does not change the belief of V.

Example

Consider the network fragment shown in FIGURE 7.31 along with the π, λ, and belief vectors, where the two CPTs for the nodes *Conversion* and *Profit* are the same as the two CPTs in TABLE 7.7 and TABLE 7.8, respectively, in our main BN example. The network is same as the one in FIGURE 7.29 with evidence posted on node *Profit*.

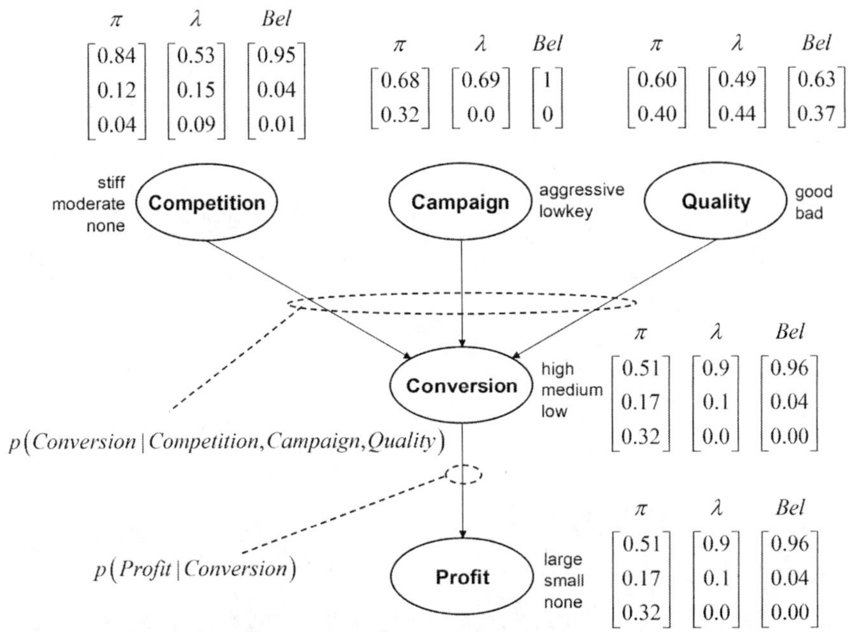

FIGURE 7.31 : Example of a polytree fragment

The downward propagation of evidence due to the posting of evidence $e_{Competition}$ at the node *Competition* is shown in FIGURE 7.32.

7.3.6 Propagation Algorithm

Now that we have illustrated different belief propagation with a series of examples, we generalize these steps to a concrete algorithm for belief propagation in polytrees.

Input:

- BN N (causal structure with associated CPTs)
- Evidence e_X on the variable X of N

Output:

- Revised belief vector for each node, i.e., $p(Y|e_X)$, for each node Y

Node Structure:

- Each node X in N with p number of states stores the following information locally in a suitable data structure (as shown in FIGURE 7.33):

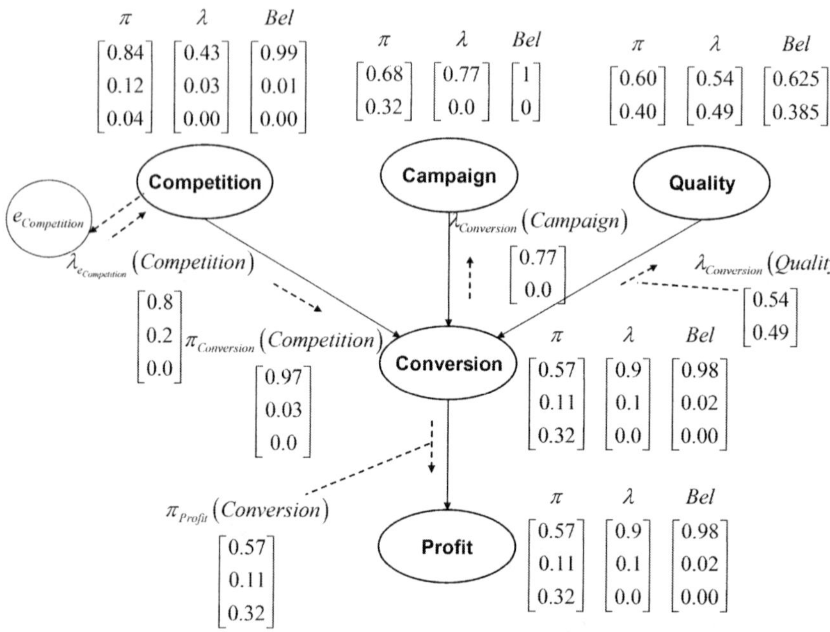

FIGURE 7.32 : Example downward propagation in a polytree fragment

- · p-ary π vector $\pi(X)$
- · p-aryλ vector $\lambda(X)$
- · p-ary belief vector $Bel(X)$
- · p-ary evidence vector $\lambda_e(X)$
- · $p \times n$ CPT $p(X|U_1, ..., U_n)$, if X has n parents $U_1, U_2, ..., U_n$
- · q-ary parent π vector $\pi_X(U_i)$, for each parent U_i with q number of states
- · p-ary child λ vector $\lambda_{Y_i}(X)$, for each child Y_i

Initial Probability Computation:

- For each node X in N with p number of states, we perform the following:
    - · If X is a root node, then set each of its π and belief vectors to its prior probability distribution.
    - · Set the evidence vector $\lambda_e(X)$, λ vector $\lambda(X)$, and each child λ vector $\lambda_{Y_i}(X)$ to $(1, ..., 1)$.
- Mark each root node and then recursively compute the π and belief vectors of the rest of the nodes through the following steps.

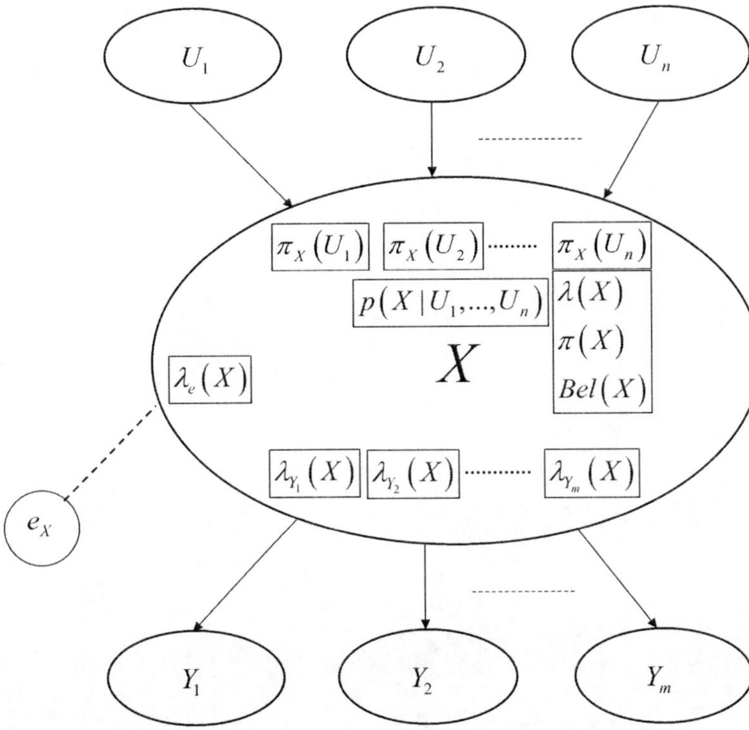

FIGURE 7.33 : Node structure

- If the parents of a node X are already marked, then perform the following:
  - Set each parent π vector $\pi_X(U_i)$ to the π vector of the parent U_i.
  - Set its π vector $\pi(X)$ to $\sum_{u_1,u_2,...,u_n} p(X|u_1,u_2,...,u_n)\prod_{i=1}^{n}\pi_X(u_i)$, if X has parents $U_1,U_2,...,U_n$.
  - Set its belief vector $Bel(X)$equal to its π vector.

Evidence Propagation:

- Set the evidence vector $\lambda_e(X)$ of X to the likelihood vector $p(e_X|X)$
- Revise the beliefs of X:
  - Compute the λ vector $\lambda(X)$ of X as the product of all its child λ vectors and the evidence vector.
  - Compute the π vector $\pi(X)$ of X as the product of all its parent π vectors.

- Compute the belief vector of X as the product of its π and λ vectors.

- Generate messages from X on the update of its evidence vector:
  - Send a message
  - $\alpha \sum_{x} \lambda(x) \sum_{\substack{u_1,...,u_{i-1},\\ u_{i+1}...,u_n}} p(x|u_1,...,u_{i-1},u_{i+1},...,u_n,U_i) \prod_{k \neq i} \pi_X(u_k)$

    to each parent U_i of X.
  - Send a message $\alpha \frac{Bel(X)}{\lambda_{Y_i}(X)}$ to each child Y_i of X.

- Generate messages from X on the update of the λ_{Y_j} vector:
  - Send a message

$$\alpha \sum_{x} \lambda(x) \sum_{\substack{u_1,...,u_{i-1},\\ u_{i+1}...,u_n}} p(x|u_1,...,u_{i-1},u_{i+1},...,u_n,U_i) \prod_{k \neq i} \pi_X(u_k)$$

to each parent U_i of X.

- Send a message $\alpha \frac{Bel(X)}{\lambda_{Y_i}(X)}$ to each child Y_i of X other than the child Y_j.

- Generate messages from X on the update of the $\pi_X(U_j)$ vector:

- Send a message

$$\alpha \sum_{x} \lambda(x) \sum_{\substack{u_1,...,u_{i-1},\\ u_{i+1}...,u_n}} p(x|u_1,...,u_{i-1},u_{i+1},...,u_n,U_i) \prod_{k \neq i} \pi_X(u_k)$$

to each parent U_i of X other than U_j.

- Send a message $\alpha \frac{Bel(X)}{\lambda_{Y_i}(X)}$ to each child Y_i of X.

If a network has already received evidence on some of its variables, then only the evidence propagation step is followed, bypassing the initial probability computation step.

7.3.7 Evidence Propagation in Directed Acyclic Graphs

The evidence propagation algorithm presented in the last section cannot usually handle DAGs (such as the one in FIGURE 7.5) because the evidence propagation on a variable in a DAG that is not a polytree may never terminate due to the recursive computation in the algorithm. This is explained in the context of the DAG shown in FIGURE 7.34.

Suppose no evidence has been posted to the variable *Demand*, making the two variables *Competition* and *Strategic* marginally independent. Now, if evidence is observed on *Competition*, then *Campaign* will receive causal evidence and will send diagnostic evidence to the *Strategic*. The node *Competition* then receives evidence from *Strategic* via *Demand*. This cyclic process of evidence propagation continues unless a stopping criterion is put in place based on repeated evidence and changes in node belief. A similar cyclic process continues in the other direction when *Competition* sends diagnostic evidence to *Demand* upon receiving evidence on itself.

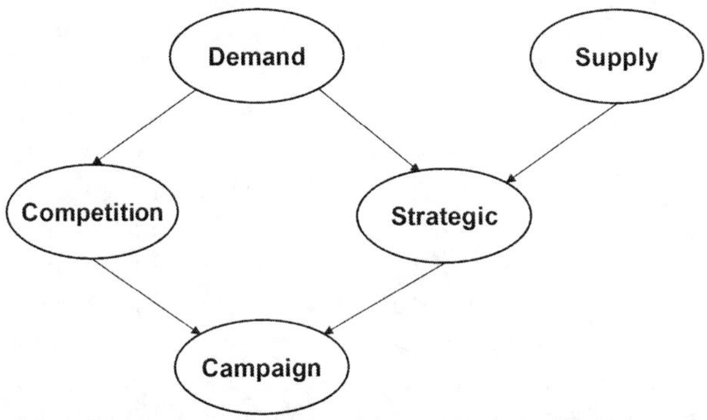

FIGURE 7.34 : Example of a DAG that is not a polytree

A solution to this problem is to deal with the joint probability distribution of the variables in the network. Although BN technology reduces the joint probability distribution of a network to merely the products of a few CPTs, we have ruled out this approach due to the large number of entries that need to be computed for a belief revision. Even for the small network in FIGURE 7.34, there are 72 entries in its joint probability distribution table that need to be computed using the following formula each time a node receives evidence.

For example, *Competition* receives evidence $e_{Competition}$:

$$
\begin{aligned}
&p\left(Demand, Supply, Competition, Strategic, Campaign | e_{Competition}\right) = \\
&\quad p\left(Demand\right) \times p\left(Supply\right) \times p\left(Competition | Demand\right) \times \\
&\quad p\left(Strategic | Demand, Supply\right) \times \\
&\quad p\left(Campaign | Competition, Strategic\right) \times p\left(e_{Competition} | Competition\right)
\end{aligned}
$$

To make use of the simple and elegant message-passing propagation algorithm while avoiding large joint probability distributions, one approach is to transform a DAG into a polytree by identifying and clustering loops into single nodes. Thus a node in a transformed cluster network is a set of nodes (also called a *clique*) instead of a single node, and joint probability distributions are computed in smaller chunks locally at the network nodes. For example, the network in FIGURE 7.34 is transformed into the network (undirected) in FIGURE 7.35 with two cliques.

Evidence on a variable in the original network is posted to the nodes in the

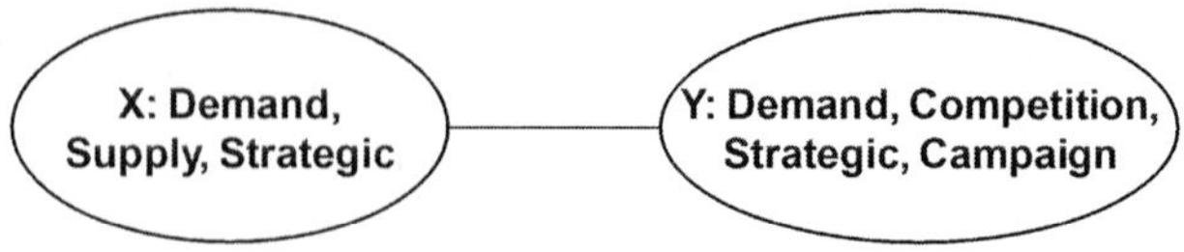

FIGURE 7.35 : Transformed network

transformed network containing the variable. The joint probability distributions are computed at the nodes, where evidence is posted and messages are passed to neighboring nodes. For example, if evidence on the variable *Demand* is observed in the cluster network in FIGURE 7.35, then the joint probability distribution $p(Demand, Competition, Strategic, Campaign)$ is computed at the node Y using some of the CPTs. *Demand* and *Strategic* are the only variables in the intersection of X and Y. Thus Y sends the change in the joint probability distribution of *Demand* and *Strategic* as a message to the variable X, which then computes the joint probability distribution of its three variables and derives the new belief of the variable *Supply* via marginalization.

In a complex network, a cycle could be very large, and local computation of joint probability distribution would still be impractical. One solution is to make smaller-sized clusters. Since the joint probability distribution of a network is derived from the CPTs, and the CPT of a variable involves only its immediate neighbors, clusters around variables can be formed using only their neighboring nodes. One such cluster network constructed from the network in FIGURE 7.34 is shown in FIGURE 7.36.

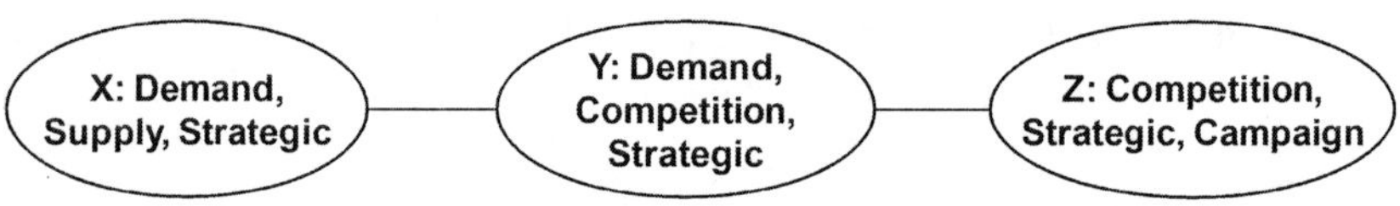

FIGURE 7.36 : Cluster network

As before, if evidence on a variable, such as *Competition*, is observed, then it is posted to one of two nodes Y and Z (say, Y) containing the variable *Competition*. Each of these nodes then computes the joint distribution locally to find the beliefs of the individual variables. The node Y then passes the revised joint probability distributions of the variables *Demand* and *Strategic* to X (respectively, *Competition* and *Strategic* to Z) to help compute the revised belief for the node *Supply* (respectively, *Campaign*) given the evidence on *Competition*.

In the following subsections, we present the *junction tree* algorithm for dealing with DAGs in general. This algorithm systematically constructs a cluster network from a BN called a *junction tree* (or *clique tree* or *join tree*). The stages of the algorithm are shown on the left side of FIGURE 7.37.

The first stage, which is the graphical transformation stage, is expanded on the right side of the figure. This stage consists of four steps: moralization,

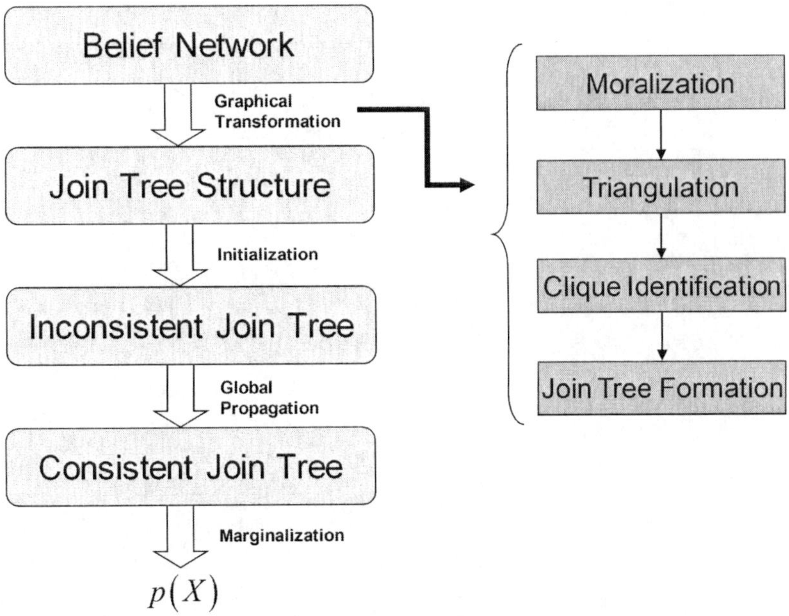

FIGURE 7.37 : Steps for constructing join trees

triangulation, clique identification, and join tree formation. These steps construct a join tree from a BN. The subsequent stages of the algorithm then compute prior beliefs of the variables in the network via an initialization of the join tree structure, followed by propagation and marginalization. The final subsection discusses how to handle evidence by computing the posterior beliefs of the variables in the network.

7.3.7.1 Graphical Transformation

The *moral graph* of a DAG is obtained by adding a link between any pair of variables with a common child, and dropping the directions of the original links in the DAG.

Example

The moral graph of the network in FIGURE 7.5 is shown in FIGURE 7.38. The dotted lines in the network in FIGURE 7.38 are the links added to the original network. For example, the nodes *Competition* and *Quality* have a common child *Conversion*, and therefore are linked with a dotted line.

An undirected graph is *triangulated* if any cycle of length greater than 3 has a chord, that is, an edge joining two nonconsecutive nodes along the cycle.

Example

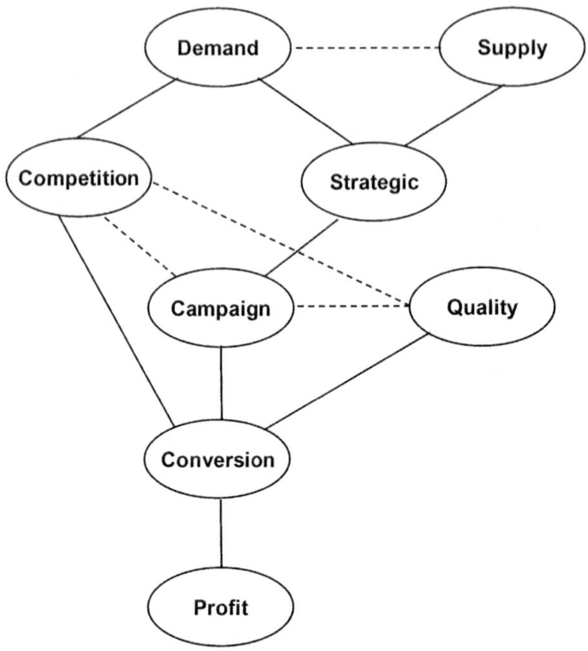

FIGURE 7.38 : The moral graph of the network in FIGURE 7.5 (added links are indicated by dotted lines)

The triangulated graph of the network in FIGURE 7.38 is shown in FIGURE 7.39. The only link added by triangulation is the link between the nodes *Competition* and *Strategic*. These two nodes are two nonconsecutive nodes along the cycle $Demand - Competition - Campaign - Strategic$ of length 4.

In general there are multiple ways to triangulate a given graph. In the case of the graph in FIGURE 7.38, we could have added a link between the nodes *Demand* and *Campaign*, instead of between the nodes *Competition* and *Strategic* along the cycle $Demand - Competition - Campaign - Strategic$, yielding a different triangulation.

The nodes of a join tree for a graph are the *cliques* in the graph (maximal sets of variables that are all pairwise linked).

Example

The five cliques in the graph in FIGURE 7.39 are listed below:

$\mathbf{C_1}$: $\{Demand, Competition, Strategic\}$
$\mathbf{C_2}$: $\{Demand, Supply, Strategic\}$
$\mathbf{C_3}$: $\{Competition, Strategic, Campaign\}$
$\mathbf{C_4}$: $\{Competition, Campaign, Quality, Conversion\}$

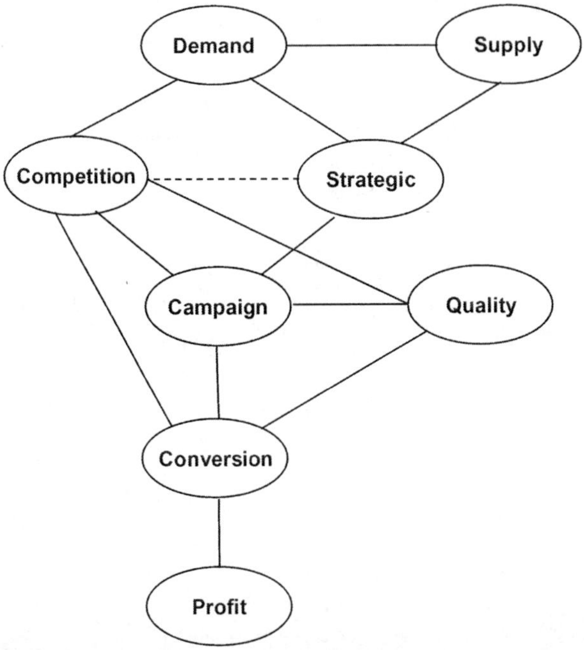

FIGURE 7.39 : A triangulated graph of the network in FIGURE 7.38 (new link is indicated by dotted lines)

$\mathbf{C}_5$: $\{Conversion, Profit\}$

The clique $\mathbf{C}_4$ is shown in FIGURE 7.40, surrounded by dotted lines. Note that the set $\{Demand, Supply, Competition, Strategic\}$ is not a clique because its nodes are not all pairwise connected since *Competition* and *Supply* are not connected. Though the nodes in the set $\{Competition, Campaign, Quality\}$ are pairwise connected, it is not a clique because the set is contained in another clique $\{Competition, Campaign, Quality, Conversion\}$, and it is therefore not maximal.

The triangulation and clique identification techniques described above are combined into a formal two-step recursive algorithm for systematically identifying cliques from an arbitrary undirected moral graph:

- Select a node X from the network N and make the cluster consisting of the node and its neighbors complete by adding the necessary edges. Choose the node that causes the least number of edges to be added. Break ties by choosing the node that induces the cluster with the smallest weight, where the *weight* of a node is the number of states, and the weight of a cluster is the product of the weights of its constituent nodes.

- Remove X along with its edges (forming a clique) and repeat the previi-

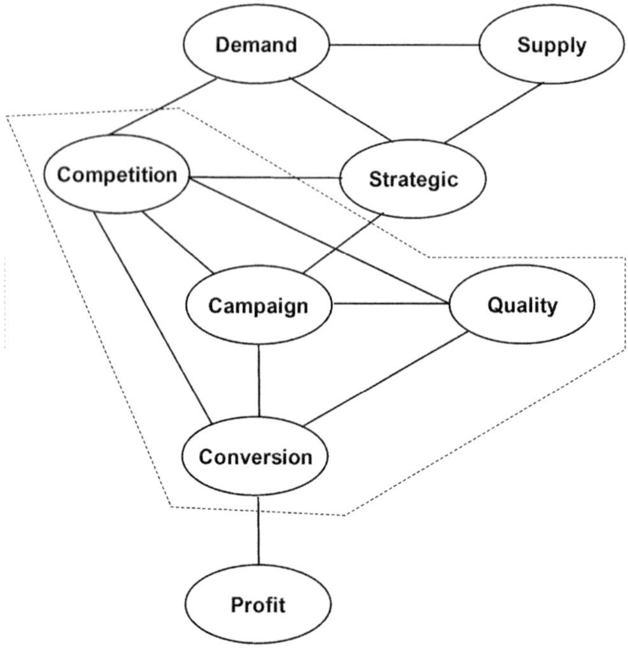

FIGURE 7.40 : An example clique (surrounded by dotted lines) in the network in FIGURE 7.39

ous step if there are still nodes left. Otherwise, if there are no nodes left, N is now triangulated. Note that a clique is formed in this stage only if it is not a subset of a subsequently induced clique.

Example

The graph in FIGURE 7.41 shows the triangulated graph obtained from the moral graph in FIGURE 7.38. The table in the figure shows the variable selection ordering in the first step of the algorithm. In each selection, the weight of the variable is computed and the induced cluster or clique is identified if it is bold and shaded.

The candidate variables to be selected first are *Supply*, *Profit*, and *Quality*, since for each of these three variables, the cluster consisting of the variable and its neighbors is already complete without the requirements for adding any edges. For example, the cluster consisting of the variable *Supply* and its two neighbors (*Demand* and *Strategic*) is complete, but the cluster consisting of the variable *Demand* and its two neighbors (*Competition* and *Strategic*) is not complete because an edge between *Competition* and *Strategic* needs to be added. The variable *Profit* is chosen among the three candidate variables because its weight 9 is the least among the three weights 12, 9, and 36 for

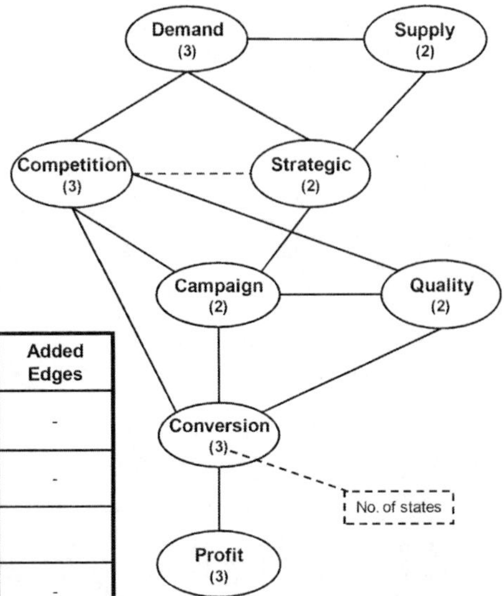

Selected Variable	Weight	Induced Cluster	Added Edges
Profit	9	**{Conversion, Profit}**	-
Supply	12	**{Demand, Supply, Strategic}**	-
Conversion	36	**{Competition, Campaign, Quality, Conversion}**	
Quality	12	{Competition, Campaign, Quality}	-
Campaign	12	**{Competition, Strategic, Campaign}**	(Competition, Strategic)
Strategic	18	**{Demand, Competition, Strategic}**	-
Demand	9	{Demand, Competition}	-
Competition	3	{Competition}	-

FIGURE 7.41 : Triangulation and clique identification

the three candidate variables, respectively. The variable *Profit* is then removed along with the edge from it leading to *Conversion*. The process then continues with the remainder of the network and the variable *Supply* is chosen next. The next variable chosen is *Conversion*. When the variable *Quality* is chosen, the corresponding induced cluster is not identified as a clique because it is a subset of a clique that is already identified.

The network is now left with the four variables *Demand*, *Competition*, *Strategic*, and *Campaign*, and the selection of any of these will require an edge to be added. The two candidate variables are *Strategic* and *Campaign* as each of these has weight 12, and each of the remaining two variables *Demand* and *Competition* has weight 18. The selection of the variable *Strategic* needs the edge from *Demand* to *Campaign* to be added, and the selection of the variable *Campaign* needs the edge from *Competition* to *Strategic* to be added.

Once we have identified cliques, we rank the nodes by assigning numbers to systematically construct a join tree out of cliques. Nodes are numbered from 1 to n in increasing order by assigning the next number to the node with the largest set of previously numbered neighbors. For example, an ordering of the nodes of the graph in FIGURE 7.5 is given below:

1 – *Demand*
2 – *Supply*
3 – *Strategic*
4 – *Competition*
5 – *Campaign*
6 – *Quality*
7 – *Conversion*
8 – *Profit*

The choice between the two nodes *Demand* and *Supply* as a starting node is arbitrary to break the tie. The node *Strategic* comes before the node *Competition* because *Strategic* has two neighbors, *Demand* and *Supply*, which have already been numbered. On the other hand, only one neighbor *Demand* of the node *Competition* has been numbered. The rest of the sequence is numbered in a similar manner.

To form a join tree based on the above ranking scheme of graph nodes, first order the cliques of the graph by rank of the highest vertex of each clique. For example, the set of five cliques $\mathbf{C}_1$, $\mathbf{C}_2$, $\mathbf{C}_3$, $\mathbf{C}_4$, and $\mathbf{C}_5$ in FIGURE 7.39 is as follows:

$\mathbf{C}_5$: $\{Conversion, Profit\}$
$\mathbf{C}_4$: $\{Competition, Campaign, Quality, Conversion\}$
$\mathbf{C}_3$: $\{Competition, Strategic, Campaign\}$
$\mathbf{C}_1$: $\{Demand, Competition, Strategic\}$
$\mathbf{C}_2$: $\{Demand, Supply, Strategic\}$

For example, the clique $\mathbf{C}_5$ comes before the clique $\mathbf{C}_4$ because $\mathbf{C}_5$ contains the node *Profit* whose rank is higher than the rank of any node in $\mathbf{C}_4$.

The join tree from an ordered set of cliques $\mathbf{C}_1$, $\mathbf{C}_2$, ..., $\mathbf{C}_n$ formed by connecting each $\mathbf{C}_i$ to a predecessor $\mathbf{C}_j$ sharing the highest number of vertices with $\mathbf{C}_i$. For example, a join tree for the above ordered set of cliques $\mathbf{C}_5$, $\mathbf{C}_4$, $\mathbf{C}_3$, $\mathbf{C}_1$, $\mathbf{C}_2$ is shown in FIGURE 7.42. Each edge in the tree is labeled with the intersection of the adjacent cliques, which is called a separator set or a *sepset*.

The following algorithm helps systematically construct a join tree as shown in FIGURE 7.42. The algorithm is optimal with respect to the mass and cost criteria adopted during the selection of sepsets.

- Create a forest of n distinct trees, where each tree consists of only one node made out of the set of n cliques produced by the triangulation and clique identification procedure above. Also, create a set $\mathbf{S}$ of $n(n-1)$ distinct sepsets obtained by intersecting all possible pairs of distinct elements in the set of cliques.

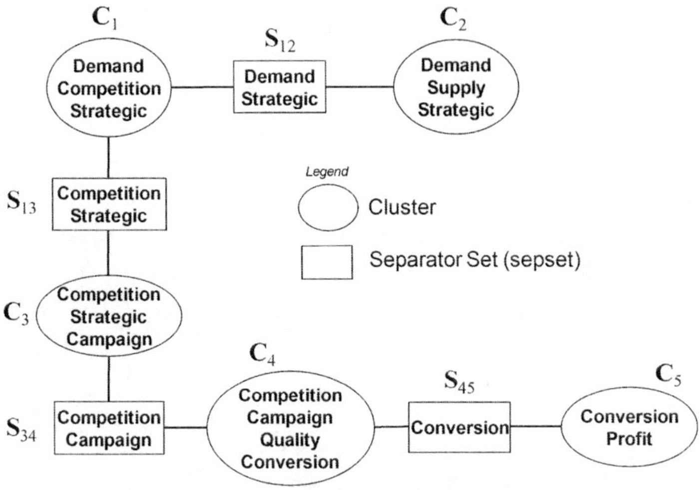

FIGURE 7.42 : Join tree for the graph in FIGURE 7.39

- Repeat the following steps $n-1$ times:
  - Select a sepset $\mathbf{S}_{ij}$ (that is, $\mathbf{C}_i \cap \mathbf{C}_j$) from $\mathbf{S}$ that has the largest mass, where mass of a sepset $\mathbf{S}_{ij}$ is the number of variables it contains. If two or more sepsets of equal mass can be chosen, then choose the candidate sepset with the smallest cost, where the *cost of a sepset* $\mathbf{S}_{ij}$ is the sum of the product of the number of states of the variables in $\mathbf{C}_i$ and the product of the number of states of the variables in $\mathbf{C}_j$.
  - Insert the selected sepset SXY between the cliques $\mathbf{C}_i$ and $\mathbf{C}_j$ only if $\mathbf{C}_i$ and $\mathbf{C}_j$ are on different trees in the forest.

Example

In the construction of the join tree in FIGURE 7.42, first the forest is formed containing all five cliques $\mathbf{C}_1$, $\mathbf{C}_2$, $\mathbf{C}_3$, $\mathbf{C}_4$, and $\mathbf{C}_5$. Each of the sepsets $\mathbf{S}_{12}$, $\mathbf{S}_{13}$, and $\mathbf{S}_{34}$ has a mass 2 and weight 6, and is therefore inserted first into the join tree. Note that the sepset $\{Strategic\}$ was not inserted between $\mathbf{C}_2$ and $\mathbf{C}_3$ before $\mathbf{S}_{12}$ or $\mathbf{S}_{13}$ as $\{Strategic\}$ has lower mass than each of $\mathbf{S}_{12}$ and $\mathbf{S}_{13}$.

7.3.7.2 Join Tree Initialization

A join tree maintains a joint probability distribution at each node, cluster, or sepset in terms of a *belief potential*, which is a function that maps each instantiation of the set of variables in the node into a real number. The belief potential of a set $\mathbf{X}$ of variables will be denoted as φ_X, and $\varphi_X(x)$ is the number onto which the potential maps x. The probability distribution of a set $\mathbf{X}$ of variables is just the special case of a potential whose elements add up to 1. In other words,

$$\sum_{x\in X} \varphi_X(x) = \sum_{x\in X} p(x) = 1$$

The marginalization and multiplication operations on potentials are defined in a manner similar to the same operations on probability distributions.

Belief potentials encode the joint distribution $p(\mathbf{X})$ of the BN according to the following:

$$p(\mathbf{X}) = \frac{\prod_i \phi_{\mathbf{C}_i}}{\prod_j \phi_{\mathbf{S}_j}}$$

where $\varphi_{\mathbf{C}_i}$ and $\varphi_{\mathbf{S}_j}$ are the cluster and sepset potentials, respectively. We have the following joint distribution for the join tree in FIGURE 7.42 (only the initial or first two letters have been used for each variable name except that *Cn* stands for *Conversion*):

$$\begin{aligned} & p\begin{pmatrix} Demand, Supply, Competition, \\ Strategic, Campaign, Quality, Conversion, Profit \end{pmatrix} \\ & = \frac{\phi_{\mathbf{C}_1}\phi_{\mathbf{C}_2}\phi_{\mathbf{C}_3}\phi_{\mathbf{C}_4}\phi_{\mathbf{C}_5}}{\phi_{\mathbf{S}_{12}}\phi_{\mathbf{S}_{13}}\phi_{\mathbf{S}_{34}}\phi_{\mathbf{S}_{45}}} \\ & = \frac{\phi_{DeCoSt}\phi_{DeSuSt}\phi_{CoStCa}\phi_{CoCaQuCn}\phi_{CnPr}}{\phi_{DeSt}\phi_{CoSt}\phi_{CoCa}\phi_{Cn}} \end{aligned}$$

It is imperative that a cluster potential agrees on the variables in common with its neighboring sepsets up to marginalization. This imperative is formalized by the concept of local consistency. A join tree is *locally consistent* if for each cluster $\mathbf{C}$ and neighboring sepset $\mathbf{S}$, the following holds:

$$\sum_{\mathbf{C}-\mathbf{S}} \phi_{\mathbf{C}} = \phi_{\mathbf{S}}$$

To start initialization, for each cluster $\mathbf{C}$ and sepset $\mathbf{S}$, set the following:

$$\phi_C \leftarrow 1, \phi_S \leftarrow 1$$

Then assign each variable X to a cluster $\mathbf{C}$ that contains X and its parents $pa(X)$. Then set the following:

$$\phi_{\mathbf{C}} \leftarrow \phi_{\mathbf{C}} p(X|pa(X))$$

Example

To illustrate the initialization process, consider the join tree in FIGURE 7.42. The allocation of prior and conditional probability tables is shown in FIGURE 7.43. The CPT for variable *Strategic* has been assigned to cluster $\mathbf{C}_2$

as it contains the variable and its parents *Demand* and *Supply*. The prior $p\,(Demand)$ could have been assigned to any of $\mathbf{C}_1$ and $\mathbf{C}_2$, but $\mathbf{C}_1$ is chosen arbitrarily.

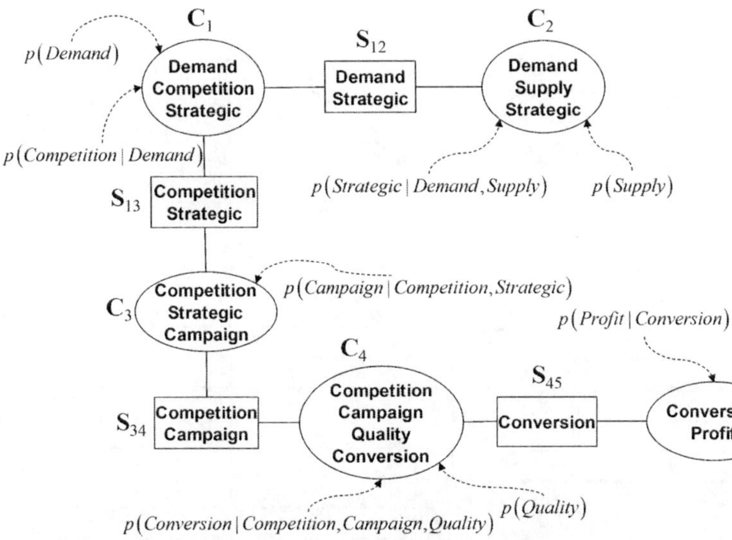

FIGURE 7.43 : Allocation of prior and conditional probability tables for join tree initialization

As an example, FIGURE 7.44 shows the computation of potential for the clique $\mathbf{C}_1$ by multiplying $p\,(Demand)$ and $p\,(Competition|Demand)$.

7.3.7.3 Propagation in Join Tree and Marginalization

The join tree thus formed is not locally consistent as, for example, $\sum\limits_{\mathrm{C}_1-\mathrm{S}_{12}} \phi_{\mathrm{C}_1} \neq \phi_{\mathrm{S}_{12}}$. An inconsistent join tree can be made consistent by using a *global propagation*. The message-passing mechanism is at the heart of global propagation.

Consider two adjacent clusters $\mathbf{C}_1$ and $\mathbf{C}_2$ with sepset $\mathbf{S}$. A message-pass from $\mathbf{C}_1$ to $\mathbf{C}_2$ consists of the following two steps:

- Projection: $\phi_{\mathrm{S}}^{old} \leftarrow \phi_{\mathrm{S}}$, $\phi_{\mathrm{S}} \leftarrow \sum\limits_{\mathrm{C}_1-\mathrm{S}} \phi_{\mathrm{C}_1}$

- Absorption: $\phi_{C_2} \leftarrow \phi_{C_2} \frac{\phi_S}{\phi_S^{old}}$

It can be easily verified that any number of messages passing as shown above

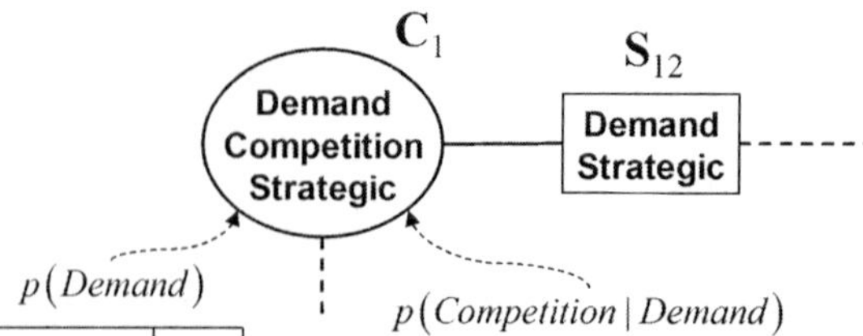

p(**Demand** = heavy)	0.55
p(**Demand** = moderate)	0.15
p(**Demand** = low)	0.30

Demand ⇒	heavy	moderate	low
p(**Competition** = stiff)	0.90	0.70	0.80
p(**Competition** = moderate)	0.09	0.20	0.15
p(**Competition** = none)	0.01	0.10	0.05

$\phi_{\mathbf{S}_{12}}$

Demand	Strategic	Initial Values
heavy	yes	1
heavy	no	1
moderate	yes	1
moderate	no	1
low	yes	1
low	no	1

$\phi_{\mathbf{C}_1}$

Demand	Competition	Strategic	Initial Values
heavy	stiff	yes	0.90 × 0.55 × 1 = 0.4950
heavy	stiff	no	0.90 × 0.55 × 1 = 0.4950
heavy	moderate	yes	0.09 × 0.55 × 1 = 0.0495
heavy	moderate	no	0.09 × 0.55 × 1 = 0.0495
heavy	none	yes	0.01 × 0.55 × 1 = 0.0055
heavy	none	no	0.01 × 0.55 × 1 = 0.0055
moderate	stiff	yes	0.70 × 0.15 × 1 = 0.1050
moderate	stiff	no	0.70 × 0.15 × 1 = 0.1050
moderate	moderate	yes	0.20 × 0.15 × 1 = 0.0300
moderate	moderate	no	0.20 × 0.15 × 1 = 0.0300
moderate	none	yes	0.10 × 0.15 × 1 = 0.0150
moderate	none	no	0.10 × 0.15 × 1 = 0.0150
low	stiff	yes	0.80 × 0.30 × 1 = 0.2400
low	stiff	no	0.80 × 0.30 × 1 = 0.2400
low	moderate	yes	0.15 × 0.30 × 1 = 0.0450
low	moderate	no	0.15 × 0.30 × 1 = 0.0450
low	none	yes	0.05 × 0.30 × 1 = 0.0150
low	none	no	0.05 × 0.30 × 1 = 0.0150

FIGURE 7.44 : Computation of potential

encodes the joint distribution $p(\mathbf{X})$ of the BN. Global propagation is a systematic collection of message-passing via the following two recursive procedures: *Collect Evidence* and *Distribute Evidence*.

- Choose an arbitrary cluster **C**.
- Unmark all clusters and call the following three steps of *Collect Evidence*(**C**):
  - Mark **C**.

- Recursively call *Collect Evidence* on each unmarked neighboring cluster of **C**.
- Pass a message from **C** to the cluster that invoked *Collect Evidence*(**C**).

- Unmark all clusters and call the following three steps of *Distribute Evidence*(**C**):
  - Mark C.
  - Pass a message from C to each of its unmarked neighboring clusters.
  - Recursively call Distribute Evidence on each unmarked neighboring cluster of C.

Example

FIGURE 7.45 shows the message flow order when the cluster $\mathbf{C}_3$ is chosen as the starting cluster in the above algorithm. First, *Collect Evidence* is called on cluster $\mathbf{C}_3$, which causes two calls of *Collect Evidence* on each of $\mathbf{C}_1$ and $\mathbf{C}_4$. The call of *Collect Evidence* on $\mathbf{C}_1$ triggers a call of *Collect Evidence* on $\mathbf{C}_2$. The node then passes message 1 to $\mathbf{C}_1$. The process continues, yielding a total of eight messages as shown in FIGURE 7.45.

Once the join tree has been made consistent, prior probabilities of variables can be obtained using marginalization. First, identify a cluster **C** that contains the variable X of interest. Then compute $p(X)$ by marginalizing ϕ_{C} as $p(X) = \sum\limits_{\mathrm{C}\backslash\{X\}} \phi_{\mathrm{C}}$.

An example of this computation for the variable *Strategic* from cluster $\mathbf{C}_2$ is shown in FIGURE 7.46.

7.3.7.4 Handling Evidence

FIGURE 7.47 shows the overall flow for using evidence in join trees to compute the variables' posterior probabilities. Compare this figure with FIGURE 7.37, which shows the flow for computing only prior probabilities. When new evidence on a variable is entered into the tree, it becomes inconsistent and requires a global propagation to make it consistent. The posterior probabilities can be computed via marginalization and normalization from the global propagation. If evidence on a variable is updated, then the tree requires initialization. Next, we present initialization, normalization, and marginalization procedures for handling evidence.

As before, to start initialization, for each cluster **C** and sepset **S**, set the following:

$$\phi_{\mathrm{C}} \leftarrow 1, \phi_{\mathrm{S}} \leftarrow 1$$

Then assign each variable X to a cluster **C** that contains X and its parents $pa(X)$, and then set the following:

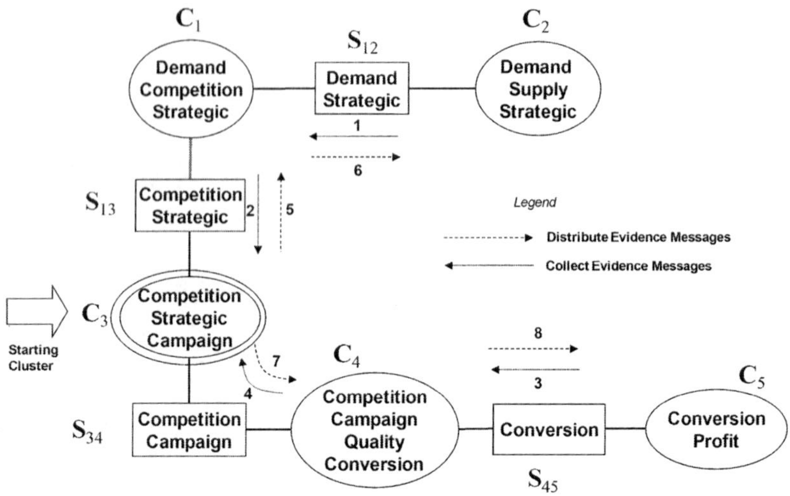

FIGURE 7.45 : Message flow in global propagation

Clique $\mathbf{C}_2 = \{Demand, Supply, Strategic\}$

Demand	Supply	Strategic	Potential ϕ_{C_2}
heavy	yes	yes	0.8
heavy	yes	no	0.2
heavy	no	yes	0.99
heavy	no	no	0.01
moderate	yes	yes	0.1
moderate	yes	no	0.9
moderate	no	yes	0.6
moderate	no	no	0.4
low	yes	yes	0.01
low	yes	no	0.99
low	no	yes	0.15
low	no	no	0.85

Sum (Shaded Rows): 2.65
Sum (Clear Rows): 3.35

p(**Strategic** = yes)	0.44 = 2.65 / (2.65 + 3.35)
p(**Strategic** = no)	0.56 = 3.35 / (2.65 + 3.35)

FIGURE 7.46 : Marginalization from potential and normalization

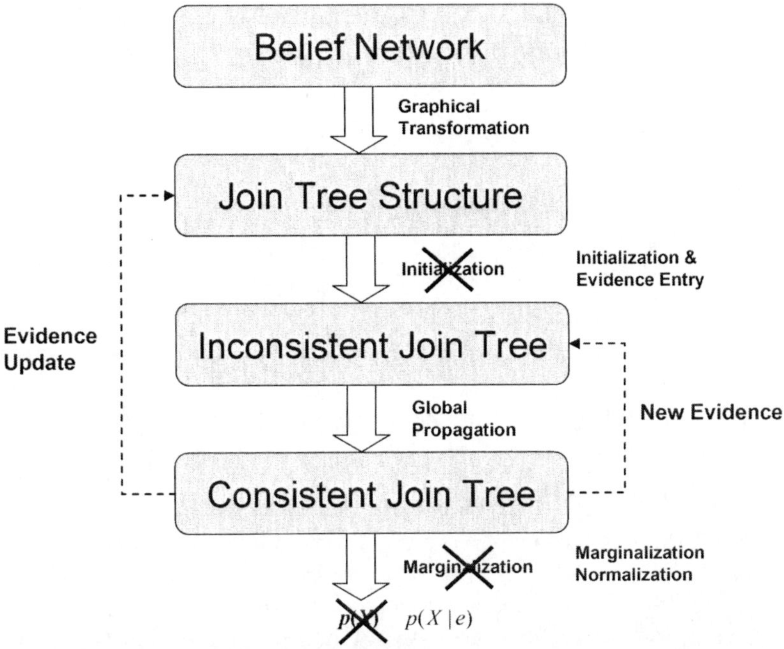

FIGURE 7.47 : Steps for handling evidence in join trees

$$\phi_{\mathbf{C}} \leftarrow \phi_{\mathbf{C}} p\left(X | pa\left(X\right)\right)$$
$$\lambda_X \leftarrow 1$$

where λ_X is the likelihood vector for the variable X. Now, perform the following steps for each piece of evidence on a variable X:

- Encode the evidence on the variable as a likelihood λ_X^{new}.
- Identify a cluster **C** that contains X (e.g., one containing the variable and its parents).
- Update as follows:

$$\phi_C \leftarrow \phi_C \frac{\lambda_X^{new}}{\lambda_X}$$
$$\lambda_X \leftarrow \lambda_X^{new}$$

Now perform a global propagation using the *Collect Evidence* and *Distribute Evidence* procedures. Note that if the belief potential of one cluster **C** is modified, then it is sufficient to unmark all clusters and call only *Distribute Evidence*(**C**).

The potential φ_C for each cluster $\mathbf{C}$ is now $p(\mathbf{C}, e)$, where e denotes evidence incorporated into the tree. Now marginalize C into the variable as

$$p(X, e) = \sum_{\mathrm{C}\backslash\{X\}} \phi_{\mathrm{C}}$$

Compute posterior $p(X|e)$ as follows:

$$p(X|e) = \frac{p(X, e)}{p(e)} = \frac{p(X, e)}{\sum_X p(X, e)}$$

To update evidence, for each variable X on which evidence has been obtained, update its likelihood vector. Then initialize the join tree by incorporating the observations. Finally, perform global propagation, marginalization, etc.

7.3.8 Complexity of Inference Algorithms

Probabilistic inference using BNs is computationally intractable, that is, it is NP-hard (Cooper, 1990). Informally, this means that if there exists an algorithm that solves our problems in polynomial time, then the polynomial-time algorithm would exist for practically all discrete problems, such as the propositional satisfiability problem. The fact that inferencing in BNs is not tractable does not mean it can never be applied; it simply means that there are cases when its inferencing time will take too long for the algorithm to be practical.

The computational complexity of Pearl's message-passing algorithm for acyclic networks (Pearl, 1988) can be shown to be $O(n \times d \times 2^d)$, where n is the number of vertices in the network and d is the network's maximal indegree. The computational complexity of Lauritzen and Spiegelhalter's junction tree algorithm (1998) equals $O(n \times 2^c)$, where n is the number of vertices in the network and c is the number of vertices in the largest clique in the clique tree that is constructed from the network. Note that the algorithm's complexity is exponential in the size of the largest clique.

If the clique sizes in the junction tree algorithm are bounded by a constant, then the algorithm takes linear time. Since the computational complexity of the junction tree algorithm relates exponentially to clique size, the best clique tree to use in practical applications is a tree inducing the smallest state space. The problem of finding such a clique tree is known to be NP-hard (Wen, 1990). Various efficient heuristic algorithms are available for finding a clique tree for an acyclic network. However, these algorithms do not exhibit any optimality properties.

It seems unlikely that an exact algorithm can be developed to perform probabilistic inference efficiently over all classes of BNs. This result suggests that research should be directed away from the search for a general, efficient, probabilistic inference algorithm, and towards the design of efficient special-case (for example, tree structure or inherently modular network), average-case, and approximation algorithms.

7.3.9 Acquisition of Probabilities

The acquisition of probabilities for BN structures involves eliciting conditional probabilities from subject-matter experts along causal directions. These probabilities can also be learned if relevant training data are available. Some of the learning techniques will be presented later in the chapter on machine learning.

Conditional probabilities are "causal" conditional probabilities of the form $p(Conversion|Competition, Campaign, Quality)$, indicating the chance of conversion given certain levels of competition and campaign and the product quality. This chance is related to market and consumer behavior, which may be best estimated by experts. Similarly, a causal probability of the form $p(Strategic|Demand,\ Supply)$ indicates the strategic value of a product to the company, given its demand and the ability to supply. The in-house strategists, together with suppliers, can best estimate this probability by taking into account additional factors such as how best the product fits into the existing product line. On the other hand, the "diagnostic" conditional probabilities in the belief context are probabilities of the form $p(Demand|Competition)$, indicating the level of demand given a certain form of competition. An experienced market analyst may best estimate in the causal direction from previous experience though both causal and diagnostic probabilities can be used to compute joint probability distributions.

The major issue related to eliciting probabilities from subject-matter experts is how to phrase questions to experts so as to accurately and efficiently determine relevant prior and conditional probabilities (Druzdzel and van der Gaag, 1995).

Example

Consider the network fragment as shown in FIGURE 7.48, which says that a campaign on television (TC), a campaign via email (EC), and phone calls (PC) together cause a high level of conversion (HC). Each variable X (TC, EC, PC, and HC) in the network is binary with two states X and $\neg X$. If we are eliciting causal probabilities, then experts will be asked questions for determining the priors $p(TC)$, $p(EC)$, and $p(PC)$ (that is, how likely it is that a company adopts a specific campaign), and the conditional $p(HC|TC, EC, PC)$.

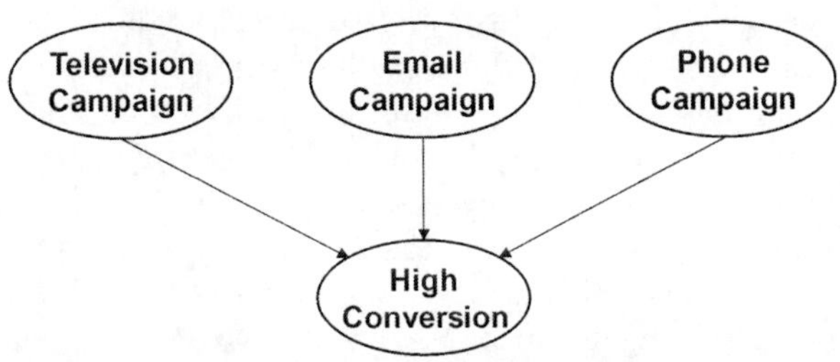

FIGURE 7.48 : BN illustrating probability acquisition

If prior probability $p(HC)$ is available, then diagnostic conditional probabilities are elicited by employing the arc reversal approach (Shachter and Heckerman, 1987). But even if the diagnostic conditional probabilities $p(TC|HC)$, $p(EC|HC)$, and $p(PC|HC)$ are known, it is not possible to uniquely determine the causal probability $p(HC|TC, EC, PC)$.

Our experience suggests that subject-matter experts, scientists, and knowledge engineers are often comfortable drawing arrows in the causal direction once the term "causality" is explained. The directionality has great impact on the resultant ease of knowledge elicitation. For example, if all three arrows in the network in FIGURE 7.48 are reversed, then the resultant network is equally effective in determining the conversion level, but now the a priori probability $p(HC)$ is required, as are the conditional probabilities$p(TC|HC)$, $p(EC|HC)$, and$p(PC|HC)$.

The number of conditional probabilities required for a node to complete its conditional probability table, like $p(HC|TC, EC, PC)$ for *HC*, grows exponentially with the number of parents. But we can employ the *noisy-or* technique to avoid building large probability tables, provided certain conditions are met (Pearl, 1988). Informally, the noisy-or technique states that any members of a set of independent conditions are likely to cause a certain event, and that this chance is not reduced when several of these conditions occur simultaneously. In the case of the node *HC*, chances for the conversion to be high can only increase when several of the three conditions, television campaign, email campaign, and phone campaign, occur simultaneously. Given this knowledge, we can generate the CPT $p(HC|TC, EC, PC)$ of eight independent entries from only three values. Formally, the noisy-or is a BN node representing an event (e.g., *Conversion*) at which the following assumptions are made:

- The *accountability* condition requires that we explicitly list as parent nodes all the conditions likely to influence the event. In the example, this assumption requires that we explicitly list all the conditions likely to cause high conversion. In other words, the condition states that an event is presumed false if all conditions listed as causes of the event are false.

- The *exception independence* condition requires that whatever inhibits each parent node from implying the event is independent of whatever inhibits other parent nodes from implying the event. For example, assume that the only factor inhibiting the high conversion when there is a television campaign is bad timing of the campaign, and the only factor inhibiting the high conversion when there is email campaign is that potential customers perceive the campaign emails as spam. The exception independence condition holds since the two inhibitory factors can be assumed independent of each other. On the other hand, the holiday season factor would have inhibited both the parent nodes for television campaign and email campaign from implying the event (because fewer people would presumably watch television or read emails), and thus it would have violated the exception independence condition.

Example

An incomplete CPT, like the one in TABLE 7.9, can be completed by deriving the missing probabilities through the noisy-or technique. Suppose only the following entries in the CPT are known:

$$p(HC|TC, \neg EC, \neg PC) = 0.7$$
$$p(HC|\neg TC, EC, \neg PC) = 0.6$$
$$p(HC|\neg TC, \neg EC, PC) = 0.9$$

Therefore, we have the following:

$$p(\neg HC|TC, \neg EC, \neg PC) = 0.3$$
$$p(\neg HC|\neg TC, EC, \neg PC) = 0.4$$
$$p(\neg HC|\neg TC, \neg EC, PC) = 0.1$$

TABLE 7.9: : An incomplete CPT to be completed by the noisy-or technique (TC – Television Campaign; EC – Email Campaign; PC – Phone Campaign; HC – High Conversion)

TC		TC				¬TC			
EC		EC		¬EC		EC		¬EC	
PC		PC	¬PC	PC	¬PC	PC	¬PC	PC	¬PC
HC	HC	?	?	?	0.7	?	0.6	0.9	?
	¬HC	?	?	?	0.3	?	0.4	0.1	?

Now,

$$p(HC|TC, EC, \neg PC) = 1 - p(\neg HC|TC, EC, \neg PC)$$

The accountability condition states that HC is false if all conditions listed as causes of HC are false. Therefore,

$$p(\neg HC|TC, \neg EC, \neg PC) = p(\neg HC|TC) = 0.3$$
$$p(\neg HC|\neg TC, EC, \neg PC) = p(\neg HC|EC) = 0.4$$
$$p(\neg HC|\neg TC, \neg EC, PC) = p(\neg HC|PC) = 0.1$$

Also,

$$p(\neg HC|TC, EC, \neg PC) = p(\neg HC|TC, EC)$$

Thus,

$$p(HC|TC, EC, \neg PC) = 1 - p(\neg HC|TC, EC)$$

Now, the exception independence condition states that the inhibitory conditions TC and EC for HC are independent of each other. Therefore,

$$p(\neg HC|TC, EC) = p(\neg HC|TC)\,p(\neg HC|EC)$$

Thus,

$$\begin{aligned} &p(HC|TC, EC, \neg PC) \\ &\quad = 1 - p(\neg HC|TC)\,p(\neg HC|EC) \\ &\quad = 1 - 0.3 \times 0.4 \\ &\quad = 0.88 \end{aligned}$$

The rest of the entries in the CPT can be computed in a similar manner.

7.3.10 Advantages and Disadvantages of Belief Networks

Like any other computational formalism, BN technology offers certain advantages and disadvantages. Advantages of BNs include:

- *Sound theoretical foundation*: The computation of beliefs using probability estimates is guaranteed to be consistent with the probability theory. This advantage stems from the Bayesian update procedure's strict derivation from the axioms of probability.

- *Graphical models*: BNs graphically depict the interdependencies that exist between related pieces of domain knowledge, enhancing understanding of the domain. The structure of a BN captures the cause-effect relationships that exist amongst the variables of the domain. The ease of causal interpretation in BN models typically makes them easier to construct than other models, minimizing the knowledge engineering costs and making them easier to modify.

- *Predictive and diagnostic reasoning*: BNs combine both deductive/predictive and abductive/diagnostic reasoning. Interdependencies among variables in a network are accurately captured, and speculative if-then-type computations can be performed.

- *Computational tractability*: BNs are computationally tractable for most practical applications. This efficiency stems principally from the exploitation of conditional independence relationships over the domain. We have presented an efficient single-pass evidence propagation algorithm for networks without loops.

- *Evidence-handling*: Evidence can be posted to any node in a BN. This means that subjective evidence can be posted at an intermediate node representing an abstract concept.

A major disadvantage of BN technology is the high level of effort required to build network models. Although it is relatively easy to build a BN structure with the help of subject-matter experts, the model will require a significant amount of probability data as the number of nodes and links in the structure increases. The size of a CPT corresponding to a node with multiple parents can potentially be huge. For example, the number of independent entries in the CPT of a binary node (a node with two states) with 8 binary parent variables is 128.

BNs are also poor at handling continuous variables. Current software handles continuous variables in a very restrictive manner (for example, they must be Gaussian and can only be children). Lerner et al. (2001) developed an inference algorithm for static hybrid BNs, which are Conditional Linear Gaussian models, where the conditional distribution of the continuous variables assigned to the discrete variables is a multivariate Gaussian. Cobb and Shenoy (2003) developed an inference algorithm in hybrid BNs using Mixtures of Truncated Potentials. These techniques have yet to be incorporated in commercial software.

7.3.11 Belief Network Tools

Various free and commercial software tools and packages are currently available incorporating some of the above functionalities for manipulating BNs. Of these, HUGIN (www.hugin.com) is the most widely used commercial package that contains a flexible, user-friendly, and comprehensive graphical user interface. The package allows modeling of decision-making problems via influence diagrams, and handles continuous variables with some restrictions. Other popular tools and packages include Netica (http://www.norsys.com/), BayesiaLab (http://www.bayesia.com/), and publicly available GeNIe/SMILE (http://genie.sis.pitt.edu/).

7.4 FURTHER READING

The book by Pearl (1988) is still the most comprehensive account on BNs, and more generally on using probabilistic reasoning to handle uncertainty. Various cases of the evidence propagation algorithms in polytrees presented here closely follow Pearl's book. Though Pearl himself developed an exact inference algorithm for DAGs, called *loop cutset conditioning* (Pearl, 1986), the junction tree algorithm of Lauritzen and Spiegelhalter (1988), as refined by Jensen et al. (1990) in HUGIN, is more general and the most popular inference algorithm for general BNs. A good comprehensive procedural account of the algorithm can be found in Huang and Darwiche (1996). Jensen's books (1996, 2002) are also useful guides in this field.

CHAPTER 8

Decision Support and Prescriptive Analytics

This chapter describes two approaches to decision support: Influence Diagrams (IDs) and Symbolic Argumentation.

Bayesian Networks (BNs) and rule-based formalisms for hypothesis evaluation do not explicitly incorporate the concepts of action and utility, which are ubiquitous in decision-making contexts. When incorporating these concepts, BNs are converted to IDs, subsuming the functionality of the normative theory of decision-making under expected utility theory (EUT) and decision trees. Decision-making based on IDs means choosing, from a set of alternative actions, the most suitable action (or hypothesis) yielding the highest utility. For inferencing in IDs, we extend the junction tree algorithm for BNs. The extended algorithm presented in this chapter compiles an ID into a strong junction tree in which the computation of maximum expected utility can be done by local message-passing in the tree.

Arguments for and against decision options in symbolic argumentation (as opposed to natural argumentation) are expressed in high-level, logical, if-then rules incorporating subjective probabilities, representing the argument strengths, provided by decision-makers. To aggregate a set of such diverse probabilistic (and possibly inconsistent) arguments for and against the decision options acquired from experts, we apply the Dempster-Shafer theory to compute degrees of belief for decision options. Incoming evidence is used to compute degrees of belief, and hence rankings, among the decision options. Decision-making using such degrees of belief is therefore based on a strong mathematical foundation.

When multiple, disparate, and uncertain knowledge sources, be they subject-matter experts or fielded sensors, are involved in making decisions, some kind of quantitative criterion is useful for measuring the quality of the consensus generated by pooling evidence from these knowledge sources. Formally, consensus in such a disparate, group-decision-making context refers to agreement on some decision by all members (experts and automated systems) of the group, rather than a majority, and the consensus process is what a group goes through to reach this agreement. The consensus process provides a way to focus on areas where experts disagree in order to initiate conflict-resolving discussions. In this chapter, we present an entropy-based criterion for measuring consensus among disparate sources when the underlying mechanism for handling uncertainty is the Dempster-Shafer theory (applicable to the Bayesian theory as a special case).

The argumentation approach (Toulmin, 1956; Fox and Das, 2000) for combining knowledge sources implicitly assumes that all sources are equally credible. This is simply not the case when there are experts of various degrees of expertise and sensors with various degrees of reliability. This chapter also presents a method for taking into account such confidence factors during the handling of uncertainty.

Both approaches to decision support are illustrated in the context of the ongoing product launching and marketing example presented in the last chapter.

8.1 EXPECTED UTILITY THEORY AND DECISION TREES

A *decision* is a choice among several alternative courses of risky or uncertain action. Expected Utility Theory (EUT) states that the decision-maker chooses among alternative courses of action by comparing their *expected utility* values, which is the weighted sum obtained by adding the utility values of possible outcomes multiplied by their respective probabilities. Formally, if $A = \{a_1, ..., a_n\}$ is the set of all possible actions as decision alternatives and $W = \{w_1, ..., w_n\}$ is the corresponding set of possible outcomes or world states, then the *expected utility* (EU) for action a_k is the following:

$$EU(a_k) = \sum_i U(w_i)\, p(w_i|a_k)$$

where $U(w_i)$ is the utility of the outcome w_i and $p(w_i|a_k)$ is the probability that the outcome is w_i if the action a_k is taken. The *maximum expected utility* (MEU) operation is used to choose the best alternative course of action:

$$MEU(A) = \max_k EU(a_k)$$

In cases where an outcome w_i depends not on the decision-maker's action but instead on other context-dependent factors over which the decision-maker has no control, the expected utility is simply defined without actions, that is,

$$EU = \sum_i U(w_i)\, p(w_i)$$

The computation of MEU is not relevant in this case.

A *decision tree* poses an ordered list of systematic questions that leads the decision-maker through a series of decisions to a logical endpoint that results in a solution. These likely outcomes of possible solutions to the problem are projected as utilities. The systematic exploration of likely outcomes is organized in a tree in which each branch node represents a choice among a number of alternatives, and each leaf node represents a solution. A branch node is either a *chance node* or an *action node*. MEUs are computed at action nodes and EUs are computed at chance nodes.

Example

FIGURE 8.1 shows an example decision tree in the context of our product launch example, in which ovals, rectangles, and diamonds represent chance nodes, decision or action nodes, and terminal nodes, respectively. The root node is a chance node representing the state of demand for the product, and branches are its uncertain outcomes. It is 80% likely that demand will be heavy and 20% likely that demand will be moderate. These two possible outcomes are represented as two branches coming out of the chance node for demand. Given either of these two alternatives of demand states, the next step is to decide whether to launch the product or not. This decision requires exploring four possible combinations of options between the demand state and the launch decision. For each of these combinations, the likely competition for the product, affecting sales, needs to be considered to compute profits for the launch of the product that is predicted as utility.

For example, two combinations corresponding to the top two branches are that the demand is heavy, the action taken is to launch the product, and that there is a 70% chance that the competition will be stiff and a 30% chance that the competition will be moderate ("moderate" includes the option "none" for no competition, for the sake of simplicity). Each of these two possibilities yields different profit as utility and is attached to the terminal node. The top branch of the tree in the figure encodes a possible outcome, which states that if the demand is heavy, a decision to launch the product is taken, and the competition is stiff, then the utility is −750. Eight possible outcomes are explored in this manner in the context of the example.

EUs and MEUs at branch nodes are computed bottom-up along the tree (right to left in the figure). For example, the EU at the *Competition* node of the topmost branch is computed using the formula $\sum_i U(w_i)\,p(w_i)$, yielding $-750 \times 0.7 + 4500 \times 0.3$, that is, 825. To compute the MEU at the node *Launch* in the upper branch of the tree, EUs of the two decisions *yes* and *no*, $EU(yes)$ and $EU(no)$, need to be computed using the formula $\sum_i U(w_i)\,p(w_i|a_k)$. Now, the EUs of the two *Competition* nodes of the upper branch are 825 and −1500. Therefore, the MEU of the node *Launch* is the maximum of 825 and −1500, that is, 825. Finally, the EU of the node *Demand* is computed using the formula $\sum_i U(w_i)\,p(w_i)$, yielding 990.

A decision-maker has no control over the outcome of a chance node. As the

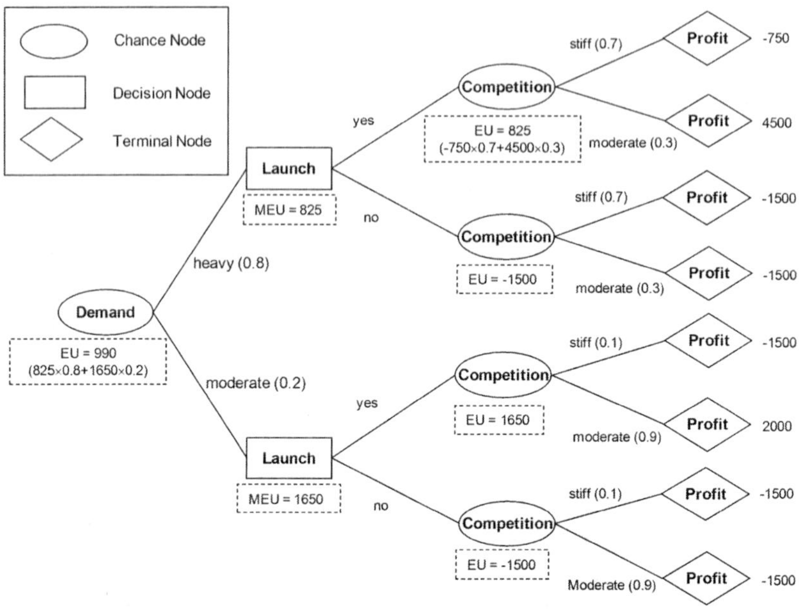

FIGURE 8.1 : An example decision tree

value of a chance node becomes known, the decision-maker makes a decision (that is, chooses a branch from a decision node) that yields the highest EU value. For example, if the demand for the product turns out to be moderate, it makes sense to launch the product, as the option is likely to yield EU 1650 which is higher than -1500.

The procedure for computing utilities using decision trees, as explained above, is a simple statistical procedure. Decision trees also provide easy-to-understand graphic representations of situations. But laying out all possible options is not feasible when there are several factors, each with multiple outcomes. Moreover, the procedure provides no mechanism for incorporating subjective knowledge. IDs address some of these issues.

8.2 INFLUENCE DIAGRAMS FOR DECISION SUPPORT

Influence diagrams (IDs) are BNs augmented with decision variables and utility functions, and are used to solve decision problems. There are three types of nodes in an ID:

- *Chance nodes* (i.e., BN nodes): represented by ovals
- *Decision nodes*: represented by rectangles
- *Value* or *utility nodes*: represented by diamonds

As opposed to chance nodes representing probabilistic variables, decision nodes represent actions that are under the full control of decision-makers and hence no CPT is attached to a decision node.

Example

FIGURE 8.2 shows an example ID from our product launch example.

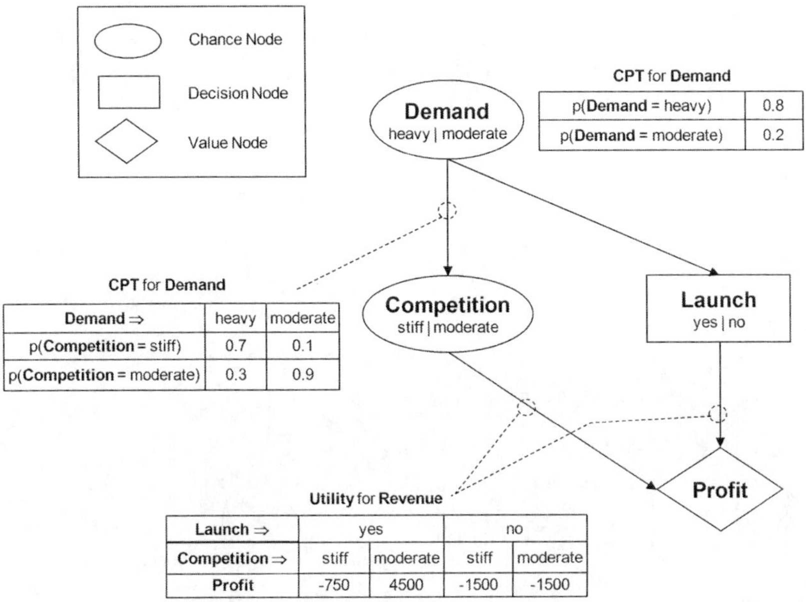

FIGURE 8.2 : An example influence diagram

There are two chance nodes (*Demand* and *Competition*), one decision node (*Launch*), and one value node (*Profit*). The arrow from the node *Demand* to the node *Competition* represents the causal influence of the state of demand on the level of competition. The CPT quantifies this causality as in usual BNs. Whether a new product is strategic to launch or not depends on its demand. As we mentioned before, there is no CPT attached to a decision node, but the arrow from the chance node *Demand* to the decision node *Launch* represents the fact that the knowledge of the state of demand for the product should be known before making the decision to launch the product. A launched product is likely to face competition and hence, in reality, the decision maker should also take into account the likely level of competition after launch. The value node *Profit* has two parents, representing the causal influence of the level of competition and the launch status on the amount of profit. The table represents a *utility function* whose definition quantifies the utilities for all possible combinations of the parent values. For example, if the decision-maker launches the product and the competition is moderate then the profit is 4500.

Inferences in IDs involve computing the EU for each of the action alternatives. This kind of computation is sensitive to the temporal order in which the decisions are made. Therefore, IDs require a directed path connecting all decision nodes sequentially. EUs are evaluated on the condition that an optimal choice has been made in all previous steps.

Suppose, $A_1, ..., A_m$ is the ordered set of actions to be decided (A_m is the last action), where each A_i is a set of mutually exclusive action options, and $V_0, ..., V_m$ is a partition of the chance variables $X_1, ..., X_n$ such that V_{i-1} is the set of variables instantiated before deciding on the action A_i. We then have the following ordering:

$$V_0 \prec A_1 \prec V_1 \prec ... \prec A_m \prec V_m$$

Next, the MEU for a chosen set of alternatives for $A_1, ..., A_m$ is given below:

$$\begin{aligned} &MEU(A_1, ..., A_m) = \\ &\quad \sum_{V_0} \max_{A_1} \sum_{V_1} ... \sum_{V_{m-1}} \max_{A_m} \sum_{V_m} \sum_{U} U \times p(V_0, V_1, ..., V_m | A_1, ..., A_m) \end{aligned}$$

The MEU for action A_k is given as

$$\begin{aligned} &MEU(A_k) = \\ &\quad \max_{A_k} \sum_{V_k} ... \sum_{V_{m-1}} \max_{A_m} \sum_{V_m} \sum_{U} U \times p(V_k, ..., V_m | V_0, ..., V_{k-1}, A_1, ..., A_m) \end{aligned}$$

Thus the computation of the MEU in an ID involves a series of alternating sum-marginalization and max-marginalization to eliminate the variables.

8.2.1 Inferencing in Influence Diagrams

In this section, we illustrate inferencing in IDs, considering the following two special cases of interactions between decisions and other types of variables:

- *Nonintervening interactions*: Actions that have no impact on variables (or probability distribution) in the network.

- *Intervening interactions*: Actions that have an impact on variables in the network that then affect the beliefs of other variables, or affect the utilities of value nodes.

Next, we present a junction tree-based algorithm for inferencing in IDs containing arbitrary sequences of interactions.

Example

FIGURE 8.3 shows an ID with one node of each type: chance, decision, and value. The decision node represents a nonintervening decision *Campaign*, which has no impact on *Competition*, i.e., $p(Competition|Campaign) = p(Competition)$. Given the likelihood e as shown in the figure, the posterior probability for *Competition* and expected utilities for each of the actions are computed as follows:

$$
\begin{aligned}
& p(Competition|e) \\
& = \begin{bmatrix} p(Competition = stiff|e) \\ p(Competition = moderate|e) \end{bmatrix} \\
& = \alpha \begin{bmatrix} 0.9 \\ 0.1 \end{bmatrix} \begin{bmatrix} 0.2 \\ 0.8 \end{bmatrix} = \begin{bmatrix} 0.692 \\ 0.308 \end{bmatrix}
\end{aligned}
$$

EUs for each of the decisions based on the posterior probabilities are computed as follows:

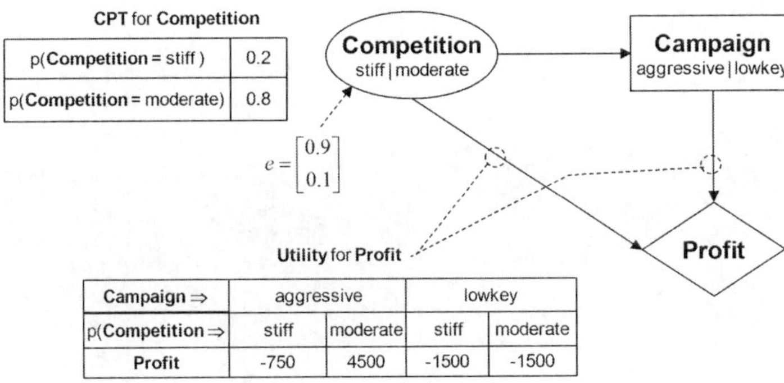

FIGURE 8.3 : ID with nonintervening action

$$
\begin{aligned}
& EU(Campaign = aggressive|e) \\
& \quad = U(Campaign = aggressive, Competition = stiff) \times \\
& \qquad\qquad p(Competition = stiff|e) + \\
& \qquad\qquad U(Campaign = aggressive, Competition = moderate) \times \\
& \qquad\qquad p(Competition = moderate|e) \\
& \quad = (-750) \times 0.692 + 4500 \times 0.308 \\
& \quad = 636.7
\end{aligned}
$$

$$
\begin{aligned}
& EU(Campaign = lowkey|e) \\
& \quad = (-1500) \times 0.692 + (-1500) \times 0.308 = -1500
\end{aligned}
$$

The MEU operation to choose the best alternative course of action is computed below:

$$
\begin{aligned}
&MEU\,(Campaign|e) \\
&\quad = \max\left\{EU\,(Campaign = aggressive|e)\,, EU\,(Campaign = lowkey|e)\right\} \\
&\quad = \max\ \{636.7, -1500\} = 636.7
\end{aligned}
$$

This MEU computation can be executed in a decision tree equivalent to the ID in FIGURE 8.3. One such tree is shown in FIGURE 8.4, where the decision and chance variables are systematically laid out (parent variables before their children) to explore all possible combinations of states. Therefore, there will be as many leaf nodes in the tree as the number of states in the joint distribution of the set of all decision and chance variables. Each branch yields some utility in terms of positive or negative credit obtained from the utility table in FIGURE 8.3. The computation of EU in the tree is performed in the usual manner starting at the leaf nodes and moving backwards.

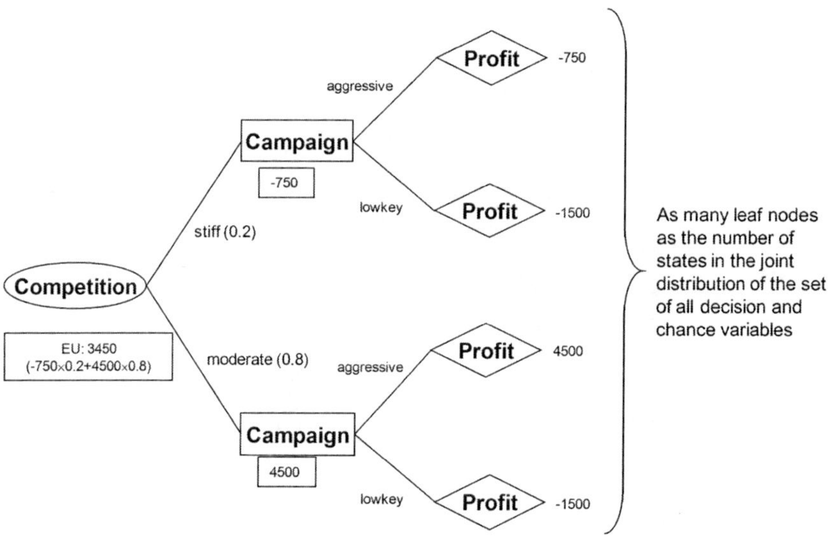

FIGURE 8.4 : Decision tree equivalent to the ID in FIGURE 8.3

When evidence on the variable *Competition* is obtained, its posterior probability is computed by component-wise multiplication followed by normalization. The EU is then computed based on the posterior probability of *Competition* as shown in FIGURE 8.5.

Example

FIGURE 8.6 shows an ID with a set of nonintervening actions. The EU is computed by summing up the MEU of each of the constituent actions. In other words,

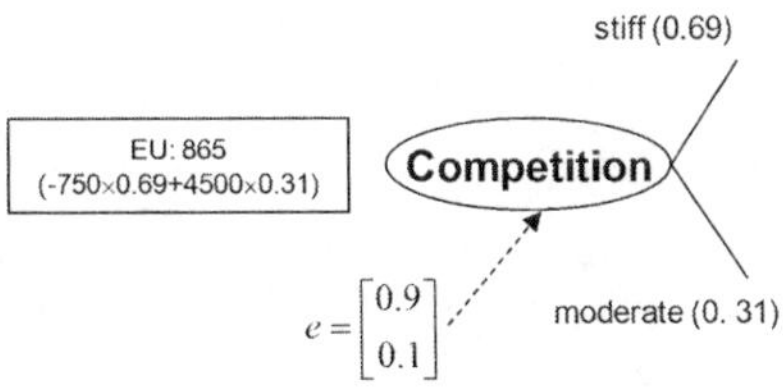

FIGURE 8.5 : Decision tree of FIGURE 8.4 with evidence entered

$$MEU\,(Television\,Ads, Phone\,Calls|e) \\ = MEU\,(Television\,Ads|e) + MEU\,(Phone\,Calls|e)$$

The MEU for the variable *Phone Calls* can be computed as follows:

$$EU\,(Phone\,Calls = aggressive|e) = (-750) \times 0.692 + 4500 \times 0.308 = 867$$
$$EU\,(Phone\,Calls = lowkey|e) = (-1500) \times 0.692 + (-1500) \times 0.308 = -1500$$

Therefore,

$$MEU\,(Phone\,Calls|e) = 867$$

Similarly, the MEU of *Television Ads* can be computed, giving

$$MEU\,(Television\,Ads|e) = -200.$$

Therefore,

$$MEU\,(Television\,Ads, Phone\,Calls|e) = 667.$$

A decision tree equivalent to the ID of FIGURE 8.6 is shown in FIGURE 8.7. The utility along a branch of the tree is computed by summing up the cost and credit corresponding to the actions specified along the branch. For example, the topmost branch states that if competition is stiff and the option *aggressive* is chosen for the decision variable *Campaign*, and the option *aggressive* is chosen for each of the two decision variables *Television Ads* and *Phone Calls*, then the overall utility is –950. This utility is obtained by adding the profit of aggressive campaign with the *Television Ads* action in the presence of competition (–200) to the profit for aggressive campaign with *Phone Calls* action in the presence of competition (–750).

Example

FIGURE 8.8 shows an ID with one decision node representing the intervening decision *Campaign* that directly influences the variable *Conversion*. In this

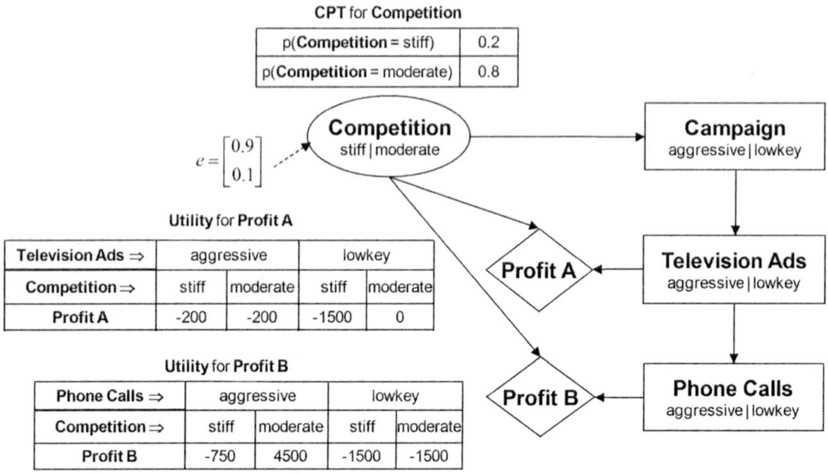

FIGURE 8.6 : ID with a set of nonintervening actions

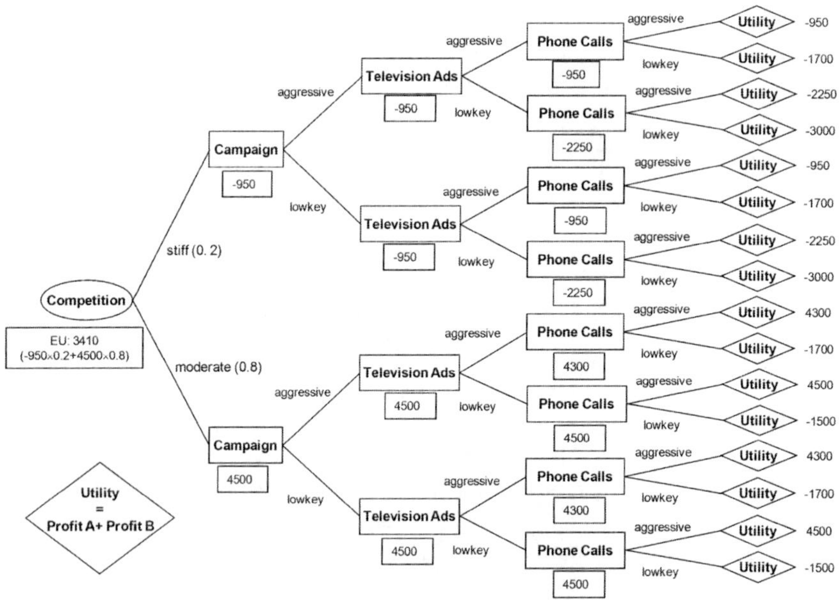

FIGURE 8.7 : Decision tree equivalence to the ID in FIGURE 8.6

example, a certain level of campaign will have some effect on the level of competition once the likelihood of the chance node *Conversion* becomes known. The posterior probability and EU for the variable *Conversion* when the option *aggressive* is chosen is computed as follows:

$$p\left(Conversion|e, Campaign = aggressive\right) = \begin{bmatrix} 0.42 \\ 0.51 \\ 0.07 \end{bmatrix}$$

$$\begin{aligned} &EU\left(Campaign = aggressive|e\right) \\ &\quad = 4500 \times 0.42 + (-500) \times 0.51 + (-1500) \times 0.07 \approx 1504 \end{aligned}$$

EU for the option *moderate* is computed similarly, yielding the following:

$$EU\left(Campaign = moderate|e\right) = -1500$$

Therefore, $MEU\left(Campaign|e\right) = 1504$

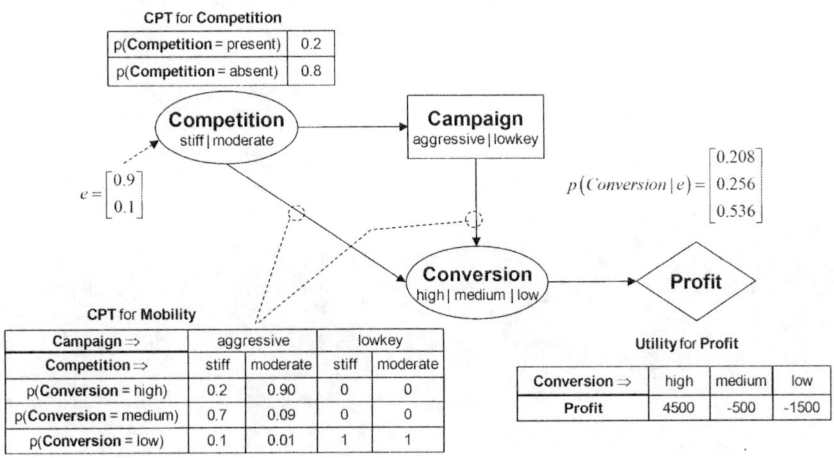

FIGURE 8.8 : ID with intervening action

A decision tree equivalent to the ID in FIGURE 8.8 is shown in FIGURE 8.9.

8.2.2 Compilation of Influence Diagrams

Compiling an ID involves transforming it to a *strong junction tree* (or *rooted junction tree*) that maintains a special ordering relative to the root clique. Recall that a *junction tree* is a tree of cliques if, for each pair $\mathbf{C}_1$ and $\mathbf{C}_2$ of cliques, $\mathbf{C}_1 \cap \mathbf{C}_2$ is contained in every clique on the path connecting $\mathbf{C}_1$ and $\mathbf{C}_2$. A *separator* of the two adjacent cliques $\mathbf{C}_1$ and $\mathbf{C}_2$ is the intersection $\mathbf{C}_1 \cap \mathbf{C}_2$.

The compilation steps for IDs are shown on the right side of FIGURE 8.10. Steps to compile BNs into junction trees are shown on the left. Details of each step are explained below.

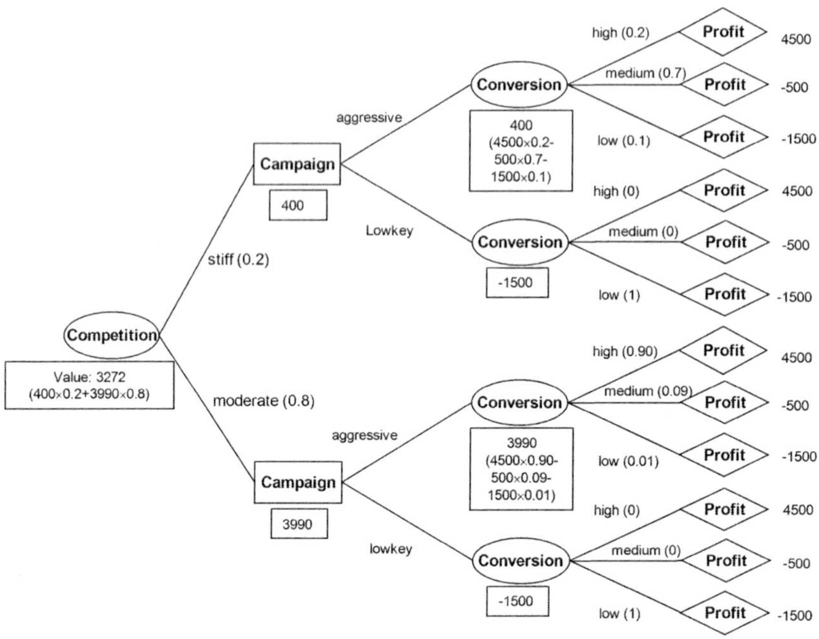

FIGURE 8.9 : Decision tree equivalent to the ID in FIGURE 8.8

- *Partitioning*: Partition the chance variables $X_1, ..., X_n$ into $V_0, ..., V_m$ such that V_{i-1} is the set of variables instantiated before deciding on the action A_i, yielding the ordering $V_0 \prec A_1 \prec V_1 \prec ... \prec A_m \prec V_m$.
- *Deletion (Arc)*: Delete edges pointing into decision nodes.
- *Moralization*: Marry parents with common children, including parents of utility nodes, and drop the directions of the original links.
- *Deletion (Node)*: Delete utility nodes along with their edges.
- *Triangulation*: Triangulate in such a way that it facilitates the computation of MEU. Do this by adopting a special elimination order based on the ordering found during partitioning. Start eliminating variables using the triangulation procedure in the following order: eliminate variables from the set V_m, then the decision variable A_m, then variables from the set V_{m-1}, then the decision variable A_{m-1}, and so on. The elimination sequence constitutes a numbering where the first eliminated variable is assigned the highest number.
- *Clique Numbering*: A clique is numbered after its variable with the highest number k (otherwise 1) such that the rest of the variables in the clique have a common neighbor outside the clique with a number lower than k.

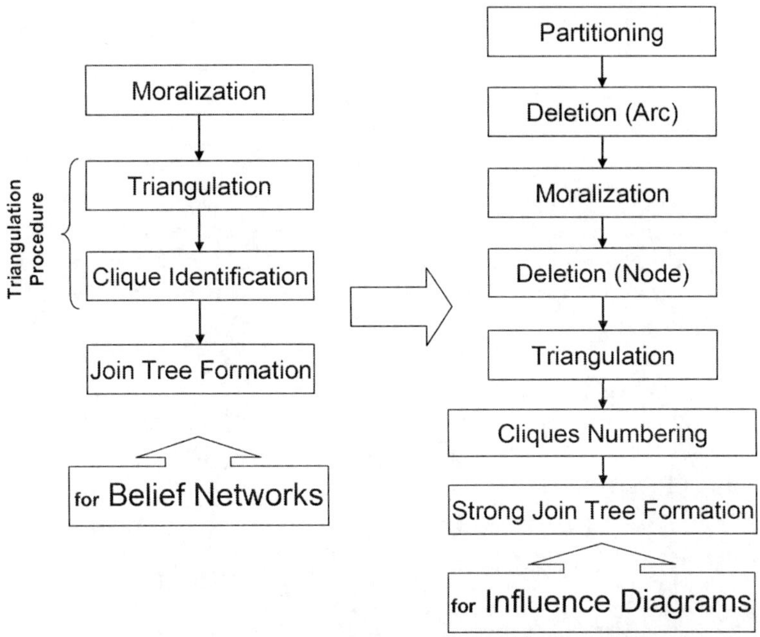

FIGURE 8.10 : Steps in the compilation process of IDs

- *Strong Join Tree Formation*: A *strong root* of a junction tree is a distinguished clique $\mathbf{R}$ such that for each pair $\mathbf{C}_1$ and $\mathbf{C}_2$ of adjacent cliques with $\mathbf{C}_1$ closer to $\mathbf{R}$ than $\mathbf{C}_2$, there is an ordering in $\mathbf{C}_2$ that respects $\prec$, where the vertices of the separator $\mathbf{C}_1 \cap \mathbf{C}_2$ preceding the vertices of $\mathbf{C}_2 - \mathbf{C}_1$. A junction tree is *strong* if it has a strong root. The ordering within a junction tree ensures that the computation of the MEU can be done by local message-passing in the tree. The following steps are followed to form a strong junction tree from the sequence $\mathbf{C}_1, ..., \mathbf{C}_n$ of cliques arranged in increasing order according to their indices:
  - Start with $\mathbf{C}_1$ as the root clique with number 1.
  - Connect the cliques as follows in the increasing order of their numbers: first, compute the following for each clique C_k $(k > 1)$:

$$S_k = C_k \cap \bigcup_{i=1}^{k-1} C_i$$

- Connect the clique C_k with another clique that contains S_k.
  - Variables that were eliminated first are placed farthest from the root in the strong junction tree.

The following example illustrates these steps to construct a strong junction tree.

Example

FIGURE 8.11 is an example ID modified from our original BN for the product launch example presented in the chapter on probabilistic graphical modeling. The chance variables *Competition* and *Strategic* are the parents of the decision variable *Campaign*, indicating that information about the market competition and company strategy are required before a decision as to the level of campaign is taken. A fixed cost will be incurred if either of the decision options is taken. If the decision is to launch an aggressive campaign, there will be a cost due to various channels to be covered. The cost is also incurred due to administrative maintenance for each conversion. The cost is therefore proportional to the total number of conversions, but credits can also be earned depending on the total number of conversions.

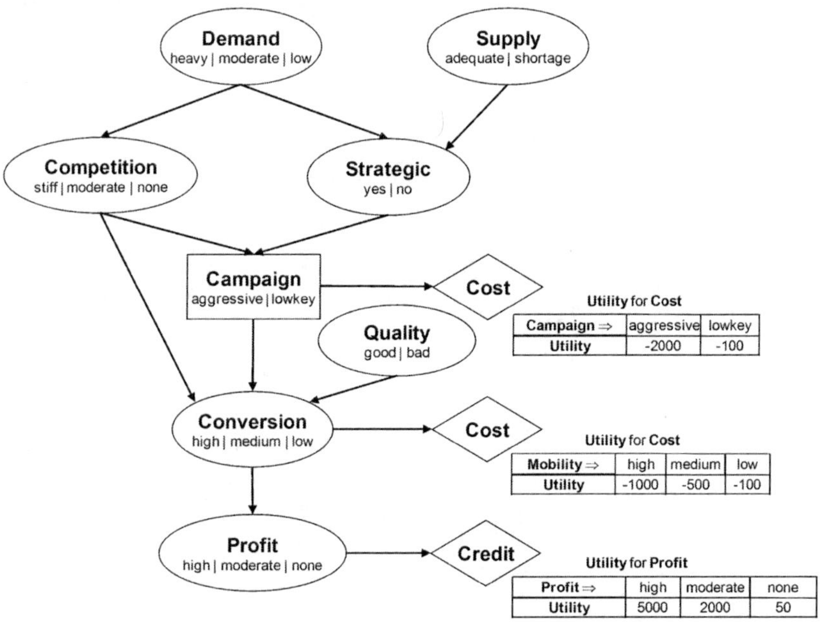

FIGURE 8.11 : An example influence diagram

Consider the following ordering of the chance and decision variables of the BN:

$$\{Supply, Demand, Competition, Strategic\} \prec \{Campaign\} \prec \\ \{Quality, Conversion, Profit\}$$

The sequence in which the variables are eliminated during the triangulation step is shown in TABLE 8.1, along with the assigned numbers.

TABLE 8.1: : Numbering of variables during triangulation

Variable	Number
Profit	8
Conversion	7
Quality	6
Campaign	5
Competition	4
Strategic	3
Demand	2
Supply	1

The five cliques identified during the triangulation step and their numbers are given below:

$\mathbf{C_1}$: $\{Demand, Supply, Strategic\} \quad \rightarrow 3$
$\mathbf{C_2}$: $\{Demand, Competition, Strategic\} \quad \rightarrow 4$
$\mathbf{C_3}$: $\{Competition, Strategic, Campaign\} \quad \rightarrow 5$
$\mathbf{C_4}$: $\{Competition, Campaign, Quality, Conversion\}\, \{\} \quad \rightarrow 7$
$\mathbf{C_5}$: $\{Conversion, Profit\} \quad \rightarrow 8$

To construct a strong junction tree, we start with $\mathbf{C_1}$ as the root. FIGURE 8.12 shows the strong junction tree based on these cliques. The variables that were eliminated first (such as *Profit* and *Conversion*) are placed farthest from the root (clique number 1) in the strong junction tree.

Inferencing in a strong junction tree employs a special collect operation from the leaves to the root of the tree. This operation is similar to the one for computing EU at the root node of a decision tree as shown in FIGURE 8.1. The difference is that a node here takes the form of a clique rather than a single variable. In addition to associating a probability potential with each clique of the tree, a utility potential is also associated with each clique. The utility potential for a clique is the sum of the utility functions assigned to it, and is a *null* function if no utility functions are assigned to it.

Example

Continuing with our earlier example, FIGURE 8.13 shows an assignment of probability distributions and utility functions. The cost utility function associated with the node *Conversion* and the credit utility function are assigned to the clique $\mathbf{C}_5$, since the parents of the corresponding two utility nodes belong to $\mathbf{C}_5$. Similarly, the cost utility function associated with the node *Campaign* could have been assigned to either of the two cliques $\mathbf{C}_3$ and $\mathbf{C}_4$ containing the variable *Campaign*, so $\mathbf{C}_3$ was chosen arbitrarily.

The computation of the utility potential for the node $\mathbf{C_5}$ is given below in FIGURE 8.14, based on the two utility functions for the two nodes for cost and credit.

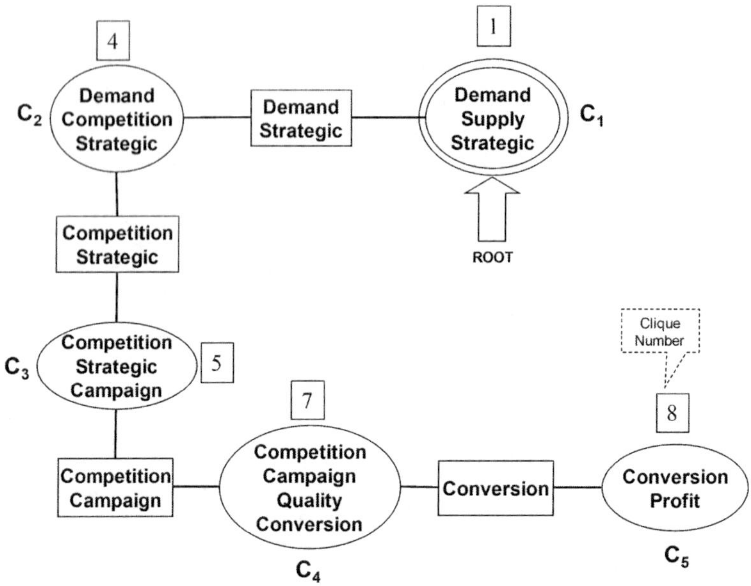

FIGURE 8.12 : Strong junction tree

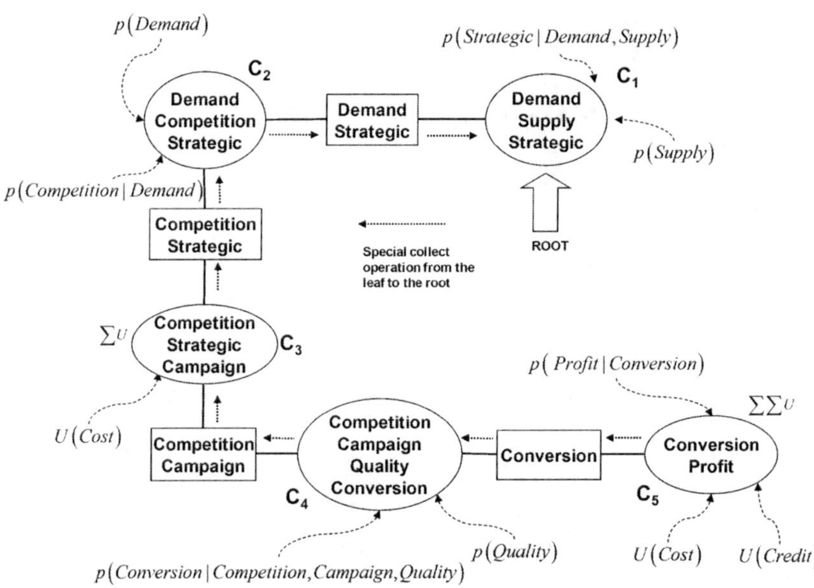

FIGURE 8.13 : Assignment of probability distributions and utility functions to cliques

Consider the following ordering of the chance and decision variables as before:

$$\{Supply, Demand, Competition, Strategic\} \prec \{Campaign\} \prec \{Quality, Conversion, Profit\}$$

Then the MEU for *Campaign* based on this ordering is (D, Su, Co, St, Ca, Q, Cn, P represent variables *Demand, Supply, Competition, Strategic, Campaign, Quality, Conversion,* and *Profit*, respectively):

$$MEU\,(Campaign) = \sum_{\{D,Su,Co,St\}} \max_{Ca} \sum_{\{Q,Cn,P\}} \sum_{U} U \times p\,(D, Su, Co, St, Q, Cn, P|Ca)$$

Utility for Cost

Conversion ⇒	high	medium	low
Utility	-1000	-500	-100

Utility for Credit

Profit ⇒	large	small	none
Utility	5000	2000	50

Conversion	Profit	Utility
high	large	4000
high	small	1000
high	none	-950
medium	large	4500
medium	small	1500
medium	none	-450
low	large	4900
low	small	1900
low	none	-50

FIGURE 8.14 : Utility potential

The special collect operation on the strong junction tree in FIGURE 8.13 allows the MEU to be computed at node 5 (clique $\mathbf{C_3}$) as follows:

$$MEU\,(Ca) = \max_{Ca} \sum_{\{Co,St\}} \left(\begin{array}{l} U\,(Cost) \times p\,(Co, St, Ca) \times \\ \sum\limits_{\{Q,Cn\}} p\,(Co, Ca, Cn, Q) \sum\limits_{P} \sum\limits_{U} U \times p\,(Cn, P) \end{array} \right)$$

where U is the sum utility as shown in FIGURE 8.14. In this example, node 5 could also have been considered as the root node.

Example

We consider the ID in FIGURE 8.15 to illustrate another product launch scenario where the objective is to minimize the overall cost. The set of three hypotheses or possible campaign recommendations are based on email and phone call campaigns, and no campaign at all. The phone call campaign is much more expensive than the email campaign, but is more effective. The total loss of existing customers as a result of increased competition depends on the campaign effect on retention and on whether a loyalty bonus to each existing customer is being offered or not. If such a bonus is not offered then it is likely that more customers will be lost than if one is offered. The state of the chance variable *Effect on Retention* should be known before the decision-maker makes a decision to offer a loyalty bonus.

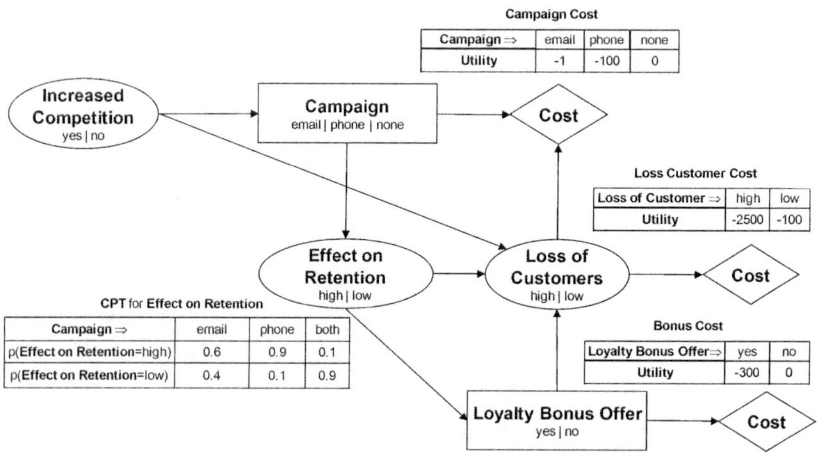

FIGURE 8.15 : An example ID in the product launch domain

FIGURE 8.16 shows an implementation of the ID in FIGURE 8.15 on the HUGIN platform. The evidence for increased competition has been propagated and the email campaign action has been taken. It shows positive expected utility for a loyalty bonus offer.

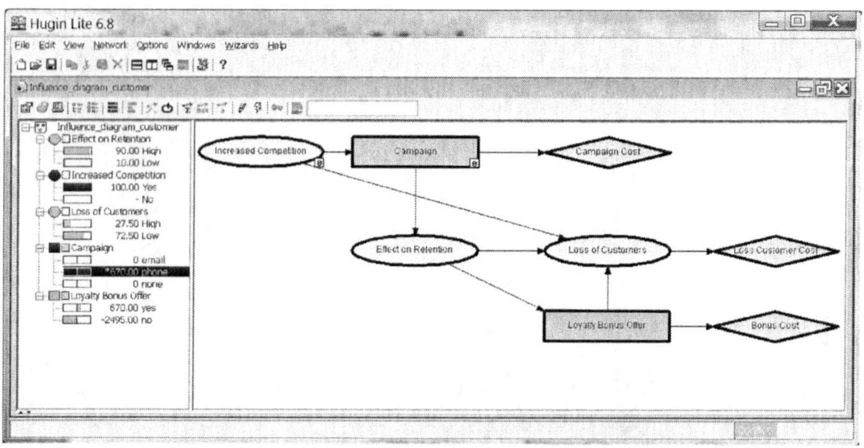

FIGURE 8.16 : An implementation of the ID in FIGURE 8.15

An alternative argumentation approach can also be employed to aid in selecting a campaign type and loyalty bonus offer. TABLE 8.2 shows a selection of arguments. The following section describes the symbolic argumentation-based approach to decision support.

TABLE 8.2: : Argumentation approach to the selection of campaign

IF there is no increase in competition AND the number of customers lost is low THEN select none WITH certainty 0.8
IF there is an increased competition AND the effect of retention is low THEN select phone WITH certainty 0.9

8.3 SYMBOLIC ARGUMENTATION FOR DECISION SUPPORT

This section presents the argumentation approach to decision-making. Arguments for and against decision options in symbolic argumentation are expressed in high-level, logical, if-then rules incorporating subjective probabilities from decision-makers representing the argument strengths. To aggregate a set of such diverse probabilistic and possibly inconsistent arguments for and against the decision options acquired from experts, we apply the Dempster-Shafer theory to compute degrees of belief for decision options. Incoming evidence is used to compute degrees of belief, and hence rankings, among the decision options. TABLE 8.3 below illustrates the symbolic argumentation in the context of our product launch scenario.

TABLE 8.3: : Summary of symbolic argumentation for a competitive product launch scenario

Situation: A competitive product is going to be launched soon The competing company has adopted an aggressive marketing campaign
Essential Elements of Information: The competing product has greater functionalities The price of the competing product is lower The competing company has larger distribution channels The competing company was successful in the past with new products The demand for this type of product is high

TABLE 8.3: : Summary of symbolic argumentation for a competitive product launch scenario

Possible Responses (hypotheses):
Upgrade the existing product
Launch a new campaign promoting the existing product
Do nothing

As shown in TABLE 8.3, a situation occurs, and sources report the essential elements of information. Possible responses are then listed and the argumentation process recommends the one with the highest support from the accumulated evidence and existing data. Knowledge from subject-matter experts used to construct and evaluate arguments is represented by rules. Example arguments for and against the candidate responses in the scenario are shown in TABLE 8.4 and TABLE 8.5, respectively. These arguments must be structured in terms of converting antecedents and consequents to propositional symbols from a well-defined ontology of the marketing domain. The values of the *strengths* of arguments for ($s1$, $s2$, $s3$, $s4$, $s5$) and against ($n1$, $n2$) can be obtained through a knowledge elicitation process with expert decision-makers.

TABLE 8.4: : Example arguments for the candidates

IF the existing product is the main source of revenue AND the demand for the existing product will continue to grow AND the competing product has greater functionalities THEN upgrade product (s1)
IF the company has the financial ability AND the existing product is a household brand THEN launch campaign (s2)
IF an upgrade to the existing product is time-consuming AND the existing product is the main source of revenue THEN launch campaign (s3)
IF the existing product contributes insignificant revenue OR upgrade is already planned THEN do nothing (s4)
IF an upgrade is easy to fit into the existing infrastructure THEN upgrade product (s5)

TABLE 8.5: : Example arguments against the candidates

IF the product is not strategic to the company AND return is low THEN NOT upgrade product or launch campaign (n1)

TABLE 8.5: : Example arguments against the candidates

IF the existing product is the main source of revenue THEN NOT do nothing (n2)

Justifications for and against candidate responses are based on the arguments in TABLE 8.4 using relevant information such as the product quality, importance of the product, financial ability to campaign, return, etc. The evaluation of these arguments is performed through a process of *aggregation*. This process includes not only an assessment of the number and strength of each independent argument and the collective force of argument for each hypothesis, but also the plausibility of the evidence and justification for each line of argument. For example, the second and third arguments for the response "launch campaign" will be aggregated to produce a combined strength that is expected to be higher than both $s2$ and $s3$, provided all the conditions in the two antecedents of the two arguments are satisfied based on the information obtained from the company's internal sources. If we use the probabilistic dictionary $[0, 1]$ to represent source reliability, then the two arguments can be aggregated by using Dempster's rule of combination as presented in the AI chapter. On the other hand, if we use the dictionary $[-1, +1]$, the arguments can be combined by using formulae from the certainty factor formalism as presented in the AI chapter. Suppose $s23$ is the combined strength after the aggregation.

All arguments for and against each response are combined in the above manner to accumulate total evidence for and against each response. Evidence against each response discounts evidence for the response. For example, total evidence for and against the response "launch campaign" (the first argument in the above table) is, respectively, $s23$ and $n1$, and therefore the aggregated evidence is $s23\,(1 - n1) \,/\, (1 - s23 * n1)$. If this aggregation process associates more weights to the response "launch campaign" than to any other response, it will be considered as the best option in the current situation.

8.3.1 Measuring Consensus

In this subsection, we present a criterion for measuring consensus among disparate sources when the underlying mechanism for handling uncertainty is the Dempster-Shafer theory. First we explain the need to measure consensus in a decision-making context with the help of a concrete example.

Example

Suppose some source of evidence heavily suggests against an *Upgrade* of the existing product (that is, either to *Launch* a new campaign or to do *Nothing*) and the values 0.9 and 0 together constitute a belief function. The focal element is $\{Launch, Nothing\}$ and the mass distribution is $m_1(\{Launch, Nothing\}) = 0.9$. We know nothing about the remaining probability 0.1, so it is allocated to the whole frame of discernment $\Omega = \{Upgrade, Launch, Nothing\}$. Another source of evidence heavily suggests against the use of *Launch*. The mass distribution in this case is $m_2(\{Upgrade, Nothing\}) = 0.9$. The remaining probability, as before, is allocated to the whole frame of discernment. Dempster's rule can then be used to combine the masses as shown in TABLE 8.6:

TABLE 8.6: : Combination of masses by Dempster's rule

La – *Launch* *Up* – *Upgrade* *No* – *Nothing*	$m_2(\{Up, No\}) = 0.90$	$m_2(\Omega) = 0.10$
$m_1(\{La, No\}) = 0.90$	$m_{1,2}(\{No\}) = 0.81$	$m_{1,2}(\{La, No\}) = 0.09$
$m_1(\Omega) = 0.10$	$m_{1,2}(\{Up, No\}) = 0.09$	$m_{1,2}(\Omega) = 0.01$

Therefore, the combined belief and plausibility are computed in the TABLE 8.7:

TABLE 8.7: : Computations of belief and plausibility

Focal Element (A)	$Bel(A)$	$Pl(A)$
$\{Nothing\}$	0.81	1.0
$\{Upgrade, Nothing\}$	0.09	0.91
$\{Launch, Nothing\}$	0.09	0.91
Ω	1.0	1.0

The above result is counterintuitive, given that neither of the two sources of evidence explicitly supported the option *Nothing*. Moreover, the table above does not reflect the underlying high level of disagreement.

The consensus metric provided below will be able to highlight the case presented above. The "entropy"-based algorithm presented here generates a very low (2.3 out of 3) degree of consensus (zero or minimum entropy is the highest consensus). The consensus-measuring criterion is based on the generalization of the concept of entropy from point function to set function (Stephanou and Lu, 1988). This generalization is composed of three measurements: belief entropy, core entropy, and partial ignorance.

Suppose Ω is a frame of discernment, m is a basic probability assignment, and $\mathbf{F} = \{A_1, ..., A_n\}$ is the set of focal elements.

The *belief entropy* of the pair $\langle m, \mathbf{F} \rangle$ is defined as follows (log is base 2):

$$E_b(m, \mathbf{F}) = -\sum_{i=1}^{n} m(A_i) \log m(A_i)$$

The belief entropy is a measure of the degree of confusion in the decision maker's knowledge about the exact fraction of belief that should be committed to each focal element in **F**. Thus, the belief entropy is naturally equal to zero if the entire belief is committed to a single focal element, that is, $m(A_k) = 1$, for some k. The maximum belief entropy occurs when belief is divided in equal fractions among the focal elements.

The *core entropy* of the pair $\langle m, \mathbf{F} \rangle$ is defined as follows:

$$E_c(m, \mathbf{F}) = -\sum_{i=1}^{n} r_i \log r_i$$

where

$$r_i = \frac{||A_i|| - 1}{\sum_{j=1}^{n} (||A_i|| - 1)}$$

and $||A_i||$ is the cardinality of A_i ($0 \log 0$ is considered 0). The core entropy is a measure of the degree of confusion in the decision-maker's knowledge of which focal elements may contain the true value. If belief is committed to a single focal element A_k, then r_k is one, and therefore the core entropy is equal to zero. The core entropy is at its maximum when belief is divided among a number of focal elements with the same cardinality.

The *partial ignorance* of the pair $\langle m, \mathbf{F} \rangle$ is defined as follows:

$$I(m, \mathbf{F}) = \sum_{i=1}^{n} m(A_i) \, s_i(A_i)$$

Where

$$s_i(A_i) = \frac{||A_i|| - 1}{||\Omega|| - 1}$$

and $||A_i||$ is the cardinality of A_i, and the assumption is that the frame of discernment has more than one element. Partial ignorance is a measure of the inability to confine the true value within a small-sized focal element. Consequently, partial ignorance is large when a large belief is committed to large focal elements. It is zero when the entire belief is committed to a singleton.

The *generalized entropy* of the pair $\langle m, \mathbf{F} \rangle$ is then defined as follows:

$$E(m, \mathbf{F}) = E_b(m, \mathbf{F}) + E_c(m, \mathbf{F}) + I(m, \mathbf{F})$$

Now suppose that we have two basic probability assignments m_1 and m_2, corresponding to two different expert knowledge sources, defining focal elements $\{A, \Omega\}$ and $\{B, \Omega\}$, respectively, where $A \subset \Omega$ and $B \subset \Omega$. Let us consider four different cases as shown in FIGURE 8.17.

It can be shown that the generalized entropy of the knowledge sources via Dempster's rule of combination for each of the first three cases is smaller than

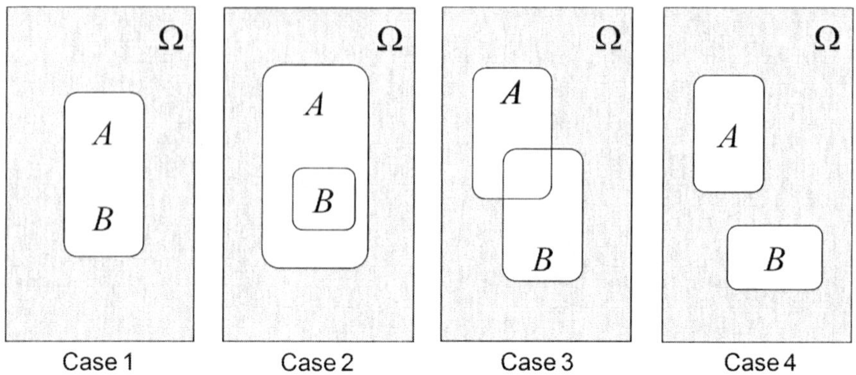

FIGURE 8.17 : Combining expert knowledge sources (Stephanou and Lu, 1988)

the sum of the individual entropies of the knowledge sources. In other words, the following relation holds for the first three cases:

$$E(m_{12}, \mathbf{F}) \le E(m_1, \mathbf{F}) + E(m_2, \mathbf{F})$$

The above implies that the pooling of two concordant bodies of evidence reduces entropy. The disjointedness between A and B in the last case indicates that there are two bodies of evidence supporting two conflicting propositions, and hence the combined generalized entropy does not necessarily get reduced.

Example

To illustrate reduction of entropy, consider the frame of discernment $\Omega = \{Upgrade, Launch, Nothing\}$, the two focal elements $\{Upgrade, Nothing\}$ and $\{Launch, Nothing\}$, and their corresponding basic probability assignments:

$$\begin{array}{l} A = \{Upgrade, Nothing\}, \quad B = \{Launch, Nothing\} \\ \mathbf{F}_1 = \{A, \Omega\}, \quad \mathbf{F}_2 = \{B, \Omega\} \\ m_1(A) = 0.7, m_1(\Omega) = 0.3, \quad m_2(B) = 0.6, m_2(\Omega) = 0.4 \end{array}$$

The entropies and ignorance are computed as follows:

Belief Entropy:

$$\begin{aligned} &E_b(m_1, \mathbf{F}_1) \\ &\quad = -m_1(A)\log m_1(A) - m_1(\Omega)\log m_1(\Omega) \\ &\quad = -0.7\log 0.7 - 0.3\log 0.3 = 0.88 \end{aligned}$$

$$\begin{aligned} &E_b(m_2, \mathbf{F}_2) \\ &\quad = -m_2(B)\log m_2(B) - m_2(\Omega)\log m_2(\Omega) \\ &\quad = -0.6\log 0.6 - 0.4\log 0.4 = 0.97 \end{aligned}$$

Core Entropy:

$$\begin{aligned} & E_c(m_1, \mathbf{F}_1) \\ & \quad = -r_1(A) \log r_1(A) - r_1(\Omega) \log r_1(\Omega) \\ & \quad = -\tfrac{1}{3} \log \tfrac{1}{3} - \tfrac{2}{3} \log \tfrac{2}{3} = 0.92 \\ & E_c(m_2, \mathbf{F}_2) \\ & \quad = -r_2(B) \log r_2(B) - r_2(\Omega) \log r_2(\Omega) \\ & \quad = -\tfrac{1}{3} \log \tfrac{1}{3} - \tfrac{2}{3} \log \tfrac{2}{3} = 0.92 \end{aligned}$$

Partial Ignorance:

$$\begin{aligned} & I(m_1, \mathbf{F}_1) = m_1(A) s_1(A) + m_1(\Omega) s_2(\Omega) \\ & \quad = 0.7 \cdot \tfrac{1}{2} + 0.3 \cdot \tfrac{2}{2} = 0.65 \\ & I(m_2, \mathbf{F}_2) = m_2(B) s_1(B) + m_2(\Omega) s_2(\Omega) \\ & \quad = 0.6 \cdot \tfrac{1}{2} + 0.4 \cdot \tfrac{2}{2} = 0.7 \end{aligned}$$

Generalized Entropy:

$$\begin{aligned} E(m_1, \mathbf{F}_1) = 0.88 + 0.92 + 0.65 = 2.45 \\ E(m_2, \mathbf{F}_2) = 0.97 + 0.92 + 0.70 = 2.59 \end{aligned}$$

Now, consider Case 3 in FIGURE 8.17. The Dempster combination rule yields a new set of focal elements and basic probability assignments as follows:

$$\begin{aligned} & A \cap B = \{Nothing\} \\ & \mathbf{F} = \{A, B, A \cap B, \Omega\} \\ & m_{1,2}(A) = 0.18, m_{1,2}(B) = 0.28, m_{1,2}(A \cap B) = 0.42, m_{1,2}(\Omega) = 0.12 \end{aligned}$$

The entropies and ignorance for the combined set of focal elements are computed as follows:

Belief Entropy:

$$\begin{aligned} E_b(m_{1,2}, \mathbf{F}) = & -0.18 \log 0.18 - 0.28 \log 0.28 \\ & -0.42 \log 0.42 - 0.12 \log 0.12 = 1.85 \end{aligned}$$

Core Entropy:

$$E_c(m_{1,2}, \mathbf{F}) = -\frac{1}{4} \log \frac{1}{4} - \frac{1}{4} \log \frac{1}{4} - \frac{0}{4} \log \frac{0}{4} - \frac{2}{4} \log \frac{2}{4} = 1.5$$

Partial Ignorance:

$$I(m_{1,2}, \mathbf{F}) = 0.18 \cdot \frac{1}{2} + 0.28 \cdot \frac{1}{2} + 0.42 \cdot \frac{0}{2} + 0.12 \cdot \frac{2}{2} = 0.35$$

Generalized Entropy:

$$E\left(m_{1,2},\mathbf{F}\right) = 1.85 + 1.50 + 0.35 = 3.70$$

Thus we observe that the relation $E\left(m_{12},\mathbf{F}\right) \leq E\left(m_{1},\mathbf{F}\right) + E\left(m_{2},\mathbf{F}\right)$ holds.

8.3.2 Combining Sources of Varying Confidence

Here we present a credibility transformation function (Yager, 2004) for combining sources with various confidences. This approach discounts the evidence with a credibility factor α and distributes remaining evidence $1-\alpha$ equally among the n elements of the frame of discernment. The transformed credibility function takes the following form:

$$m_{\alpha}\left(A\right) = m\left(A\right)\cdot\alpha + \frac{1-\alpha}{n}$$

In the Bayesian formalism where each focal element A is a singleton set, we distribute the remaining evidence $1-\alpha$ as per their prior probabilities. In other words, we modify the credibility function as the following:

$$p_{\alpha}\left(A\right) = p\left(A\right)\cdot\alpha + p_{0}\left(A\right)\cdot\frac{1-\alpha}{n}$$

When prior probabilities are uniformly distributed among elements of the frame of discernment, this becomes a special case of the credibility function for the Dempster-Shafer case. Moreover, if the prior probability of A is zero, then it remains zero after the transformation via the credibility function.

Example

$$\begin{aligned}&\Omega = \{Upgrade, Launch, Nothing\}\\&A = \{Upgrade, Launch\}\\&m_{1}\left(A\right) = 0.7\end{aligned}$$

If the reliability of the source of m_1 is 0.8, then

$$m_{0.8}\left(A\right) = 0.7\cdot 0.8 + \frac{1-0.8}{2} = 0.66$$

$$m_{0.8}\left(\Omega\right) = 0.3\cdot 0.8 + \frac{1-0.8}{2} = 0.34$$

8.4 FURTHER READING

More details on the strong junction tree algorithm presented in this chapter can be found in Jensen et al. (1994) and Shenoy (1992). From the historical perspective, Howard and Matheson (1981) first introduced IDs, and their ability to model decision problems with uncertainty by transforming them into decision trees, for a single decision-maker. Shachter (1986) described a reduction-based approach for evaluating IDs. More details on symbolic argumentation, and the underlying theoretical foundation, can be found in Fox and Das (2000) and Das (2005 & 2008a). The paper by Stephanou and Lu (1988) is the source of the entropy-based consensus measurement presented here.

CHAPTER 9

Time Series Modeling and Forecasting

This chapter presents temporal model-based approaches to analytics in dynamic, fast-changing environments such as the financial market. Temporal approaches, as opposed to static- or snapshot-based approaches, handle time formally, in that random variables in a temporal model change their values as time changes to form a time series. Temporal models are therefore appropriate for modeling the stochastic nature of a dynamic environment such as the financial market. We present the Kalman Filter (KF) technique for estimating the state of a dynamic system where transition from one state to another is assumed to be linear. We then discuss nonlinear transition via the Extended Kalman Filter (EKF).

We next present two graphical approaches to temporal modeling, namely, Hidden Markov Models (HMMs) and the Dynamic Bayesian Networks (DBNs). HMMs are also useful for sequence recognition, such as understanding semantics of word sequences in text data and patterns in the financial market over time. DBNs generalize HMMs, and DBNs are temporal extensions of Bayesian Belief Networks (BNs) presented earlier in the book. Readers are therefore advised to understand the BN technology before reading the section on DBNs in this chapter. We cover various approaches to learning HMMs and DBNs. Note that the concepts of states and state transitions, and models of transition and observation, underlie all of these temporal models.

9.1 PROBLEM MODELING

A *time-series* is a sequence $X_0, X_1, X_2, ...$ of data points representing the state of a "system" as it evolves over time. Each X_k represents the system's state at time step k. The definition of a system in this context is very broad; it could be any physical system or even an abstract phenomenon. The state is composed of a set of attributes of the system modeling its behavior. Hence X_k

is a vector of attribute values. For example, one can represent the state of a vehicle in terms of its location, speed, fuel status, engine temperature, and so on. The state of a financial market can be modeled in terms of its trend (bear or bull) and values of various indices. Some of these attributes may not be directly observable. If we say that a vehicle is healthy, the attribute "health" is not directly observable, but is inferred from other observables such as engine temperature, noise, and emissions. Similarly, financial market trends are not directly observable but can be inferred from other observables such as the values of various indices and stock prices of major companies.

Modeling a time-series problem involves deciding on what attributes constitute X_k and then defining state transition and observation models. The state transition model infers X_{k+1} from X_k. In other words, we can use such a model to predict market trends, for example. The observation model indicates what one expects to observe at time t when the system is in state X_k. The actual and expected observations are used to adjust the parameters of the model. Model adjustments and predictions are part of the model estimation problem.

9.1.1 State Transition and Observation Models

A discrete-time state-space model of a dynamical system consists of the following two equations of transition (or motion) and observation (or measurement) models:

$$\left.\begin{aligned} X_{k+1} &= f\left(X_k, U_k\right) + W_k \\ Z_k &= h\left(X_k\right) + V_k \end{aligned}\right\} k = 0, 1, 2, ...$$

where

- $X_k \in \mathrm{R}^{n_x}$ is the system state at the time step k (actual time is t_k);
- $Z_k \in \mathrm{R}^{n_z}$ is the measurement or observed output state at the time step k;
- $U_k \in \mathrm{R}^{n_u}$ is the known input at the time step k;
- $W_k \in \mathrm{R}^{n_w}$ is the process or state white noise;
- $V_k \in \mathrm{R}^{n_v}$ is the measurement white noise;
- $f : \mathrm{R}^{n_x} \rightarrow \mathrm{R}^{n_x}$ is the known state transition function to predict the system state one-step ahead; and
- $h : \mathrm{R}^{n_x} \rightarrow \mathrm{R}^{n_x}$ is the known observations function to relate system states to observations.

Note that the attributes of a system state vector X_k are continuous-valued in this section and the next, but they may also be categorical in a hybrid model

(Pfeffer et al., 2007). The noise variables W_k and V_k are assumed to be independent of each other, and with zero-mean normal probability distributions as

$$\begin{array}{l} p(W_k) \sim N(0, Q_k) \\ p(V_k) \sim N(0, R_k) \end{array}$$

where Q_k and R_k are, respectively, the process and measurement noise covariance matrices at time step k. Therefore,

$$\begin{array}{l} E[W_k] = E[V_k] = 0, \ \ k = 0, 1, 2, ... \\ \left. \begin{array}{l} E\left[W_i W_j^T\right] = \delta_{ij} Q_i \\ E\left[V_i V_j^T\right] = \delta_{ij} R_i \end{array} \right\} \ i, j = 0, 1, 2, ... \end{array}$$

Since the process and observation noises are independent, we have

$$E\left[W_i V_j^T\right] = 0 \quad i, j = 0, 1, 2, ...$$

The values of the initial state and the noise variables at each time step k are uncertain and are described by probability models. The transition and observation equations along with these probability models prescribe the following transition and measurement PDFs, providing a complete description of the system:

$$\begin{array}{l} p(X_0) \\ \left. \begin{array}{l} p(X_{k+1} | X_k, U_k) \\ p(Z_k | X_k) \end{array} \right\} k = 0, 1, 2, ... \end{array}$$

9.1.2 Estimation Problem

The estimate of the system state X_k at time step k is represented by the posterior conditional PDF $p(X_k | Z_{1:i}, U_{1:k})$, where $Z_{1:i} = \{Z_1, ..., Z_i\}$ is the cumulative measurements up to time i and $U_{1:k} = \{U_1, ..., U_k\}$ is the cumulative known inputs up to the time step k. Various types of the *estimation problem* are then listed below:

- If $i = k$ then the problem of estimating $p(X_k | Z_{1:k}, U_{1:k})$ is called *filtering*.
- If $i < k$ then the problem is called *prediction*.
- If $i > k$ then the problem is called *smoothing*.

Often we will evaluate the filtering problem at every time step k in a Markovian fashion, that is, sequentially update $p(X_k | Z_{1:k}, U_{1:k})$ as $p(X_k | Z_k, U_k)$. In other words, the update is conditional on the observed system input and output up to the current time, but only by using the following information: 1) $p(X_k | Z_{k-1}, U_{k-1})$ produced at the end of the previous time step; 2) observation data from the current time step; and 3) the prescribed probabilistic noise models W_k and V_k. Unless otherwise stated, the conditioning of every PDF on the input variable U_k is left implicit.

The Bayesian approach to the solution of the prediction, filtering, and smoothing problems is specified below:

$$p\left(X_k|Z_{1:k-1}\right) = \int\limits_{R^{n_x}} p\left(X_k|X_{k-1}\right) p\left(X_{k-1}|Z_{1:k-1}\right) dX_{k-1}$$

$$\begin{aligned} & p\left(X_k|Z_{1:k}\right) \\ & = p\left(X_k|Z_k, Z_{1:k-1}\right) \\ & = \frac{p(Z_k|X_k)p(X_k|Z_{1:k-1})}{p(Z_k|Z_{1:k-1})} \\ & = \frac{p(Z_k|X_k)p(X_k|Z_{1:k-1})}{\int\limits_{R^{n_x}} p(Z_k|X_k)p(X_k|Z_{1:k-1})\, dX_k} \end{aligned}$$

where the current observations are independent of the past observations given the system state, that is, $p\left(Z_k|X_k, Z_{1:k-1}\right) = p\left(Z_k|X_k\right)$. Now,

$$\begin{aligned} & p\left(X_k|Z_{1:i}\right) \\ & = p\left(X_k|Z_{1:k}, Z_{k+1:i}\right) \\ & = p\left(X_k|Z_{1:k}\right) \frac{p(Z_{k+1:i}|X_k, Z_{1:k})}{p(Z_{k+1:i}|Z_{1:k})} \\ & = p\left(X_k|Z_{1:k}\right) \int\limits_{R^{n_x}} \frac{p(Z_{k+1:i}|X_{k+1}, Z_{1:k})p(X_{k+1}|X_k, Z_{1:k})}{p(Z_{k+1:i}|Z_{1:k})} dX_{k+1} \\ & = p\left(X_k|Z_{1:k}\right) \int\limits_{R^{n_x}} \frac{p(X_{k+1}|Z_{1:i})}{p(X_{k+1}|Z_{1:k})} p\left(X_{k+1}|X_k\right) dX_{k+1} \end{aligned}$$

where the future states are independent of the current observations given the system's current state, that is, $p\left(X_{k+1}|X_k, Z_{1:k}\right) = p\left(X_{k+1}|X_k\right)$
The major challenge to the Bayesian approach is that the above estimation problems involving high-dimensional integrals usually do not have a closed-form solution. (If an equation, expressed in terms of generally accepted functions and mathematical operations, is a solution to a given problem, then the equation is a *closed-form solution* to the problem.) A closed-form solution exists when the transition and observation models are linear and uncertainties are Gaussian. A linear system can be described by the following equations:

$$\left.\begin{aligned} X_{k+1} &= F_k X_k + G_k U_k + W_k \\ Z_k &= H_k X_k + V_k \end{aligned}\right\} k = 0, 1, 2, \ldots$$

where F_k, G_k, and H_k are, respectively, transition, input, and observation model matrices.

Example

Suppose we want to predict the opening price of a stock and assume that x_k is the price at time step k. The state vector comprised is defined as follows:

$$X_k = \begin{bmatrix} x_k \\ x_{k-1} \\ x_{k-2} \end{bmatrix}$$

where x_i is the opening price at time point i. An example predicted opening price model is the weighted sum of the previous three days:

$$x_{k+1} = 0.6 * x_k + 0.3 * x_{k-1} + 0.1 * x_{k-2}$$

Hence the transition matrix is F for in the transition equation $X_{k+1} = FX_k + W_k$ is defined as follows:

$$\begin{bmatrix} x_{k+1} \\ x_k \\ x_{k-1} \end{bmatrix} = \begin{bmatrix} 0.6 & 0.3 & 0.1 \\ 1 & 0 & 0 \\ 0 & 1 & 0 \end{bmatrix} \begin{bmatrix} x_k \\ x_{k-1} \\ x_{k-2} \end{bmatrix} + W_k$$

where W_k is Gaussian with zero mean and process noise covariance as defined in the above problem modeling section. Note that there is no input to control the state. We assume the noise-free measurement as the observation model:

$$Z_k = X_k$$

Later we will apply a Kalman filter to estimate X_{k+1} upon observation at time step $k + 1$.

Example

Suppose we want to track accumulated spending on a single account, and its state vector is composed of the amount a_k spent so far and the rate r_k per day as:

$$X_k = \begin{bmatrix} a_k \\ r_k \end{bmatrix}$$

We are able to measure the amount spent and the rate every T days (i.e., $T = t_{k+1} - t_k$ is the sampling or observation interval period). The spending at time step k is controlled via input u_k, which could be zero, positive, or negative, representing respectively, no change, increase, and decrease in spending. Therefore, the transition and observation models can be encoded as the following linear equations:

$$X_{k+1} = \begin{bmatrix} 1 & T \\ 0 & 1 \end{bmatrix} X_k + \begin{bmatrix} 0 \\ u_k \end{bmatrix} + W_k$$

$$Z_k = \begin{bmatrix} 1 & 0 \end{bmatrix} X_k + V_k$$

The noise is due to some unexpected spending that could be budgeted for in advance.

9.2 KALMAN FILTER (KF)

The Kalman Filter (KF) (Kalman, 1960; Bar-Shalom and Fortmann, 1988) is based on a state-space formulation of a continuous or discrete-time system.

Here we focus our attention on discrete-time KF. The system must be linear, but may be time-variant. Recall that the transition and observation models for a linear system have the following form:

$$\left.\begin{array}{c} X_k = F_{k-1}X_{k-1} + G_{k-1}U_{k-1} + W_{k-1} \\ Z_k = H_k X_k + V_k \end{array}\right\} k = 1, 2, ...$$

Given a set of observations, KF gives an estimate of the state of the dynamical system. We provide a detailed derivation of the KF, as it is the most dominant and fundamental filtering technique. Readers who are not interested in this level of detail may go directly to FIGURE 9.1 to check the overall KF steps.

For the case of Gaussian signals, and given the assumed linear model, the state estimate is optimum in the sense that it minimizes the norm of the difference between the estimate and the actual state. Symbolically,

$$\hat{X}_{i|j} = \underset{\hat{X}_{i|j}}{\arg\min}\, E\left[\left(X_i - \hat{X}_{i|j}\right)\left(X_i - \hat{X}_{i|j}\right)^T |Z_{1:j}\right]$$

where $\hat{X}_{i|j}$ is the estimate of the state at time step i given all the observations up to time step j. The solution to this minimization problem can be obtained by differentiating with respect to the expected value and equating the resultant expression to zero:

$$\begin{aligned} &\frac{\partial}{\partial \hat{X}_{i|j}} E\left[\left(X_i - \hat{X}_{i|j}\right)\left(X_i - \hat{X}_{i|j}\right)^T |Z_{1:j}\right] \\ &= \frac{\partial}{\partial \hat{X}_{i|j}}\left[\int_{X_i} \left(X_i - \hat{X}_{i|j}\right)\left(X_i - \hat{X}_{i|j}\right)^T p\left(X_i|Z_{1:j}\right) dX_i\right] \\ &= 2\int_{X_i} \left(X_i - \hat{X}_{i|j}\right) p\left(X_i|Z_{1:j}\right) dX_i \\ &= 0 \end{aligned}$$

Therefore,

$$\hat{X}_{i|j} \int_{X_i} p\left(X_i|Z_{1:j}\right) dX_i = \int_{X_i} X_i p\left(X_i|Z_{1:j}\right) dX_i$$

$$\text{i.e., } \hat{X}_{i|j} = E\left[X_i|Z_{1:j}\right]$$

Specifically,

$$\begin{aligned} &\hat{X}_{k|k-1} \\ &= E\left[X_k|Z_{1:k-1}\right] \\ &= E\left[F_{k-1}X_{k-1} + G_{k-1}U_{k-1} + W_{k-1}|Z_{1:k-1}\right] \\ &= F_{k-1}E\left[X_{k-1}|Z_{1:k-1}\right] + G_{k-1}U_{k-1} + E\left[W_{k-1}|Z_{1:k-1}\right] \\ &= F_{k-1}\hat{X}_{k-1|k-1} + G_{k-1}U_{k-1} \end{aligned}$$

since the input is independent of observations, and the noise is of zero-mean.

For a liner filtering of the prediction $\hat{X}_{k|k-1}$ based on the current observation Z_k, the filtered estimate $\hat{X}_{k|k}$ can be written as a linear weighted sum of the prediction and observation as the following:

$$\hat{X}_{k|k} = K_k Z_k + \bar{K}_k \hat{X}_{k|k-1}$$

for some matrices K_k and $\bar{K}_k$, and their relationship is derived as follows.

First, $E\left[\left(X_k - \hat{X}_{k|k}\right) Z_i^T\right] = 0,\ i = 1, ..., k,$

[applying the orthogonality principle]

i.e., $E\left[\left(F_{k-1}X_{k-1} + G_{k-1}U_{k-1} + W_{k-1} - K_k Z_k - \bar{K}_k \hat{X}_{k|k-1}\right) Z_i^T\right] = 0$

[substituting the values of X_k and $\hat{X}_{k|k}$]

i.e., $F_{k-1}E\left[X_{k-1}\right] Z_i^T + G_{k-1}U_{k-1}Z_i^T - K_k E\left[Z_k\right] Z_i^T - \bar{K}_k E\left[\hat{X}_{k|k-1}\right] Z_i^T = 0$

[using $E\left[W_k\right] = 0$]

i.e., $F_{k-1}E\left[X_{k-1}\right] Z_i^T + G_{k-1}U_{k-1}Z_i^T - K_k E\left[H_k X_k + V_k\right] Z_i^T - \bar{K}_k E\left[\hat{X}_{k|k-1}\right] Z_i^T = 0$

[substituting the values of Z_k]

i.e., $F_{k-1}E\left[X_{k-1}\right] Z_i^T + G_{k-1}U_{k-1}Z_i^T - K_k H_k E\left[X_k\right] Z_i^T - \bar{K}_k E\left[\hat{X}_{k|k-1}\right] Z_i^T = 0$

[using $E\left[V_k\right] = 0$]

i.e., $E\left[X_k\right] Z_i^T - K_k H_k E\left[X_k\right] Z_i^T - \bar{K}_k E\left[\hat{X}_{k|k-1}\right] Z_i^T = 0$

[$X_k = F_{k-1}X_{k-1} + G_{k-1}U_{k-1} + W_{k-1}$ gives
$F_{k-1}E\left[X_{k-1}\right] = E\left[X_k\right] - G_{k-1}U_{k-1}$, since $E\left[W_k\right] = 0$]

i.e., $E\left[X_k - K_k H_k X_k - \bar{K}_k \hat{X}_{k|k-1}\right] Z_i^T = 0$

i.e., $E\left[\left(X_k - K_k H_k X_k - \bar{K}_k X_k\right) + \bar{K}_k\left(X_k - \hat{X}_{k|k-1}\right)\right] Z_i^T = 0$

i.e., $E\left[\begin{array}{l}\left(X_k - K_k H_k X_k - \bar{K}_k X_k\right) + \\ \bar{K}_k\left(X_k - F_{k-1}\hat{X}_{k-1|k-1} - G_{k-1}U_{k-1}\right)\end{array}\right] Z_i^T = 0$

[since $\hat{X}_{k|k-1} = F_{k-1}\hat{X}_{k-1|k-1} + G_{k-1}U_{k-1}$]

i.e., $E\left[\begin{array}{l}\left(X_k - K_k H_k X_k - \bar{K}_k X_k\right) + \\ \bar{K}_k\left(F_{k-1}X_{k-1} - F_{k-1}\hat{X}_{k-1|k-1} + W_{k-1}\right)\end{array}\right] Z_i^T = 0$

[since $X_k = F_{k-1}X_{k-1} + G_{k-1}U_{k-1} + W_{k-1}$]

i.e., $\left(I - K_k H_k - \bar{K}_k\right) E\left[X_k\right] Z_i^T = 0$

[since $E\left[W_{k-1}\right] = 0$ and $E\left[\left(X_k - \hat{X}_{k|k}\right) Z_i^T\right] = 0,\ i = 1, ..., k$]

i.e., $I - K_k H_k - \bar{K}_k = 0$ [for any given X_k]

i.e., $\bar{K}_k = I - K_k H_k$

Therefore,

$$
\begin{aligned}
&\hat{X}_{k|k} \\
&\quad = K_k Z_k + (I - K_k H_k)\,\hat{X}_{k|k-1} \\
&\quad = \hat{X}_{k|k-1} + K_k\left(Z_k - H_k \hat{X}_{k|k-1}\right)
\end{aligned}
$$

The above result states that the estimation is the sum of the prediction plus some fraction K_k of the difference between the actual and the predicted observation. The value of the constant K_k, known as *Kalman gain*, is yet to be derived. The estimation of the error covariance matrix is:

$$
P_{i|j} = E\left[\left(X_i - \hat{X}_{i|j}\right)\left(X_i - \hat{X}_{i|j}\right)^T |Z_{1:j}\right]
$$

Specifically, $P_{k|k-1} = E\left[\left(X_k - \hat{X}_{k|k-1}\right)\left(X_k - \hat{X}_{k|k-1}\right)^T |Z_{1:k-1}\right]$

Since $\hat{X}_{k|k-1} = F_{k-1}\hat{X}_{k-1|k-1} + G_{k-1}U_{k-1}$ and $X_k = F_{k-1}X_{k-1} + G_{k-1}U_{k-1} + W_{k-1}$, we have the following derivation:

$$
\begin{aligned}
&P_{k|k-1} \\
&\quad = E\left[\left(X_k - \hat{X}_{k|k-1}\right)\left(X_k - \hat{X}_{k|k-1}\right)^T |Z_{1:k-1}\right] \\
&\quad = F_{k-1}E\left[\left(X_{k-1} - \hat{X}_{k-1|k-1}\right)\left(X_{k-1} - \hat{X}_{k-1|k-1}\right)^T |Z_{1:k-1}\right] F_{k-1}^T \\
&\qquad\quad + E\left[W_{k-1}W_{k-1}^T\right]
\end{aligned}
$$

Therefore, $P_{k|k-1} = F_{k-1}\hat{P}_{k-1|k-1}F_{k-1}^T + Q_{k-1}$

Moreover, $P_{k|k} = E\left[\left(X_k - \hat{X}_{k|k}\right)\left(X_k - \hat{X}_{k|k}\right)^T |Z_{1:k}\right]$

Since $\hat{X}_{k|k} = \hat{X}_{k|k-1} + K_k\left(Z_k - H_k\hat{X}_{k|k-1}\right)$ and $Z_k = H_k X_k + V_k$, we have the following derivation:

$$
\begin{aligned}
P_{k|k} &= E\left[\left(X_k - \hat{X}_{k|k}\right)\left(X_k - \hat{X}_{k|k}\right)^T |Z_{1:k}\right] \\
&= E\Big[\left(X_k - \hat{X}_{k|k-1} - K_k\left(Z_k - H_k\hat{X}_{k|k-1}\right)\right) \\
&\qquad \left(X_k - \hat{X}_{k|k-1} - K_k\left(Z_k - H_k\hat{X}_{k|k-1}\right)\right)^T |Z_{1:k}\Big] \\
&= E\Big[\left(X_k - \hat{X}_{k|k-1} - K_k\left(H_k X_k + V_k - H_k\hat{X}_{k|k-1}\right)\right) \\
&\qquad \left(X_k - \hat{X}_{k|k-1} - K_k\left(H_k X_k + V_k - H_k\hat{X}_{k|k-1}\right)\right)^T |Z_{1:k-1}\Big]
\end{aligned}
$$

$$
\begin{aligned}
&= E\left[\left((I - K_k H_k)\left(X_k - \hat{X}_{k|k-1}\right) - K_k V_k\right)\right. \\
&\qquad \left.\left((I - K_k H_k)\left(X_k - \hat{X}_{k|k-1}\right) - K_k V_k\right)^T |Z_{1:k-1}\right] \\
&= (I - K_k H_k) E\left[\left(X_k - \hat{X}_{k|k-1}\right)\left(X_k - \hat{X}_{k|k-1}\right)^T |Z_{1:k-1}\right] \\
&\qquad (I - K_k H_k)^T + K_k E\left[V_k V_k^T\right] K_k^T
\end{aligned}
$$

Since $P_{k|k-1} = E\left[\left(X_k - \hat{X}_{k|k-1}\right)\left(X_k - \hat{X}_{k|k-1}\right)^T |Z_{1:k-1}\right]$, we have the a posteriori estimation of error covariance:

$$
P_{k|k} = (I - K_k H_k) P_{k|k-1} (I - K_k H_k)^T + K_k R_k K_k^T
$$

We are interested in the value of the gain K_k that minimizes $P_{k|k}$. We want to partially differentiate $P_{k|k}$ with respect to K_k, so $P_{k|k}$ needs to be rewritten to make use of the following matrix formulae:

$\frac{\partial}{\partial X}\left[YX^T\right] = Y$, where X and Y are square
$\frac{\partial}{\partial X}\left[XY\right] = Y^T$, where X and Y are square
$\frac{\partial}{\partial X}\left[XYX^T\right] = 2XY^T$, where Y is symmetric

Now we rewrite $P_{k|k}$ to contain terms only of the form XY and XYX^T:

$$
\begin{aligned}
P_{k|k} &= (I - K_k H_k) P_{k|k-1} (I - K_k H_k)^T + K_k R_k K_k^T \\
&= P_{k|k-1} - K_k H_k P_{k|k-1} - P_{k|k-1} H_k^T K_k^T + K_k \left(H_k P_{k|k-1} H_k^T + R_k\right) K_k^T \\
\frac{\partial P_{k|k}}{\partial K_k} &= -\left(H_k P_{k|k-1}\right)^T - P_{k|k-1} H_k^T + 2K_k \left(H_k P_{k|k-1} H_k^T + R_k\right)^T \\
&= -2P_{k|k-1} H_k^T + 2K_k \left(H_k P_{k|k-1} H_k^T + R_k\right)
\end{aligned}
$$

Therefore, $K_k = P_{k|k-1} H_k^T \left(H_k P_{k|k-1} H_k^T + R_k\right)^{-1}$. FIGURE 9.1 summarizes the Kalman Filter steps as derived above.

Example

Here we apply a Kalman filter to our earlier stock price prediction example with the following transition and observables equations:

$$
\begin{aligned}
X_{k+1} &= X_k + W_k \\
Z_k &= X_k
\end{aligned}
$$

where the state vector X_k and the transition matrix F are

$$
X_k = \begin{bmatrix} x_k \\ x_{k-1} \\ x_{k-2} \end{bmatrix}, F = \begin{bmatrix} 0.6 & 0.3 & 0.1 \\ 1 & 0 & 0 \\ 0 & 1 & 0 \end{bmatrix}
$$

FIGURE 9.2 shows a plot of the actual Microsoft stock prices over 100 days from Jan 3, 2012, along with predicted and filtered prices from a MATLAB implementation of the two-stage Kalman filter in FIGURE 9.1. The predicted

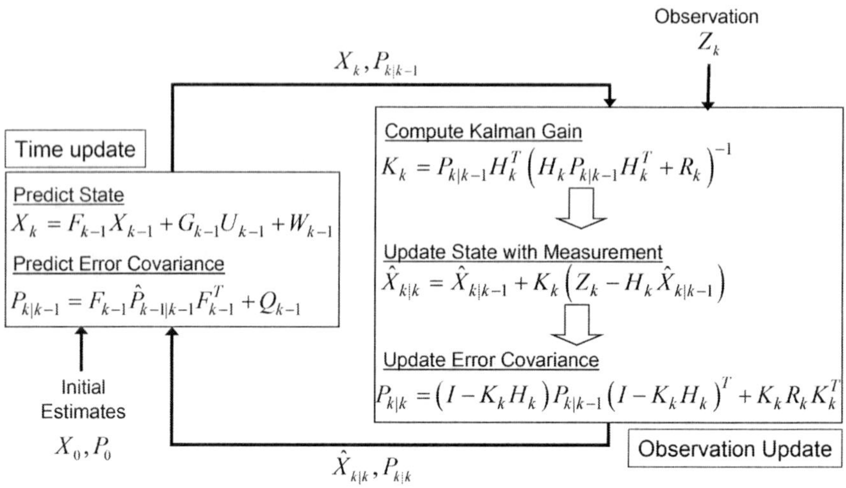

FIGURE 9.1 : Kalman Filter steps

price change and its standard deviation from the filter's first-stage can be used to determine buy-sell signals. It is clear from the plot that the filter algorithm requires certain number of stages to catch up with an upward or downward trend in the stock price. A filtered value at any time point is always in between the corresponding predicted and observed values. We provide a listing of the code for this implementation in Appendix C.

Example

Here is another example application of the Kalman filter but with simpler scalar-type state transition equation and observations are assumed to be without noise:

$$
\begin{aligned}
x_{k+1} &= x_k + w_k \\
z_k &= x_k
\end{aligned}
$$

The plot on the left of FIGURE 9.3 shows the actual Microsoft stock prices over a period of one year, along with the predicted and filtered prices from an R implementation of the two-stage Kalman filter in FIGURE 9.1. For a closer comparison, the plot on the right of FIGURE 9.3 shows the actual prices over a period of 25 days, along with the predicted prices using the same implementation. The code listing is given in Appendix C.

Example

We consider a generalization of our earlier example on tracking spending in an account to two accounts. The transition equation $X_{k+1} = F_k X_k + W_k$ without an input can be formulated as follows:

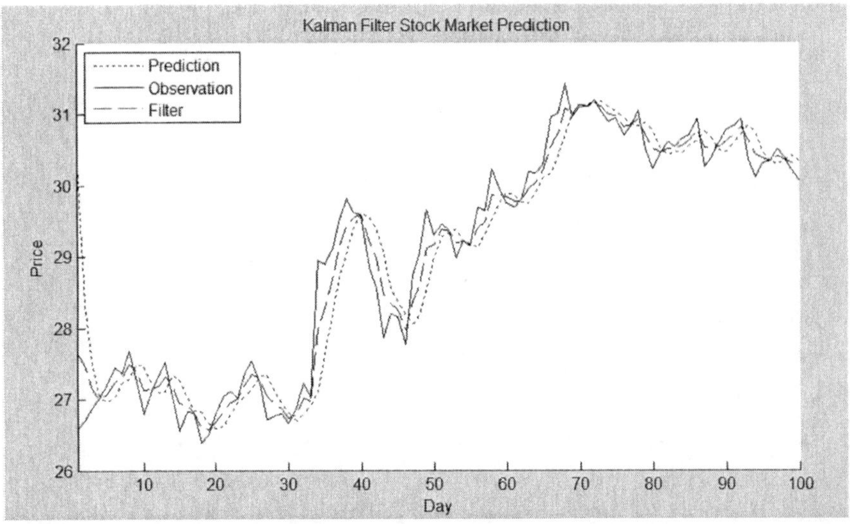

FIGURE 9.2 : Predicted, observed, and filtered stock prices via a Kalman filter over a period of 100 days

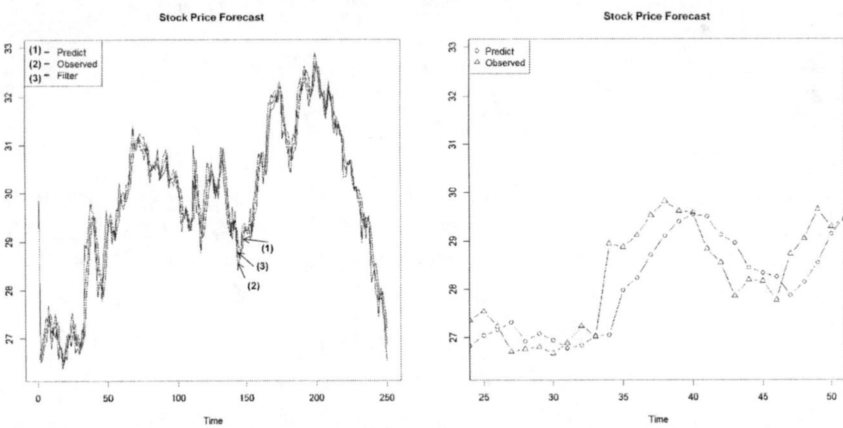

FIGURE 9.3 : (left) Predicted, observed, and filtered stock prices via a scalar Kalman filter over a period of one year; (right) Predicted and observed stock prices over a period of 25 days

$$\begin{bmatrix} a_{k+1} \\ r_{x(k+1)} \\ b_{k+1} \\ r_{y(k+1)} \end{bmatrix} = \begin{bmatrix} 1 & T & 0 & 0 \\ 0 & 1 & 0 & 0 \\ 0 & 0 & 1 & T \\ 0 & 0 & 0 & 1 \end{bmatrix} \begin{bmatrix} a_k \\ r_{xk} \\ b_k \\ r_{yk} \end{bmatrix} + W_k$$

where a_k and b_k in the state vector are, respectively, the accumulated spending in accounts one and two at time step k, and r_{xk} and r_{yk} are, respectively, the rates of spending in each of those two accounts. The variable T is the observation interval $t_{k+1} - t_k$. The measurement model $Z_k = H_k X_k + V_k$ is

$$\begin{bmatrix} z_{xk} \\ z_{yk} \end{bmatrix} = \begin{bmatrix} 1 & 0 & 0 & 0 \\ 0 & 0 & 1 & 0 \end{bmatrix} \begin{bmatrix} a_k \\ r_{xk} \\ b_k \\ r_{yk} \end{bmatrix} + V_k$$

The process noise W_k and the measurement noise V_k are assumed to be zero-mean, white, Gaussian, and independent of each other:

$$W_k \sim N(0, Q_k)$$
$$V_k \sim N(0, R_k)$$

where the process covariance matrix Q_k and the noise covariance matrix R_k are derived as

$$Q_k = \begin{bmatrix} T^3/3 & T^2/2 & 0 & 0 \\ T^2/2 & T & 0 & 0 \\ 0 & 0 & T^3/3 & T^2/2 \\ 0 & 0 & T^2/2 & T \end{bmatrix} \begin{bmatrix} \sigma_x \\ \sigma_{vx} \\ \sigma_y \\ \sigma_{vy} \end{bmatrix}$$
$$R_k = \begin{bmatrix} \sigma_x^2 & 0 \\ 0 & \sigma_y^2 \end{bmatrix}$$

9.2.1 Extended Kalman Filter (EKF)

The Kalman Filter (KF), as presented earlier, is a Bayesian optimal Minimum Mean Square Error (MMSE) estimator for linear systems with Gaussian noise. The Extended Kalman Filter (EKF) replaces the nonlinear transition and observation equation

$$X_k = f(X_{k-1}, U_{k-1}) + W_{k-1}$$
$$Z_k = h(X_k) + V_k$$

with an approximate linear system obtained via the Taylor series expansion of the transition equation about mean $\bar{X}$ of the random variable X:

$$\begin{aligned} & f(X) \\ & \quad = f(\bar{X} + \delta X) \\ & \quad = f(\bar{X}) + \nabla f \delta X + \tfrac{1}{2}\nabla^2 f \delta X^2 + \tfrac{1}{3!}\nabla^3 f \delta X^3 + \tfrac{1}{4!}\nabla^4 f \delta X^4 + ... \end{aligned}$$

where δX is a zero-mean Gaussain variable with covariance P_{XX}, and ∇f is the Jacobian of f (the matrix of all first-order partial derivatives of a vector-valued function) evaluated at $\bar{X}$. So, if f has the form

$$f(x,y,z) = \begin{bmatrix} f_1(x,y,z) \\ f_2(x,y,z) \end{bmatrix}$$

then its *Jacobian* has the form

$$\nabla f = \begin{bmatrix} \frac{\partial f_1}{\partial x} & \frac{\partial f_1}{\partial y} & \frac{\partial f_1}{\partial z} \\ \frac{\partial f_2}{\partial x} & \frac{\partial f_2}{\partial y} & \frac{\partial f_2}{\partial z} \end{bmatrix}$$

Taking expectations of the equation of $f(X)$ on both sides, it can be shown that the transformed mean and covariance are as follows:

$$\begin{aligned} \bar{Y} &= f(\bar{X}) + \tfrac{1}{2}\nabla^2 f P_{XX} + \tfrac{1}{2}\nabla^4 f E\left[\delta_X^4\right] + ... \\ P_{YY} &= \nabla F P_{XX}(\nabla f)^T + \tfrac{1}{2\times 4!}\nabla^2 f\left(E\left[\delta_X^4\right] - ...\right)\left(\nabla^2 f\right)^T + \\ &\quad \tfrac{1}{3!}\nabla^3 f E\left[\delta_X^4\right]\left(\nabla^3 f\right)^T + ... \end{aligned}$$

If the moments and derivatives can be evaluated correctly up to the n-th order, the mean and covariance are correct up to the n-th order as well. Each term in the series is scaled by a progressively smaller and smaller term due to an increasing power of δX. Therefore, the prediction procedure should be concentrated on evaluating the lower-order terms. From this point of view, linearization assumes the second and higher terms of δX can be neglected to obtain

$$\begin{aligned} \bar{Y} &= f(\bar{X}) \\ P_{YY} &= \nabla f P_{XX}(\nabla f)^T \end{aligned}$$

Considering, $\hat{X}_{k-1|k-1}$ for $\bar{X}$, $\hat{X}_{k|k-1}$ for $\bar{Y}$, $P_{k-1|k-1}$ for P_{XX}, and $P_{k|k-1}$ for P_{YY}, we formulate the following recursive estimation for EKF:

Prediction:

$$\begin{aligned} \hat{X}_{k|k-1} &= f\left(\hat{X}_{k-1|k-1}, U_{k-1}\right) + W_{k-1} \\ P_{k|k-1} &= \tilde{F}_{k-1} P_{k-1|k-1} \tilde{F}_{k-1}^T + Q_{k-1} \end{aligned}$$

Observation Update:

$$\begin{aligned} K_k &= P_{k|k-1}\tilde{H}_k^T\left(\tilde{H}_k P_{k|k-1}\tilde{H}_k^T + R_k\right)^{-1} \\ \hat{X}_{k|k} &= \hat{X}_{k|k-1} + K_k\left(Z_k - H_k\hat{X}_{k|k-1}\right) \\ P_{k|k} &= \left(1 - K_k\tilde{H}_k\right)P_{k|k-1}\left(1 - K_k\tilde{H}_k\right)^T + K_k R_k K_k^T \end{aligned}$$

where $\tilde{F}_{k-1} = \nabla f\left(\hat{X}_{k-1|k-1}\right)$ and $\tilde{H}_k = \nabla h\left(\hat{X}_{k|k-1}\right)$. The following example illustrates an estimation via EKF.

Example

Consider the following state vector of spending from two different accounts in a company, where the spending rates are determined by two independent parameters:

$$X_k = \begin{bmatrix} a_k \\ b_k \\ p_1 \\ p_2 \end{bmatrix}$$

where a_k and b_k represent spending from the two accounts at time step k, and p_1 and p_2 are two parameters used to compute the accumulated spending as defined by the following nonlinear transition equation:

$$\begin{aligned} X_{k+1} &= f(X_k) + W_k \\ &= \begin{bmatrix} f_1(X_k) \\ f_2(X_k) \\ f_3(X_k) \\ f_4(X_k) \end{bmatrix} + \begin{bmatrix} w_{1k} \\ w_{2k} \\ w_{3k} \\ w_{4k} \end{bmatrix} = \begin{bmatrix} \frac{p_1 a_k + p_2 b_k}{p_1 + p_2} \\ \frac{p_2 a_k + p_1 b_k}{p_1 + p_2} \\ \sqrt{p_1 p_2} \\ p_2 \end{bmatrix} + \begin{bmatrix} w_{1k} \\ w_{2k} \\ w_{3k} \\ w_{4k} \end{bmatrix} \end{aligned}$$

Therefore,

$$\begin{aligned} \tilde{F}_k = \nabla f\left(\hat{X}_{k|k}\right) &= \left.\frac{\partial f\left(X_{k|k}\right)}{\partial X_k}\right|_{X_k = \hat{X}_{k|k}} \\ &= \begin{bmatrix} \frac{\partial f_1}{\partial a_k} & \frac{\partial f_1}{\partial b_k} & \frac{\partial f_1}{\partial p_1} & \frac{\partial f_1}{\partial p_2} \\ \frac{\partial f_2}{\partial a_k} & \frac{\partial f_2}{\partial b_k} & \frac{\partial f_2}{\partial p_1} & \frac{\partial f_2}{\partial p_2} \\ \frac{\partial f_3}{\partial a_k} & \frac{\partial f_3}{\partial b_k} & \frac{\partial f_3}{\partial p_1} & \frac{\partial f_3}{\partial p_2} \\ \frac{\partial f_4}{\partial a_k} & \frac{\partial f_4}{\partial b_k} & \frac{\partial f_4}{\partial p_1} & \frac{\partial f_4}{\partial p_2} \end{bmatrix} \\ &= \begin{bmatrix} \frac{p_1}{p_1+p_2} & \frac{p_2}{p_1+p_2} & \frac{p_2(a_k - b_k)}{(p_1+p_2)^2} & ? \\ \frac{p_2}{p_1+p_2} & \frac{p_1}{p_1+p_2} & ? & ? \\ 0 & 0 & -\frac{1}{2}\sqrt{\frac{p_2}{p_1}} & -\frac{1}{2}\sqrt{\frac{p_1}{p_2}} \\ 0 & 0 & 0 & 1 \end{bmatrix} \end{aligned}$$

The measurement equation is

$$Z_k = X_k + V_k$$

9.3 MARKOV MODELS

A simple Markov model of a stochastic process is specified as a triplet $\langle S, A, \Pi \rangle$ defined as follows:

- A set $S = \{s_1, ..., s_n\}$ of n distinct *states*, one of which is assumed to be the state of the process at time step t. The process undergoes a change of state at regularly spaced discrete time steps $t = 1, 2, ...$
- A set $A = \{a_{ij}\}_{i,j=1,...,n}$ of *state transition probabilities*, where each a_{ij} represents the probability of transitioning from state s_i to state s_j. Symbolically, $p(X_t = s_j | X_{t-1} = s_i) = a_{ij}$, where X_t is the random variable representing the state at time step t.
- An initial probability distribution $\Pi = \{\pi_1, ..., \pi_n\}$, respectively, over the states $S = \{s_1, ..., s_n\}$, where π_i is the probability that the model will start in state s_i.

The total sum of initial distribution probabilities must be equal to 1:

$$\sum_{i=1}^{n} \pi_i = 1$$

The total sum of the outgoing transition probabilities from a given state must also sum to 1:

$$\sum_{j=1}^{n} a_{ij} = 1$$

The above Markov model can be represented as a probabilistic graphical model with states representing nodes and directed arcs representing transitions. FIGURE 9.4 represents a Markov model with four states along with its transition matrix shown on the right. Note that the transitions with the zero probability are not shown.

In a *first-order Markov model*, the probability of a particular state is dependent only on the previous state:

$$p(X_t = s_i | X_{t-1} = s_j, X_{t-2} = s_k, ...) = p(X_t = s_i | X_{t-1} = s_j)$$

The model above will be called ***observable*** if each state corresponds to a physical observable event.

Example

Given a Markov model in FIGURE 9.4, we can then ask such questions as: What is the probability that the observation sequence $\{s_3, s_4, s_1, s_3, s_2\}$ of states corresponding to $t = 1, 2, 3, 4, 5$ will be observed? This probability is evaluated as follows:

$$\begin{aligned}
&p(\{s_3, s_4, s_1, s_3, s_2\}) \\
&\quad = p(s_3) \cdot p(s_4 | s_3) \cdot p(s_1 | \{s_3, s_4\}) \cdot \\
&\qquad\qquad p(s_3 | \{s_3, s_4, s_1\}) \cdot p(s_2 | \{s_3, s_4, s_1, s_3\}) \\
&\quad = p(s_3) \cdot p(s_4 | s_3) \cdot p(s_1 | s_4) \cdot p(s_3 | s_1) \cdot p(s_2 | s_3) \\
&\quad = \pi_3 \cdot a_{43} \cdot a_{14} \cdot a_{31} \cdot a_{23}
\end{aligned}$$

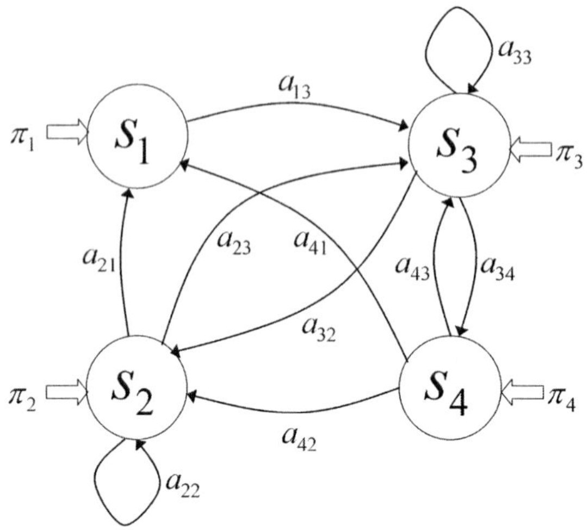

$$A = \begin{bmatrix} 0 & 0 & a_{13} & 0 \\ a_{21} & a_{22} & a_{23} & 0 \\ 0 & a_{32} & a_{33} & a_{34} \\ a_{41} & a_{42} & a_{43} & 0 \end{bmatrix}$$

FIGURE 9.4 : Markov model and transition matrix with four states

Example

Consider a three-state Markov model for financial market trends over short time frames. The terms used here for describing the states are the following:

$$\begin{aligned} s_1 &= \text{Upward market trend } (\textit{bull}) \\ s_2 &= \text{Downward market trend } (\textit{bear}) \\ s_3 &= \text{No change } (\textit{static}) \end{aligned}$$

The model and the transition probability matrix A are given in FIGURE 9.5. As an example, the probability of the observation sequence

$$\{bear, bull, static, static, bear\}$$

can be computed as below:

$$\begin{aligned} & p\left(\{bear, bull, static, static, bear\}\right) \\ & \quad = p\left(bear\right) \cdot p\left(bull|bear\right) \cdot p\left(static|bull\right) \cdot \\ & \qquad\qquad p\left(static|static\right) \cdot p\left(bear|static\right) \\ & \quad = 0.2 \cdot 0.5 \cdot 0.2 \cdot 0.5 \cdot 0.1 \\ & \quad = 0.001 \end{aligned}$$

9.3.1 Hidden Markov Models (HMM)

In a Markov model, each state corresponds to an observable event. However, the events we are interested in are not observable in many applications. For example, exact trends are not observable, but various financial indices are

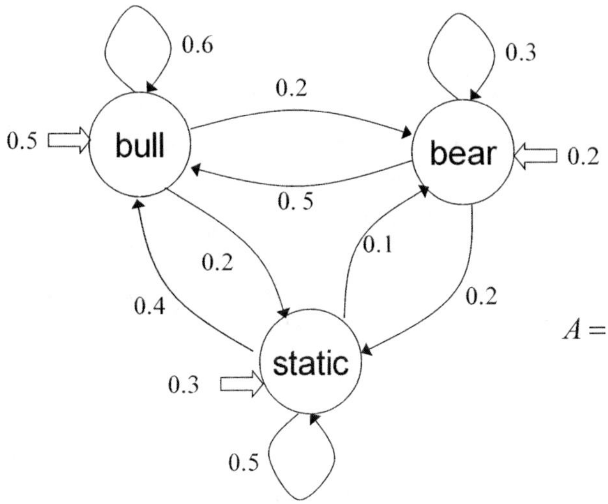

$$A = \begin{bmatrix} 0.6 & 0.2 & 0.2 \\ 0.5 & 0.3 & 0.2 \\ 0.4 & 0.1 & 0.5 \end{bmatrix}$$

FIGURE 9.5 : Example Markov model and transition matrix with three states

observables that indicate whether the market is up, down or flat. In this case, the motion models are *hidden* because they are not observed. The notion of the Markov model is extended to the Hidden Markov Model (HMM) to encode both hidden and observed events. Formally, an HMM is a quintuplet $\langle S, O, A, B, \Pi \rangle$ defined as follows:

- A set $S = \{s_1, ..., s_n\}$ of n distinct *states*, one of which is assumed to be the state of the process at time step t.
- A set $O = \{o_1, ..., o_m\}$ of m distinct *observation symbols* corresponding to the physical output of the system or process being modeled.
- A set $A = \{a_{ij}\}_{i,j=1,...,n}$ of *state transition probabilities*, where each a_{ij} represents the probability of transitioning from state s_i to state s_j. Symbolically, $p(X_t = s_j | X_{t-1} = s_i) = a_{ij}$, where X_t is the random variable representing the state at time point step t.
- A set $B = \{b_i(o_j)\}_{i=1,...,n; j=1,...,m}$ of *observation likelihoods*, where each $b_i(o_j)$ represents the probability of observing o_j at state s_i. Symbolically, $p(Y_t = o_j | X_t = s_i) = b_{ij}$, where Y_t is the random variable representing the observation at time step t.
- An initial probability distribution $\Pi = \{\pi_1, ..., \pi_n\}$, respectively, over the states $S = \{s_1, ..., s_n\}$, where π_i is the probability that the model will start in state s_i.

As before, we have the following constraints for a Markov model:

$$\sum_{i=1}^{n} \pi_i = 1, \quad \sum_{j=1}^{n} a_{ij} = 1$$

In a *first-order HMM*, as in the case of a first-order Markov model, the probability of a particular state is dependent only on the previous state:

$$p\left(X_t = s_i | X_{t-1} = s_j, X_{t-2} = s_k, ...\right) = p\left(X_t = s_i | X_{t-1} = s_j\right)$$

Finally, in a first-order HMM, the probability of an output observation is dependent only on the state that produced the observation. Symbolically,

$$p\left(Y_t = o_i | X_i = s_j, ..., X_t = s_k, ...\right) = p\left(Y_t = o_i | X_t = s_k\right)$$

Example

FIGURE 9.6 represents an HMM, extended from the simple Markov model shown in FIGURE 9.4 with four states, along with its observation matrix shown on the right. The transition is as before in FIGURE 9.4. Note that the observations with zero probability are not shown.

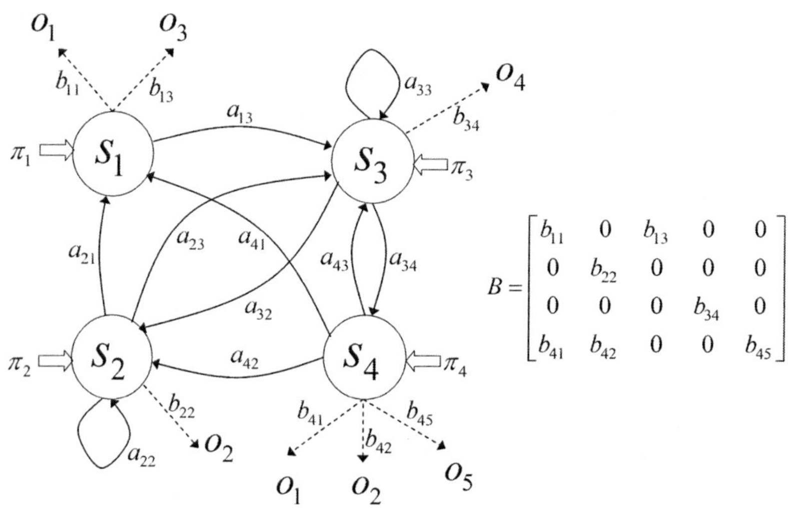

FIGURE 9.6 : HMM with four states along with its observation matrix

An HMM $\langle S, O, A, B, \Pi \rangle$ can be used as a generator to give an observation sequence $Y_1 Y_2 ... Y_t ...$ as follows:

1. Choose an initial state X_1 from S according to the initial state distribution Π.

2. Set $t = 1$.
3. Choose Y_t from O according to the observation likelihood in state X_t.
4. Transit to a new state X_{t+1} from S according to the state transition distribution for state X_t.
5. Set $t = t + 1$ and return to Step 3.

FIGURE 9.7 shows the evolution of this generator around the time step t.

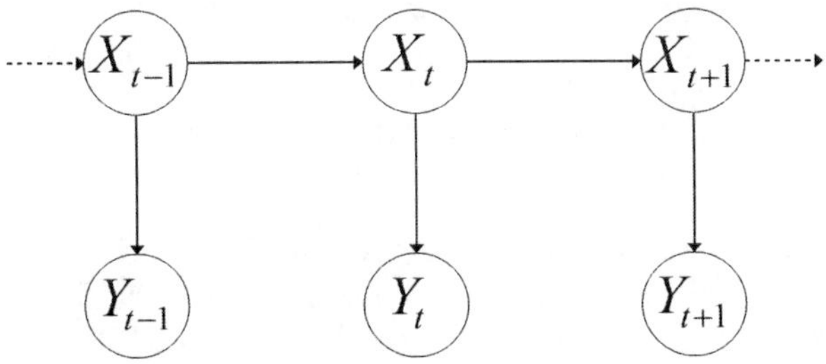

FIGURE 9.7 : Evolution of the HMM

Example

Continuing with our financial market prediction example, the set of hidden states is $\{bull, bear, static\}$ and the observables are the trend of the market index value considered from the set $\{up, down, flat\}$. The prior and transition probabilities are as before, and the observable likelihoods are shown in FIGURE 9.8.

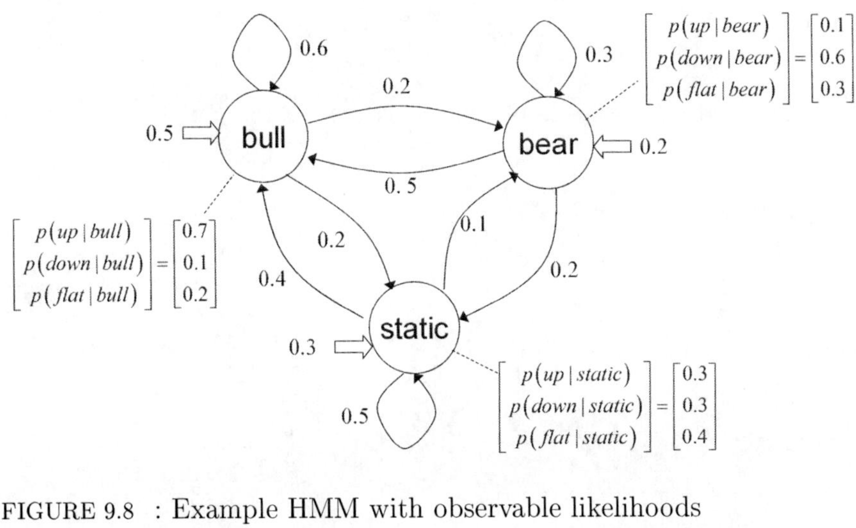

FIGURE 9.8 : Example HMM with observable likelihoods

Note that the HMM in FIGURE 9.8 is *fully connected* in the sense that the transition probability between any two states is nonzero.

Three natural problems typically arise in applications that use HMM:

- Computing the likelihood of an observation sequence (*the forward algorithm*): Find the probability of a given sequence of observations to be generated by the model.
- Computing the most probable state sequence (*the Viterbi algorithm*): Find the most probable sequence of states that is likely to generate a given observation sequence.
- Estimating the parameters of a model (*the Baum-Welch algorithm*): Find the most probable parameter set of a model given its structure and one or more observation sequences.

The forward, Viterbi algorithms, and Baum-Welch algorithm are detailed in the following three subsections. The Baum-Welch algorithm, because of its machine learning slant, is better placed in Chapter 10 on model learning.

9.3.2 The Forward Algorithm

Given an HMM $\langle S, O, A, B, \Pi \rangle$ and an observation sequence $Y_1...Y_T$, we want to compute the probability $p(Y_1...Y_T)$, which can be obtained by summing over all possible state sequences of length T as follows:

$$p(Y_1...Y_T) = \sum_{X_1...X_T} p(Y_1...Y_T | X_1...X_T) p(X_1...X_T)$$

Since the observations are independent,

$$p(Y_1...Y_T | X_1...X_T) = \prod_{t=1}^{T} p(Y_t | X_1...X_T)$$

Since an output observation is dependent only on the state that produced the observation, for every t,

$$p(Y_t | X_1...X_T) = p(Y_t | X_t) = b_{X_t}(Y_t)$$

Moreover,

$$\begin{aligned} & p(X_1...X_T) \\ & \quad = p(X_1) p(X_2|X_1) p(X_3|X_1, X_2) ... p(X_T|X_1, ..., X_{T-1}) \\ & \quad = p(X_1) p(X_2|X_1) p(X_3|X_2) ... p(X_T|X_{T-1}) \\ & \quad = \pi_{X_1} a_{X_1 X_2} a_{X_2 X_3} ... a_{X_{T-1} X_T} \\ & \quad = \pi_{X_1} \prod_{t=1}^{T-1} a_{X_t X_{t+1}} \end{aligned}$$

Therefore,

$$
\begin{aligned}
& p(Y_1...Y_T) \\
&= \sum_{X_1...X_T} \left(\prod_{t=1}^{T} b_{X_t}(Y_t)\right)\left(\pi_{X_1}\prod_{t=1}^{T-1} a_{X_t X_{t+1}}\right) \\
&= \sum_{X_1...X_T} \pi_{X_1} b_{X_1}(Y_1)\, a_{X_1 X_2} b_{X_2}(Y_2) ... a_{X_{T-1} X_T} b_{X_T}(Y_T)
\end{aligned}
$$

The above probability computation for each sequence $X_1...X_T$ of states can be interpreted as follows. First at time-step 1 in the process we are in state X_1 with probability π_{X_1}. The symbol Y_1 is generated at this state with probability $b_{X_1}(Y_1)$. When the time changes, a transition takes place from state X_1 to state X_2 with probability $a_{X_1X_2}$. The symbol Y_2 at this state is generated with probability $b_{X_2}(Y_2)$. The process continues until the final transition takes place from state X_{t-1} to state X_t with probability $a_{X_{T-1}X_T}$, and the symbol Y_t is generated with probability $b_{X_T}(Y_T)$.

The simplest way of computing $p(Y_1...Y_T)$ is to enumerate all possible state sequences and then, for each such sequence $X_1...X_T$, compute the term in the summation by following the above interpretation.

Example

Consider an evolution (shown in FIGURE 9.9) of the HMM in FIGURE 9.8. This evolution provides a term in the summation for computing $p(up\, down\, down)$:

$$
\begin{aligned}
& \pi_{static} b_{static}(up)\, a_{static\, bull} b_{bull}(down)\, a_{bull\, bear} b_{bear}(down) \\
&= 0.3 \times 0.3 \times 0.4 \times 0.1 \times 0.2 \times 0.6 \\
&= 0.000432
\end{aligned}
$$

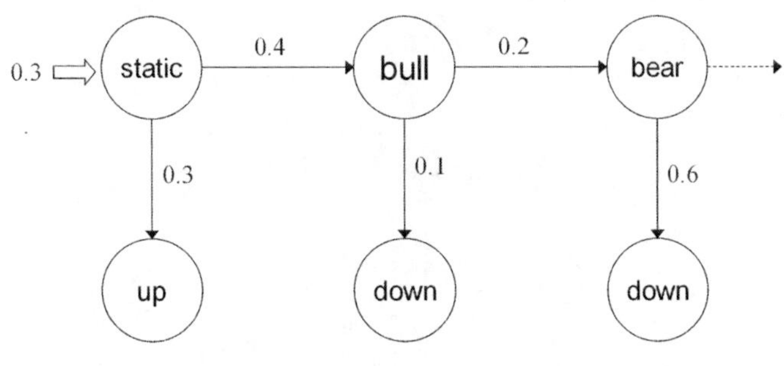

FIGURE 9.9 : An evolution of the HMM in FIGURE 9.8

The total number of sequences to be handled in this way can be very large (e.g., 3^{100} for four states and 100 time steps). The forward algorithm below is a more efficient implementation for computing $p(Y_1...Y_T)$.

The algorithm considers the forward variable $\alpha_t(s_i)$ as defined below:

$$\alpha_t(s_i) = p(Y_1...Y_t, X_t = s_i)$$

The variable represents the joint probability of the partial observation sequence $Y_1...Y_t$ and state s_i at time t. The three-step forward algorithm is developed via an inductive computation of $\alpha_t(s_i)$.

Step 1: Initialization

$$\alpha_1(s_i) = \pi_i b_i(Y_1), 1 \le i \le n$$

Step 2: Induction

$$\alpha_{t+1}(s_j) = \left(\sum_{i=1}^{n} \alpha_t(s_i) a_{ij}\right) b_j(Y_{t+1}), 1 \le t \le T-1;\ 1 \le j \le n$$

Step 3: Termination

$$p(Y_1...Y_T) = \sum_{i=1}^{n} \alpha_T(s_i)$$

FIGURE 9.10 generically illustrates the computation of a forward variable.

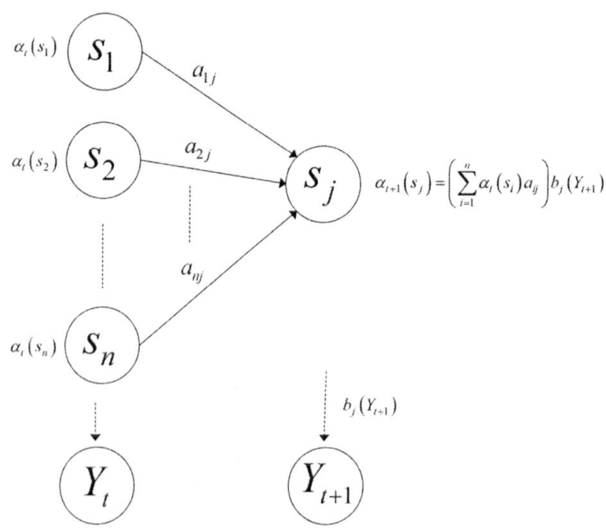

FIGURE 9.10 : Illustration of the computation of a forward variable

Example

Consider the HMM in FIGURE 9.8. FIGURE 9.11 illustrates the forward algorithm with the following computation of values of α-variables at various stages (*bu* – *bull*; *be* – *bear*; *st* – *static*).

$$\begin{aligned}\alpha_1(bu) &= \pi_{bu} p(up|bu) = 0.5 \cdot 0.7 = 0.35 \\ \alpha_1(be) &= \pi_{be} p(up|be) = 0.2 \cdot 0.1 = 0.02 \\ \alpha_1(st) &= \pi_{st} p(up|st) = 0.3 \cdot 0.3 = 0.09\end{aligned}$$

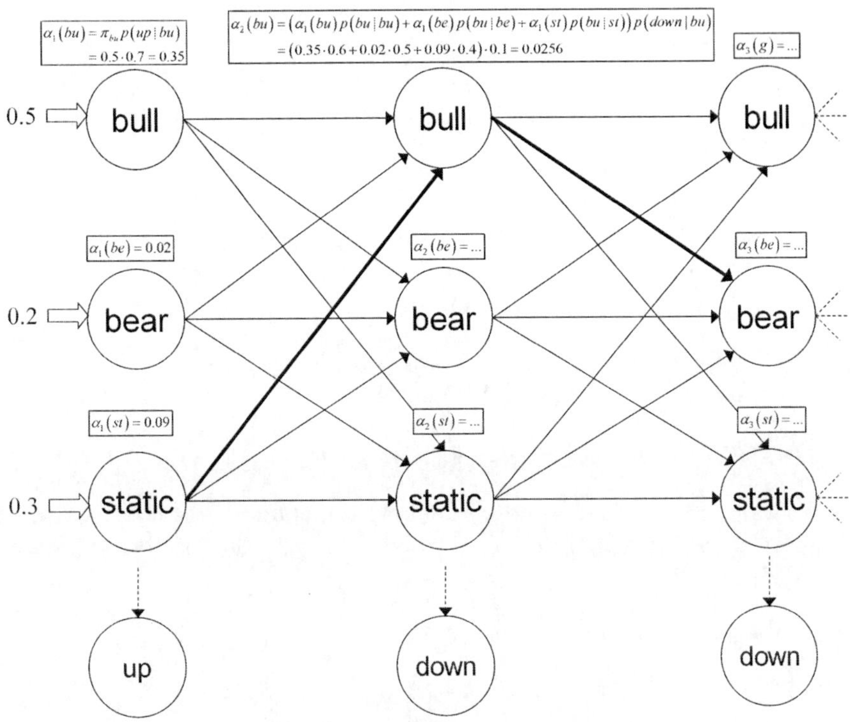

FIGURE 9.11 : Illustration of the forward algorithm (bu – bull; be – bear; st – static)

$$\begin{aligned}&\alpha_2(bu) \\ &\quad = (\alpha_1(bu)\, p(bu|bu) + \alpha_1(be)\, p(bu|be) + \alpha_1(st)\, p(bu|st))\, p(down|bu) \\ &\quad = (0.35 \cdot 0.6 + 0.02 \cdot 0.5 + 0.09 \cdot 0.4) \cdot 0.1 = 0.0256\end{aligned}$$

$$\begin{aligned}&\alpha_2(be) \\ &\quad = (\alpha_1(bu)\, p(be|bu) + \alpha_1(be)\, p(be|be) + \alpha_1(st)\, p(be|st))\, p(down|be) \\ &\quad = (0.35 \cdot 0.2 + 0.02 \cdot 0.3 + 0.09 \cdot 0.1) \cdot 0.6 = 0.0510\end{aligned}$$

$$\begin{aligned}&\alpha_2(st) \\ &\quad = (\alpha_1(bu)\, p(st|bu) + \alpha_1(be)\, p(st|be) + \alpha_1(st)\, p(st|st))\, p(down|st) \\ &\quad = (0.35 \cdot 0.2 + 0.02 \cdot 0.2 + 0.09 \cdot 0.5) \cdot 0.3 = 0.0357\end{aligned}$$

9.3.3 The Viterbi Algorithm

Given an HMM $\langle S, O, A, B, \Pi \rangle$ and an observation sequence $Y_1 ... Y_T$, we want to find the most probable sequence $X_1 ... X_T$ of states that is likely to generate the observation sequence. In other words, we have the following maximization problem at hand:

$$\max_{X_1 ... X_T} p\left(X_1 ... X_T | Y_1 ... Y_T\right)$$

which is equivalent to the maximization problem

$$\max_{X_1 ... X_T} p\left(X_1 ... X_T, Y_1 ... Y_T\right)$$

To compute this, let us define the following inductive variable:

$$\delta_t\left(s_i\right) = \max_{X_1 ... X_T} p\left(X_1 ... X_t = s_i, Y_1 ... Y_t\right)$$

which is the highest probability along a single path that ends in state s_i. The induction principle provides the following:

$$\delta_{t+1}\left(s_j\right) = \left(\max_i \delta_t\left(s_i\right) a_{ij}\right) b_j\left(Y_{t+1}\right)$$

We want to keep track of the argument that maximized the induction principle above at each time point t via the variable $\psi_t\left(s_j\right)$. The Viterbi algorithm steps are given below:

Step 1: Initialization

$$\begin{array}{ll} \delta_1\left(s_i\right) = \pi_i b_i\left(Y_1\right) & 1 \leq i \leq n \\ \psi_1\left(i\right) = start & 1 \leq i \leq n \end{array}$$

Step 2: Recursion

$$\begin{array}{ll} \delta_t\left(s_j\right) = \left(\max\limits_{1 \leq i \leq n} \delta_{t-1}\left(s_i\right) a_{ij}\right) b_j\left(Y_t\right) & 1 \leq j \leq n;\ 2 \leq t \leq T \\ \psi_t\left(s_j\right) = \left(\arg\max\limits_{1 \leq i \leq n} \delta_{t-1}\left(s_i\right) a_{ij}\right) & 1 \leq j \leq n;\ 2 \leq t \leq T \end{array}$$

Step 3: Termination

$$\text{Best score } P^* = \max_{1 \leq i \leq n} \delta_T\left(s_i\right)$$

$$\text{Path backtracking start } X_T^* = \arg\max_{1 \leq i \leq n} \delta_T\left(s_i\right)$$

Step 4: State sequence

$$X_t^* = \psi_{t+1}\left(X_{t+1}^*\right) \qquad t = T-1, T-2, ..., 1$$

The Viterbi algorithm is similar to the forward algorithm except that it maintains the ψ-variable for backtracking and employs maximization in Step 2 instead of a summation.

Example

Consider the HMM in FIGURE 9.8. FIGURE 9.12 illustrates the Viterbi algorithm with the computation of values of δ- and ψ-variables at various stages.

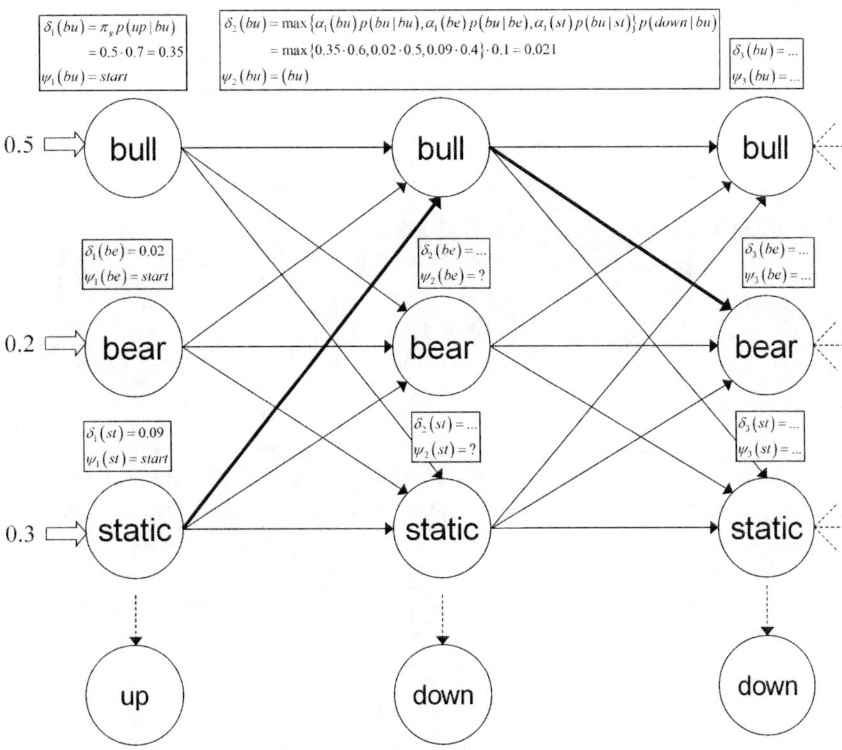

FIGURE 9.12 : Illustration of a Viterbi algorithm

9.3.4 Baum-Welch Algorithm for Learning HMM

Given an HMM $M = \langle S, O, A, B, \Pi \rangle$ and an observation sequence $Y_1...Y_T$, we want to re-estimate M as $\bar{M} = \langle S, O, \bar{A}, \bar{B}, \bar{\Pi} \rangle$ so that $\bar{M}$ is more likely than M in the sense that $p(Y_1...Y_T|M) > p(Y_1...Y_T|\bar{M})$. In other words, the new model is more likely to produce the given observation sequence. This is done via an iterative Baum-Welch or forward-backward algorithm.

The forward algorithm considers a forward variable $\alpha_t(s_i)$ as defined below:

$$\alpha_t(s_i) = p(Y_1...Y_t, X_t = s_i)$$

The forward variable represents the joint probability of the partial observation sequence $Y_1...Y_t$ and state s_i at time t. The forward algorithm computes the forward variable iteratively. In a similar manner, we define a backward variable $\beta_t(s_i)$ as follows:

$$\beta_t(s_i) = p(Y_{t+1}...Y_T | X_t = s_i)$$

The backward variable represents the probability of the partial observation sequence from $t+1$ to the end given that the state at time point t is s_i. The variable is inductively computed as follows:

Step 1: Initialization

$$\beta_T(s_i) = 1 \qquad 1 \leq i \leq n$$

Step 2: Induction

$$\beta_t(s_i) = \sum_{j=1}^{n} a_{ij} b_j(Y_{t+1}) \beta_{t+1}(s_j) \qquad t = T-1, T-2, ..., 1;\ 1 \leq i \leq n$$

FIGURE 9.13 illustrates the computation of a backward variable.

Given the sequence $Y_1...Y_T$ of observations and any two states s_i and s_j, the re-estimation $\bar{a}_{ij}$ of the parameter is simply the ratio of the expected number of transitions from state s_i to state s_j and the expected number of transitions from state s_i as a whole. Therefore, we define the following variable representing the posterior probability of transition from state s_i to state s_j given the observation sequence:

$$\xi_t(s_i, s_j) = p(X_t = s_i, X_{t+1} = s_j | Y_1...Y_T)$$

Then the expected number of transitions from state s_i has to be computed for every time point between 1 and $T-1$ as follows:

Expected number of transitions from state s_i to s_j is $\sum_{t=1}^{T-1} \xi_t(s_i, s_j)$.

In a similar argument,

Expected number of transitions from state s_i is $\sum_{t=1}^{T-1} \sum_{j=1}^{n} \xi_t(s_i, s_j)$.

Application of Bayes' rule converts $\xi_t(s_i, s_j)$ as follows:

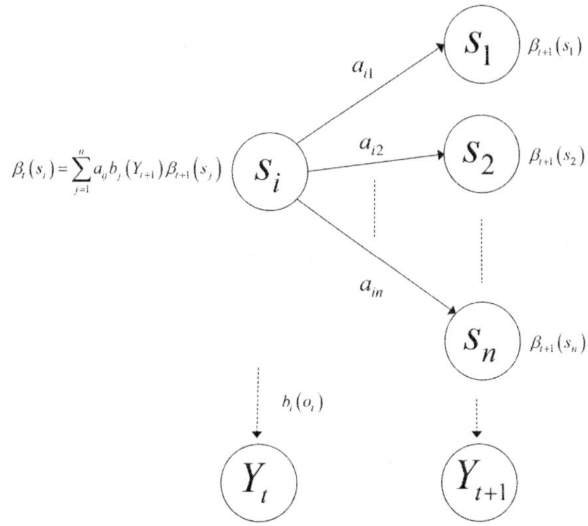

FIGURE 9.13 : Illustration of the computation of a backward variable

$$
\begin{aligned}
&\xi_t(s_i, s_j) \\
&= \frac{p(X_t=s_i, X_{t+1}=s_j, Y_1 \ldots Y_T)}{p(Y_1 \ldots Y_T)} \\
&= \frac{p(X_t=s_i, X_{t+1}=s_j, Y_1 \ldots Y_T)}{\sum_{i=1}^{n} \sum_{j=1}^{n} p(X_t=s_i, X_{t+1}=s_j, Y_1 \ldots Y_T)}
\end{aligned}
$$

Now the computation of the numerator of the above expression, as illustrated in FIGURE 9.14, is the following:

$$
\begin{aligned}
&p(X_t = s_i, X_{t+1} = s_j, Y_1 \ldots Y_T) \\
&\quad = p(Y_1 \ldots Y_t, X_t = s_i) a_{ij} b_j(Y_{t+1}) p(Y_{t+2} \ldots Y_T | X_{t+1} = s_j) \\
&\quad = \alpha_t(s_i) a_{ij} b_j(Y_{t+1}) \beta_{t+1}(s_j)
\end{aligned}
$$

Therefore,

$$
\xi_t(s_i, s_j) = \frac{\alpha_t(s_i) a_{ij} b_j(Y_{t+1}) \beta_{t+1}(s_j)}{\sum_{i=1}^{n} \sum_{j=1}^{n} \alpha_t(s_i) a_{ij} b_j(Y_{t+1}) \beta_{t+1}(s_j)}
$$

Define the following variable $\gamma_t(s_i)$ as the expected number of transitions from the state s_i at time t:

$$
\gamma_t(s_i) = \sum_{j=1}^{n} \xi_t(s_i, s_j)
$$

The re-estimated model parameters are the following:

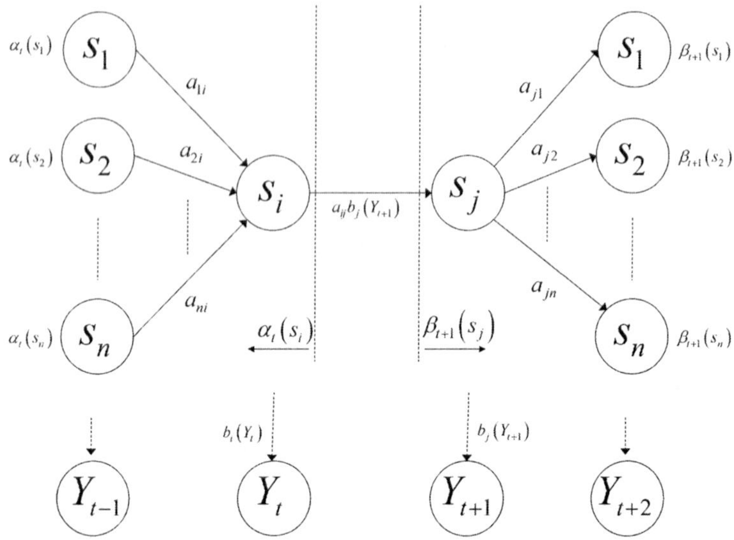

FIGURE 9.14 : Computation of the joint probability of being in state $\mathbf{s_i}$ at time $\mathbf{t}$ and state $\mathbf{s_j}$ at time $\mathbf{t+1}$

$$\bar{\pi}_i = \text{expected number of times in state } s_i \text{ at the state (i.e., } t = 1) = \gamma_1(s_i) \; 1 \le i \le n$$

$$\bar{a}_{ij} = \frac{\text{expected number of transitions from state } s_i \text{ to state } s_j}{\text{expected number of transitions from state } s_i} = \frac{\sum_{t=1}^{T-1} \xi_t(s_i, s_j)}{\sum_{t=1}^{T-1} \sum_{j=1}^{n} \xi_t(s_i, s_j)} = \frac{\sum_{t=1}^{T-1} \xi_t(s_i, s_j)}{\sum_{t=1}^{T-1} \gamma_t(s_i)}$$

$$\bar{b}_{s_i}(o_k) = \frac{\text{expected number of times in state } s_i \text{ and observing symbol } o_k}{\text{expected number of times in state } s_i} = \frac{\sum_{t=1}^{T-1} \gamma_t(s_i, o_k)}{\sum_{t=1}^{T-1} \gamma_t(s_i)}$$

where $\gamma_t(s_i, o_k)$ is $\gamma_t(s_i)$ for the observation sequence $Y_1 ... Y_{t-1} o_k Y_t ... Y_T$.

The probability of the observation sequence can be improved by recursively re-estimating the parameters $\bar{A}, \bar{B}, \bar{\Pi}$ until some limiting point is reached.

9.4 DYNAMIC BAYESIAN NETWORKS (DBNS)

One limitation of BNs presented earlier in the chapter on probabilistic graphical models is that they do not explicitly or adequately model temporal information that may be required when modeling a dynamic operational environment. This limitation can decrease overall assessment accuracy and thereby reduce operational utility. To illustrate, consider the BN shown in FIGURE 9.15.

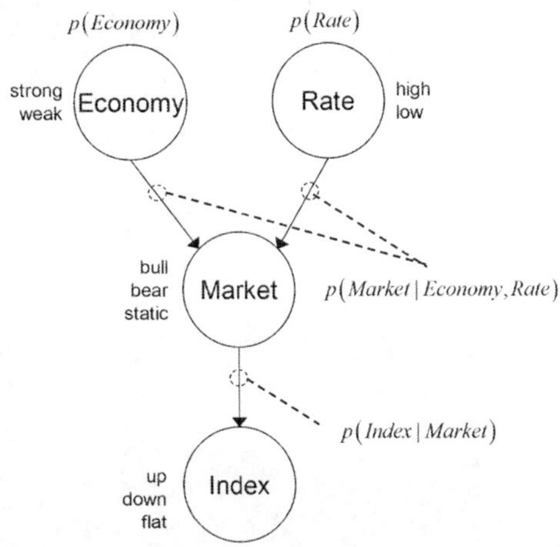

FIGURE 9.15 : An example static BN

There are many factors on which the financial market trends depend – economy, consumer spending, economic policies of the government, industrial output, unemployment rate, GDP, interest rate, and stability of the currency, just to name a few. We have considered economy and unemployment rate only just for the purpose of illustration. The financial market trend then determines the market index trend which is observable.

The economy and the unemployment rate in the current time period together affect the market trend, which is one of bull, bear, or static, at this period of time. The market trend then determines the trend in the market index value defined by the CPT shown in FIGURE 9.8. The fact that a sustained good economy or low unemployment rate may affect the market trend differently than in just a single period of time (which is considered here) is not modeled in this BN.

To address this problem, we introduce Dynamic Bayesian Networks (DBNs) (Murphy, 2002; Ghahramani, 2001), which are simply BNs for modeling time series data. There are two key ideas behind the extension of a BN to a DBN:

- All nodes of the BN are associated with particular time steps, simply by indexing the nodes with a time step value.

- Some BN nodes for a given time step may have causal dependencies on nodes from earlier time steps (in addition to the usual causal dependencies on nodes from their own time step); such dependencies are called *temporal dependencies*.

The result is a DBN. FIGURE 9.16 illustrates the general case of time indexing and temporal dependency: variable X_t from time step t has causal dependencies on some variables X_t^i from its own time step t; it also has causal dependencies on X_{t-j}^i from earlier time steps. When dependencies between nodes are only from the time step immediately prior, we say we have a Markovian model.

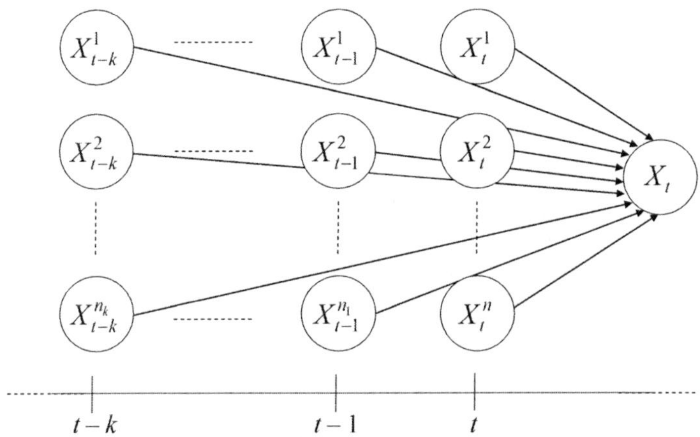

FIGURE 9.16 : General temporal dependency in DBNs

As a concrete illustration, consider a temporal extension of the static BN of FIGURE 9.15 to the DBN in FIGURE 9.17. The economy node at time step t depends on the economy node at the previous time point. The market node at time step t not only depends on the economy and unemployment rate nodes at t, but also on the economy at one and two time periods before. Therefore, the CPT of the economy node at time step t is $p(E_t|E_{t-1})$, and the CPT of the market node at time step t is $p(M_t|R_t, E_t, E_{t-1}, E_{t-2})$, where M and E represent market and economy, respectively. In the case of a Markovian model, the CPT of the market node is $p(M_t|R_t, E_t, E_{t-1})$. Note that the exact length of the time period is defined as needed by the specific application at hand, which could be, for example, a minute, an hour, or a day.

We assume that both current and past economic conditions affect the market. An alternative modeling strategy would be to account for all the past economic effects via the market node in the immediate past, thus yielding a Markovian model as shown in FIGURE 9.18. In other words, an overall effect of the past economy on the market node at time step t is summarized by the market node at time step $t-1$.

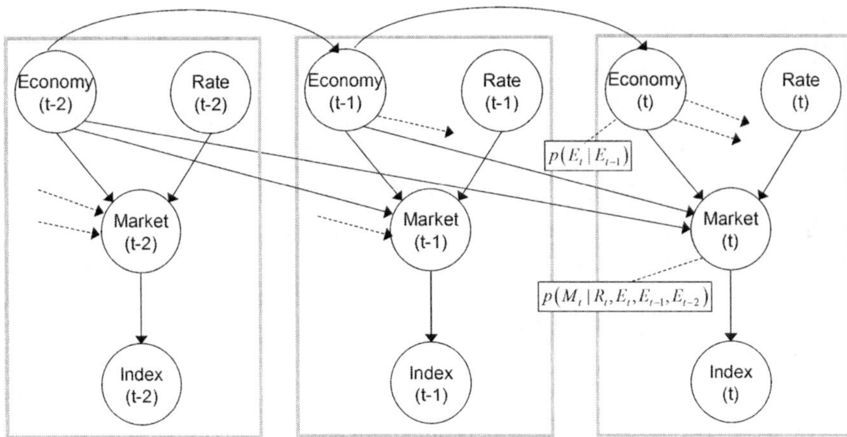

FIGURE 9.17 : An example DBN based on the BN in FIGURE 9.15

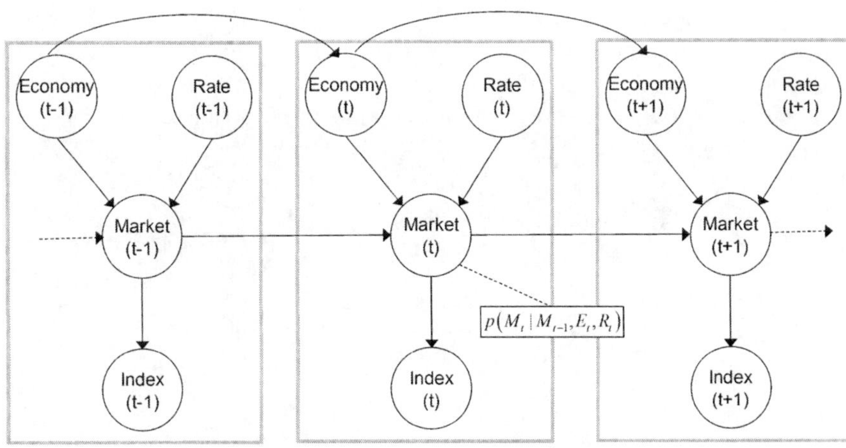

FIGURE 9.18 : A Markovian version of the DBN in FIGURE 9.17

A DBN is assumed to be *stationary* in the sense that the node relationships within a time step t and the transition probabilities from time step t to time step $t+1$ (both expressed in CPTs) do not vary with t. Therefore, we can carry out inference in a DBN using just a 2TBN, which considers only the nodes from two consecutive time steps.

A fragment of the evolution of an HMM can be considered a DBN. For example, the fragment in FIGURE 9.7 is a DBN with six nodes, where the members of the sets S and O in the definition of the HMM form the mutually exclusive and exhaustive set of states of nodes X_is and Y_js respectively. The CPTs $p(X_0)$, $p(X_i|X_{i-1})$, and $p(Y_i|X_i)$ can be constructed, respectively, from Π, A, and B in the definition of the HMM. DBNs model problems at a finer level than HMMs. The concept of a state in a DBN is a possible combination of the states of its variables. So, an example state for the DBN in FIGURE 9.18 is

$$\langle Economy = weak, Rate = high, Market = bull, Index = down \rangle$$

All variables considered here are categorical. There will be an infinite number of states if one or more variables is continuous in nature (e.g., *Rate*); otherwise, the number of states that can be composed from a DBN consisting of only categorical variables is finite. For example, there will be 36 states for the network. These states then constitute the states of an HMM equivalent to the DBN. The transition probabilities $p(X_t|X_{t-1})$ in this HMM can be computed from the CPTs of the DBN.

9.4.1 Inference Algorithms for DBNs

A naïve approach to inference in a DBN is to evolve it for a desired number of time steps and then to treat it as a static BN. FIGURE 9.19 shows an unrolled version of the DBN in FIGURE 9.18 up to time step 5. Evidence can be posted at any time step to obtain the necessary prediction. So if the current time step is 3 and evidence has been posted, then querying at time step 4 or 5 provides prediction. Smoothing can be done by reposting any evidence in the past time step 1 or 2.

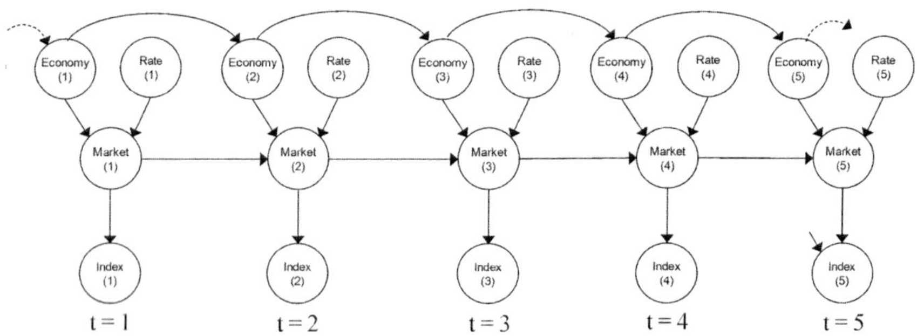

FIGURE 9.19 : Unrolled up to time step 5 for the DBN in FIGURE 9.18

Though a naïve approach to inference in DBNs is simple to implement, the size of an unrolled DBN becomes large with many time steps. What we need is a process to maintain a simple 2TBN by advancing forward one step at a time and dynamically trimming past BN slices. The following two algorithms leverage the junction tree algorithm on the 2TBN:

- Frontier algorithm (Zweig, 1998), and
- Interface algorithm (Murphy, 2002).

We will present the interface algorithm as it is known to be more efficient than the frontier algorithm. The algorithm uses the interface to d-separate the past from the present during the evolution of a DBN process. We consider a simplified version of the algorithm that does one-step prediction and filtering.

Inference in hybrid DBNs involving both discrete and continuous variables requires the particle filtering technique (to be presented in the next section). Here we consider the BN in FIGURE 9.20, a discrete and extended version of the BN in FIGURE 9.15, to illustrate an exact inference algorithm for DBNs involving only discrete variables. The added node *Output* represents industrial output.

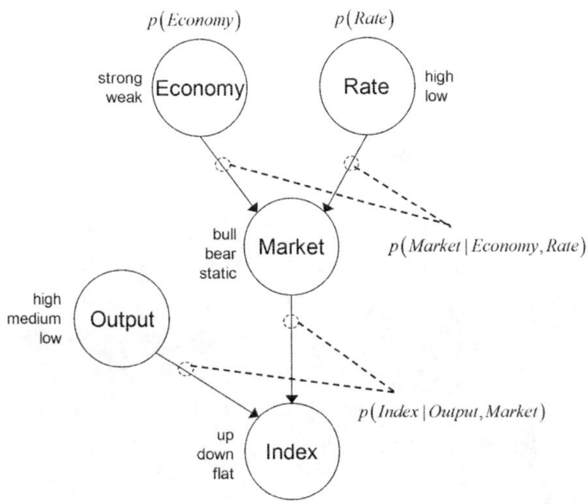

FIGURE 9.20 : An example BN to illustrate a DBN inference algorithm

FIGURE 9.21 is a 2TBN of the BN in FIGURE 9.20. The shaded nodes are the outgoing interface $\mathbf{I}_t = \{Economy\,(E)\,, Market\,(M)\,, Output\,(O)\}$, that is, the set of nodes in the current time step t with children in time step $t+1$. Interface $\mathbf{I}_t$ d-separates past from future and encapsulates all the historical information necessary to carry out prediction and filtering.

As part of the initialization step of the interface algorithm, we create the following two junction trees J_1 and J_t;

- J_1 is the junction tree created from time slice 1 of the 2TBN and used for inferencing at time step $t = 1$.

- J_t is the junction tree for each subsequent time step and is created from time slice 2 of the 2TBN and the outgoing interface of time slice 1.

The steps in creating J_1 are same as the steps for building junction trees from static BNs, except that necessary edges are added during the moralization stage to guarantee that the interface $\mathbf{I}_1$ falls completely within a single clique.

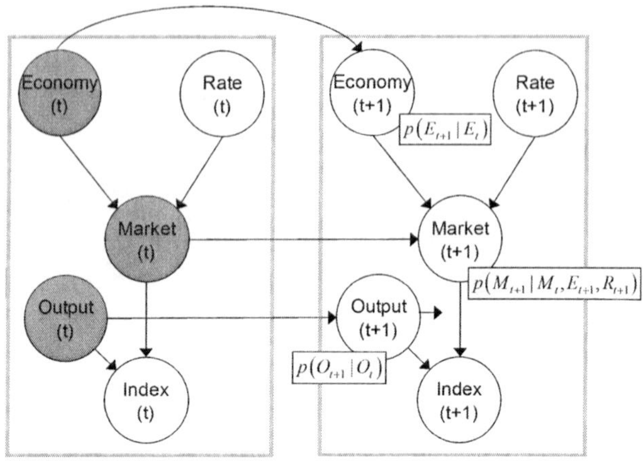

FIGURE 9.21 : 2TBN based on the BN in FIGURE 9.20

For example, FIGURE 9.22 shows the steps involved in creating junction tree J_1 from time slice 1 of 2TBN in FIGURE 9.21. The figure also shows that an additional edge has been added between the two nodes *Economy* and *Output*. The clique that contains $\mathbf{I}_1$ is called *in-clique*, and also *out-clique* in J_1.

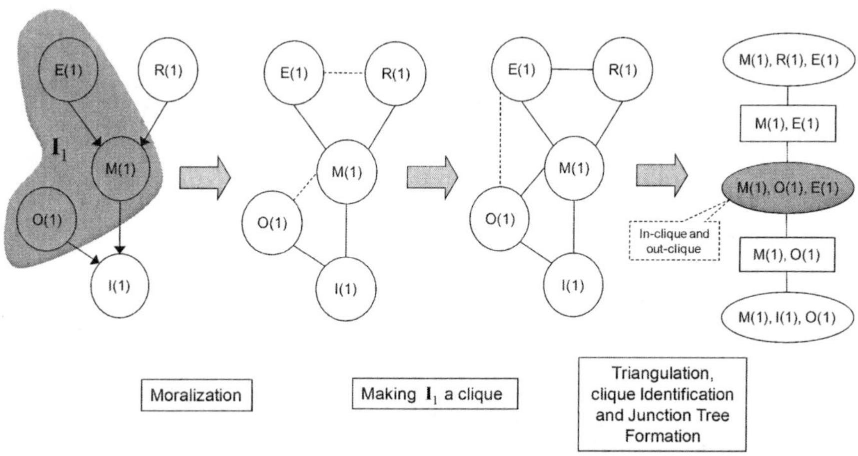

FIGURE 9.22 : Junction tree for the slice at **t=1** of the 2TBN in FIGURE 9.21 with nodes E (Economy), R (Rate), O (Output), I (Index), and M (Market)

To form J_t, start with the whole 2TBN, and then identify nodes $\mathbf{I}_t$ and $\mathbf{I}_{t+1}$ in the outgoing interfaces of time slices t and $t+1$, respectively. The resulting 2TBN is then converted to 1.5TBN by removing noninterface nodes in time slice t. FIGURE 9.23 shows these two steps starting from the 2TBN in FIGURE 9.21.

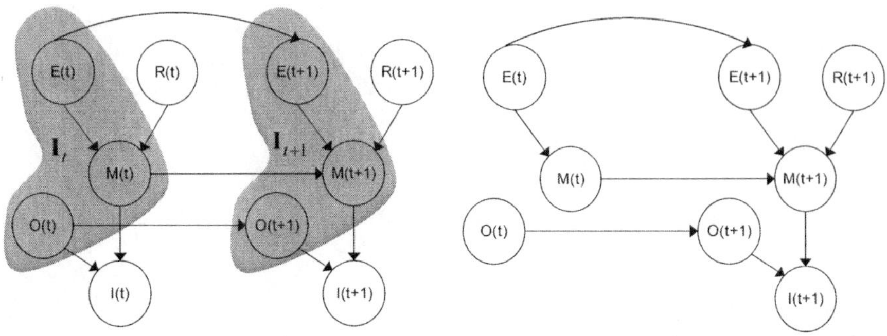

FIGURE 9.23 : (left) Identification of outgoing interfaces in 2TBN, and (right) construction of 1.5TBN from 2TBN

The next step is to moralize the resulting 1.5TBN the same way as in static BNs, adding in edges in $\mathbf{I}_t$ and $\mathbf{I}_{t+1}$ as necessary to make them complete. FIGURE 9.24 shows these two steps applied to the 1.5TBN from FIGURE 9.23.

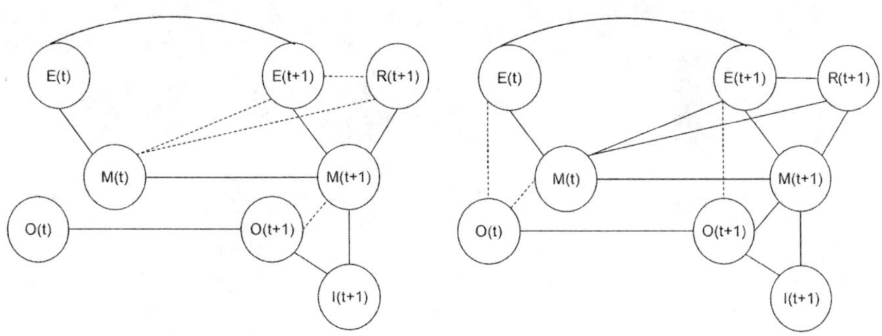

FIGURE 9.24 : (left) Moralization of 1.5TBN in FIGURE 9.23, and (right) making outgoing interfaces complete

The moralized 1.5TBN is then triangulated the same way as in static BNs, and cliques are identified to form the junction tree J_t. The cliques in the junction tree containing outgoing interface $\mathbf{I}_t$ and $\mathbf{I}_{t+1}$ are called in-clique and out-clique, respectively. The DBN on the left side of FIGURE 9.25 is the triangulation of the resulting DBN of FIGURE 9.24, and the corresponding junction tree is shown on the right of FIGURE 9.25.

In the beginning ($t = 0$), J_1 is initialized to obtain clique potentials by multiplying CPTs in the same way as in static BNs, and the potential for its in-clique and out-clique is determined. The potential ϕ_1 of interface $\mathbf{I}_1$ is obtained by marginalizing the out-clique potential in J_1. Then the time is

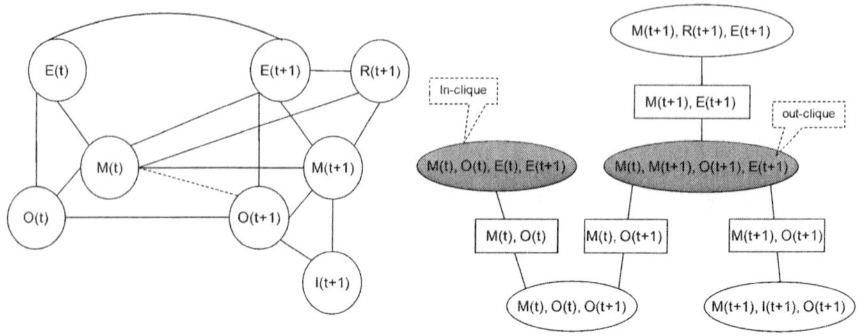

FIGURE 9.25 : (left) Triangulation of the DBN on the right of FIGURE 9.24, and (right) clique identification from the triangulated DBN

forwarded ($t = 1$) as shown, for example, in FIGURE 9.26 for our running example.

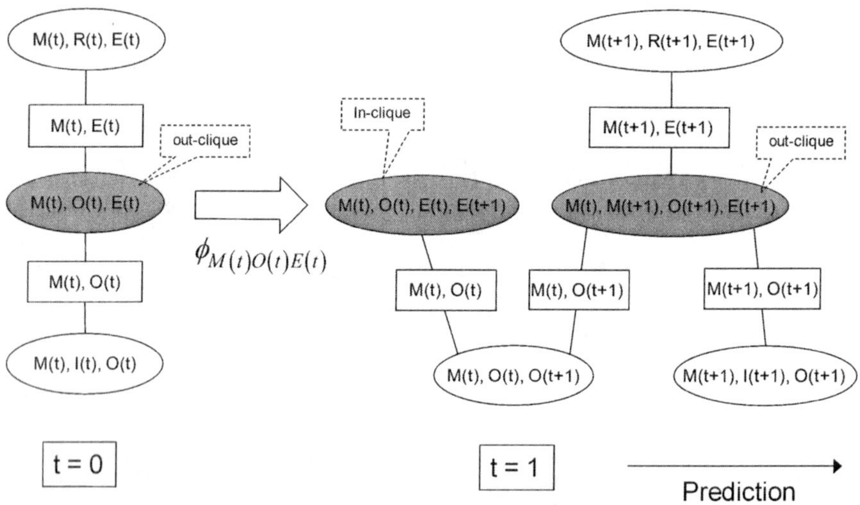

FIGURE 9.26 : Advancing DBN inference form **t=0** to **t=1**

J_2 is initialized the same way as in static BNs except we multiply only the second time slice nodes' CPTs from a clique onto that clique's potential. Considering the DBN in FIGURE 9.25, none of the CPTs for the nodes $M(t)$, $O(t)$, and $E(t)$ is multiplied. Potential ϕ_1 is multiplied onto the in-clique of J_2. Any evidence at $t = 1$ can be posted to J_2, which can then be used to make a one-step prediction.

Time is then forwarded ($t = 2$) as shown for our running example in FIGURE 9.27. The interface potential ϕ_2 is computed from the out-clique potential of J_2 and multiplied with the in-clique potential of J_3. The filtering and prediction from J_3 are computed as before, and the process continues.

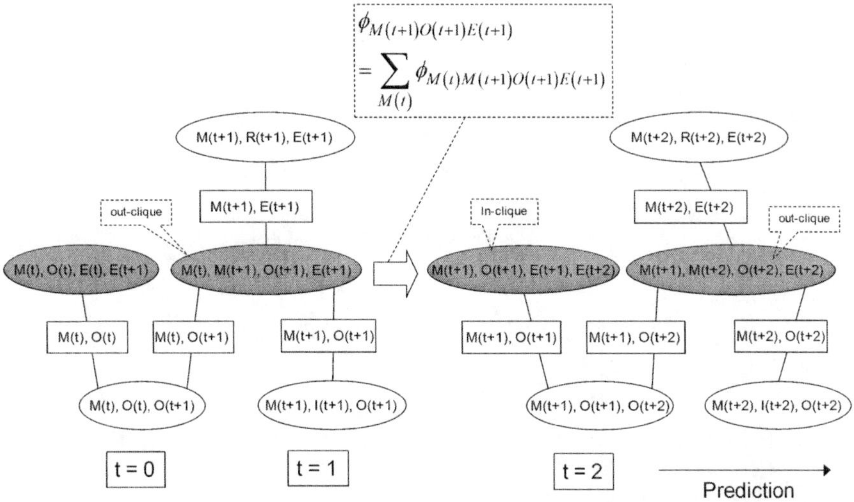

FIGURE 9.27 : Advancing the DBN inference form **t=1** to **t=2**

9.5 FURTHER READING

A seminal paper containing good background information on HMMs is Rabiner (1989). The discussion on HHMMs in this chapter largely follows Fine et al. (1998). Murphy (2002) provides a good introduction on DBNs and inference algorithms.

CHAPTER 10

Monte Carlo Simulation

Monte Carlo Sampling

This chapter presents nonparametric sampling-based algorithms to handle function nonlinearities and multimodal distributions by approximating them via a finite weighted sum of N samples, called *particles*. With a sufficient number of particles, an approximate distribution can be obtained that is close to the corresponding true distribution. Sampling-based algorithms will be able to handle, for example, temporal models with nonlinear transition and observation functions. They are also useful for Bayesian updates in models involving integrations that cannot be solved analytically or models with both numerical and categorical variables. In this chapter, we cover Markov Chain Monte Carlo (MCMC) sampling algorithms, including Gibbs sampling, the Metropolis-Hastings algorithm, and the particle filter (PF). The PF is especially effective for handling hybrid Dynamic Bayesian Networks (DBNs) containing continuous and discrete variables.

10.1 MONTE CARLO APPROXIMATION

As we have seen before, integrals are vital for computing the expected values and marginalization of continuous probability distributions. However, many functions representing distributions cannot be integrated analytically and instead rely on approximate numerical methods. The Monte Carlo sampling approach is such a method, and was originally developed to use random number generation to compute integrals.

Suppose we need to compute the following integral that cannot be computed analytically:

$$\int_a^b h(x)\,dx$$

If the function $h(x)$ can be decomposed into another function $g(x)$ and a probability density function $f(x)$ defined over the interval (a, b) then the integral can be expressed as an expectation of $g(x)$ over the density $f(x)$ of a probability distribution as follows:

$$\int_a^b h(x)\,dx = \int_a^b g(x)\,f(x)\,dx = E_{f(x)}\left(g(x)\right)$$

Now we can draw a large number of samples $x_1, ..., x_n$ of the variable x as per the density $f(x)$ to approximate the integral as follows:

$$\int_a^b h(x)\,dx = E_{f(x)}\left(g(x)\right) \cong \frac{1}{n}\sum_{i=1}^{n} g(x)$$

Since $f(x)$ is a probability density function with domain (a, b), $f(x) \geq 0,\ x \in (a, b)$, and $\int_a^b f(x)\,dx = 1$. If the latter condition is not satisfied, we normalize $f(x)$ and consider $f^*(x) = \frac{f(x)}{M}$ instead of $f(x)$, where $\int_a^b f(x)\,dx = M < \infty$. So the integral becomes

$$\int_a^b h(x)\,dx = \int_a^b g(x)\,f(x)\,dx = \int_a^b Mg(x)\,f^*(x)\,dx = ME_{f^*(x)}\left(g(x)\right)$$

It is often difficult to generate random samples from the distribution $p(X)$ defined by the density $f(x)$. MC-based methods provide a way of sampling from the distribution $p(X)$. Any probability of interest can then be computed from the generated samples.

Example

Consider the following integration:

$$\int_0^1 \left(1 + 2e^{-x}\right) e^{-x} dx$$

The analytical solution for this problem provides the true value of the above expectation as $2 - \frac{1}{e}\left(1 + \frac{1}{e}\right) \approx 1.4967$. Now we apply Monte Carlo approximation to solve this problem. Note that the integration limits are 0 and 1. Drawing samples $x_1, ..., x_n$ uniformly from $(0, 1)$, we obtain

$$\int_0^1 \left(1 + 2e^{-x}\right) e^{-x} dx \cong \frac{1}{n}\sum_{i=1}^{n} \left(1 + 2e^{-x_i}\right) e^{-x_i}$$

In the simulation, the approximate value of the integral is 1.5032 when $n = 1000$. Alternatively, we can view the integral as

$$\int_0^1 \left(1+2e^{-x}\right) e^{-x} dx = E_{e^{-x}} \left[1+2e^{-x}\right]$$

So we draw samples from the exponential distribution e^{-x} to apply Monte Carlo. But we consider $\frac{e^{-x}}{M}$ as the density function, where $M = \int_0^1 e^{-x} dx$, instead of e^{-x} since $\int_0^1 e^{-x} dx \neq 1$. But how do we draw samples from $f^* = \frac{e^{-x}}{M}$? Note that for the distribution $f^*(x)$, the CDF is $F(x) = t = \frac{1}{M}(1 - e^x)$, and its inverse is $x = F^{-1}(t) = \ln \frac{1}{1-tM}$, $0 \le t \le 1$. If t is selected uniformly from $(0, 1)$ then x follows the distribution $f^*(x)$. Thus if we draw a large number of samples $x_1, ..., x_n$ of the variable x as per the density $f^*(x)$ to approximate the integral as follows, the integral can be computed by applying Monte Carlo as

$$\int_0^1 \left(1+2e^{-x}\right) e^{-x} dx = M E_{f^*(x)} \left[1+2e^{-x}\right] \cong \frac{M}{n} \sum_1^n \left(1+2e^{-t_i}\right)$$

In the simulation, the approximate value of the integral is 1.4957 when $n = 1000$.

Here is an application of Monte Carlo to make a prediction of the state of the variable X at the next time $t+1$ based on the observations $Z_1, ..., Z_t$ until the current time t:

$$\begin{aligned} &p(X_{t+1}|Z_{1:t}) \\ &\quad = \int_{R^{n_x}} p(X_{t+1}|X_t = x, Z_{1:t})\, p(X_t = x|Z_{1:t})\, dx \\ &\quad \cong \frac{1}{n} \sum_{i=1}^{n} p(X_{t+1}|s_i, Z_{1:t}), \;\; where \;\; s_i \sim p(X_t = x|Z_{1:t}) \end{aligned}$$

Though Monte Carlo sampling is generally simple and easy to use, generating samples from a complex distribution is often quite difficult, since most of the probability is concentrated in regions whose volume is a tiny fraction of the total (Neal, 1993). These regions must be searched and covered by a proper sampling procedure.

The *Markov Chain Monte Carlo* (MCMC) sampling method is based on the fact that the correct distribution $p(X)$ of the random variable X is generated in the limit as the length of the chain grows. Let $X^{(t)}$ denote the value of X at time t, and let the state space refer to the range of possible X values. The random variable is a *Markov process* if the transition probabilities between different values in the state space depend only on the current state of the random variable, i.e.,

$$p\left(X^{(t+1)}|X^{(t)},....,X^{(1)},X^{(0)}\right)=p\left(X^{(t+1)}|X^{(t)}\right)$$

Thus for a Markov random variable, the only information about the past required to predict the future is the current state of the random variable, and knowledge of the values of earlier states does not change the transition probability. A *Markov chain* refers to a sequence of random variables $\{X^{(0)},X^{(1)},...,X^{(t)},...\}$, which is defined by giving an initial distribution for $X^{(0)}$ and the transition probabilities $p\left(X^{(t+1)}|X^{(t)}\right)$. These probabilities are chosen so that the distribution of $X^{(t)}$ converges to the correct distribution for X as t increases; that is, the stationary distribution of the Markov chain is in fact $p(X)$. The Markov chain can feasibly be simulated by sampling from the initial distribution and then, in succession, from the conditional transition distributions. For a sufficiently long chain, a Markov chain can then be used to estimate expectations. There are many different ways of setting up a Markov chain that has this desired property, including Gibbs sampling, Metropolis-Hastings algorithm, and PF algorithm.

10.2 GIBBS SAMPLING

Given a mixed set $\{X_1,...,X_n\}$ of discrete and continuous random variables, suppose we want to sample from the joint distribution $p(X_1,...,X_n)$ in order to compute one or more of the marginals $p(X_i)$. The Gibbs sampling technique samples repeatedly, replacing each component with a value picked from its distribution that is conditional on the current values of all other components. The intuition is that it is easier to consider a sequence of conditional distributions $p\left(X_k|\{X_i\}_{i\neq k}\right)$ than it is to obtain the marginals by integration of the joint density. The algorithm can be viewed as simulating a Markov chain $X^{(0)},X^{(1)},X^{(2)},....$ At step 0, the sampler starts with some initial values $\left\{x_1^{(0)},...,x_n^{(0)}\right\}$ of the variables $\{X_1,...,X_n\}$ and the following procedure is followed for transitioning to $X^{(t)}$ from $X^{(t-1)}$, $t=1,2,...$:

Draw sample x_1^t from the conditional $p\left(X_1|x_2^{t-1},x_3^{t-1},...,x_n^{t-1}\right)$
Draw sample x_2^t from the conditional $p\left(X_2|x_1^t,x_3^{t-1},...,x_n^{t-1}\right)$
...
Draw sample x_i^t from the conditional $p\left(X_i|x_1^t,...,x_{i-1}^t,x_{i+1}^{t-1},...,x_n^{t-1}\right)$
...
Draw sample x_n^t from the conditional $p\left(X_n|x_1^t,x_2^t,...,x_{n-1}^t\right)$

The sequence converges on a stationary or target distribution that is independent of the starting values. Note that the new value x_i^t is used immediately after it is generated to obtain the next value x_{i+1}^t. An entry of the transition matrix $T\left(X^{(t-1)}, X^{(t)}\right)$ of the above Markov chain can be defined as $B_1\left(X^{(t-1)}, X^{(t)}\right)...B_n\left(X^{(t-1)}, X^{(t)}\right)$ where

$$B_k\left(X^{(t-1)}, X^{(t)}\right) = p\left(X_k | \left\{x_i^t\right\}_{i \neq k}\right) \times \prod_{i \neq k} \delta\left(x_i^{t-1}, x_i^t\right)$$

$B_k\left(X^{(t-1)}, X^{(t)}\right)$ leaves all the components except x_k^{t-1} unchanged and draws a new x_k^{t-1} from its distribution, conditional on the current values of all the other components.

When we sample from $p\left(X_i | x_1^t, ..., x_{i-1}^t, x_{i+1}^{t-1}, ..., x_n^{t-1}\right)$ we can take advantage of conditional independence. For example, a conditional on the immediate neighbors of a target node X_i (called a *Markov Blanket*) in a Bayesian network is independent of all other variables, so their current values are irrelevant and constructing the right sampling distribution becomes much simpler. In general, the Markov Blanket of a target variable is the minimum conditioning set of variables that makes the target independent of all other variables. The Markov Blanket allows rapid Gibbs sampling in very large distributions. Later in the machine learning chapter we provide a procedure to apply Gibbs sampling in order to learn the parameters of a Bayesian network from an incomplete data set. Here we provide an example of learning parameters of general statistical distributions.

Example

Suppose the data set $\mathbf{D}$ comprises N observations (i.i.d.) $x_1, ..., x_N$ of variable $X \sim N\left(\mu, \sigma^2\right)$. The posterior $p\left(\mu, \sigma^2 | \mathbf{D}\right)$ does not belong to a standard family. We want to apply Gibbs sampling to estimate the posterior value of μ and σ^2. Consider first the case when the variance σ is given. The likelihood function for μ is

$$p(\mathbf{D}|\mu) = \prod_{n=1}^{N} p\left(x_n | \mu, \sigma^2\right) = \frac{1}{\left(2\pi\sigma^2\right)^{\frac{N}{2}}} Exp\left\{-\frac{1}{2\sigma^2} \sum_{n=1}^{N} \left(x_n - \mu\right)^2\right\}$$

The following Gaussian prior of μ, such as $\mu \sim N\left(\mu_*, \sigma_*^2\right)$, is a conjugate one:

$$p\left(\mu | \mu_*\right) = \frac{1}{\left(2\pi\sigma_*^2\right)^{\frac{1}{2}}} Exp\left\{-\frac{1}{2\sigma_*^2} \left(\mu - \mu_*\right)^2\right\}$$

Hence the posterior $p(\mu|\mathbf{D})$ is also Gaussian $\mu \sim N\left(\mu_N, \sigma_N^2\right)$ where

$$\frac{1}{\sigma_N^2} = \frac{1}{\sigma_*^2} + \frac{N}{\sigma^2}$$
$$\mu_N = \sigma_N^2 \left(\frac{\mu_*}{\sigma_*^2} + \frac{N}{\sigma^2}\left(\frac{1}{N}\sum_{n=1}^{N} x_n\right)\right)$$

Note that σ_*^2 is the variance of the prior of μ whereas σ^2 is the variance of the observation noise.

Next consider the case when the mean μ is given. The likelihood function for σ^2 is

$$p\left(\mathbf{D}|\sigma^2\right) = \prod_{n=1}^{N} p\left(x_n|\mu,\sigma^2\right) \propto \left(\frac{1}{\sigma^2}\right)^{\frac{N}{2}} Exp\left\{-\frac{1}{2\sigma^2}\sum_{n=1}^{N}\left(x_n-\mu\right)^2\right\}$$

An Inverse-Gamma prior of σ^2, such as $\sigma^2 \sim IGam\left(\alpha,\beta\right)$, is a conjugate one:

$$\begin{aligned} & IGam\left(\sigma^2|\alpha,\beta\right) \\ & = \tfrac{\beta^\alpha}{\Gamma(\alpha)}\left(\sigma^2\right)^{-\alpha-1} Exp\left\{-\tfrac{\beta}{\sigma^2}\right\} \\ & \propto \left(\sigma^2\right)^{-\alpha-1} Exp\left\{-\tfrac{\beta}{\sigma^2}\right\} \end{aligned}$$

The posterior is also Inverse-Gamma $IGam\left(\alpha+\frac{N}{2},\beta+\frac{1}{2}\sum\limits_{n=1}^{N}\left(x_n-\mu\right)^2\right)$ as follows:

$$\begin{aligned} & p\left(\sigma^2|\mathbf{D}\right) \\ & \propto \left(\sigma^2\right)^{-\alpha-1}\left(\tfrac{1}{\sigma^2}\right)^{\frac{N}{2}} Exp\left\{-\tfrac{\beta}{\sigma^2}-\tfrac{1}{2\sigma^2}\sum_{n=1}^{N}\left(x_n-\mu\right)^2\right\} \\ & \propto \left(\sigma^2\right)^{-\left(\alpha+\frac{N}{2}\right)-1} Exp\left\{-\frac{\beta+\frac{1}{2}\sum_{n=1}^{N}\left(x_n-\mu\right)^2}{\sigma^2}\right\} \end{aligned}$$

Hence the Gibbs sampler for simulating the posterior of $p\left(\mu,\sigma^2|\mathbf{D}\right)$ is as follows:

Initialize, $\mu_0 = \frac{1}{N}\sum\limits_{n=1}^{N} x_n,\ \alpha = 1,\ \beta = 0$

For i $= 0$ to 1000

Draw sample σ_i^2 from $IGam\left(1+\frac{N}{2},\frac{1}{2}\sum\limits_{n=1}^{N}\left(x_n-\mu\right)^2\right)$

Compute $\frac{1}{\sigma_N^2} = \frac{1}{\sigma_*^2}+\frac{N}{\sigma^2},\ \mu_N = \sigma_N^2\left(\frac{\mu_*}{\sigma_*^2}+\frac{N}{\sigma^2}\left(\frac{1}{N}\sum\limits_{n=1}^{N} x_n\right)\right)$

with $\sigma^2 = \sigma_i^2$

Draw sample μ_{i+1} from $N\left(\mu_N,\sigma_N^2\right)$

End.

10.3 METROPOLIS-HASTINGS ALGORITHM

The Metropolis-Hastings algorithm is a popular MCMC method. The generation of X_{t+1} for the distribution $p\left(X\right)$ is a two-stage process. The first stage generates a candidate X^* from the proposal distribution $q\left(X^*|X_t\right)$, and the second stage is the accept-reject step of the candidate. A typical proposal distribution is to use a normal distribution centered on the current state X_t and for some standard deviation σ:

$$X^*|X_t \sim N\left(X_t,\sigma^2\right)$$

The accept-reject state calculates the following acceptance probability:

$$\alpha\left(X_t, X^*\right) = \min\left(1, \frac{p\left(X^*\right)}{p\left(X_t\right)} \times \frac{q\left(X_t | X^*\right)}{q\left(X^* | X_t\right)}\right)$$

Note that the form of the distribution $p(X)$ may contain an integral as a normalizing constant which cannot be computed analytically in its denominator. This integral gets cancelled out in the expression $\frac{p(X^*)}{p(X_t)}$. Moreover, the proposal distribution $q\left(X^* | X_t\right)$ is the probability of generating a X^* as the candidate given that the current state is X_t and, conversely, $q\left(X_t | X^*\right)$ is the probability of generating a X_t as the candidate given that the current state is X^*. If the form of the proposal distribution $q\left(X^* | X_t\right)$ is symmetric, such as the normal distribution

$$q\left(X | Y\right) = \frac{1}{\sqrt{2\pi}\sigma} \exp\left(\frac{1}{2\sigma^2}\left(X - Y\right)^2\right)$$

then the two probabilities $q\left(X^* | X_t\right)$ and $q\left(X_t | X^*\right)$ will be equal and thus the value of $\frac{q(X_t | X^*)}{q(X^* | X_t)}$ is 1. This is a special case of the Metropolis-Hastings algorithm and is called the *Metropolis algorithm.*

Having proposed the candidate X^* and calculated the acceptance probability, the following rule is used to decide whether to accept or reject the candidate:

Set $X_{t+1} = X^*$ with probability $\alpha\left(X_t, X^*\right)$ (acceptance)
Set $X_{t+1} = X_t$ with probability $1 - \alpha\left(X_t, X^*\right)$ (rejection)

The Metropolis-Hastings algorithm is a widely used MCMC algorithm for large distributions. It is simple to understand and is easy to implement, but it can sometimes be difficult to choose and sample from proposed conditional distributions.

10.4 PARTICLE FILTER (PF)

The Particle Filter (PF) algorithm is a simple and effective MCMC algorithm for estimating the state of a stochastic process or a dynamic system over time, where the state cannot be measured directly but may be inferred from a set of observations at each time. PF is also known as a sequential Monte Carlo (introduced in Handschin and Mayne, 1969), Condensation (CONditional DENSity propagATION) (Isard and Blake, 1998), Sampling Importance Resampling (SIR) (Doucet et al., 2001), the bootstrap filter (Gordon et al., 1993), the survival of the fittest (Kanazawa et al., 1995), etc. PF handles nonlinearities and multimodal distributions by approximating them via a finite weighted sum of N samples, called *particles.* With a sufficient number of particles, an approximate conditional distribution can be obtained that is arbitrarily close to the true conditional distribution.

In this section, we present PF to estimate states of nonlinear dynamical systems and to inference in Dynamic Bayesian Networks (DBNs).

10.4.1 Particle Filter for Dynamical Systems

PF is based on propagating a probability density function for the state $X_t \in R^{n_x}$ of a dynamic system over time using the state equation

$$X_t = f(X_{t-1}, V_t)$$

and a set of observations $Y_t \in R^{n_y}$ at each time step governed by the measurement equation

$$Z_t = h(X_t, W_t)$$

where $V_t \in R^{n_v}$ and $W_t \in R^{n_w}$ are independent white noise (f and h could be time-variant). The PF algorithm computes the conditional density $L_t = p(X_t|Z_{1:t})$ and also any functional of the state by the expectation $E(g(X_t)|Z_{1:t})$. The prediction step is done according to the following equation:

$$\begin{aligned} & p(X_t|Z_{1:t-1}) \\ & \quad = \int_{R^{n_x}} p(X_t|X_{t-1} = x)\, p(X_{t-1} = x|Z_{1:t-1})\, dx \\ & \quad = \int_{R^{n_x}} p(X_t|X_{t-1} = x)\, L_{t-1} dx \end{aligned}$$

The term $p(X_t|X_{t-1})$ can be calculated using $X_t = f(X_{t-1}, V_t)$ as follows:

$$\begin{aligned} & p(X_t|X_{t-1}) \\ & \quad = \int_{R^{n_v}} p(X_t|X_{t-1}, V_t = v)\, p(V_t = v|X_{t-1} = x)\, dv \\ & \quad = \int_{R^{n_v}} \delta(X_t - f(X_{t-1}, v))\, p(V_t = v)\, dv \end{aligned}$$

where $\delta(x)$ denotes the Dirac delta function[1]. In the filtering step, the conditional density L_t is computed by applying Bayes's rule as follows:

$$L_t(X_t) = p(X_t|Z_{1:t}) = \frac{p(Z_t|X_t)\, p(X_t|Z_{1:t-1})}{p(Z_t|Z_{1:t-1})}$$

The term $p(Z_t|X_t)$ can be calculated using $Z_t = h(X_t, W_t)$ as follows:

$$\begin{aligned} & p(Z_t|X_t) \\ & \quad = \int_{R^{n_w}} p(Z_t|X_t, W_t = w)\, p(W_t = w|X_{t-1})\, dw \\ & \quad = \int_{R^{n_w}} \delta(Z_t - h(X_t, w))\, p(W_t = w)\, dw \end{aligned}$$

[1] A function that has the value everywhere except at $x = 0$ where its value is infinitely large in such a way that $\int_{-\infty}^{+\infty} \delta(x)\, dx = 1$.

The normalizing denominator $p(Z_t|Z_{1:t-1})$ is given by the following integral:

$$p(Z_t|Z_{0:t-1}) = \int_{\mathrm{R}^{n_x}} p(Z_t|X_t = x)\, p(X_t = x|Z_{0:t-1})\, dx$$

The above integrals cannot be solved analytically for many problems, and thus numerical methods must be used. The PF approach is to approximate these densities by a finite weighted sum of N samples, called *particles.* These particles are Dirac densities centered on elements of R^{n_x}. Thus we have the following:

$$L_t = p(X_t|Z_{1:t}) \approx \sum_{i=1}^{N} w_t^i \delta\left(X_t - x_t^i\right)$$

where x_t^i is the i-th sample of X_t. The above discretization makes the PF adaptive, placing more particles in places where the probability density is higher. The target distribution $p(X_t|Z_{1:t})$ is hard to sample from; instead, we sample from a proposal or importance distribution $q(X_t|Z_{1:t})$, and weight the sample according to

$$\begin{aligned} q_t^i &\propto \frac{p(X_t^i|Z_{1:t})}{q(X_t^i|Z_{1:t})} \\ &\propto \frac{p(Z_t|X_t^i)p(X_t^i|X_{t-1}^i)p(X_{t-1}^i|Z_{1:t-1})}{q(X_t^i|X_{t-1}^i,Z_{1:t})q(X_{t-1}^i|Z_{1:t-1})} \\ &\propto \frac{p(Z_t|X_t^i)p(X_t^i|X_{t-1}^i)}{q(X_t^i|X_{t-1}^i,Z_{1:t})} q_{t-1}^i \end{aligned}$$

The weights must be normalized using the relation $\sum_i q_t^i = 1$. The most common proposal is to sample from the transition prior:

$$q\left(X_t^i|X_{t-1}^i, Y_{1:t}\right) = p\left(X_t^i|X_{t-1}^i\right)$$

Thus, $q_t^i \propto p\left(Z_t|X_t^i\right) q_{t-1}^i$. With importance sampling, each and every sample drawn from importance distribution q was used to calculate the conditional density $L_t = p(X_t|Z_{1:t})$, but a fraction of the samples are rejected for sampling in the Metropolis-Hastings algorithm.

The application of the PF requires the following steps:

- Create the first particle set S_0 by drawing N independent samples from an initial prior marginal $p(X_0)$ and assign uniform weight $q_0^n = \frac{1}{N}$ to each sample x_0^n.
- Sample from $p(V_t)$ for all t.
- Compute $p(Z_t|X_t)$ via a known function $l(Z_t; X_t) \propto p(Z_t|X_t)$ for all t.

Based on the above, prediction, filtering, and estimation are recursively computed via the following algorithm:

ALGORITHM: Basic Particle Filter

Initialization

$$\begin{cases} x_0^n \sim p(X_0) \\ q_0^n = \frac{1}{N} \end{cases} \qquad n = 1, ..., N$$

Prediction:

$$\begin{cases} v_t^n \sim p(V_t) \\ x_{t|t-1}^n = f\left(x_{t-1}^n, v_t^n\right) \end{cases} \qquad n = 1, ..., N$$

Filter:

$$\begin{cases} q_t^n = \frac{l\left(z_t; x_{t|t-1}^n\right) q_{t-1}^n}{\sum\limits_{i=1}^{N} l\left(z_t; x_{t|t-1}^i\right) q_{t-1}^i} \\ x_t^n = x_{t|t-1}^n \end{cases} \qquad n = 1, ..., N$$

Estimation:

Estimate $\mathrm{E}(X_t)$ by $\sum\limits_{n=1}^{N} q_t^n x_t^n$

The major drawback of the above algorithm is that after several steps, only a few particles keep high weights and the rest have very small ones that do not carry any information. One solution to avoid this problem of degeneracy of the particle set, adopted in Gordon et al. (1993), is to apply the following resampling step at each time period:

ALGORITHM: Resampling of a Basic Particle Filter

Resampling:

$$\begin{cases} x_t^n \sim \sum\limits_{i=0}^{N} q_t^i \delta\left(X_t - x_{t|t-1}^i\right) \\ q_t^n = \frac{1}{N} \end{cases} \qquad n = 1, ..., N$$

Instead of applying the resampling step at each time period, period resampling has been introduced (Kong et al., 1994) based on the effective sample size N_{eff}, which can be estimated as

$$\frac{1}{\sum\limits_{n=1}^{N} \left(q_t^n\right)^2}$$

representing the number of meaningful particles. The modified resampling algorithm based on the degeneracy measure is given below:

ALGORITHM: Degeneracy Measure-Based Resampling

Resampling:

Calculate $N_{eff} = \frac{1}{\sum_{i=1}^{N} (q_t^n)^2}$

If $N_{eff} < N_{threshold}$ then

$$\begin{cases} x_t^n \sim \sum_{i=0}^{N} q_t^i \delta\left(X_t - x_{t|t-1}^i\right) \\ q_t^n = \frac{1}{N} \end{cases} \qquad n = 1, ..., N$$

Else

$$x_t^n = x_{t|t-1}^n \qquad n = 1, ..., N$$

10.4.2 Particle Filter for DBN

The transition and observation models can also be represented by a complex DBN, exploiting the underlying causal structure among the random variables instead of using parametric functions f and h. The following algorithm can be used to apply PF to a DBN.

ALGORITHM: Particle Filter for DBN

Initialization:

$$\begin{cases} x_0^n \sim p(X_0) \\ q_0^n = \frac{1}{n} \end{cases} \qquad n = 1, ..., N$$

Prediction & Filter:

For $n = 1 : N$
  Set x_t^n = empty vector of length equal to the number of nodes in a time slice of the DBN.
  Set $q_t^n = 1$.
  For each node i in topological order in time slice t (ordering guarantees that parent node values are known).
  Let u be the value of $pa\left(X_t^i\right)$ from x_{t-1}^n .
    If X_t^i not in the observation Z_t
      Sample $x_t^{n,i} \sim p\left(X_t^i | pa\left(X_t^i\right) = u\right)$
    Else
      Set $x_t^{n,i}$ = value X_t^i in Z_t.
      Set $q_t^n = q_t^n \times p\left(X_t^i = x_t^{n,i} | pa\left(X_t^i\right) = u\right)$.

Estimation:

Estimate (for continuous variables): $E(X_t)$ by $\sum_{n=1}^{N} q_t^n x_t^n$.

Example

Consider the example Markovian DBN (Doucet et al., 2000a and 2000b) in FIGURE 10.1 containing three temporal Boolean variables A (*Market*), B (*Output*), and C (*Rate*) representing, respectively, the stock market (*up*, *down*), the industrial output (*up*, *down*), and the unemployment rate (*up*, *down*). The Z-variables are observations. There are temporal dependencies among the variables; for example, the industrial output at the current time step affects both the stock market and the employment rate at the next time step. We estimate variable states via exact Bayesian filter and via approximate PF.

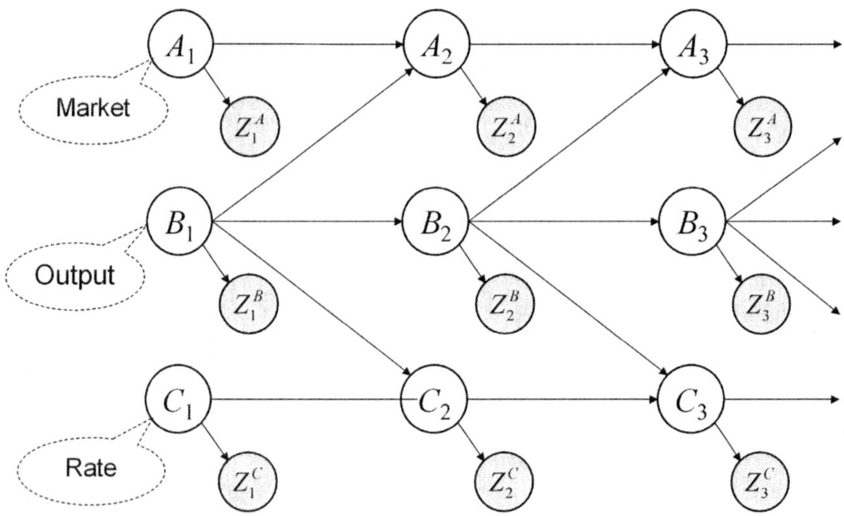

FIGURE 10.1 : Example DBN

For the Bayesian filter, given the initial prior $p(A_0, B_0, C_0)$ for the joint distribution, the following pair of recursive prediction and filtering equations can be derived by applying a combination of Bayes' and marginalization rules:

$$\begin{aligned}
&p(A_t, B_t, C_t|Z_{1:t-1})\\
&\quad = \sum_{A_{t-1}} \sum_{B_{t-1}} \sum_{C_{t-1}} p(A_t, B_t, C_t|A_{t-1}, B_{t-1}C_{t-1})\, p(A_{t-1}, B_{t-1}, C_{t-1}|Z_{1:t-1})\\
&\quad = \sum_{A_{t-1}} \sum_{B_{t-1}} \sum_{C_{t-1}} p(A_t|A_{t-1}, B_{t-1}) p(B_t|B_{t-1})\\
&\qquad\qquad p(C_t|B_{t-1}C_{t-1})\, p(A_{t-1}, B_{t-1}, C_{t-1}|Z_{1:t-1})\\
&\quad = \sum_{B_{t-1}} p(B_t|B_{t-1}) \sum_{A_{t-1}} p(A_t|A_{t-1}, B_{t-1})\\
&\qquad\qquad \sum_{C_{t-1}} p(C_t|B_{t-1}C_{t-1})\, p(A_{t-1}, B_{t-1}, C_{t-1}|Z_{1:t-1})
\end{aligned}$$

$$\begin{aligned}
p(A_t, B_t, C_t|Z_{1:t}) &= \frac{p(Z_t|A_t,B_t,C_t)p(A_t,B_t,C_t|Z_{1:t-1})}{\sum\limits_{A_t}\sum\limits_{B_t}\sum\limits_{C_t} p(Z_t|A_t,B_t,C_t)p(A_t,B_t,C_t|Z_{1:t-1})}\\
&= \frac{p(Z_t^A|A_t)p(Z_t^B|B_t)p(Z_t^C|C_t)p(A_t,B_t,C_t|Z_{1:t-1})}{\sum\limits_{A_t}\sum\limits_{B_t}\sum\limits_{C_t} p(Z_t|A_t,B_t,C_t)p(A_t,B_t,C_t|Z_{1:t-1})}
\end{aligned}$$

For PF, the following transition priors are used to sample particles at time t:

$$p(B_t|B_{t-1}), p(A_t|A_{t-1}, B_{t-1}), p(C_t|C_{t-1}, B_{t-1})$$

Then evaluate the importance weight as

$$w_t \,\alpha\, p(Z_t|A_t, B_t, C_t)$$

10.4.3 Particle Filter Issues

One problem of the PF is that its state vector-based formalism is usually very high in dimension. The higher the dimension in an application domain, the larger the number of particles required to cover the area in the high-dimensional space (which increases exponentially). Consequently, there is a need for a large number of particles to approximate conditional distributions from high-dimensional spaces.

The Rao-Blackwellised Particle Filter (RBPF) algorithm exploits some of the analytical structure of the model by dividing the set of random variables into two: one subset is handled by the PF and the other subset by a bank of KFs. Sometimes a partitioned or factored sampling approach is adopted when the underlying system dynamics can be separated into several independent components (Das et al., 2005; Pfeffer et al., 2007).

If the conditional distribution $p(Z_t|X_t)$ has severe outliers, many samples will be allocated to parts of the distribution with high predicted probability but low observational probability, and relatively few samples will be allocated to parts of the distribution with low predicted probability but high observational probability. Consequently, a large number of samples are needed for approximation accuracy, which creates a problem as dimensionality increases.

10.5 FURTHER READING

For an overview of the state of the art in PF, see Doucet et al. (2001), Arulampalam et al. (2002), and Djuric et al. (2003). More details on UKF can be found in Julier and Uhlmann (1997).

CHAPTER 11

Cluster Analysis and Segmentation

Segmentation of data is a fundamental requirement for analytics when dealing with customer background, sales transactions, customer surveys, and similar data. An appropriate segmentation of customer data can provide insights to enhance a company's performance by identifying the most valuable customers or the customers that are likely to leave the company. *Cluster analysis* (Duda et al., 2001; Jain et al., 1999; Jain and Dubes, 1988) attempts to segment a dataset of items or instances into clusters, where instances correspond to points in an n-dimensional Euclidean space. A cluster is a set of points in a dataset that are similar to each other but are dissimilar to other points in the dataset. Most traditional clustering techniques, such as feed-forward and supervised neural networks, rely on carefully crafted data points in terms of fixed-length vector structures of ordered n-tuples. Each component in a vector represents some feature of an object from the underlying problem domain.

The similarity between two data points is quantified by measuring the distance between them with respect to a selected set of data attributes or features. A typical way of measuring distance between two data points $X = (x_1, ..., x_n)$ and $Y = (y_1, ..., y_n)$ in the feature space is the Euclidean distance

$$\sqrt{\sum_{i=1}^{n} (x_i - y_i)^2}$$

where all n attributes are selected and considered numeric. A user must define their own distance when the selected set of attributes is a mixture of categorical and numerical types or as needed by the application at hand.

This chapter covers some of the most popular and powerful clustering techniques for segmenting data sets, namely, Hierarchical, k-Means, k-Nearest Neighbor (kNN), Support Vector Machine (SVM), and multi-layer feed-forward Neural Networks (NNs). The first three have their roots in traditional statistics, whereas the latter two grew out of machine learning research.

k-means, kNN, and SVM feature in the top ten algorithms for data mining (Wu and Kumar, 2009). kNN, SVM, and NN are *supervised clustering* techniques, meaning the instances are given with known labels. Instances are unlabeled in *unsupervised clustering* techniques, and Hierarchical and k-Means fall into this category.

SVM is meant to handle very large dimensional data and hence is naturally suitable for clustering unstructured text documents where records are built using parsed words and phrases from documents. Unsupervised text classification and topic extraction techniques, such as Latent Semantics Analysis (LSA), Probabilistic LSA (PLSA), and Latent Dirichlet Allocation (LDA), to be introduced in the section on text classification, can be used for segmenting both structured and unstructured textual corpus. Various generative models introduced in the chapter on machine learning, such as Naïve Bayesian Classifier and Bayesian Networks, can also be used to segment data.

11.1 HIERARCHICAL CLUSTERING

Hierarchical clustering (Johnson, 1967) is an unsupervised technique that builds clusters wherein each node is a subset of its ancestors. Visualizing this hierarchy provides a useful summary of the data, as the hierarchy may correspond to a meaningful taxonomy. There are two approaches to hierarchical clustering:

- Bottom-up or agglomerative clustering (Jung and Kim, 2001), with the approach of grouping small clusters into larger ones.
- Top-down or divisive clustering, with the approach of splitting big clusters into smaller ones.

The bottom-up approach is the most popular hierarchical clustering. The idea is to use the data to build a binary tree that successively merges similar groups of points. It requires a measure of similarity among groups of data points, but does not require that the number of clusters be specified in advance.

Bottom-up Hierarchical Clustering Algorithm

Input: N items to cluster.

Output: Hierarchical partitions of items.

Step 1: Assign each item to a separate cluster, so initially there will be N clusters, each containing just one item. Compute "distances" (similarities) between clusters as defined below.

Step 2: Find the closest pair of clusters and merge them into a single cluster, so there will be one cluster less.

Step 3: Compute distances between the new cluster and each of the old clusters.

Step 4: Repeat steps 2 and 3 until all items are clustered into a single cluster of size N.

Given a distance measure between two data points, three types of distances between clusters can be defined:

- *Single-linkage clustering* (connectedness or minimum): Distance between two clusters to be equal to the shortest distance from any member of one cluster to any member of the other cluster. Single-linkage can produce "chaining," where a sequence of close observations in different clusters causes early merges of those clusters.
- *Complete-linkage clustering* (diameter or maximum): Distance between two clusters to be equal to the greatest distance from any member of one cluster to any member of the other cluster. Complete-linkage has the opposite problem of single-linkage, in that it might not merge close clusters because of outlier members that are far apart.
- *Average-linkage clustering*: Distance between two clusters to be equal to the average distance from any member of one cluster to any member of the other cluster. Average-linkage represents a natural compromise, but depends on the scale of the similarities.

Ward's distance, for example, between two clusters A and B depends on by how much the sum of squares will increase if the two clusters are merged. The distance $\Delta(A,B)$ is the difference between the total within-cluster sum of squares for the two clusters A and B separately, and the within-cluster sum of squares resulting from merging the two clusters in cluster $A \cup B$:

$$\begin{aligned}\Delta(A,B) \\ &= \sum_{z_i \in A\cup B} \|z_i - \bar{z}\|^2 - \sum_{x_j \in A} \|x_j - \bar{x}\|^2 - \sum_{y_j \in B} \|y_j - \bar{y}\|^2 \\ &= \frac{n(A)+n(B)}{n(A)n(B)} \|\bar{x} - \bar{y}\|^2\end{aligned}$$

where $\bar{x}$ represents cluster-centers and $n(*)$ represents the number of elements in the cluster. The sum of squares of any two clusters that can be formed at each step can then be minimized. Ward's distance is less susceptible to the effects of noise and outliers than other methods of clustering.

Example

TABLE 11.1 is a dataset containing items of the three attributes Temperature, Humidity, and Decision, extracted from the play-tennis dataset in Appendix B (ignore the Decision attribute for this example). The Id column has been added for the purpose of illustration.

TABLE 11.1: : Temperature-Humidity table

Id	Temperature	Humidity	Decision
1	75	70	don't play
2	80	90	don't play
3	85	85	play
4	72	95	play
5	69	70	play
6	72	90	don't play
7	83	78	play
8	64	65	don't play
9	81	75	play
10	71	80	play
11	65	70	play
12	75	80	play
13	68	80	play
14	70	96	don't play

FIGURE 11.1 displays the output from SAS hierarchical clustering based on this table as input with average-linkage as the distance between clusters. The items with Ids 4, 6, and 14 in TABLE 11.1 correspond to the encircled cluster at level three in the hierarchy. A closer look at these items in the table reveals their similarity with respect to both Temperature and Humidity attributes.

Hierarchical structures are informative but are not suitable for large datasets. The algorithm imposes a hierarchical structure on data, even when such a structure is not appropriate. The crucial question is how many clusters are to be considered. The complexity of hierarchical clustering is higher than k-means (introduced next).

11.2 K-MEANS CLUSTERING

The k-Means algorithm (Hartigan and Wang, 1979) is an unsupervised clustering technique that classifies the input data points into k number of clusters based on their inherent distance from each other. The principle is to minimize the sum of squares of the distances between data and the corresponding cluster centroids:

$$\sum_{i=1}^{k} \sum_{x_j \in S_i} (x_j - \mu_i)^2$$

where $S_1, ..., S_K$ are k clusters with centroids $\mu_1, ..., \mu_k$ respectively. This technique is non-deterministic, since the output clusters depend on the initial

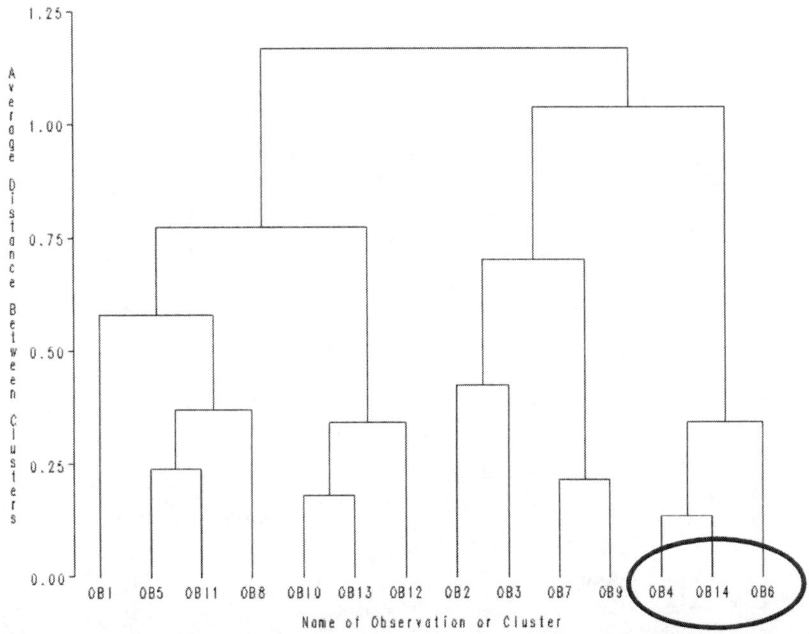

FIGURE 11.1 : Hierarchical clustering of TABLE 11.1 using SAS

choice of k points. It is also a flat (non-hierarchical) clustering technique because it gives us a single set of clusters with no particular organization or structure within them.

k-Means Algorithm

Input: Set of N items and number k of centroids.

Output: k clusters

Step 1: Place k points into the space represented by the items that are being clustered. These points represent initial cluster centroids. Good practice is to place them as far from each other as possible.

Step 2: Assign each object to the cluster that has the closest centroid.

Step 3: When all objects have been assigned, recalculate the positions of the k centroids.

Step 4: Repeat Steps 2 and 3 until the centroids no longer change.

Note that different initial positions of centroids yield different final clusters.

Example

We consider the dataset in TABLE 11.1 for attributes Temperature and Humidity. FIGURE 11.2 displays the output from SAS k-means clustering on this dataset with $k = 4$. The clusters that were generated are the ones circled at the bottom of the figure. The hierarchy of FIGURE 11.1 is shown here for the purpose of comparison. Some statistics of the generated clusters are shown at the upper half of the FIGURE 11.2. In comparison between the hierarchical and k-means clustering, two of the four clusters at level two of the hierarchy exactly correspond to two of the four clusters generated by k-means clustering.

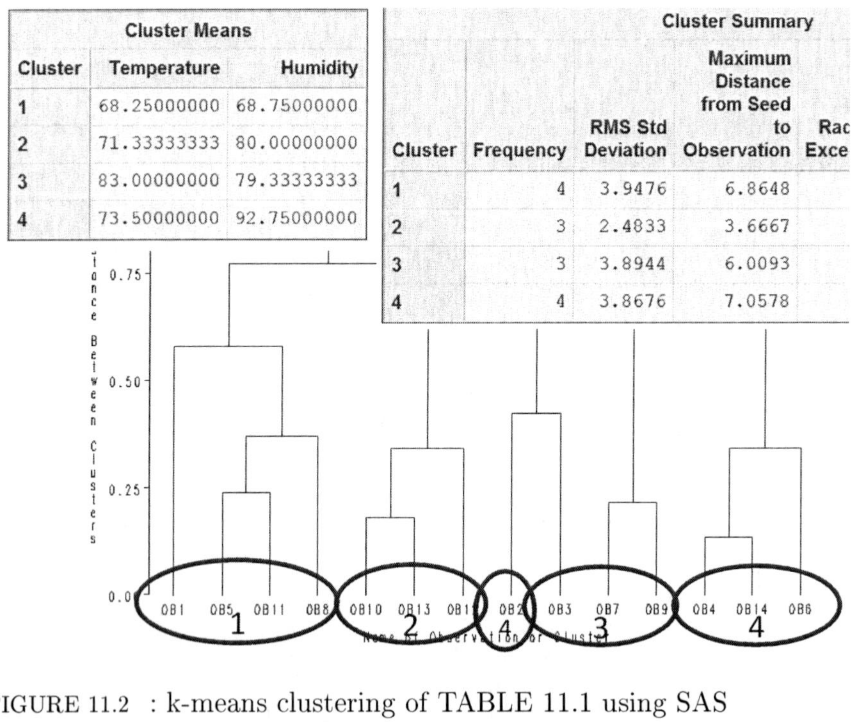

Cluster Means

Cluster	Temperature	Humidity
1	68.25000000	68.75000000
2	71.33333333	80.00000000
3	83.00000000	79.33333333
4	73.50000000	92.75000000

Cluster Summary

Cluster	Frequency	RMS Std Deviation	Maximum Distance from Seed to Observation	Rac Exce
1	4	3.9476	6.8648	
2	3	2.4833	3.6667	
3	3	3.8944	6.0093	
4	4	3.8676	7.0578	

FIGURE 11.2 : k-means clustering of TABLE 11.1 using SAS

k-means clustering is faster than hierarchical clustering, although determining the value of k in advance is often difficult, and the technique does not handle non-convex clusters effectively.

11.3 K-NEAREST NEIGHBORS

The k-Nearest Neighbor (kNN) algorithm (Cover and Hart, 1967) is a supervised technique for classifying objects based on closest training instances in the feature space. For a given unlabeled instance, kNN finds the k "closest" labeled instances in the training dataset and then assigns to the unlabeled instance the class that appears most frequently within the k-subset. kNN is therefore making decisions from past experience, and is behaving in the manner of a loan expert for credit risk assessment (Henley and Hand, 1996) or a physician for clinical assessment (Zhu et al., 2007).

A physician will likely recommend a particular treatment program to a new patient if the new patient's clinical profile matches those patients who have been successfully treated by the physician in the past with the same program. Similarly, a loan officer will be likely to approve credit to a new applicant if the new applicant's credit profile matches those applicants who have successfully repaid loans without defaulting. Hence, a physician's past patients or a loan officer's past cases can be regarded as their training set. Matching the clinical or credit profile of a new patient or applicant to those of the expert's past patients or applicants is similar to finding a number of nearest neighbors from the training set.

kNN Algorithm

Input and output:

- Dataset of n training-instance set $\{(X_1, y_1), ..., (X_n, y_n)\}$, where each X_i is a feature vector and y_i is the corresponding decision outcome, which is a value from the set $\{o_1, ..., o_m\}$ of all possible outcomes.
- Number of nearest neighbor k.
- Distance measurement function $d(X_i, X_j)$ and a strategy to break a tie.
- New feature vector X_0 for which the decision outcome y_0 needs to be determined.
- Decision threshold c.

Step 1: Identify k observations in the training dataset that are most similar to X_0 based on the distance measurement function.

Step 2: Estimate the probabilities $p(y_0 = o_i)$, $i = 1, ..., m$, by the average responses of these k neighbors. If k_1 is the number out of K responses for which $y_0 = o_j$ then $p(y_0 = o_j)$ is the ratio k_1/k after breaking any tie. Note that weights of the neighbors based on their distance from y_0 (e.g., inverse square of the distances) can be assigned while computing the ratio.

Step 3: Assign $y_0 = o_j$ for which $p(y_0 = o_j)$ is the largest and crosses the threshold c.

Example

We consider the dataset in TABLE 11.1. We have $n = 14$, $m = 2$, and $X_i =$

(t_i, h_i), $i = 1, ..., 14$, where t_i is the value of the attribute Temperature of the instance with Id i, h_i is the corresponding value of the attribute Humidity, and y_i is the corresponding value of the attribute Decision. For example, $X_4 = (72, 95)$ and $y_4 = play$. Suppose $k = 4$, $X_0 = (70, 92)$, and $c = 0$.

As shown in TABLE 11.2, X_2, X_4, X_6, and X_{14} are the closest four points from X_0. Now, $p(y_0 = play) = 1/4 = 0.25$, $p(y_0 = don't\, play) = 3/4 = 0.75$. Hence, $y_0 = don't\, play$.

TABLE 11.2: : Data points X_1 to X_{14} and their distances from $X_0 = (70, 92)$

Temperature	**Humidity**	**Distance**	**Play Tennis**
75	70	22.56	don't play
80	90	10.20	don't play
85	85	16.55	play
72	95	3.61	play
69	70	22.02	play
72	90	2.83	don't play
83	78	19.10	play
64	65	27.66	don't play
81	75	20.25	play
71	80	12.04	play
65	70	22.56	play
75	80	13.0	play
68	80	12.16	play
70	96	4.0	don't play

11.4 SUPPORT VECTOR MACHINES

Support Vector Machine (SVM) is a state-of-the-art classification method (Vapnik, 1998 & 2010) suitable for dealing with very high-dimensional data. We introduce various cases of SVM classifiers. Then we explain the concept of Vapnik-Chervonekis (VC) dimension, which offers some theoretical insights into SVM's maximum margin classifier and expected risk in terms of test errors.

11.4.1 Linearly Separable Data

This section explains the mathematical formulation of SVM for linearly separable data, that is, when the training data points can be separated by a hyperplane. The classification problem is restricted to the two-class problem without loss of generality. The data for a two-class classification problem consists of objects labeled with one of two labels corresponding to the two classes, say +1 (positive examples) and −1 (negative examples). In general, as shown in FIGURE 11.3, there are many linear classifiers (hyperplanes) that separate the data, but only one optimal separating hyperplane provides maximum separation, yielding the *maximum margin classifier*. The points that influence optimality are called *support vectors*, which are the data points that lie closest to the hyperplane representing the decision boundary. These points are the most difficult to classify, but help to determine the decision boundary.

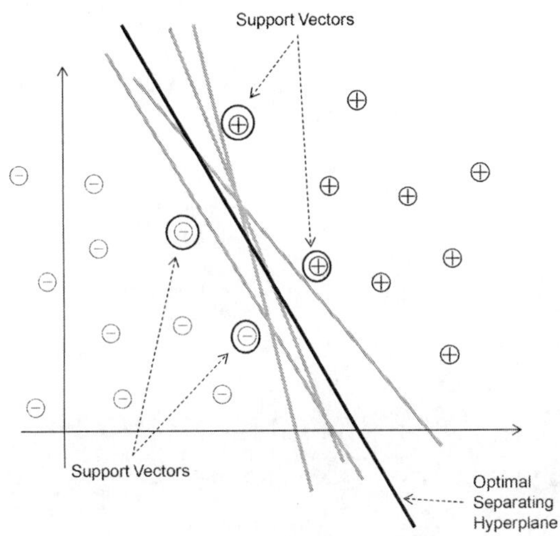

FIGURE 11.3 : Many hyperplanes separating two classes of data points

Suppose boldface $\mathbf{x}$ denotes a vector with components x_i as features. Consider a set of N linearly separable data points $(\mathbf{x}_1, y_1), ..., (\mathbf{x}_N, y_N)$, where each y_i is either $+1$ or -1. As shown in FIGURE 11.4, we choose a decision boundary $\mathbf{w}.\mathbf{x} + b = 0$ such that the plus and minus hyperplanes containing support vectors are as follows:

$$\begin{array}{l}\text{Plus Hyperplane: } \mathbf{w}.\mathbf{x}_i + b = +1 \\ \text{Minus Hyperplane: } \mathbf{w}.\mathbf{x}_i + b = -1\end{array}$$

The plus and minus hyperplanes are parallel to each other and are equidistant from the decision boundary. The vector $\mathbf{w}$ is perpendicular to both plus and minus hyperplanes. It can be verified easily that the width of the margin is

$$\frac{2}{\sqrt{\mathbf{w}.\mathbf{w}}} \text{ or } \frac{2}{\|\mathbf{w}\|}$$

For positive examples ($y_i = +1$) and negative examples ($y_i = -1$), we have the following:

$$\begin{array}{l}\mathbf{w}.\mathbf{x}_i + b \geq +1 \text{ when } y_i = +1 \\ \mathbf{w}.\mathbf{x}_i + b \leq -1 \text{ when } y_i = -1\end{array}$$

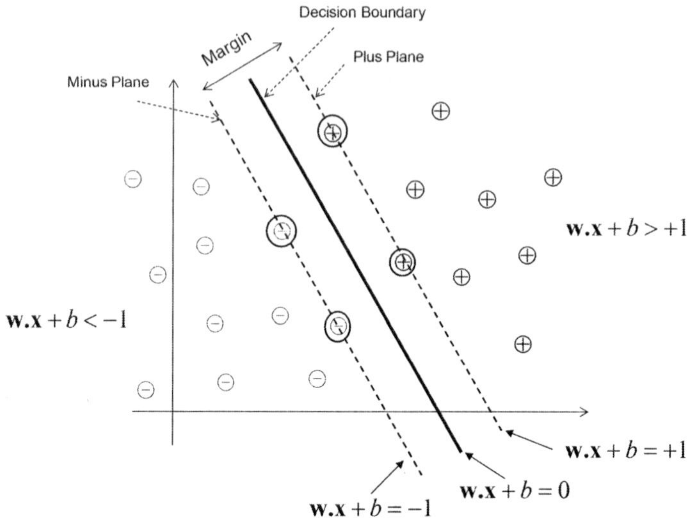

FIGURE 11.4 : Maximum margin classifier

The above two together yields the following relation:

$$y_i\left(\mathbf{w}.\mathbf{x}_i + b\right) \geq 1 \quad i = 1, ..., N$$

The optimal hyperplane $(\mathbf{w}, b)$ solves the following equivalent quadratic programming problem (maximization of the geometric margin $\frac{1}{\|\mathbf{w}\|}$ is equivalent to minimizing $\|\mathbf{w}\|^2$):

Minimize: $\frac{1}{2}\|\mathbf{w}\|^2$
Subject to the constraints: $y_i\left(\mathbf{w}.\mathbf{x}_i + b\right) \geq 1 \quad i = 1, ..., N$

To solve the problem, we introduce positive Lagrangian multipliers $\alpha_i, i = 1, ..., N$, for each inequality constraint. The constraint equations are multiplied by positive Lagrange multipliers (see the Wikipedia article) and subtracted from the objective function to form the following Lagrangian:

$$L\left(\mathbf{w}, b, \alpha\right) = \frac{1}{2}\|\mathbf{w}\|^2 - \sum_{i=1}^{N} \alpha_i y_i \left(\mathbf{w}.\mathbf{x}_i + b\right) + \sum_{i=1}^{N} \alpha_i$$

$L\left(\mathbf{w}, b, \alpha\right)$ is to be minimized with respect to $\mathbf{w}$ and b, and simultaneously requires that the derivative with respect to each α_i is zero. Since the objective function is convex and the constraints are linear (defining a convex set as their solutions), the following dual problem can be solved for the above optimization problem:

Maximize: $L(\alpha) = \sum_{i=1}^{N} \alpha_i - \frac{1}{2} \sum_{i=1}^{N} \sum_{j=1}^{N} \alpha_i \alpha_j y_i y_j (\mathbf{x}_i . \mathbf{x}_j)$
Subject to the constraints: $\alpha_i \geq 0 \quad i = 1, ..., N$

$$\sum_{i=1}^{N} \alpha_i y_i = 0$$

Once an optimal solution α^* is found, corresponding $\mathbf{w}^*$ and b^* can be obtained as the following:

$$\mathbf{w}^* = \sum_{i=1}^{N} \alpha_i y_i \mathbf{x}_i$$
$$b^* = y_{k^*} - \mathbf{w}^* . \mathbf{x}_{k^*}, \ \textit{where}\ k^* = \arg\max_{k} \alpha_k$$

Note that α_is are non-zeros only for the training data points representing the support vectors. For all other training data points $\alpha_i = 0$. The decision function is therefore

$$f^*(\mathbf{x}) = \mathbf{w}^* . \mathbf{x} + b^*$$

Therefore, only support vectors are relevant for classifications.

11.4.2 Preparation of Data and Packages

SVM requires that each training instance is represented as a vector of real numbers. Categorical attributes have to be converted to their equivalent numerical representation via, for example, 1-of-C coding. If a categorical attribute takes n possible values then it can be represented as an ordered n-tuple of numbers, only one of which is one and the rest are zeros (Hsu et al., 2010). For example, the categorical variable Outlook in the play-tennis example in Appendix B can be represented as 3-tuple. The representation of the values sunny, overcast and rain are (1, 0, 0), (0, 1, 0), and (0, 0, 1), respectively.

It is also recommended that each numerical attribute is scaled to the range of [-1, +1] or [0, 1], and both training and test instances are transformed accordingly. The scaling avoids attributes in greater numeric ranges dominating those in smaller numeric ranges.

LIBSVM is a library for Support Vector Machines (SVMs) with source code in C++ and Java (http://www.csie.ntu.edu.tw/~cjlin/libsvm/).

11.4.3 Non-Separable Data

The objective function of the dual Lagrangian problem described in the previous subsection grows arbitrarily large when applied to non-separable data as shown in FIGURE 11.5. To address this problem, the original linear constraints are relaxed as follows:

$$\mathbf{w}.\mathbf{x}_i + b \geq +1 - \varepsilon_i \text{ when } y_i = +1$$
$$\mathbf{w}.\mathbf{x}_i + b \leq -1 + \varepsilon_i \text{ when } y_i = -1$$
$$\varepsilon_i \geq 0$$

The corresponding optimization criterion is to minimize $\frac{1}{2}\|\mathbf{w}\|^2 + C\sum_{i=1}^{N}\varepsilon_i$, where C represents the penalty of error.

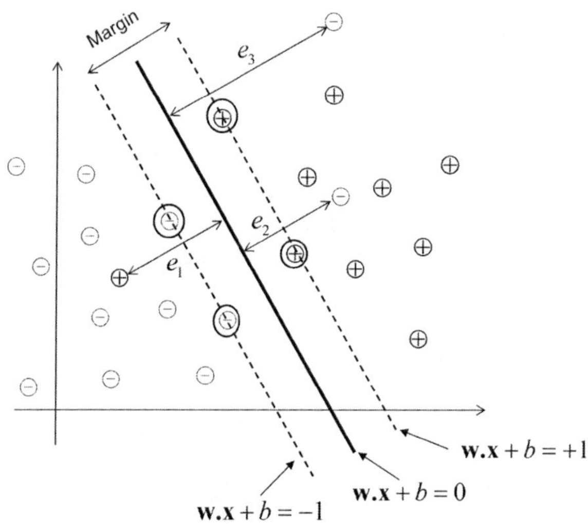

FIGURE 11.5 : Maximum margin classifier for non-separable data

As before, we have the following dual Lagrangian problem:

Maximize: $L(\alpha) = \sum_{i=1}^{N}\alpha_i - \frac{1}{2}\sum_{i=1}^{N}\sum_{j=1}^{N}\alpha_i\alpha_j y_i y_j (\mathbf{x}_i.\mathbf{x}_j)$

Subject to the constraints:

$$0 \leq \alpha_i \leq C \quad i = 1, ..., N$$
$$\sum_{i=1}^{N}\alpha_i y_i = 0$$

Again the solution is given by

$$\mathbf{w}^* = \sum_{i=1}^{N}\alpha_i y_i \mathbf{x}_i$$
$$b^* = y_{k^*}(1 - \varepsilon_{k^*}) - \mathbf{w}^*.\mathbf{x}_{k^*}, \text{ where } k^* \text{ is } \arg\max_k \alpha_k$$

where only the support vectors have non-zero α_i values.

11.4.4 Non-Linear Classifier

A separating hyperplane cannot always be used to divide the data, as shown in FIGURE 11.6. On the left of the figure, all the negative data points are enclosed within a circle, and on the right the negative points are enclosed within a parabola. In other words, the decision function $\phi(\mathbf{x})$ is a non-linear function and the labeling decision is

$$f(\mathbf{x}, \alpha) = \begin{cases} +1, & \text{if } sign\,(\phi(\mathbf{x})) \text{ is positive} \\ -1, & \text{if } sign\,(\phi(\mathbf{x})) \text{ is negative} \end{cases}$$

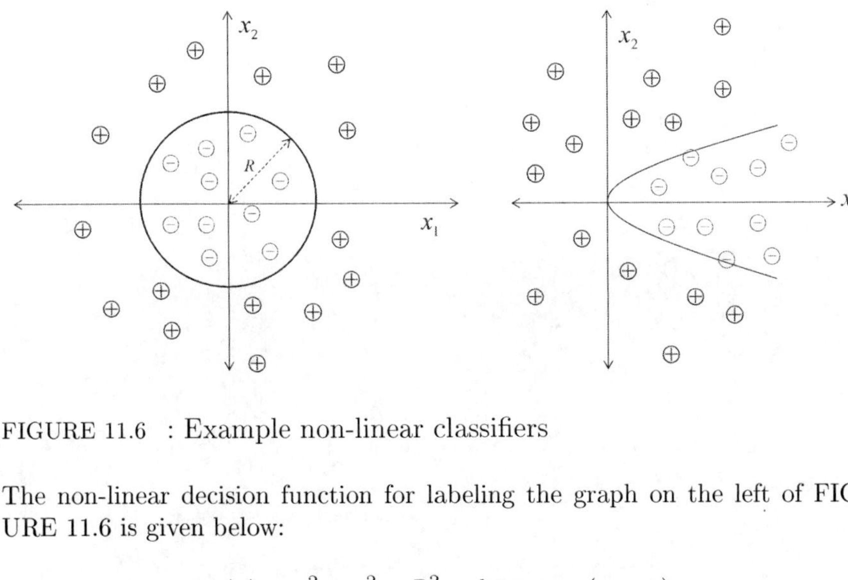

FIGURE 11.6 : Example non-linear classifiers

The non-linear decision function for labeling the graph on the left of FIGURE 11.6 is given below:

$$\phi(\mathbf{x}) = x_1^2 + x_2^2 - R^2, \text{ where } \mathbf{x} = (x_1, x_2)$$

The non-linear decision function for labeling the graph on the right is:

$$\phi(\mathbf{x}) = |x_1| - x_2^2, \text{ where } \mathbf{x} = (x_1, x_2)$$

In both cases, if $\phi(\mathbf{x}) \geq 0$ then classify $\mathbf{x}$ as positive; else negative. We need to generalize SVM to handle cases when the decision function is a non-linear function of the data.

To allow for the classification problems as shown in FIGURE 11.6, the input data points are non-linearly mapped to a high-dimensional space. The points in the new space then become linearly separable. Two very simple illustrations of this are shown in FIGURE 11.7.

The data points on the horizontal axis of the plot at the top-left of FIGURE 11.7 cannot be separated by a simple line. But if the points are transformed to a two-dimensional space via the non-linear transformation function $\phi(x_1) = (x_1, x_1^2)$ then, as shown in the plot at the top-right of FIGURE 11.7, the points in the transformed space are linearly separable by a

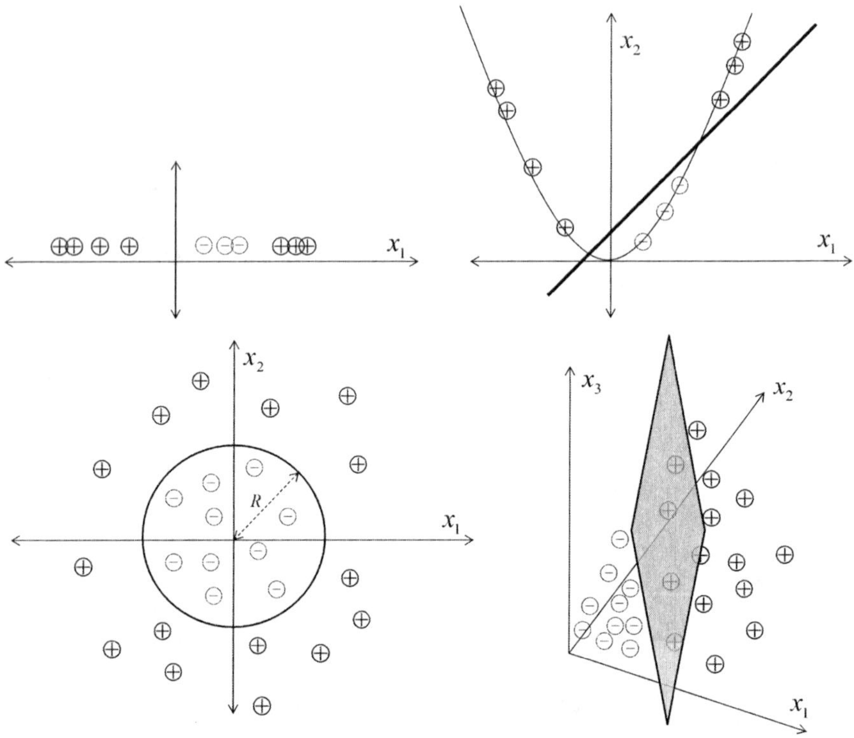

FIGURE 11.7 : Non-linear transformation of data points to higher dimensional feature space

line. Similarly, the data points in the two-dimensional space at the bottom-left of FIGURE 11.7 cannot be separated by a simple line. But if the points are transformed to a three-dimensional space via the non-linear transformation function $\phi(x_1, x_2) = \left(x_1^2, \sqrt{2}x_1x_2, x_2^2\right)$ then, as shown in the plot at the bottom-right of FIGURE 11.7, the points in the transformed space are linearly separable by a hyperplane.

So we preprocess the input data by transforming $\mathbf{x}$ to $\phi(\mathbf{x})$ and then learn the decision function $f(\mathbf{x}) = \mathbf{w} \cdot \phi(\mathbf{x}) + b$. But the dimensionality of $\phi(\mathbf{x})$ can be very large, making the transformed data points hard to represent explicitly in memory, and even harder for the quadratic programming to solve, as the large dot product of nonlinearly mapped data can be expensive. The "kernel" approach picks a suitable function that corresponds to dot product of some nonlinear mapping instead.

In the linearly separable case, the decision rule was

$$f^*(\mathbf{x}) = \sum_{i=1}^{N} \alpha_i y_i (\mathbf{x}_i . \mathbf{x}) + b^*$$

The decision rule is now

$$\begin{aligned} f^*(\mathbf{x}) & \\ &= \sum_{i=1}^{N} \alpha_i y_i \left(\phi(\mathbf{x}_i) . \phi(\mathbf{x})\right) + b^* \\ &= \sum_{i=1}^{N} \alpha_i y_i K(\mathbf{x}_i, \mathbf{x}) + b^* \end{aligned}$$

We call $K(\mathbf{x}_i, \mathbf{x}) = \phi(\mathbf{x}_i) . \phi(\mathbf{x})$ the *kernel function.* The explicit computation of $\phi(\mathbf{x})$ is not necessary. It is sometimes possible to easily compute $K(\mathbf{x}_i, \mathbf{x})$ directly in the original feature space that corresponds to computing the kernel in complex large-dimensional feature spaces. For example, consider the following mapping of $\mathbf{x} = (x_1, x_2)$ from the two-dimensional space into the six-dimensional space:

$$\phi(\mathbf{x}) = \left(x_1^2, x_2^2, \sqrt{2}x_1 x_2, \sqrt{2}x_1, \sqrt{2}x_2, 1\right)$$

The kernel is computed in the original two-dimensional space as follows:

$$\begin{aligned} K(\mathbf{x}, \mathbf{x}') & \\ &= \phi(\mathbf{x}) . \phi(\mathbf{x}') \\ &= (x_1 x_1' + x_2 x_2' + 1)^2 \\ &= (\mathbf{x}.\mathbf{x}' + 1)^2 \end{aligned}$$

This is a polynomial kernel of degree 2. The dual problem when a kernel function is used now takes the following form:

Maximize:

$$L(\alpha) = \sum_{i=1}^{N} \alpha_i - \frac{1}{2} \sum_{i=1}^{N} \sum_{j=1}^{N} \alpha_i \alpha_j y_i y_j K(\mathbf{x}_i, \mathbf{x}_j)$$

Subject to the constraints:

$$\begin{aligned} & 0 \leq \alpha_i \leq C \quad i = 1, ..., N \\ & \sum_{i=1}^{N} \alpha_i y_i = 0 \end{aligned}$$

The decision function is $f^*(\mathbf{x}) = \sum_{i=1}^{N} \alpha_i y_i K(\mathbf{x}_i, \mathbf{x}) + b^*$. The different kernel functions are listed below.

- Polynomial of degree p: $K(\mathbf{x}, \mathbf{x}') = (\mathbf{x}.\mathbf{x}' + 1)^p$
- Gaussian Radial Basis Function: $K(\mathbf{x}, \mathbf{x}') = e^{-\frac{\|\mathbf{x}-\mathbf{x}'\|^2}{2\sigma^2}}$
- Multi-Layer Perceptron: $K(\mathbf{x}, \mathbf{x}') = \tanh(\rho\mathbf{x}.\mathbf{x}' - \delta)$

A polynomial kernel is popular for non-linear modeling. There are many other types of kernels, including Fourier, splines, additive kernels, and tensor products.

SVM does not offer any concrete guidance on the choice of a kernel. The effect of choosing a certain kernel in the feature space is often unclear. It is always possible to make a mapping into a potentially very high dimensional space to produce a classifier with no classification errors on the training set. However, this kind of classifier may suffer from overfitting and may not generalize well for the new data set.

11.4.5 VC Dimension and Maximum Margin Classifier

The Vapnik-Chervonekis (VC) dimension can be defined for various classes of functions, but for our purpose here we consider only those functions $\{f(\mathbf{x}, \alpha)\}_{\alpha}$ with variables $\mathbf{x}$, parameters α, and range $\{+1, -1\}$ representing two classes, that is, $f(\mathbf{x}, \alpha) \in \{+1, -1\}$, for each f. A given set of N points can be labeled with +1 and –1 in 2^N different ways. For each labeling, a member of $\{f(\mathbf{x}, \alpha)\}$ can be found which correctly assigns those labels. The set of points in that case is said to be *shattered* by $\{f(\mathbf{x}, \alpha)\}$. The *VC dimension* for the set of functions $\{f(\mathbf{x}, \alpha)\}$ is the maximum number of points that can be shattered by $\{f(\mathbf{x}, \alpha)\}$.

Consider each function $f(\mathbf{x}, \alpha)$ as linear, that is, as hyperplanes of the form $\mathbf{w}.\mathbf{x} + b$ with $\mathbf{x}$ as the vector $(x_1, ..., x_n)$ and $\mathbf{w}$ as $(w_1, ..., w_n)$ and $\mathbf{w}.\mathbf{x} = \sum_{i=1}^{n} w_i x_i$. Then the decision function for assigning labels is

$$f(\mathbf{x}, \mathbf{w}, b) = \begin{cases} +1, & \text{if}\, sign(\mathbf{w}.\mathbf{x} + b) \text{ is positive} \\ -1, & \text{if}\, sign(\mathbf{w}.\mathbf{x} + b) \text{ is negative} \end{cases}$$

As shown in FIGURE 11.8, we can shatter two points in R^1 by $\{wx + b\}_{w,b}$ (i.e., $\{x = k\}_k$) as separating hyperplanes, but we can never shatter three points in R^1 (see the left of FIGURE 11.10). Hence the VC dimension is two.

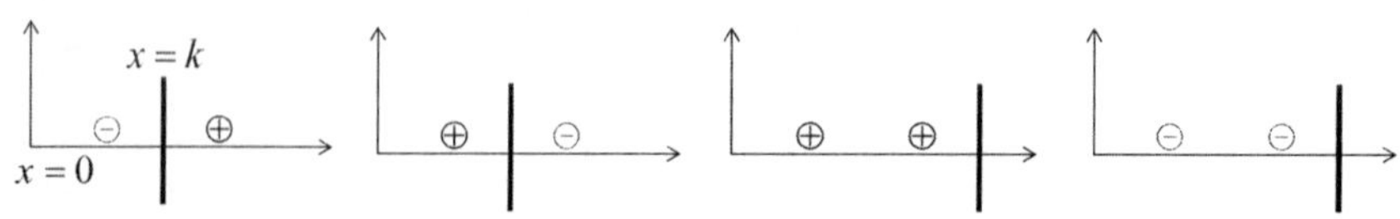

FIGURE 11.8 : Shattering two points in R^1

Similarly, as shown in FIGURE 11.9, we can shatter three non-collinear points in R^2 by lines $\{w_1 x_1 + w_2 x_2 + b\}_{w_1, w_2, b}$ as separating hyperplanes but we can never shatter four points (see the right of FIGURE 11.10). Hence the VC dimension is three. More generally, separating hyperplanes in R^n have a VC dimension of $n + 1$. Thus separating hyperplanes in high-dimension feature

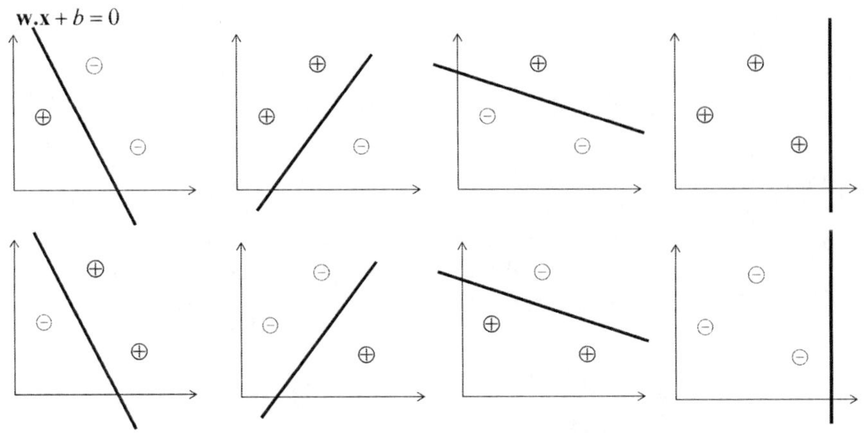

FIGURE 11.9 : Shattering three non-collinear points in R^2

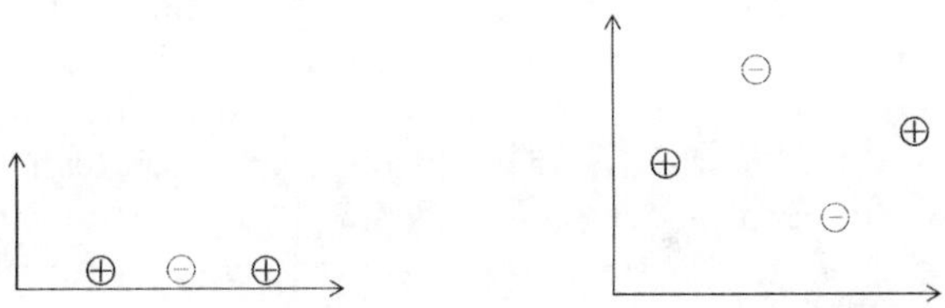

FIGURE 11.10 : Cases when shattering is not possible in R^1 (left) and R^2(right) by hyperplanes

spaces have a very large VC dimension and therefore may not generalize well. But margin hyperplanes can still have a small VC dimension.

It may seem that the VC dimension of separating hyperplanes in R^n is almost identical to the number of parameters it takes to define a hyperplane in R^n. This is not always the case, however, as Sine waves of the form $f(x) = a\sin(bx)$ have infinite VC dimension but only 2 parameters a and b (Vapnik, 1998). By choosing the phase and period carefully, we can shatter any random collection of one-dimensional data points. In the two-dimensional space, an axis-aligned rectangle can shatter four points. Therefore, the VC dimension of the class of axis-aligned rectangles in two dimensions is four.

VC dimension can be stated as the maximal number of training examples that can be learned by a machine without error, for all possible binary labelings of the training data. The concept, for example, tells us that using the class of axis-aligned rectangles, we can learn only datasets containing four points and not more in the two-dimensional space. But a learning algorithm that can learn datasets of four points is not very useful. This is because the VC dimension is independent of the probability distribution from which instances are drawn. In reality, training instances that are close to each other are likely to have the same labels, and we need not consider all possible labelings. There are many datasets with large number of points that can be classified by the class of lines.

The optimal hyperplane stems from the function class with the lowest VC dimension, and the lower the VC dimension the larger the margin. The construction of decision boundaries based on support vectors contrasts with Naïve Bayesian Classifier and logistics regression, where a decision boundary is obtained by utilizing all of the available training data points.

The VC dimension of SVM with polynomial kernel of degree 2 is 6 since $\phi(\mathbf{x}) = \left(x_1^2, x_2^2, \sqrt{2}x_1x_2, \sqrt{2}x_1, \sqrt{2}x_2, 1\right)$ is a separating hyperplane in R^5.

11.5 NEURAL NETWORKS

The network model we present here is a general multi-layer feed-forward Neural Network (NN). Each layer has a number of nodes. FIGURE 11.11 illustrates such an NN consisting of three layers. The first layer serves as the *input layer* and receives input from some source for its three nodes. The pattern of the outputs from the third layer (the *output layer*) is the network's response to the input. The layers between the input layer and the output layer are called *hidden layers*. For example, if we want to classify good loan applications versus bad loan applications, the network input is the applicant's background information (such as job type, earning, credit score, etc). In our example, the output will be either accept or reject for any input. Inputs are usually normalized in the $[0, 1]$ scale.

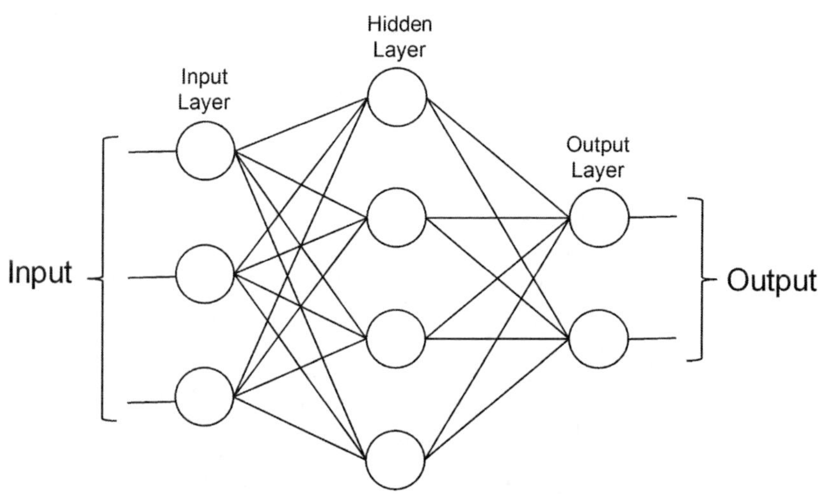

FIGURE 11.11 : A 3-layer neural network

As shown in FIGURE 11.12, each node (or neuron) i in a network is associated with a state variable x_i and a real-valued bias of the neuron v_i.

Links (or synapses) connect nodes from two successive layers. Each such link ij from node i to node j is associated with a real-valued weight w_{ij}. The aggregated input to the node i after the necessary bias adjustment is the following:

$$x = \sum_j w_{ji}x_j - v_i$$

For each node i, an activation function f is defined, where f is usually of the form of either a discontinuous step function or its smoothly increasing generalization (known as a *sigmoid function*) as defined below:

$$f(x) = \frac{1}{1 + e^{-x}}$$

The output from any unit depends on the activation function.

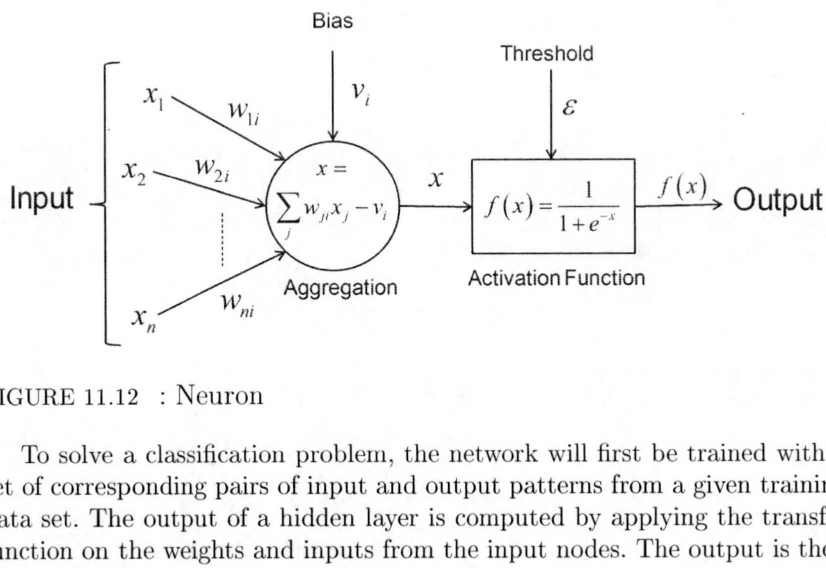

FIGURE 11.12 : Neuron

To solve a classification problem, the network will first be trained with a set of corresponding pairs of input and output patterns from a given training data set. The output of a hidden layer is computed by applying the transfer function on the weights and inputs from the input nodes. The output is then compared against the expected output and the weights are adjusted according to the error through a *back propagation* algorithm.

For every input pattern in the training set, the actual output is compared with the desired output to produce the following cost function which needs to be minimized:

$$E = \frac{1}{2}\sum_i (e_i - o_i)^2$$

where e_i and o_i are the expected and observed outputs of unit i respectively. Gradient descent is a common method applied to the above optimization problem in the weight space. For each input pattern, the weights are updated proportionately to the negative of the gradient of the cost E in the weight space as follows:

$$\Delta w_{ij} = -\lambda \frac{\partial E}{\partial w_{ij}}$$

where λ is the learning rate. The subsection below derives Δw_{ij} to be used for the following back-propagation algorithm without biases and considering only three layers.

Back-Propagation Algorithm

Input:

- Numbers of input, hidden, and output layers (and hence the topology).
- Learning rate λ between 0 and 1.
- Maximum number of cycles N.
- Error tolerance e.

Algorithm Steps:

Step 1: Initialize network weights w_{ij} to small random values. Set the number of cycles to zero.

Step 2: Select an instance from the training data set.

Step 3: Propagate the instance through the input and the hidden layers according to the equations as shown in FIGURE 11.12.

Step 4: Use Δw_{ij} and Δw_{jk} as derived in the subsection below to update every connection as $w_{ij} = w_{ij} + \Delta w_{ij}$.

Step 5: Compute the error E in the network according to $E = \frac{1}{2}\sum_{i}(e_i - o_i)^2$ and increase the number of cycles by 1.

Step 6: If the total number of cycles exceeds N or if E exceeds e then return to step 2 and cycle.

11.5.1 Model Building and Data Preparation

A neural network can be thought of as a continuous valued function. One question often asked is regarding the number of hidden layers required. If the data is linearly separable, no hidden layers are needed at all. If the data is not linearly separable then some theoretical results will help to provide guidance. According to Hornik et al. (1990), every real-valued continuous function with domain [0, 1] can be approximated by functions computable in three layers with nodes capable of linear processing such as $\sum_j w_{ji}x_j$. According to Kolmogorov (1957), every real-valued continuous function can be computed in four layers. In other words, a three-layer computer is a universal approximator, in that it can approximate an arbitrary continuous function, and a four-layer computer is a universal representer, in that it can compute an arbitrary continuous function.

So what about the size of the hidden layer(s), and how many neurons each layer will contain? There are some empirically derived rules-of-thumb. The most commonly used rule is that the size of the hidden layer falls between the size of the input and size of the output layers. As mentioned earlier, the number of neurons comprising the input layer is usually equal to the number of dimensions or columns in the data minus one, as one is left out for the output layer. In some cases one might leave out some input columns as well, if they are considered irrelevant to the output column.

It is recommended that a continuous value input (e.g., height) is normalized in the scale [0, 1]or [−1, 1], but preferably in the latter with center 0. The categorical variables are to be transformed via 1-of-C coding as detailed in the data preparation subsection of the SVM section above. A categorical variable takes on a finite number of unordered distinct values. The simplest way to represent a categorical variable to neural networks is by using a dummy variable with one 0/1 flag for each possible value. For example, if the domain of the categorical variable *Quantity* is $\{Small, Medium, Large\}$ then an input node is created for each of the values, thus creating three input nodes for the variable. An output attribute must be scaled to the range that the activation function can produce. Sigmoid functions, for example, can produce values in the range from 0 to 1. In the case of the loan applications, the training data will consist of a set of good and bad customers in terms of historical records of their loan repayment.

11.5.2 Gradient Descent for Updating Weights

Let us assume here that indices i, j, and k represent, respectively, the input, the hidden, and the output layers of a 3-layer neural network as shown in FIGURE 11.11. We start with the following weight change for a hidden to output weight, which is proportional to the negative of the gradient of the error E in the weight space:

$$\Delta w_{jk} = -\lambda \frac{\partial E}{\partial w_{jk}}$$

where $E = \frac{1}{2}\sum_i (e_i - o_i)^2$. The error E is not directly a function of the weight and hence we rewrite the above weight update as follows:

$$\Delta w_{jk} = -\lambda \frac{\partial E}{\partial e_k} \frac{\partial e_k}{\partial s_k} \frac{\partial s_k}{\partial w_{jk}}$$

where $s_k = \sum_j w_{jk} e_j$, and $e_k = f(s_k) = \frac{1}{1+e^{-s_k}}$. Hence,

$$\frac{\partial E}{\partial e_k} = e_k - o_k$$
$$\frac{\partial e_k}{\partial s_k} = \frac{e^{-s_k}}{\left(1+e^{-s_k}\right)^2} = \frac{1}{1+e^{-s_k}}\left(1 - \frac{1}{1+e^{-s_k}}\right) = e_k\left(1 - e_k\right)$$
$$\frac{\partial s_k}{\partial w_{jk}} = e_j$$

Therefore,

$$\begin{aligned} &\Delta w_{jk} \\ &= -\lambda \left(e_k - o_k\right) e_k \left(1 - e_k\right) e_j \\ &= -\lambda \delta_k e_j, \text{ where } \delta_k = \left(e_k - o_k\right) e_k \left(1 - e_k\right) \end{aligned}$$

To compute the weight change for an input to hidden weight, we consider the following:

$$\Delta w_{ij} = -\lambda \frac{\partial E}{\partial w_{ij}} = -\lambda \frac{\partial E}{\partial e_j} \frac{\partial e_j}{\partial s_j} \frac{\partial s_j}{\partial w_{ij}}$$

The weight change in this case depends on the error at all of the nodes this weighted connection can lead to. Hence, we can rewrite as

$$\begin{aligned} &\Delta w_{ij} \\ &= -\lambda \frac{\partial E}{\partial e_j} \frac{\partial e_j}{\partial s_j} \frac{\partial s_j}{\partial w_{ij}} \\ &= -\lambda \left(\sum_k \frac{\partial E}{\partial e_k} \frac{\partial e_k}{\partial s_k} \frac{\partial s_k}{\partial e_j} \right) \frac{\partial e_j}{\partial s_j} \frac{\partial s_j}{\partial w_{ij}} \\ &= -\lambda \left(\sum_k \left(e_k - o_k\right) e_k \left(1 - e_k\right) w_{jk} \right) e_j \left(1 - e_j\right) e_i \\ &= -\lambda \left(\sum_k \delta_k w_{jk} \right) e_j \left(1 - e_j\right) e_i \\ &= -\lambda \Delta_j e_i, \text{ where } \Delta_j = \left(\sum_k \delta_k w_{jk} \right) e_j \left(1 - e_j\right) \end{aligned}$$

11.6 FURTHER READING

There is an abundance of books on cluster analyses. A good introductory book is by Jain and Dubes (1988). Two very comprehensive books on clustering are (Duda et al., 2001) and (Xu and Wunsch, 2008). A good overview paper on clustering is by Jain et al. (1999). Das et al. (2006) and Kanjilal et al. (2007) introduce the concept of spatiotemporal clustering applied on time-series data on multiple different entities. Cristianini and Shaw-Taylor (2000) and Burgess (1998) provide a comprehensive introduction to SVM.

CHAPTER 12

Machine Learning for Analytics Models

This chapter presents Machine Learning (ML)[1] techniques for learning analytics models in the form of networks, trees, and rules. We start with algorithms for learning Decision Trees (DTs). Next we learn various probabilistic graphical models, namely, Naïve Bayesian Classifier (NBC), k-dependence NBC (kNBC), and Bayesian Belief Networks (BN). Finally, we present a general rule-induction technique, called Inductive Logic Programming (ILP). Each of these models has a structural component easily comprehensible to end users, and thus provides users with an opportunity to tweak models using subjective knowledge. In contrast, a feed-forward Neural Network (NN) is black-box in nature, exhibiting only the input-output interface and certain learning parameters. NN models (presented in the last chapter) are learned directly from the data and are then used for classification. In contrast, DTs, ILP rules, and graphical NBC, kNBC, and BN models can be produced in consultation with subject-matter experts even without having any observational data from which to learn.

The algorithms for learning DTs that are presented here are ID3 (Quinlan, 1986) and C4.5 (Quinlan, 1993), where the latter is an extension of ID3 to account for unavailable values, continuous attribute value ranges, pruning of DTs, rule derivation, and so on. Note that the DT learning method Classification and Regression Tree (CART) (Breiman et al., 1984) differs from ID3 in the way splits are preformed. CART is a binary tree whereas ID3 and C4.5 are not. Once a DT has been constructed from training data, propositional probabilistic rules can be extracted from the tree.

Most of the learning techniques presented here are *supervised*, meaning

[1]Somewhat-related phrases are Knowledge Discovery and Data Mining. Knowledge Discovery is the whole "process" of identifying patterns, which includes data selection, preprocessing, and transformation steps before the application of ML techniques. Data Mining sometimes refers to the whole process of knowledge discovery and sometimes to the specific ML technique. Note that an analytics model is a collection of patterns.

that instances are given with known labels (the corresponding correct outputs). In many decision-making or classification problems, obtaining labeled training instances for learning is expensive and time-consuming, as they require the efforts of experienced human annotators, while large quantities of unlabeled instances are readily available. *Semi-supervised learning* addresses this problem by using large amounts of unlabeled data, together with the available labeled data, to build better classifiers. This chapter presents a semi-supervised algorithm for learning NBC from labeled and unlabeled instances via the Expectation-Maximization (EM) algorithm. In fact, the learning of BNs from incomplete observations via EM algorithms that we present in this chapter is also semi-supervised because there is no designated classifier node in a BN. Hence an unlabeled instance can be considered as an incomplete observation, and vice versa. In the case of BNs, we learn both parameters and structures by considering cases for complete and incomplete data sets.

The graphical NBC, kNBC, and BN models are *generative* in that they provide full probabilistic models of all variables (conditional and priors), and sampling using these models can generate synthetic data points. In contrast, a *discriminative* model provides a model only for the target variable(s) conditional on the observed variables (to directly estimate posterior probabilities or estimate functions between input and output). Examples of discriminative models include linear and logistic regression, SVMs, NNs, and kNNs. In general, discriminative techniques perform better than generative ones by learning only classifier functions, as opposed to learning explicit relations among variables via joint probability distributions to facilitate sampling.

12.1 DECISION TREES

Learning of Decision Trees (DTs) is probably the most widely used machine-learning technique. Learning works by building a DT from a set of instances where the input decision variables and the correct decision (or classification) are known. Once built, a DT can be reinterpreted as a set of "if-then" rules if required. One rule is generated for each leaf node in the tree. Each node in a DT specifies a test of some attribute, and each branch descending from the node corresponds to one possible value of the node. Each leaf node corresponds to a classification of instances. A newly arrived instance is classified by tracking it down the tree from the root to some leaf.

Example

We apply DT technique to an example related to the product-launch example adopted in the chapter on probabilistic graphical models. We construct a DT to classify circumstances under which a high or a low conversion takes place. We make use of past product records containing the following four attributes: product demand, strategic importance of the product within the company, level of campaign, and the level of conversion. TABLE 12.1 presents historical sample records.

TABLE 12.1: : Records for classifying the level of conversion

Demand	Strategic	Campaign	Conversion
heavy	yes	aggressive	high
moderate	no	aggressive	high
heavy	yes	aggressive	medium
low	no	lowkey	medium
heavy	yes	aggressive	low
low	yes	lowkey	low
moderate	yes	aggressive	medium
low	no	aggressive	medium
heavy	yes	lowkey	low
moderate	no	lowkey	low
heavy	yes	aggressive	high
moderate	no	lowkey	high
low	no	lowkey	low
heavy	yes	aggressive	high
heavy	yes	aggressive	medium
low	no	lowkey	low

Each row in the table represents a classification to a level of conversion whose value is *high*, *medium* or *low*. Thus the first row is interpreted as a high conversion took place for a product with heavy demand and strategic importance to the company and via an aggressive campaign. Given these past results, one problem is to predict the level of conversion (i.e., the *Conversion* column as the output) given the demand, strategic importance, and the level of campaign. In other words, the learning algorithm has to discover patterns in the form of rules by learning from the past records as shown in the table. The learned DT will help to analyze the effect of a certain level of campaign given the values of a product's demand and its strategic importance.

12.1.1 Algorithms for Constructing Decision Trees

ID3 (Quinlan, 1986) is a basic DT learning algorithm, and C4.5 (Quinlan, 1993) is an extension of ID3 to account for unavailable values, continuous attribute value ranges, pruning of DTs, rule derivation, and so on. ID3 is a top-down, "greedy" search algorithm moving through the space of possible DTs. The algorithm is given below.

ID3 Algorithm

Inputs:

- *Training Set*: The training examples (e.g., the records in TABLE 12.1).
- *Target Attribute*: The attribute whose value is to be predicted by the learned DT (e.g., *Conversion*).
- *Input Attributes*: A list of other attributes that may be tested by the learned DT (e.g., *Demand*, *Strategic*, and *Campaign*).

Output:

- A learned DT that classifies the given training set

Algorithm:

Create a new node *Root* for the tree;
If all members of *Training Set* are in the same class C
  Set *Root* = single node tree with label C;
Else If *Input Attributes* is empty
  Set *Root* = single node tree with label as the most common
    value of Target Attribute in Training Set;
Else
  Set A = member of *Input Attributes* that maximizes information
    gain $Gain\,(Training\,Set, A)$ (explained below);
A is the decision attribute for *Root*;
  For each possible value v of A
    Add a new branch below *Root*, testing for $A = v$;
    Set $Training\,Set\,(v)$ = subset of *Training Set* with $A = v$;
    If $Training\,Set\,(v)$ is empty
      Add a leaf below the new branch with label that is most
      common value of Target Attribute in Training Set;
    Else
      Below the new branch add sub-tree obtained by the
      following recursive call:

$$ID3\,(Training\,Set\,(v)\,, Target\,Attribute, Input\,Attributes - \{A\})\,;$$

Return *Root*;

Within the above algorithm, a measure of effectiveness, called *information gain*, of an attribute A is computed via the procedure $Gain\,(Training\,Set, A)$. The attribute that provides the maximum information gain is placed at the root of the DT. The information gain metric is an information theoretic measure of how much "entropy" is revealed by a specific attribute. Given a collection S of c class labels, the entropy is defined as

$$Entropy\,(S) = -\sum_{i=1}^{c} p_i \log_2 (p_i)$$

where p_i is the proportion of S belonging to class i. The formula for computing information gain for an attribute A with respect to a set of instances$S$ is

$$Gain\,(S, A) = Entropy\,(S) - \sum_{v \in Values(A)} \frac{|S_v|}{|S|} Entropy\,(S_v)$$

where the sum is taken over all possible values of the attribute A, and S_v is the subset of A for which the attribute A has the value v.

Information gain has a natural bias toward attributes with a large domain (i.e., the "date" attribute). This can result in the selection of an attribute that works well with training data but will not generalize. One alternative approach is to use the following *GainRatio* function (Quinlan, 1986):

$$SplitInformation\,(S, A) = -\sum_{i=1}^{c} \frac{|S_i|}{|S|} \log_2 \frac{|S_i|}{|S|}$$

$$GainRatio\,(S, A) = \frac{Gain\,(S, A)}{SplitInformation\,(S, A)}$$

where S_i is the subset of S for which A has value v_i.

Example

For the problem at hand, we have three attributes that are candidates for the root node. The attribute with the highest information gain will be selected. We first consider A as *Strategic*, S as the instances in the table, and compute the information gain for S.

$$\begin{array}{l} Values\,(Strategic) = \{yes, no\} \\ S = \{high\,(5)\,, medium\,(5)\,, low\,(6)\} \\ Entropy\,(S) = -\frac{5}{16} \log_2 \frac{5}{16} - \frac{5}{16} \log_2 \frac{5}{16} - \frac{6}{16} \log_2 \frac{6}{16} = 1.579 \end{array}$$

where *high* (5) means 5 instances of *high*, *medium* (5) means 5 instances of *medium*, and *low* (6) means 6 instances of *low* in the set S. Similarly,

$$\begin{array}{l} S_{yes} = \{high\,(3)\,, medium\,(3)\,, low\,(3)\} \\ Entropy\,(S_{yes}) = -\frac{3}{9} \log_2 \frac{3}{9} - \frac{3}{9} \log_2 \frac{3}{9} - \frac{3}{9} \log_2 \frac{3}{9} = 1.584 \end{array}$$

$$\begin{array}{l} S_{no} = \{high\,(2)\,, medium\,(2)\,, low\,(3)\} \\ Entropy\,(S_{no}) = -\frac{2}{7} \log_2 \frac{2}{7} - \frac{2}{7} \log_2 \frac{2}{7} - \frac{3}{7} \log_2 \frac{3}{7} = 1.556 \end{array}$$

$$\begin{array}{l} Gain\,(S, Strategic) \\ \quad = Entropy\,(S) - \frac{9}{16} Entropy\,(S_{yes}) - \frac{7}{16} Entropy\,(S_{no}) \\ \quad = 1.579 - \frac{9}{16} \times 1.584 - \frac{7}{16} \times 1.556 \\ \quad = 0.006 \end{array}$$

Similarly,

$$
\begin{aligned}
&Gain\,(S, Demand)\\
&\quad = Entropy\,(S) - \tfrac{7}{16} Entropy\,(S_{heavy}) - \\
&\qquad\qquad \tfrac{4}{16} Entropy\,(S_{moderate}) - \tfrac{5}{16} Entropy\,(S_{low})\\
&\quad = Entropy\,(S) - \tfrac{7}{16}\left(-\tfrac{3}{7}\log_2\tfrac{3}{7} - \tfrac{2}{7}\log_2\tfrac{2}{7} - \tfrac{2}{7}\log_2\tfrac{2}{7}\right) - \\
&\qquad\qquad \tfrac{4}{16}\left(-\tfrac{2}{4}\log_2\tfrac{2}{4} - \tfrac{1}{4}\log_2\tfrac{1}{4} - \tfrac{1}{4}\log_2\tfrac{1}{4}\right) - \\
&\qquad\qquad \tfrac{5}{16}\left(-\tfrac{0}{5}\log_2\tfrac{0}{5} - \tfrac{2}{5}\log_2\tfrac{2}{5} - \tfrac{3}{5}\log_2\tfrac{3}{5}\right)\\
&\quad = 1.579 - \tfrac{7}{16} \times 1.556 - \tfrac{4}{16} \times 1.5 - \tfrac{5}{16} \times 0.97\\
&\quad = 0.220
\end{aligned}
$$

$$
\begin{aligned}
&Gain\,(S, Campaign)\\
&\quad = Entropy\,(S) - \tfrac{9}{16} Entropy\,(S_{aggressive}) - \tfrac{7}{16} Entropy\,(S_{lowkey})\\
&\quad = Entropy\,(S) - \tfrac{9}{16}\left(-\tfrac{4}{9}\log_2\tfrac{4}{9} - \tfrac{4}{9}\log_2\tfrac{4}{9} - \tfrac{1}{9}\log_2\tfrac{1}{9}\right) - \\
&\qquad\qquad \tfrac{7}{16}\left(-\tfrac{1}{7}\log_2\tfrac{1}{7} - \tfrac{1}{7}\log_2\tfrac{1}{7} - \tfrac{5}{7}\log_2\tfrac{5}{7}\right)\\
&\quad = 1.579 - \tfrac{9}{16} \times 1.392 - \tfrac{7}{16} \times 1.148\\
&\quad = 0.293
\end{aligned}
$$

The attribute *Campaign* achieves the highest information gain and should be used as the root for the DT. In fact, inspecting the partial trees in FIGURE 12.1, it makes the most sense to include *Campaign* at the root since it discriminates most of the samples split along its branches. Intuitively, the level of campaign has the highest impact on the conversion.

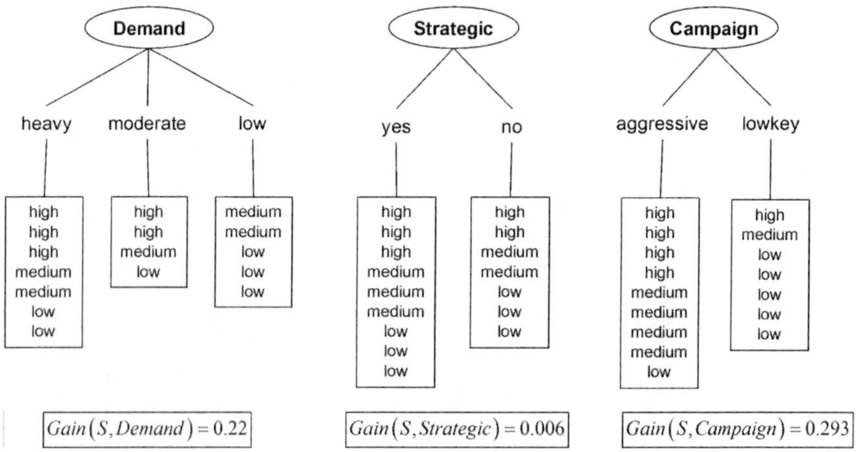

FIGURE 12.1 : Alternative splits from the root node of a DT and information gains

Having found the best split, the whole procedure is repeated with each subset of the example training set. As shown in FIGURE 12.2, the information gain for each of the two attributes *Demand* and *Strategic* will be computed

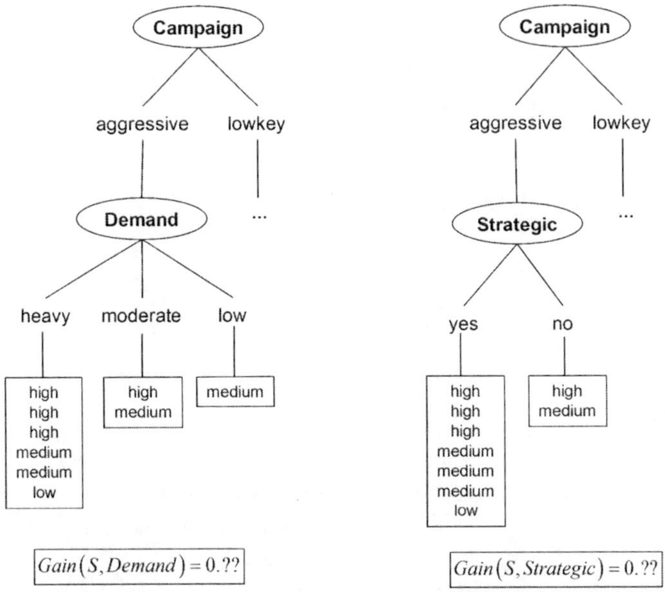

FIGURE 12.2 : DT alternative splits and information gains

next and one of them can be used to split the DT further for *Campaign* = *aggressive* depending on gain (the computation of gain is left as an exercise).

The splitting process continues for those branches containing samples from different classes (i.e., containing at least two of *high, medium* and *low*). One can now easily extract rules from the tree constructed so far. The rightmost branch yields the following rule (assuming that *Demand* is chosen for splitting the branch for *aggressive*):

IF *Campaign* = *aggressive*
AND *Demand* = *low*
THEN *Conversion* = *medium*

The support value in this case is 1.0 as no counterexample has been considered for the specific conditions of the rule above, but one can easily extract support from the probability scale [0, 1] by taking the ratio between the number of correct classification cases to the total number of cases. For example, the support values are 0.50 and 0.33 for the following two rules:

IF *Campaign* = *aggressive*
AND *Demand* = *heavy*
THEN *Conversion* = *high* (0.50)

IF *Campaign* = *aggressive*
AND *Demand* = *heavy*

THEN *Conversion* = *medium* (0.33)

On the other hand, if the tree is pruned (to be introduced later) after the *Campaign* node, as in the rightmost tree in FIGURE 12.1, then the following two rules are generated:

IF *Campaign* = *lowkey*
THEN *Conversion* = *low* (0.71)

IF *Campaign* = *aggressive*
THEN *Conversion* = *high* (0.44)

Example

The problem here is to predict the performance of individual students or groups of students, given their backgrounds. We assume a set of six sample students (in reality there will be many thousands) with their backgrounds in Philosophy, Mathematics or Computer Science. A student's background identifies a natural "population" or "community" and facts learned in this example may apply to an individual student or to the population to which a student belongs. TABLE 12.2 presents sample test results of these students. Each row in the table represents an answer to a question whose type is either General Knowledge or Reasoning. Thus the first row is interpreted as: a student with a background in Philosophy has answered a Reasoning type question correctly. In other words, the learning algorithm has to discover patterns (possibly in the form of rules) by learning the performance of existing students shown in the table.

TABLE 12.2: : Student answer table joined from two separate normalized tables Student(Id, Background) and Answer(Id, Question Type, Answer Code) on the common attribute Id.

Id	**Background**	**Question Type**	**Answer Code**
1	Philosophy	Reasoning	True
1	Philosophy	General Knowledge	True
2	Mathematics	Reasoning	True
2	Mathematics	General Knowledge	False
3	Computer Science	Reasoning	True
3	Computer Science	General Knowledge	True
4	Mathematics	Reasoning	True
4	Mathematics	General Knowledge	True
5	Computer Science	Reasoning	False
5	Computer Science	General Knowledge	True
6	Philosophy	Reasoning	True
6	Philosophy	General Knowledge	True

Before we compute the information gain for all attributes, we have to pick the attribute that "makes the most sense" to include at the root of the decision tree. To explain this point, it suffices to note that according to the information gain measure, the Id attribute provides the best prediction for the student performance (but with very little "support" as defined later in the ILP section). However, this does not help predict the performance of a new student based on their background, because the identification of the new student will not match any of the existing ones and therefore will not allow branching from the root. Alternatively, if we consider Background as the root then the corresponding decision tree is shown in FIGURE 12.3.

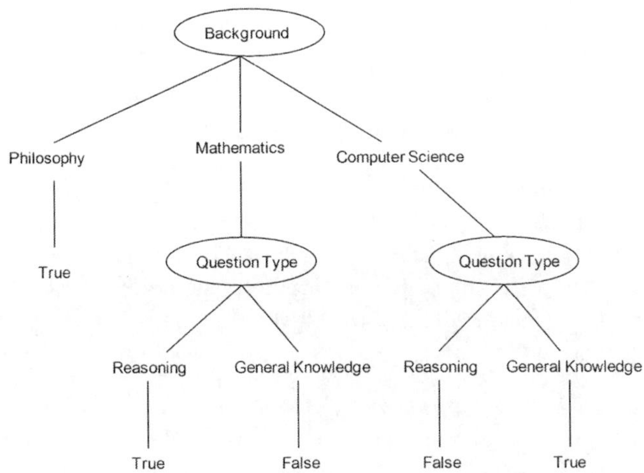

FIGURE 12.3 : DT for student answers

Note that we followed the same information gain procedure as in the last example for choosing nodes at the next level. One can now easily extract rules from the tree in FIGURE 12.3. The two leftmost branches yield the following two rules:

IF Background = Philosophy THEN Answer = True
IF Background = Mathematics AND Question Type = Reasoning
THEN Answer = True

The usual pruning can be made to avoid overfitting.

12.1.2 Overfitting in Decision Trees

During the construction of a DT from a training data set, there is always a danger that the process is learning only the characteristics of the specific training set, as opposed to the general concepts involved. If that is indeed the case then the tree "overfits" to the training set, that is, the tree has been specialized to the training set as opposed to what will occur generally. Formally, suppose H is the hypotheses set of all possible DTs. Then a hypothesis h in H *overfits* training data if there is an alternative hypothesis h_1 in H such that h has a smaller error than h_1 over the training data set, but h_1 has a smaller error than h over the entire distribution of instances. There are two ways to prevent overfitting:

- Stop growing the tree when splitting data is no longer statistically significant.
- Grow a full tree and then post-prune to remove the parts that overfit.

In the first case, all available data for training are used and a statistical test is applied to estimate whether pruning or expanding is likely to produce improvement. In the second case, a separate test data set is used to evaluate the utility of post-pruning. There are various types of pruning:

- *Reduced-Error Pruning*: Decision nodes are pruned from the full tree. Pruning a node removes the sub-tree rooted at the node and makes it a leaf node. The most common classification of the training examples associated with the node is assigned to the node. In reduced-error pruning, the resulting pruned tree has to perform better than the original tree over the test set.
- *Reduced-Error Pruning with Prune Factor*: In the reduced-error pruning as defined above, we prune a node if the error before pruning is greater than the error after pruning. But if we want to improve by a certain fraction of the error before pruning, we introduce a pruning factor. If this factor times the error before pruning is greater than the error after pruning then the node is pruned. If the factor is 1 then it becomes the reduced-error pruning.
- *Confidence-based Pruning*: Confidence represents a threshold of inherent error allowed in the data while pruning a node of the decision tree. By increasing this threshold, one applies more pruning, and consequently generates more general models. The confidence value of 100% means pruning always, whereas 0% means no pruning.
- *Rule Postpruning*: We convert the full tree into an equivalent set of rules and then prune each rule by removing preconditions, resulting in improved estimated accuracy over the test set.

Note that one advantage of converting a DT to rules before pruning is that the distinction between attribute tests that occur near the root of the tree and those that occur near the leaves is removed.

Example

FIGURE 12.4 is a screenshot of an implementation of the above product-launch example in *i*DAS (a tool explained later in the penultimate chapter). The two trees before and after pruning are shown. Note that the branch along the condition "*Campaign – lowkey*" has been pruned. This makes sense according to the rightmost branch of the rightmost tree in FIGURE 12.1, which is dominated by the attribute value *low*.

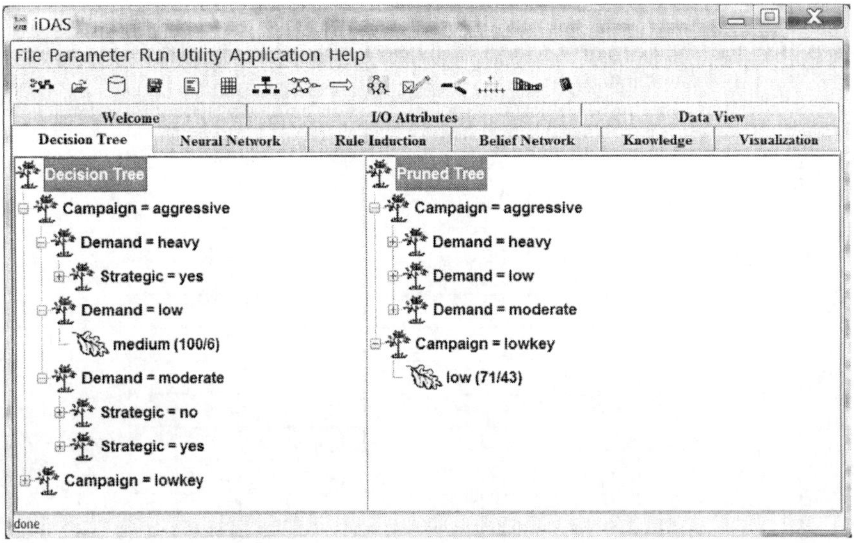

FIGURE 12.4 : iDAS implementation of the product-launch example

12.1.3 Handling Continuous Attributes

For a classification problem with only discrete attributes, each non-leaf node of a constructed DT is a test and its number of descendants is equal to the domain size of the attribute (i.e., the number of possible values for the discrete attribute). But for a continuous attribute A, its range is partitioned into a discrete set of intervals. A new Boolean attribute A_c is created to test if the value of A is less than a threshold c or not $(A < c)$. To choose c, instances of A are sorted first and then the boundaries where the output or target classification changes are identified. Candidate thresholds are then generated between two boundaries, and the information gains for different choices of thresholds are computed.

Example

Consider the records in TABLE 12.3 created with the discrete attributed *Campaign* and *Conversion* columns from TABLE 12.1, and adding the continuous counterpart of *Campaign*, *Campaign* (C), which is the amount spent for campaigning by the company in thousands of dollars. TABLE 12.4 is the sorted version of the table based on the continuous attribute *Campaign* (*C*).

TABLE 12.3: : Discrete attributes Campaign and Conversion from TABLE 12.1 and the continuous counterpart Campaign (C) of the attribute Campaign

Campaign	**Campaign (C)**	**Conversion**
aggressive	5000	high
aggressive	3000	high
aggressive	1000	medium
lowkey	400	medium
aggressive	750	low
lowkey	50	low
aggressive	800	medium
aggressive	600	medium
lowkey	100	low
lowkey	40	low
aggressive	4500	high
lowkey	200	high
lowkey	25	low
aggressive	4500	high
aggressive	2500	medium
lowkey	30	low

TABLE 12.4: : Sorting by the continuous attribute Campaign (C) in TABLE 12.3

Campaign (C)	25	30	40	50	100	200	400	600
Campaign	l	l	l	l	l	l	l	a
Conversion	l	l	l	l	l	h	m	m
Campaign (C)	750	800	1000	2500	3000	4500	4500	5000
Campaign	a	a	a	a	a	a	a	a
Conversion	l	m	m	m	h	h	h	h

The discrete values of *Campaign* have been obtained from its continuous counterpart based on the threshold \$400K (i.e., if campaign dollars spent are less than or equal to \$400K then it is a low-key campaign, otherwise it is aggressive). Now if the continuous attribute *Campaign* (*C*) is given instead of the discrete attribute *Campaign* then, for example, a list of thresholds between boundaries where the value of the attribute *Conversion* changes is 100, 200, 600, 750, and 2500. Therefore, the test intervals for the new discretized attribute are:

$$Campaign_c = \begin{cases} Campaign \leq 100 \\ 100 < Campaign \leq 200 \\ 200 < Campaign \leq 600 \\ 600 < Campaign \leq 750 \\ 750 < Campaign \leq 2500 \\ Campaign > 2500 \end{cases}$$

The information gains for these choices of thresholds are then computed.

12.1.4 Advantages and Disadvantages of Decision Tree Techniques

The advantages of DT techniques are that they:

- Employ a fast learning process;
- Generate intuitive rules in natural language-like syntax;
- Handle both continuous and discrete variables;
- Indicate clearly which fields are most important for prediction.

The disadvantages of DT techniques are the following:

- They are not suitable for prediction tasks where the output attribute is continuous;
- They are linear rectangular classifier and do not handle nonlinear data sets well;
- There is no backtracking in core ID3 during the construction of a tree.

12.2 LEARNING NAIVE BAYESIAN CLASSIFIERS

This section describes how to learn Naïve Bayesian Classifiers (NBCs) from structured records. Later in the section on text analytics, we will learn NBCs from a text corpus to classify documents. Learning NBCs from structured relational databases of records is just a special case of learning from unstructured documents. Each child node in an NBC corresponds to an attribute or feature. For text-based document indexing, these attributes usually indicate the presence or absence of a word in a text document. The parent node determines the output of the discriminant function, which is the class to which the record or document belongs.

Let D be a relational table of all training records. One discrete attribute C of D is designated as the class or output attribute and the rest of the attributes $V_1, V_2, \ldots$ that are discrete are considered as the input attributes. Suppose the set $c_1, \ldots, c_n$ is all the values that the class attribute C can take, and thus is a training record that is labeled with members from the set $\{c_1, ..., c_n\}$ of classes. Consider an NBC as shown in FIGURE 12.5 with root node C whose states are $c_1, ..., c_n$. We denote $C = \{c_1, ..., c_n\}$ for convenience. For each V_j, add a child node of C with as many states v_{jl}s as the number of values the discrete attribute V_j can take. For example, if V_j is the node Outlook in our play-tennis example, then $v_{j1} = sunny, v_{j2} = overcast, v_{j3} = rain$.

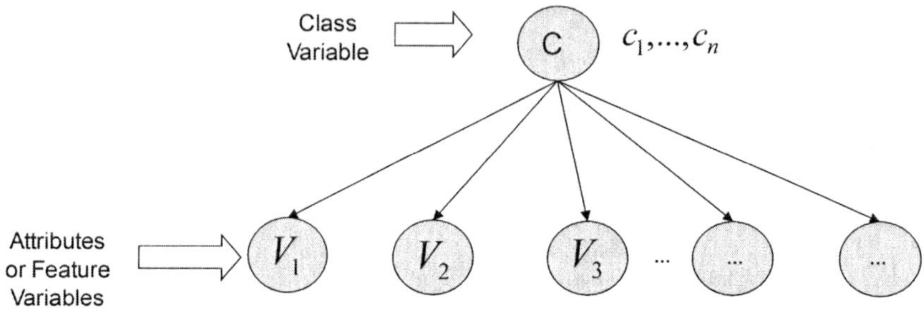

FIGURE 12.5 : Generic structure of an NBC

In order to compute the following probabilities, we apply the Maximum Likelihood Estimate (MLE), which is simply the relative frequency and corresponds to the most likely value of each parameter given the training data:

$$p(c_i) = \frac{\text{Number of records in } D \text{ for which the label is } c_i}{\text{Total number of records in } D} = \frac{N(c_i)}{|D|}$$

$$p(v_{jl}|c_i) = \frac{\left[\begin{array}{c}\text{Number of times } v_{jl} \text{ occurs in the column of } V_j \text{ of} \\ \text{all the training records labeled } c_i\end{array}\right]}{\text{Total number of records in all the training documents labeled } c_i}$$
$$= \frac{N(v_{jl}, c_i)}{\sum_j N(v_{jl}, c_i)}$$

The problem with the MLE estimate is that $p(v_{jl}|c_i)$ is zero if v_{jl} did not occur in any record labeled c_i in the training data. So a record with occurrences of v_{jl}, and perhaps genuinely belonging to the class c_i, will get a conditional probability of zero for c_i since we multiply the conditional probabilities for all words. To avoid this, Laplace smoothing, which simply adds 1 to each count, is applied as follows:

$$p(v_{jl}|c_i) = \frac{1 + N(v_{jl}, c_i)}{\sum_j (1 + N(v_{jl}, c_i))} = \frac{1 + N(v_{jl}, c_i)}{|V| + \sum_j N(v_{jl}, c_i)}$$

The probability of a record d containing v_js given a class c_i is

$$p(d|c_i) = \prod_j p(v_j|c_i)$$

The class probabilities are estimated in the same manner, involving the ratio of count to smoothing:

$$p(c_i) = \frac{1 + N(c_i)}{|C| + |D|}$$

Let d be a record that we want to classify, and the given set of classes is $C = \{c_1, ..., c_n\}$. We want to compute $p(c_i|d)$, for every i:

$$p(c_i|d) = \frac{p(c_i)\,p(d|c_i)}{p(d)} = \frac{p(c_i)\prod\limits_j p(v_j|c_i)}{\sum\limits_{k=1}^{n} p(c_k)\prod\limits_j p(v_j|c_k)}$$

where v_js are attribute values in record d. The product of conditional probabilities comes from the assumption that attributes in a record are independent, given the record class. Note that the conditional independence assumption of features does not hold in most cases, as attributes are often correlated.

Here we don't need the estimated posterior $p(c_i|d)$ to be correct. Instead, we only need

$$\arg\max_{c_i} p(c_i|d) = \arg\max_{c_i} p(c_i)\prod_j p(v_j|c_i)$$

The score for each class can be expressed in the following tractable form for analytical purposes:

$$\log(p(c_i)) + \sum\nolimits_j \log(p(v_j|c_i))$$

The score is not a probability value, but is sufficient for the purpose of determining the most probable class. It reduces the round-off errors due to a product of small fractions caused by a large number of tokens.

Example

Consider the play-tennis data in Appendix B. We discretize the attributes Temperature and Humidity with the following rule:

$$\begin{array}{ll} High & if > 80 \\ Medium & if > 70 \text{ and } \leq 80 \\ Low & if \leq 70 \end{array}$$

TABLE 12.5 shows the table after discretization. The learned NBC from the table with the variable Decision as the root node is shown in FIGURE 12.6.

TABLE 12.5: : The play-tennis data in Appendix B after discretization of the attributes Temperature and Humidity

Outlook	Temperature	Humidity	Windy	Decision
sunny	high	high	weak	don't play
sunny	medium	high	strong	don't play

TABLE 12.5: : The play-tennis data in Appendix B after discretization of the attributes Temperature and Humidity

overcast	high	medium	weak	play
rain	low	high	weak	play
rain	low	medium	weak	play
rain	low	low	strong	don't play
overcast	low	low	strong	play
sunny	medium	high	weak	don't play
sunny	low	low	weak	play
rain	medium	medium	weak	play
sunny	medium	low	strong	play
overcast	medium	high	strong	play
overcast	high	medium	weak	play
rain	medium	medium	strong	don't play

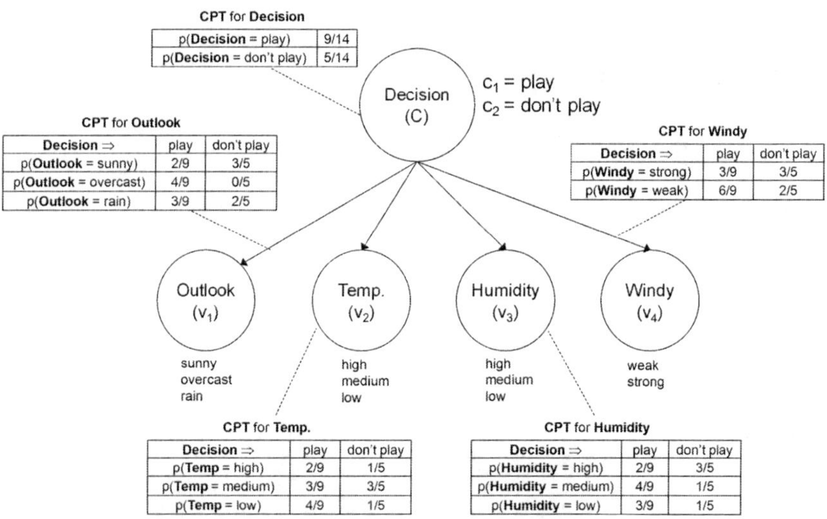

FIGURE 12.6 : The learned NBC from TABLE 12.5

12.2.1 Semi-Supervised Learning of NBC via EM

Traditional supervised learning can make use of training records in order to learn a classifier. The preparation of such a training set is a time-consuming and expensive manual effort, however. The obvious need is to build a model based on a limited number of labeled training instances and an abundance of unlabeled instances, which is called *semi-supervised learning* (Zhu and Goldberg, 2009; Chapelle et al., 2006). We introduce a semi-supervised algorithm for learning NBC from labeled and unlabeled instances via the Expectation-Maximization (EM) algorithm (Nigam et al., 2000). For an easy transfer of the following semi-supervised algorithm to text document classification, we assume that each child node V_j in the NBC model is binary with states $\{v_j, \neg v_j\}$. We will simply denote the node as v_j while V is the set of all nodes $v_1, v_2, \ldots$. Thus, $p(v_j|c_i) = 1 - p(\neg v_j|c_i)$.

The EM algorithm is an iterative procedure for maximizing the log likelihood function $p(\theta|D)$, where D is the union of the collections D_l of labeled training records and D_u of unlabeled records, and θ is the set of all parameters in NBC that are to be estimated. The probability of all data is:

$$\begin{aligned} & p(D|\theta) \\ & \quad = \prod_{d\in D} p(d|\theta) \\ & \quad = \prod_{d\in D} \sum_{i=1}^{|C|} p(c_i|\theta)\, p(d|c_i,\theta) \\ & \quad = \prod_{d\in D_l} \sum_{i=1}^{|C|} p(c_i|\theta)\, p(d|c_i,\theta) \times \prod_{d\in D_u} \sum_{i=1}^{|C|} p(c_i|\theta)\, p(d|c_i,\theta) \end{aligned}$$

where $p(c_i|\theta)$ is either 0 or 1 for each labeled instance in D_l. Instead of maximizing $p(\theta|D)$ directly, we work with $\log(p(\theta|D))$, which is maximizing $\log(p(\theta)\, p(D|\theta))$:

$$\begin{aligned} & \log(p(\theta)\, p(D|\theta)) \\ & \quad = \log(p(\theta)) + \sum_{d\in D_l} \log\left(\sum_{i=1}^{|C|} p(c_i|\theta)\, p(d|c_i,\theta)\right) \\ & \qquad \times \sum_{d\in D_u} \log\left(\sum_{i=1}^{|C|} p(c_i|\theta)\, p(d|c_i,\theta)\right) \end{aligned}$$

The prior probability distribution $p(\theta)$ over parameters θ can be represented as a Dirichlet distribution:

$$p(\theta) \propto \prod_{c_i\in C} \left((p(c_i))^{\alpha-1} \prod_{v_j\in V} (p(v_j|c_i))^{\alpha-1} \right)$$

where α is a parameter greater than 0. Assuming that after the nth iteration the current estimate for parameters θ is θ_n, the estimation at the next step can be derived as

$$\theta^{n+1} = \arg\max_{\theta} \{\log(p(\theta)\, p(D|\theta))\}$$

The above recursive formula yields the following two-step algorithm iterated a certain number of times or upon changes below a certain threshold.

EM Algorithm for Semi-Supervised Learning of NBC

Initial Step: Build an initial NBC from the labeled records D_l only using the formulae for $p(c_i)$ and $p(d|c_i)$ as derived above.

Iteration Step: Loop through the E- and M-steps while classifier parameters improve, as measured by the change in the complete log probability $\log(p(\theta)p(D|\theta))$ of the labeled and unlabeled data, and the prior.

E-step: Use the current NBC to estimate the class probabilities c_i of each unlabeled record d using the following equation:

$$p(c_i|d) = \frac{p(c_i)\,p(d|c_i)}{p(d)} = \frac{p(c_i)\prod_j p(v_j|c_i)}{\sum_{k=1}^{n} p(c_k)\prod_j p(v_j|c_k)}$$

Note that $p(c_i|d)$ is either 0 or 1 for every labeled record.

M-step: Re-estimate the probabilities the NBC using the following formulae:

$$p(v_j|c_i) = \frac{1+\sum_{d\in D} N(v_j,d)p(c_i|d)}{|V|+\sum_{k=1}^{|V|}\sum_{d\in D} N(v_k,d)p(c_i|d)}$$

$$p(c_i) = \frac{1+\sum_{d\in D} p(c_i|d)}{|C|+|D|}$$

where $N(v_j, d)$ is the number of occurrences of v_j in d.

As before, the output NBC takes an unlabeled record and predicts a class label for it. FIGURE 12.7 shows a high-level architecture for semi-supervised learning. We assume the existence of some historical or human-labeled instances (top-left in the figure) to start with, but these will be expanded over time. We train and build an initial NBC model based on these labeled instances. This is simple one-step training without requiring an iteration loop for convergence (as required in EM learning).

Given a data stream with both labeled and unlabeled instances (bottom-right in the figure), we make use of the initial model to label automatically. These machine-labeled instances from the initial model, along with the historical labeled instances, are used together to train a model via EM learning to produce the final model. Those machine-labeled instances with a high threshold confidence from the initial model are output immediately. The rest are candidates for human-labeling.

The above process is an iterative real-time one. As it receives labeled and unlabeled instances, it puts the unlabeled instances through the latest trained classifier and creates a buffer for those that fail to cross the threshold. Once the number of unmarked instances in the buffer exceeds a certain pre-specified number, it triggers the EM learning as a background process and replaces the current classifier model when finished. The steps of the algorithm are given below:

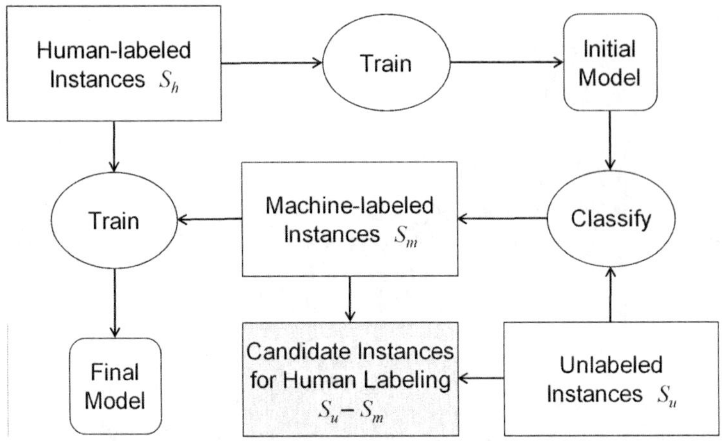

FIGURE 12.7 : Semi-supervised learning algorithm

Semi-Supervised Learning of NBC with Human Labeling

Input:

- Some human-labeled training instances S_h
- A large number of unlabeled data instances in the pool $S_u = \{s_1, ..., s_N\}$

Step 1: Train an NBC classifier using the current training instances S_h

Step 2: Classify the unlabeled training instances in S_u using the trained classifier

Step 3: Let $S_m \, (\subseteq S_u)$ be the set of machine-labeled instances that cross the threshold set for the classifier

Step 4: Apply the EM algorithm to fit both the initial classifier and new machine-labeled data S_m

Step 5: Modify the unlabeled instance set $S_u = S_u - S_m$ as a candidate for human-labeling

Step 6: Add newly arrived unlabeled instances into the instances left in S_u after human-labeling.

In the above algorithm, if a trained NBC model is not able to classify an unmarked instance because the instance does not cross a pre-defined threshold, the instance becomes a candidate for labeling by a human operator. The decision whether to send it to the human operator depends on the computed amount of information gain via an entropy measure for example, thus implementing an optional combination of semi-supervised and *active learning* (Sarawagi and Bhamidipaty, 2002; Tur et al., 2005).

12.3 LEARNING OF KNBC

The algorithm for constructing kNBC is provided with a set of input labeled training instances belonging to a class C and with the value of k for the maximum allowable degree of feature dependence. It outputs a kNBC model with conditional probability tables determined from the input data. The structural simplicity of kNBC (and hence NBC) and the completeness of the input labeled instances avoid the need for complex algorithms used for learning structure and parameters in BNs (to be detailed in the next section). The algorithm here makes use of the following *mutual information* between two variables X and Y when selecting the order of child nodes and the k parent nodes of a child:

$$I(X;Y) = \sum_{X,Y} p(X,Y) \times \log\left(\frac{p(X,Y)}{p(X)\,p(Y)}\right)$$

The probabilities in this formula are determined by counting the number of individual and pair-wise joint occurrences of the variables in the articles.

kNBC Algorithm

- Let the used variable list $\mathbf{S}$ be empty. Let the k-dependence network *BN* being constructed begin with a single class node C.
- Repeat until $\mathbf{S}$ includes all domain features (i.e., the vocabulary containing all the terms):
    - · Select feature $X_{\max}$which is not in $\mathbf{S}$ and has the largest value $I(X_{\max};C)$.
    - · Add a node to *BN* representing $X_{\max}$.
    - · Add an arc from C to $X_{\max}$ in *BN*.
    - · Add $m = \min(|\mathbf{S}|, k)$ arcs from m distinct features X_j in $\mathbf{S}$ with the highest value for $I(X_{\max}; X_j|C)$.
    - · Add $X_{\max}$ to $\mathbf{S}$.
- Compute the conditional probability tables inferred from the structure of *BN* by using counts from input instances and output *BN*.

kNBC requires the computation of $p(v_{jl}|c_i, \Pi(V_j))$, as opposed to the requirement in NBC of $p(v_{jl}|c_i)$, using the following, where $\Pi(V_j)$ is an instance of the parent variables of V_j (not including C):

$$\frac{\left[\begin{array}{c}\text{Number of times } v_{jl} \text{ occurs in the column of } V_j \text{ of all the training} \\ \text{instances labeled } c_i \text{ and in each such instance has occurrenecs} \\ \text{of all the values in } \Pi(V_j)\end{array}\right]}{\left[\begin{array}{c}\text{Total number of training instances labeled } c_i \text{ and each such} \\ \text{instance has occurrenecs of all the values in } \Pi(V_j)\end{array}\right]}$$

The formula to be used to classify instances is the same as the one specified in the graphical modeling chapter.

Example

Consider the discretized version of the play-tennis example of Appendix B, presented in the NBC section of the probabilistic graphical modeling chapter. FIGURE 12.8 shows a kNBC ($k = 1$) (extension of the NBC in FIGURE 12.6) where the variable Windy is influenced by Outlook in addition to the root variable. The learned CPT for the variable Windy from the data is also shown in the figure. Note that some of the entries in the CPT are zero or undefined due to not having enough number of instances covering all possible values of variables. A uniform prior can be assumed for the column of undefined values. One can also assume a small value close to zero in place of a zero and then normalize the column appropriately.

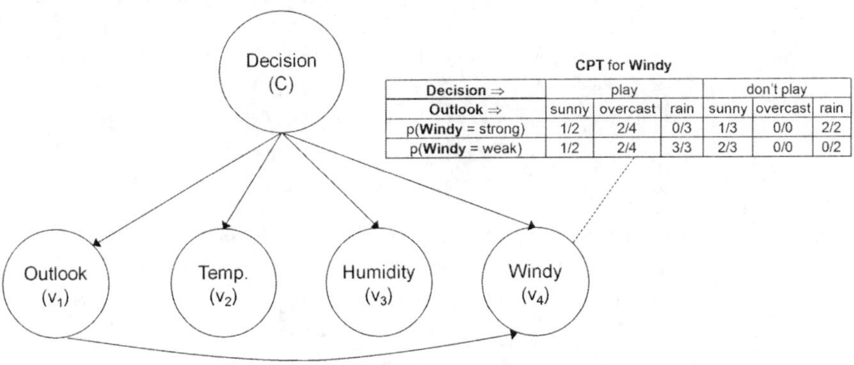

Decision ⇒	play			don't play		
Outlook ⇒	sunny	overcast	rain	sunny	overcast	rain
p(Windy = strong)	1/2	2/4	0/3	1/3	0/0	2/2
p(Windy = weak)	1/2	2/4	3/3	2/3	0/0	0/2

FIGURE 12.8 : The learned kNBC from TABLE 12.5

12.4 LEARNING OF BAYESIAN BELIEF NETWORKS

Modeling an analytics problem based on Bayesian Belief Networks (BNs) requires a specification of the network structure and a set of probabilities (or parameters) for each node (or variable), called a Conditional Probability Table (CPT). Therefore, the task of defining a BN model can be divided into two subtasks: 1) defining or learning the structure of the network, and 2) defining or learning the set of probabilities. Usually, learning structure is much harder than learning probabilities. However, a structure is much easier to elicit from experts than are probabilities. Eliciting probabilities is especially difficult for a node with a large number of parents (in which case its CPT becomes very complex). Also, since the world is rarely fully observable, we must consider cases where we have to derive a BN structure when some of the nodes are hidden, or some of the data are missing. Deriving the structure is much harder when everything we wish to model is only partially observed.

We identify various cases of learning BNs depending on the prior knowledge of network structures and observability on variables.

12.4.1 Cases for Learning Bayesian Networks

In general, the framework for learning structure and/or probabilities for BNs given some data set gives rise to the following four cases:

- *Known Structure and Fully Observable Variables*: The network structure is given and assumed to be complete, and the given data set is complete in the sense that it includes observations of all the variables in the network. The goal here is to learn the probabilities of the variables from the data set.

- *Known Structure and Partially Observable Variables*: The network structure is given and assumed to be complete, and the data set includes observations of some (but not all) of the variables in the network. The variables whose observations are not specified in the data set are either *missing* or *hidden*. A variable is hidden because it cannot be explicitly measured. The goal here is to learn the probabilities of the network from the data set, in spite of the missing data. Some observations of a variable could be missing due to a bad collection procedure.

- *Unknown Structure and Fully Observable Variables*: Neither the network structure nor the probabilities of the network are known. But the network that is to be learned will contain only those variables that are in the data set; there are no hidden variables. The goal here is to learn both the structure and the probabilities of the network.

- *Unknown Structure and Partially Observable Variables*: Neither the network structure nor the probabilities of the network are known, and the network may contain hidden variables that are not in the data set. The goal here is to learn both the structure and the probabilities of the network.

In the rest of this section, we summarize the most widely used techniques for deriving BNs with only discrete variables (a discrete variable can take on one of a limited number of values, which are often referred to as the *states* of that variable). These techniques are summarized in FIGURE 12.9.

Structure ⇒ Observability ⇓	Known Network Structure	Unknown Network Structure
Fully Observable Variables	**Parameter Estimation** Maximum Likelihood (ML) Estimation Bayesian Dirichlet (BD)	**Discrete Search** Entropy, Bayesian, or MDL Score-Based (e.g., K2) Dependency Constraint-Based
Partially Observable Variables	**Parametric Optimization** Expectation Maximization (EM) Gibbs' Sampling Gradient Descent-Based (e.g., APN)	**Search and Optimizaton** Expectation Maximization (EM) (e.g., Structural EM)

FIGURE 12.9 : Cases for learning BNs

12.4.2 Learning Probabilities

12.4.2.1 Brief Survey

Learning probabilities from a complete data set is discussed in Spiegelhalter and Lauritzen (1990) and Buntine (1991). Lauritzen (1995) describes how to apply the Expectation Maximization (EM) algorithm (Dempster et al., 1977) to BNs. Learning using Gibbs' sampling (Geman and Geman, 1984) is discussed in Thomas et al. (1992) and Gilks et al. (1996). Learning probabilities from incomplete data using gradient methods is discussed by Thiesson (1995), Russel et al. (1995), and Binder et al. (1997).

12.4.2.2 Learning Probabilities from Fully Observable Variables

A common approach here is to use the Maximum Likelihood (ML) estimates for the probabilities, which reduces to simple counting of relative frequencies of the values of the variable (Spiegelhalter and Lauritzen, 1990). To illustrate the technique, let $\mathbf{X} = \{X_1, ..., X_n\}$ (or $(X_1, ..., X_n)$, based on an ordering) be the set of all variables in the given network structure S. The vector $\theta_S = (\theta_1, ..., \theta_n)$ denotes the probability distribution in the structure, and its corresponding vector of variables is $\mathbf{\Theta}_S = (\Theta_1, ..., \Theta_n)$. Each X_i is discrete with states $x_i^1, ..., x_i^{r_i}$, and the variable θ_{ijk} represents a specific CPT entry, the probability that variable X_i takes on its k-th possible value assignment given that its parents pa_i take on their j-th possible value assignment. Therefore,

$$\sum_{k=1}^{r_i} \theta_{ijk} = 1$$

where r_i is the number of states in the variable X_i. To learn the probabilities given the structure S and data set $\mathbf{D} = \{D_1, ..., D_N\}$, we need to compute the posterior distribution $p(\theta_S|D, S)$. Two assumptions are made to compute this distribution. The first assumption is that the data set $\mathbf{D}$ is complete, and the second assumption is that the parameter vectors $\theta_{ij} = (\theta_{ij1}, ..., \theta_{ijr_i})$ are mutually independent as follows:

$$p(\theta_S|S) = \prod_{i=1}^{n} \prod_{j=1}^{q_i} p(\theta_{ij}|S)$$

where q_i is the number of possible parent states for the node X_i, and θ_{ij} are the parameters for the local likelihood function. These parameters remain independent given the data set $\mathbf{D}$ as follows:

$$p(\theta_S|D, S) = \prod_{i=1}^{n} \prod_{j=1}^{q_i} p(\theta_{ij}|D, S)$$

Therefore, the parameters θ_{ij} can be updated independently, and a Dirichlet distribution is often used to estimate these parameters. In general, the probability density of the Dirichlet distribution for variables $\mathbf{p} = (p_1, ..., p_n)$ with parameters $\mathbf{u} = (u_1, ..., u_n)$ is defined by

$$p(\mathbf{p}) = Dirichlet(\mathbf{p}; \mathbf{u}) = \frac{\Gamma\left(\sum_{i=1}^{n} u_i\right)}{\prod_{i=1}^{n} \Gamma(u_i)} \prod_{i=1}^{n} p_i^{u_i - 1}$$

where each $p_i \geq 0$, $\sum_{i=1}^{n} p_i = 1$, and each $u_i > 0$ is interpreted as the prior observation counts for events governed by p_i. Γ represents the Gamma function, which satisfies $\Gamma(n+1) = n\Gamma(n)$ and $\Gamma(1) = 1$. In our case, we assume that each vector θ_{ij} has a Dirichlet distribution with the prior observation counts α_{ijk}, that is,

$$p(\theta_{ij}|S) = c \cdot \prod_{k=1}^{r_i} \theta_{ijk}^{\alpha_{ijk} - 1}$$

where c is a normalization constant. If N_{ijk} is the number of times in $\mathbf{D}$ the variable X_i takes on its k-th possible value assignment $X_i = v_{ik}$, given that its parents pa_i take on their j-th possible value assignment, then

$$p(\theta_{ij}|D, S) = c \cdot \prod_{k=1}^{r_i} \theta_{ijk}^{\alpha_{ijk} + N_{ijk} - 1}$$

Therefore, learning probabilities from a complete data set is based on simple counting of relative frequencies of occurrences of the values of the variable.

12.4.2.3 Learning Probabilities from Partially Observable Variables

Various approaches exist to maximize the posterior distribution $p(\mathbf{D}|\theta_S, S)$, the probability assigned by the network to the observed data set when the CPT parameters are set to θ_S. The Adaptive Probabilistic Network (APN) (Russel et al., 1995) is an approach that uses a gradient descent algorithm for maximization. A widely studied stochastic method is Gibbs' sampling, which can be used to approximate any function of an initial joint distribution $p(\mathbf{X})$, provided certain conditions are met. An alternative approximation algorithm is the Expectation-Maximization (EM) algorithm, which can be viewed as a deterministic version of Gibbs' sampling.

Gradient Descent Algorithm

The gradient-based algorithms view the probability $p(\mathbf{D}|\theta_S, S)$ as a function of the CPT entries θ_S, thereby reducing the probability learning problem to one of finding the maximum of a multivariate nonlinear function. Equivalently, the log-likelihood function of $p(\mathbf{D}|\theta_S, S)$ is maximized via the gradient-ascent approach, where a small step is taken in the direction of the gradient to the point $\theta_S + \alpha\Delta\theta_S$, for some step-size parameter α.

The gradient-ascent approach is modified to take into account the constraint that θ_S consists of conditional probability values $\theta_{ijk} \in [0,1]$ and $\sum_k \theta_{ijk} = 1$. The contribution of each data case D_l to the gradient can be computed separately, and the results are summed as illustrated below:

$$\begin{aligned}
&\frac{\partial}{\partial\theta_{ijk}} \ln p(\mathbf{D}|\theta_S, S) \\
&= \frac{\partial}{\partial\theta_{ijk}} \ln \prod_{l=1}^{N} p(D_l|\theta_S, S) \quad \text{[data points are independent]} \\
&= \sum_{l=1}^{N} \frac{\partial}{\partial\theta_{ijk}} \ln p(D_l|\theta_S, S) \\
&= \sum_{l=1}^{N} \frac{\frac{\partial}{\partial\theta_{ijk}} p(D_l|\theta_S, S)}{p(D_l|\theta_S, S)}
\end{aligned}$$

Thus, we have

$$\begin{aligned}
&\frac{\partial}{\partial\theta_{ijk}} \ln p(\mathbf{D}|\theta_S, S) \\
&= \sum_{l=1}^{N} \frac{\frac{\partial}{\partial\theta_{ijk}} \left(\sum_{u,v} p(D_l|x_{iv}, pa_{iu}, \theta_S, S) p(x_{iv}|pa_{iu}, \theta_S, S) p(pa_{iu}, \theta_S, S) \right)}{p(D_l|\theta_S, S)}
\end{aligned}$$

Since θ_{ijk} appears once in the above expression and $\theta_{ijk} = p(x_{iv}|pa_{iu}, \theta_S, S)$

$$\begin{aligned}
&\frac{\partial}{\partial\theta_{ijk}} \ln p(\mathbf{D}|\theta_S, S) \\
&= \sum_{l=1}^{N} \frac{p(D_l|x_{ik}, pa_{ij}, \theta_S, S) p(pa_{ij}, \theta_S, S)}{p(D_l|\theta_S, S)} \\
&= \sum_{l=1}^{N} \frac{p(x_{ik}, pa_{ij}|D_l, \theta_S, S) p(D_l|\theta_S, S) p(pa_{ij}, \theta_S, S)}{p(x_{ik}, pa_{ij}, \theta_S, S) p(D_l|\theta_S, S)}
\end{aligned}$$

Thus,

$$\frac{\partial}{\partial \theta_{ijk}} \ln p(\mathbf{D}|\theta_S, S) = \sum_{l=1}^{N} \frac{p(x_{ik}, pa_{ij}|D_l, \theta_S, S)}{\theta_{ijk}}$$

Each term $p(x_{ik}, pa_{ij}|D_l, \theta_S, S)/\theta_{ijk}$ in the summation gets computed in a network when the evidence D_l is posted. In a junction tree implementation of evidence propagation (discussed in the chapter on probabilistic graphical models), a node and its parents always appear together in at least one clique (*cliques* are groupings of nodes formed when performing graph transformations on a BN, as called for by the junction tree algorithm), and the required probability can be found by marginalizing the other variables in the clique.

Gibbs' Sampling

Please refer to the chapter on Monte Carlo sampling for a detailed discussion on Gibbs' sampling techniques. Here we outline the technique specifically to learn the parameters θ_S of a Bayesian network with structure S from the incomplete data set $\mathbf{D}$. To approximate θ_S via Gibbs' sampling, first the values of θ_S and the states of unobserved variables in $\mathbf{D}$ are initialized, producing a complete data set $\mathbf{U}$. Then, for each variable X_i in D_l that is not observed in the original data set $\mathbf{D}$, that variable's state is reassigned according to the distribution $p(x_{il}|\mathbf{U}\backslash x_{il}, \theta_S, S)$. This produces another complete dataset $\mathbf{V}$. Next, the posterior distribution $p(\theta_S|V, S)$ is computed as in the case of learning probabilities using a complete data set, and finally the values of $\theta_S$are reassigned. These two steps are iterated to compute the average of $p(\theta_S|V, S)$ as an approximation.

EM Algorithm

The EM algorithm is an iterative procedure for maximizing the log likelihood function $p(\theta_S|D, \mathbf{S})$ or $p(\theta|\mathbf{D})$, when network structure S is assumed implicitly. Assuming that after the nth iteration the current estimate for parameters θ is θ_n, the estimation at the next step can be derived as

$$\begin{aligned} &\theta^{n+1} \\ &= \arg\max_{\theta} \sum_{D \in \mathbf{D}} \sum_{\mathbf{z}} p(\mathbf{z}|D, \theta^n) \ln p(D, \mathbf{z}|\theta) \\ &= \arg\max_{\theta} \sum_{D \in \mathbf{D}} E_{\mathbf{Z}|D,\theta^n} \{\ln p(D, \mathbf{Z}|\theta)\} \end{aligned}$$

where $\mathbf{Z}$ is the set of those variables in the network structure S for which the values in D are missing or unobserved, and $\mathbf{z}$ is a realization of the variables in $\mathbf{Z}$. The above recursive formula yields the following two-step algorithm iterated a certain number of times or when the change in the log likelihood is below a certain threshold:

E-step: For each case D in the data set $\mathbf{D}$ with missing values of variables $\mathbf{Z}$, compute the probability (expectation) $p(\mathbf{z}|D, \theta^n)$ of each possible completion

$\mathbf{z}$ of D by assuming θ^n. Replace the original data point with all of these completions, weighted by probabilities.

M-step: Compute new θ_{ijk}^{n+1} to maximize $E_{\mathbf{Z}|D,\theta^n}\{\ln p(D,\mathbf{Z}|\theta)\}$ where D and $\mathbf{Z}$ together are realizations of both observed and unobserved variables. The new θ_{ijk}^{n+1} defines the new θ^{n+1}.

In the case of no missing values (i.e., $\mathbf{Z}$ is empty), the new probability values that maximize the simplified log likelihood $\arg\max_{\theta}\left\{\sum_{\mathbf{D}\in\mathbf{D}} \ln p(\mathbf{D}|\theta)\right\}$ for a complete data set are as follows:

$$\theta_{ijk}^{n+1} = \frac{N_{ijk}}{N_{ij}}$$

where N_{ijk} is the number of times in $\mathbf{D}$ the variable X_i takes on its k-th possible value assignment $X_i = v_{ik}$ given that its parents pa_i take on their j-th possible value assignment, and N_{ij} is the number of times the parents take on the j-th value assignment. In the case of maximization within the M-step above, these counts are fractional since we consider expectations. Incomplete data cases are counted according to their associated weights as follows:

$$\theta_{ijk}^{n+1} = \frac{\sum\limits_{D\in D} p(X_i = v_{ik}, pa_{ij}|D,\theta^n)}{\sum\limits_{D\in D} p(pa_{ij}|D,\theta^n)}$$

Now the sum in the numerator can be replaced by the sum $\sum_{\mathbf{u}} p(\mathbf{u}|D,\theta^n)$ over the index $\mathbf{u}$ where v_{ik} belongs to, and pa_{ij} is a subset of, the completed D with $\mathbf{u}$.

The Dirichlet prior is commonly used for a variable X_i. In particular, the Dirichlet for random variable X_i is specified by the parameters $\alpha_1, ..., \alpha_n$, leading to a density proportional to $\theta_{i1}^{\alpha_1 - 1}, ..., \theta_{in}^{\alpha_n - 1}$, where $\sum_{l=1}^{n} \theta_{il} = 1$. The above EM parameter estimation then becomes

$$\theta_{ijk}^{n+1} = \frac{\alpha_i + \sum\limits_{D\in D} p(X_i = v_{ik}, pa_{ij}|D,\theta^n)}{\sum\limits_{l}\alpha_l + \sum\limits_{D\in D} p(pa_{ij}|D,\theta^n)}$$

In the case of an uninformative prior, each α_i is 0. It is a common technique to assume each $\alpha_i > 0$ to deal with the problem of insufficient counts (i.e., instantiations that never appear in the dataset, leading to zero probabilities and division by zero).

Generally, EM for BN learning works well when the fraction of missing information is small. If not then EM will be inefficient for higher-dimensional data.

Example

Consider the BN in FIGURE 12.10. The structure indicates that supply and demand together affect the price of a certain commodity, which in turn affects the profit of a company. Each of the four variables is binary, capturing the upward and downward trends of the state of the variable. We have assumed a Beta prior for probabilities θ_0 as indicated in the CPTs, though they could have been uniform. The figure also displays some of the revised CPT entries by applying the EM learning algorithm as described below.

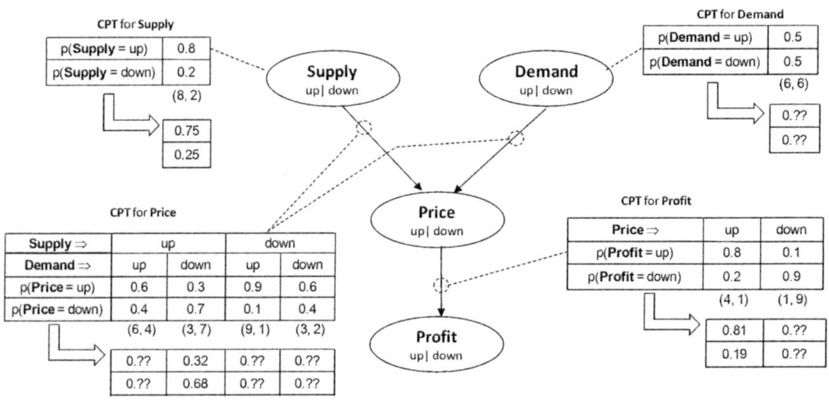

FIGURE 12.10 : Example Bayesian network for parameter learning

So the variable set **X** is $\{Supply, Demand, Price, Profit\}$. TABLE 12.6 is the input data set **D** with some missing information in all three data items. As an example, the missing variable set **Z** for the first, second, and third record is $\{Demand, Price\}$, $\{Supply, Price\}$, and $\{Profit\}$, respectively. The completed data set is shown in TABLE 12.7 along with the computed probabilities for each case.

TABLE 12.6: : An incomplete data set for parameter learning

Supply	**Demand**	**Price**	**Profit**
up	?	?	down
?	down	?	up
down	down	up	?

TABLE 12.7: : The completed data set of the incomplete data set in TABLE 12.6

Supply	**Demand**	**Price**	**Profit**	**p(D,z|θ)**	**p(z|D,θ)**
up	up	up	down	0.8*0.5*0.6*0.2 = 0.048	0.10

TABLE 12.7: : The completed data set of the incomplete data set in TABLE 12.6

up	up	down	down	0.8*0.5*0.4*0.9 = 0.144	0.31
up	down	up	down	0.8*0.5*0.3*0.2 = 0.024	0.05
up	down	down	down	0.8*0.5*0.7*0.9 = 0.252	0.54
up	down	up	up	0.8*0.5*0.3*0.8 = 0.096	0.55
up	down	down	up	0.8*0.5*0.7*0.1 = 0.028	0.16
down	down	up	up	0.2*0.5*0.6*0.8 = 0.048	0.27
down	down	down	up	0.2*0.5*0.4*0.1 = 0.004	0.02
down	down	up	up	0.2*0.5*0.6*0.8 = 0.048	0.8
down	down	up	down	0.2*0.5*0.6*0.2 = 0.012	0.2

θ_1 can now be computed from TABLE 12.7 as follows:

$$p\left(Supply = up\right) = \frac{8+0.10+0.31+0.05+0.54+0.55+0.16}{10+3} = 0.75$$
$$p\left(Supply = down\right) = 0.25$$

$$p\left(Price = up\,|Supply = up\&\ Demand = down\right)$$
$$= \frac{3+0.05+0.55}{10+0.05+0.54+0.55+0.16} = 0.32$$
$$p\left(Price = down\,|Supply = up\&\ Demand = down\right)$$
$$= \frac{3+0.54+0.16}{10+0.05+0.54+0.55+0.16} = 0.68$$

$$p\left(Profit = up\,|Price = up\right)$$
$$= \frac{4+0.55+0.27+0.8}{5+0.1+0.05+0.55+0.27+0.8+0.2} = 0.81$$
$$p\left(Profit = down\,|Price = up\right) = 0.19$$

and so on.

12.4.2.4 Online Adjustment of Parameters

Unlike the EM technique, there is no iterative process for convergence in online learning and adaptation of BN parameters. Here, for evidence at time t, the algorithm is run over the network nodes once and the CPTs are updated with the new values.

$$\theta_{ijk}^{t+1} = \eta \frac{p_{\theta_t}\left(x_{ik} pa_{ij} | z_t\right)}{p_{\theta_t}\left(pa_{ij} | z_t\right)} + \left(1 - \eta\right) \theta_{ijk}^{t}$$

where

- θ_{ijk}^{t} represents the state of a specific CPT entry at the current time t;
- z_t is evidence at time t;
- η is the learning rate (e.g., values of 0.05 and lower); and
- $p_{\theta_t}(.)$ represents the probability value at time t.

12.4.3 Structure Learning

12.4.3.1 Brief Survey

Approaches to learning the structure of a BN can be broadly classified into two categories:

- A *dependency analysis*-based approach captures dependencies among nodes, and more importantly, leaves unconnected nodes that are independent of each other. Some of the approaches in this category are in Srinivas et al. (1990), Fung and Crawford (1990), Spirtes et al. (1990), and Verma and Pearl (1992).
- A *searching and scoring*-based approach defines a "score" that describes the fitness of each possible searched structure to the observed data. Commonly used scores include Entropy (Chow and Liu, 1968; Rebane and Pearl, 1987; Herskovits and Cooper, 1990), Bayesian (Cooper and Herskovits, 1992; Heckerman et al., 1995; Singh and Valtorta, 1995), and MDL (Lam and Bacchus, 1994; Suzuki, 1996; Friedman and Goldszmidt, 1996).

In cases when the number of variables is large, the dependency analysis-based methods are usually more efficient. However, when the sample size is small and the data are noisy, the searching- and scoring-based algorithms can often give more accurate results via an exhaustive search of the whole model space to find the optimal model. There are also algorithms that can handle data sets with missing values (Ramoni and Sebastiani, 1997; Singh, 1997; Friedman, 1998).

The notion of equivalence of network structures is important and should be kept in mind when pruning the search for structures. Consider the networks in FIGURE 12.11 constructed from the domain of three variables X, Y, and Z. All are equivalent in that they can capture the same set of data, given appropriate conditional probability tables.

The joint probability distributions decompose respectively as the following:

$$\begin{aligned} p(X,Y,Z) &= p(X)\,p(Y|X)\,p(Z|Y) \\ p(X,Y,Z) &= p(Y)\,p(X|Y)\,p(Z|Y) \\ p(X,Y,Z) &= p(Z)\,p(Y|Z)\,p(X|Y) \end{aligned}$$

Applying Bayes' rule repeatedly, we can derive the following:

$$\begin{aligned} & p(X)\,p(Y|X)\,p(Z|Y) \\ & = p(Y,X)\,p(Z|Y) = p(Y)\,p(X|Y)\,p(Z|Y) \\ & = p(Z,Y)\,p(X|Y) = p(Z)\,p(Y|Z)\,p(X|Y) \end{aligned}$$

The above network structures are shown to be distribution-equivalent, as the variable probabilities must be equal at any state of information. The methods for learning equivalent classes of network structures can be found in Chickering (2002).

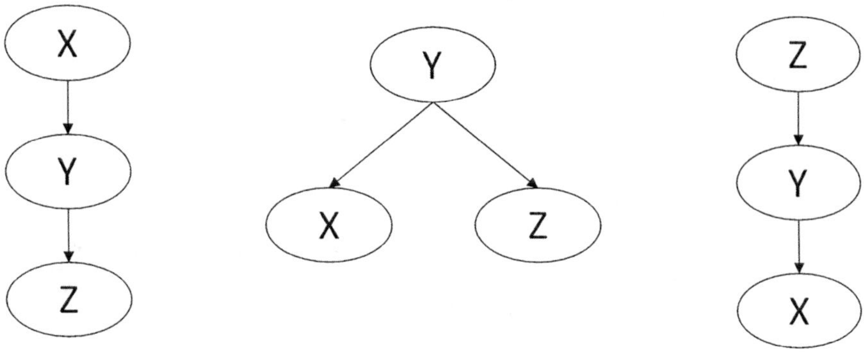

FIGURE 12.11 : Equivalent network structures

It is also important here to contrast statistical correlation and causal semantics in BNs to illustrate ambiguities in BN learning. The BN fragment in FIGURE 12.12 illustrates that the country's economic condition, represented by the variable *Economy*, will cause the demand for various products such as the products *A* and *B*. The two children nodes *Demand Product A* and *Demand Product B* are correlated, but one does not cause the other.

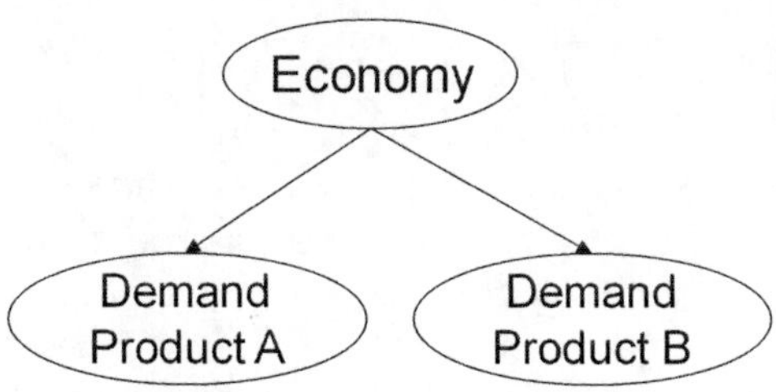

FIGURE 12.12 : Correlated BN nodes

FIGURE 12.13 shows a sample data set and possible BN structures. The data set clearly shows that the two variables are perfectly correlated. In other words, a low key campaign (resp. aggressive) causes low (resp. high) conversion, and vice versa, but only the first relationship is a causal one.

These ambiguities can be resolved effectively in a mixed-initiative learning system with human-in-the-loop.

12.4.3.2 Learning Structure from Fully Observable Variables

The technique proposed in Cooper and Herskovits (1992) to learn structure from a complete data set uses a "greedy" search algorithm through a space of all possible BN structures. Aliferis and Cooper (1994) evaluate the accuracy of K2, a specific instantiation of a greedy search algorithm. To select the most probable structure *S* of conditional dependencies among the variables in a

Campaign	Conversion
aggressive	high
lowkey	low
lowkey	low
lowkey	low
lowkey	low
aggressive	high
aggressive	high

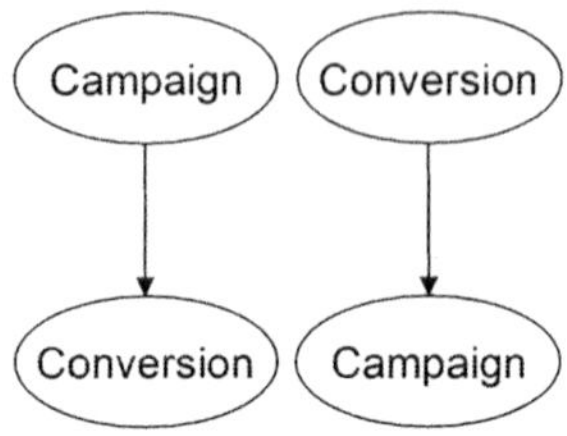

FIGURE 12.13 : BNs representing data sets

complete data set $\mathbf{D}$ of m independent cases $D_1, ..., D_m$, the selection of the structure is based on the evaluation of

$$p(S, \mathbf{D}) = c \cdot p(S)\, p(\mathbf{D}|S)$$

where $p(\mathbf{D}|S)$ is the marginal likelihood of $\mathbf{D}$ given S, derived in Cooper and Herskovits (1992), as follows:

$$p(\mathbf{D}|S) = \prod_{i=1}^{n} \prod_{j=1}^{q_i} \frac{\Gamma(\alpha_{ij})}{\Gamma(\alpha_{ij} + N_{ij})} \cdot \prod_{k=1}^{r_i} \frac{\Gamma(\alpha_{ijk} + N_{ijk})}{\Gamma(\alpha_{ijk})}$$

The above marginal likelihood is also known as the Bayesian-Dirichlet scoring function. Suppose that the possible models are equally likely a priori, and that the user can formulate a partial ordering of the variables so that if $X_i \prec X_j$ then X_i cannot be a parent of X_j. Let pa_i be the current set of parents of the node X_i. Then the local contribution of a node X_i and its parents to the joint probability $p(S, \mathbf{D})$ is measured by the local marginal likelihood as follows:

$$g(X_i, pa_i) = \prod_{j=1}^{q_i} \frac{\Gamma(\alpha_{ij})}{\Gamma(\alpha_{ij} + N_{ij})} \cdot \prod_{k=1}^{r_i} \frac{\Gamma(\alpha_{ijk} + N_{ijk})}{\Gamma(\alpha_{ijk})}$$

where $N_{ij} = \sum_{k=1}^{r_i} N_{ijk}$. If we assume a uniform distribution of the prior observation counts (i.e., $\alpha_{ijk} = c$, for some c) then the above expression can be simplified to

$$g(X_i, pa_i) = \prod_{j=1}^{q_i} \frac{(r_i - 1)!}{(N_{ij} + r_i - 1)!} \cdot \prod_{k=1}^{r_i} N_{ijk}!$$

Here we describe how this expression is derived. If P is the vector whose values denote the conditional probability assignments associated with the BN structure S, and f is the conditional density function over P given S, then

$$
\begin{aligned}
& p(S,\mathbf{D}) \\
& = \int_P p(\mathbf{D}|P,S) f(P|S) p(S)\, dP \\
& = p(S) \int_P p(\mathbf{D}|P,S) f(P|S)\, dP \\
& = p(S) \int_P \left[\prod_{l=1}^{N} p(D_l|P,S) \right] f(P|S)\, dP \\
& = p(S) \int_P \left[\prod_{l=1}^{N} \prod_{i=1}^{n} p\left(X_i = D_{il}|P, pa_{i\sigma(i,l)}\right) \right] f(P|S)\, dP
\end{aligned}
$$

where pa_{ij} is the j-th possible value assignment of parents pa_i, and $\sigma(i,l)$ is an index function such that the instantiation of parents in case l is the $\sigma(i,l)$-th possible value assignment of pa_i. Supposing the possible values of variable X_i are $v_{i1},...,v_{ir_i}$, we can rewrite the above equation by grouping terms as

$$
p(S,\mathbf{D}) = p(S) \int_P \left[\prod_{i=1}^{n} \prod_{j=1}^{q_i} \prod_{k=1}^{r_i} p(X_i = v_{ik}|P, pa_{ij})^{N_{ijk}} \right] f(P|S)\, dP
$$

Recall that N_{ijk} is the number of times in $\mathbf{D}$ the variable X_i takes on its k-th possible value assignment $X_i = v_{ik}$ given that its parents pa_i take on their j-th possible value assignment. Since $f(p(X_i|pa_{ij}))$ is independent of $f(p(X_u|pa_{uv}))$, we have

$$
f(P|S) = \prod_{i=1}^{n} \prod_{j=1}^{q_i} f(\theta_{ij1},...,\theta_{ijr_i})
$$

Therefore,

$$
\begin{aligned}
& p(S,\mathbf{D}) \\
& = p(S) \int_{\theta_{111}} \cdots \int_{\theta_{ijk}} \cdots \int_{\theta_{nq_n r_n}} \left[\prod_{i=1}^{n} \prod_{j=1}^{q_i} \prod_{k=1}^{r_i} \theta_{ijk}^{N_{ijk}} \right] \\
& \qquad \left[\prod_{i=1}^{n} \prod_{j=1}^{q_i} f(\theta_{ij1},...,\theta_{ijr_i}) \right] d\theta_{111}...\theta_{ijk}...\theta_{nq_n r_n} \\
& = p(S) \prod_{i=1}^{n} \prod_{j=1}^{q_i} \int_{\theta_{ij1}} \cdots \int_{\theta_{ijr_i}} \left[\prod_{k=1}^{r_i} \theta_{ijk}^{N_{ijk}} \right] f(\theta_{ij1},...,\theta_{ijr_i})\, d\theta_{ij1}...\theta_{ijr_i} \\
& = p(S) \prod_{i=1}^{n} \prod_{j=1}^{q_i} C_{ij} \int_{\theta_{ij1}} \cdots \int_{\theta_{ijr_i}} \prod_{k=1}^{r_i} \theta_{ijk}^{N_{ijk}}\, d\theta_{ij1}...\theta_{ijr_i}
\end{aligned}
$$

where the distribution $f(\theta_{ij1},...,\theta_{ijr_i})$ is assumed to be uniform and is equal to some constant C_{ij}. Since $f(\theta_{ij1},...,\theta_{ijr_i})$ is a probability density function, we have

$$\int_{\theta_{ij1}} \cdots \int_{\theta_{ijr_i}} C_{ij} d\theta_{ij1} ... \theta_{ijr_i} = 1$$

$$i.e., \; C_{ij} = \frac{1}{\int_{\theta_{ij1}} \cdots \int_{\theta_{ijr_i}} d\theta_{ij1} ... \theta_{ijr_i}}$$

But we have the following Dirichlet's integral:

$$\int_{\theta_{ij1}} \cdots \int_{\theta_{ijr_i}} \prod_{k=1}^{r_i} \theta_{ijk}^{N_{ijk}} d\theta_{ij1} ... \theta_{ijr_i} = \frac{\prod_{k=1}^{r_i} N_{ijk}!}{(N_{ij} + r_i - 1)!}$$

Substituting, $N_{ijk} = 0$, we obtain

$$\int_{\theta_{ij1}} \cdots \int_{\theta_{ijr_i}} d\theta_{ij1} ... \theta_{ijr_i} = \frac{1}{(r_i - 1)!}$$

$$i.e., \; C_{ij} = (r_i - 1)!$$

Therefore,

$$p(S, \mathbf{D}) = p(S) \prod_{i=1}^{n} \prod_{j=1}^{q_i} \frac{(r_i - 1)!}{(N_{ij} + r_i - 1)!} \prod_{k=1}^{r_i} N_{ijk}!$$

Example

Consider the data **D** in TABLE 12.8 to illustrate the computation of $p(S, \mathbf{D})$.

TABLE 12.8: : Records for deriving BN structures

Competition	**Campaign**	**Profit**
moderate	lowkey	large
stiff	aggressive	large
moderate	lowkey	large
moderate	lowkey	large
moderate	aggressive	large
moderate	lowkey	small
stiff	aggressive	small
moderate	lowkey	large
stiff	aggressive	small
moderate	lowkey	large
moderate	lowkey	large

We consider the two structures S_1 and S_2 as shown in FIGURE 12.14.

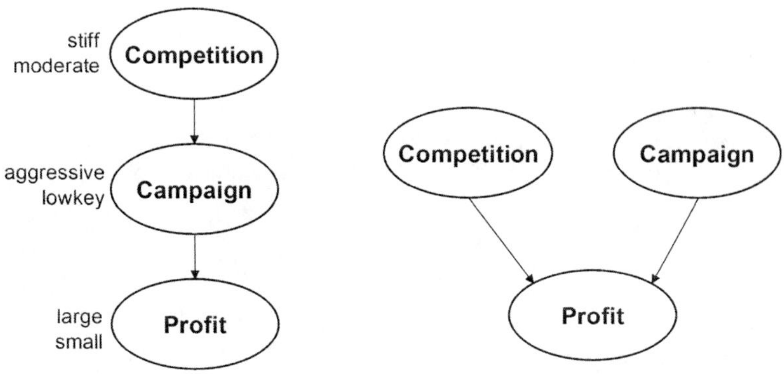

FIGURE 12.14 : Possible BN structures for records in TABLE 12.8

$$
\begin{aligned}
&n = 3 \\
&X_1 = Competition, X_2 = Campaign, X_3 = Profit
\end{aligned}
$$

There are 25 possible structures and thus $p(S_1) = p(S_2) = \frac{1}{25}$. The probabilities of the two structures $p(S_1, \mathbf{D})$ and $p(S_2, \mathbf{D})$ are computed as follows:

$$
\begin{aligned}
q_1 = 0, q_2 = 2, q_3 = 2 \\
r_1 = 2, r_2 = 2, r_3 = 2
\end{aligned}
$$

$$
\begin{aligned}
&N_{211} = 7; N_{212} = 0; N_{221} = 1; N_{222} = 3; \\
&N_{311} = 7; N_{312} = 1; N_{321} = 1; N_{322} = 2 \\
&N_{21} = 7; N_{22} = 4; N_{31} = 8; N_{32} = 3
\end{aligned}
$$

$$
\begin{aligned}
&p(S_1, \mathbf{D}) \\
&= p(S_1) \prod_{i=1}^{n} \prod_{j=1}^{q_i} \frac{(r_i - 1)!}{(N_{ij} + r_i - 1)!} \prod_{k=1}^{r_i} N_{ijk}! \\
&= \frac{1}{25} \frac{(2-1)!\ 7!\ 0!}{(7+2-1)!} \frac{(2-1)!\ 1!\ 3!}{(4+2-1)!} \frac{(2-1)!\ 7!\ 1!}{(8+2-1)!} \frac{(2-1)!\ 1!\ 2!}{(3+2-1)!} \\
&= 0.3 \times 10^{-8}
\end{aligned}
$$

$$
\begin{aligned}
q_1 = 0, q_2 = 0, q_3 = 4 \\
r_1 = 2, r_2 = 2, r_3 = 2
\end{aligned}
$$

$$
\begin{aligned}
&N_{311} = 6; N_{312} = 1; N_{321} = 0; N_{322} = 0; N_{331} = 1; N_{332} = 0; N_{341} = 1; N_{342} = 2 \\
&N_{31} = 7; N_{32} = 0; N_{33} = 1; N_{34} = 3
\end{aligned}
$$

$$
\begin{aligned}
&p(S_2, \mathbf{D}) = p(S_2) \prod_{i=1}^{n} \prod_{j=1}^{q_i} \frac{(r_i - 1)!}{(N_{ij} + r_i - 1)!} \prod_{k=1}^{r_i} N_{ijk}! \\
&= \frac{1}{25} \frac{(2-1)!\ 6!\ 1!}{(7+2-1)!} \frac{(2-1)!\ 0!\ 0!}{(0+2-1)!} \frac{(2-1)!\ 1!\ 0!}{(1+2-1)!} \frac{(2-1)!\ 1!\ 2!}{(3+2-1)!} \\
&= 0.3 \times 10^{-6}
\end{aligned}
$$

Therefore, the second structure is 100 times more likely than the first structure.

K2 Algorithm

The K2 algorithm proceeds by adding one parent at a time and computing $g(X_i, pa_i)$. The set pa_i is expanded to include the parent nodes that give the largest contribution to $g(X_i, pa_i)$ and stops inclusion when the probability settles.

Input:

- An ordered set of nodes $X_1, ..., X_n$, such that if $i < j$ $(1 \leq i, j \leq n)$ then a structure with X_j as an ancestor of X_i is not allowed.
- An upper bound u on the number of parents a node can have.
- A data set $\mathbf{D}$ of m cases.

Output:

- A BN structure specifying the parents, if any, of each node

Steps:

For each node $X_i, i = 1, ..., n$, perform the following steps:
  Set $pa_i = \emptyset$, where pa_i is the set of parents of the node X_i.
  Set $g_{old} = g(X_i, pa_i)$.
  While $|pa_i| < u$, perform the following steps:
    Set node X from $\{X_1, ..., X_{i-1}\} - pa_i$
    that maximizes $g(X_i, pa_i \cup \{X\})$.
    If $g(X_i, pa_i \cup \{X\}) > g_{old}$ then

$$g_{old} = g(X_i, pa_i \cup \{X\})$$
$$pa_i = pa_i \cup \{X\}$$

  Else
    Break out of the while loop
  End
End

12.4.3.3 Learning Structure from Partially Observable Variables

The most difficult case occurs when the structure is unknown and there are hidden variables and/or missing data. Most of the above techniques could be adapted to discover variables, but with a high search cost. The hidden nodes have to be marginalized to compute the Bayesian score. Since this is usually intractable, it is common to use an asymptotic approximation to the posterior called BIC (Bayesian Information Criterion), which is easy to use and does not require the evaluation of prior distribution. Friedman (1998) developed a Structural EM algorithm that combines the standard EM algorithm to optimize parameters with a structure search for model selection. Structural EM learns networks based on penalized likelihood scores, which include the BIC/MDL score.

12.4.4 Use of Prior Knowledge from Experts

There are approaches to include prior knowledge from experts in BN structure learning to reduce the search space of all possible models. The simplest choice is a uniform prior over structures (Heckerman, 1996), but an expert can provide structural knowledge of the following kind (Srinivas et al., 1990) that can constrain the search space:

- Declaring that a variable must be a root node;
- Declaring that a variable must be a leaf node;
- Declaring that one variable must be a parent or ancestor of another node;
- Declaring conditional independence among variables.

A common constraint is a total ordering on variables (Buntine, 1991; Cooper and Herskovits, 1992). As an alternative to total ordering on variables, Hojsgaard and Thiesson (1995) use a partition of the available variables into "blocks" provided by an expert. Another common constraint is to limit the number of parents any variable may have (Cooper and Herskovits, 1992; Friedman and Koller, 2003).

12.5 INDUCTIVE LOGIC PROGRAMMING

The Inductive Logic Programming (ILP) approach to rule induction constructs a program, consisting of rules and facts (together known as clauses), that computes the desired result. Starting from a simple program, the technique modifies the program from a set of instances through the process of specialization and generalization of the clauses. Roughly, the generalization process replaces an attribute value with a variable, or converts the antecedent of an if-then rule to a more general form. Analogously, the specialization process replaces a variable with an attribute value or converts the antecedent of an if-then rule to a more restrictive form.

We illustrate how this learning technique works using the example on student test results presented earlier. Our goal is to derive a program that will help us to compute the performance of an arbitrary student, and especially to predict the value of the column *Answer Code* of the *Answer* table given a student's background. Let us illustrate the specialization process. We introduce the so-called literals for two normalized tables of TABLE 12.2 as shown in FIGURE 12.15:

2-place predicate $Student\,(Id, Background)$, and

3-place predicate $Answer\,(Id, Question\,Type, Answer\,Code)$

STUDENT	
Id	**Background**
1	Philosophy
2	Mathematics
3	Computer Science
4	Mathematics
5	Computer Science
6	Philosophy

ANSWER		
Id	**Question Type**	**Answer Code**
1	Reasoning	True
1	General Knowledge	True
2	Reasoning	True
2	General Knowledge	False
3	Reasoning	True
3	General Knowledge	True
4	Reasoning	True
4	General Knowledge	True
5	Reasoning	False
5	General Knowledge	True
6	Reasoning	True
6	General Knowledge	True

FIGURE 12.15 : Two normalized tables of TABLE 12.2

We start with a simple program consisting of only the following general rule:

$$\rightarrow Answer\,(X, Y, Z)$$

where X, Y, and Z are variables. The above rule has an empty antecedent. This rule states that for every combination of values of the variables X, Y, and Z is in the relation *Answer*. The rule certainly covers all the tuples in the *Answer* table but it also covers the ones that are not in the table, like, $(1, Reasoning, False)$ (or even $(1, False, Reasoning)$ if data type is not considered). So we need to specialize the rule by adding literals to the antecedent. To avoid generating $(1, Reasoning, False)$, we can add an equality constraint on the variable Z as follows:

$$Z = True \rightarrow Answer\,(X, Y, Z)$$

But the above rule still covers $(2, General\,Knowledge, True)$ which is not in the *Answer* table. To avoid this, we can specialize by instantiating the variable Y as follows:

$$Y = Reasoning \wedge Z = True \rightarrow Answer\,(X, Y, Z)$$

But the above rule still covers $(5, Reasoning, True)$ which is not in the *Answer* table. At this stage we can further specialize the rule to cater to individual students. The objective here is to infer general performance across students. Adding the *Student* predicate to the antecedent yields:

$$Student\,(X,U) \wedge Z = True \rightarrow Answer\,(X,Y,Z)$$

This rule is no different from the original rule as far as its cover to positive and negative instances are concerned. The rule above does not specialize and still covers facts that are not in the table *Answer*, such as $(2, General\ Knowledge, True)$.

Here we have two choices. Either we introduce a new literal or restrict the variables to constants. For example, if we restrict the variable X, which corresponds to the Id attribute, to a particular student (say, 1) then the rule becomes

$$Student\,(X,U) \wedge Z = True \wedge X = 1 \rightarrow Answer\,(X,Y,Z)$$

This rule states that each answer from student 1 is True. The program is now necessary as it validates only the correct instances. We can derive similar rules for students 3, 4, and 6. Therefore, the rules learned so far are the following:

$$\begin{array}{l} Student\,(X,U) \wedge Z = True \wedge X = 1 \rightarrow Answer\,(X,Y,Z) \\ Student\,(X,U) \wedge Z = True \wedge X = 3 \rightarrow Answer\,(X,Y,Z) \\ Student\,(X,U) \wedge Z = True \wedge X = 4 \rightarrow Answer\,(X,Y,Z) \\ Student\,(X,U) \wedge Z = True \wedge X = 6 \rightarrow Answer\,(X,Y,Z) \end{array}$$

But the program consisting of the above four rules is not sufficient as it does not cover two positive instances of students 2 and 5.

An option here is to bind the variable U representing a student's background. One such specialization is as follows:

$$Student\,(X,U) \wedge U = Philosophy \wedge Z = True \rightarrow Answer\,(X,Y,Z)$$

The rule above covers only part of the table *Answer*. Addition of the above rule to our program does not make it sufficient as the positive instances of students 2,3, 4 and 5 are still not covered. Binding $U$to Mathematics and Y to Reasoning will cover one of these two as follows:

$$\begin{array}{l} Student\,(X,U) \wedge U = Mathematics \wedge \\ \quad Y = Reasoning \wedge Z = True \rightarrow Answer\,(X,Y,Z) \end{array}$$

We need to generate more such rules to cover all of the tuples in the table *Answer*. The process continues until the program becomes sufficient.

The inefficiency of ILP techniques lies within the combinatorial generalization and specialization process to obtain a new program from the current one. The FOIL algorithm (Quinlan, 1990) to be presented here learns positive Horn clauses without function symbols. The input consists of information about the predicates, one of which is the *target predicate* to be the consequent of each clause of a Horn clause program. For each predicate there is a set of facts or ground atoms that belong to the predicate. We follow the Closed World Assumption (CWA) rule (or program completion semantics) to determine the facts other than those specified belonging to the target predicate.

Facts in the training data set that are known to be under the target predicate will be referred to as $\oplus$ (positive training instances) and those not in the predicate as $\otimes$ (negative training instances). For example, if the set of facts under the target predicate P is $\oplus = \{P(a,b)\}$ then CWA rule provides $\otimes = \{P(a,a), P(b,b), P(b,a)\}$.

The algorithm starts with a training set containing all $\oplus$ and $\otimes$ facts and then learns a function-free Horn clause to explain some of the $\oplus$ facts, removes the covered $\oplus$ facts from the training set, and continues with the search for the next clause. When rules covering all the $\oplus$ facts have been found, they are reviewed to eliminate any redundant clauses and reordered so that any recursive clauses come after the non-recursive base cases.

Perfect definitions that exactly match the data are not always possible due to outliers, exceptions, and missing facts in real data, and this is to be expected. A gain measure is used to limit the complexity of clauses and programs. The final clauses produced by the algorithm may cover most rather than all of the $\oplus$ facts while covering a few rather than none of the $\otimes$ facts.

Algorithm

Input:

- An n-ary predicate P called the target predicate.
- Training set of facts **F**.

Output:

- RULES - a set of learned rules.

Steps:

Set RULES = {}.
Set $\oplus$ = Facts in **F** that are under the target predicate P.
Set $\otimes$ = Facts under P obtained via CWA that are not in $\oplus$.
While $\oplus$ is non-empty, perform the following steps to learn a new rule:
  Set *Rule* $= \rightarrow P(X_1, ..., X_n)$, i.e., *Rule* has empty condition.
  Set TEMP = $\otimes$
  While TEMP is non-empty, perform the following steps:
    Generate a literal L to be added to the antecedent of *Rule*. See the discussion below on how to choose L from a set of candidate literals. Add L to the antecedent of *Rule*.
    Set TEMP = Subset of the facts in TEMP that satisfies the antecedent of *Rule*. Note that the facts that satisfy the antecedent can still be generated by the rule constructed so far and thus one or more conditions need to be

added to the antecedent in the next steps to stop
producing negative instances by the rule.
Add *Rule* to RULES.
Delete those members of $\oplus$ that are covered by *Rule*.
Return RULES.

Following types of literals can be generated as candidate literals to add to the antecedent of a rule that is being learned:

- If Q is an m-ary predicate occurring in the training data set $\mathbf{F}$ then $Q(Y_1, ..., Y_m)$ or its negation is a candidate literal where one or more of the variables $Y_1, ..., Y_m$ are occurring in the variables present in *Rule*.

- $Z_i = c$ or $Z_i \neq c$, where Z_i is a variablea occurring in *Rule* and c is a constant.

Since there will be more than one candidate literal to add to the antecedent of a rule, an information gain criterion will be used to select a literal. Suppose L is a candidate literal that might be added to the antecedent of *Rule*. Then the information gained by adding a literal L to rule *Rule* is defined as follows:

$$Gain\,(L, Rule) = s * \left(\log_2 \frac{p_1}{p_1 + n_1} - \log_2 \frac{p}{p+n} \right)$$

where p and n are the sizes of $\oplus$ and $\otimes$, respectively, before adding L to the antecedent of R, and p_1 and n_1 are the sizes of $\oplus$ and $\otimes$, respectively, when the new rule is obtained from *Rule* by adding L to its antecedent.

There are two parameters to be considered in order to measure the validity of a rule – the *support* and *confidence* of the rule (Roberto et al., 1999). Confidence denotes the strength of a rule, and support describes the quality of the rule. Suppose N is the total number of instances in the training set $\mathbf{F}$, and N_C denotes the number of instances that satisfy the condition C. Then the values of the two parameters for the rule are defined as follows:

$$\begin{array}{l} Support = \frac{N_{\mathbf{X}\&\mathbf{Y}}}{N} = p\,(\mathbf{X}\&\mathbf{Y}) \\ Confidence = \frac{N_{\mathbf{X}\&\mathbf{Y}}}{N_{\mathbf{X}}} = p\,(\mathbf{Y}|\mathbf{X}) \end{array}$$

The higher the confidence of rule, the more accurate a prediction the rule can make. Before adding a rule to the set RULES in the above algorithm, the values of these two parameters should be calculated. The rule is added if the values of the parameters exceed the set thresholds.

12.6 FURTHER READING

Mitchell's book (1997) is a good introduction to both DT and machine learning. See (Zhu, 2005) for a survey on semi-supervised learning. The book discusses ILP technique to extract rules in first-order logic syntax. For surveys on

BN learning, please consult Buntine (1996), Heckerman (1996), and Krause (1998). Neapolitan (2003) discusses the Bayesian method for learning the values of discrete and continuous parameters, and both the Bayesian and constraint-based methods for learning structure. For a discussion on HMM and HHMM learning, see Rabiner (1989) and Fine et al. (1998), respectively.

CHAPTER 13

Unstructured Data and Text Analytics

Text analytics is a process for analyzing large text corpii to help discover information that is strategic to an organization. Sources of text include customer feedback, blogs, reviews, and interactions on social networks, some of which are openly available while the rest are company proprietary. For example, text analytics will discover people's opinions on various blog sites about a company's new product, or analyze customers' sentiment from text surveys. Text analytics applications include sentiment analysis, business and military intelligence analyses, e-service, scientific discovery, and search and information access.

The two most fundamental tasks that provide foundations for text analytics are: 1) information structuring and extraction; and 2) text classification and topic extraction. In this chapter, we give a brief introduction to some well-known Natural Language Processing (NLP) techniques for information structuring and then extraction in the form of subject-predicate-object Resource Description Framework (RDF) triples. We then present an array of approaches to text document classification and topic extraction, all of which (including RDF triple extraction) are part of the text analytics tool aText, discussed in the penultimate chapter on analytics tools.

We begin with the supervised Naïve Bayesian Classifier (NBC), which we introduced earlier as a graphical classification and decision-making model using structured data. We then present its generalization, k-dependence NBC (kNBC). Note that this topics are in fact the labels of the training instances for these supervised techniques. We compare the performances of these techniques in the context of a well-known text corpus and with Support Vector Machine (SVM)-based discriminative classification as a baseline in the final chapter.

Latent Semantic Analysis (LSA) is one of the early approaches to text classification, with successful applications in information retrieval (Dumais et al., 1988). LSA can be used effectively for unsupervised text classification in conjunction with SVM, which was introduced earlier in the cluster analysis chapter. LSA constructs feature vectors from the terms occurring in documents. Such vectors become "very high-" dimensional to account for every term occurring in the text corpus. LSA transforms high-dimensional data into a much smaller-dimensional latent topic space where the clustering is performed, and it attempts to solve the synonomy and polysemy problems to match documents by taking advantage of the implicit higher-order structure of the association of terms with articles to create a multi-dimensional semantic structure.

We present two powerful unsupervised text classification techniques. One is a probabilistic variation of algebraic LSA, called probabilistic LSA (PLSA) (Hofmann, 1999), and the other is called Latent Dirichlet Allocation (LDA) (Blei et al., 2003). Both PLSA and LDA produce generative models and are useful in suggesting latent topics in corpii by projecting their most representative words.

13.1 INFORMATION STRUCTURING AND EXTRACTION

The following definition of unstructured data is perhaps the most succinct among those found on the web:

"Unstructured Data (or unstructured information) refers to information that either does not have a pre-defined data model and/or does not fit well into relational tables."

– Wikipedia, 2013

There are several points to be noted here. First, the above definition itself is full of "information" as absorbed by you while reading, but is certainly not "usable" by a computer program. Second, the concept of data needs to be distinguished from that of information, as the former is not usable by humans without a proper context (or meta-information). Information is the semantic interpretation of data, and represents relationships among data with meaning and purpose. These relationships can be captured well in unstructured natural languages or figures. Structured data have become synonymous with relational data. Structured relational data are organized and searchable by data type within the actual content to be queried by SQL, and highly unstructured data is commonly associated with file servers, bitmap images/objects, and document management systems. Data "in-between," which includes XML data, HTML pages, PDF documents, emails, HTTP traffic and clickstream data, search results and application log files, is in a state of transition to a structured form. According to some recent estimates, unstructured data represents approximately 85% of enterprise data.

The structure of some data may not be defined formally, but can still be implied by exploiting linguistics and auditory and visual structures present in the data. Moreover, data with some form of structure may still be characterized as unstructured if the structure is not helpful for the desired processing task. One should also be aware of the data-information-knowledge continuum/hierarchy, and the concept of unstructuredness is applicable at every level of the hierarchy. So what is structuring and what do structures look like?

A concrete example of structuring is shown in FIGURE 13.1. A textual description of the picture is "Homer is sitting in a chair drinking beer." A human observer may discover more objects in the picture than just Homer and a beer bottle, and may infer a lot more information from the "context" of this picture, including the possibility that Homer is depressed. Structuring involves representing this information using a suitable syntax. The example here uses both RDF triples and relational tables. Note that an added advantage of such syntax being declarative is that a human is able to read, add, and update, if necessary, in addition to the machine. Once we have a structured representation, a machine can interpret and reason with it based on its semantic interpretation and positional knowledge of attributes. For example, the name of a person would appear in the first position of an RDF-representation, and in the column headed by "Person" of a relational representation. This type of position-based convention is not feasible for unstructured texts, since the same picture can be described in multiple ways due to the free-form nature of natural languages.

⇐ Increasingly suitable for human consumption

Image

Text

Homer is sitting on a chair drinking beer.

An alternative:

Homer is drinking beer while sitting on a chair.

Representation

RDF Triplets:
(homer, sitting, chair)
(homer, drinking, beer)

Relational table:

Action	*Person*	*Object*
sitting	homer	chair
drinking	homer	beer

Increasingly suitable for machine processing ⇒

FIGURE 13.1 : Data structuring continuum

Let us now turn our attention towards structuring more complex media such as audio and video. Consider the information in FIGURE 13.2. The video is not even embedded into this document, but an informed reader familiar with this famous scene already has a context much richer than what has been expressed by a fragment of the full discourse between Steiger and Brando. How do we represent such discourses found in audio, video, and documents, and make them useful for extracting events, text aggregation and summarization, information filtering, etc.? Two things are certainly required

– one for capturing and interpreting rich discourse structure, and the other for representing uncertainty. Both object (in dialogues) and meta-level (in the process) uncertainties need to be captured.

		⇐ Increasingly suitable for human consumption
Audio and Video	Discourse	Representation
	*Steiger (Charley)*: "Oh, I had some bets down for you. You saw some money." *Brando(Terry)*: "You don't understand! I coulda had class. I coulda been a contender. I could've been somebody, instead of a bum, which is what I am, let's face it. It was you, Charley."	Perhaps a declarative logical syntax for representing dialogues and discourse and embedded in it a formalism for handling uncertainty.
Increasingly suitable for machine processing ⇒		

FIGURE 13.2 : Complex structuring of discourse

This dialog in FIGURE 13.2 is representative of the complexity involved in structuring. It uses dialects, arguments, uncertainty, assertion, co-reference, named entities, and so on. The application of deep linguistics processing in analyzing unstructured textual data therefore is essential.

13.2 BRIEF INTRODUCTION TO NLP

Natural Language Processing (NLP) techniques provide a rich paradigm for semantic interpretation of events and text queries. This process will allow us to analyze and structure unstructured text data. To apply such a technique to transcribed speech, some additional preprocessing is necessary, since transcribed texts from speech are without punctuation and capital letters. This section provides a brief introduction to NLP with examples (Ait-Mokhtar et al., 2010). We do not detail state-of-the-art approaches to NLP. Readers are encouraged to look for other sources of NLP background materials if interested in a deeper exploration of the area.

As shown in FIGURE 13.3, the levels of NLP can be grouped into the following two stages: Syntactic Analysis and Semantic Analysis.

We make use of the Stanford parser (http://nlp.stanford.edu/software/lex-parser.shtml) to illustrate these stages in the next two subsections.

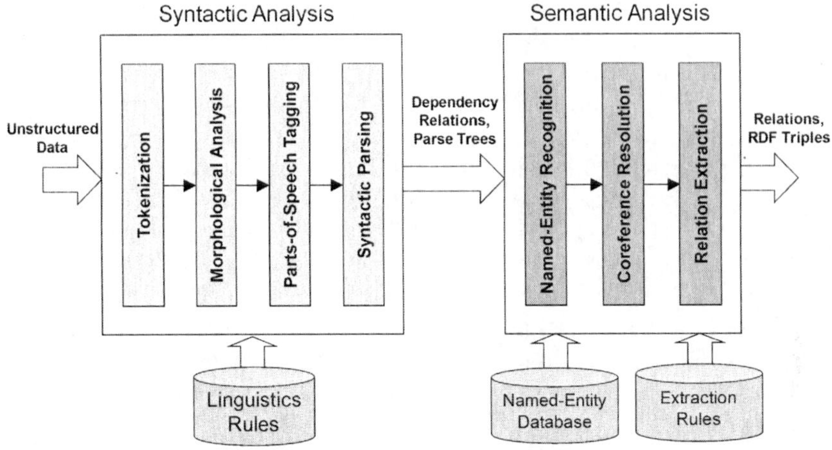

FIGURE 13.3 : Steps in NLP and Relation Extraction

13.2.1 Syntactic Analysis

As shown in FIGURE 13.3, the Syntactic Analysis stage has the following steps in an increasing level of structuring and abstraction from the text surface: Tokenization, Morphological Analysis, Parts-of-Speech Tagging, and Syntactic Parsing.

13.2.1.1 Tokenization

The Tokenization step produces lexical tokens as words and symbols in the input unstructured text. Tokenization segments a sequence of character codes (the input text) into a sequence of basic tokens (mostly word forms, but also punctuation symbols and numbers). Consider the following example sentence as input unstructured text:

He got the job in spite of not having all the necessary qualifications.

The tokenized text is the following:

He /got /the /job /in spite of /not /having /all /the /necessary /qualifications /.

Tokens that lead to alternative tokenizations are marked as ambiguous in the lexicon. Techniques that are used for tokenization include regular expression and finite state automata.

13.2.1.2 Morphological Analysis

Morphology is the study of the relationships between word surface forms (i.e., words as they appear in texts) and their lexical forms (lemmas and morphosyntactic features). Morphological analysis assigns each token all its possible morphosyntactic readings (base forms, part-of-speech categories, morphological features such as number or gender, etc.). For example, the token "hands" is mapped into its base form "hand," the part-of-speech Noun, and the morphosyntactic feature Pl, which stands for plural. A single pass algorithm is used to perform tokenization and morphological analysis. TABLE 13.1 is the output of tokenization and morphological analysis of the example input sentence (Open Xerox tags convention: 123SP – any person singular or plural, 3P – third person, Adj – adjective, Aux - auxiliary, Def – definite, Det – determiner, NomObl – nominative or oblique case, Non3Sg – not third person singular, PastBoth – past participle and past tense, Pers – Person, Pl – plural, Pres – present tense, Prog – progressive, Pron – pronoun, Punct – punctuation, Quant – quantifier, Sent – sentence, Sg – Singular, SP – singular or plural).

TABLE 13.1: : An example morphological analysis

Sequence of Tokens	**Lemma (base form) + POS and Morphosyntactic Features**
He	**he** + Pron + Pers + Nom + 3P + Sg
got	**get** + Verb + PastBoth + 123SP
the	**the** + Det + Def + SP
job	**job** + Noun + Sg **job** + Verb + Pres + Non3sg
in spite of	**in_spite_of** + Prep
not	**not** + Adv + Neg
having	**have** + Verb + Prog **have** + Aux + Prog
all	**all** + Det + Pl + Quant **all** + Pron + NomObl + 3P + Pl
the	**the** + Det + Def + SP
necessary	**necessary** + Adj
qualifications	**qualification** + Noun + Pl
.	**.** + Punct + Sent

13.2.1.3 Part-of-Speech (POS) Tagging

POS tagging selects one morphosyntactic reading for each token according to context (i.e., disambiguating the morpholosyntactic readings of words). Rule-based methods disambiguate grammatical constraints in order to eliminate incorrect tags depending on context, such as "a verb cannot follow a determiner" and "an auxiliary must be followed by a verb." Statistical and machine learning based techniques are also used. TABLE 13.2 is an example POS tagging obtained from TABLE 13.1.

TABLE 13.2: : An example parts-of-speech tagging

Sequence of Tokens	**Lemma (base form) + POS and Morphosyntactic Features**
He	**he** + Pron + Pers + Nom + 3P + Sg
got	**get** + Verb + PastBoth + 123SP
the	**the** + Det + Def + SP
job	**job** + Noun + Sg **INVALID: job** + Verb + Pres + Non3sg
in spite of	**in_spite_of** + Prep
not	**not** + Adv + Neg
having	**have** + Verb + Prog **INVALID: have** + Aux + Prog
all	**all** + Det + Pl + Quant **INVALID: all** + Pron + NomObl + 3P + Pl
the	**the** + Det + Def + SP
necessary	**necessary** + Adj
qualifications	**qualification** + Noun + Pl
.	. + Punct + Sent

13.2.1.4 Syntactic Parsing

Syntactic parsing is the assignment of syntactic (i.e., grammatical) structures to sentences where words are grouped into syntactic constituents and/or interconnected with grammatical relations. The input of a parsing process is usually a sequence of tokens with disambiguated morphosyntactic information (POS-tagged input). There are two types of parsing: *constituent-based parsing* (Chomsky, 1957) to produce constituent-based or phrase-based structures, and *dependency-based parsing* (Tesniere, 1959) to produce dependency structures.

The constituent-based parsing produces a constituent-based structure that groups words into hierarchical labeled constituents (phrases). The parsing result is a phrase structure tree where nodes are phrases/constituents and leaves are wordforms. FIGURE 13.4 shows a constituent-based tree structure of the input sentence and FIGURE 13.5 shows the interface of the Stanford parser to run the same.

Linking words with grammatical relations (e.g., subject, object, and attribute) are called *dependencies*. The result of dependency-based parsing is a set of dependency relations. The output from the parser on the input sentence is shown in FIGURE 13.6, where the dependency relations for the input sentence are nsubj(got, He), dobj(got, job), det(job, the), prepc_in_spite_of(job, having), neg(having, not), dobj(having, qualifications), predet(qualifications, the), amod(qualifications, necessary), and

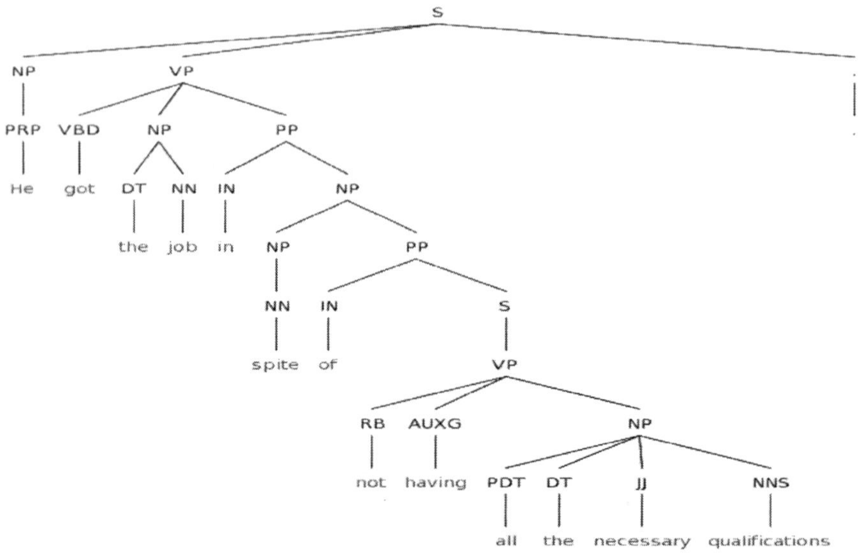

FIGURE 13.4 : An example constituent-based structure

FIGURE 13.5 : Stanford parser producing a constituent-based structure

det(the, all). The Stanford parser defines an extensive set of 56 dependency relations. These relations are organized in a hierarchy, thereby permitting the specification of the relationship between a node and its dependent.

The dependence relations from an input sentence form a dependency structure known as a Stanford Dependency (SD) graph (de Marneffe et al., 2006 & 2010). SD graphs are syntactic dependency graphs where nodes are words and

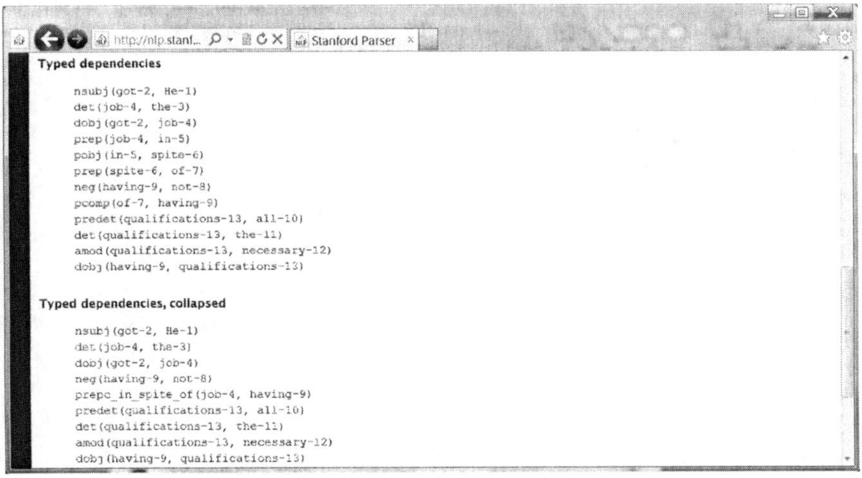

FIGURE 13.6 : Generated dependency relations from Stanford parser

the edges are labeled with the syntactic relations between words. The dependency graph structure corresponding to the collapsed dependency relations in FIGURE 13.6 is shown in FIGURE 13.7.

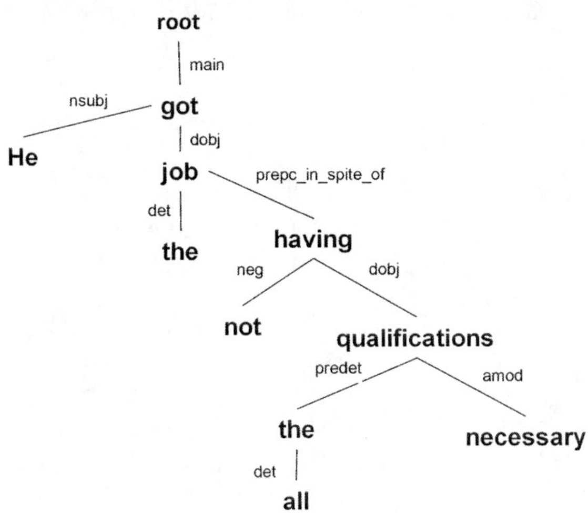

FIGURE 13.7 : An example dependency graph

13.2.2 Semantic Analysis

The Semantic Analysis stage builds a formal representation of the meaning of sentences from their syntactic structures and the basis meanings of words. As shown in FIGURE 13.3, this stage has the following three steps: Named Entity Recognition, Co-reference Resolution, and Relation Extraction.

13.2.2.1 Named Entity Recognition

A Named Entity (NE) refers to a person's name, location name, organization name, etc., occurring in a text. Dates and numerical data are often considered as NEs. NEs are also extended to basic semantic elements of a specific domain, e.g., gene names in biology. The Named Entity Recognition step enriches the NE database by identifying names, places, dates, and other words and phrases that establish the meaning of a body of text. Consider the text in FIGURE 13.8:

> Barack Hussein Obama II (born August 4, 1961) is the 44th and current President of the United States. He is the first African American to hold the office. Obama previously served as a United States Senator from Illinois, from January 2005 until he resigned after his election to the presidency in November 2008.
>
> A native of Honolulu, Hawaii, Obama is a graduate of Columbia University and Harvard Law School, where he was the president of the Harvard Law Review...

FIGURE 13.8 : Example text for named entity recognition

In this text, Barack Hussein Obama II and Obama are person names. The fact that they refer to the same person will be detected via co-reference resolution as described below. The text also contains various location and organization names and dates.

Ambiguities frequently occur in the process of recognizing NEs. For example, Washington could be a person or a city depending on the context. Similarly, Turner could be a person or a city or an organization or a common noun. The use of the word Britain in the sentence "The prestigious Wimbledon tournament takes place in Britain" is a location, whereas the word is an organizational representative in the sentence "Britain presented a draft UN resolution last month." Handcrafted NE recognition systems are dependent on human intuition, but there are machine learning approaches.

13.2.2.2 Co-reference Resolution

A co-reference is a relation among linguistic expressions that refers to the same entity. It occurs when the same thing is referred to with multiple and possibly different expressions in a document. There are two types of co-references:

anaphora and cataphora. FIGURE 13.9 shows an example block of text and various types of co-references.

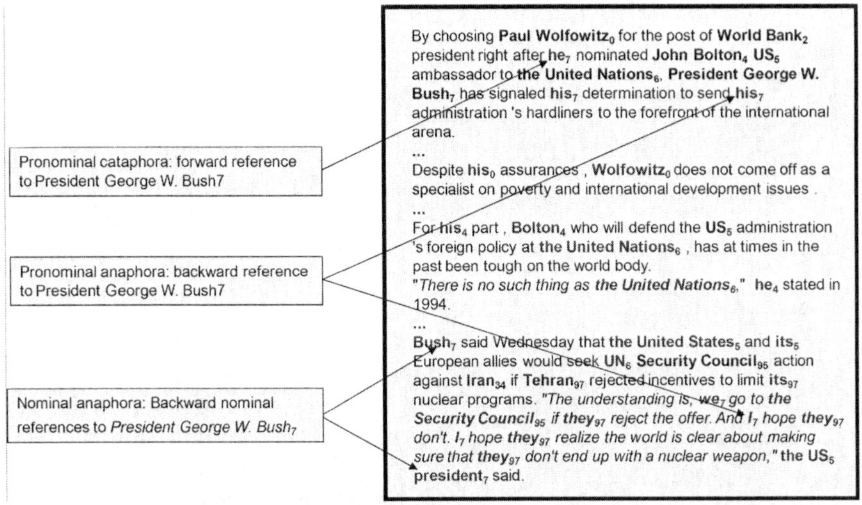

FIGURE 13.9 : Example co-references

13.2.2.3 Relation Extraction

Our approach to relation extraction is in the form of RDF triples and is essentially along the line of (Bedaride and Gardent, 2009) by making use of the SD graphs that the Stanford parser produces. From the SDs produced by the Stanford parser, our approach produces labeled SDs (LSDs) where the syntactic relations among a verb and its arguments are replaced by the roles. LSD graphs carry more semantic meaning than SD graphs and are richer than predicate-argument structures.

FIGURE 13.10 shows a graphical depiction of the RDF triple extraction process from two different, but semantically equivalent, dependency graphs. Our in-house tool *a*Text implements rules encoding such extraction processes.

13.3 TEXT CLASSIFICATION AND TOPIC EXTRACTION

This section presents two supervised and three unsupervised approaches to text classification, all of which are part of aText. The supervised approaches are NBC and kNBC, and the unsupervised approaches are LSA, PLSA and LDA.

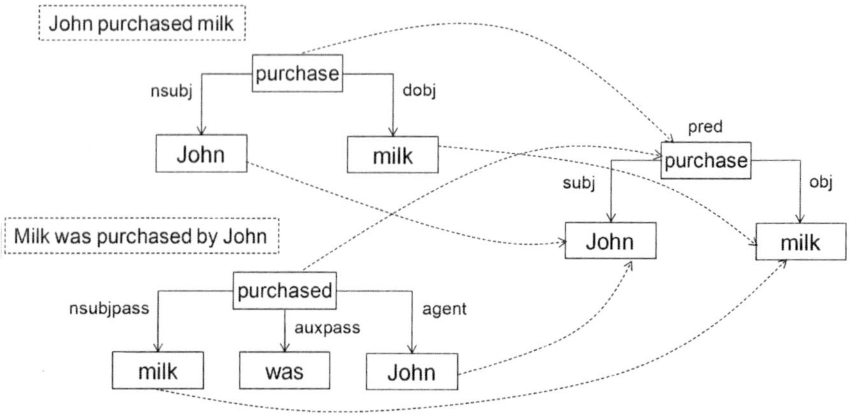

FIGURE 13.10 : Dependency relation to RDF triple

13.3.1 Naïve Bayesian Classifiers (NBC)

This subsection describes how to learn Naïve Bayesian Classifiers (NBCs) from text documents to be used for classifying or indexing unstructured customer surveys, for example. Learning NBCs from structured relational databases is just a special case of learning from unstructured documents. Each child node in an NBC corresponds to an attribute or feature. For text-based document indexing, these attributes usually indicate the presence or absence of a word in a text document. The parent node determines the output of the discriminant function, which is the class to which the document belongs.

To index items within a document, the child nodes in an NBC correspond to "tokens," or words, in a set of items. The selection of tokens is generally accomplished in three steps:

- *Stop words* are removed from the set of documents. Stop words are those words that carry little semantic content (e.g., a, and, the, that, it).
- Documents are *stemmed*. Stemming refers to a process by which words are replaced with their root; thus raining, rains, and rained would all be replaced with the common root "rain."
- *Tokens* are selected to omit both low-frequency and high-frequency words. This is generally done by computing the TF/IDF (term frequency/inverse document frequency) value for each word, as described in Quinlan (1986). Cutoff values are employed to select the set of tokens to be used.

Let D be the set of all training documents that are labeled with members from the set $C = \{c_1, ..., c_n\}$ of classes. Following the above steps, collect all distinct words and other tokens that occur in D and call them $V = \{v_1, ..., v_m\}$.

Consider an NBC as shown in FIGURE 13.11 with root node C whose states are $c_1, ..., c_n$. For each member v_j of V, add a binary child node of C.

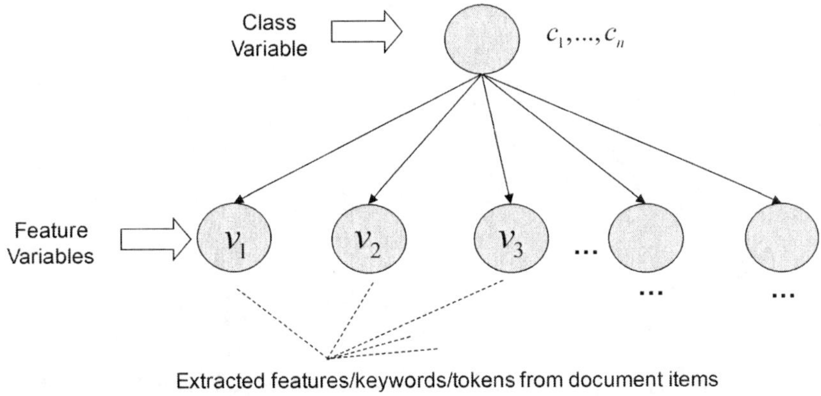

FIGURE 13.11 : Generic structure of an NBC

Compute the following probabilities by applying the Maximum Likelihood Estimate (MLE), which is simply the relative frequency and corresponds to the most likely value of each parameter given the training data:

$$p(c_i) = \frac{\text{Number of elements in } D \text{ for which the label is } c_i}{\text{Total number of elements in } D}$$

$$p(v_j|c_i) = \frac{\left[\begin{array}{c}\text{Number of times } v_j \text{ occurs in all the training} \\ \text{documents labeled } c_i\end{array}\right]}{\left[\begin{array}{c}\text{Total number of words that occur in all the training} \\ \text{documents labeled } c_i\end{array}\right]} = \frac{N(v_j, c_i)}{\sum_j N(v_j, c_i)}$$

where $N(v_j, c_i)$ is the number of times v_j occurs in all the training documents labeled c_i.

The problem with the MLE estimate is that $p(v_j|c_i)$ is zero if v_j did not occur in any document labeled c_i in the training data. So a document with occurrences of v_j, and perhaps genuinely belonging to the class c_i, will get a conditional probability of zero for c_i since we multiply the conditional probabilities for all words. To avoid this, Laplace smoothing, which simply adds one to each count, is applied as follows:

$$p(v_j|c_i) = \frac{1 + N(v_j, c_i)}{\sum_j (1 + N(v_j, c_i))} = \frac{1 + N(v_j, c_i)}{|V| + \sum_j N(v_j, c_i)}$$

Let d be a document that we want to classify, and the given set of classes is $C = \{c_1, ..., c_n\}$. We want to compute $p(c_i|d)$, for every i.

$$p\left(c_i|d\right) = \frac{p\left(c_i\right)p\left(d|c_i\right)}{p\left(d\right)} = \frac{p\left(c_i\right)\prod\limits_j p\left(v_j|c_i\right)}{\sum\limits_{k=1}^{n} p\left(c_k\right)\prod\limits_j p\left(v_j|c_k\right)}$$

where v_js are tokens in document d. The product of conditional probabilities comes from the assumption that tokens in a document are independent given the document class. Note that the conditional independence assumption of features does not hold in most cases. For example, the word co-occurrence is a commonly used feature for text classification.

We don't need the estimated posterior $p\left(c_i|d\right)$ to be correct. Instead, we only need

$$\arg\max_{c_i} p\left(c_i|d\right) = \arg\max_{c_i} p\left(c_i\right)\prod_j p\left(v_j|c_i\right)$$

The score for each class can be expressed in the following tractable form for analytical purposes:

$$\log\left(p\left(c_i\right)\right) + \sum\nolimits_j \log\left(p\left(v_j|c_i\right)\right)$$

The score is not a probability value, but is sufficient for the purpose of determining the most probable class. It reduces the round-off errors due to a product of small fractions caused by a large number of tokens.

Example

An example NBC is shown in FIGURE 13.12, which is based on a ski-related document corpus of web pages. Some pages are advertisements for "shops," some are describing "resorts," and the rest are categorized as "other," containing articles, events, results, etc. The mutually exclusive and exhaustive set of hypotheses is the three classification classes of documents, and each child node of the network corresponds to a keyword as target attribute.

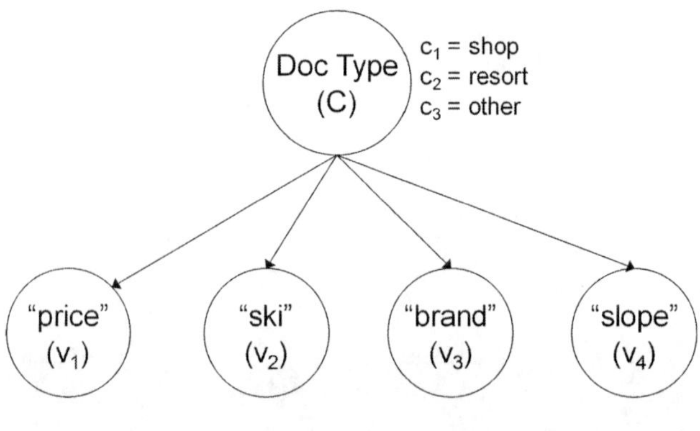

FIGURE 13.12 : NBC for document classification

Categorical or boolean observations (i.e., when we know for certain whether a term appears in a document d or not) of some vocabulary V (say, $V = \{v_1, v_2, v_3, v_4\}$) provide the following posteriors of the hypotheses:

$$p(c_i|d) \;\alpha\; p(c_i) \prod_{j=1,2,3,4} p(v_j|c_i), \;\; i = 1, 2, 3$$

The decision regarding the identification of the most likely target can then use

$$\arg\max_{c_i} p(c_i|d), \text{ i.e., } \arg\max_{c_i} p(c_i) \prod_{j=1,2,3,4} p(v_j|c_i)$$

But if the observations generate likelihoods $p(z_i|v_j)$ then the above decision criteria become

$$\arg\max_{c_i} p(c_i) \prod_{j=1,2,3,4} \sum_{k=1,2} p(z_j|v_j = v_{jk}) \, p(v_j = v_{jk}|c_i)$$

where v_{jk}s are the binary states of the feature v_j. In a suitably constructed corpus with a distribution of documents among the three categories *shop*, *resort* and *other* as 60%, 30% and 10%, the posterior probability distribution of the class variable given that a document has only "ski" and "brand" keywords is as follows:

$$\begin{aligned} p(DocType = shop|ski, brand, \neg slope) &= 0.91 \\ p(DocType = resort|ski, brand, \neg slope) &= 0.08 \\ p(DocType = other|ski, brand, \neg slope) &= 0.01 \end{aligned}$$

A kNBC model of the same corpus provides enhanced disambiguation among classes.

13.3.2 k-Dependence Naïve Bayesian Classifier (kNBC)

We have detailed kNBC models from structured data earlier in the probabilistic graphical modeling chapter. We have also detailed the above NBC models for structured data. Generalizing these two types, a generic kNBC structure is shown in FIGURE 13.13. We have described how to learn kNBC models from structured data earlier in the machine learning chapter. We have also detailed above how to learn NBC models from unstructured data. The procedure for learning kNBC from unstructured data is a generalization of both techniques.

kNBC requires the computation of $p(v_j|c_i, \Pi(v_j))$, as opposed to the requirement of $p(v_j|c_i)$ by NBC, using the following:

$$\frac{\left[\begin{array}{c}\text{Number of times } v_j \text{ occurs in all the training documents labeled } c_i \\ \text{and have ocurrenecs of each of the words in } \Pi(v_j)\end{array}\right]}{\left[\begin{array}{c}\text{Total number of words that occur in all the training documents labeled } c_i \\ \text{and have ocurrenecs of each of the words in } \Pi(v_j)\end{array}\right]}$$

The formulae to be used to classify is the same as the one specified in the probabilistic graphical modeling chapter.

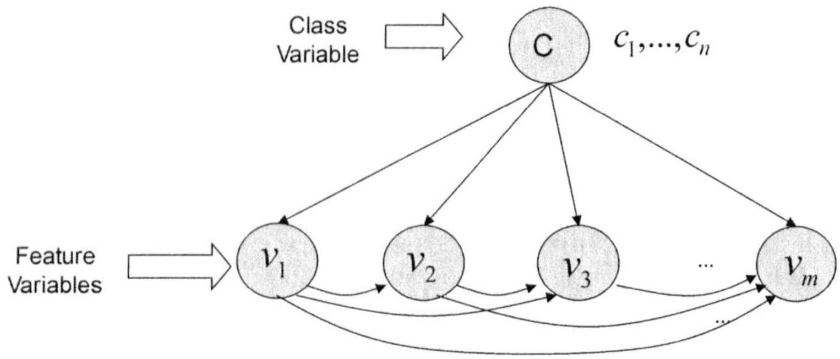

FIGURE 13.13 : Generic structure of a kNBC

Example

An example kNBC is shown in FIGURE 13.14, which is based on a ski-related document corpus of web pages as defined in the previous example.

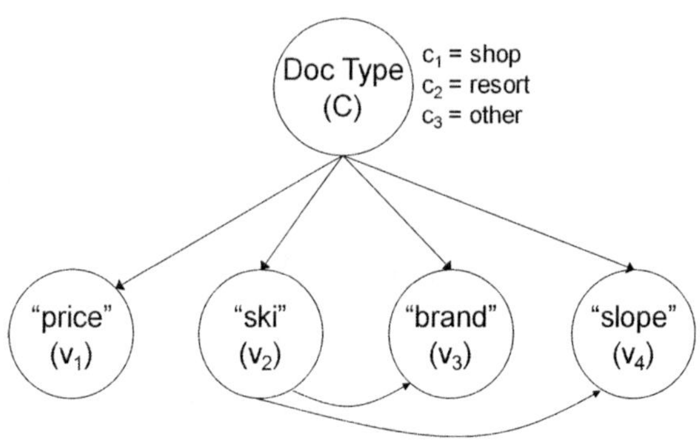

FIGURE 13.14 : kNBC for document classification

In a kNBC structure of FIGURE 13.13, an edge from v_i to v_j implies that the influence of v_i on the assessment of the class variable also depends on the value of v_j. For example, in FIGURE 13.14, the influence of the attribute "brand" on the class *DocType* (C) depends on the value of "ski," while in the equivalent NBC (i.e., without the edges among children) the influence of each attribute on the class variable is independent of other attributes. These additional edges among children in a kNBC affect the classification process in that NBC will overpenalize the probability of the class variable by considering two unlikely observations, while the augmented network of FIGURE 13.14 will not.

More concretely, in a suitably constructed corpus with distribution of documents among the three categories *shop*, *resort* and *other* as 60%, 30% and 10%, the posterior probability distribution of the class variable in the equivalent NBC given that a document has only "ski" and "brand" keywords is as follows:

$$p(DocType = shop|ski, brand, \neg slope) = 0.91$$
$$p(DocType = resort|ski, brand, \neg slope) = 0.08$$
$$p(DocType = other|ski, brand, \neg slope) = 0.01$$

While computing conditional probabilities from the frequency of occurrences, one would expect $p(brand|shop, ski)$ to be higher than $p(brand|resort, ski)$ since a web page for a ski shop is more likely to mention the keyword "brand" than a web page of a ski resort. Similarly, $p(slope|resort, ski)$ is likely to be higher than $p(slope|shop, ski)$. These kinds of dependencies are not captured in an NBC. In the kNBC, the probability distribution among the hypotheses is as follows, due to the presence of the keywords *ski* and *brand* in a web page but the absence of the keyword *slope*:

$$p(DocType = shop|ski, brand, \neg slope) = 0.99$$
$$p(DocType = resort|ski, brand, \neg slope) \approx 0.01$$
$$p(DocType = other|ski, brand, \neg slope) \approx 0.00$$

Note here the enhanced disambiguation in classification as compared to (0.91, 0.08, 0.01) obtained from the NBC presented earlier for the same evidence.

13.3.3 Latent Semantic Analysis

Latent Semantic Analysis (LSA) (Dumais et al., 1988; Deerwester et al., 1990) maps high-dimensional-count vector space representations of text documents (articles, for example) to a lower-dimensional representation in a latent semantic space. *Latent Semantic Indexing* (LSI) refers to using LSA for indexing for applications to information retrieval. LSA finds a data mapping which provides information beyond the lexical level and reveals semantic relations between the entities of interest. It attempts to solve the synonomy[1] and polysemy[2] problems to match documents by taking advantage of the implicit higher-order structure of the association of terms with articles. LSA also transforms high-dimensional data into a latent topic space of much smaller dimension where the clustering is performed. A similarity measure between two vectors (usually the cosine of their contained angle in the semantic space) is defined to cluster the vectors representing a text corpus of documents.

Terms and documents in the LSA model are represented by an incidence matrix $\mathbf{M}_{t\times d} = [a_{ij}]_{t\times d}$ of size $t \times d$. Each of the t unique terms in the document collection is assigned a row in the matrix, while each of the d documents in the collection is assigned a column in the matrix. A non-zero element a_{ij} indicates that term i occurs in document j as well as the number of times the term appears in that document. Since the number of terms in a given document is typically far less than the number of terms in the entire document collection, $\mathbf{M}_{t\times d}$ is usually very sparse.

---

[1]Two words are synonymous if they have the same meaning.

[2]A polysemy is a word or phrase with multiple meanings.

Each entry (i, j) in $\mathbf{M}_{t\times d}$is the frequency of term i in document j. The terms that appear only once in the corpus are usually pruned. A weighting function is then generally applied to increase the amount of information in $\mathbf{M}_{t\times d}$. An example weighting function of the elements of the matrix is *term frequency–inverse document frequency* (*tf-idf*). The tf-idf value increases proportionally to the number of times a word appears in the document, but is offset by the frequency of the word in the corpus. The offsetting is meant to address the fact that some words are more common than others.

A Singular Value Decomposition (SVD) (introduced in the chapter on mathematical and statistical preliminaries) of the term by article association matrix is computed, producing a matrix with reduced dimensionality to approximate the original matrix as the model of "semantic" space for the collection. To measure whether a given document closely matches the documents in a collection, the document is first projected into the term-document space. Then, one of several similarity measures can be applied to compare the projected document with the ones in the reduced term-document space of incidence matrix for collection.

As shown in FIGURE 13.15, SVD on a matrix $\mathbf{M}_{t\times d}$ results in three matrices: $\mathbf{T}_{t\times p}$ and $\mathbf{D}_{d\times p}$ which are orthonormal (has orthogonal, unit-length columns), and $\mathbf{S}_{p\times p}$, which is a diagonal matrix of singular values, such that $\mathbf{M}_{t\times d} = \mathbf{T}_{t\times p} \times \mathbf{S}_{p\times p} \times \mathbf{D}^T_{d\times p}$, where $\mathbf{X}^T$ is the transpose of $\mathbf{X}$. Row vectors in matrix $\mathbf{T}$ represent terms in the latent space and column vectors in $\mathbf{D}$ represent documents in the latent space.

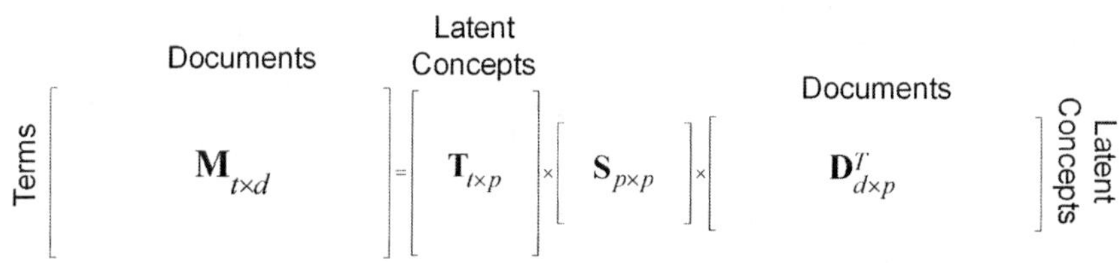

FIGURE 13.15 : SVD decomposition of a term-document matrix

The resultant matrices are truncated such that only the first k singular values in $\mathbf{S}_{p\times p}$, where $k << rank(M)$ along with the corresponding columns in $\mathbf{T}_{t\times p}$and $\mathbf{D}_{d\times p}$, are kept. In the truncated space, $\mathbf{M}_k = \mathbf{T}_k \times \mathbf{S}_k \times \mathbf{D}_k^T$, which is a unique matrix that is the least-squares best approximation of rank k to $\mathbf{M}_{t\times d}$.

After performing these initial transformations, the column vectors in $\mathbf{T}_k$ and $\mathbf{D}_k^T$ may be used for information retrieval purposes. Document and term vector representations in the latent space can be clustered based on traditional clustering algorithms like k-means using similarity measures like cosine. A query is viewed as a mini document to translate it to the latent space to compare to the existing documents in a given corpus for retrieval. We first represent the query as a term vector $Q_{t\times 1}$, similar to the way each document is represented by a term vector. The expression

$$Q_{t\times 1}^{T} \times \mathbf{T}_{t\times p} \times \mathbf{S}^{-1}$$

is just like a row of $\mathbf{D}_k$ and can be employed like a usual document's vector in the latent space for making comparisons with other documents.

Because LSA results in a space based on underlying semantic similarity, documents on similar topics should tend to cluster in the space. This feature is the basis for using LSA for filtering out irrelevant documents. We provide here a concrete example of LSA to demonstrate some of its advantages in clustering and information retrieval.

Example

TABLE 13.3 provides a sample dataset consisting of the titles of some articles from leading US newspapers on May 4, 2012. There are two classes of titles: the articles labeled j-1 through j-6 are related to the US unemployment figure for the month of April, and the articles a-1 thorough a-4 are on the record auction amount of Edvard Munch's painting *The Scream.* Words occurring in more than one title are italicized and selected for indexing. Named entities are recognized and words are stemmed before indexing.

TABLE 13.3: : Titles of articles on the topics of unemployment and art auction

ID	**Article Title**
j-1	*Labor* department says job *market* shows *signs* of *improvement*
j-2	*Jobless claims* show *improvement* in the *labor market*
j-3	US applications for *unemployment* aid *drop sharply*, a good *sign* for future hiring
j-4	*Unemployment claims drop sharply*
j-5	*Jobless claims* fall *sharply* after three weeks of increases
j-6	The 86 *million* invisible *unemployed*
a-1	*Edvard Munch*'s '*The Scream*' goes for \$119.9 *million* at Sotheby's
a-2	*Edvard Munch*'s '*The Scream*' *sells* for *record* \$119.9 *million* at *auction*
a-3	'*The Scream*' *sells* at *auction* for \$119.9 *million*, a *record* at an *auction*
a-4	'*The Scream*' *auctioned* for *record* \$119.9 *million*

The entries in the term by document matrix in FIGURE 13.16 are simply the frequencies with which each term actually occurred in each document. Such a matrix could be used directly for keyword-based retrievals or for some distance-based clustering of the columns representing vectors. But here the matrix is an initial input of the SVD analysis as explained technically above.

Term	Document									
	j-1	j-2	j-3	j-4	j-5	j-6	a-1	a-2	a-3	a-4
labor	1	1	0	0	0	0	0	0	0	0
market	1	1	0	0	0	0	0	0	0	0
sign	1	0	1	0	0	0	0	0	0	0
improv	1	1	0	0	0	0	0	0	0	0
jobless	0	1	0	0	1	0	0	0	0	0
claim	0	1	0	1	1	0	0	0	0	0
unemploy	0	0	1	1	0	1	0	0	0	0
drop	0	0	1	1	0	0	0	0	0	0
sharply	0	0	1	1	1	0	0	0	0	0
million	0	0	0	0	0	1	1	1	1	1
Edvard Munch	0	0	0	0	0	0	1	1	0	0
The Scream	0	0	0	0	0	0	1	1	1	1
sell	0	0	0	0	0	0	0	1	1	0
record	0	0	0	0	0	0	0	1	1	1
auction	0	0	0	0	0	0	0	1	2	1

FIGURE 13.16 : A term by document matrix for the article titles in TABLE 13.3

So the input matrix $\mathbf{M}_{15\times 10}$, a 15-term by 10-document matrix from FIGURE 13.16, is presented in FIGURE 13.17.

$$\mathbf{M}_{15\times 10} = \begin{bmatrix}
1.00 & 1.00 & 0.00 & 0.00 & 0.00 & 0.00 & 0.00 & 0.00 & 0.00 & 0.00 \\
1.00 & 1.00 & 0.00 & 0.00 & 0.00 & 0.00 & 0.00 & 0.00 & 0.00 & 0.00 \\
1.00 & 0.00 & 1.00 & 0.00 & 0.00 & 0.00 & 0.00 & 0.00 & 0.00 & 0.00 \\
1.00 & 1.00 & 0.00 & 0.00 & 0.00 & 0.00 & 0.00 & 0.00 & 0.00 & 0.00 \\
0.00 & 1.00 & 0.00 & 0.00 & 1.00 & 0.00 & 0.00 & 0.00 & 0.00 & 0.00 \\
0.00 & 1.00 & 0.00 & 1.00 & 1.00 & 0.00 & 0.00 & 0.00 & 0.00 & 0.00 \\
0.00 & 0.00 & 1.00 & 1.00 & 0.00 & 1.00 & 0.00 & 0.00 & 0.00 & 0.00 \\
0.00 & 0.00 & 1.00 & 1.00 & 0.00 & 0.00 & 0.00 & 0.00 & 0.00 & 0.00 \\
0.00 & 0.00 & 1.00 & 1.00 & 1.00 & 0.00 & 0.00 & 0.00 & 0.00 & 0.00 \\
0.00 & 0.00 & 0.00 & 0.00 & 0.00 & 1.00 & 1.00 & 1.00 & 1.00 & 1.00 \\
0.00 & 0.00 & 0.00 & 0.00 & 0.00 & 0.00 & 1.00 & 1.00 & 0.00 & 0.00 \\
0.00 & 0.00 & 0.00 & 0.00 & 0.00 & 0.00 & 1.00 & 1.00 & 1.00 & 1.00 \\
0.00 & 0.00 & 0.00 & 0.00 & 0.00 & 0.00 & 0.00 & 1.00 & 1.00 & 0.00 \\
0.00 & 0.00 & 0.00 & 0.00 & 0.00 & 0.00 & 0.00 & 1.00 & 1.00 & 1.00 \\
0.00 & 0.00 & 0.00 & 0.00 & 0.00 & 0.00 & 0.00 & 1.00 & 2.00 & 1.00
\end{bmatrix}$$

FIGURE 13.17 : Matrix $\mathbf{M}_{15\times 10}$

Computing the SVD of the matrix $\mathbf{M}_{15\times 10}$ above results in the following three matrices:

- $\mathbf{T}_{15\times10}$: 10–dimensional left-singular vectors for 15 terms (FIGURE 13.18).
- $\mathbf{S}_{10\times10}$: Diagonal matrix of 10 singular values (FIGURE 13.19).
- $\mathbf{D}_{10\times10}$: 10–dimensional right-singular vectors for 10 documents (FIGURE 13.20).

$$\mathbf{T}_{15\times10} = \begin{bmatrix} 0.00 & 0.29 & -0.41 & 0.17 & 0.00 & -0.06 & 0.09 & -0.09 & -0.01 & -0.04 \\ 0.00 & 0.29 & -0.41 & 0.17 & 0.00 & -0.06 & 0.09 & -0.09 & -0.01 & -0.04 \\ 0.00 & 0.26 & -0.01 & 0.53 & -0.15 & 0.33 & -0.35 & 0.29 & 0.00 & -0.07 \\ 0.00 & 0.29 & -0.41 & 0.17 & 0.00 & -0.06 & 0.09 & -0.09 & -0.01 & -0.04 \\ 0.00 & 0.30 & -0.19 & -0.45 & 0.08 & -0.01 & -0.26 & 0.43 & 0.11 & 0.63 \\ 0.00 & 0.46 & -0.01 & -0.52 & 0.07 & -0.07 & 0.17 & -0.24 & -0.06 & -0.35 \\ -0.03 & 0.34 & 0.43 & 0.27 & 0.09 & -0.49 & 0.25 & 0.14 & 0.11 & 0.14 \\ -0.01 & 0.30 & 0.36 & 0.16 & -0.11 & 0.15 & 0.20 & -0.43 & -0.04 & 0.48 \\ -0.01 & 0.42 & 0.39 & -0.16 & -0.08 & 0.32 & -0.27 & 0.14 & -0.05 & -0.38 \\ -0.48 & 0.02 & 0.06 & 0.11 & 0.43 & -0.43 & -0.21 & 0.19 & -0.08 & -0.18 \\ -0.20 & -0.01 & 0.00 & 0.04 & 0.57 & 0.49 & 0.33 & 0.07 & 0.10 & 0.04 \\ -0.45 & -0.02 & -0.02 & 0.00 & 0.24 & 0.21 & -0.26 & -0.38 & -0.23 & 0.17 \\ -0.28 & -0.01 & -0.02 & -0.04 & -0.19 & 0.21 & 0.60 & 0.46 & -0.04 & -0.06 \\ -0.39 & -0.02 & -0.02 & -0.04 & -0.23 & 0.02 & -0.08 & -0.17 & 0.87 & -0.07 \\ -0.54 & -0.02 & -0.04 & -0.08 & -0.53 & -0.07 & 0.01 & 0.00 & -0.38 & 0.08 \end{bmatrix}$$

FIGURE 13.18 : Matrix $\mathbf{T}_{15\times10}$

$$\mathbf{S}_{10\times10} = \begin{bmatrix} 4.21 & 0.00 & 0.00 & 0.00 & 0.00 & 0.00 & 0.00 & 0.00 & 0.00 & 0.00 \\ 0.00 & 3.08 & 0.00 & 0.00 & 0.00 & 0.00 & 0.00 & 0.00 & 0.00 & 0.00 \\ 0.00 & 0.00 & 2.55 & 0.00 & 0.00 & 0.00 & 0.00 & 0.00 & 0.00 & 0.00 \\ 0.00 & 0.00 & 0.00 & 1.87 & 0.00 & 0.00 & 0.00 & 0.00 & 0.00 & 0.00 \\ 0.00 & 0.00 & 0.00 & 0.00 & 1.64 & 0.00 & 0.00 & 0.00 & 0.00 & 0.00 \\ 0.00 & 0.00 & 0.00 & 0.00 & 0.00 & 1.20 & 0.00 & 0.00 & 0.00 & 0.00 \\ 0.00 & 0.00 & 0.00 & 0.00 & 0.00 & 0.00 & 0.89 & 0.00 & 0.00 & 0.00 \\ 0.00 & 0.00 & 0.00 & 0.00 & 0.00 & 0.00 & 0.00 & 0.76 & 0.00 & 0.00 \\ 0.00 & 0.00 & 0.00 & 0.00 & 0.00 & 0.00 & 0.00 & 0.00 & 0.44 & 0.00 \\ 0.00 & 0.00 & 0.00 & 0.00 & 0.00 & 0.00 & 0.00 & 0.00 & 0.00 & 0.34 \end{bmatrix}$$

FIGURE 13.19 : Matrix $\mathbf{S}_{10\times10}$

The following relationship holds: $\mathbf{M}_{15\times10} = \mathbf{T}_{15\times10} \times \mathbf{S}_{10\times10} \times \mathbf{D}^T_{10\times10}$. Since $\mathbf{T}_{15\times10}$ and $\mathbf{D}_{10\times10}$ have orthogonal, unit length columns, $\mathbf{T}_{15\times10} \times \mathbf{T}^T_{15\times10} = \mathbf{I}$ and $\mathbf{D}_{10\times10} \times \mathbf{D}^T_{10\times10} = \mathbf{I}$. We now approximate $\mathbf{M}_{15\times10}$ as $\mathbf{M}_2$ keeping only the first two singular values and the corresponding columns from the matrices $\mathbf{T}_{15\times10}$ and $\mathbf{D}_{10\times10}$. In this reduced model, $\mathbf{M}_2 = \mathbf{T}_2 \times \mathbf{S}_2 \times \mathbf{D}^T_2$ and $\mathbf{M}_{15\times10} \approx \mathbf{M}_2$, where $\mathbf{T}_2$, $\mathbf{S}_2$, **and** $\mathbf{D}_2$ are shown in FIGURE 13.21, and matrix $\mathbf{M}_2$ is shown in FIGURE 13.22.

$$\mathbf{D}^{T}_{10\times 10} = \begin{bmatrix} 0.00 & 0.00 & -0.01 & -0.01 & 0.00 & -0.12 & -0.27 & -0.56 & -0.64 & -0.44 \\ 0.37 & 0.53 & 0.43 & 0.49 & 0.38 & 0.12 & 0.00 & -0.02 & -0.02 & -0.01 \\ -0.48 & -0.56 & 0.46 & 0.46 & 0.07 & 0.19 & 0.01 & -0.02 & -0.03 & -0.01 \\ 0.56 & -0.24 & 0.43 & -0.13 & -0.60 & 0.21 & 0.08 & 0.00 & -0.07 & -0.01 \\ -0.09 & 0.09 & -0.15 & -0.02 & 0.04 & 0.32 & 0.76 & 0.18 & -0.50 & -0.05 \\ 0.14 & -0.21 & 0.26 & -0.08 & 0.20 & -0.76 & 0.23 & 0.36 & -0.11 & -0.22 \\ -0.11 & 0.18 & -0.21 & 0.38 & -0.42 & 0.04 & -0.15 & 0.44 & 0.09 & -0.60 \\ 0.03 & -0.10 & 0.19 & -0.51 & 0.43 & 0.43 & -0.16 & 0.22 & 0.13 & -0.47 \\ -0.06 & 0.05 & 0.06 & -0.07 & -0.01 & 0.07 & -0.49 & 0.53 & -0.55 & 0.40 \\ -0.52 & 0.51 & 0.50 & -0.33 & -0.29 & -0.12 & 0.08 & -0.07 & 0.05 & 0.00 \end{bmatrix}$$

FIGURE 13.20 : Matrix $\mathbf{D}_{10\times 10}$

$$\mathbf{T}_2 = \begin{bmatrix} 0.00 & 0.29 \\ 0.00 & 0.29 \\ 0.00 & 0.26 \\ 0.00 & 0.29 \\ 0.00 & 0.30 \\ 0.00 & 0.46 \\ -0.03 & 0.34 \\ -0.01 & 0.30 \\ -0.01 & 0.42 \\ -0.48 & 0.02 \\ -0.20 & -0.01 \\ -0.45 & -0.02 \\ -0.28 & -0.01 \\ -0.39 & -0.02 \\ -0.54 & -0.02 \end{bmatrix} \qquad \mathbf{S}_2 = \begin{bmatrix} 4.21 & 0.00 \\ 0.00 & 3.08 \end{bmatrix}$$

$$\mathbf{D}^{T}_{2} = \begin{bmatrix} 0.00 & 0.00 & -0.01 & -0.01 & 0.00 & -0.12 & -0.27 & -0.56 & -0.64 & -0.44 \\ 0.37 & 0.53 & 0.43 & 0.49 & 0.38 & 0.12 & 0.00 & -0.02 & -0.02 & -0.01 \end{bmatrix}$$

FIGURE 13.21 : Matrices $\mathbf{T}_2$, $\mathbf{S}_2$, and $\mathbf{D}_2$

The matrix $\mathbf{M}_2$ does not exactly match the original term by document matrix $\mathbf{M}_{15\times 10}$ but it draws closer and closer as the number of singular values increases.

FIGURE 13.23 shows the two-dimensional geometric representation for terms and documents that resulted from the above SVD analysis, where each term and document is described by its position in this two-dimensional factor space. Terms are shown as filled diamonds and article titles are represented by filled squares.

Nearly all of the titles j-1 to j-5 are located along the Latent Dimension 2, and the titles a-1 to a-4 are located along the Latent Dimension 1. This division clearly reflects the two classes of documents that have been selected. The title j-6 is located somewhere along the line in between the two axes. This is because j-6 contains the word "million," which is predominant in one class,

$$
\mathbf{M}_2 = \begin{bmatrix}
0.33 & 0.47 & 0.38 & 0.44 & 0.34 & 0.11 & 0.00 & -0.02 & -0.02 & -0.01 \\
0.33 & 0.47 & 0.38 & 0.44 & 0.34 & 0.11 & 0.00 & -0.02 & -0.02 & -0.01 \\
0.30 & 0.42 & 0.34 & 0.39 & 0.30 & 0.10 & 0.00 & -0.02 & -0.02 & -0.01 \\
0.33 & 0.47 & 0.38 & 0.44 & 0.34 & 0.11 & 0.00 & -0.02 & -0.02 & -0.01 \\
0.34 & 0.49 & 0.40 & 0.45 & 0.35 & 0.11 & 0.00 & -0.02 & -0.02 & -0.01 \\
0.52 & 0.75 & 0.61 & 0.69 & 0.54 & 0.17 & 0.00 & -0.03 & -0.03 & -0.01 \\
0.39 & 0.55 & 0.45 & 0.51 & 0.40 & 0.14 & 0.03 & 0.05 & 0.06 & 0.04 \\
0.34 & 0.49 & 0.40 & 0.45 & 0.35 & 0.12 & 0.01 & 0.01 & 0.01 & 0.01 \\
0.48 & 0.69 & 0.56 & 0.63 & 0.49 & 0.16 & 0.01 & 0.00 & 0.00 & 0.01 \\
0.02 & 0.03 & 0.05 & 0.05 & 0.02 & 0.25 & 0.55 & 1.13 & 1.29 & 0.89 \\
-0.01 & -0.02 & 0.00 & -0.01 & -0.01 & 0.10 & 0.23 & 0.47 & 0.54 & 0.37 \\
-0.02 & -0.03 & -0.01 & -0.01 & -0.02 & 0.22 & 0.51 & 1.06 & 1.21 & 0.83 \\
-0.01 & -0.02 & 0.00 & 0.00 & -0.01 & 0.14 & 0.32 & 0.66 & 0.76 & 0.52 \\
-0.02 & -0.03 & -0.01 & -0.01 & -0.02 & 0.19 & 0.44 & 0.92 & 1.05 & 0.72 \\
-0.02 & -0.03 & 0.00 & -0.01 & -0.02 & 0.27 & 0.61 & 1.27 & 1.46 & 1.00
\end{bmatrix}
$$

FIGURE 13.22 : Matrix $\mathbf{M}_2$

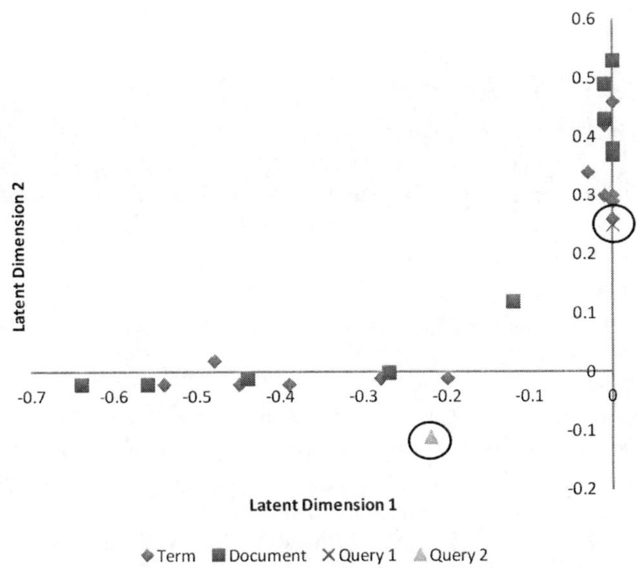

FIGURE 13.23 : Excel implementation of a plot of 15 terms, 10 documents, and 2 queries along the two latent dimensions

and also contains the word "unemployed," which is predominant is the other class. A clustering algorithm based on the cosine-based distance computation will accurately classify the set of titles with the exception of j-6.

Now consider the search queries "record auction amount" and "Jobless claims figure." Simple keyword-based matching of one or more words would return a-2, a-3, and a-4 for the first query, but not a-1, and j-2, j-4, and j-5 for the second query, but not j-1, j-3, and j-6. But with the LSA, the two queries are first placed in the latent space as shown by an X and a solid triangle (both encircled) based on the following computation for two queries:

Query = "record auction amount"
$Q^T_{15\times 1} = (0\ 0\ 0\ 0\ 0\ 0\ 0\ 0\ 0\ 0\ 0\ 0\ 0\ 1\ 1)$
$Q^T_{15\times 1} \times \mathbf{T}_2 \times \mathbf{S}_2^{-1} = (-0.22\ -0.11)$

Query = "jobless claims figure"
$Q^T_{15\times 1} = (0\ 0\ 0\ 0\ 1\ 1\ 0\ 0\ 0\ 0\ 0\ 0\ 0\ 0\ 0)$
$Q^T_{15\times 1} \times \mathbf{T}_2 \times \mathbf{S}_2^{-1} = (0.00\ 0.25)$

It is clear from FIGURE 13.23 that the articles within a reasonable cosine of the first query would retrieve a-1 to a-4 and maybe j-6, but not any of j-1 to j-5 Similarly, the second query would retrieve j-1 to j-5 and maybe j-6 but not any of a-1 to a-4.

13.3.4 Probabilistic Latent Semantic Analysis (PLSA)

PLSA (Hofmann, 1999) is an unsupervised learning technique based on a statistical latent class generative model. The main difference between PLSA and LSA is the objective function utilized to determine the optimal decomposition. As opposed to an algebraic approach in LSA, PLSA relies on the likelihood function of multinomial sampling and aims for an explicit maximization, via the expectation maximization (EM) algorithm, of the predictive power of the model. Moreover, the mixture approximation of the co-occurrence table in PLSA is a well-defined probability distribution and factors are probabilistically well-defined. In contrast, LSA does not define a properly normalized probability distribution, and the term-document matrix above may even contain negative entries. In addition, there is no obvious interpretation of the directions in the LSA latent space, while the directions in the PLSA space are interpretable as multinomial word distributions.

Suppose, $D = \{d_1, ..., d_N\}$ is a collection of text documents containing terms from vocabulary $W = \{w_1, ..., w_M\}$. A latent variable model for co-occurrence data associates the unobserved topic variable $Z = \{z_1, ..., z_K\}$ with each observation. The joint probability model over $D \times W$ is the following:

$$p(d,w) = p(d)\,p(w|d) = p(d)\sum_{z} p(w|z)\,p(z|d)$$

The recursive two steps of the EM algorithm for PLSA are the following:

E-Step: $p(z|d,w) = \frac{p(z)p(d|z)p(w|z)}{\sum\limits_{z' \in Z} p(z')p(d|z')p(w|z')}$

$$\textbf{M-Step:}\quad \begin{aligned} p(w|z) &\propto \sum_{d\in D} n(d,w)p(z|d,w) \\ p(d|z) &\propto \sum_{w\in W} n(d,w)p(z|d,w) \\ p(z) &\propto \sum_{d\in D}\sum_{w\in W} n(d,w)p(z|d,w) \end{aligned}$$

where $n(d,w)$is the number of times w occurred in document d. The tool aText contains an implementation of the above EM algorithm.

Hierarchical PLSA (Gaussier et al., 2002) is a hierarchical generative model of textual data, where words may be generated by topic-specific distributions at any level of the hierarchy, and the model can automatically generate hierarchies. In a typical hierarchy, one can assign documents to classes at the leaves of the hierarchy, while words are sampled from topics that are in any node of the hierarchy. This therefore allows classes to be linguistically related when sharing common ancestor topics.

13.3.5 Latent Dirichlet Allocation (LDA)

LDA (Blei et al., 2003) is an unsupervised latent topic detection and text segmentation technique. An LDA model is a fully generative graphical model in which every topic is a distribution over the terms of the vocabulary, and every document is a distribution over the topics. These distributions are sampled from Dirichlet distributions. LDA models the words in the documents under the "bag-of-words" assumption, thus ignoring the orders of the words in the documents. Each document in LDA is generated by choosing a distribution over topics and then choosing each word in the document from a topic selected according to the topic distribution. The words of the documents are drawn from the term-distribution of a topic which was just drawn for this word from the topic-distribution of the document. FIGURE 13.24 shows the process of how LDA generates the words.

The boxes are "plates" representing replicates. With this plate notation, the dependencies among the many variables can be captured concisely. The outer plate represents documents, while the inner plate represents the repeated choice of topics and words within a document. The following notations further explain the diagram.

- M is number of documents in **D** to classify.
- K is the number of topics / mixture components **K**.
- V is the number of unique terms w in vocabulary **W**.
- $\vec{\alpha}$ is the Dirichlet parameter on the topic mixture proportions. $\vec{\alpha}$ is a K-vector $[\alpha_1, ..., \alpha_K]^T$, where α_k refers to the prior of topic k. If $\vec{\alpha}$ is symmetric then each α_k is assigned to the same scalar value.
- $\vec{\beta}$ is the parameter on the topic mixture components. $\vec{\beta}$ is a V-vector

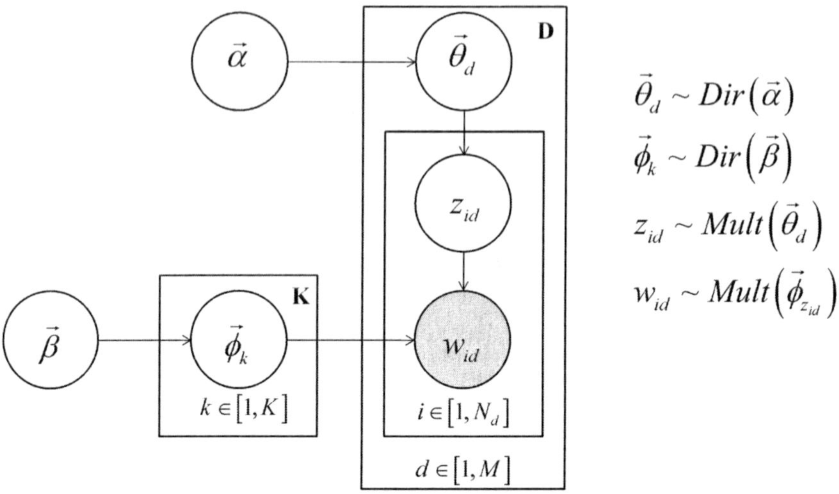

FIGURE 13.24 : LDA model

$[\beta_{k1}, ..., \beta_{kV}]^T$, where β_{kv} refers to the prior to the prior for the vth word in the vocabulary **V** under the topic k. If $\vec{\beta}$ is symmetric then each β_{kv} is assigned to the same scalar value.

- Θ is the multinomial distributions of topics for the documents in corpus **D**. $\Theta = \left\{\vec{\theta}_d\right\}_1^M$ ($M \times K$ matrix), one proportion $\vec{\theta}_d$ for each document d. $\vec{\theta}_d$ is a K-vector $[\theta_{d1}, ..., \theta_{dK}]^T$, where θ_{dk} denotes the probability $p(z = k|d)$ of assigning words in d to topic k.

- Φ is the multinomial distributions of word values under certain topic. $\Phi = \left\{\vec{\phi}_k\right\}_1^K$ ($K \times V$ matrix), one component for each topic. $\vec{\phi}_k$ is a V-vector $[\phi_{k1}, ..., \phi_{kV}]^T$, where ϕ_{kv} denotes the probability $p(w|z = k)$ of generating the vth word in the vocabulary under topic k.

- N_m is the document length (document-specific), modeled with a Poisson distribution with constant parameters.

- **z** represent topic indices; z_{id} is the topic mixture indicator that chooses the topic for the ith word in document d.

- **w** represents the words in the corpus;w_{id} is the term indicator for the ith word in document d.

- n represents word counts in the corpus. n_{dvk} is the number of times in document d word v has been assigned to topic k in the vector of assignments **z**,. Use of "(.)" in the subscripts or superscripts denotes summation. For example, $n_{d(.)k} = \sum_v n_{dvk}$ and $n_{(.)vk} = \sum_d n_{dvk}$.

Here is how a document d is generated in LDA. First the length is obtained via Poisson distribution. The LDA model first picks a multinomial distribution $\vec{\theta}_d = [\theta_{d1}, ..., \theta_{dK}]^T$ from the Dirichlet distribution $\vec{\alpha} = [\alpha_1, ..., \alpha_K]^T$, where θ_{dk} denotes the probability $p(z = k|d)$ of assigning words in d to topic k . Hence,

$$p\left(\vec{\theta}_d|\vec{\alpha}\right) = \frac{\Gamma\left(\sum_{k=1}^{K} \alpha_k\right)}{\prod_{k=1}^{K} \Gamma(\alpha_k)} \prod_{k=1}^{K} \theta_{dk}^{\alpha_k - 1} = \frac{\Gamma(\alpha_{(.)})}{\prod_{k=1}^{K} \Gamma(\alpha_k)} \prod_{k=1}^{K} \theta_{dk}^{\alpha_k - 1}$$

The model then assigns a topic $z_{id} = k$ to the ith word in the document according to the multinomial distribution $\vec{\theta}_d$. Given the topic $z_{id} = k$, the model then picks a word w_{id} from the vocabulary of $\mathbf{V}$ words according to the multinomial distribution $\vec{\phi}_k = [\varphi_{k1}, ..., \varphi_{kV}]^T$, where φ_{kv} denotes the probability $p(w|z = k)$ of generating the vth word in the vocabulary under topic k. $\vec{\phi}_k$ is generated from the Dirichlet distribution $[\beta_{k1}, ..., \beta_{kV}]^T$ for each topic k. Hence,

$$p\left(\vec{\phi}_k|\vec{\beta}\right) = \frac{\Gamma\left(\sum_{v=1}^{V} \beta_{kv}\right)}{\prod_{v=1}^{V} \Gamma(\beta_{kv})} \prod_{v=1}^{V} \varphi_{kv}^{\beta_{kv} - 1} = \frac{\Gamma(\beta_{k(.)})}{\prod_{v=1}^{V} \Gamma(\beta_{kv})} \prod_{v=1}^{V} \varphi_{kv}^{\beta_{kv} - 1}$$

There are several methods developed for making inferences in LDA, including variational, expectation maximization, and MCMC with Gibbs sampling. The approach in *a*Text is the Gibbs sampling approach. We need the full joint probability distribution $p\left(\mathbf{z}, \mathbf{w}, \Theta, \Phi|\vec{\alpha}, \vec{\beta}\right)$ to derive the conditional probability $p(z_{id} = k|\mathbf{z}_{-i}, \mathbf{w})$ for the Gibbs sampler. Now,

$$\begin{aligned}
&p\left(\mathbf{w}, \mathbf{z}, \Theta, \Phi|\vec{\alpha}, \vec{\beta}\right) \\
&= p(\Theta|\vec{\alpha})\, p(\mathbf{z}|\Theta)\, p\left(\Phi|\vec{\beta}\right) p(\mathbf{w}|\mathbf{z}, \Phi) \\
&= \prod_{d=1}^{D} p\left(\vec{\theta}_d|\vec{\alpha}\right) \times \prod_{d=1}^{D} p\left(\vec{\theta}_d\right) \times \prod_{k=1}^{K} p\left(\vec{\phi}_k|\vec{\beta}\right) \times \prod_{k=1}^{K} p\left(\vec{\phi}_k\right) \\
&= \prod_{d=1}^{D} \frac{\Gamma(\alpha_{(.)})}{\prod_{k=1}^{K} \Gamma(\alpha_k)} \prod_{k=1}^{K} \theta_{dk}^{\alpha_k - 1} \times \prod_{d=1}^{D} \prod_{k=1}^{K} \theta_{dk}^{n_{d(.)k}} \\
&\quad \times \prod_{k=1}^{K} \frac{\Gamma(\beta_{k(.)})}{\prod_{v=1}^{V} \Gamma(\beta_{kv})} \prod_{v=1}^{V} \varphi_{kv}^{\beta_{kv} - 1} \times \prod_{k=1}^{K} \prod_{v=1}^{V} \varphi_{kv}^{n_{(.)vk}} \\
&= \prod_{d=1}^{D} \frac{\Gamma(\alpha_{(.)})}{\prod_{k=1}^{K} \Gamma(\alpha_k)} \prod_{k=1}^{K} \theta_{dk}^{\alpha_k + n_{d(.)k} - 1} \times \prod_{k=1}^{K} \frac{\Gamma(\beta_{k(.)})}{\prod_{v=1}^{V} \Gamma(\beta_{kv})} \prod_{v=1}^{V} \varphi_{kv}^{\beta_{kv} + n_{(.)vk} - 1}
\end{aligned}$$

$$
\begin{aligned}
& p\left(\mathbf{w},\mathbf{z}|\vec{\alpha},\vec{\beta}\right) \\
& = \int\limits_{\Theta}\int\limits_{\Phi} p\left(\mathbf{w},\mathbf{z},\Theta,\Phi|\vec{\alpha},\vec{\beta}\right) d\Theta d\Phi \\
& = \prod_{d=1}^{D} \frac{\Gamma\left(\alpha_{(.)}\right)}{\prod_{k=1}^{K}\Gamma(\alpha_k)} \frac{\prod_{k=1}^{K}\Gamma\left(\alpha_k + n_{d(.)k}\right)}{\Gamma\left(\alpha_{(.)} + n_{d(.)(.)}\right)} \times \prod_{k=1}^{K} \frac{\Gamma\left(\beta_{k(.)}\right)}{\prod_{v=1}^{V}\Gamma(\beta_{kv})} \frac{\prod_{v=1}^{V}\Gamma\left(\beta_{kv} + n_{(.)kv}\right)}{\Gamma\left(\beta_{k(.)} + n_{(.)(.)k}\right)}
\end{aligned}
$$

When the priors $\vec{\alpha}$ and $\vec{\beta}$ are symmetric, the conditional probability for the Gibbs sampler is

$$
p\left(z_{id} = k|\mathbf{z}_{-i},\mathbf{w}\right) \alpha \frac{n_{(.)w_i k}^{-i} + \beta}{n_{(.)(.)k}^{-i} + V\beta} \cdot \frac{n_{dw_{id}k}^{-i} + \alpha}{n_{dw_{id}(.)} + K\alpha}
$$

where $n_{(.)(.)(.)}^{-i}$ is a count that does not include the current assignment of z_i. The first ratio expresses the probability of w_i under topic k, and the second ratio expresses the probability of topic k in document d. The approach samples the latent variables according to the posterior probability given the data and the model parameters. It then makes inferences based on the sampled values. Given a sample z, we can estimate the values of the other latent variables by

$$
\begin{aligned}
\phi_{kv} &= \frac{n_{(.)vk} + \beta_{kv}}{n_{(.)(.)k} + \sum\limits_{v}\beta_{kv}} \\
\theta_{dk} &= \frac{n_{d(.)k} + \alpha_k}{n_{d(.)(.)} + \sum\limits_{k}\alpha_k}
\end{aligned}
$$

Now, ϕ_{kv}, which denotes the probability $p\left(w|z = k\right)$ of generating the vth word in the vocabulary under topic k, and θ_{dk}, which denotes the probability $p\left(z = k|d\right)$ of assigning words in d to topic k. If we are interested in assigning a topic to each word in a document (i.e., $p\left(z|d,w\right)$) then it is the product of the above two.

13.4 FURTHER READING

The seminal papers on kNBC, PLSA, and LDA are (Sahami, 1996), (Hofmann, 1999), and (Blei et al., 2003), respectively.

CHAPTER 14

Semantic Web

The exchange of information is vital to analytics involving the interplay among distributed computer-based processes, physical systems, and human operators. Therefore there is a need for a standardized semantics of the information content to be exchanged, so as to be comprehended by the various entities involved. The Semantic Web (http://www.semanticweb.org/) is an extension of the current web, in which information is given well-defined meaning via ontology, better enabling computers and people to work cooperatively. The Semantic Web builds on the W3C's (http://www.w3.org) standard model Resource Description Framework (RDF) (http://www.w3.org/RDF/) for data interchange on the web. RDF integrates a variety of applications using XML for syntax and Uniform Resource Identifier (URI) for naming. This chapter describes RDF, RDF Schema (RDFS) that provides a framework to describe application-specific classes and properties, and Ontology Web Language (OWL) that extends RDFS with additional modeling primitives for enhanced expressivity. Finally, we detail a family of Description Logic (DL) as the underlying theoretical foundation of these frameworks.

14.1 RESOURCE DESCRIPTION FRAMEWORK (RDF)

Resource Description Framework (RDF) is a way of representing machine-readable Web metadata to allow interoperability among applications. The basic RDF model has three fundamental concepts:

- **Resources** are "things" that we want to talk about, such as web pages, websites, customers, authors, books, publishers, places, machines, buildings, and products. Every resource has a Universal Resource Identifier (URI), which is a web address or some other kind of unique identifier.
- **Properties,** or predicates, describe relations between resources, such as "name," "color," "designed by," and "purchased." Properties are also identified by URIs.
- **Statements** assert the properties of resources. An RDF statement is a

subject-predicate-object triple. The subject or object of a statement can be another resource, or it can be a literal or an atomic value such as a string. The predicate establishes the relationship between a subject and an object and makes the object value a characteristic of the subject.

As shown in FIGURE 14.1, the subject-predicate-object triple of an RDF statement can be represented as a directed RDF graph with labeled nodes and arcs, where the subject and object of the statement are represented as nodes, and an arc is drawn from the subject to the object labeled with a property. Such graphs are fundamental constructs of a *semantic network.* As shown in the figure, RDF statements are written in platform-independent XML. The XML language used by RDF is called RDF/XML. RDF documents thus offer semantic network representation.

RDF Triple	`subject predicate object`
Graphical form	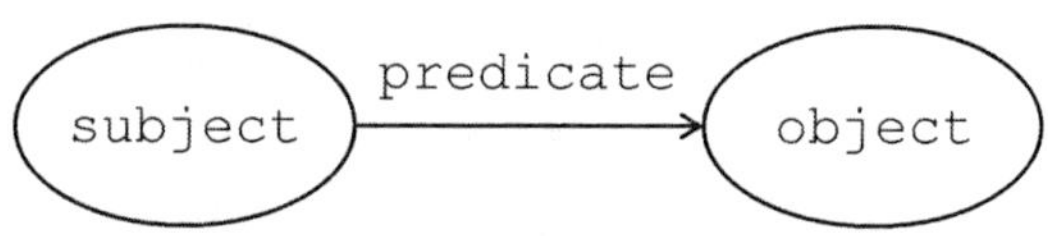
Relational form	`predicate(subject, object)`
RDF/XML form	<rdf:Description rdf:about="subject"> <ex:predicate>"object"</ex:predicate> </rdf:Description>

FIGURE 14.1 : Various forms of a statement

In an RDF/XML document there are two types of nodes: resource nodes and property nodes. *Resource nodes* are the subjects and objects of statements, and they usually have an rdf:about attribute on them, giving the URI of the resource they represent. The rdf:Description tag in the RDF/XML representation in FIGURE 14.1 is a resource node for the description of a subject with the unique ID "subject." Resource nodes contain only property nodes, which represent statements. *Property nodes* contain literal values, like "object" or a reference to an object resource using the rdf:resource attribute, or they may contain a full resource node as their object. Here is a concrete example of RDF/XML representation.

Example

Consider the sentence "Mary Parker purchased milk," which has the following parts:

Subject: Mary Parker

Predicate: purchased
Object: milk

The complete XML document containing the description above would be:

```
<?xml version="1.0"?>
<rdf:RDF
    xmlns:rdf="http://www.w3.org/
       1999/02/22-rdf-syntax-ns#"
    xmlns:ma="http://machineanalytics.com/schema/">
    <rdf:Description about="Mary Parker">
       <ma:purchase>milk</ma:purchase>
    </rdf:Description>
</rdf:RDF>
```

The representation has only one resource node. The only property node contains the literal value “milk.” Unlike a subject or object, a predicate must always be a URI. Here the namespace prefix “ma” refers to a specific prefix chosen by the creator of the above RDF/XML expression and defined in the XML namespace declaration xmlns:ma=http://machineanalytics.com/schema/

Example

This example illustrates a representation of general relations in RDF/XML beyond just RDF triples which are binary relations. Consider the relational tables, TABLE 14.1, TABLE 14.2, TABLE 14.3, and TABLE 14.4, containing some customer records and example sale transactions.

TABLE 14.1: : Example customer relational table

Customer				
Cust ID	**Name**	**Email**	**SSN**	**Gender**
C-123	Mary Parker	mary@abc.zom	707-77-3176	F
C-456	John Smith	john@def.hom	304-73-5241	M
C-789	Jack Bunn	jack@ghi.zom	770-78-0355	M
C-135	Sandra Searle	sand@jkl.def	617-88-0452	F
C-246	Betsy Dodson	bd@mno.zom	978-44-1267	F

TABLE 14.2: : Example product table

Product	
Prod ID	**Name**
D-1	Milk
D-2	Cheese
D-3	Yogurt
D-4	Ice Cream

TABLE 14.2: : Example product table

M-1	Chicken
V-1	Spinach

TABLE 14.3: : Example dairy product table

Dairy Product	
Prod ID	**Lactose (g)**
D-1	11
D-2	1
D-3	5
D-4	6

TABLE 14.4: : Example purchase table

Purchased	
Cust ID	**Prod ID**
C-123	D-1
C-123	D-3
C-123	D-4
C-456	M-1
C-456	D-1
C-246	V-1

For each table there are as many resource nodes as the number of rows. Each resource node contains only property nodes, which represent statements. For each row in the first table, there are four statements (and hence four property nodes). The first resource node has the subject "C-123" and predicates "cust:name," "cust:email," "cust:phone," and "cust:gender." Property nodes, in turn, contain literal values, like "Mary Parker," "mary@abc.zom," "707-774-3176," and "F." Following is an RDF/XML representation of the schema of the TABLE 14.1.

```
<?xml version="1.0"?>
<rdf:RDF
    xmlns:rdf="http://www.w3.org/1999/02/
       22-rdf-syntax-ns#"
    xmlns:cust="http://www.machineanalytics.com/cust#">

    <rdf:Description
       rdf:about="http://www.machineanalytics.com/
          cust/C-123">
```

```
        <cust:name>Mary Parker</cust:name>
        <cust:email>mary@abc.zom</cust:email>
        <cust:phone>707-774-3176</cust:phone>
        <cust:gender>F</cust:gender>
    </rdf:Description>

    <rdf:Description
        rdf:about="http://www.machineanalytics.com/
            cust/C-456">
        <cust:name>John Smith</cust:name>
        <cust:email>john@def.hom</cust:email>
        <cust:phone>304-731-5241</cust:phone>
        <cust:gender>M</cust:gender>
    </rdf:Description>
    .
    .
    .
</rdf:RDF>
```

The other tables can be represented in RDF/XML in a similar manner. RDF can be further formalized by ontology modeling languages such as RDF Schema (RDFS) and the Ontology Web Language (OWL) as detailed in the next two sections.

14.1.1 RDF Schema (RDFS)

RDFS provides a framework to describe application-specific classes and properties. Classes in RDFS are much like classes in object-oriented programming languages, allowing resources to be defined as instances of classes and subclasses of classes. FIGURE 14.2 is a graphical depiction of the schema of the four relational tables, namely, TABLE 14.1, TABLE 14.2, TABLE 14.3, and TABLE 14.4.

Classes are represented in ovals, and properties (i.e., predicates) are represented in rectangles. There are four classes, namely, Customer, Product, DairyProduct, and Literal, of which DairyProduct is a subclass of the class Product and Literal is the class of all values of literals. The equivalent XML representation of the graphical RDFS in FIGURE 14.2 is shown below.

```
<?xml version="1.0"?>
<rdf:RDF
    xmlns:rdf="http://www.w3.org/1999/02/
        22-rdf-syntax-ns#"
    xmlns:rdfs=http://www.w3.org/2000/01/rdf-schema#

    <rdfs:Class rdf:ID="Class">
        <rdfs:comment>The Customer OWL</rdfs:comment>
```

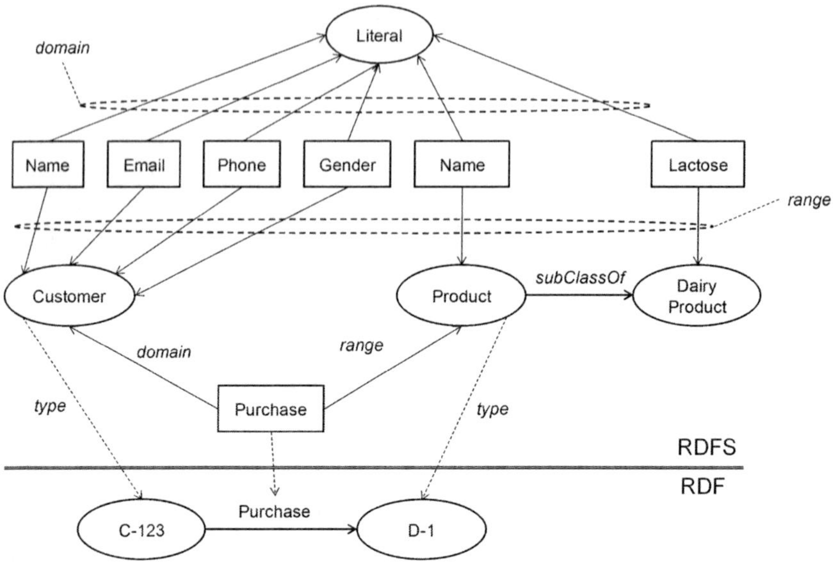

FIGURE 14.2 : A graphical depiction of the schema of the four relational tables, namely, TABLE 14.1, TABLE 14.2, TABLE 14.3, and TABLE 14.4

```
</rdfs:Class>
<!-
   Defining classes and subclasses
->
<rdf:Description rdf:ID="Customer">
   <rdf:type rdf:resource=
      "http://www.w3.org/2000/01/rdf-schema#Class"/>
</rdf:Description>

<rdfs:Class rdf:ID="Product">
   <rdfs:subClassOf
      rdf:resource="http://www.w3.org/2002/07/
      owl#Thing"/>
</rdfs:Class>

<!-
   Abbreviated syntax for classes
   <rdfs:Class rdf:ID="Product" />
->

<rdfs:Class rdf:ID="DairyProduct">
   <rdfs:subClassOf rdf:resource="#Product"/>
```

```
    </rdfs:Class>

    <!-
       Defining Property Purchase
    ->
    <rdf:Property rdf:ID="Purchased"
         rdfs:comment="Customers purchase products">
       <rdfs:domain rdf:resource="#Customer"/>
       <rdfs:range rdf:resource="#Product"/>
    </rdf:Property>
</rdf:RDF>
```

In the XML representation, rdf:type declares a resource to be an instance of a class (e.g., D-1 is a Product). rdfs:domain specifies the domain of a property which is the class of those resources that may appear as subjects in a triple with the property (i.e., predicate). rdfs:range specifies the range of a property which is the class of those resources that may appear as values in a triple with property (i.e. predicate).

14.1.2 Ontology Web Language (OWL)

RDF and RDFS provide basic capabilities for describing vocabularies that describe resources. OWL extends RDFS with additional modeling primitives for enhanced expressivity, including the ability to describe new classes by combining existing classes using intersections, unions, negation, cardinality constraints, and transitive closure. The complete OWL language (OWL Full) provides two specific subsets, namely, OWL Lite and OWL DL (DL stands for Description Logic), where OWL Lite is a sub-language of OWL DL.

Following is an OWL/XML representation of the schema of the four tables – TABLE 14.1, TABLE 14.2, TABLE 14.3, and TABLE 14.4.

```
<?xml version="1.0"?>
<!DOCTYPE rdf:RDF [
    <!ENTITY xsd "http://www.w3.org/2001/XMLSchema#">
]>
<rdf:RDF
    xmlns:rdf ="http://www.w3.org/1999/02/
       22-rdf-syntax-ns#"
    xmlns:rdfs="http://www.w3.org/2000/01/rdf-schema#"
    xmlns:owl="http://www.w3.org/2002/07/owl#"
    xmlns="http://www.machineanalytics.com/customer/#"
    xmlns:customer="http://www.machineanalytics.com/
       customer/#"
    xmlns:xsd=" http://www.w3.org/2001/XMLSchema#"
    xml:base="http://www.machineanalytics.com/
       customer/">
```

```
<owl:Ontology rdf:about="">
   <owl:versionInfo>V 1.0</owl:versionInfo>
   <rdfs:label>Customer-Product Ontology
      </rdfs:label>
</owl:Ontology>

<owl:Class rdf:ID="Customer"/>
<owl:Class rdf:ID="Product"/>
<owl:Class rdf:ID="DairyProduct">
   <rdfs:subClassOf rdf:resource="#Product"/>
</owl:Class>
<owl:Class rdf:ID="SSN"/>
<owl:ObjectProperty rdf:ID="hasSSN"
   <rdfs:domain rdf:resource="#Customer"/>
   <rdfs:range rdf:resource="#SSN"/>
</owl:ObjectProperty>

<owl:ObjectProperty rdf:ID="hasPurchased"
   <rdfs:domain rdf:resource="#Customer"/>
   <rdfs:range rdf:resource="#Product"/>
</owl:ObjectProperty>

<owl:Class rdf:ID="Customer">
   <rdfs:subClassOf>
      <owl:Restriction>
      <owl:onProperty rdf:resource="#hasSSN"/>
      <owl:allValuesFrom rdf:resource="#SSN"/>
      </owl:Restriction>
   </rdfs:subClassOf>
   <rdfs:subClassOf>
      <owl:Restriction>
      <owl:onProperty rdf:resource="#hasSSN"/>
      <owl:maxCardinality rdf:datatype="&xsd;
      nonNegativeInteger">1</owl:maxCardinality>
      </owl:Restriction>
   </rdfs:subClassOf>
</owl:Class>

<owl:ObjectProperty rdf:ID="hasCustomer">
   <owl:inverseOf rdf:resource="#hasSSN"/>
</owl:ObjectProperty>

<owl:Class rdf:ID="SSN">
   <rdfs:subClassOf>
      <owl:Restriction>
      <owl:onProperty rdf:resource=
```

```
            "#hasCustomer"/>
            <owl:maxCardinality rdf:datatype=
            "&xsd; nonNegativeInteger">1</owl:maxCardinality>
            </owl:Restriction>
        </rdfs:subClassOf>
    </owl:Class>

    <owl:DatatypeProperty rdf:ID="hasName"/>
        <rdfs:domain rdf:resource="#Customer"/>
        <rdfs:range rdf:resource="&xsd;string">
    <owl:DatatypeProperty>

    <owl:DatatypeProperty rdf:ID="hasEmail"/>
        <rdfs:domain rdf:resource="#Customer"/>
        <rdfs:range rdf:resource="&xsd;string">
    <owl:DatatypeProperty>

    <owl:DatatypeProperty rdf:ID="hasPhone"/>
        <rdfs:domain rdf:resource="#Customer"/>
        <rdfs:range rdf:resource="&xsd;string">
    <owl:DatatypeProperty>

    <owl:DatatypeProperty rdf:ID="hasGender"/>
        <rdfs:domain rdf:resource="#Customer"/>
        <rdfs:range rdf:resource="#GenderOption">
    <owl:DatatypeProperty>

    <GenderOption rdf:ID="M"/>
    <GenderOption rdf:ID="F"/>
</rdf:RDF>
```

This XML representation is self-explanatory. In the representation, property owl:ObjectProperty defines a relation between instances of two classes. owl:DatatypeProperty defines relations among instances of classes and RDF literals and XML Schema datatypes. owl:Restriction adds a restriction to a statement. The OWL built-in properties like owl:maxCardinality, including the ones used here, will be defined formally in terms of DL syntax.

14.2 DESCRIPTION LOGICS

Description Logics (DLs) are decidable fragments of first-order logic with only unary and binary predicates, and individual constants are termed as *individual names*. A unary predicate represents a *concept* which is a set of individuals, and a binary predicate represents a *role* which is a binary relation between the individuals. Example concepts are Customer and Person representing, respectively, the set of all customers and the set of all persons. An example role is CustomerOf, representing the relationship between customers and various services provided by a company.

14.2.1 Description Logic Syntax

We first define the basic DL, Attributive Concept Language with Complements (ALC) (Schmidt-Schauß and Smolka, 1991), and then describe a number of extensions. Assume that a countably infinite supply of concept names, usually denoted C and D, and of role names, usually denoted R and S, are available. Roles are used to express relationships between concepts. Concept descriptions in ALC DL are formed according to the following recursive rules:

$$C, D := A, R, \top, \bot, \neg C, C \sqcap D, C \sqcup D, \exists R.C, \forall R.C$$

For example, the intersection of the two concepts C and D, denoted as $C \sqcap D$, is the set of individuals that belong to both C and D. For example,

$$Customer \sqcap Female$$

denotes the set of individuals that are both customers and female. The join of the two concepts C and D, denoted as $C \sqcup D$, is the set of all individuals that belong to either C or D. For example,

$$PremierCustomer \sqcup Female$$

denotes the set of individuals that are premier or female customers. The negation of a concept C, denoted as $\neg C$, is the set of all individuals that do not belong to C. For example, the set of individuals that are non-premier customers can be represented as

$$\neg PremierCustomer$$

DL allows value or role restriction constructs. The universal role restriction construct $\forall R.C$ requires that all the individuals that are in a specified relationship R with the concept being described belong to the concept C. For example,

$$\forall CustomerOf.DairyProduct$$

denotes all individual customers who purchase only dairy products. Note that the concept above also includes those individuals that are not customers of dairy products at all. The existential role restriction construct $\exists R.C$ requires that there is at least one individual in a specified relationship R with the concept being described who belongs to the concept C. The concept

$$\exists CustomerOf.DairyProduct$$

describes those individuals that are customers of at least one dairy product. The existential role construct allows us to define the concept *Customer* in terms of *CustomerOf* as

$$Customer \equiv \exists CustomerOf.\top$$

because the definition of a customer is of someone who is a customer of at least one product.

Number restriction constructs in DL allow us to restrict the number of individuals that can be reached via a given role. For example, the at-least restriction

$$\geq 6\, CustomerOf.Product$$

represents the set of individuals that are customers of at least six products. Conversely, the at-most restriction

$$\leq 6\, CustomerOf.Product$$

represents the set of individuals that are customers of at most six products. Now every customer of "half dozen" type who is a customer of exactly six products can be represented as

$$HalfDozenCustomer \sqsubseteq$$
$$\leq 6\, CustomerOf.Product \sqcap \geq 6\, CustomerOf.Product$$

Domain and range constraints on roles are stated as axioms asserting that if an individual x is related to an individual y by a role R, then x must be an instance of the concept that is the domain of R and y must be an instance of the concept that is the range of R. To restrict the domain of *CustomerOf* to female individuals we can use the axiom

$$\exists CustomerOf.\top \sqsubseteq Female$$

and to restrict the range of *CustomerOf* to *DairyProduct*, we can write

$$\top \sqsubseteq \forall CustomerOf.DairyProduct$$

Note that these restrictions are different from the notion of integrity constraints in databases (or knowledge bases) (Das, 1992), which are properties that a database must satisfy. If we have the role assertion

$$CustomerOf\,(Mary,\ Cheese)$$

in a knowledge base in the presence of the above two restrictions then $Female\,(Mary)$ and $DairyProduct\,(Cheese)$ will be inferred from the knowledge base. But if the two restrictions are treated as integrity constraints then those would have been violated since neither the concept assertion $Female\,(Mary)$ nor $DairyProduct\,(Cheese)$ is present or in the knowledge base.

Note that concept expressions in the syntax of DL are variable-free. In fact, a concept expression denotes the set of all individuals satisfying the properties specified in the expression. Therefore, $C \sqcap D$ can be regarded as the first-order logic sentence $C(x) \wedge D(x)$, where the variable ranges over all individuals in the interpretation domain and $C(x)$ and $D(x)$ are true for those individuals that belong to the concept C and D respectively. See TABLE 14.5 for all other interpretations.

In DL, a *nominal* is a concept that has exactly one individual. For example, {john} is the concept which has only one individual, John. A concept can be defined by enumerating individuals such as

$$DairyProduct \equiv \{milk\} \sqcup \{cheese\} \sqcup \{yogurt\}$$

14.2.2 Description Logic Axioms

DL axioms are divided into three groups: assertional (ABox) axioms, terminological (TBox) axioms, and relational (RBox) axioms. These axioms together constitute a knowledge base of the domain in context. From the point of view of logic, these axioms are just sentences of the underlying logical language.

ABox axioms capture knowledge about named individuals. For example, $john.Customer$, or equivalently $Customer(john)$ in a first-order language, asserts that John is a customer and that the individual named John is an instance of the concept Customer. Role assertions describe binary relations between named individuals. The assertion $\langle wireless,\ john\rangle : CustomerOf$or $CustomerOf(wireless,\ john)$ states that *john* is a *wireless* customer and that the individual named John is in the relation with the individual named *john* via the relation Customer.

TBox axioms describe subsumption and equivalence relationships between concepts. For example, the fact that all premier customers are customers can be expressed by the concept inclusion

$$PremierCustomerOf \ \sqsubseteq CustomerOf$$

The concept PremierCustomerOf is subsumed by the concept Customer. Such knowledge can be used to infer implicit facts about individuals. For example, if Jack is a premier customer then Jack is also a customer by virtue of the above subsumption relation. The equivalence between two concepts asserts that they have the same instances. For example, for some companies all gold members are premier customers, and vice versa, as in

$$GoldMemberOf \ \equiv \ PremierCustomerOf$$

Synonyms are, by definition, equivalent concepts.

14.2.3 Description Logic Constructs and Subsystems

TABLE 14.5 presents the fundamental constructs of DL categorized into its subsystems and their equivalent representation in first-order logic.

TABLE 14.5: : Subsystems of Description Logics

System	Descriptions	DL Const.	Equivalent FOL Syntax
S (ALC)	Atomic Concept	A	A
	Individual Name	$a : C$	$C(a)$
	Top Concept	$\top$	$\top$
	Bottom Concept	$\bot$	$\bot$
	Subsumption	$C \sqsubseteq D$	$\forall x (C(x) \to D(x))$
	Equivalence	$C \equiv D$	$\forall x (C(x) \leftrightarrow D(x))$
	Role	$\langle a, b \rangle : R$	$R(a, b)$
	Intersection	$C \sqcap D$	$C(x) \wedge D(x)$
	Join	$C \sqcup D$	$C(x) \vee D(x)$
	Complement or Negation	$\neg C$	$\neg C(x)$
	Existential Restriction	$\exists R.C$	$\exists y (R(x, y) \wedge C(y))$
	Universal Restriction	$\forall R.C$	$\forall y (R(x, y) \to C(y))$
H	Subsumption of Roles	$R \sqsubseteq S$	$\forall x \forall y (R(x, y) \to S(x, y))$
	Equivalence of Roles	$R \equiv S$	$\forall x \forall y (R(x, y) \leftrightarrow S(x, y))$
O	Nominal	$\{a\}$	
	Value Restriction	$\exists R. \{a\}$	$R(x, a)$
	Enumeration	$\{a_1, ..., a_n\}$	$x = a_1 \vee ... \vee x = a_n$
I	Inverse Roles	$R \equiv S^-$	$\forall x \forall y (R(x, y) \leftrightarrow S(y, x))$
Q	Qualified Cardinality	$= nR.C$	$\leq nR.C \sqcap \geq nR.C$
	Qualified Max Cardinality	$\leq nR.C$	$\forall y_1 ... \forall y_{n+1} \left(\bigwedge_{1 \leq i \leq n+1} (R(x, y_i) \wedge C(y_i)) \to \bigvee_{\substack{1 \leq i < n+1; \\ i < j \leq n+1}} y_i = y_j \right)$

TABLE 14.5: : Subsystems of Description Logics

	Qualified Min Cardinality	$\geq nR.C$	$\exists y_1 ... \exists y_n \left(\bigwedge_{1 \leq i \leq n} (R(x, y_i) \wedge C(y_i)) \wedge \bigwedge_{1 \leq i < n; i < j \leq n} y_i \neq y_j \right)$
N	Cardinality	$= nR.\top$	$\leq nR.\top \sqcap \geq nR.\top$
	Max Cardinality	$\leq nR.\top$	$\forall y_1 ... \forall y_{n+1} \left(\bigwedge_{1 \leq i \leq n+1} R(x, y_i) \rightarrow \bigvee_{\substack{1 \leq i < n+1 \\ i < j \leq n+1}} y_i = y_j \right)$
	Min Cardinality	$\geq nR.\top$	$\exists y_1 ... \exists y_n \left(\bigwedge_{1 \leq i \leq n} R(x, y_i) \wedge \bigwedge_{\substack{1 \leq i < n \\ i < j \leq n}} y_i \neq y_j \right)$

The system SHOIQ extends S (ALC) with several expressive means, namely H, O, I, and Q, as shown in the table. SHOIQ is the foundation for reasoning in the semantic web. The constructs in N are special cases of those in S. The fragment SHOIN of SHOIQ roughly corresponds to the ontology language OWL DL, which was recommended by the W3C as the standard web ontology language. The well-known DAML (DARPA Agent Markup Language) together with OIL (Ontology Inference Layer) correspond to SHIQ.

14.2.4 Description Logic and OWL Constructs in Relational Database

TABLE 14.6 shows a list of DL constructs and their equivalent OWL constructs, some of which have been used in the OWL/XML representation in the previous section.

TABLE 14.6: : Description Logic and OWL constructs

DL Construct	**OWL Construct**
$C \sqsubseteq D$	subClassOf
$C \equiv D$	equivalentClasses
$C \sqcap D$	intersectionOf
$C \sqcup D$	unionOf
$\neg C$	complementOf
$\exists R.C$	someValuesFrom
$\forall R.C$	allValuesFrom

TABLE 14.6: : Description Logic and OWL constructs

$R \sqsubseteq S$	subPropertyOf
$R \equiv S$	equivalentProperties
$R^+ \sqsubseteq R$	transitiveProperty
$\exists R.\{a\}$	value
$\{a_1, ..., a_n\}$	oneOf
$R \equiv S^-$	inverseOf
$= nR.C$	cardinality
$\leq nR.C$	maxCardinality
$\geq nR.C$	minCardinality
$= nR.\top$	cardinality
$\leq nR.\top$	maxCardinality
$\geq nR.\top$	minCardinality

14.2.5 Description Logic as First-Order Logic

The schema of a relational database is defined in terms of relations, view, and the integrity constraints among them. The schema can be transformed as a set of TBox axioms. For example, one can state the integrity constraint that each customer has a unique social security number and that each SSN can be associated with at most one customer. This can be expressed by the following TBox axioms (Motik et al., 2007):

$$\begin{array}{l} Customer \sqsubseteq \exists hasSSN.SSN \\ Customer \sqsubseteq \leq 1?hasSSN.SSN \\ SSN \sqsubseteq \leq 1?hasSSN.SSN^- \end{array}$$

The above axioms can be translated to first-order axiom as follows:

$$\begin{array}{l} \forall x \left(Customer\left(x\right) \rightarrow \exists y \left(hasSSN\left(x,y\right) \wedge SSN\left(y\right)\right)\right) \\ \forall x \forall y_1 \forall y_2 \left(\begin{array}{l} Customer\left(x\right) \wedge hasSSN\left(x,y_1\right) \wedge SSN\left(y_1\right) \wedge \\ hasSSN\left(x,y_2\right) \wedge SSN\left(y_2\right) \rightarrow y_1 = y_2 \end{array} \right) \\ \forall x_1 \forall x_2 \forall y \left(\begin{array}{l} SSN\left(y\right) \wedge hasSSN\left(x_1,y\right) \wedge Customer\left(x_1\right) \wedge \\ hasSSN\left(x_2,y\right) \wedge Customer\left(x_2\right) \rightarrow x_1 = x_2 \end{array} \right) \end{array}$$

A view can be thought of as a definite rule in first order logic. For example, the definite rule

$$\begin{array}{l} P\left(x\right) \wedge Q\left(x\right) \rightarrow R\left(x\right) \\ i.e., \ \forall x \left(P\left(x\right) \wedge Q\left(x\right) \rightarrow R\left(x\right)\right) \end{array}$$

is equivalent to the DL axiom

$$P \sqcap Q \sqsubseteq R$$

A more complex definite rule of the form

$$P(x) \wedge Q(x,y) \wedge R(y) \to S(x)$$
$$i.e.\ \forall x\,(P(x) \wedge \exists y\,(Q(x,y) \wedge R(y)) \to S(x))$$

is equivalent to the DL axiom

$$P \sqcap \exists Q.R \sqsubseteq S$$

14.3 FURTHER READING

The W3C document on RDF Primer (2004) provides the reader with the basic knowledge required to effectively use RDF. The W3 document on OWL (2004) demonstrates the use of the OWL. A good read on semantic web in general is (Antoniou and van Harmelen, 2004). Good resources on DLs include (Baader et al., 2003; Baader and Nutt, 2003; Nardi and Brachman, 2002).

CHAPTER 15

Analytics Tools

This chapter describes three tools designed and implemented by the author, namely, *i*DAS, E5, and *a*Text. The chapter also describes very briefly a handful of commercial and publicly available tools for analytics.

Intelligent Decision Aiding System (*i*DAS) provides implementations of a set of machine learning techniques introduced in Chapter 10 and a calculus for combining supports for decision options from these individual techniques. Environment for 5th Generation Applications (E5) provides a development environment in declarative languages with an embedded expert system shell. Analysis of Text (*a*Text) is a tool for information extraction and classification of text documents, implementing the techniques introduced earlier in the text analytics chapter. Various features of each of these tools are explained with hand-crafted data sets, and realistic case studies are carried out in the next chapter. Both *i*DAS and *a*Text have been developed in platform-independent Java, whereas E5 has been developed in Visual C++ and provides a graphical user interface for the expert system. Please contact the author directly to obtain the demonstration versions of these tools. Although the demonstration versions have reduced functionalities, do not provide APIs, and do not allow users to save results, they are furnished with the full example data sets used here. Consult the online usage manual wherever available.

As for publicly available tools, we describe the popular scripting language R to program and solve analytical problems. We also introduce the popular machine learning tool WEKA, though some of the techniques in it can be found in the three tools above. As for popular commercial tools, we present MATLAB as a counterpart of R. Both R and MATLAB functionalities are illustrated using two implementations of market prediction via Kalman filters. Many examples in the descriptive and inferential chapters have been illustrated using the commercial tool SAS. Here we briefly describe the problem modeling methodology in SAS. Note that detailed descriptions of these tools are beyond the scope of this book. Readers are advised to consult relevant manuals and numerous online tutorials that are available for each of these tools.

15.1 INTELLIGENT DECISION AIDING SYSTEM (IDAS)

*i*DAS is an interactive decision-making platform (logo is in FIGURE 15.1) to help in choosing the most suitable action based on past experience and observations. It applies four methods to generate decision-making models automatically from historical training data:

- Decision Tree as a linear method
- Neural Network as a non-linear method
- Rule Induction as a symbolic method
- Bayesian Belief Network as a graphical method

FIGURE 15.1 : iDAS logo

As shown in FIGURE 15.2, decision making by *i*DAS involves four stages:

1. Preparation of data from ODBC compliant data sources or from plain text files in certain format.
2. Automatic building of the above four decision-making models from data, applying the methods detailed in previous chapters.
3. Preparation of an input and feeding into the system.
4. Generation and aggregation of assessments from individual models.

Each model outputs its own decision based on the input. The Evidence Aggregation module then applies a proprietary algorithm to aggregate four decisions and come up with a combined single decision.

The *i*DAS interface is shown in FIGURE 15.3. It has multiple tabbed panes, with one pane for each of the four methods, the welcome pane as shown in the figure, one pane for obtaining input from user and display decisions, and one pane for visualization of data and decisions. Selection of a tabbed pane for a method enables viewing of the corresponding model once constructed. The interface provides a button panel and a set of menus. Users can see a short text description of the function of a button by placing the cursor on it. Each method button constructs the corresponding model after preparation of the

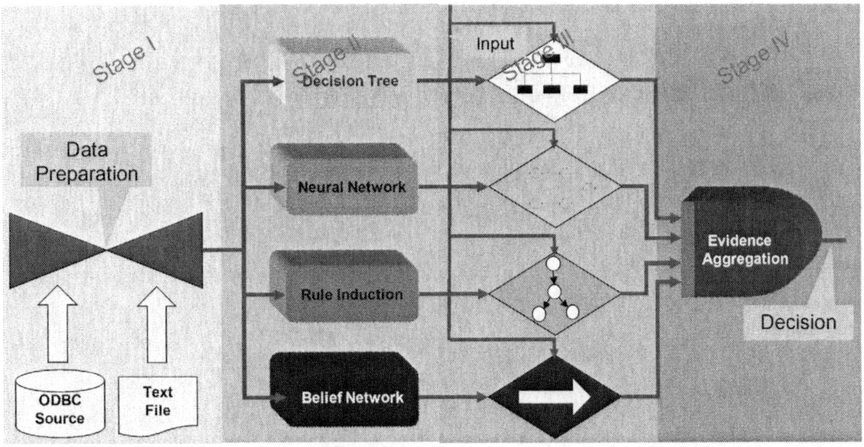

FIGURE 15.2 : iDAS overall process

data. The menu items are for managing data files, setting method parameters, and invoking various in-built applications. The welcome pane contains some data-flow animations of the methods.

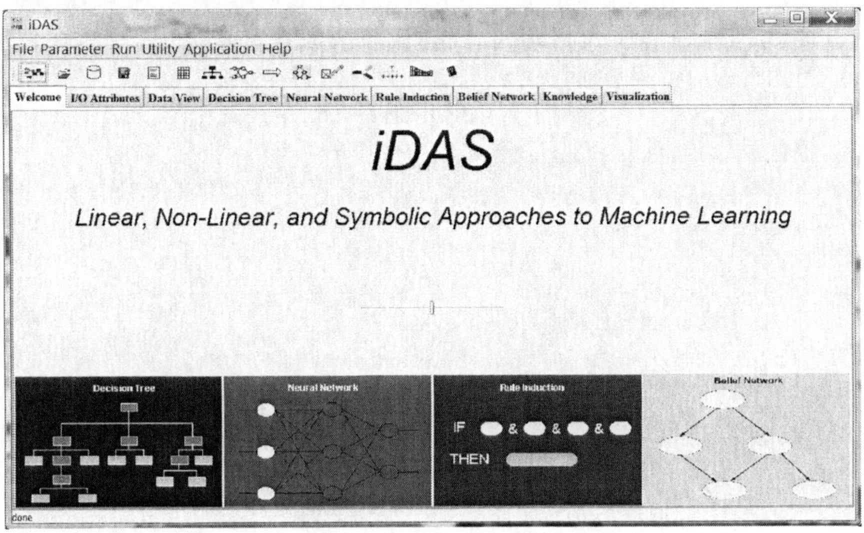

FIGURE 15.3 : iDAS interface

The first-step in *i*DAS is the preparation of training data containing labeled instances. Selecting the menu item File |Open Database or File |Text File opens up a dialog window as shown in FIGURE 15.4 with the appropriately highlighted button.

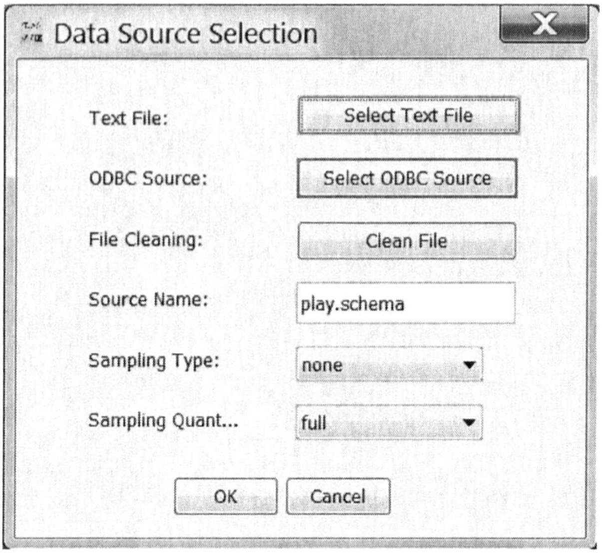

FIGURE 15.4 : Selection of data source

Select ODBC or text data source as appropriate. The schema file name should also be the data source name for a text data set. The play-tennis example in Appendix B is in a text file and the loan case study is in an Excel file, which is ODBC-compliant. The schema file for the play-tennis example is the following:

```
|attribute descriptions
Outlook: discrete
Temperature: integer
Humidity: float
Windy: discrete
Class: discrete
```

The user can sample from the data file instead of dealing with the whole data set. The sampling type and quantity can be selected accordingly. Choose the default sampling type and full sampling quantity for the play-tennis example since we only have a handful of instances. The number of training instances should ideally be sampled from very large data sets.

*i*DAS automatically reads the schema information from the data source, and the database attributes are displayed on its I/O Attributes tabbed pane as shown in FIGURE 15.5.

For a discrete-valued attribute, the Value column indicates the finite set of possible values an attribute can take. *i*DAS automatically constructs the set from the values of the attribute in training instances. For example, the set of all possible values for the attribute Outlook has the elements overcast, rainy,

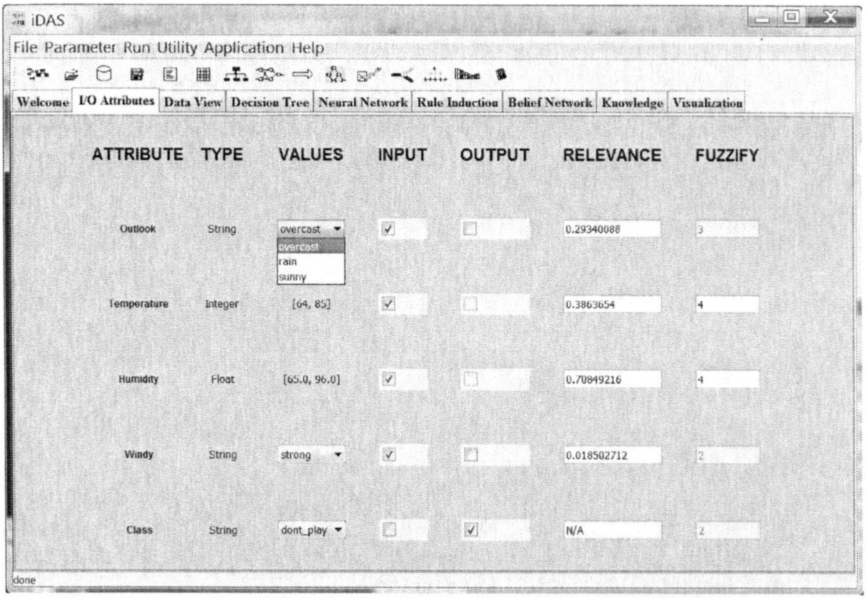

FIGURE 15.5 : Selection of relevant attributes

and sunny. For a continuous-valued attribute, this value is a range within which all the values of the attribute belong. For example, this range is 64-85 for Temperature. For a decision-making problem, one of the attributes is considered as the output attribute and a subset or all of the rest are input. The user can choose input-output attributes by checking the relevant boxes. Note that a user may consider only a subset of the attributes relevant to the decision-making problem guided by the values in the Relevance column. A value in the Fuzzify column indicates the number of values the corresponding attribute can take. For a discrete attribute, this is the size of the set of possible values the attribute can take. A continuous-values attribute is discretized by equally dividing its range interval into the number of times equal to the value the user specifies in the Fuzzify column. Select the menu item File |Save Schema once the attribute properties are adjusted.

Once the attribute properties are adjusted, the training instances can be viewed in the Data View pane, as shown in FIGURE 15.6, by pressing the button with a table icon in the tool bar. By pressing the same button the test instances can be viewed.

To generate a decision tree model, select the Decision Tree tabbed pane. Get the parameter dialog window, as shown in FIGURE 15.7, by selecting the menu Parameter |Decision Tree. Then accept the default values by pressing the OK button of the dialog and then the Yes button of the Previously Generated Tree dialog. The confidence and prune factor values can be customized by the user as needed. The confidence value indicates the minimum percentage of

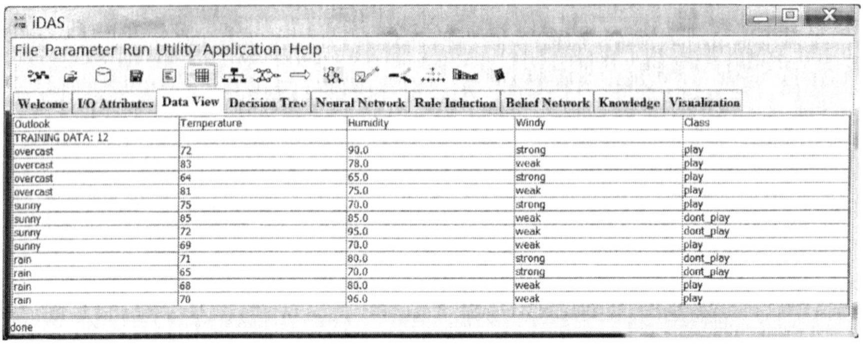

FIGURE 15.6 : View of Selected Historical Data

instances needed along each branch. The prune factor controls the size of the decision tree.

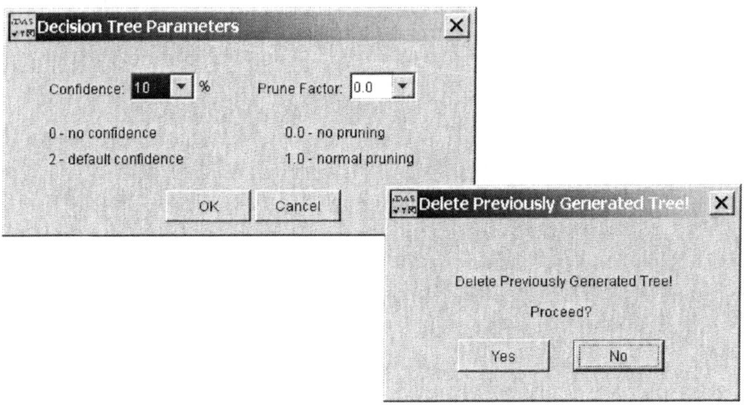

FIGURE 15.7 : Dialog for setting decision tree parameters

Generate the tree, as shown in FIGURE 15.8, by selecting the menu Run |Construct Tree. Unfold the root node to see its branches.

To generate a neural network model, first select the Neural Network tabbed pane. Get the parameter dialog window, as shown in FIGURE 15.9, by selecting the menu Parameter |Neural Network. Accept the default values by pressing the OK button and then the Yes button on the dialog with the question "Delete previously trained network?" These parameters have been discussed previously when introducing the neural network model in the machine learning chapter.

Generate the network, as shown in FIGURE 15.10, by selecting the menu Run |Train Network. Then train the network by selecting the menu Run |Train Network again. The training might take several minutes depending on the parameter values.

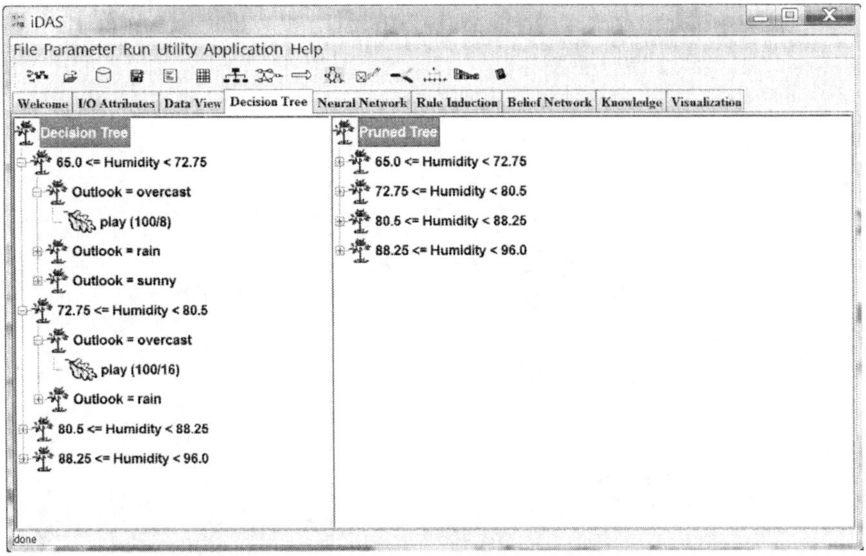

FIGURE 15.8 : iDAS generated decision tree model

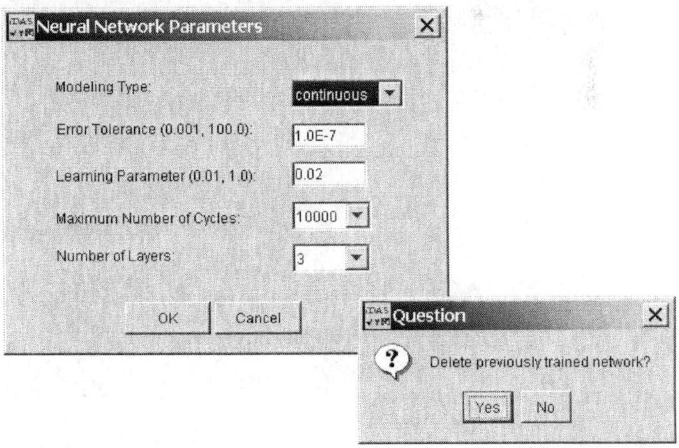

FIGURE 15.9 : Dialog for setting neural network parameters

To generating a rule-induction model via Inductive Logic Programming, select the Rule Induction tabbed pane. Get the parameter dialog window, as shown in FIGURE 15.11, by selecting the menu item Parameter |Rule Induction. Then accept the default values of the parameters by pressing the OK button and the Yes button to the dialog for the question "Delete previously generated rules?" The support and confidence parameters have been discussed at the end of the rule induction section of the machine learning chapter.

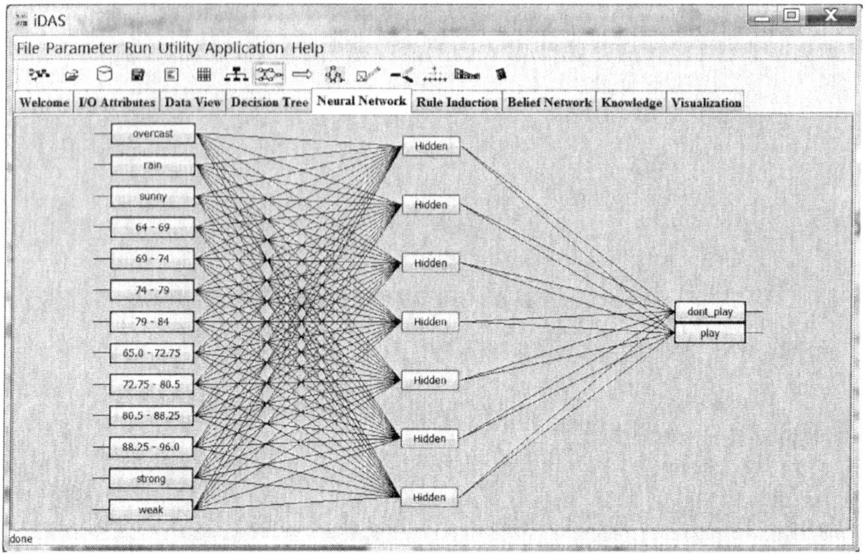

FIGURE 15.10 : iDAS generated neural network model

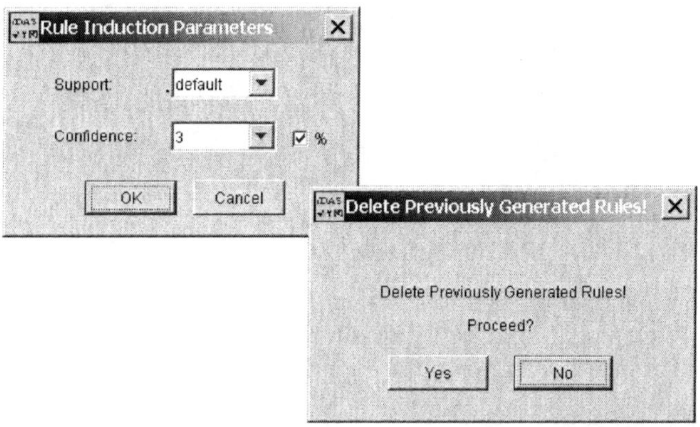

FIGURE 15.11 : Dialog for setting parameters for rule induction

Generate rules, as shown in FIGURE 15.12, by selecting the menu item Run |Generate Rules. The rule generation process for each candidate may take several minutes depending on the size of the input data and the number of attributes selected as input. Once a sufficient number of rules are generated for a candidate, the rule generation process for the next candidate can be started by pressing the Cancel button on the progress dialog window. Click on a rule to see its details in a dialog window. The dialog shows the antecedent, the consequent, and the support and confidence values of the selected rule. The rest of the rules can be navigated sequentially through the same dialog. A specific rule can be activated/deactivated as seen fit by the user.

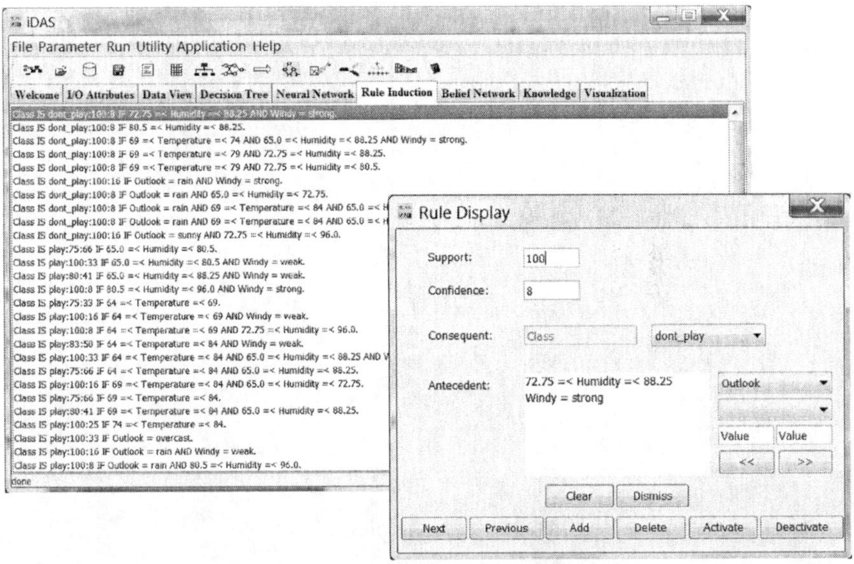

FIGURE 15.12 : Generated rules via rule induction

To generate a Bayesian Belief Network (BN) model, select the Belief Network tabbed pane. Get the parameter dialog window, as shown in FIGURE 15.13, by selecting the menu item Parameter |Belief Network. Accept the default values by pressing the OK button and the Yes button of the dialog window for the question "Delete previously generated network?"

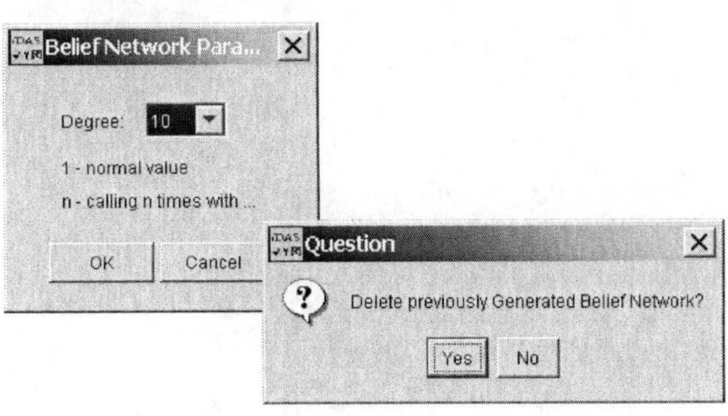

FIGURE 15.13 : Dialog for setting parameters for belief network model

Then construct the BN, as shown in FIGURE 15.14, by clicking the menu Run |Learn BeliefNet. Learn the BN model from training instances by selecting the same menu again. The learning process may take a few minutes.

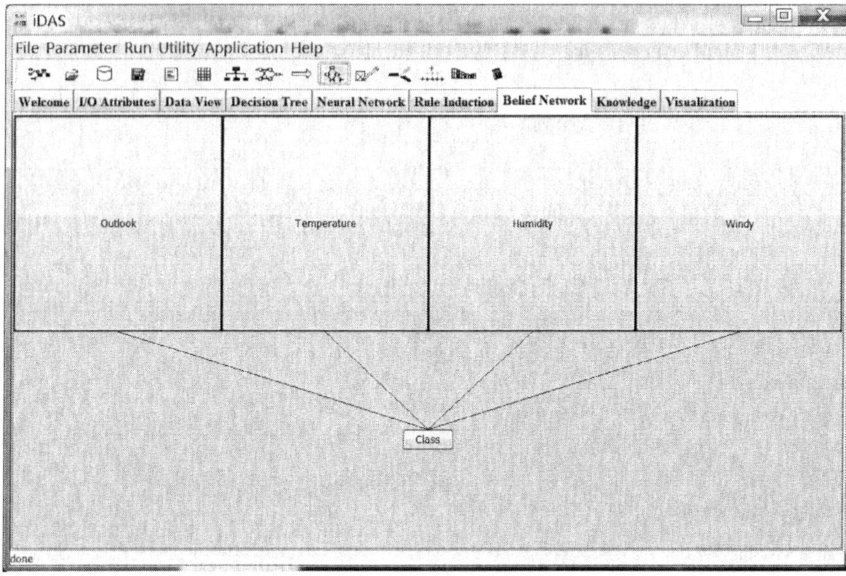

FIGURE 15.14 : iDAS generated belief network model

Now that all four models are built, the value of the output attributes can be determined based on selected values of the input attributes. Select the Knowledge tabbed pane and then select the menu Run |Make Decision to obtain an interactive input-output interface embedded within the pane as shown in FIGURE 15.15.

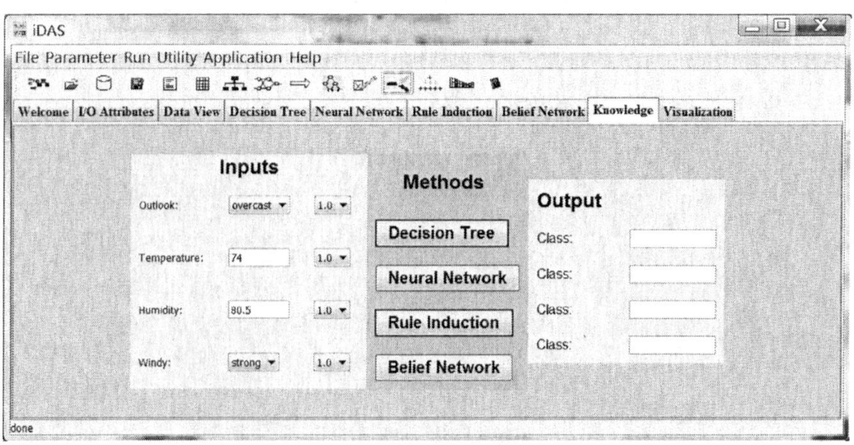

FIGURE 15.15 : Prediction by four generated models

In the input panel of the interface, select values for the input attribute. Press the buttons in the Methods panel to obtain the values of the output attributed by the four methods individually. As shown in the figure, with input values of the four attributes as overcast, 74, 80.5, and strong, respectively, the values of the output attribute by the four models will be shown in the output column.

To combine the four values of the output attribute to obtain a single overall assessment, press the Evidence Aggregation button (three layers of plus signs in the shape of a pyramid) to obtain a dialog displaying the individual and aggregated assessment results as shown in FIGURE 15.16. The overall assessment is shown in the Accumulation column.

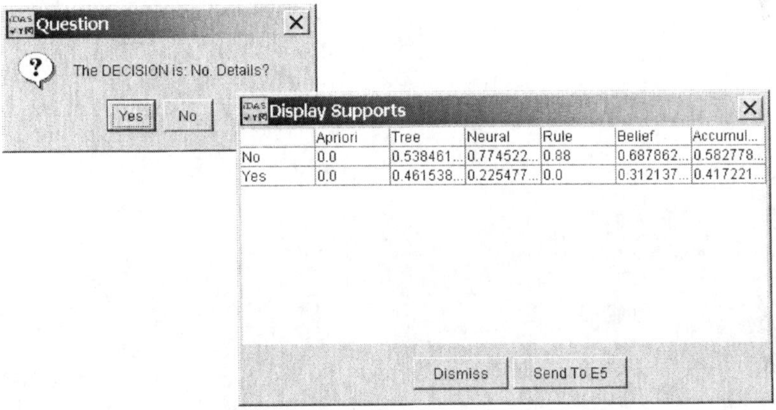

FIGURE 15.16 : Aggregation of assessments by models

To visualize the distribution of the output class for each of the input attribute values, press the Visualization tab. Get the parameter dialog window, as shown in FIGURE 15.17, by selecting the menu Parameter |Visualization. Accept the default values by pressing the OK button.

Generate the visualization by selecting the menu Run |Visualization Chart (or pressing the visualization button in the form of a bar graph). The output is shown FIGURE 15.18 in the Visualization tabbed pane. As seen in the figure, the distribution of instances among the values of the output attribute (i.e., play, don't play) is almost equal when the input value is "overcast" of the attribute Outlook, whereas this is not the case for the value "strong" of the attribute Windy.

Finally, to evaluate the performance of the four models on the test data set, press the Test button (the shape of a stylus) and the dialog window that will appear is similar to the one shown in FIGURE 15.19. For each of the methods, the dialog window shows the distribution of the test cases among correct classification (Positive), incorrect classification (Negative), and no conclusion (Unknown).

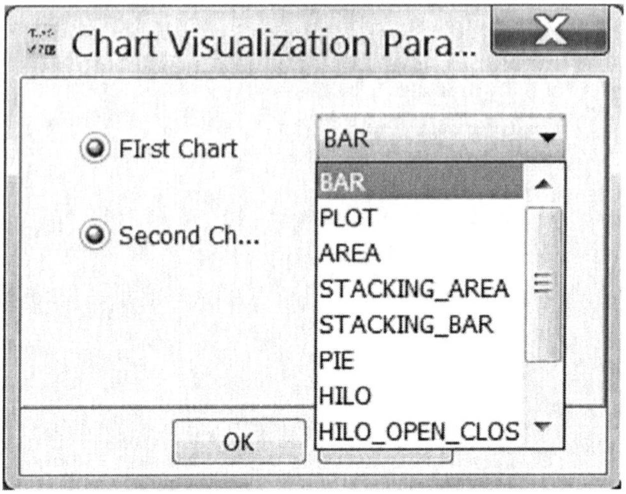

FIGURE 15.17 : Dialog for setting parameters for visualization

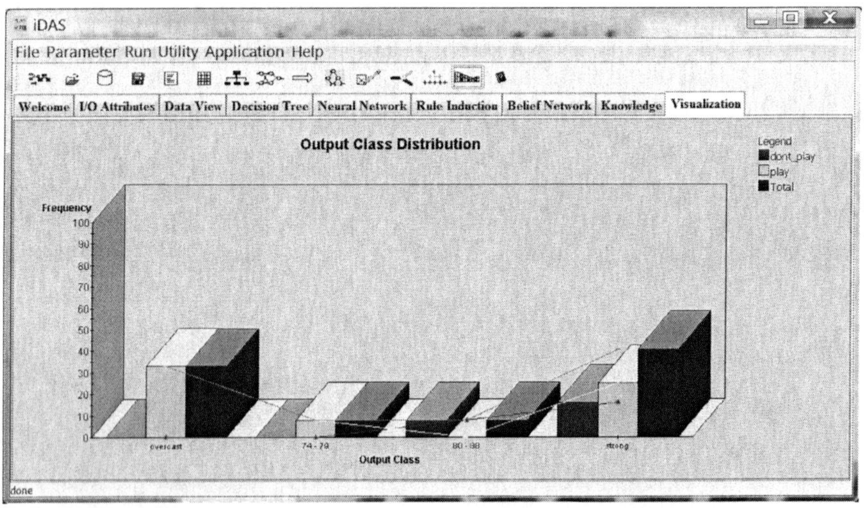

FIGURE 15.18 : iDAS visualization

15.2 ENVIRONMENT FOR 5TH GENERATION APPLICATIONS (E5)

E5 is an integrated and interactive development environment (logo is in FIGURE 15.20) written in Visual C++. It has the following three modes of operation along with several in-built ready-to-go applications:

- Rule-based expert system shell

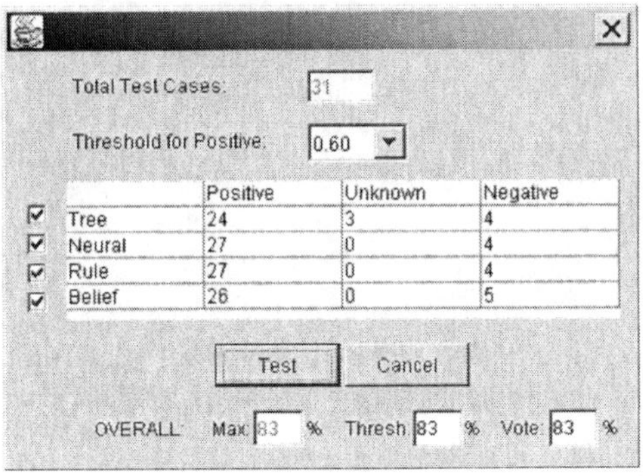

FIGURE 15.19 : Evaluation of the models

- Prolog interpreter
- Lisp interpreter

FIGURE 15.20 : E5 logo

The two interpreters allow users to develop multi-document applications with graphical user interfaces. For example, the expert system shell itself has been developed in E5 Prolog. The visual interface of E5 is shown in FIGURE 15.21. Various buttons and menu items of E5 allow invoking of the interpreters and applications, access to files, databases, and DLLs, and in-built language-specific commands to the interpreter.

As shown in FIGURE 15.22, E5 allows creation of projects and maintenance of individual files like any other integrated development environment. Users can create, open, close, save, and delete both projects and individual files for any application created in Prolog and Lisp.

15.2.1 Rule-based Expert System Shell

The expert system shell is written entirely in E5 Prolog and the interface provides all functions necessary to create and maintain a knowledge base and query it. Users can define their own operators to create a customized syntax for knowledge elements in the forms of facts and rules. The shell implements a

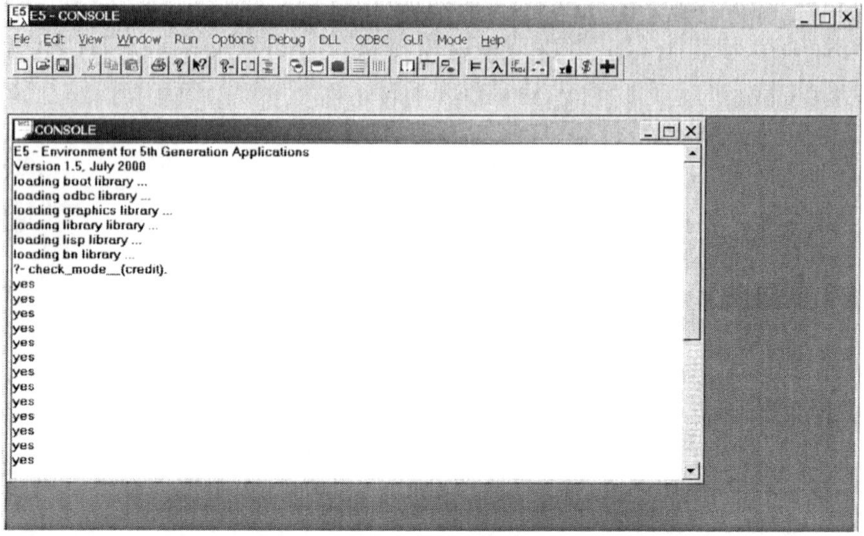

FIGURE 15.21 : E5 visual interface

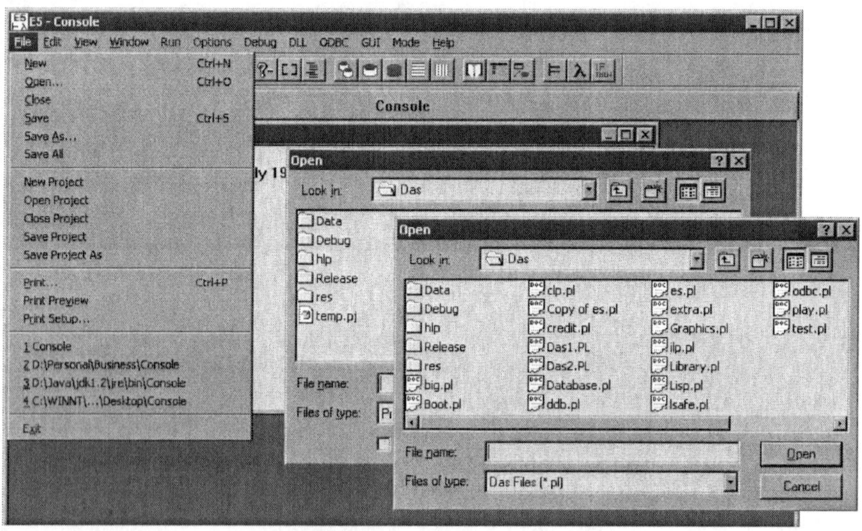

FIGURE 15.22 : E5 projects and files maintenance

backward chain reasoning with Certainty Factor as the underlying formalism for handling uncertainty. Certainty Factor has been introduced earlier in the artificial intelligence chapter. The expert systems shell is invoked by clicking the "IF-THEN" button on the E5 interface. The interface for the shell is shown in FIGURE 15.23.

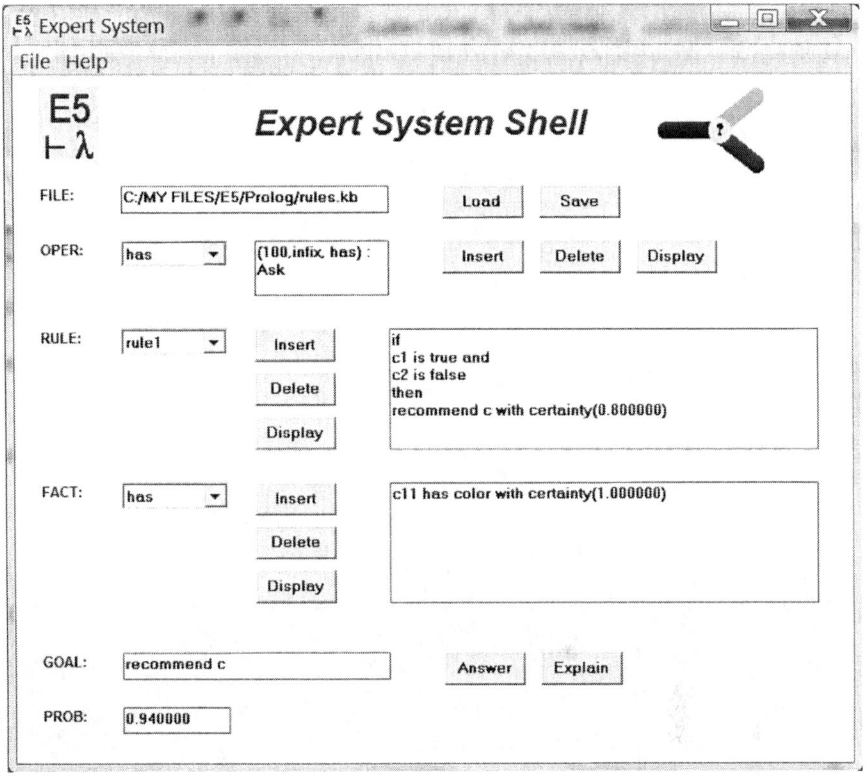

FIGURE 15.23 : E5 interface for the expert system shell

The interface accepts a file containing some knowledge base facts and rules as input and loads it into the system. An example knowledge base file is shown in FIGURE 15.24. Once the file has been loaded, individual facts, rules and operators can be viewed by selecting them from the drop-down lists.

A knowledge base typically contains a set of user-defined operators, a set of rules, and a set of facts. User-defined operators enhance the readability of knowledge base facts and rules. In FIGURE 15.24, for example, the two user-defined operators are the infix operator 'has' and the prefix operator 'recommend.' The operators 'if', 'and', 'then', 'with', and ':' are system-defined. There are three rules and three facts that are defined using these operators.

As shown in FIGURE 15.23, the query 'recommend c' has been posed to the shell and certainty is computed as 0.94. The explanation in FIGURE 15.25 says that the answer has been derived by combining answers from rule 3 and rule 1 as each of these rules has 'recommend c' in its consequent. For resolving 'c1 is true' in the antecedent of rule 1, the backward chaining process uses rule 2 since it has 'c1 is true' in its consequent. The required evidence aggregation in the process uses the certainty factor calculus.

```
operator(100, infix, has).
operator(100, prefix, recommend).
% system defined operators: if, and, then, with, ':'
rule1:
        if      c1 is true
        and     c2 is false
        then    recommend c
        with    certainty(0.8).
rule2:
        if      c11 has color
        then    c1 is true
        with    certainty(1.0).
rule3:
        if      c3 is true
        then    recommend c
        with    certainty(0.7).
fact:   c11 has color with certainty(1.0).
fact:   c2 is false with certainty(1.0).
fact:   c3 is true with certainty(1.0).
```

FIGURE 15.24 : Example knowledge base

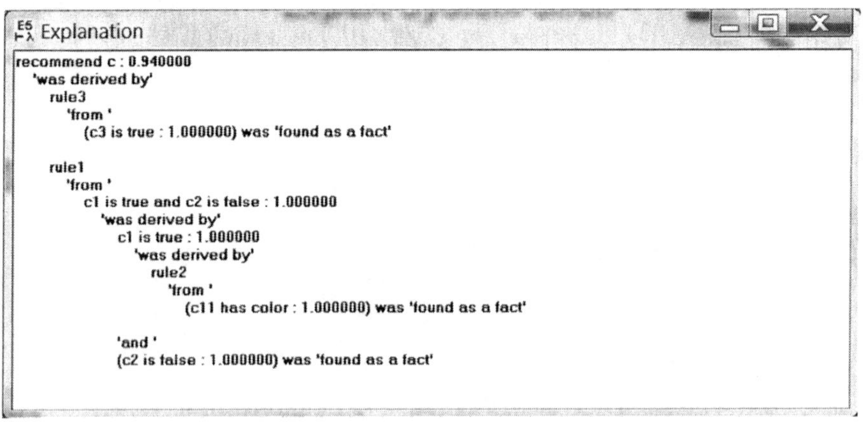

FIGURE 15.25 : Query explanation

15.2.2 Prolog Interpreter

*i*DAS offers a full implementation of ANSI Prolog and LISP. The prolog interpreter supports graphical application development and integration of ODBC-compliant data sources as facts. The interpreter has a complete debugging facility. We provide a series of self-explanatory screen shots of various functionalities of the Prolog interpreter, but users are advised to consult the manual for further information.

- Prolog interpreter and backtracking (FIGURE 15.26)
- Multi-document interface for the interpreter (FIGURE 15.27)
- Consulting files, listing predicates and facts, querying (FIGURE 15.28)
- Environment options (FIGURE 15.29)
- Debugging in E5 Prolog (FIGURE 15.30)
- Loading of Dynamic Link Library (DLL) (FIGURE 15.31)
- Open Data Base Connectivity (ODBC) dialog (FIGURE 15.32)
- Interactive creation of frame for graphical interface (FIGURE 15.33)
- Interactive creation of graphical control elements (FIGURE 15.34)
- Interactive creation of graphics (FIGURE 15.35)
- Setting up graphical environment (FIGURE 15.36)

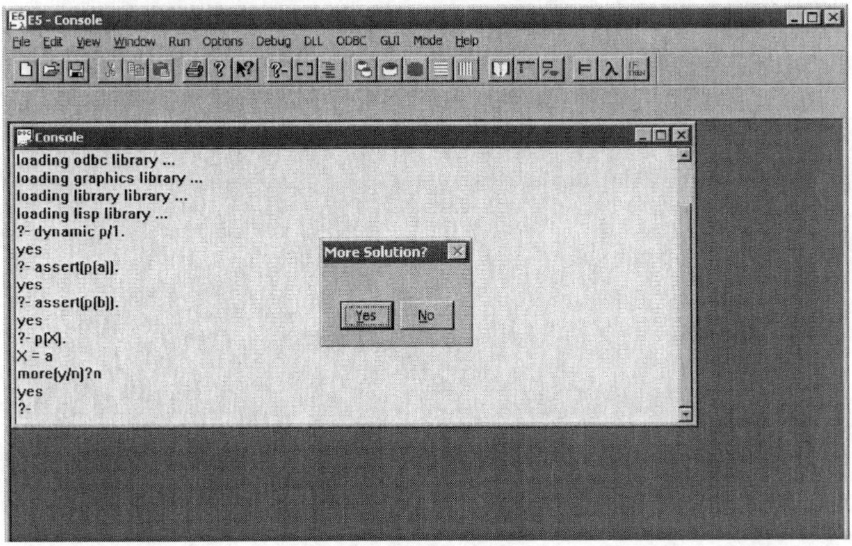

FIGURE 15.26 : E5 Prolog interpreter and backtracking

15.2.3 Lisp Interpreter

The E5 Lisp interpreter currently has a limited functionality but is envisioned to grow with future demand. The interface is shown in FIGURE 15.37.

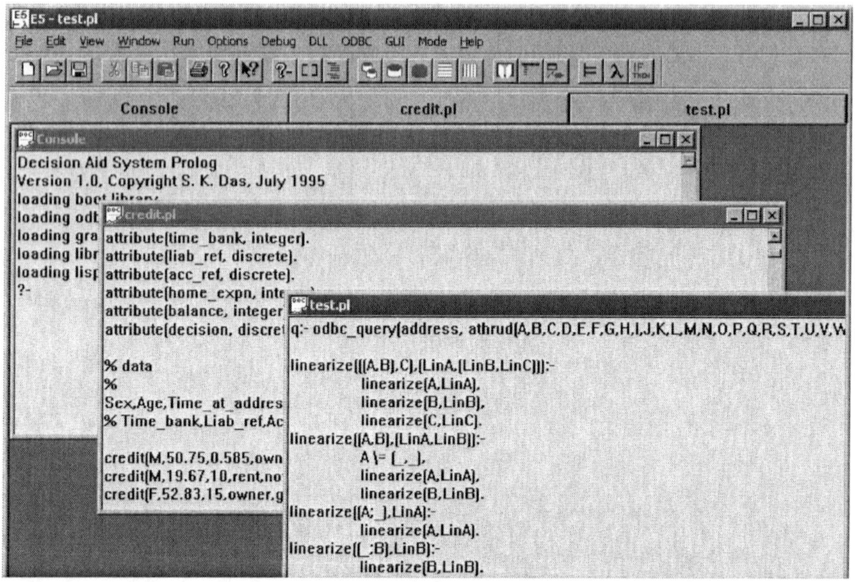

FIGURE 15.27 : E5 multi-document interface for the interpreter

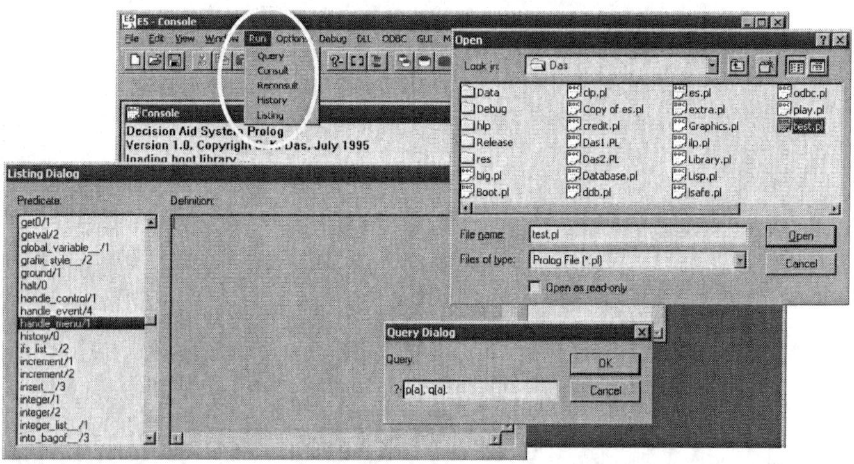

FIGURE 15.28 : Consulting files, listing predicates and facts, querying

15.3 ANALYSIS OF TEXT (ATEXT)

*a*Text is a text analytics tool (logo is in FIGURE 15.38) to automatically extract information from text corpii and to categorize text documents as described in the text analytics chapter earlier. Text processing includes tokenization, stemming, tagging, named-entity recognition, co-reference resolu-

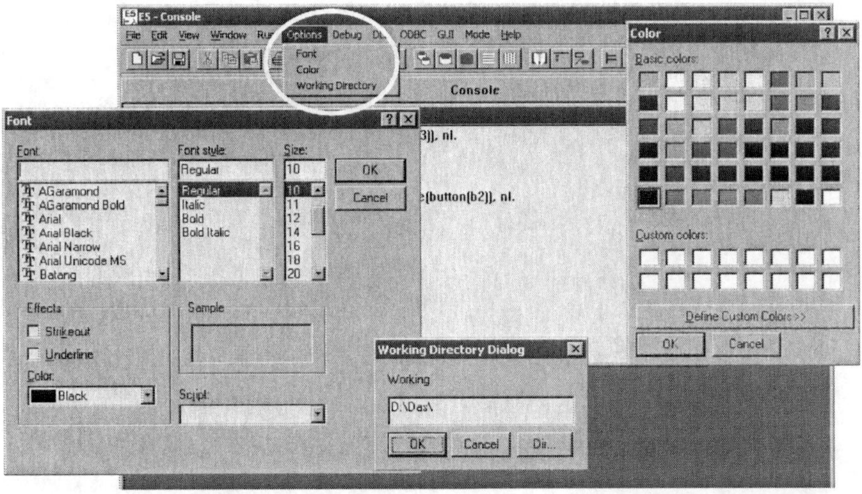

FIGURE 15.29 : Environment options

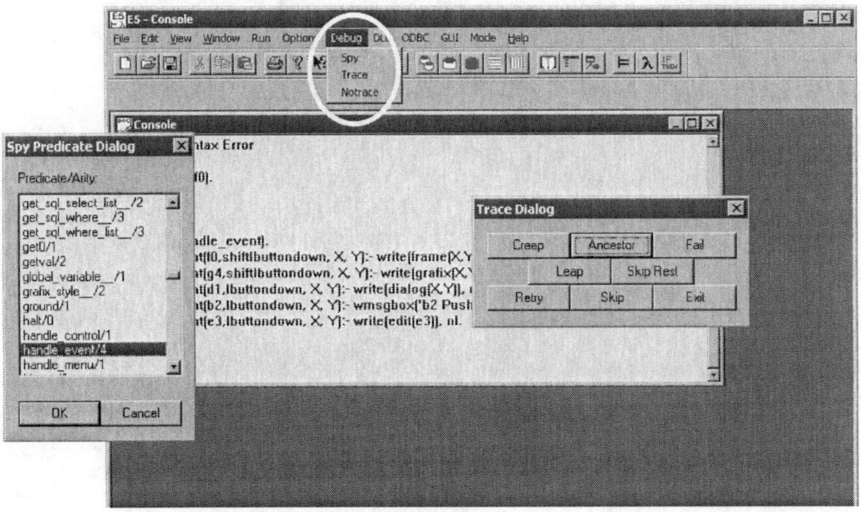

FIGURE 15.30 : Debugging in E5 Prolog

tion, and relations extraction and representation in Resource Description Format (RDF) triples via deep linguistics processing. Categorization techniques include the following mixture of supervised and unsupervised techniques:

- Naïve Bayesian Classifier (NBC)
- k-dependence NBC (kNBC)
- SVM Classifier on Fisher Kernel (FK)

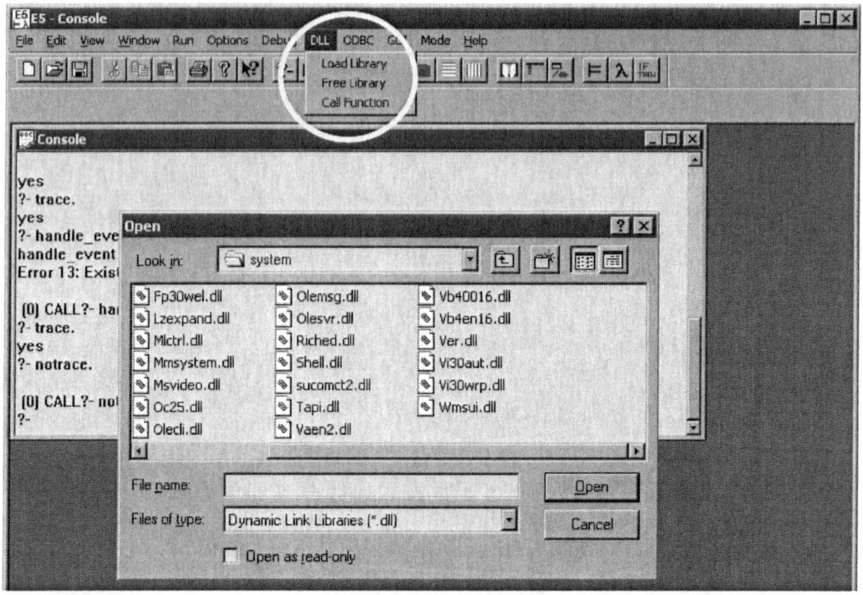

FIGURE 15.31 : Loading of Dynamic Link Library (DLL)

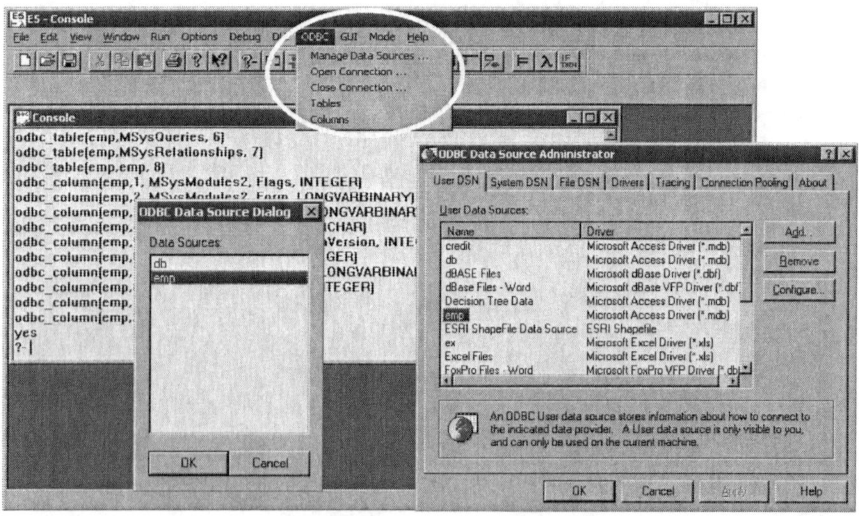

FIGURE 15.32 : Open Data Base Connectivity (ODBC) dialog

- Latent Semantic Analysis (LSA)
- Probabilistic LSA (PLSA)
- Latent Dirichlet Allocation (LDA)

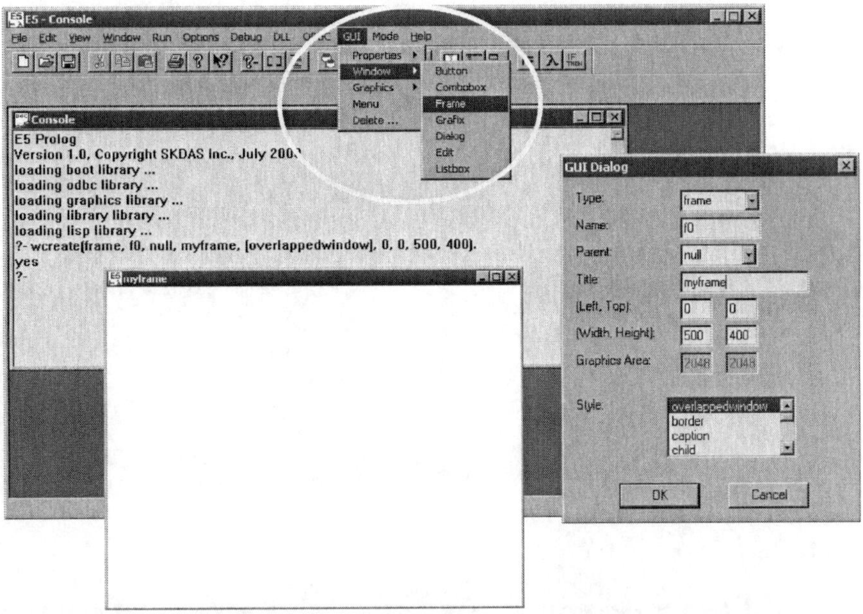

FIGURE 15.33 : Interactive creation of frame for graphical interface

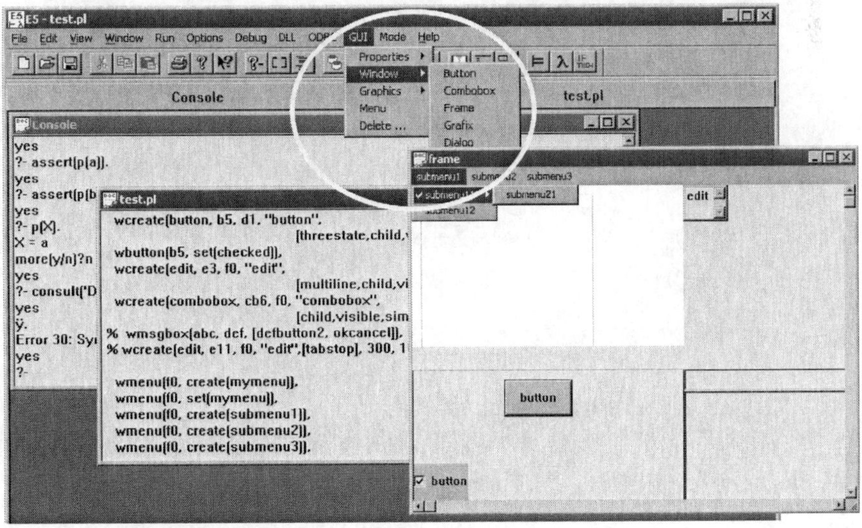

FIGURE 15.34 : Interactive creation of graphical control elements

FKs are derived from NBC and kNBC models. The main interface of aText is shown in FIGURE 15.39. The buttons on the left are for setting and running the classification and extraction methods.

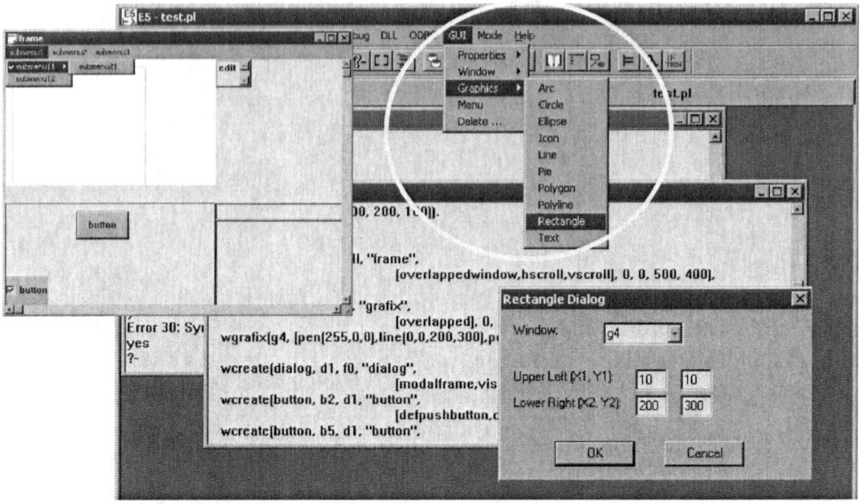

FIGURE 15.35 : Interactive creation of graphics

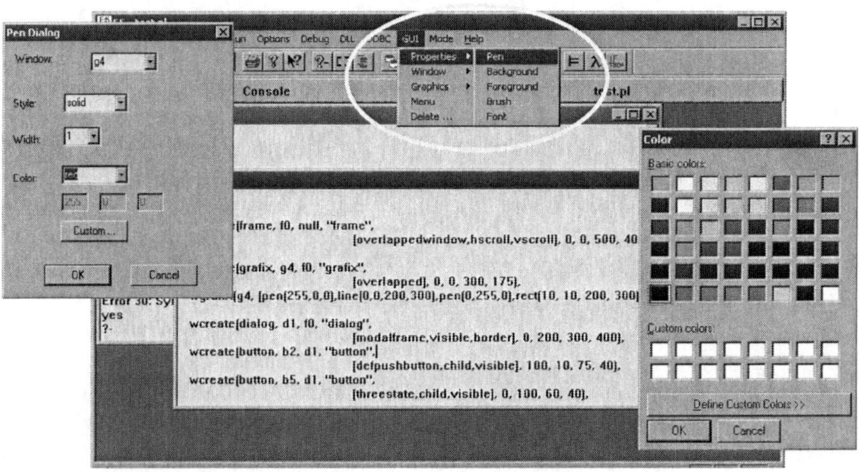

FIGURE 15.36 : Setting up graphical environment

Given a set of articles and a number N of latent topics, aText automatically classifies those documents into N topic categories. The parameters relevant to a method can be set. aText does not write anything on the local disk to save any temporary results during the running of it. The sample version comes with a set of preloaded demos. To run a demo, select the item by name under the Demo menu and then reconfigure the default parameters and run the method. To run aText on a dataset of text articles, follow these steps.

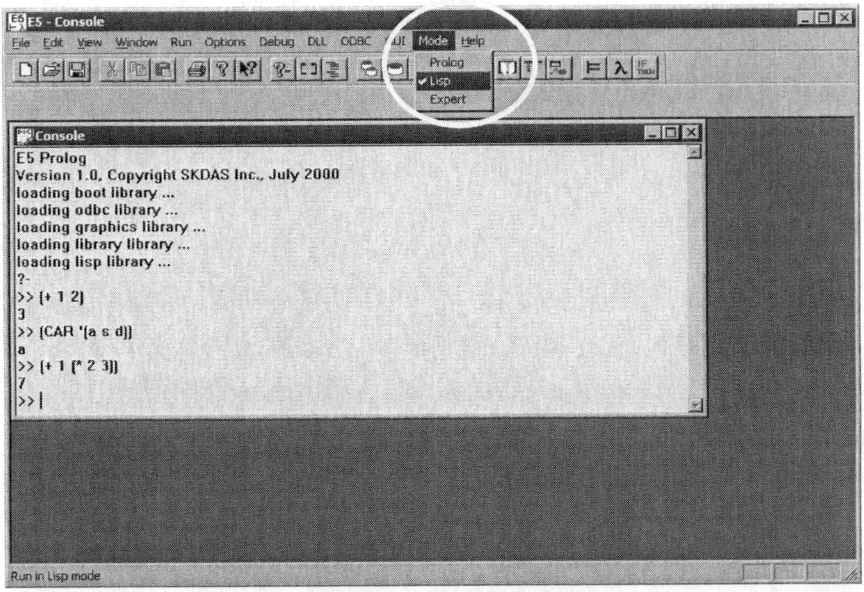

FIGURE 15.37 : Lisp interpreter

FIGURE 15.38 : aText logo

The data preparation step, input training and test articles are created and organized in a folder. The simplest approach is to create a file for each article. The file name of an article will be considered its unique identifier. NBC, kNBC and FK are supervised methods and therefore require topic names. Create a subfolder for each topic containing all the articles belonging to the topic. The subfolder names will be considered as the topic names. However, there are other ways to organize topics to input to aText:

- **Individual**: Each training/test article is a file. All the N files corresponding to N articles are placed within a folder which then becomes the input folder. The files may be organized into subfolders as needed. The file reader recursively reads all the files in a specified directory for

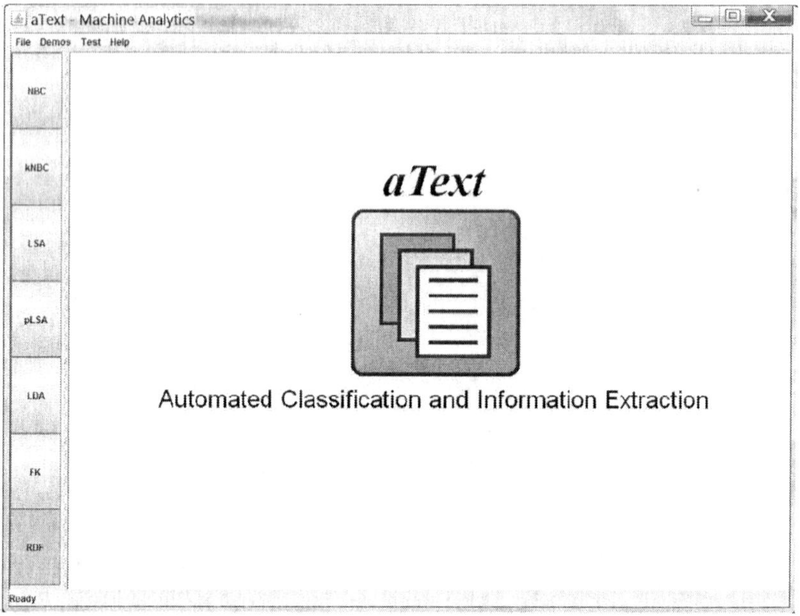

FIGURE 15.39 : aText interface

training/test articles. The full path containing the file name of an article becomes the unique identification for the article.

- **Individual Topic**: Same as Individual except the first non-empty line in each file corresponding to an article is the topic name of the article.
- **Individual Clustered**: As in the case of Individual, each training/test article is a file. In the supervised mode, the files corresponding to a specific topic are grouped together to put in a directory with the topic name. So each directory contains all the files on a specific topic. The full path containing the file name of an article becomes the unique identification for the article. If there are M topics, then M subdirectories are to be created under a directory. The name of the directory is then the input directory for training/test articles. In an unsupervised mode, files do not need to be grouped together in topics. The file reader recursively reads all the files in a specified directory for training/test articles. Here is an example folder structure:

```
[input dir]
   [topic directory 1]
      [article file 1]
      [article file 2]
      [article file 3]
```

```
    ...
[topic directory 2]
   [article file 1]
   [article file 2]
   [article file 3]
   ...
[topic directory 3]
...
```

- **Delimited**: Same as Individual except a file may contain more than one article with empty lines separating them. Any folder organization can be adopted in the input directory.
- **Delimited Topic**: Same as Individual Topic except a file may contain more than one article with empty lines separating them. Any folder organization can be adopted in the input directory.
- **Delimited Clustered**: Same as Individual Clustered except a file may contain more than one article with empty lines separating them. Any folder organization can be adopted in the input directory.
- **XML:** Not available in the demo version.
- **Custom:** Not available in the demo version.

The user can choose any of these modes after selecting the menu Mode |Input. The test records can be specified by choosing one of two options after selecting the menu Mode |Test:

- **File**: Choosing this option means test records come from files in an input directory with the same structure as the training data.
- **Sampling**: This option assumes that test records will be created by sampling a certain percentage from the training records.

Note that only the supervised methods require specification of test records. By selecting the menu Mode |Training, one of the following three training modes can be selected:

- **Supervised**: If instances are given with known labels or topics (the corresponding correct outputs) then the learning is called supervised. The methods NBC, kNBC and FK/SVM fall into this category. The rest of the methods will be disabled if this option is chosen.
- **Unsupervised learning**: If instances are without topics then the training is called unsupervised. The methods LDA, PLSA and LSA fall into this category. The rest of the methods will be disabled if this option is chosen.

- **Both**: The labeled input will be expected but the unsupervised methods will still be run by ignoring the topic names.

Once the input and test records have been prepared, they can be loaded by specifying the folder location via the selection of menu File |Open. A list of articles and corresponding stemmed versions can then be browsed as shown in FIGURE 15.40. Stemming (Frakes, 1992) is the conflation of the morphological variants of the same word (e.g., application, applied, applying) into a common stem (apply). In most cases, stemming leads to an improvement in the classification performance. *a*Text incorporates a Porter stemmer (Porter, 1980) for preprocessing text files.

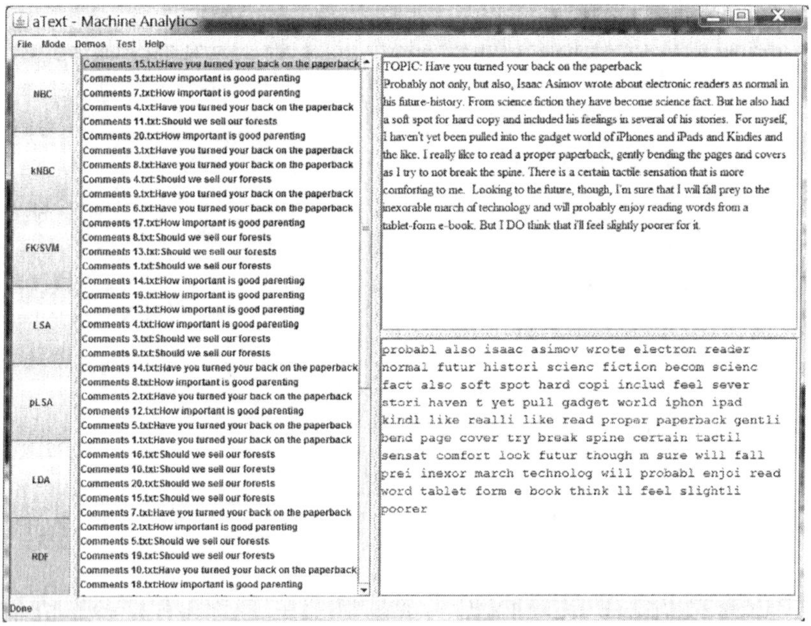

FIGURE 15.40 : Stemmed articles

Once textual records have been loaded, FIGURE 15.41 shows the extracted statistics from the loaded records, which are obtained by selecting the menu File |Param. These parameters are applicable across all the methods:

- **Number of Topics**: This parameter is the number of topics extracted by parsing the input directory. Its value depends on the input mode as follows:
  - **Individual, Delimited**: The default value is one after the input is read, and the topic name is the input folder.
  - **Individual Clustered, Delimited Clustered**: The value is the

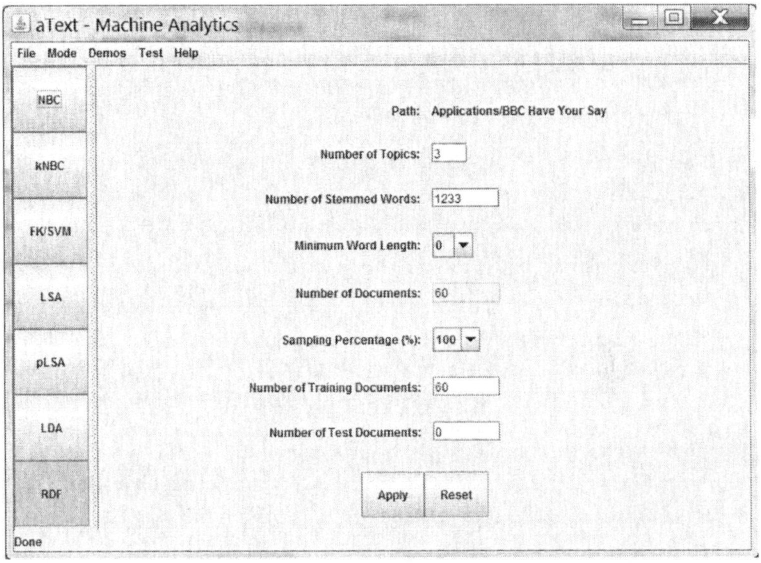

FIGURE 15.41 : Data parameter setting

number of subfolders in which the articles are organized. The topics are the subfolder names.

- **Individual Topic, Delimited Topic**: The value is the number of unique topic names extracted by parsing.

In an unsupervised mode this value can be set to the desired number of latent topics.

- **Number of Stemmed Words**: This parameter is the number of unique stemmed words obtained by parsing all the input documents. This value can be set to a smaller number to reduce the training time. The system automatically samples the required number of stemmed words based on an average tf/idf measure which keeps the most relevant words for classification.

- **Minimum Word Length**: This parameter represents the minimum length of the stemmed words kept after parsing. The default value is zero, meaning all the parsed and stemmed words are kept, but the value can be changed to another number to reduce the number of stemmed words and hence to reduce the time complexity.

- **Number of Documents**: Total number of documents read from the input directory. This parameter cannot be modified. In an unsupervised mode, all the articles read are initially training articles.

- **Sampling Percentage**: This parameter value is the percentage of documents to be considered for training. By default 100% of all the documents will be considered. Selection of another value causes a change in the field for training documents just under it.
- **Number of Training Documents**: The parameter value is the number of training documents read from the input directory. This can be set to any number, if not specified by the sampling percentage field, up to the total number of documents.
- **Number of Test Documents**: Total number of test documents is the difference between the number of documents and the number of training documents. The test documents do not contribute to the training performance and hence its value is irrelevant to the training model quality.

As mentioned, values of some of the above data parameters can be changed. For example, one can reduce the parameter value of the number of stemmed words, minimum word length, or training documents if the problem size is too large. *a*Text samples articles and words accordingly.

To run one of the six methods, push the corresponding method button displayed on the left panel (RDF is described later). A panel containing buttons and dropdown lists will appear as shown in FIGURE 15.42.

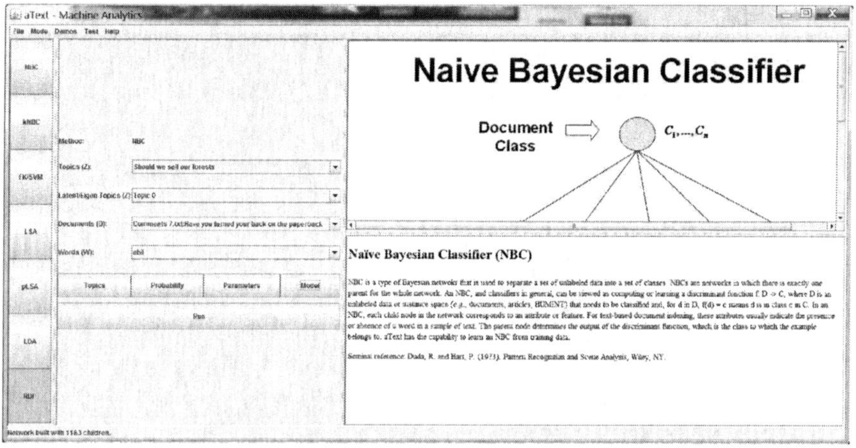

FIGURE 15.42 : Running a method

Push the Parameter button to obtain the interface for setting parameters for a selected method as shown on the rightmost panel in FIGURE 15.43.

Not all parameters are relevant to all methods. At a minimum, the number of latent topics, which is common across all the methods, must be specified. The default parameters for each method can then be changed. These parameters are explained below, but please consult individual methods for detailed explanations:

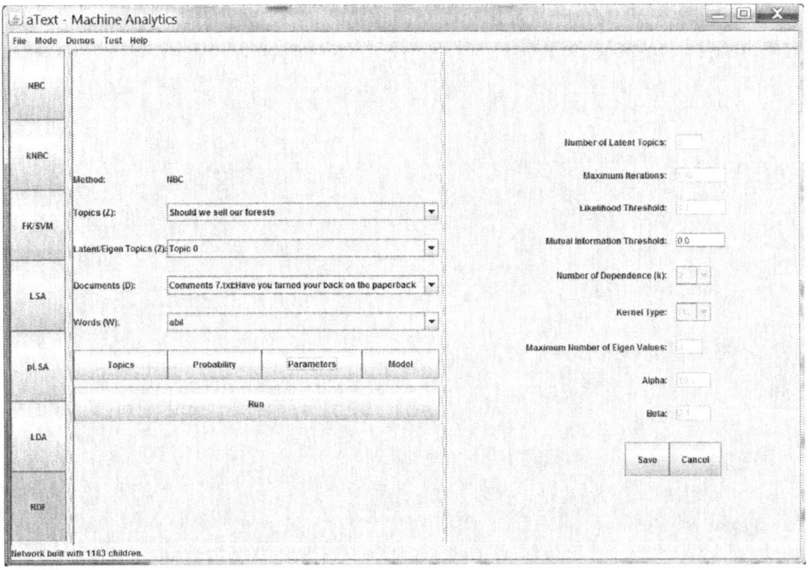

FIGURE 15.43 : Interface for setting method parameters

- **Kernel Type**: This parameter is relevant to the FK/SVM method. There are four types of kernels to choose from: 1) Linear; 2) Polynomial; 3) RBF; and 4) Sigmoid. The default is Linear.

- **Number of Dependences**: The parameter is relevant to the kNBC method. The value of k is an integer greater than equal to 0. For $k = 0$, kNBC is just NBC. The default value of k is 2.

- **Maximum Number of Eigenvalues**: This parameter is relevant to LSA. This should be the same as the number of latent topics expected.

- **Number of Latent Topics**: This value must be chosen by the user for each unsupervised method. The value represents the number of latent topics.

- **Maximum Iterations**: This parameter is relevant to the methods LSA and LDA. The value is a stopping criterion for the iterative convergence procedures employed in the Gibbs sampling and EM techniques. The selected procedure continues to loop until the specified likelihood threshold value exceeds the computed likelihood, or the number of iterations exceeds the specified number of maximum iterations, whichever of these two conditions is met first.

- **Likelihood Threshold**: This is the log likelihood threshold value as a stopping point for the iterative convergence procedures employed in

Gibbs sampling and EM techniques. The log likelihood value is the log of the products of all $p(Z|W)p(W)$ varying Z and W.

- **Mutual Information Threshold**: This parameter is relevant to the method NBC and hence also to kNBC and FK/SVM. If the mutual information between a child node representing a word and the parent node exceeds the threshold value, then the child is included in the NBC model. This means that the higher the threshold, the fewer the number of children nodes. This is a way to cut the modeling complexity without sacrificing performance.

- **Alpha**: The parameter is for the prior of document distribution in LDA. The default is 10.0.

- **Beta**: The parameter is for the prior of word distribution in LDA. The default is 0.1.

After the records are loaded, a method is selected, and corresponding parameters are set, the method can now be run by pressing the Run button. The panel at the bottom of the aText interface displays the state. The stemmed words will be divided into a number of categories (as many as the number of latent topics) and can be viewed by pressing the Topic button as shown in FIGURE 15.44. Each stemmed word is associated with the corresponding root word and its probability of belonging into the topic.

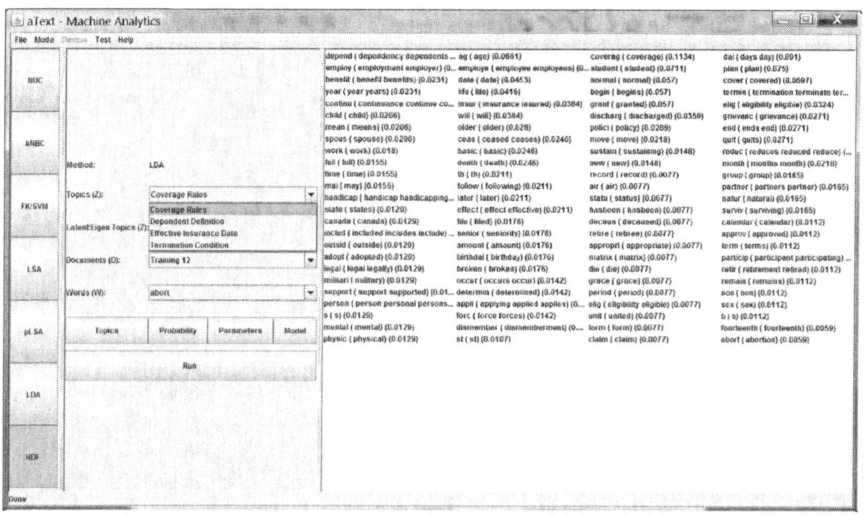

FIGURE 15.44 : Extracted topics

Various probabilities as defined for each method can be displayed as in FIGURE 15.45 by pressing the Probability button. The panel on the right displays method-specific probabilities corresponding to the selected values of topic, document and word as shown in the panel on the left.

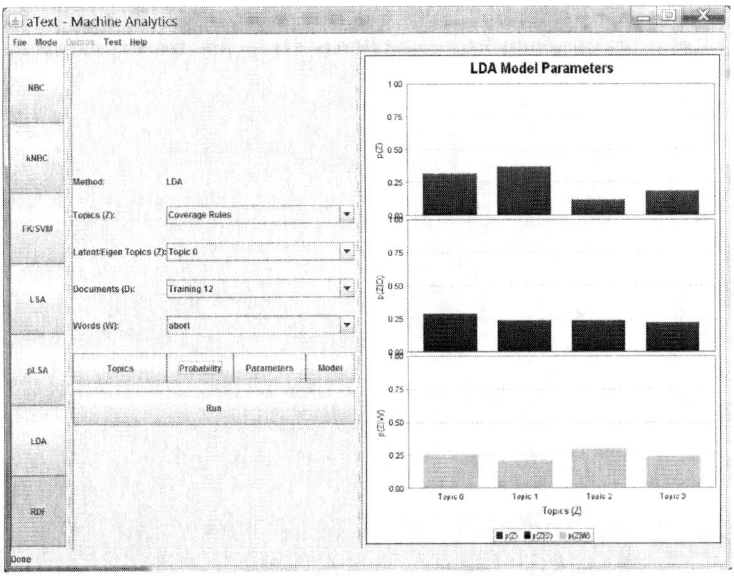

FIGURE 15.45 : Display of probabilities

A method can now be tested by selecting menu Test |Method and then the corresponding method. The topic distribution of each document (i.e., the probability of a document belonging to a topic) as determined by the method can be displayed as in FIGURE 15.46.

Finally, RDF triples from an article can be obtained by pressing the RDF button (this feature is limited in the demo version of *a*Text). A list of the articles will appear. If an article is selected from the list then the text in the article is displayed along with extracted relations from the articles as shown in FIGURE 15.47.

Only a limited number of rules for extracting relations have been incorporated into this demo version of *a*Text. Consequently, the number of extracted rules is not exhaustive in the sense that are many more relations in the text outside of the ones displayed at the lower panel.

15.4 R AND MATLAB

MATLAB (http://www.mathworks.com/products/matlab/) is a high-level language and interactive technical computing environment. The environment combines comprehensive built-in math and graphics functions with a powerful high-level language. The most basic MATLAB data structure is the matrix whose elements can be numbers, characters, Boolean values, or even other

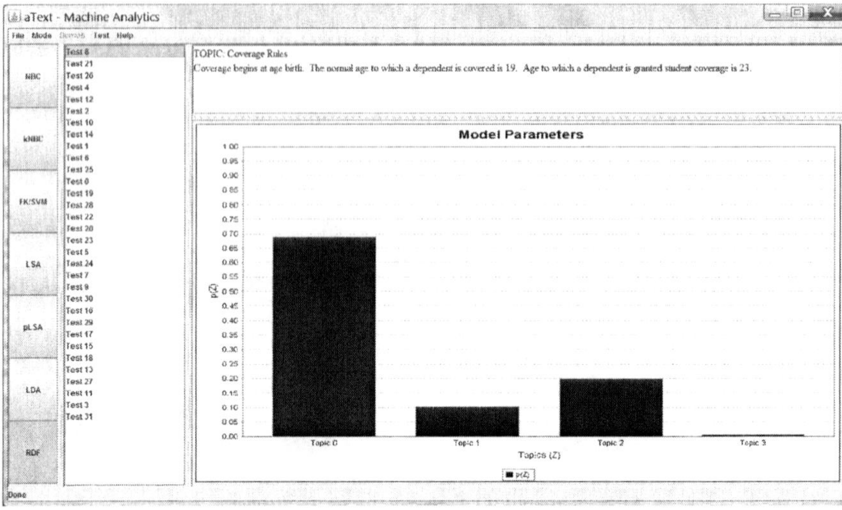

FIGURE 15.46 : Topic distribution as determined by a method

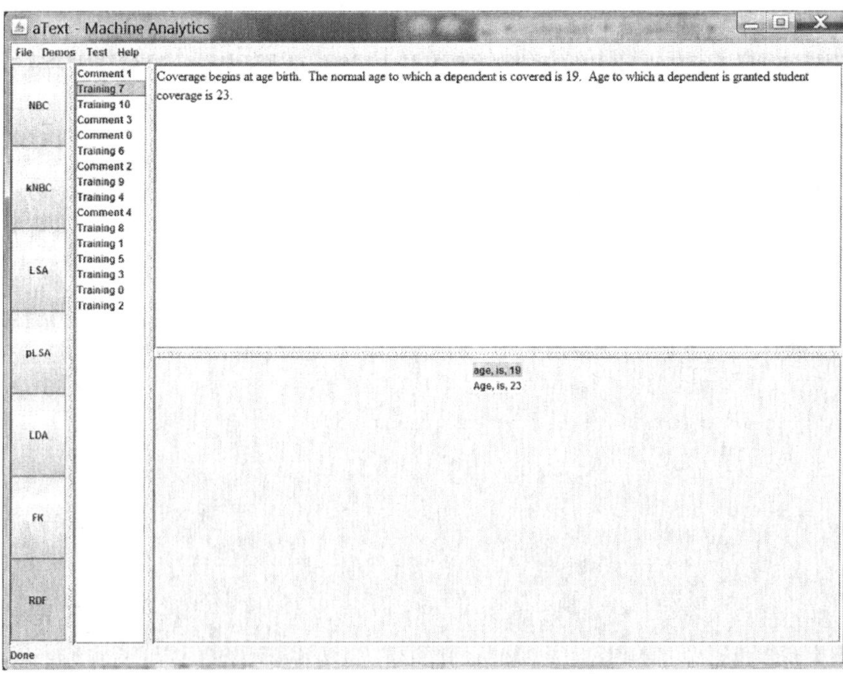

FIGURE 15.47 : Extracted RDF triples

MATLAB structure types. MATLAB provides very efficient operations on matrices, and uses two-dimensional 1-by-n matrices to store arrays of numbers as well. MATLAB also supports data structures that have more than two dimensions.

R (http://www.r-project.org/) is a free publicly available software environment for statistical computing and graphics. The basic data structure in R is the vector. Computations in R happen by evaluating functions which can be created, stored and invoked. R uses lazy evaluation by default for all arguments.

There are similarities and differences in the syntax for MATLAB and R. Appendix C contain the codes of two different Kalman filters for stock market opening price prediction as illustrated earlier in the chapter on time series modeling. The first filter is implemented in MATLAB and the second is implemented in R. If a line of code in R is not syntactically complete, the interpreter looks for that code to continue on the next line. On the other hand, MATLAB requires the line to end in "..." if the code is to be continued on the next line. Readers are encouraged to consult online manuals that are available at the product sites.

The stock price data required to run the code can be downloaded from the Yahoo! Finance site (http://finance.yahoo.com/q?s=MSFT). The data is assumed to be stored in the file "Microsoft 2012.csv." To run the MATLAB code in Appendix C, copy the code for the function "noise_cov_matrix" to a file named "noise_cov_matrix.m" and the rest of the code to the file "kalman.m," and then type "kalman" at the interpreter command prompt. It is assumed that the code and data files are in the same directory. To run the R code, copy the code to the file "kalman.r" in the same directory and then type "source("kalman.r")" at the R command prompt.

15.5 SAS AND WEKA

SAS (www.sas.com) is a leading provider of commercial statistical, clustering and data mining software packages. SAS Enterprise Guide is a point-and-click, menu- and wizard-driven tool that empowers users to analyze data and publish results. Earlier in many places in the book we have screenshots of SAS Enterprise Guide. The learning-edition version is no longer supported. A typical SAS interface performing cluster analyses is shown in FIGURE 15.48.

The panel on the right of the interface in FIGURE 15.48 displays the Project Designer, which shows a process flow for the current project, and the panel on the left displays the Project Explorer, which displays a hierarchical view of the active projects. The Project Designer shows a data and information network or grid, where a node is a data, processing, algorithm, or output type element. A data type node represents input data stored in various formats, including Excel, plain text, and ODBC-compliant data files. All or a subset of attributes in input data can be imported to the SAS format. An algorithm node allows a user to set (by double-clicking on the node) parameters relevant to the algorithm that the node represents. Various charts and statistics can then be generated as per user specifications.

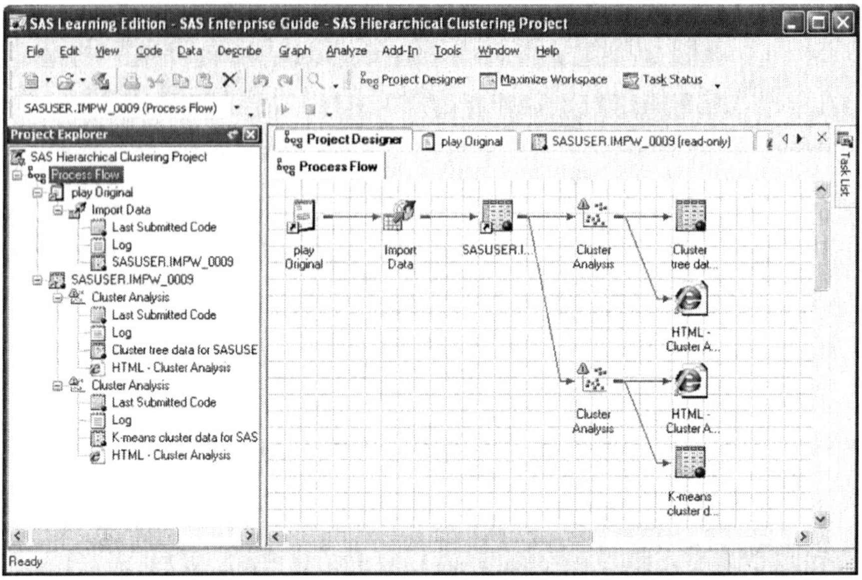

FIGURE 15.48 : SAS Visualization interface

Weka (http://www.cs.waikato.ac.nz/ml/weka/) is a machine learning tool with algorithms that can be applied directly using a visualization interface or can be called via Java code using APIs. Weka tools implement algorithms for data pre-processing, classification, regression, clustering, and association rule mining. There are four different application processing interfaces of Weka (see FIGURE 15.49):

- Explorer interface for preprocessing, attribute selection, learning, and visualization, which is like *i*DAS interface as presented above.
- Experimenter for testing and evaluating machine learning algorithms.
- KnowledgeFlow for visual design of data mining processes, which is very much like the SAS interface for modeling processes.
- Simple Command Line Interface for typing commands.

Data can be imported from a file in various formats, including ARFF (Attribute Relation File Format), CSV (Comma Separated Values in text file), and C4.5 (which is also an *i*DAS text file format that requires two separated files). Weka can also read from a URL or from an SQL database using JDBC. The ARFF representation of the play-tennis example in Appendix B is shown below.

```
@relation play-tennis
@attribute Outlook {overcast, sunny, rain}
```

FIGURE 15.49 : Weka interface

```
@attribute Temperature numeric
@attribute Humidity numeric
@attribute Windy {weak, strong}
@attribute Decision {play, dont_play}
@data
overcast,72,90,strong,play
overcast,83,78,weak,play
overcast,64,65,strong,play
overcast,81,75,weak,play
sunny,75,70,strong,play
sunny,80,90,strong,dont_play
sunny,85,85,weak,dont_play
sunny,72,95,weak,dont_play
sunny,69,70,weak,play
rain,71,80,strong,dont_play
rain,65,70,strong,dont_play
rain,75,80,weak,play
rain,68,80,weak,play
rain,70,96,weak,play
```

FIGURE 15.50 is the Weka explorer interface once the data above is loaded. The user can then select relevant input-output attributes for applying many regression, classification, and association rule-mining algorithms that Weka provides. Readers are encouraged to download and start using the tool.

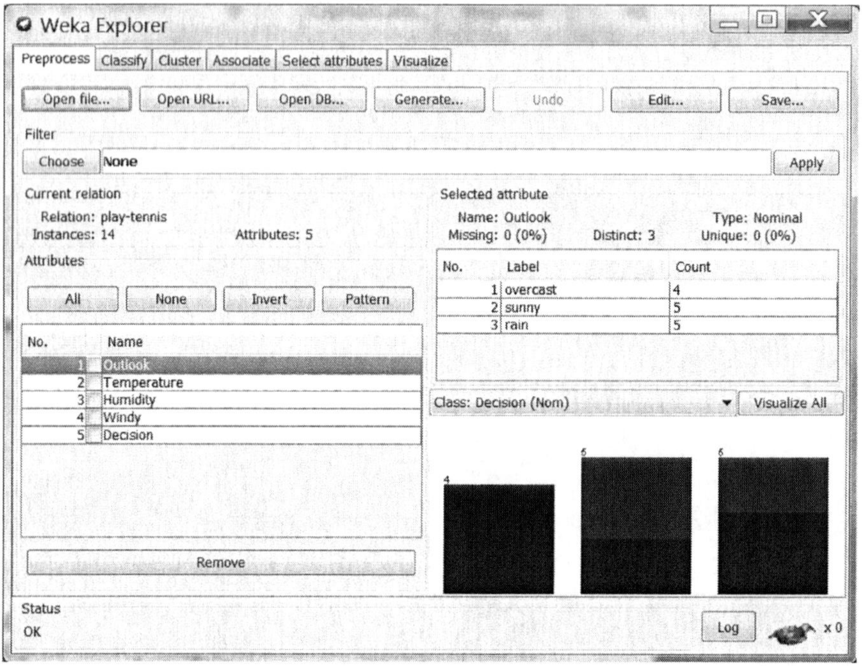

FIGURE 15.50 : Weka Explorer interface

Many of the algorithms that the Weka tool incorporates have been presented in this book, including linear and logistics regression analyses, Bayesian networks and NBC, SVM, decision trees, neural networks, kNN, k-means clustering, and so on.

CHAPTER 16

Analytics Case Studies

This chapter presents four case studies, namely, risk assessment, fraud detection, sentiment analysis, and life status estimation, based on both real and simulated datasets and events. The implementations make use of all three tools, *i*DAS, E5, and *a*Text, described in the last section. The risk assessment case study takes a hybrid model-based/machine learning approach, whereas the life status estimation case study, which is temporal in nature, is purely model-based. Many generative/discriminative models and supervised/unsupervised clustering techniques presented in this book are suitable for detecting various types of fraud, and we provide overall guidelines instead of one detailed modeling approach. The sentiment analysis case study makes use of an unstructured textual corpus of customer surveys.

16.1 RISK ASSESSMENT MODEL I3

Merriam-Webster defines risk as the "possibility of loss or injury." We are constantly exposed to risk - at work, on vacation, even at home. We try to avoid risk by choosing the best possible course of action, based primarily on our own judgments, provided by our cognitive decision-making processes. Risk assessment is the process by which individuals evaluate the potential of risk. The goal of risk assessment is to capture this mental process in order to provide individuals (who might be investment managers, investors, or health and safety directors, for example) with a rational basis for making decisions that minimize loss or injury.

Here we assess risk in three different scenarios, which we call the I3 (Institution-Industry-Individual) scenarios, as shown in FIGURE 16.1:

1. Mortgage and consumer lending to individuals by institutions
2. Individuals buying industrial stocks and bonds
3. Financial institutions providing credits to industries

In the first I3 scenario, there is an abundance of mortgage and consumer lending cases for which detailed credit histories are available. It is impossible for human loan officers to analyze the vast amount of historical data, and thus the first I3 scenario calls for a machine learning approach to evaluating mortgages and consumer lending from credit histories (Shirata, 1998; Sung et al., 1999).

The second I3 scenario is similar to the first, as there is an abundance of historical market data about stock purchases that can be analyzed via a machine learning approach.

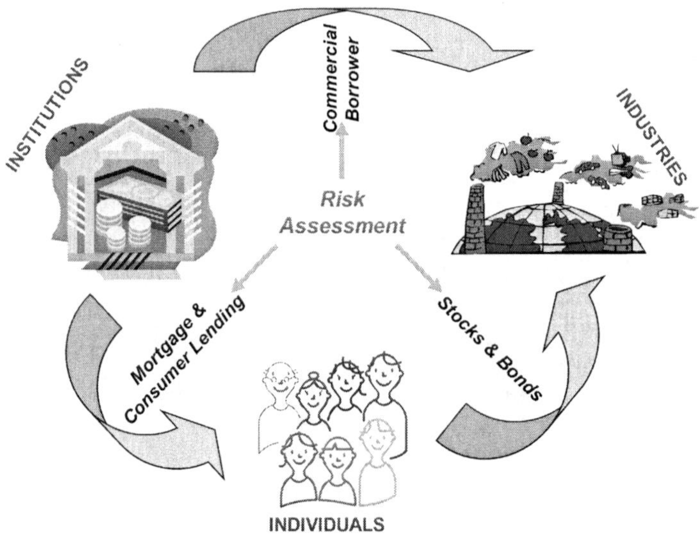

FIGURE 16.1 : I3 scenarios for credit risk assessment

In the third I3 scenario, credit risk is the possibility that a financial institution's loan portfolio will lose value if its borrowers become unable to pay back their debts. It is the largest risk faced by commercial banks, since loans and other debt instruments constitute the bulk of their assets, and large loans make up a substantial percentage of total banking assets. Data for the third I3 scenario may include only handful of large loan cases, unlike in the two other I3 scenarios. The human judgment exercised by experienced bank staff is central to the assignment of rating (Treacy and Carey, 1998). Human judgments are not always quantifiable (e.g., management ability and integrity) and hence the symbolic modeling based on knowledge from subject-matter experts. Moreover, a bank's rating systems differ significantly from those of the credit agencies, are assigned by bank personnel, and are usually not revealed to outsiders (Treacy and Carey, 1998). Hence there is a requirement for customizable systems incorporating individual experts' knowledge.

16.2 RISK ASSESSMENT IN INDIVIDUAL LENDING USING IDAS

This case study demonstrates an application of *i*DAS to determine the likelihood of eligibility for a mortgage or consumer loan based on job status, occupation, income, etc. A similar risk assessment application in the insurance domain is the analysis of demographical trends in order to help agents understand what role an individual's age, gender, occupation, etc., may play in their overall risk factor. This type of analysis can help insurers to determine premium rates more accurately.

The approach here is to create profiles of existing customers already approved for loans, and then use the created profiles for assessing the risk of loans to new customers. This application is ideal for day-to-day banking operations or for any online form-processing environment to determine eligibility within verticals such as insurance and healthcare. The case study demonstrates the successful application of traditional, well-established, and effective statistical and data mining techniques of *i*DAS, namely, decision trees, neural networks, rule induction, and Bayesian classification.

Loan applications to a financial institution (a bank or a home loan business) can be categorized into good applications and bad applications. Good applications are the applications that are worthy of receiving a loan, and bad applications are the ones that should be rejected due to the high likelihood of loan payment default. A financial institution usually employs loan officers to make credit decisions, and in many cases the process becomes purely mechanical based on some well-defined rules and policies of the institution. The loan officers gain knowledge over time, and some flexibility can be introduced to avoid rejecting genuinely good applications if their knowledge can be captured properly.

Our objective here is to determine the likelihood of eligibility based on job status, occupation, income, etc. We first create profiles or models of existing customers already approved for loans, and then use these profiles for assessing the risk of providing credit to new customers. The models are built in *i*DAS as before, using past records of customers stored in an ODBC-compliant Microsoft Access database named loan.mdb. The dialog in FIGURE 16.2 shows the loading of the schema and data from the database.

FIGURE 16.3 shows the tabbed pane with all the attributes that are automatically extracted along with their properties. The analyst may decide to choose only a subset of these attributes that are considered relevant in making loan decisions. As an example, for the set of factors relevant to loan decision, check the following five attributes as input: Res_status, Occupation, Job_status, Liab_ref, and Acc_ref. Check the attribute Decision as the output attribute. Select on the menu item File |Save Schema. FIGURE 16.4 shows the training instances in the Data View tabbed pane.

FIGURE 16.5, FIGURE 16.6, FIGURE 16.7, and FIGURE 16.8 show,

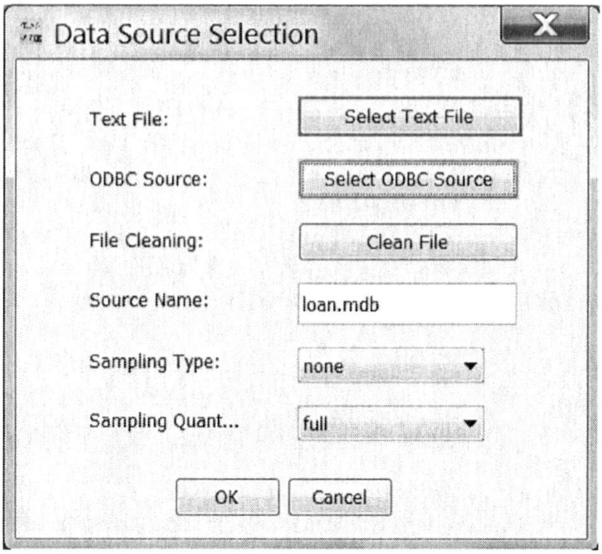

FIGURE 16.2 : Selection of the loan data source

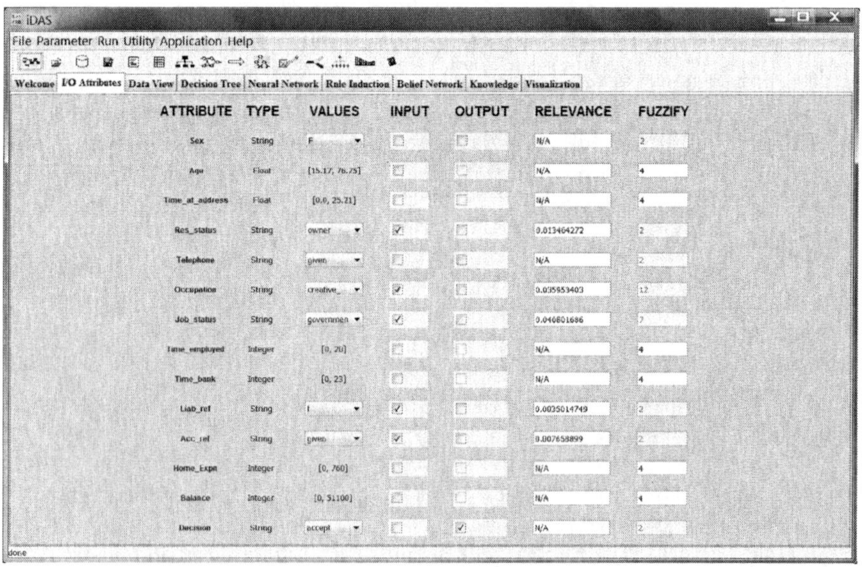

FIGURE 16.3 : Selection of relevant attributes

respectively, the output decision tree, neural network, rule induction, and Bayesian network models generated by *i*DAS running on the training data.

FIGURE 16.9 shows the interface for interactive loan decision prediction

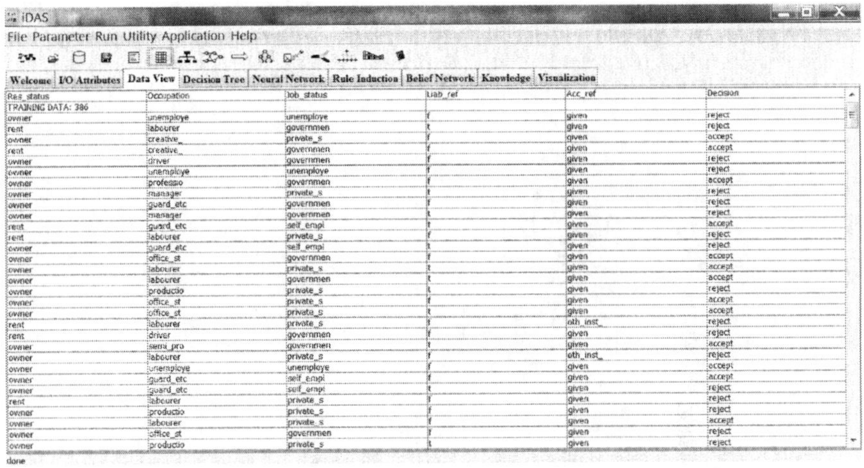

FIGURE 16.4 : View of selected historical training data

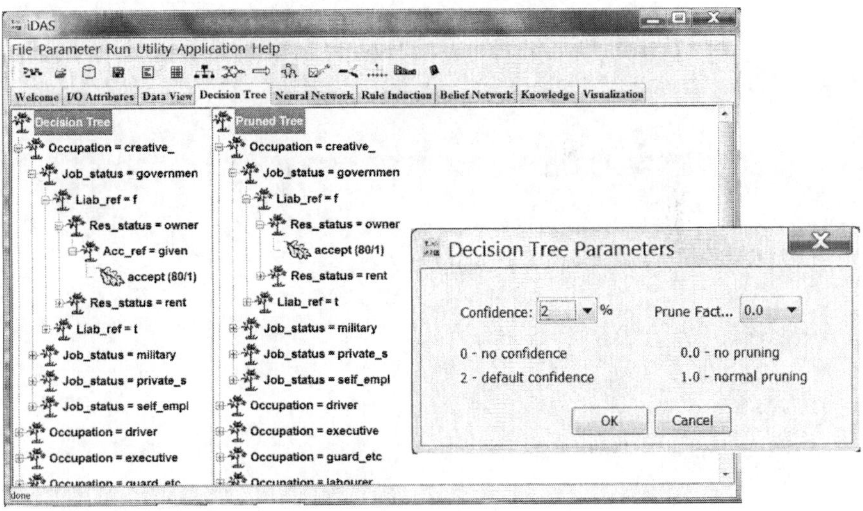

FIGURE 16.5 : Decision Tree model

given the input of an applicant. FIGURE 16.10 shows the overall decision based on an aggregation of the individual decisions.

A visualization of the distributions of the output attributes is shown in FIGURE 16.11. As shown in FIGURE 16.12, the performance on the test cases with 60% threshold is about 83%. The decision by a method is considered positive if the confidence crosses this threshold.

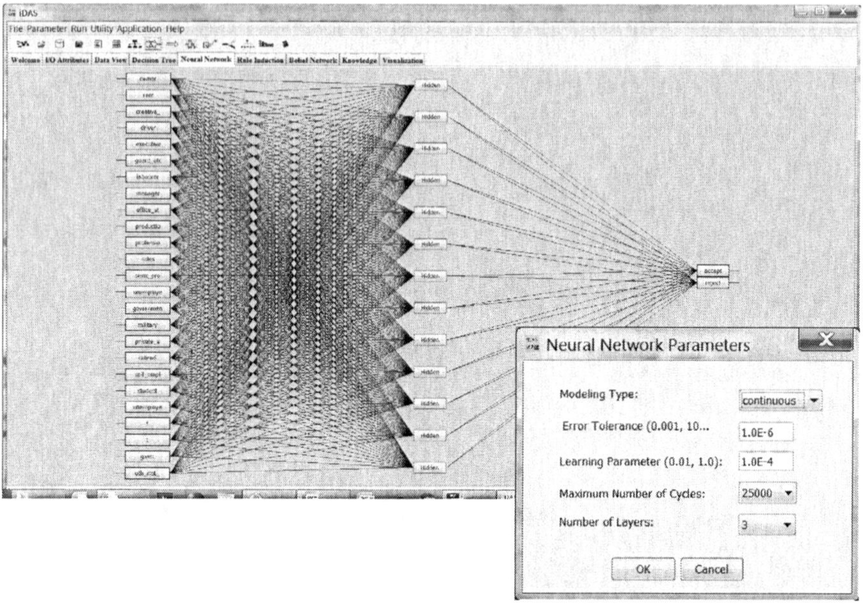

FIGURE 16.6 : Neural network model

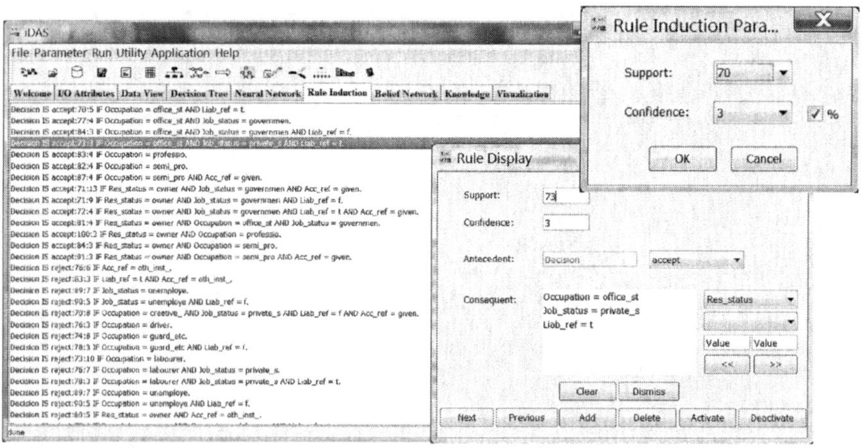

FIGURE 16.7 : Generated rules

16.3 RISK ASSESSMENT IN COMMERCIAL LENDING USING E5 AND IDAS

This case study demonstrates risk assessment in commercial lending using the tool RiskAid, which is developed within E5 and also makes use of *i*DAS. RiskAid implements a hybrid knowledge-based/data mining approach.

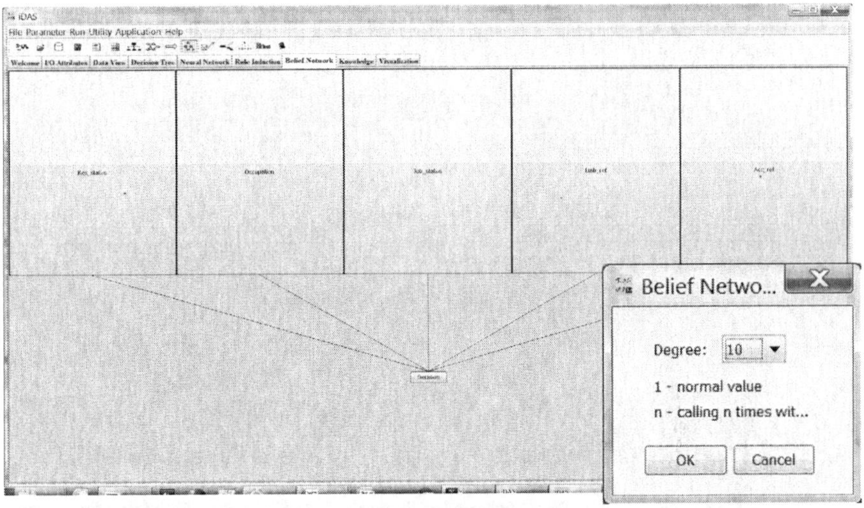

FIGURE 16.8 : Bayesian network model

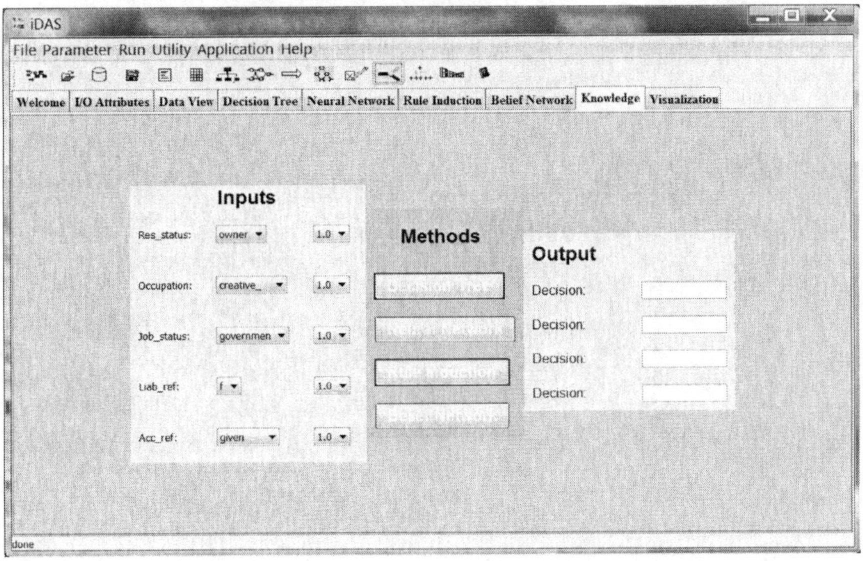

FIGURE 16.9 : Loan decision prediction by the four models

RiskAid uses *i*DAS to make decisions based on historical data, and applies the symbolic argumentation and Bayesian network technologies to process acquired subjective knowledge from experts. The overall decision is obtained by aggregating three individual output decisions.

RiskAid's approach makes subjective assessment consistent, explainable,

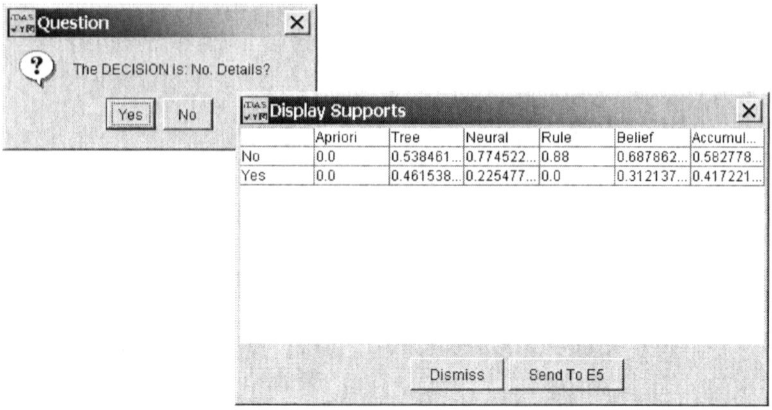

FIGURE 16.10 : Aggregation of assessments by individual models

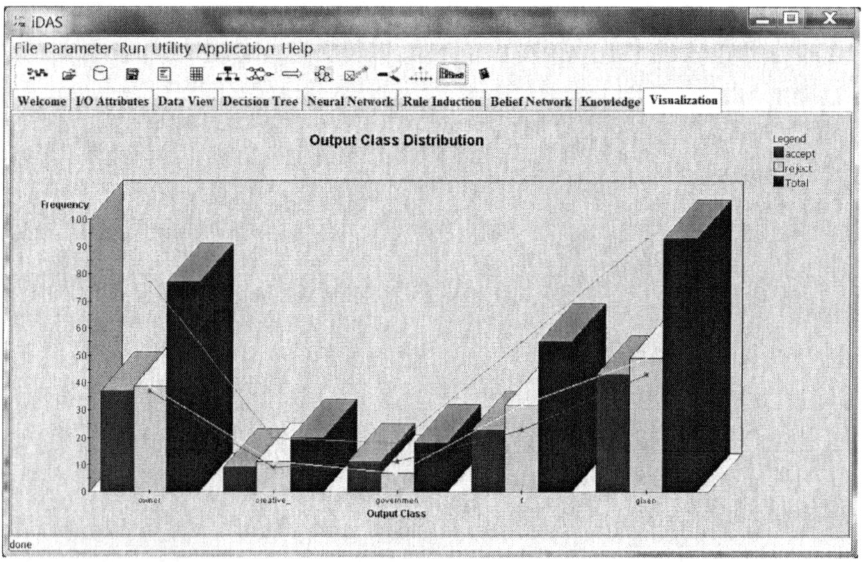

FIGURE 16.11 : Visualization of distribution of the output attributes

auditable, efficient, and extensible. It makes use of non-quantifiable subjective judgments and integrates with quantitative assessments from historical data in a mathematically well-founded manner. The approach is customizable based on specific requirements of an organization and helps with compliance with regulations (e.g., state and federal fair lending laws, Sarbanes-Oxley Act 2002).

The architecture of RiskAid is shown in FIGURE 16.13. The architecture and problem modeling methodology of RiskAid lend itself to applicability across any other domains involving risks caused by a variety of factors.

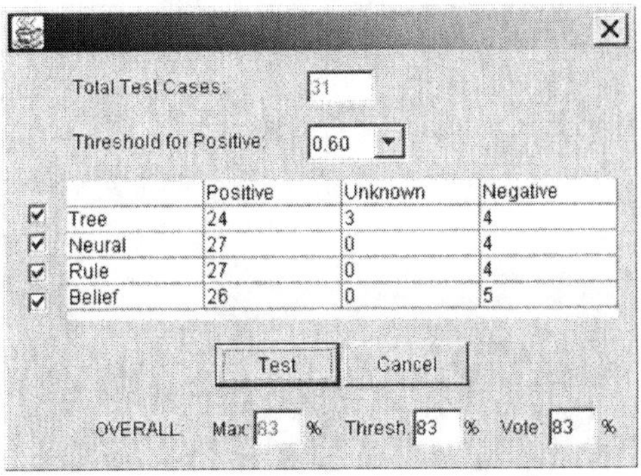

FIGURE 16.12 : Performance evaluation on test records

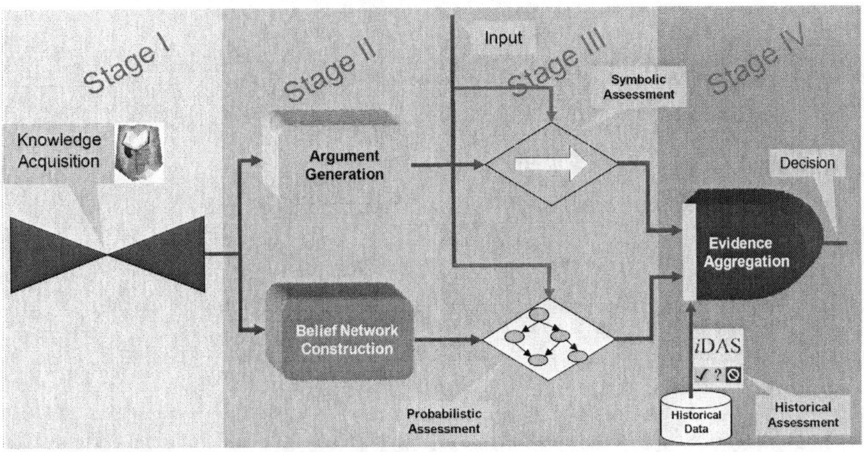

FIGURE 16.13 : RiskAid architecture

RiskAid provides an interface (FIGURE 16.14) to acquire expert knowledge to model problems and to assess risk in specific cases. An expert's knowledge is captured in terms of factors and subfactors affecting the credit risk assessment task at hand. The overall credit risk or default assessment is represented by a degree of proximity which shows the borrower's closeness to an 'ideal' form that the expert considers creditworthy. The expert establishes the ideal context by choosing the relevant factors and their degrees of relevance to the credit risk assessment.

The default set of factors can be loaded by selecting the menu File |Load Default. The interface for managing factors displaying the default set is shown in FIGURE 16.15. The degree of relevance of each factor is chosen from its drop-down menu. If a factor is not relevant to the risk assessment then Not Relevant is chosen.

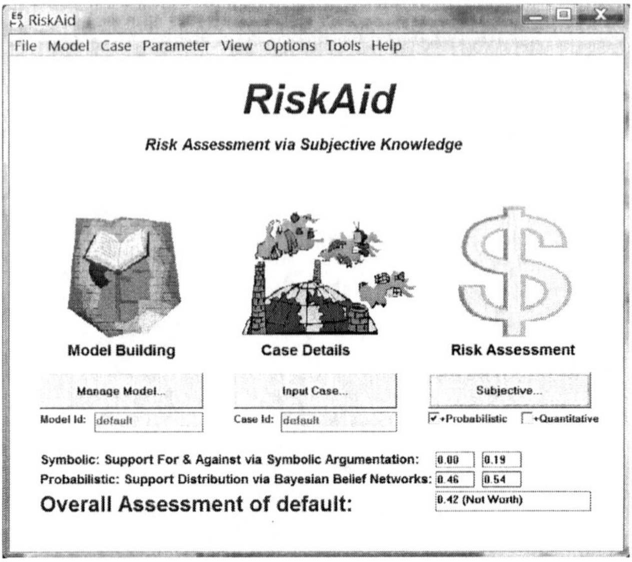

FIGURE 16.14 : RiskAid interface

The subfactor interface of each factor can be obtained by pressing its View button. FIGURE 16.16 shows the subfactors of the factor Management Organization. The following values are chosen for each subfactor:

- Subfactor name
- Degree of relevance to the risk assessment task at hand.
- Dictionary of symbolic values from which the subfactor chooses its value.
- Ideal value of the subfactor.
- Minimum value of the subfactor (can be thought of as the average).
- Unacceptable value of the subfactor.

If the value of a subfactor is equal to the value set as its minimum, it does not contribute anything to the overall score. As the score becomes higher, approaching the ideal value, the subfactor contributes positively to the overall score. On the other hand, as the score becomes lower, approaching the unacceptable value, the subfactor contributes negatively to the overall score

The case study here will show the downward trend of the overall assessment of Kmart, based on the values of some of the factors available in open source, prior to its bankruptcy declaration in early 2002. FIGURE 16.17 shows some of the important events in the history of Kmart since 2000 (except its foundation event). If an expert believes that any of the events has an effect

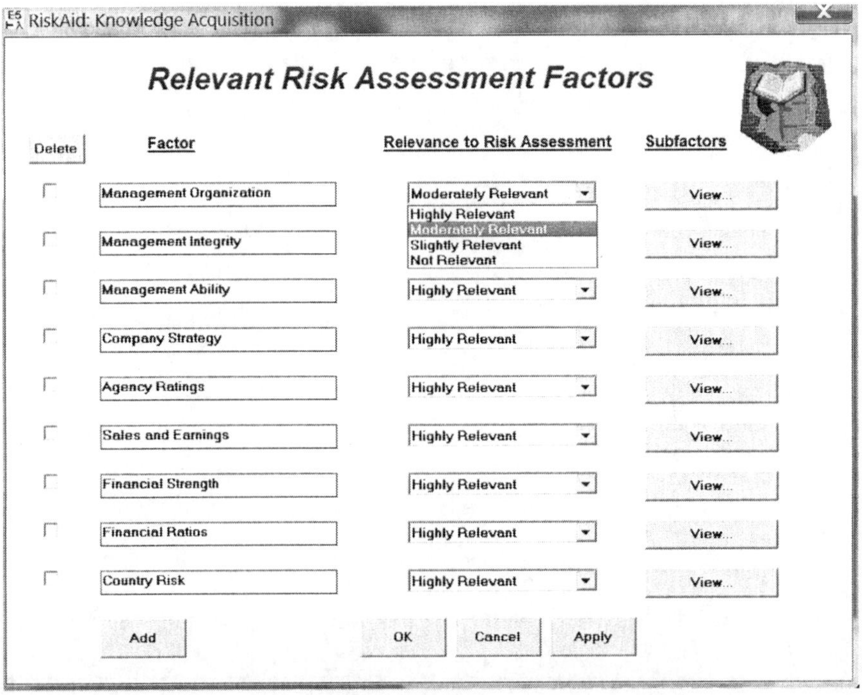

FIGURE 16.15 : Example factors for credit risk assessment

on determining the credit-worthiness of Kmart, then a factor corresponding to the event should be created by specifying its degree of relevance, dictionary from which it takes value, and the ideal, minimum and unacceptable values. For example, if the monthly sales are a relevant factor then the user defines its degree of relevance, creates an appropriate numeric dictionary (if not already in-built) by selecting the menu Tools |Construct Dictionary, and then selects the ideal, minimum and acceptable values.

Once a risk assessment model has been built, the user can provide input to the model as values of the relevant subfactors become known, to obtain the overall assessment. For example, FIGURE 16.18 shows the interface for providing input to the subfactors of the Management Organization factor.

FIGURE 16.19 shows the changing overall credit risk assessment of Kmart by RiskAid as we input the values of the subfactors in FIGURE 16.17 to the model.

The confidence on the overall assessment is boosted with the probability of Kmart heading towards bankruptcy that was computed by *i*DAS using historical bankruptcy data from the SEC. As shown in FIGURE 16.20, Bankruptcy Prediction is considered a subfactor of the Agency Ratings factor in the Kmart model. We compute this value via *i*DAS.

To run *i*DAS, we load a pre-constructed Access data source as shown

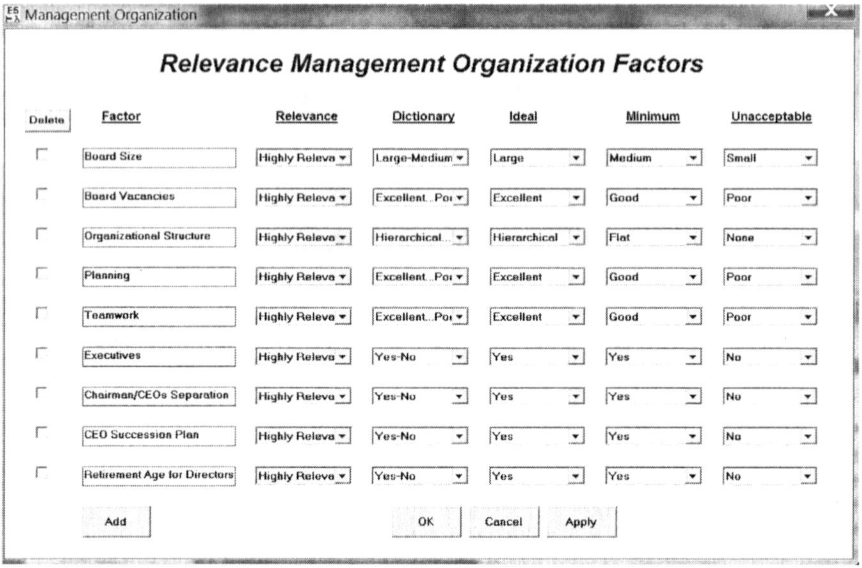

FIGURE 16.16 : Example subfactors of a factor for credit risk assessment

Date	Significant Event
1899	S. S. Kresge Co. founded (later to become Kmart)
Jan 2000	Kmart's credit rating is BB by both Moody's and S&P
May 2000	Charles C. Conaway was elected chairman and CEO
2001	72 stores close
2001	Kmart announced it would develop, produce and sell a new exclusive line of Disney children's clothing under a direct-to-retail licensing agreement
2001	Kmart announced the acquisition of BlueLight.com, the company's e-commerce subsidiary
Nov 8, 2001	October's same-store sales fall 4.4 percent
Nov 27, 2001	Kmart reports a loss of $224 million for its third quarter that ended Oct 31
Dec 14, 2001	Moody's cuts Kmart debt of $4.7 billion in bond to junk status
Jan 10, 2002	Kmart reports December same-store sales fell 1 percent
Jan 11, 2002	Moody's lowered Kmart's credit rating two notches
Jan 16, 2002	S&P dropped Kmart's corporate credit rating from a BB to B-
Jan 22, 2002	Kmart files for Chapter 11 bankruptcy protection

FIGURE 16.17 : Important events in the history of Kmart since 2000

in FIGURE 16.21. Various derived financial ratio attributes from the original SEC data is shown in FIGURE 16.22, of which only five are considered relevant to determine the likelihood of bankruptcy of Kmart by *i*DAS. Note that all of the attributes are numerical.

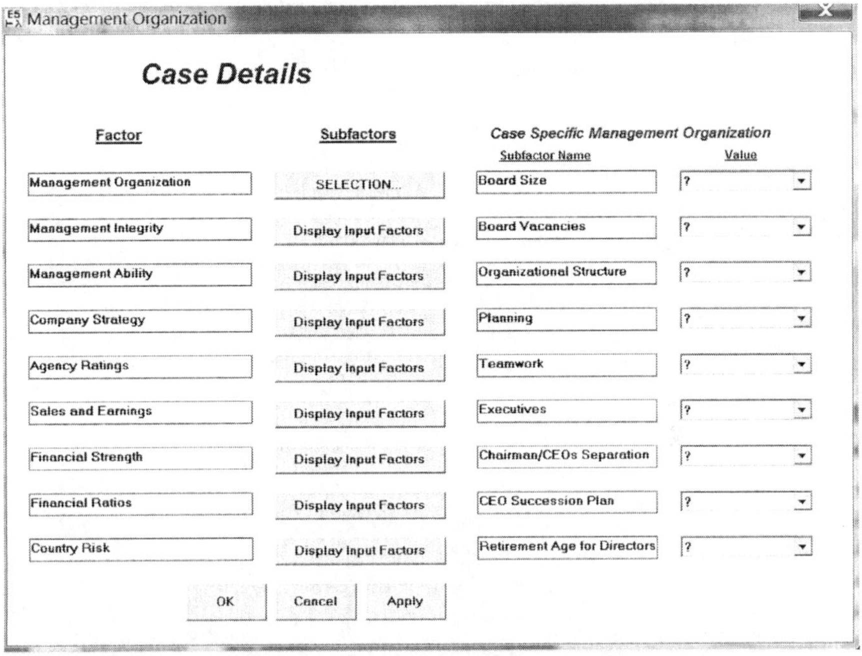

FIGURE 16.18 : Input to subfactors

Date	Event	RiskAid (E5) Factor	Assessment
1899	S. S. Kresge Co. founded	Years in Relevant Business	0.44 (Not Worth)
Jan 2000	Moody's and S&P ratings	Agency Ratings	0.72 (Moderately)
May 2000	Charles C. Conaway CEO	Management Ability	0.77 (Highly)
2001	Stores close	Company Strategy/Decrease Market Share	0.70 (Moderately)
2001	Disney agreement	Company Strategy/Joint Venture	0.77 (Highly)
2001	BlueLight.com acquisition	Company Strategy/Additional Business Acquisition	0.82 (Highly)
Nov 8, 2001	Sales fall	Sales & Earnings	0.70 (Moderately)
Nov 27, 2001	Third quarter loss	Sales & Earnings	0.58 (Slightly)
Dec 14, 2001	Moody's cuts rating	Agency Ratings	0.39 (Not Worth)
Jan 10, 2002	Sales fall	Sales & Earnings	0.39 (Not Worth)
Jan 11, 2002	Moody's lowered rating	Agency Ratings	0.31 (Not Worth)
Jan 16, 2002	S&P dropped rating	Agency Ratings	0.14 (Not Worth)
Jan 22, 2002	Files chapter 11	Financial Strengths	0.08 (Not Worth)

Subjective Factors

Instantaneous ratings by RiskAid that agencies never produce

FIGURE 16.19 : Significant events and associated factors and assessments

FIGURE 16.23 shows the bankruptcy training data loaded by *i*DAS. Some amount of data has been set aside for testing.

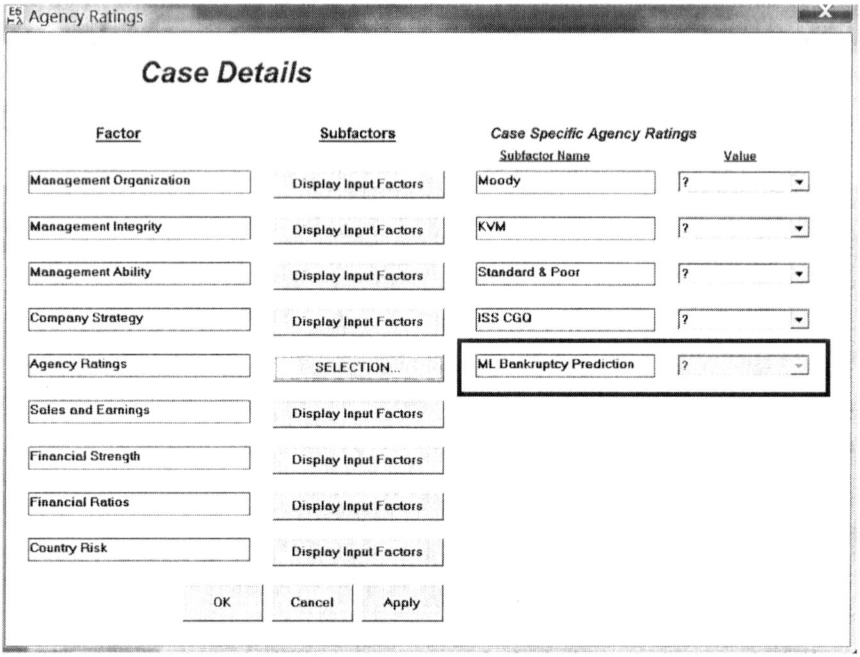

FIGURE 16.20 : Example factors and subfactors in RiskAid

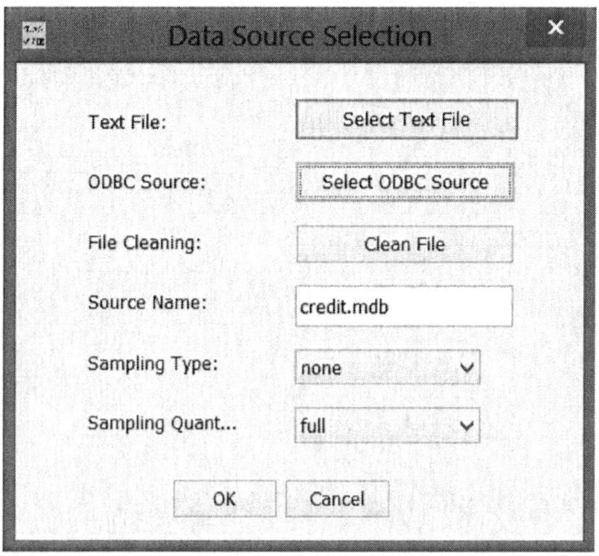

FIGURE 16.21 : Selection of data source

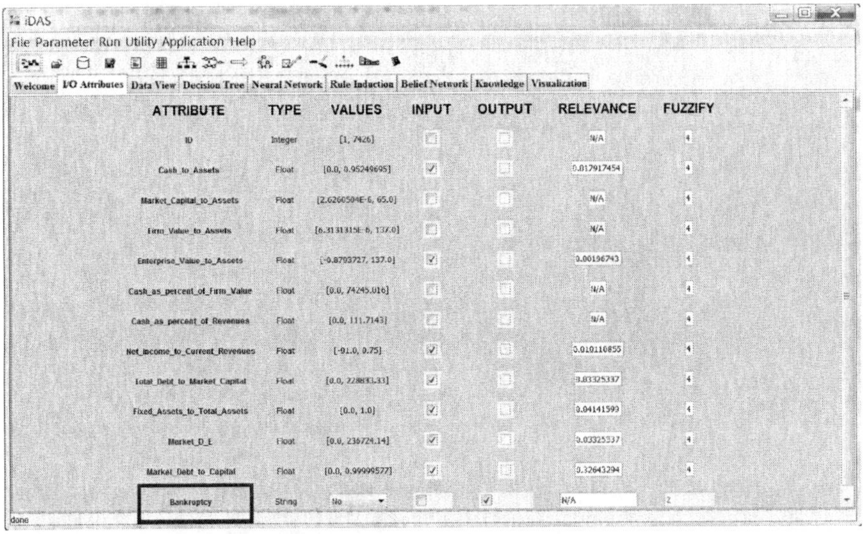

FIGURE 16.22 : SEC bankruptcy schema loaded into iDAS

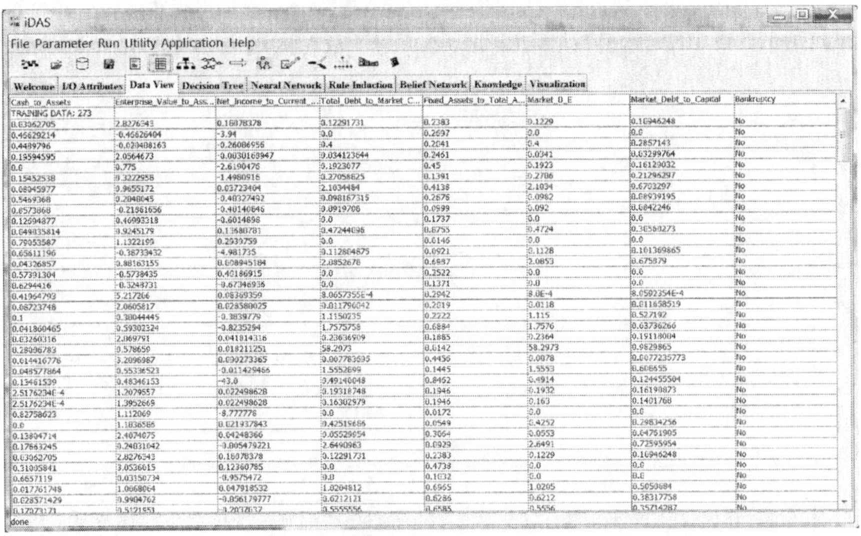

FIGURE 16.23 : SEC bankruptcy data loaded into iDAS

We then generate various models as described in the last chapter and evaluate the performance with the test data. The result is shown in FIGURE 16.24.

FIGURE 16.25 shows the values of financial ratio attributes for Kmart (in contrasted with that of Walmart) which are to be input via the Decision tabbed pane as shown in FIGURE 16.26. The pane can be filled with the

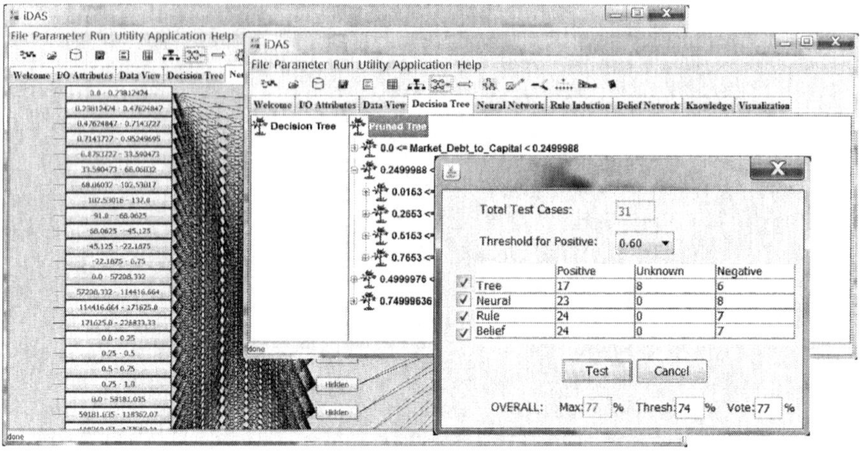

FIGURE 16.24 : Performance of the methods on the bankruptcy data

prepared input for Kmart by selecting the menu item Application |Credit |Prepare Input |Kmart. The overall assessment is also shown in the dialog of FIGURE 16.26. To incorporate the aggregated result to the overall assessment being carried out by the subjective process of RiskAid, press the Send to E5 button in the dialog.

Financial Ratios	Kmart	Walmart
Id – Ticker - Year	3845 – KMRTQ – Jan/30/2002	7169 – WMT- Jan/31/2002
Cash_to_Assets	0.087	0.026
Market_Capital_to_Assets	0.006	2.676
Firm_Value_to_Assets	0.151	2.938
Enterprise_Value_to_Assets	0.064	2.912
Cash_as_Percent_of_Firm_Value	0.577	0.009
Cash_as_Percent_of_Revenues	0.034	0.009
Net_Income_to_Current_Revenues	-0.025	0.031
Total_Debt_to_Market_Capital	14.546	0.098
Fixed_Assets_to_Total_Assets	0.431	0.548
Market_D_E	14.545	0.098
Market_Debt_to_Capital	0.550	0.089
Bankruptcy	Yes	No

FIGURE 16.25 : Comparison of the financial ratios of Kmart and Walmart

After the Send to E5 button is pressed on the dialog window shown in

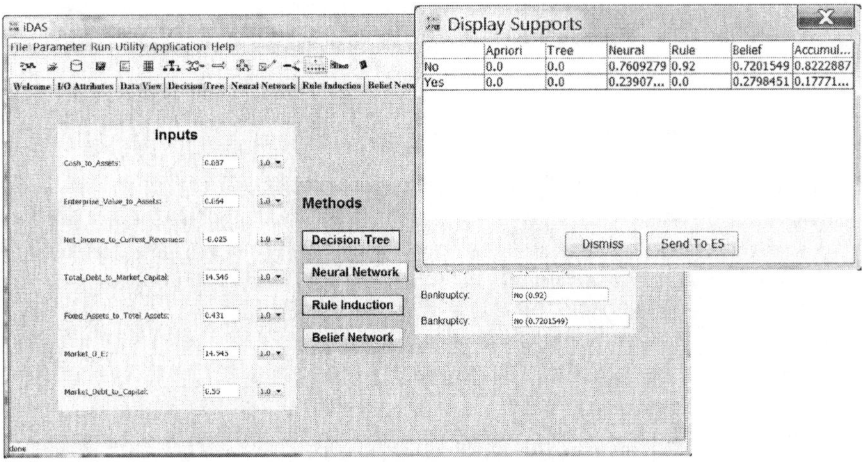

FIGURE 16.26 : Overall assessment of bankruptcy prediction by the four RiskAid quantitative generated models

FIGURE 16.26., the overall Quantitative assessment of Kmart's bankruptcy likelihood is sent to RiskAid as a message. RiskAid then incorporates this into its overall assessment using the input interface for the Agency Ratings subfactors as shown in FIGURE 16.20. The result of the overall assessment will be displayed on the RiskAid main interface shown in FIGURE 16.14.

16.4 FRAUD DETECTION

Fraud is unlawful and criminally deceptive activity intended to result in financial or personal gain at the expense of others. *Fraud detection* refers to detection of such activities occurring in commercial organizations such as banks, credit card companies, insurance agencies, cell phone companies, stock market, etc. (Chandola et al., 2009). *Fraud prevention* describes measures to stop fraud from occurring in the first place. Fraud detection comes into play once fraud prevention has failed and tries to identify a fraud as quickly as possible once it has been perpetrated (Bolton and Hand, 2002). Many types of fraud can be found in a variety of application domains:

- Credit card fraud
- Money laundering
- Insurance claim fraud
- Loan application fraud
- Insider trading

- Medical billing fraud
- Network intrusion detection
- Telecommunication fraud

Fraud detection for credit card fraud, for example, involves the process of classifying transactions into two classes – a class of legitimate and a class of fraudulent transactions. In general, the objective of fraud detection is to maximize correct predictions (i.e., true positives) and minimize incorrect predictions (i.e., false positives and missed detections) to an acceptable level of cost.

A general approach to fraud detection is to build a supervised two-class classifier where some portion (preferably half) of the training data represents normal transactions and the rest is fraudulent. Many clustering and classification technologies presented in this book are suitable for detecting fraud, including decision trees, SVM, regression analyses, and neural networks.

In some domains, fraud is quite rare, although large amounts of money may be lost from this as a result. For example, credit card fraud amounts to less than 0.05% of the total number of transactions. Hence there is an abundance of transactional data that are "normal" (i.e., not fraudulent) in comparison to fraudulent transactions. Often an approach is to build a profile of the normal behavior, which can be patterns or summary statistics for the overall population. Then we use the normal profile to detect anomalies that are observations with characteristics significantly different from the normal profile. The approach is related to building one-sided classifiers that are suitable for situations where labeled data exist for only one of the classes in a two-class problem.

The calculation of various statistical parameters such as averages, quantiles, probability distributions, and so on, can also be considered as building normal models of observations. For example, in terms of building normal models representing a customer profile, the averages may include average spending per months, average length of call, and average number of calls per month. Customer profile may also include the types of items usually purchased and their purchase locations. If an observed transaction falls outside the accepted level of significance then it is considered to be an outlier and is suspected to be fraud. Many outlier detection technologies (Hodge and Austin, 2004) are pertinent for fraud detection. Anomaly detection (Chandola et al., 2009) is a closely related topic area which refers to the problem of finding patterns in data that do not conform to expected behavior.

Credit card fraud is divided into two types – offline fraud and online fraud. Offline fraud is committed by using a stolen physical card at storefront or call center. Online fraud is committed via web and phone shopping. In online fraud only the card's details are needed, and a manual signature and card imprint are not required at the time of purchase. One effective way to detect fraud is to build a profile of usage patterns for each user. A profile can be a set of simple if-then-type rules which are triggered when certain conditions are met. Such conditions include when a transaction exceeds a certain amount, a series of frequent small transactions, and the purchase of an unusual item or a purchase at an unusual location.

Money-laundering is a way to "cleanse" or validate money that was earned through criminal activities, typically via three phases – placement, layering and integration. Money-laundering actions can be inspected at two levels. At the individual account or person-level inspection, the transactions of an account or person are examined to identify irregularities. Rare transactional patterns are categorized as anomalous in order to recognize money-laundering. Hence the fraud detection problem can be reduced to an outlier detection problem or a two-class pattern classification problem. Often it is also necessary to detect a series of similar transactions, which is a temporal pattern classification problem, to detect money-laundering.

At a network level inspection for money-laundering, all accounts and customers are looked at to identify suspicious loops. Link analysis is a technique to explore associations among a large number of objects of different types. In the case of money-laundering, these objects might include people, bank accounts, businesses, wire transfers, and cash deposits. Exploring relationships among these different objects helps indicate networks of activity, both legal and illegal. Link analysis can indicate where to focus investigations. A detailed account of link analysis is out of the scope of this book.

Fraudulent auto insurance claims involve staged accidents and injuries, fake car repairs, and fake driver and passenger medical treatment. For detecting application fraud, two different situations have to be classified. When applications come from one user with the same details, it is classified as "duplicates," and when applications come from different individuals with similar details, it is classified as "identity fraudsters." Machine learning techniques can help make distinctions between legitimate and fraudulent applications and insurance claims in the auto, property and medical domains. The problem of detecting unauthorized access in computer networks or an attack on a network is in the cyber security domain. Telecommunication fraud detection involves finding fraudulent usage of cellular telephones based on profiling customer behavior.

In summary, if there is an abundance of data for both genuine and fraudulent transactions, a supervised approach to classification and clustering is applicable. The suitability of a specific supervised approach depends on the type, volume, and dimensionality of data. If there is not enough representative data available for fraudulent transactions, an outlier or anomaly detection approach is most suitable. A semi-supervised approach is appropriate in a situation when there is a dearth of representative fraudulent transactions. The classifier is adjusted as more and more fraudulent transactions become available. Note that an unsupervised approach is suitable when the nature of fraudulent transactions is not known in advance.

16.5 SENTIMENT ANALYSIS USING ATEXT

Sentiment analysis involves classification of opinions expressed by consumers and customers. The classification is supervised when training data is available, otherwise it is unsupervised. This case study demonstrates how *a*Text can be applied to a popular text corpus, TripAdvisor (Baccianella et al., 2009), to analyze consumer sentiments (Das, 2013). The case study demonstrates the application of the powerful supervised and unsupervised classification techniques of *a*Text. Little or no manual effort is required to prepare the text corpus before processing, except for an automated stemming (Frakes, 1992). We show a comparable and sometimes improved performance over the baseline discriminative SVM-based classification.

16.5.1 Text Corpus Classification

TripAdvisor (2007) corpus has been built by Baccianella et al. (2009), consisting of 15,763 hotel reviews from the TripAdvisor website[1], a popular site to review tourism-related activities. Each review is labeled with a score of one to five "stars." FIGURE 16.27 shows three samples with 5, 3 and 1 stars:

203223_3024338 ***Fantastic*** For the money the location is fantastic It is about 300 yards from a metro station From the hotel you can walk to the colosseum you can practically see it when you leave the hotel Yes the rooms are small but the hotel has ***great*** character I would definitely stay there again and would recommend it to others _PROS_Nothing _CONS_Nothing **5**
274573_3994017 Perfectly ***okay*** The Hotel Suisse was just okay Daniela was very helpful but the other people at the front desk were not We found their attitude less than desirable The rooms were clean and spacious Breakfast delivered to the room was a bit ackward but certainly doable The location to the Spanish steps was quite helpful easy access to the Metro and a taxi stand They also asked for 1 night stay in cash which we thought was odd _PROS_Nothing _CONS_Nothing **3**
253154_3638452 ***Terrible*** experience The twin room booked turned out to be a single with single bed and camp bed By our third night we had an ant infestation which the management were unwilling to deal with Eventually I had to spray the room and wait till 1 30am before being able to return We left _PROS_Nothing _CONS_Nothing **1**

FIGURE 16.27 : Example TripAdvisor Reviews

Note the usage of highly discriminatory words like "fantastic," "okay," and "terrible" in coherence with the degree of ratings. We have used 10,508 doc-

[1]http://www.tripadvisor.com

uments for training and used 5,255 documents for testing. The training set contains 23,341 unique stemmed words.

Number of articles (or reviews): 15763
Number of stemmed words: 23341
Number of topics: 5
Total number of training articles: 10508
Total number of test articles: 5255

The distribution of labels, as shown in TABLE 16.1, is highly skewed, since 44% of all the training articles have a global score of 5 stars, 34.8% a global score of 4 stars, 10% 3 stars, 7.1% 2 stars and only 4.1% 1 star. Test articles have a similar distribution.

TABLE 16.1: : Distribution of TripAdvisor training articles

Topic	#
5	4630
4	3643
3	1052
2	752
1	431

This kind of skewed distribution tends to make the classification task for the least frequent scores difficult. FIGURE 16.28 shows a fragment of the learned kNBC for the TripAdvisor corpus showing dependencies among stemmed words. As expected, the word "terrible" has dependence on words such as "rude" and "worst" and the word "comfort" has dependence on words such as "clean" and "walk."

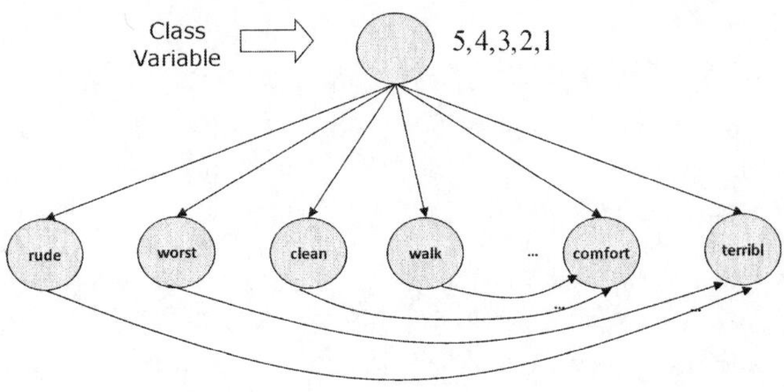

FIGURE 16.28 : Example kNBC ($k = 2$) dependencies for the TripAdvisor corpus

The learned kNBC model can then be used to classify test instances to obtain a probability distribution among the five topics as shown in FIGURE 16.29.

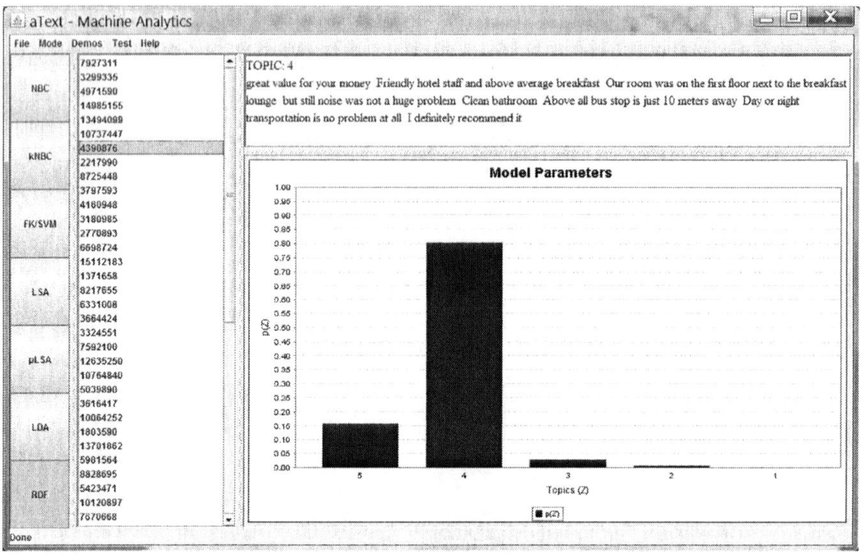

FIGURE 16.29 : Text classification by kNBC

Both PLSA and LDA can be used to obtain topic classification in an unsupervised manner. If the desired number of topics is specified as two then FIGURE 16.30 shows the suggested two topics by *a*Text with weighted words. Note that the first topic has words like "great," "good," "clean," "nice," "recommend," "excel," "comfort," and "quiet," all of which can be associated with a good hotel experience.

16.5.2 Evaluation Results

The performance analyses of kNBC (and NBC with $k = 0$) on TripAdvisor are presented in this section. To reduce the complexity of dealing with thousands of children in a kNBC model, we have discarded all children sharing very low mutual information with the root node. First we used the formula for $I(X;Y)$ for mutual information presented in the machine learning chapter. In this process we have experimentally shown that discarded children nodes indeed contribute very little or nothing to improved performance. We then computed the performances of kNBC by varying the value of the dependence degree k, and compared them against the baseline SVM.

As shown in the table in FIGURE 16.31, the performance for kNBC ($k = 0$) does not degrade with the progressive reduction of the number of child nodes by increasing the mutual information threshold. The table suggests

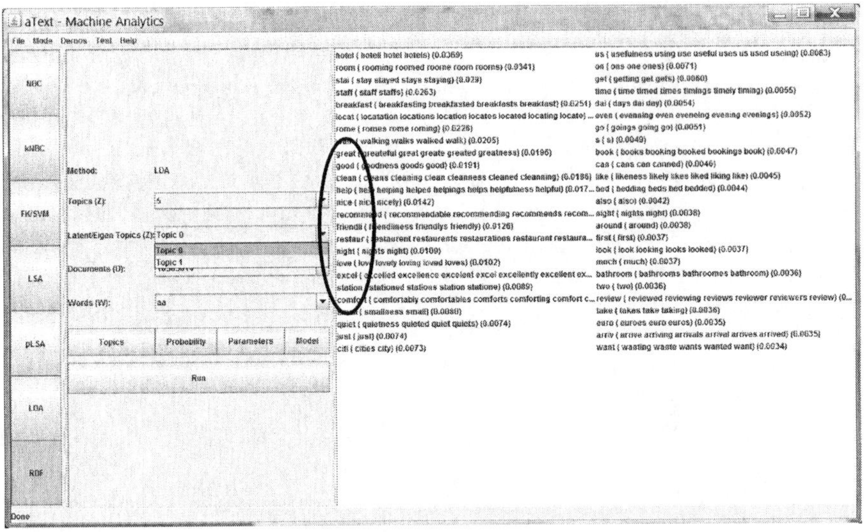

FIGURE 16.30 : Topic extracted from TripAdvisor reviews with weighted representative words

that performance stabilizes after the threshold value 0.005. The baseline SVM performance for this value is as follows:

Mutual information threshold: 0.005
Reduced number of children nodes: 117
Baseline SVM performance: 58.2%

NBC Model	Mutual Information Threshold						
	0.001	0.002	0.003	0.004	0.005	0.006	0.007
No of Children	3521	401	237	160	117	79	61
Hit Rate	57.9	57.1	57.7	57.1	58.2	57.8	57.0
F-Measure	89.8	89.6	90.5	90.7	91.3	91.7	91.6

FIGURE 16.31 : Performance of a kNBC model by varying its number of children

With a kNBC consisting of 117 children and $k = 2$, the confusion matrix is shown in the table in FIGURE 16.32. In this table, we have computed the "hit rate," i.e., the percentage of the total number of diagonal elements compared to the total number of reports. This is equal to 58.9%. A plausible explanation of the low performance of the TripAdvisor corpus is the blurriness between two consecutive ratings. Many words in reports from satisfied customers rating 4 and 5 are likely to be common; as will be the case with ratings of 1 and 2. If we now transform the classification as a binary classification problem with ratings 4 and 5 in the "positive" class and ratings 1-3 in the "negative" class, performance becomes acceptable. We then follow the usual precision, recall, and F-measure definitions.

Dependency k: 2
Hit Rate: 58.9%
Precision: 90.9%
Recall: 92.2%
F-Measure: 91.5%

*k*NBC Model	5	4	3	2	1
5	1662	602	56	25	10
4	535	996	220	61	9
3	49	167	153	83	9
2	25	60	80	138	71
1	12	6	15	71	140

FIGURE 16.32 : TripAdvisor Confusion Matrix

We now have varied the dependencies, and TABLE 16.2 shows the hit rate (first row) and F-measure (second row) by varying the value of k between 0 and 3.

TABLE 16.2: : Comparison of performances of kNBC by varying k

	$k = 0$ (NBC)	$k = 1$	$k = 2$	$k = 3$
kNBC	57.7% 90.5%	58.8% 91.2%	58.9% 91.5%	57.8% 91.5%

It is clear that $k = 2$ yields the optimal performance.

16.6 LIFE STATUS ESTIMATION USING DYNAMIC BAYESIAN NETWORKS

The life status estimation task involves determining the status of a subject on the basis of remote sensor data. This has applications in areas wherever remote monitoring is involved, including home patient care and device and plant monitoring. In this particular status estimation task, overcoming possible sensor failures and determining where such failures lie is far more difficult than the clinical assessment itself.

We developed the Probabilistic Unit Life States Estimation (PULSE) architecture (Das et al., 2004). The PULSE system applies Dynamic Bayesian Networks (DBNs) to produce dynamic clinical assessments. As a by-product of the clinical assessment, the PULSE system also produces an assessment of reliability of the underlying hardware, and supports fault isolation analysis techniques.

We have developed a modular architecture for the development and testing of DBNs for life status estimation. A schematic of this architecture is shown in FIGURE 16.33. As seen in the diagram, there are three major functional components to the PULSE system:

- *Simulation Layer*: Creates and/or provides the various biometric measurements to be used;
- *Sensor Layer*: Retrieves biometric measurements from the simulation layer, and adds noise depending on the type of sensor failure to be simulated. These parameters can be modified at run time;
- *Status Estimation Layer*: Takes sensor readings and performs assessments using DBNs to deliver clinical status estimates along with confidence estimates and sensor error alerts.

In order to develop an assessment network for mortality assessment, knowledge elicitation sessions were held with medical experts. In these elicitation sessions, we sought to accumulate two types of information:

- Physiological patterns indicating likely trauma, thus providing information for assessment; and
- Physiological patterns unlikely to appear, providing information for sensor validation.

The elicited information was transcribed into a Markovian DBN that uses two sensors: systolic blood pressure and pulse. FIGURE 16.34 is a screenshot of the Mortality Assessment Network in three time slices. The network covers three distinct time slices, has two history nodes that accumulate state in the network, and has four input nodes that are posted with trend and absolute evidence from the sensors. The network spans 90 seconds (i.e., there are 30

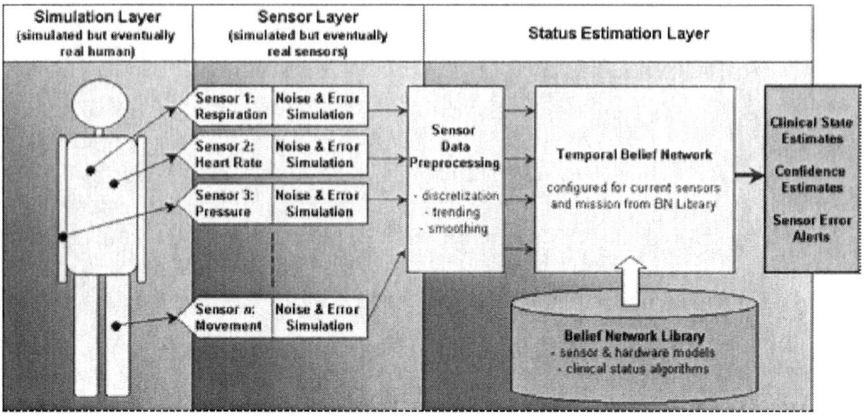

FIGURE 16.33 : PULSE architecture

seconds between two time steps) including history nodes, as this is a useful time span to keep in view when trying to detect the physiological patterns that accompany serious trauma (discussed farther below). The output is read from the Confidence and Alive nodes. The existing implementation of PULSE makes use of a history node-based inference algorithm developed by the author but the DBN inferencing algorithm presented in the time-series modeling chapter can also be used.

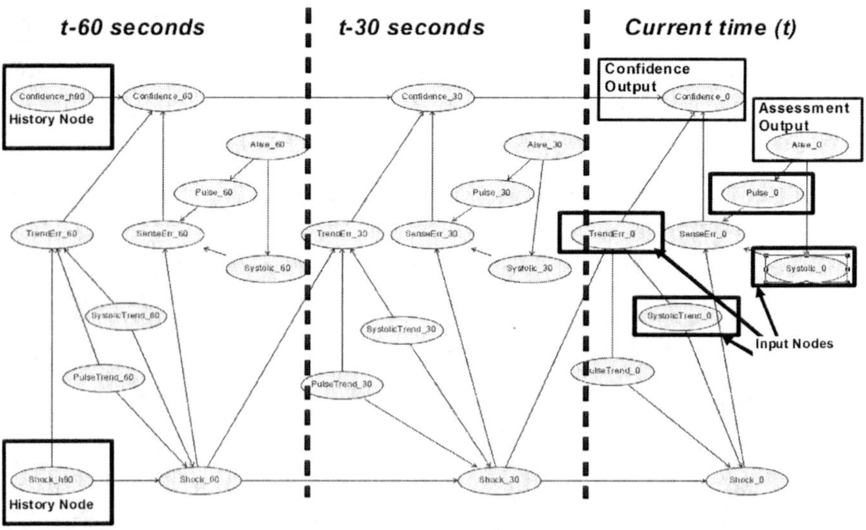

FIGURE 16.34 : The assessment network

FIGURE 16.35 provides a conceptual breakdown of a single slice of the above network. There are three "modules" within a time slice. These modules are:

- *Physiological Module*: Provides a confidence component according to how well-observed metrics match known physiological trends (in this case, shock or normal physiological states);
- *Hardware Module*: Provides a confidence given the operating parameters of the sensor hardware (maximum and minimum values allowed for each sensor);
- *Clinical Module*: Provides an assessment of a subject's mortality on the basis of current readings from the sensor hardware.

There is no direct connection between the physiological module and the clinical module in this network; thus, the goodness of fit between the known physiological patterns and the observed sensor readings contributes to the confidence in the hardware, but does not influence the assessment directly. This separation was useful in the development of this network, but is not a necessary feature.

Note the direct connection between the "Shock" nodes in each time slice. The probability tables at these nodes define an expected evolution of shock, that is, once in shock, it is likely the person will remain in shock and in fact, shock will become more severe. The shock nodes, in turn, constrain the trends we would expect to see for each monitored metric, and deviations from these patterns are determined at the "TrendErr" node, which in turn reduces the "Confidence" in the hardware.

The mortality assessment is made by detecting whether or not the monitored unit has both a pulse and viable blood pressure reading (hence causal links from the node Alive to the Pulse and Systolic nodes). Illegal states (impossible values on either heart rate or blood pressure sensors), or states that are unlikely given the current stage of shock, register an error at the "SenseErr" node, and this also reduces confidence in the hardware.

As shown in FIGURE 16.35, the network has two outputs, a clinical assessment (the Alive node), and a hardware confidence (the Confidence node). These are to be interpreted as follows:

- Alive_0 – The current best estimate as to whether or not the unit is still alive. In general, this value should be either "yes" or "no" (with some very small deviance from certainty). Occasionally, when the clinical state is not recognizable (e.g., no blood pressure yet continued heart beat, which is possible due to sensor error) each state will have a nonnegligible probability. This may be interpreted as an "indeterminate" state, in which an assessment is not really possible.
- Confidence_0 – The current estimate as to the reliability of the underlying hardware. The interpretation of this node is fairly straightforward.

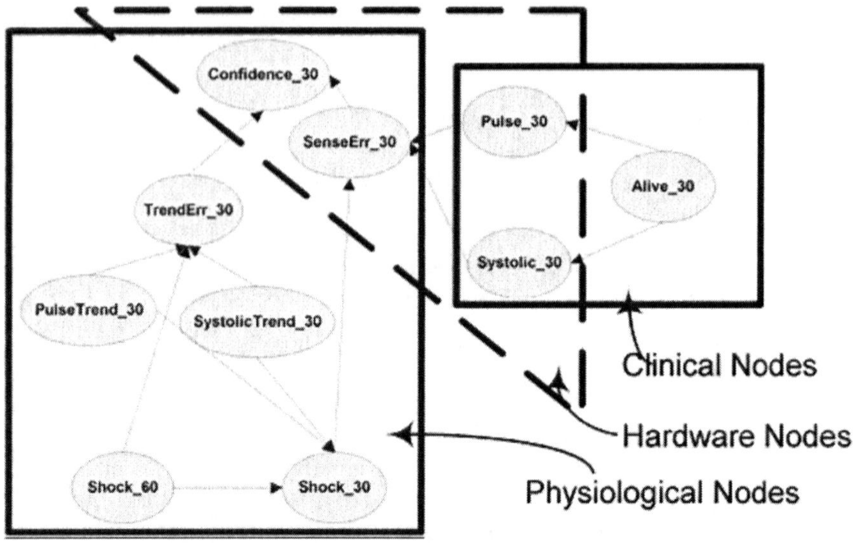

FIGURE 16.35 : Conceptual breakdown of mortality network

Ultimately, the output from these nodes should be used to drive a "user-friendly" layer that interprets the output so as to provide a well-tuned decision support tool. Our network performed very well for simulated data over a variety of sensor conditions.

APPENDIX A

Usage of Symbols

A.1 SYMBOLS USED IN THE BOOK

In general, the conventions in TABLE A.1 below are used for symbols representing terms, random variables, clauses, sets, and so on:

TABLE A.1: : Symbols used in the book

Item	**Convention**	**Example**
Random variable states or variables in a logical language	Italicized, lowercase letters	$x, y, z, ..., x_1, y_1, z_1, ...$
Probabilistic random variables, vectors or graph nodes	Italicized, uppercase letters or italicized string starting with an uppercase letter	$X, Y, Z, N, U, V, W, ...,$ $X_1, Y_1, Z_1, N_1, U_1, V_1, W_1, ...$ Weather, Mobility, ...
Logical predicate symbols	Italicized uppercase letters or italicized string starting with an uppercase letter	$P, Q, R, ..., P_1, Q_1, R_1, ...$ Weather, Mobility, ...
Random variable states or constant symbols in a logical language	Italicized, lowercase letters or italicized string starting with a lowercase letter	$a, b, c, ..., a_1, b_1, c_1, ...$ medium, yes, john, canceled, ...
Function symbols	Italicized, lowercase letters or italicized string starting with a lowercase letter	$f, g, h, ..., f_1, g_1, h_1, ...$ *succ*
Atoms, Literals	Italicized, uppercase letters	$A, B, L, M, ...,$ $A_1, B_1, L_1, M_1, ...$

TABLE A.1: : Symbols used in the book

Formulae, Goals, Clauses	Italicized, uppercase letters	$F, G, H, F_1, G_1, H_1, ...$
Sets, matrices, and clusters	Bold or italicized, Times-Roman typeface, uppercase letters	$\mathbf{A}, \mathbf{B}, \mathbf{S}, ..., A, B, S, ...$

New terminology is italicized on its first use. Figures and tables are sequentially numbered by including chapter numbers. A vector with n attributes will be represented by an $n \times 1$ matrix.

APPENDIX B

Examples and Sample Data

B.1 PLAY-TENNIS EXAMPLE

TABLE B.1 below depicts a small structured relational dataset (Mitchell, 1997) that is widely used within the machine learning community to illustrate algorithm concepts and steps. We make use of the dataset for the same purpose, but across all three paradigms, covered in the book, namely, statistics, AI, and ML. Our selection of this dataset is deliberate, because its manageable size will allow us to: 1) convey concepts in a very precise manner without requiring much space; and 2) compare the internal steps of different algorithms, for the same purpose, across the three paradigms.

TABLE B.1: : Example relational dataset

Outlook	**Temperature**	**Humidity**	**Windy**	**Decision**
sunny	85	85	weak	don't play
sunny	80	90	strong	don't play
overcast	83	78	weak	play
rain	70	96	weak	play
rain	68	80	weak	play
rain	65	70	strong	don't play
overcast	64	65	strong	play
sunny	72	95	weak	don't play
sunny	69	70	weak	play
rain	75	80	weak	play
sunny	75	70	strong	play
overcast	72	90	strong	play
overcast	81	75	weak	play
rain	71	80	strong	don't play

B.2 UNITED STATES ELECTORAL COLLEGE DATA

FIGURE B.1 below provides an example relational dataset of US electoral college votes, population, and area by state.

Microsoft Excel - ElectoralPopArea.xls [Compatibility Mode]

	A	B	C	D	E	F	G	H
1	State	Electoral Votes	Population	Total Area	Water Area	Land Area	Density per Square Mile of	
2	Alabama	9	4,447,100	52,419.02	1,675.01	50,744.00	87.6	
3	Alaska	3	626,932	663,267.26	91,316.00	571,951.26	1.1	
4	Arizona	10	5,130,632	113,998.30	363.73	113,634.57	45.2	
5	Arkansas	6	2,673,400	53,178.62	1,110.45	52,068.17	51.3	
6	California	55	33,871,648	163,695.57	7,736.23	155,959.34	217.2	
7	Colorado	9	4,301,261	104,093.57	376.04	103,717.53	41.5	
8	Connecticut	7	3,405,565	5,543.33	698.53	4,844.80	702.9	
9	Delaware	3	783,600	2,489.27	535.71	1,953.56	401.1	
10	District of Columbia	3	572,059	68.34	6.94	61.4	9316.9	
11	Florida	27	15,982,378	65,754.59	11,827.77	53,926.82	296.4	
12	Georgia	15	8,186,453	59,424.77	1,518.63	57,906.14	141.4	
13	Hawaii	4	1,211,537	10,930.98	4,508.36	6,422.62	188.6	
14	Idaho	4	1,293,953	83,570.08	822.87	82,747.21	15.6	
15	Illinois	21	12,419,293	57,914.38	2,330.79	55,583.58	223.4	
16	Indiana	11	6,080,485	36,417.73	550.83	35,866.90	169.5	
17	Iowa	7	2,926,324	56,271.55	402.2	55,869.36	52.4	
18	Kansas	6	2,688,418	82,276.84	461.96	81,814.88	32.9	
19	Kentucky	8	4,041,769	40,409.02	680.85	39,728.18	101.7	
20	Louisiana	9	4,468,976	51,839.70	8,277.85	43,561.85	102.6	
21	Maine	4	1,274,923	35,384.65	4,523.10	30,861.55	41.3	
22	Maryland	10	5,296,486	12,406.68	2,632.86	9,773.82	541.9	
23	Massachusetts	12	6,349,097	10,554.57	2,714.55	7,840.02	809.8	
24	Michigan	17	9,938,444	96,716.11	39,912.28	56,803.82	175.0	
25	Minnesota	10	4,919,479	86,938.87	7,328.79	79,610.08	61.8	
26	Mississippi	6	2,844,658	48,430.19	1,523.24	46,906.96	60.6	
27	Missouri	11	5,595,211	69,704.31	818.39	68,885.93	81.2	
28	Montana	3	902,195	147,042.40	1,489.96	145,552.43	6.2	
29	Nebraska	5	1,711,263	77,353.73	481.31	76,872.41	22.3	
30	Nevada	5	1,998,257	110,560.71	734.71	109,825.99	18.2	
31	New Hampshire	4	1,235,786	9,349.94	381.84	8,968.10	137.8	
32	New Jersey	15	8,414,350	8,721.30	1,303.96	7,417.34	1134.4	
33	New Mexico	5	1,819,046	121,589.48	233.96	121,355.53	15.0	
34	New York	31	18,976,457	54,556.00	7,342.22	47,213.79	401.9	
35	North Carolina	15	8,049,313	53,818.51	5,107.63	48,710.88	165.2	
36	North Dakota	3	642,200	70,699.79	1,723.86	68,975.93	9.3	
37	Ohio	20	11,353,140	44,824.90	3,876.53	40,948.38	277.3	
38	Oklahoma	7	3,450,654	69,898.19	1,231.13	68,667.06	50.3	
39	Oregon	7	3,421,399	98,380.64	2,383.85	95,996.79	35.6	
40	Pennsylvania	21	12,281,054	46,055.24	1,238.63	44,816.61	274.0	
41	Rhode Island	4	1,048,319	1,545.05	500.12	1,044.93	1003.2	
42	South Carolina	8	4,012,012	32,020.20	1,910.73	30,109.47	133.2	
43	South Dakota	3	754,844	77,116.49	1,231.85	75,884.64	9.9	
44	Tennessee	11	5,689,283	42,143.27	926.15	41,217.12	138.0	
45	Texas	34	20,851,820	268,580.82	6,783.70	261,797.12	79.6	
46	Utah	5	2,233,169	84,898.83	2,755.18	82,143.65	27.2	
47	Vermont	3	608,827	9,614.26	364.7	9,249.56	65.8	
48	Virginia	13	7,078,515	42,774.20	3,180.13	39,594.07	178.8	
49	Washington	11	5,894,121	71,299.64	4,755.58	66,544.06	88.6	
50	West Virginia	5	1,808,344	24,229.76	152.03	24,077.73	75.1	
51	Wisconsin	10	5,363,675	65,497.82	11,187.72	54,310.10	98.8	
52	Wyoming	3	493,782	97,813.56	713.16	97,100.40	5.1	

Sheet1 Sheet2 Sheet3

FIGURE B.1 : Ref: http://mathforum.org/workshops/sum96/data.collections/datalibrary/data.set6.html

APPENDIX C

Matlab and R Code Examples

C.1 MATLAB CODE FOR STOCK PREDICTION USING KALMAN FILTER

```
% Read the stock market data from an Excel file
DATA = xlsread('Microsoft 2012.csv');

% A is 252x7, but extract the field 2nd column 'Open'
Open = DATA(:, 1)';
MO = mean(Open);
N = 100; % Number of steps; N = length(Open) means all the
data
Z = [];
Z = [Z [Open(1) MO MO]'];
Z = [Z [Open(2) Open(1) MO]'];
for k = 3:1:N
    Z = [Z [Open(k) Open(k-1) Open(k-2)]']; %#ok<AGROW>
end

F = [[0.6 0.3 0.1]; [1 0 0]; [0 1 0]]; % Transition matrix
I = eye(3); % Identity matrix
H = I;

% Define the noise covariances factors
[Q] = noise_cov_matrix(N, 0.01);
[R] = noise_cov_matrix(N, 0.02);

% Set initial values of state and covariance matrices
```

```
X_FILTER_0 = [MO + rand() MO + rand() MO + rand()]';
P_FILTER_0 = noise_cov_matrix(N, 1.0);

W_0 = mvnrnd(zeros(3,1), Q)';
X_PREDICT = F * X_FILTER_0 + W_0;
P_PREDICT = F * P_FILTER_0 * F' + Q;

K = P_PREDICT * H' * inv(H * P_PREDICT * H' + R);
X_FILTER = X_PREDICT(:, 1) + K * (Z(:, 1) - H * X_PREDICT(:,
1));
P_FILTER = (I - K * H) * P_PREDICT * (I - K * H)' + K * R
* K';

% Prediction-filter loop
for k = 2:1:N
    W = mvnrnd(zeros(3,1), Q)'; % Noise vector
    % Predict state
    X_PREDICT = [X_PREDICT (F * X_FILTER(:, k-1) + W)];
    % Predict error covariance
    P_PREDICT = F * P_FILTER * F' + Q;

    % Compute Kalman gain
    K = P_PREDICT * H' * inv(H * P_PREDICT * H' + R);
    % Update state with measurements
    X_FILTER = [X_FILTER (X_PREDICT(:, k) + ...
    K * (Z(:, k) - H * X_PREDICT(:, k)))];

    % Update error covariance
    P_FILTER = (I - K * H) * P_PREDICT * ...
    (I - K * H)' + K * R * K';
end
% Plot of predicted and observed stock prices
L1=line(1:N, X_PREDICT(1, :), 'color', 'k', 'linestyle',
':');
hold on
L2=line(1:N, Z(1, :), 'color', 'k', 'linestyle', '-');
hold on
L3=line(1:N, X_FILTER(1, :), 'color', 'k', 'linestyle', '-');
legend([L1(1) L2(1) L3(1)],
    'Prediction','Observation','Filter');
legend('Location', 'NorthWest');
title('Kalman Filter Stock Market Prediction');
xlabel('Day');
ylabel('Price');
xlim=[1 N];
set(gca,'XLim',xlim);
```

```
% Generates noise randomly in a vector of size N and
% then returns the covariance matrix the vector of three
% time-shifted variables x(k), x(k-1), and x(k-2).
function [A] = noise_cov_matrix(N, factor)
    Noise = rand(1, N);
    a11 = factor * var(Noise);
    a12 = factor * cov(Noise(3:N), Noise(2:N-1));
    a13 = factor * cov(Noise(3:N), Noise(1:N-2));
    a23 = factor * cov(Noise(2:N-1), Noise(1:N-2));
    A = [[a11, a12(1,2), a13(1,2)]; ...
    [a12(1,2), a11, a23(1,2)]; [a13(1,2), a23(1,2), a11]];

end
```

C.2 R CODE FOR STOCK PREDICTION USING KALMAN FILTER

```
# R Kalman filter source code to predict stock opening price
# File name: kalman.r; run as source("kalman.r")

# Read the stock market data from Excel
DATA <- read.csv('Microsoft 2012.csv');

# DATA is 252x7, but extract 2nd column 'Open' as observation
Z
Z <- DATA[ , 2]

# Define the length of the simulation.
N <- length(Z)

# Define the system. Change these to change the system.
F <- 1 # F=1 for a constant, |F|<1 for a first order system.
H <- 1

# Define the noise covariances.
Q <- 0.01
R <- 0.02

# Preallocate memory for all arrays initialized with zeros
X_PREDICT <- rep(1, N)
X_FILTER <- rep(1, N)
P_PREDICT <- rep(1, N)
P_FILTER <- rep(1, N)
K <- rep(1, N)

# Calculate the process and measurement noise.
w1 <- rnorm(N)

# Noise (for better comparison).
W_0 <- runif(1) * sqrt(Q)
W <- w1 * sqrt(Q)

# Initial guesses for state and a posteriori covariance.
X_FILTER_0 <- mean(Z)
P_FILTER_0 <- 4

# Calculate the first estimates for all values based upon
the
# initial guess of the state and the a posteriori covariance.
# The rest of the steps will be calculated in a loop.
```

```
# Predictor equations
X_PREDICT[1] <- F * X_FILTER_0 + W_0
P_PREDICT[1] <- F * P_FILTER_0 * F + Q

# Filter equations
K[1] <- P_PREDICT[1] * H / (H * P_PREDICT[1] * H + R)
X_FILTER[1] <- X_PREDICT[1] + K[1] * (Z[1] - H * X_PREDICT[1]
P_FILTER[1] <- (1 - K[1] * H) * P_PREDICT[1] *
    (1 - K[1] * H) + K[1] * R * K[1]

# % Prediction-filter loop
for (k in 2:N) {
    # Predictor equations
    X_PREDICT[k] <- F * X_FILTER[k-1] + W[k-1]
    P_PREDICT[k] <- F * P_FILTER[k-1] * F + Q;

    # Compute Kalman gain
    K[k] <- P_PREDICT[k] * H / (H * P_PREDICT[k] * H + R)

    # Update state with measurements
    X_FILTER[k] <- X_PREDICT[k] + K[k] *
    (Z[k] - H * X_PREDICT[k])

    # Update error covariance
    P_FILTER[k] <- (1 - K[k] * H) * P_PREDICT[k] *
    (1 - K[k] * H) + K[k] * R * K[k]
}

# Plot prediction, observation and filter states
interval <- c(rep(1:N)) # interval is the vector [1, 2, ...,
N]
x11(width=12, height=6, pointsize=12)
par(mfrow=c(1,2))
#matrix <- cbind(X, Z, X_FILTER)
#ts.plot(matrix)
#ts.plot(xlim=range(interval),ylim=range(Z))
ts.plot(X_PREDICT, col="red", xlab="Time", ylab="",
    xlim=range(interval), ylim=range(Z))
par(new = TRUE)
ts.plot(Z, col="black", xlab="Time", ylab="",
    xlim=range(interval), ylim=range(Z))
par(new = TRUE)
ts.plot(X_FILTER, col="blue", xlab="Time", ylab="",
    xlim=range(interval), ylim=range(Z))
title(main="Stock Price Forecast")
legend("topleft", c("Predict", "Observed", "Filter"),
```

```
    lty=c(1,1), lwd=c(2.5,2.5), col=c("red", "black", "blue"

par(new = FALSE)

# Plot prediction and observation with 25 points
interval <- c(rep(25:50))
plot(X_PREDICT, type = "b", pch = 1, col="red",
    xlab="Time", ylab="", xlim=range(interval), ylim=range(

par(new = TRUE)
plot(Z, type = "b", pch = 2, col="black",
    xlab="Time", ylab="", xlim=range(interval), ylim=range(

title(main="Stock Price Forecast")
legend("topleft", c("Predict", "Observed"), pch=c(1, 2))
par(new = FALSE)
```

References

Ait-Mokhtar, S., Brun, C., and Das, S. (2010). "The Role of Natural Language Processing in High-Level Fusion," Xerox Research Centre Europe, Tutorial Slides, *International Conference on Information Fusion*, Edinburgh, Scotland.

Aliferis, C., and Cooper, G. (1994). "An evaluation of an algorithm for inductive learning of Bayesian Belief Networks using simulated datasets," *Proceedings of the 10th Conference on Uncertainty in Artificial Intelligence* (*UAI*), Seattle, WA.

Anderson, T. (2003). *An Introduction to Multivariate Statistical Analysis*, Wiley-Interscience, Third Edition.

Antoniou, G. and van Harmelen, F. (2004). *A Semantic Web Primer*, The MIT Press.

Arulampalam, S., Maskell, S., Gordon, N., and Clapp, T. (2002). "A tutorial on particle filters for on-line nonlinear/non-Gaussian Bayesian tracking," *IEEE Transactions on Signal Processing*, 50:174–188.

Baader, F., Goble, C., McGuinness, D., Nardi, D., and Patel-Schneider, P. (eds.). (2003). *The Description Logic Handbook*, Cambridge University Press.

Baader, F. and Nutt, W. (2003). "Basic Description Logics," http://www.inf.unibz.it/ ~franconi/dl/course/dlhb/dlhb-02.pdf

Baccianella, S., Esuli, A., and F. Sebastiani. (2009). "Multifacet rating of product reviews.," *Proceedings of the 31st European Conference on Information Retrieval*, Lecture Notes in Computer Science, pp. 461–472. Springer.

Bar-Shalom, Y., and Fortmann, T. (1988). *Tracking and Data Association*, Mathematics in Science and Engineering Series, Vol. 179, Academic Press, NY.

Bedaride, P. and Gardent, C. (2009). "Semantic normalisation: a framework and an experiment." *8th International Conference on Computational Semantics* (IWCS), Tilburg, Netherlands.

Berger, J. and Bernardo, J. (1992). "On the development of reference priors," In Bayesian Statistics 4: *Proceedings of the Fourth Valencia International Meeting*. Clarendon Press, Oxford. 35–60.

Bernardo, J. (1979). "Reference posterior distributions for Bayesian inference," *Journal of Royal Statistical Society*, B 41, pp. 113–147.

Binder, J., Koller, D., Russell, S., and Kanazawa, K. (1997). "Adaptive probabilistic networks with hidden variables," *Machine Learning*, 29:213–244.

Blasch, E., and Plano, S. (2002). "JDL Level 5 fusion model: User refinement issues and applications in group tracking," *Proceedings of the SPIE*, 4729:270–279, Signal Processing, Sensor Fusion, and Target Recognition XI.

Blasch, E., and Plano, S. (2003). "Level 5: User refinement to aid the fusion process," *Proceedings of the SPIE*, 5099, Multisensor, Multisource Information Fusion: Architectures, Algorithms, and Applications.

Blei, D., Ng, A., and Jordan, M. (2003). "Latent Dirichlet allocation," *Journal of Machine Learning Research*, 3(5):993–1022.

Bolton, R. and Hand, D. (2002). "Statistical Fraud Detection: A Review," *Statistical Science*, Vol. 17, Issue 3, pp. 235–255.

Bonissone, P., and Tong, R. (1985). "Reasoning with uncertainty in expert systems (editorial)," *International Journal of Man-Machine Studies*, 241–250.

Bratko, I. (2000). *Prolog Programming for Artificial Intelligence*, 3rd edition, Wokingham, Addison-Wesley, England.

Breiman, L., Friedman, J., Stone, C., and Olshen, R. (1984). *Classification and Regression Tress*, Chapman and Hall/CRC.

Brooks, R. A. (1986). "A robust layered control system for a mobile robot," *IEEE Journal of Robotics and Automation*, RA-2:14–23.

Buntine, W. (1991). "Theory refinement on Bayesian networks," *Proceedings of the 7th Annual Conference on Uncertainty in Artificial Intelligence (UAI)*, Los Angeles, CA.

Buntine, W. (1996). "A guide to literature on learning probabilistic network from data," *IEEE Transactions on Knowledge and Data Engineering*, 8:195–210.

Burgess, C. (1998). "A tutorial on support vector machines for pattern recognition," *Data Mining and Knowledge Discovery*, Vol. 2(2), pp. 955–974.

Chandola, V., Banerjee, A., and Kumar, A. (2009). "Anomaly detection: A survey," *ACM Computing Surveys*, Vol. 41, Issue 3, pp. 1–58.

Chang, C. L., and Lee, R. C. T. (1973). *Symbolic Logic and Mechanical Theorem Proving*, Academic Press, NY.

Chapelle, O., Schölkopf, B., and Zien, A. (2006). *Semi-Supervised Learning*, MIT Press, Cambridge, MA.

Chellas, B. F. (1980). *Modal Logic: An Introduction*, Cambridge University Press, Cambridge, England.

Chickering, D. (2002). "Learning equivalence classes on Bayesian network structures," *Journal of Machine Learning Research*, 2:445–498.

Chomsky, N. (2002). *Syntactic Structures*, Walter de Gruyter, 2nd Edition, Berlin and NY.

Chow, C. K., and Liu, C. N. (1968). "Approximating discrete probability distributions with dependence trees," *IEEE Transactions on Information Theory*, 14:462–467.

Chung, K. L. (2000). *A Course in Probability Theory*, Academic Press, NY.

Clark, K. L. (1978). "Negation as failure," *Logic and Databases*, 293–322, Plenum Press, NY.

Clocksin, W. F., and Mellish, C. S. (2003). *Programming in Prolog*, 5th edition, Springer-Verlag, Berlin, Germany.

Cobb, B., and Shenoy, P. (2003). "Inference in hybrid Bayesian networks with mixtures of truncated exponentials," *Proceedings of the 6th Workshop on Uncertainty Processing*, 47–63, Czech Republic.

Cook, S. A. (1971). "The complexity of theorem proving procedures," *Proceedings of the 3rd Annual ACM Symposium on the Theory of Computing*, ACM Press, NY, 151–158.

Cooper, G. (1990). "The computational complexity of probabilistic inference using Bayesian Belief Networks," *Artificial Intelligence*, 42.

Cooper, G., and Herskovits, E. (1992). "A Bayesian method for the induction of probabilistic networks from data," *Machine Learning*, 9:309–347.

Copi, I. M. (1979). *Symbolic Logic*, Macmillan, New York.

Cover, T. and Hart, P. (1967). "Nearest neighbor pattern classification," *IEEE Transaction on Information Theory*, Vol. 13, No. 1, pp. :21e7.

Cristianini, N. and Shaw-Taylor, J. (2000). *An Introduction to Support Vector Machines and Other Kernel-based Learning Methods*, Cambridge University Press.

Das, S. (1992). *Deductive Databases and Logic Programming*, Addison-Wesley, Wokingham, England.

Das, S., and Grecu, D. (2000). "COGENT: Cognitive agent to amplify human perception and cognition," *Proceedings of the 4th International Conference on Autonomous Agents*, Barcelona.

Das, S., Grey, R., and Gonsalves, P. (2002). "Situation assessment via Bayesian Belief Networks," *Proceedings of the 5th International Conference on Information Fusion*, Annapolis, Maryland.

Das, S., Introne, J., Lawless, D., Hoyt, R., and Muza, S. (2004). "Probabilistic Unit Life Status Estimation (PULSE)," *Proceedings of the 7th International Conference on Information Fusion*, Stockholm, Sweden.

Das, S. (2005). "Symbolic argumentation for decision making under uncertainty," *Proceedings of the 8th International Conference on Information Fusion*, Philadelphia, PA.

Das, S., Lawless, D., Ng, B., and Pfeffer, A. (2005). "Factored particle filtering for situation assessment in urban environments," *Proceedings of the 8th International Conference on Information Fusion*, Philadelphia, PA.

Das, S., Kanjilal, P., and Lawless, D. (2006). "Spatiotemporal clustering for aggregating hostile units in cluttered environments," *Proceedings of the 9th International Conference on Information Fusion*, Florence, Italy (July).

Das, S. (2008a). *Foundations of Decision-Making Agents: Logic, Probability, and Modality*, World Scientific/Imperial College Press, Singapore/London.

Das, S. (2008b). *High-Level Data Fusion*, Artech House, Norwood, MA.

Das, S. (2013). "Feature Dependencies and Fisher Kernel in Text Classification." *Proceedings of the European Conference on Data Analysis*, Luxembourg.

de Marneffe, M-C, MacCartney, B., and Manning, C. (2006). "Generating typed dependency parses from phrase structure parses." *Proceedings of LREC-06.*

de Marneffe, M-C et al. (2010). "Stanford typed dependencies manual: Revised for Stanford Parser v. 1.6.5," Stanford University.

Deerwester, S., Dumais, S. T., Furnas, G. W., Landauer, T. K., and Harshman R. (1990). "A. Indexing by latent semantic analysis," *Journal of the Society for Information Science*, 41(6):391–407.

Dempster, A. P. (1966). "New methods for reasoning towards posterior distributions based on sample data," *Annals of Mathematical Statistics*, 37:355–374.

Dempster, A., Laird, N., and Rubin, D. (1977). "Maximum likelihood from incomplete data via the EM algorithm," *Journal of Royal Statistical Society B*, 39:1–38.

Deo, N. (1974). *Graph Theory with Applications to Engineering and Computer Science*, Prentice Hall, Englewood Cliffs, NJ.

Djuric, P., Kotecha, J., Zhang, J., Huang, Y., Ghirmai, T., Bugallo, M., and Miguez, J. (2003). "Particle filtering," *IEEE Signal Processing Magazine*, 20(5):19–38.

Doucet, A., de Freitas, N., Murphy, K., and Russel, S. (2000a). "Rao-Blackwellised particle filtering for dynamic Bayesian networks," *Proceedings of the 16th Conference on Uncertainty in Artificial Intelligence (UAI)*, Stanford, CA.

Doucet, A., de Freitas, N., Murphy, K., and Russel, S. (2000b). "A simple tutorial on RBPF for DBNs," *http://www.cs.ubc.ca/~nando/software.html*

Doucet, A., de Freitas, N., and Gordon, N. (eds.). (2001). *Sequential Monte Carlo Methods in Practice*, Springer-Verlag, NY.

Druzdzel, M. J., and van der Gaag, L. C. (1995). "Elicitation of probabilities for belief networks: Combining qualitative and quantitative information," *Proceedings of the 11th Conference on Uncertainty in Artificial Intelligence (UAI)*, Montreal, Canada.

Dubois, D., and Prade, H. (1988). *Possibility Theory*, Plenum Press, NY.

Duda, R., and Hart, P. (1973). *Pattern Recognition and Scene Analysis*, Wiley, NY.

Duda, R. O., Hart, P. E., and Stork, D. G. (2001). *Pattern Classification*, 2nd edition, John Wiley & Sons, NY.

Dumais, S. T., Furnas, G. W., Landauer, T. K., and Deerwester, S. (1988). "Using latent semantic analysis to improve information retrieval," *Proceedings of CHI'88: Conference on Human Factors in Computing*, Washington, DC.

Feller, W. (1968). *An Introduction to Probability Theory and Its Applications*, Vol. 1, John Wiley & Sons, NY.

Fine, S., Singer, Y., and Tishby, N. (1998). "The hierarchical hidden Markov model: Analysis and applications," *Machine Learning*, 32:42–62.

Fox, J., and Das, S. (2000). *Safe and Sound: Artificial Intelligence in Hazardous Applications*, AAAI-MIT Press, Cambridge, MA.

Frakes, W. (1992). "Stemming Algorithms," In: W.B. Frakes and R. Baeza-Yates (eds), *Information Retrieval. Data Structures and Algorithms*, pp. 131-160, Prentice Hall, 1992.

Friedman, N. (1998). "The Bayesian structural EM algorithm," *Proceedings of the 14th International Conference on Uncertainty in Artificial Intelligence (UAI)*, Madison, WI.

Friedman, N., Getoor, L., Koller, D., Pfeffer, A. (1999). "Learning Probabilistic Relational Models," *Proceedings of the 16th International Joint Conference on Artificial Intelligence* (IJCAI), pp. 1300–1309.

Friedman, N., and Goldszmidt, M. (1996). "Learning Bayesian networks with local structure," *Proceedings of the 12th International Conference on Uncertainty in Artificial Intelligence (UAI)*, Portland, OR.

Friedman, N., and Koller, D. (2003). "Being Bayesian about network structure: A Bayesian approach to structure discovery in Bayesian networks," *Machine Learning*, 50:95–126.

Fung, R. M., and Crawford, S. L. (1990). "Constructor: A system for the induction of probabilistic models," *Proceedings of the 8th National Conference on Artificial Intelligence (AAAI)*, Boston, MA.

Gallier, J. H. (2003). *Logic for Computer Science*, John Wiley & Sons, NY. Revised online version, *http://www.cis.upenn.edu/~jean/gbooks/ logic.html*

Gaussier, E., Goutte, C., Popat, K., and Chen, F. (2002). "A Hierarchical Model for Clustering and Categorising Documents," in Advances in Information Retrieval, *Proceedings of the 24th BCS-IRSG European Colloquium on IR Research* (ECIR).

Gelman, A., Carlin, J., Stern, H., and Rubin, D. (2003). *Bayesian Data Analysis*, Chapman and Hall/CRC Press.

Gelman, A., and Hill, J. (2006). *Data Analysis Using Regression and Multilevel/Hierarchical Models*, Cambridge University Press.

Geman, S., and Geman, D. (1984). "Stochastic relaxation, Gibbs distributions and the Bayesian restoration of images," *IEEE Transaction on Pattern Analysis & Machine Intelligence*, 6:721–742.

Ghahramani, Z. (2001). "An introduction to Hidden Markov Models and Bayesian networks," *International Journal of Pattern Recognition and Artificial Inteligence*, 15(1):9–42.

Gilks, W., Richardson, S., and Spiegelhalter, D. (eds.). (1996). *Markov Chain Monte Carlo in Practice*, Chapman and Hall, London.

Ginsberg, M. L. (ed.). (1987). *Readings in Nonmonotonic Reasoning*, Morgan Kaufmann, Los Altos, CA.

Golub, G., and Van Loan, C. F. (1996). *Matrix Computations*, 3rd edition, The Johns Hopkins University Press, Baltimore.

Gordon, N., Salmond, D., and Smith, A. (1993). "Novel approach to nonlinear/non-Gaussian Bayesian state estimation," *IEE Proceedings on Radar and Signal Processing*, 140(2):107–113.

Gorsuch, R. (1983). *Factor Analysis*, Lawrence Earlbaum, New Jersey.

Grimmett, G., and Stirzaker, D. (2001). *Probability and Random Processes*, Oxford University Press.

Grime, S. (2011). "Unstructured Data and the 80 Percent Rule," at web site http:// clarabridge.com/default.aspx?tabid=137& ModuleID=635& ArticleID=551

Hall, D., and Llinas, J. (2001). *Handbook of Multisensor Data Fusion*, CRC Press, Boca Raton, FL.

Handschin, J., and Mayne, D. (1969). "Monte Carlo technique to estimate the conditional expectation in multi-stage nonlinear filtering," *International Journal of Control*, 9(5):547–559.

Hartigan, J. and Wang, M. (1979). "A K-means clustering algorithm," *Applied Statistics*, Vol. 28, pp. 100–108.

Heckerman, D. E. (1996). "A tutorial on learning Bayesian networks," *Technical Report: MSR-TR-95-06*, Microsoft Corporation, Redmond, WA.

Heckerman, D. E., Geiger, D., and Chickering, D. M. (1995). "Learning Bayesian networks: The combination of knowledge and statistical data," *Machine Learning*, 20(3).

Heckerman, D. E., and Shortliffe, E. H. (1992). "From certainty factors to belief networks," *Artificial Intelligence in Medicine*, 4:35–52.

Henley, W. and Hand D. (1996). "The k-Nearest-Neighbor classifier for assessing consumer credit risk," *The Statistician*, Vol. 45, Issue 1, pp. 77–95.

Herskovits, E., and Cooper, G. (1990). "Kutato: An entropy-driven system for construction of probabilistic expert systems from databases," *Proceedings of the 6th International Conference on Uncertainty in Artificial Intelligence (UAI)*, Cambridge, MA.

Hintikka, J. (1962). *Knowledge and Belief: An Introduction to the Logic of the Two Notions*, Cornell University Press, NY.

Hodge, V. and Austin, J. (2004). "A survey of outlier detection methodologies," *Artificial Intelligence Review*, Vol. 22, No. 2, pp. 85–126.

Hofmann T. (1999). "Probabilistic Latent Semantic Analysis," *Proceedings of the Conference on Uncertainty in Artificial Intelligence* (UAI), Stockholm.

Hojsgaard, S., and Thiesson, B. (1995). "BIFROST: Block recursive models induced from relevant knowledge, observations, and statistical techniques," *Computational Statistics and Data Analysis*, 19:155–175.

Hornik, K., Stinchcombe, M, and White, H. (1990). "Universal approximation of an unknown mapping and its derivative using multilayer feed forward networks," *Neural Networks*, Vol. 3, No. 5, pp. 551-560.

Hosmer, D., Lemeshow, S., and May, S. (2008). *Applied Survival Analysis: Regression Modeling of Time to Event Data*, Wiley-Interscience.

Howard, R. A., and Matheson, J. E. (1981). "Influence diagrams," *Readings on the Principles and Applications of Decision Analysis*, 721–762, Strategic Decisions Group, Menlo Park, CA.

Hsu, C-W., Chang, C-C., and Lin, C-J. (2010). "A Practical Guide to Support Vector Classification," http://www.csie.ntu.edu.tw/~cjlin.

Huang, C., and Darwiche, A. (1996). "Inference in Belief Networks: A procedural guide," *International Journal of Approximate Reasoning*, 15(3):225–263.

Hughes, G. E., and Cresswell, M. J. (1996). *A New Introduction to Modal Logic*, Routledge, London.

Isard, M., and Blake, A. (1998). "Condensation – Conditional density propagation for visual tracking," *International Journal of Computer Vision*, 29:5–28.

Jackson, P. (1998). *Introduction to Expert Systems*, Addison-Wesley, Wokingham, England.

Jain, A. and Dubes, R (1988). *Algorithms for Clustering Data*, Prentice Hall, NJ.

Jain, A., Murthy, M., and Flynn, P. (1999). "Data clustering: A review," *ACM Computing Surveys*, 31(3):264–323.

Jeffreys, H. (1946). "An invariant form for the prior probability in estimation problems," *Proceedings of the Royal Society of London*, Series A, Mathematical and Physical Sciences, Vol. 186, pp. 453–461.

Jeffreys, H. (1961), *Theory of Probability*, Oxford University Press.

Jensen, F. V., Lauritzen, S. L., and Olesen. K. G. (1990). "Bayesian updating in causal probabilistic networks by local computations," *Computational Statistics*, Q. 4, 269–282.

Jensen, F., Jensen, F. V., and Dittmer, S. L. (1994). "From influence diagrams to junction trees," *Proceedings of the 10th Conference on Uncertainty in Artificial Intelligence* (*UAI*), Seattle, WA.

Jensen, F. V. (1996). *An Introduction to Bayesian Networks*, Springer-Verlag, NY.

Jensen, F. V. (2002). *Bayesian Networks and Decision Graphs*, Springer-Verlag, NY.

Johnson, S. (1967). "Hierarchical Clustering Schemes," *Psychometrika*, Vol. 32, pp. 241–254.

Julier, S. J., and J. K. Uhlmann. (1997). "A new extension of the Kalman filter to nonlinear systems," *Proceedings of the 11th International Symposium on Aerospace/Defense Sensing*, Simulation and Controls, Multi Sensor Fusion, Tracking and Resource Management II, SPIE.

Jung, S. and Kim, T-S. (2001). "An agglomerative hierarchical clustering using partial maximum array and incremental similarity computation method," *Proceedings of the IEEE International Conference on Data Mining*, pp. 265–272.

Kalman, R. (1960). "A new approach to linear filtering and prediction problems," *Journal of Basic Engineering*, 82:35–45.

Kanazawa, K., Koller, D., and Russell, S. (1995). "Stochastic simulation algorithms for dynamic probabilistic networks," *Proceedings of the 11th Conference on Uncertainty in Artificial Intelligence* (UAI), Montreal, Canada.

Kanjilal, P., Das, S., and Lawless, D. (2007). "Spatiotemporal clustering from noisy data," *Proceedings of the IJCAI Workshop on Spatial and Temporal Reasoning*, Hyderabad, India.

Kaplan, L. and Meier, P. (1958). "Nonparametric estimation from incomplete observations," *Journal of American Statistical Association*, Vol. 53, pp. 457–481.

Karp, R. (1972). "Reducibility among combinatorial problems," *Complexity of Computer Computations*, 85–103, Plenum Press, NY.

Kirk, J. (2006). "Analytics buzzword needs careful definition," InfoWorld. Also available at: http://www.infoworld.com/t/data-management/analytics-buzzword- needs-careful-definition-567

Kleinbaum, D. and Klein, M. (2005). *Survival Analysis: A Self-Learning Text*, Springer-Verlag, New York.

Kleinbaum, D., Kupper, L., Nizam, A., and Muller, K. (2007). *Applied Regression Analysis and Other Multivariable Methods*, Duxbury Press.

Klir, G. J., and Yuan, B. (1995). *Fuzzy Sets and Fuzzy Logic: Theory and Applications*, Prentice Hall, Upper Saddle River, NJ.

Kolmogorov, A. (1957). "On the representation of continuous functions of several variables by superpositions of continuous functions of one variable and addition," *Doklady*, Vol. 114, pp. 679–681.

Kong, A., Liu, J. S., and Wong, W. H. (1994). "Sequential imputation method and Bayesian missing data problems," *Journal of the American Statistical Association*, 89:278–288.

Kowalski, R. A. (1979). "Algorithm = Logic + Control," *Communications of the ACM*, 22(7):424–435.

Krause, P. (1998). "Learning probabilistic networks," *The Knowledge Engineering Review*, 13:321–351.

Kripke, S. A. (1963). "Semantical analysis of modal logic I: Normal modal propositional calculi," *Zeitschrift fur Mathematische Logik und Grundladen der Mathematik* (*ZMLGM*), 9:67–96.

Lam, W., and Bacchus, F. (1994). "Learning Bayesian Belief Networks: An approach based on the MDL principle," *Computational Intelligence,* 10(4).

Lauritzen, S. (1995). "The EM algorithm for graphical association models with missing data," *Computational Statistics and Data Analysis*, 19:191–201.

Lauritzen, S., and Spiegelhalter, D. (1988). "Local computations with probabilities on graphical structures and their applications to experts systems," *Journal of Royal Statistical Society B*, 50(2):154–227.

Leake, D. B. (ed.). (1996). *Case-Based Reasoning: Experiences, Lessons, and Future Directions*, AAAI Press/MIT Press, Cambridge, MA.

Lemmon, E. J. (1977). "*An introduction to modal logic*," American Philosophical Quarterly, Monograph No. 11, University of Illinois Press, Champaign, IL.

Lerner, U., Segal, E., and Koller, D. (2001). "Exact inference in networks with discrete children of continuous parents," *Proceedings of the 17th Annual Conference on Uncertainty in Artificial Intelligence (UAI)*, Seattle, WA.

Lloyd, J. W. (1987). *Foundations of Logic Programming*, 2nd edition, Springer-Verlag, Berlin, Germany.

Llinas, J., Bowman, C., Rogova, G., Steinberg, A., Waltz, E., and White, F. (2004). "Revisiting the JDL data fusion model II," *Proceedings of the 7th International Conference on Information Fusion*, Sweden.

Łukasiewicz, J. (1970). *Selected Works* (ed.: L. Borkowski), North-Holland Publication Company, Amsterdam and PWN, Warsaw.

McCarthy, J. (1980). "Circumscription: A form of nonmonotonic reasoning," *Artificial Intelligence*, 13:27–39.

Mendelson, E. (1987). *Introduction to Mathematical Logic*, Wadsworth & Brooks/Cole Advanced Books and Software, Pacific Grove, CA.

Meyer, J.-J. Ch., and van der Hoek, W. (1995). "Epistemic logic for AI and computer science," *Cambridge Tracts in Theoretical Computer Science*, 41, Cambridge University Press, Cambridge, England.

Mitchell, T. (1997). *Machine Learning.* McGraw-Hill, NY.

Motik, B., Horrocks, I., and Sattler, U. (2007). "Bridging the Gap Between OWL and Relational Databases," *WWW Conference.*

Murphy, K. (2002). *Dynamic Bayesian Networks: Representation, Inference and Learning*, Ph.D. thesis, University of California, Berkeley.

Nardi, D. and Brachman, R. (2002). "An Introduction to Description Logics," http://www.inf.unibz.it/~franconi/dl/course/dlhb/dlhb-01.pdf

Neal, R. (1993). "Probabilistic Inference Using Markov Chain Monte Carlo Methods," Technical Report CRG-TR-93-1, Department of Computer Science, University of Toronto.

Neapolitan, R. E. (2003). *Learning Bayesian Networks*, Prentice Hall, Upper Saddle River, NJ.

Nigam, K., McCallum, A., Thurn, S., and Mitchell, T. (2000). "Text classification from labeled and unlabeled documents using EM," *Machine Learning*, Vol. 39, pp. 103-134.

O'Keefe, R. A. (1990). *Craft of Prolog*, MIT Press, Cambridge, MA.

OODA Loop. (2001). *http://www.d-n-i.net/fcs/ppt/boyds_ooda_loop.ppt*

OWL. (2004). OWL Web Ontology Language Guide, http://www.w3.org/TR/ owl-guide/; OWL Web Ontology Language Reference. http://www.w3.org/TR/owl-ref/

Papadimitriou, C. H. (1993). *Computational Complexity*, Addison Wesley, Reading, MA.

Pearl, J. (1986). "A constraint-propagation approach to probabilistic reasoning," *Proceedings of the 2nd Conference on Uncertainty in Artificial Intelligence* (UAI), Philadelphia, PA.

Pearl, J. (1988). *Probabilistic Reasoning in Intelligent Systems: Networks of Plausible Inference*, Morgan Kaufmann, San Mateo, CA.

Pearl, J. (1990). "Reasoning under uncertainty," *Annual Review of Computer Science*, 4:37–72.

Pfeffer, A., Das, S., Lawless, D., and Ng, B. (2007). "Global/local dynamic models," *Proceedings of the 20th International Joint Conference on Artificial Intelligence (IJCAI)*, Hyderabad, India.

Porter, M. (1980). "An algorithm for suffix stripping," *Program*, Vol. 14, No. 3, pp. 130−137.

Quinlan, J. R. (1986). "Induction of decision trees," *Machine Learning*, 1(1):81–106.

Quinlan, J. R. (1993). *C4.5: Programs for Machine Learning*, Morgan Kaufmann, San Francisco, CA.

Quinlan, J. R. (1990). "Learning logical definitions from relations," *Machine Learning*, Vol. 5, pp. 239–266.

Rabiner, L. (1989). "A tutorial on Hidden Markov Models and selected applications in speech recognition," *Proceedings of the IEEE* 77, 257–286.

Ramoni, M., and Sebastiani, P. (1997). "Discovering Bayesian Networks in incomplete databases," *Technical Report KMI-TR-46*, Knowledge Media Institute, The Open University, Milton Keynes, UK.

Rasmussen, J. (1983). "Skills, rules and knowledge: Signals, signs and symbolism, and other distinctions in human performance models," *IEEE Transactions on Systems, Man, and Cybernetics*, 12:257–266.

Rasmussen, J. (1986). *Information Processing and Human Machine Interaction: An Approach to Cognitive Engineering*, North Holland, NY, 1986.

RDF-Primer. (2004). RDF Primer 1.0: RDF Schema, http://www.w3.org/TR/ rdf-primer/.

Reason, J. (1990). *Human Error*, Cambridge University Press, Cambridge, UK.

Rebane, G., and Pearl, J. (1987). "The recovery of causal poly-trees from statistical data," *Proceedings of the Uncertainty in Artificial Intelligence (UAI)*, Seattle, WA.

Reiter, R. (1978). "On closed world databases," *Logic and Databases*, 55−76, Plenum Press, NY.

Reiter, R. (1980). "A logic for default reasoning," *Artificial Intelligence*, 13:81–132.

Richardson, M. and Domingos, P. (2006). "Markov Logic Networks," *Machine Learning*, Vol. 62, No. 1–2, pp. 107–136.

Roberto, J., Bayardo, J., and Agrawal, R. (1999). "Mining the most interesting rules," *Proceedings of the ACM SIGKOD International Confenece on Knowledge Discovery and Data Mining in USA*, pp. 145–154.

Robinson, J. A. (1965). "A machine-oriented logic based on the resolution principle," *Journal of the Association for Computing Machinery*, 12:23–41.

Russel, J., Binder, J. Koller, D., and Kanazawa, K. (1995). "Local learning in probabilistic networks with hidden variables," *Proceedings of the 14th International Joint Conference on Artificial Intelligence* (IJCAI), Montreal, Canada.

Russell, S. J., and Norvig, P. (2009). *Artificial Intelligence: A Modern Approach*, 3rd Edition, Prentice Hall, NJ.

Sahami, M. (1996). "Learning limited dependence Bayesian classifiers," *Proceedings of the 2nd International Conference on Knowledge Discovery and Data Mining*, pp. 335–338, Portland, OR.

Schmidt-Schaubß, M. and Smolka, G. (1991). "Attributive concept descriptions with complements," *Artificial Intelligence*, Vol. 48, No. 1, pp. 1–26.

Sarawagi, S. and Bhamidipaty, A. (2002), "Interactive Deduplication Using Active Learning, *International Conference on Very Large Data Bases* (VLDB), pp. 269–278.

Shachter, R. D. (1986). "Evaluating influence diagrams," *Operations Research*, 34:871–882.

Shachter, R. D., and Heckerman, D. (1987). "Thinking backward for knowledge acquisition," *AI Magazine*, 8(3):55–61.

Shafer, G. (1976). *Mathematical Theory of Evidence*, Princeton University Press, Princeton, NJ.

Shenoy, P. P. (1992). "Valuation-based systems for Bayesian decision analysis," *Operations Research*, 40(3):463–484.

Shirata, C. (1998). "Financial ratios as predictor of bankruptcy in Japan: An empirical research," *Proceedings of the Second Asian Pacific Interdisciplinary Research in Accounting Conference*, pp. 437–445.

Shortliffe, E. H. (1976). *Computer-based Medical Consultations: MYCIN*, Elsevier, NY.

Shortliffe, E. H., and Buchanan, B. G. (1975). "A Model of Inexact Reasoning in Medicine," *Mathematical Biosciences*, 23(3/4):351–379.

Singh, M. (1997). "Learning Bayesian networks from incomplete data,"

Proceedings of the 14th National Conference on Artificial Intelligence (AAAI), Providence, RI.

Singh, M., and Valtorta, M. (1995). "Construction of Bayesian network structures from data: A brief survey and an efficient algorithm," *International Journal of Approximate Reasoning*, 12:111–131.

Smets, P. (1991). "Varieties of ignorance and the need for well-founded theories," *Information Sciences*, 57–58:135–144.

Smets, P. (1994). "Non standard probabilistic and non probabilistic representations of uncertainty," *Proceedings of the 5th International Conference on Information Processing and Management of Uncertainty in Knowledge-Based Systems* (IPMU), Paris, France.

Spiegelhalter, D., and Lauritzen, S. (1990). "Sequential updating of conditional probabilities on directed graphical structures," *Networks*, 20:579–605.

Spirtes, P., Glymour, C., and Scheines, R. (1990). "Causality from probability," *Proceedings of Advanced Computing for the Social Sciences*, Williamsburg, VA.

Srinivas, S., Russell, S., and Agogino, A. M. (1990). "Automated construction of sparse Bayesian networks from unstructured probabilistic models and domain information," *Proceedings of the 5th Conference on Uncertainty in Artificial Intelligence (UAI)*, New York, NY.

Steinberg, A. N., Bowman, C. L., and White, Jr., F. E. (1998). "Revisions to the JDL data fusions models," *Proceedings of the 3rd NATO/IRIS Conference*, Quebec City, Canada.

Stephanou, H. E., and Lu, S.-Y. (1988). "Measuring consensus effectiveness by a generalized entropy criterion," *IEEE Transactions on Pattern Analysis and Machine Intelligence*, 10(4):544–554.

Sterling, L., and Shapiro, E. (1994). *The Art of Prolog*, MIT Press, Cambridge, MA.

Stoll, R. R. (1963). *Set Theory and Logic*, W. H. Freeman and Company, NY (Reprint edition (1979) by Dover Publications).

Strang, G. (2009). *Introduction to Linear Algebra*, Wellesley-Cambridge Press.

Sung et al. (1999). Dynamics in modeling in data mining: Interpretive approach to bankruptcy prediction, JMIS.

Suzuki, J. (1996). "Learning Bayesian Belief Networks based on the MDL principle: An efficient algorithm using the branch and bound technique," *Proceedings of the International Conference on Machine Learning*, Italy.

Tesniere, L. (1969). *Elements de syntaxe structurale*, Klincksieck, 2nd Edition, Paris.

Thiesson, B. (1995). "Accelerated quantification of Bayesian networks with incomplete data," *Proceedings of First International Conference on Knowledge Discovery and Data Mining*, Montreal, QU.

Thomas, A., Spiegelhalter, D., and Gilks, W. (1992). "Bugs: A program to perform Bayesian inference using Gibbs' sampling," *Bayesian Statistics* 4, 837–842, Oxford University Press, UK.

Thurstone, L. (1947). *Multiple Factor Analysis*. University of Chicago Press.

Toulmin, S. (1956). *The Uses of Argument*, Cambridge University Press, Cambridge, England.

Treacy, W. and Carey, M. (1998). "Credit Risk Rating at Large U.S. Banks," Board's Division of Banking Supervision and Regulation, and Board's Division of Research and Statistics, Federal Reserve Bulletin.

Tur, G., Tur, D., and Schapire, R. (2005). "Combining active and semi-supervised learning for spoken language understanding," *Speech Communication*, Vol. 45, pp. 171–186.

Van Emden, M. H., and Kowalski, R. A. (1976). "The semantics of predicate logic as a programming language," *Journal of the Association for Computing Machinery*, 23(4):733–742.

Vapnik, V. (1998). *Statistical Learning Theory*, Wiley-Interscience.

Vapnik, V. (2010). *The Nature of Statistical Learning Theory*, Springer.

Verma, T. S., and Pearl, J. (1992). "An algorithm for deciding if a set of observed independencies has a causal explanation," *Proceedings of the 8th International Conference on Uncertainty in Artificial Intelligence* (*UAI*), Stanford, CA.

Wen, W. X. (1990). "Optimal decomposition of Belief Networks," *Proceedings of the 6th Conference on Uncertainty in Artificial Intelligence* (*UAI*), Cambridge, MA.

White, Jr., F. E. (1987). "Data fusion lexicon," Joint Directors of Laboratories, Technical Panel for C3, Data Fusion Sub-Panel, Naval Ocean Systems Center, San Diego.

White, Jr., F. E. (1988). "A model for data fusion," *Proceedings of the 1st National Symposium on Sensor Fusion*, Vol. 2.

Wilson, R. (1996). *Introduction to Graph Theory*, Addison-Wesley, Reading, MA.

Wu, X. and Kumar, V. (eds.) (2009). *The Top Ten Algorithms in Data Mining*, Chapman & Hall/CRC.

Xu, R. and Wunsch, D. (2008). *Clustering*, Wiley-IEEE Press.

Yager, R. R. (2004). "On the determination of strength of belief for decision support under uncertainty – Part II: Fusing strengths of belief," *Fuzzy Sets and Systems*, 142:129–142.

Yager, R. R., Kacprzyk, J., and Fedrizzi, M. (eds.) (1994). *Advances in the Dempster-Shafer Theory of Evidence*, John Wiley & Sons.

Zadeh, L. A. (1965). "Fuzzy sets," *Information and Control*, 8:338–353.

Zadeh, L. A. (1978). "Fuzzy sets as the basis for a theory of possibility," *Fuzzy Sets and Systems*, 1:3–28.

Zadeh, L. A. (2002). "What is fuzzy logic and what are its applications?" PowerPoint Presentation.

Zhu, M., Chen, W., Hirdes, J., and Stolee, P. (2007). "The K-nearest neighbor algorithm predicted rehabilitation potential better than current Clinical Assessment Protocol," *Journal of Clinical Epidemiology*, Vol. 60, pp. 1015–1021.

Zhu, X. (2005). "Semi-Supervised Learning Literature Survey," Report No. 1530, Computer Sciences, University of Wisconsin-Madison.

Zhu, X. and Goldberg, A. (2009). *Introduction to Semi-Supervised Learning*, Morgan & Claypool Publisher.

Zweig, G. (1998). *Speech Recognition with Dynamic Bayesian Networks*, Ph.D. thesis, University of California, Berkeley.

Index

06/01/14